MW00990045

Networking
Fundamentals
Third Edition

Richard M. Roberts • Chuck Easttom

Publisher

The Goodheart-Willcox Company, Inc.

Tinley Park, IL

www.g-w.com

Copyright © 2020

by

The Goodheart-Willcox Company, Inc.

All rights reserved. No part of this work may be reproduced, stored, or transmitted in any form or by any electronic or mechanical means, including information storage and retrieval systems, without the prior written permission of The Goodheart-Willcox Company, Inc.

Manufactured in the United States of America.

Library of Congress Catalog Card Number 2018005849

ISBN 978-1-63563-443-3

1 2 3 4 5 6 7 8 9 10 – 20 – 24 23 22 21 20 19 18

The Goodheart-Willcox Company, Inc. Brand Disclaimer: Brand names, company names, and illustrations for products and services included in this text are provided for educational purposes only and do not represent or imply endorsement or recommendation by the author or the publisher.

The Goodheart-Willcox Company, Inc. Safety Notice: The reader is expressly advised to carefully read, understand, and apply all safety precautions and warnings described in this book or that might also be indicated in undertaking the activities and exercises described herein to minimize risk of personal injury or injury to others. Common sense and good judgment should also be exercised and applied to help avoid all potential hazards. The reader should always refer to the appropriate manufacturer's technical information, directions, and recommendations; then proceed with care to follow specific equipment operating instructions. The reader should understand these notices and cautions are not exhaustive.

The publisher makes no warranty or representation whatsoever, either expressed or implied, including but not limited to equipment, procedures, and applications described or referred to herein, their quality, performance, merchantability, or fitness for a particular purpose. The publisher assumes no responsibility for any changes, errors, or omissions in this book. The publisher specifically disclaims any liability whatsoever, including any direct, indirect, incidental, consequential, special, or exemplary damages resulting, in whole or in part, from the reader's use or reliance upon the information, instructions, procedures, warnings, cautions, applications, or other matter contained in this book. The publisher assumes no responsibility for the activities of the reader.

The Goodheart-Willcox Company, Inc. Internet Disclaimer: The Internet resources and listings in this Goodheart-Willcox Publisher product are provided solely as a convenience to you. These resources and listings were reviewed at the time of publication to provide you with accurate, safe, and appropriate information. Goodheart-Willcox Publisher has no control over the referenced websites and, due to the dynamic nature of the Internet, is not responsible or liable for the content, products, or performance of links to other websites or resources. Goodheart-Willcox Publisher makes no representation, either expressed or implied, regarding the content of these websites, and such references do not constitute an endorsement or recommendation of the information or content presented. It is your responsibility to take all protective measures to guard against inappropriate content, viruses, or other destructive elements.

Cover image: alphaspirit/shutterstock.com

Library of Congress Cataloging-in-Publication Data
Names: Roberts, Richard M., author. | Easttom, Chuck, author.
Title: Networking fundamentals / by Richard M. Roberts, Chuck Easttom.
Description: Third edition. | Tinley Park, IL : The Goodheart-Willcox Company, Inc., [2020] |
Includes index.
Identifiers: LCCN 2018005849 | ISBN 9781635634433
Subjects: LCSH: Computer networks.
Classification: LCC TK5105.5 .R625 2020 | DDC 004.6--dc23 LC record available at
https://lccn.loc.gov/2018005849

Preface

Networking Fundamentals was written for individuals wishing to pursue a career in information technology with a specific focus on networking and network administration. The text provides specific content about information technology as well as career information that is needed for employment. It is an introductory text, so no previous networking experience is required.

This text is aligned to the most recent CompTIA Network+ Certification Exam objectives. By studying *Networking Fundamentals* and using the ancillary study guide and lab manual, you can improve your chances of earning an industry-recognized certification. Upon completing this course, you will able to:

- recall the foundational concepts of networking, including topologies, classifications, and the OSI model;
- understand copper-core transmissions, categorize Ethernet cable, and terminate twisted-pair cable;
- describe fiber-optic transmissions and characteristics;
- differentiate among wireless communication technologies and wireless networks;
- provide examples of digital signals and encoding;
- explain the use of network operating systems and the evolution of networking protocols;
- identify and use various Microsoft operating systems;
- compare and contrast Unix/Linux-based software with Microsoft-based software;
- define the function of a server and describe server types and services;
- differentiate between IPv4 and IPv6 addresses, understand DNS operation, and list TCP/IP utilities;
- understand the concept of subnetting a network;
- describe the mechanics of voice, audio, and video transmission;
- discuss the function of a web server and describe specific web services, such as NNTP and e-mail;
- compare and contrast remote networking technologies;
- assess the security of a network and mitigate breaches and vulnerabilities;
- perform regular maintenance of a network;
- apply the CompTIA network troubleshooting strategy and diagnose and treat common network problems;
- summarize the processes for designing and installing a new network;
- complete and pass a CompTIA Network+ practice exam; and
- analyze networking employment opportunities in the information technology industry.

Information technology is an ever-changing landscape. A successful career in the IT industry requires you to continually learn and stay current with new information about networking, as well as every facet of computing. Earning certifications in IT and other specialty areas will help you stay current with hardware, software, and security changes. More importantly, it will help you further your information technology career.

About the Authors

Richard M. Roberts has designed curriculum; taught electricity, electronics, and computer technology; and supervised technical teachers for 45 years. He is currently an adjunct instructor at South Florida Community College. His time is divided between consulting, teaching students and instructors, and writing instructional materials. He also authored the *Computer Service and Repair* textbook and coauthored the *Electricity and Electronics* textbook.

Chuck Easttom has over 25 years of IT experience, holds two master degrees, has 42 industry certifications, and 13 computer science patents. In addition to his two master degrees, he is currently working on a third and a doctorate. He is also the author of 25 computer science books aside from *Networking Fundamentals*. Chuck is a frequent speaker at cybersecurity and computer science conferences.

Student Resources

Student Text

Networking Fundamentals is an up-to-date text that covers computer networks as well as networking theory and concepts. It provides the skills and basic knowledge required for pursuing studies in specific networking fields such as administration, design, and support. The text content is aligned to the CompTIA Network+ Certification Exam objectives and will prepare students for certification.

Online Text

The G-W Online Textbook platform gives students instant access to the textbook and resources with browser-based devices including iPads®, notebooks, PCs, and Mac computers. Textbook pages look exactly the same as the printed text, and all materials are located on a convenient online bookshelf and accessible at home, at school, or on the go. A linked table of contents provides quick access to each chapter. A search tool enables the user to locate a specific topic or word within the text. Students can enlarge or compress a page and print individual pages for off-line reading.

Online Learning Suite

The G-W Online Learning Suite includes the online text, study guide, lab manual, and CompTIA Network+ Reference Guide, creating a complete learning package. It is accessible through any Internet-enabled device, including computers, smartphones, and tablets. All instructional materials are found on a convenient online bookshelf and accessible at home, in school, or on the go.

Study Guide

The supplemental study guide provides students with a valuable means of review and practice essential for mastery of basic network knowledge and skills. The first half of the study guide contains practice exercises that reinforce concepts and skills learned in the corresponding textbook chapters. The completion of these activities greatly enhances the opportunity for students to earn Network+ Certification. The second half of the study guide contains a CompTIA Network+ Reference Guide to help students study and prepare for the CompTIA Network+ Exam. The reference guide includes a detailed review of each CompTIA objective. This review provides a more student-friendly description of the objective's coverage, examples of the objective, and related concepts.

Laboratory Manual

The supplemental laboratory manual encourages students to apply the concepts they have learned in the text. It provides an opportunity to perform many of the tasks required in a typical networking employment setting and incorporates review questions at the end of each lab to reinforce understanding of the practicality and purpose of the activities. For ease of reference, the table of contents shows both the topic covered and the corresponding textbook chapter.

Instructor Resources

LMS Integration

Integrate Goodheart-Willcox content within your Learning Management System for a seamless user experience for both you and your students. LMS-ready content in Common Cartridge® format facilitates single sign-on integration and gives you control of student enrollment and data. With a Common Cartridge® integration, you can access the LMS features and tools you are accustomed to using and G-W course resources in one convenient location—your LMS.

In order to provide a complete learning package for you and your students, G-W Common Cartridge® includes the Online Learning Suite and Online Instructor Resources. When you incorporate G-W content into your courses via Common Cartridge®, you have the flexibility to customize and structure the content to meet the educational needs of your students. You may also choose to add your own content to the course.

QTI® assessment files are available within the Online Instructor Resources for import into your LMS. These pre-built assessments help you measure student knowledge and track results in your LMS gradebook. Questions and tests can be customized to meet your assessment needs.

Online Instructor Resources (OIR)

Online Instructor Resources provide all the support needed to make preparation and classroom instruction easier than ever. Available in one accessible location, the OIR includes instructor's resources, instructor's presentations for PowerPoint®, and Assessment Software with Question Banks. These resources are available as a subscription and can be accessed at school, at home, or on the go.

Instructor's Resources

One resource provides instructors with time-saving preparation tools such as answer keys, lesson plans, chapter reviews and quizzes, pretests, posttests, and other teaching aids.

Instructor's Presentations for PowerPoint®

Instructor's Presentations for PowerPoint® provide a useful teaching tool when presenting the lessons. These fully customizable slides help you teach and visually reinforce the key concepts from each chapter. Slides include the list of Outcomes and Key Terms from each chapter, definitions for each Key Term, talking points for important concepts, and selected Review and Sample Network+ Questions.

Assessment Software with Question Banks

Administer and manage assessments to meet your classroom needs. The following options are available through the Respondus Test Bank Network. The Respondus Test Bank Network contains test question banks to use with Respondus 4.0 and Respondus LE (Limited Edition).

- A Respondus 4.0 license can be purchased directly from Respondus, which enables you to easily create tests that can be printed on paper or published directly to a variety of Learning Management Systems. Once the question files are published to an LMS, exams may be distributed to students with results reported directly to the LMS gradebook.

- Respondus LE is a limited version of Respondus 4.0. and is free with purchase of the Instructor Resources. It allows you to download test banks and create assessments that can be printed or saved as a paper test.

Focus on Certification

Networking Fundamentals is designed with certification in mind. This text has been updated to reflect current programs, systems, and practices in the information technology industry. It also adheres to the newest objectives of the CompTIA Network+ Exam, ensuring students are up to date with the most recent testing domains.

Outcomes

At the beginning of each chapter, a list of outcomes guide student learning as they read the material presented. Each outcome is aligned with the content headings, as well as with the summary bullet points and review questions at the end of the chapter. This alignment provides a logical flow through each page of the material so that students may build on individual knowledge as they progress through the chapters.

Network+ Objectives

Network+ Objectives are listed on each chapter opener to engage students and highlight important testing points presented in the content. Students can use the list of objectives as a checklist, verifying their understanding of the Network+ standards as they are presented in the material. In addition, the objectives are noted by an icon in the margin where the material is covered. This provides a visual clue as to where each objective is met in the chapter.

Tech Tip

The Tech Tip feature highlights supplemental information about practical application of networking concepts. These tips vary in their scope, ranging from simple synonyms or definitions of discussed material to real-world advice that provides students with insight that will help in their assignments and careers.

Note

The Note feature provides information that may not be tested on the CompTIA exam, but will be helpful for students to know as they begin their careers. This information provides valuable insight to real-word situations in the workplace.

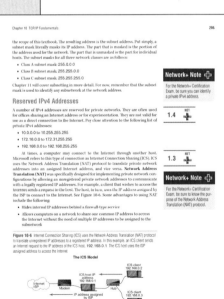

Network+ Note

The Network+ Note feature provides students with tips and facts regarding the CompTIA Network+ Certification Exam. These tips will help students study for the certification exam.

Caution

The Caution feature highlights important personal- and machine-safety information students need to know before performing networking tasks. These alert students to actions that may cause personal injury or damage to a computer or electronic device.

Visuals

Chapter figures have been strategically created to highlight important information. Illustrations, photos, diagrams, and screen captures help students visualize the concepts discussed in the text for better understanding and retention of the material, as well as future application of the content.

End-of-Chapter Content

End-of-chapter material provides an opportunity for review and application of concepts.

- A concise **Summary** reiterates the chapter outcomes and provides a brief review of the content for student reference. This helps students focus on important concepts presented in the text.

- **Review Questions** highlight basic concepts presented in the chapter so students can evaluate their understanding of the material.

- **Sample Network+ Exam Questions** challenge students to answer questions similar to those they will face on the CompTIA exam, providing a sample of what to expect on the exam.

Organization

The text is divided into 20 chapters to accommodate classes that are presented online or face-to-face. Theoretically, the chapters may be covered in any order that meets the requirements of the class. However, it is suggested that instructors follow the order presented in the text.

- **Chapter 1 Introduction to Networking** provides a definition for networking, explains its uses and practicalities, and offers categories and topologies for various network types. Communication methods, protocols, the OSI model, networking media, and industry organizations are also covered, albeit in a cursory fashion. Many of these topics are also discussed at length throughout the text.

- **Chapter 2 Network Media—Copper-Core Cable** discusses analog and digital signals, data transmission, and provides a foundation of electronic terms that will be used throughout the text. The bulk of the chapter is dedicated to coverage of copper-core cables. IEEE standards are introduced, as are types of wiring faults.

- **Chapter 3 Fiber-Optic Cable** is dedicated to discussion of the characteristics of light. Construction of cabling and transmission methods are also covered, as are IEEE standards and contributing factors to data loss.

- **Chapter 4 Wireless Technology** covers various types and methods for wireless technology. Wi-Fi and the IEEE 802.11 standards are discussed at length. In addition, information about radio, microwave, satellite, and infrared transmissions, technologies, and interference is also provided.

- **Chapter 5 Digital Encoding and Data Transmission** enables students to learn about digital signals and encoding, data packaging and codes, and UDP frames. Additionally, a more in-depth look of the OSI model is provided.

- **Chapter 6 Network Operating Systems and Network Communication** describes networking protocols and their functions in various operating systems. Information about common networking operating systems is also discussed.

- **Chapter 7 Microsoft Network Operating Systems** presents Microsoft-created software used to facilitate network operation. Microsoft Server 2016 is included, but focus is given to universal information, such as common features, Active Directory structure, POSIX, and interoperability.

- **Chapter 8 Unix/Linux Operating Systems** details a brief history of Unix and Linux. Students will also learn about the advantages and disadvantages of open-source systems and how Unix/Linux can communicate with Microsoft systems.

- **Chapter 9 Introduction to Servers** offers an in-depth review of server types and services. Students learn about the characteristics of SCSI, types of RAID systems, and external-storage systems. Also covered are ACPI and ACPICA standards, system resources, Fibre Channel, IQN addresses, virtualization, hypervisors, and resources for further study.

- **Chapter 10 TCP/IP Fundamentals** looks at IPv4 and IPv6 addressing, DNS, IP, TCP, UDP, ports and sockets, DHCP, and broadcast versus multicast addresses. Students will also learn about TCP/IP-based troubleshooting utilities that can be used in most networking environments.

- **Chapter 11 Subnetting** describes the binary number system; dotted decimal notation; purposes, advantages, and disadvantages of subnetting; and network segmenting devices. Students will also learn about VLANs, link aggregation, and CIDR notation.

- **Chapter 12 Additional Transmission Modalities** focuses on the basics of audio and voice transmission and the compression and decompression of video. Transmission protocols are discussed at length, and students will learn VoIP troubleshooting methods.

- **Chapter 13 Web Servers and Services** details the differences among the Internet, an intranet, and an extranet; the parts and functions of a URL; and information about markup languages. A more in-depth look at FTP and NNTP is provided in this chapter as well.

- **Chapter 14 Remote Access and Long-Distance Communication** highlights components of telecommunication systems and provides a comparison of remote-connection technologies. Also covered in this chapter is dial-up networking and VPNs.

- **Chapter 15 Network Security** focuses on the types of hacking and common network breaches and vulnerabilities. This chapter also covers common mitigation techniques.

- **Chapter 16 Maintaining the Network** includes methods for monitoring servers and networks, maintenance software, proper maintenance of hardware, ensuring system integrity, and tools used to maintain stable electrical power.

- **Chapter 17 Fundamentals of Troubleshooting a Network** outlines the CompTIA-suggested network troubleshooting strategies. It also describes the stages of computer operation and methods for diagnosing problems at each stage. Startup processes; tools; and strategies used to troubleshoot dual-boot systems, connection problems, and recovery methods are also discussed.

- **Chapter 18 Designing and Installing a New Network** offers a cursory view of network design and installation. Full coverage spans outside the scope of this text, but this chapter provides students with enough information to get them started and to help them determine if this is an area in which they would like to specialize.

- **Chapter 19 Network+ Certification Exam Preparation** provides strategies for scheduling, preparing for, and taking the CompTIA Network+ Certification Exam. This chapter also features a 50-question practice exam that can be scored by the instructor.

- **Chapter 20 Employment in the Field of Networking Technology** provides students with information they will need as they look toward employment in the IT industry. Various networking-based careers are explored, as are sources of career information. Important topics such as digital citizenship and soft skills are also discussed at length. It is important to gain insight into this information because students will need these skills for a successful career.

New to this Edition

The third edition of *Networking Fundamentals* has been revised to align to current CompTIA Network+ Exam objectives. Additionally, updates were made in each chapter to provide coverage of the newest operating systems and networking technologies.

The most noticeable change to this edition is a minor reorganization of the chapters, resulting in 20 chapters rather than 21 as in the last edition. In the previous edition, a chapter was dedicated to a close inspection of the OSI model. This information has been relocated into chapters that provide similar or related content. This was done to streamline student progression and enhance comprehension by grouping related content together.

- **Chapter 1 Introduction to Networking** was revised to include a detailed discussion of the OSI model previously found in Chapter 16 of the second edition. This change was made in an effort to allow students the ability to apply the OSI model to subsequent lessons in a more meaningful way.

- **Chapter 2 Network Media—Copper-Core Cable** was updated and streamlined to highlight the most important information while making the material more accurate in regard to what students will encounter in the real world.

- **Chapter 3 Fiber-Optic Cable** has been given minor updates and revisions.

- **Chapter 4 Wireless Technology** was streamlined and revised to bring the chapter up to date with new wireless technology.

- **Chapter 5 Digital Encoding and Data Transmission** now includes detailed information about encapsulation formerly found in Chapter 16 of the previous edition.

- **Chapter 6 Network Operating Systems and Network Communication** has been brought up to date and now aligns closer to CompTIA objectives.

- **Chapter 7 Microsoft Network Operating Systems** was revised to make it current with CompTIA objectives and recent software released.

- **Chapter 8 Unix/Linux Operating Systems** is largely intact as originally presented in the previous edition, but was given minor revisions and updates.

- **Chapter 9 Introduction to Servers** was revised for accuracy and for inclusion of the topic of virtualization.

- **Chapter 10 TCP/IP Fundamentals** was revised for accuracy and relevance to make it more current with industry standards.

- **Chapter 11 Subnetting** was given minor revisions and updates.

- **Chapter 12 Additional Transmission Modalities** has been retitled and updated for accuracy and relevance.

- **Chapter 13 Web Servers and Services** was revised to provide content that aligns with current Network+ Exam objectives.

- **Chapter 14 Remote Access and Long-Distance Communication** is largely intact as it was in the previous edition, but has been revised with updates and information regarding IPsec.

- **Chapter 15 Network Security** was heavily revised and reorganized to include a dedicated section to malware, increased discussion of cryptography and vulnerabilities, device hardening, and current authentication methods.

- **Chapter 16 Maintaining the Network**, formerly Chapter 17, now includes new information about network documentation and diagrams and networking monitoring.

- **Chapter 17 Fundamentals of Troubleshooting a Network** was previously Chapter 18. It features CompTIA's newly revised troubleshooting guidelines, information about new troubleshooting tools, and a discussion of the boot processes of newer operating systems.

- **Chapter 18 Designing and Installing a New Network**, formerly Chapter 19, received minor revisions and updates.

- **Chapter 19 Network+ Certification Exam Preparation**, formerly Chapter 20, has been updated to align with the CompTIA N10-007 Network+ Exam objectives.

- **Chapter 20 Employment in the Field of Networking Technology** was Chapter 21 in the previous edition. It now includes coverage of digital citizenship and soft skills. Digital citizenship is important for all occupations and even more important for IT careers. Soft skills are equally important, as these are the skills employers look for when hiring and promoting employees.

How to Use this Text

The *Networking Fundamentals* text and accompanying resources will help you prepare for and pass the CompTIA Network+ Certification Exam. You will learn about the foundations of computer networking, network media and devices, transmission methods, protocols, security, maintenance, and other important topics. These are concepts that you will need to understand not only for the certification exam, but for your career as a networking professional. Each chapter in *Networking Fundamentals* begins with a set of learning outcomes. These are the goals you should focus on accomplishing by the time you complete each chapter. For each outcome, there is a corresponding top-level heading, review question, and summary bullet point to help ensure you understand the topics covered in the chapter. There is also a list of CompTIA Network+ Certification Exam objectives listed at the beginning of each chapter that outline the CompTIA content that will be discussed.

In addition to learning outcomes, the chapter-opening material also lists a set of key terms that will be discussed throughout the material. These terms are printed in boldface when they appear in the content. This makes them easily distinguished from the rest of the text. There are also important words or phrases printed in italic text to which you should pay special attention and consideration. Studying these terms will help you understand the material and better prepare you for your certification and employment.

Each chapter concludes with a summary of important points to remember, organized by level-one heading. This summary will help you review important topics from each section of the chapter.

Following the suggested guidelines will help you make the most of your introduction to networking.

- Read the outcomes listed in the chapter opener. Each outcome is tied directly to the headings within the content. In addition, they are repeated in the chapter summary and applied in the end-of-chapter review questions. The connection of outcomes throughout the content helps you focus and apply important information as you read each chapter.

- Read the list of CompTIA objectives in the chapter-opening material. These objectives are also called out in the margin with an icon where the material is covered. Use the list of objectives in the chapter opener as a checklist to take inventory of CompTIA standards you understand as well as information you need to review. The icons in the margins are there to direct you to the coverage of each objective for review.

- Pay attention to the illustrations. Each illustration is strategically created to highlight important information. By studying these, you will extend your learning and improve retention and application of the content.

- Read all Network+ Note, Tech Tip, and Caution features as you progress through the material. This information helps supplement your learning by highlighting study tips, providing useful industry information, and helping you ensure personal and machine safety when working with networking devices.

- Review the summary at the end of each chapter. This will help you retain important information from the chapter.

- Answer the review questions and sample Network+ questions in the end-of-chapter material. These questions provide exposure to the types of questions likely to be on the CompTIA Network+ Certification Exam. By practicing these questions, you increase your chances of successfully earning a Network+ certification.

Reviewers

Goodheart-Willcox Publisher would like to thank the following individuals for their honest and valuable input in the development of *Networking Fundamentals*.

Dr. Adam Beatty, Director of Computer Information Technology Programs, West Virginia Northern Community College, Wheeling, West Virginia

James Burton Browning, Ed.D., Chair, Business, Engineering, and Technology, Brunswick Community College, Supply, North Carolina

James C. Church, Assistant Professor, Department of Computer Science and Information Technology, Austin Peay State University, Clarksville, Tennessee

David C. Dellacca, MS, Associate Professor, Department of Computer Information and Graphics Technology, Indiana University–Purdue University Indianapolis, Indianapolis, Indiana

J.B. Groves III, Instructor of Computer Science, Wharton County Junior College, Richmond, Texas

Ron Hutain, Department Head of Automation Technology, Arkansas Tech University, Ozark Campus, Ozark, Arkansas

Dr. Ola Jobi, CISSP, Adjunct Faculty Staff, Computer Science and Computer Information Technology, Austin Community College, Austin, Texas

Stephan S. Jones, Ph.D., Professor of Information and Communication Sciences, Ball State University, Muncie, Indiana

Ronald Kovac, Professor of Information and Communication Sciences, Ball State University, Muncie, Indiana

Dennis M. Lutz, Network Manager, Sumitomo Drive Technologies, Chesapeake, Virginia

Debra McCusker, M.S.E.E., CCNA1, CCNA2, Faculty Instructor, Information Technology, Alamance Community College, Graham, North Carolina

Kevin Mess, Professor/CIT Academic Linux Server Administrator, School of Advanced & Applied Technologies, College of Southern Nevada, Las Vegas, Nevada

Robert C. Nelson, Information Technology Program Coordinator, Blinn College, Bryan, Texas

Ron Price, Instructor, Information Systems/Computer Science, Spokane Falls Community College, Spokane, Washington

Gregg Tennefoss, Professor of Computer Science & IT, Tidewater Community College, Virginia Beach, Virginia

Brief Contents

Contents

CHAPTER 20

Employment in the Field of Networking Technology 630

APPENDIX A

APPENDIX B

APPENDIX C

APPENDIX D

1 Introduction to Networking

✚ Network+ Certification Exam Objectives

The following subject areas are introduced in this chapter. Many of them appear in more detail later in the textbook. Begin studying them now as simple concepts, and you will be better prepared to comprehend the information presented in later chapters.

Objectives

1.1: Protocols and Ports—SMTP 25; FTP 20, 21; NTP 123

Protocol Types

1.2: Explain devices, applications, protocols, and services at their appropriate OSI layers

1.3: Software-Defined Networking

1.5: Wired Topologies

Types—LAN, WAN, CAN, PAN

1.7: Summarize cloud concepts and their purposes

1.8: NTP

2.2: Router, Switch, Hub, Media Converter

2.3: Multilayer Switch

2.5: ATM

3.1: Logical vs. Physical Diagrams

3.4: Out-of-Band Management—Router

5.2: Software Tools—Bandwidth Speed Tester

5.5: Incorrect Time

Learning Outcomes

- Summarize the advantages and disadvantages of a network system.
- Classify a network as a LAN, MAN, or WAN.
- Identify basic network topologies.
- Compare and contrast a peer-to-peer network with a client/server network.
- Summarize cloud concepts and their purposes.
- Define *network operating system*.
- Describe how devices communicate on a network.
- Recall the common networking protocols.
- Differentiate between network addresses.
- Describe various network media and devices.
- Identify the major standards organizations.
- Recall the layers of the OSI model.

Copyright Goodheart-Willcox Co., Inc.

Key Terms

access port

active hub

administrative server

American National Standards Institute (ANSI)

application layer

asynchronous transfer mode (ATM)

attenuation

bridge

brouter

bus topology

cell

centralized administration

client/server network

copper-core cable

database server

data link layer

decentralized administration

dedicated server

driver

fiber-optic cable

file server

gateway

hosts

hub

hybrid topology

Infrastructure as a Service (IaaS)

Institute of Electrical and Electronic Engineers (IEEE)

International Organization for Standardization (ISO)

Internet protocol (IP) address

layer 1 device

layer 2 device

layer 3 device

local area network (LAN)

logical identification

media

media access control (MAC) address

media converter

mesh topology

metropolitan area network (MAN)

multilayer switch

multistation access unit (MAU)

network

network address

network administrator

network interface card (NIC)

network layer

network operating system (NOS)

network topology

node

Open Systems Interconnection (OSI) model

passive hub

peer-to-peer network

physical layer

Platform as a Service (PaaS)

presentation layer

print server

protocol

repeater

ring topology

router

server

session layer

Software as a Service (SaaS)

standard

star topology

switch

Telecommunications Industry Association (TIA)

Transmission Control Protocol/ Internet Protocol (TCP/IP)

transport layer

wide area network (WAN)

wireless topology

World Wide Web Consortium (W3C)

Overview

This chapter presents a general overview of networking and introduces basic networking concepts. Each topic presented is expanded and explained in detail in later chapters. For full comprehension of the concepts presented throughout the textbook, it is essential that you complete the correlating labs in the lab manual for a valuable learning experience.

Definition of a Network

A **network** is an interconnected collection of computers, computer-related equipment, and communication devices. Any device that can be attached to a network and given a network address is called a **node**. Computers on a network are called **hosts**. This collection could include a PC, laptop computer, tablet PC, printer, cell phone, telephone, pager, fax machine, or other device, as shown in Figure 1-1. A network can be as simple as two computers in one room or as large as thousands of computers, computer equipment, and communication devices spread across the entire globe.

Figure 1-1 Various devices that can be part of a network.

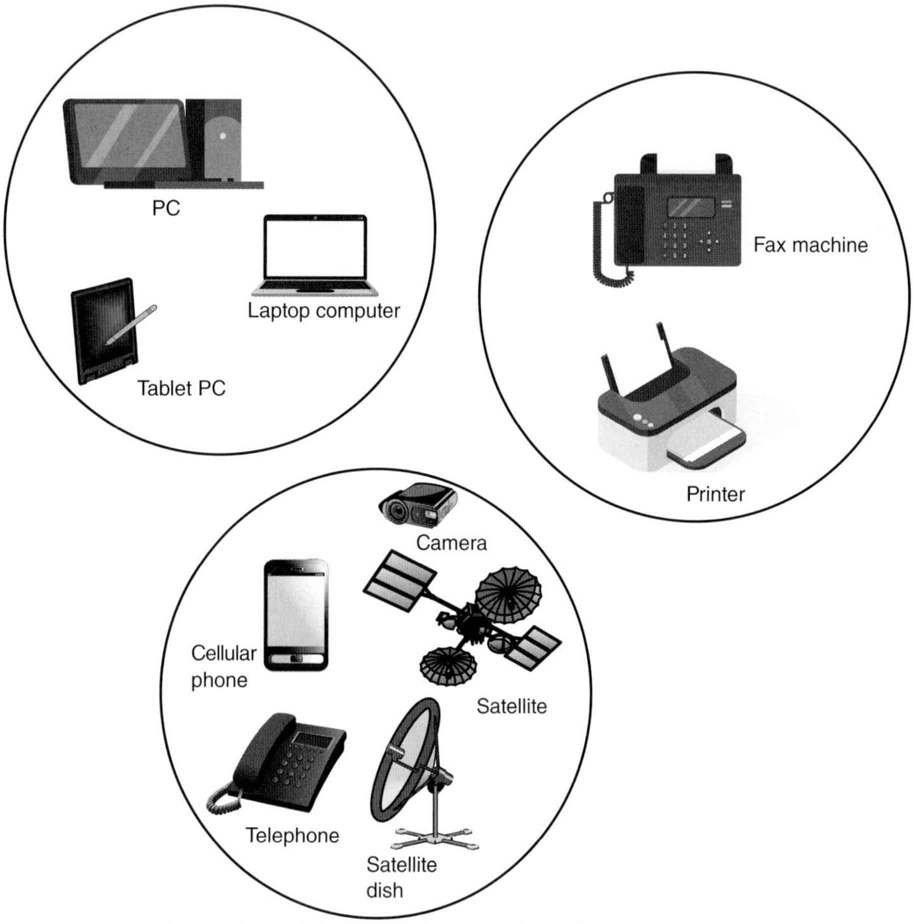

(workstation icon) RedlineVector/Shutterstock.com; (laptop icon) Jemastock/Shutterstock.com; (phone icons) Tetiana Yurchenko/Shutterstock.com; (fax machine icon) KittyVector/Shutterstock.com; (printer icon) Vectors Bang/Shutterstock.com; Goodheart-Willcox Publisher

The purpose of a network is to share computer-related equipment and data. Examples of data are text files, spreadsheets, database information, images, video, music, and voice. Examples of computer-related equipment are printers, Internet-enabled devices, and fax machines.

A network is not the best answer for every situation and should be justified. You must compare the need versus the cost. Next, we will look at the advantages and disadvantages of networking.

Copyright Goodheart-Willcox Co., Inc.

Advantages of Networking

Networks provide a means to share software, data, equipment, and communication quickly, easily, and inexpensively. A corporate network saves time and money by providing quick access to files and resources throughout the corporation. By using a network system to its full potential, data and communication can be exchanged in the same day in a series of e-mails, phone conversations, and networking conferences. Network meetings can take place quickly and easily between individuals from all over the world, costing only a fraction of what it would cost if the participants had to travel. A small- or a home-office network can easily share a single printer or data, eliminating the need to transport files via a USB flash drive or CD.

A network can facilitate the delivery of a file to anyone on the network in a short time and at very little cost. Prior to the use of the Internet, editors and writers were required to exchange work via the US Postal Service. A manuscript would be mailed and delivered in two or three days. The manuscript would be read, edited, and returned within a few days via the public mail system. The writer would review the remarks, changes would be made, and the manuscript would be mailed once again. This process was slow and would typically take a week or more for each chapter. Today, material indicating corrections or clarifications can be exchanged via computer network in the same day, saving time and shipping costs.

The ability to share network devices can also save a company a significant amount of time and money. Consider a very expensive poster printer used in commercial advertising and art. If this printer were installed on a network, a person located at another PC on the network could simply send his or her artwork to that printer via the network. In fact, everyone in the art department could do the same. There would be no need to buy multiple printers. If the printer were not networked, printing a graphic would be much more difficult and would consume a significant amount of time. The file would have to be copied to a USB flash drive or a CD-RW disc and physically transported to the PC attached to the printer.

Another advantage of networking is security. Security is a vital part of an organization's structure. It protects information such as customer lists, patient records, legal material, and ideas from being stolen or destroyed. Networks can keep data more secure than a traditional paper system. In an old hard-copy system, data can be photocopied and distributed without the company's permission by anyone having access to the original documents. Customer lists, patient files, financial records, and such can all be copied. A network can be structured to allow users to access only what they need to use for their individual jobs. Users can be added to a network as individuals or groups to access particular files, collections of files, and equipment. Allowing specific access is known as assigning user rights or permissions. Security will be covered in detail in Chapter 15.

Disadvantages of Networking

Although networking has many advantages, it has its disadvantages as well. These disadvantages include needing additional personnel; losing access to files when the network is down; and vulnerability to cyberattacks, malware, and disgruntled workers.

Additional personnel are often needed to maintain and modify the network. This adds to the business's operational costs. The number of staff is directly related to the size of the network and the complexity of its design. A small, peer-to-peer net-

Copyright Goodheart-Willcox Co., Inc.

work is cost-effective and requires few network administration skills for installation and maintenance. A large, client/server-type network can be very expensive and requires users to have specialized training prior to its installation and operation. This type of network typically requires a network administrator and additional networking staff. The original cost of installing a network, as well as overcoming the complexity of its usage, can be a disadvantage. However, after long-term use and training, the costs can be justified.

One of the largest disadvantages of a network depends on how it is designed and configured. Often, when a network goes down, files may not be accessible. Unless a backup system is in place, files that are shared from the file server cannot be retrieved until the administrator repairs the network.

Security can be a double-edged sword. A network can provide an excellent means of security, yet fail to provide security because of the many variables involved. A network can be susceptible to hackers, viruses, and disgruntled workers. The security issues associated with networks will be discussed in detail in later chapters.

Network Classifications

The size and function of a network not only drives the required manpower, but dictates its classification as well. A *network classification* is the category of a network based on its physical size, management, and usage. Three commonly known classifications include local area network, metropolitan area network, and wide area network. A **local area network (LAN)** is a network that is usually confined to a single building and managed by a single entity. An example of a LAN is an office building. A **metropolitan area network (MAN)** consists of two or more LANs connected with private or public communication lined within the same geographic area—for example, a computer network used by governmental employees of an entire city. MANs are also typically managed by a single entity. A **wide area network (WAN)** consists of a large number of networks and PCs connected with private and public communication lines throughout many geographic areas; for example, computers used by the US government may be on a WAN.

While most professionals use the terms LAN, MAN, and WAN in practice, some organizations, such as CompTIA and their Network+ certification, further divide networks into many more categories. The first of these categories is *personal area network (PAN)*. A PAN is a small network, perhaps consisting of a single computer and mobile device. A *campus area network (CAN)* is a network spread across multiple buildings in the same geographical location, much like a college campus. Finally, a *global area network (GAN)* is any network that spans multiple countries, for example, the Internet.

Network Topologies

The physical arrangement of computers, computer-related devices, communication devices, and cabling in a network is referred to as **network topology**. The four major topologies are bus, ring, star, and mesh. Combining two or more of the four major topologies creates a hybrid topology.

The physical network topology tells you how the nodes are arranged and connected on a network. Recall that a *node* is any device attached to a network and given a network address that is capable of processing and forwarding data. Some of these devices could be a PC, hub, switch, router, server, and repeater. Computers on a network are called *hosts*, as demonstrated in Figure 1-2. In a wireless network, cabling is not used, and nodes do not have to be arranged in a set pattern; however, each network device in a wireless network is capable of processing and forwarding data.

Copyright Goodheart-Willcox Co., Inc.

Figure 1-2 A node denotes any device on the network that is capable of processing and forwarding data.

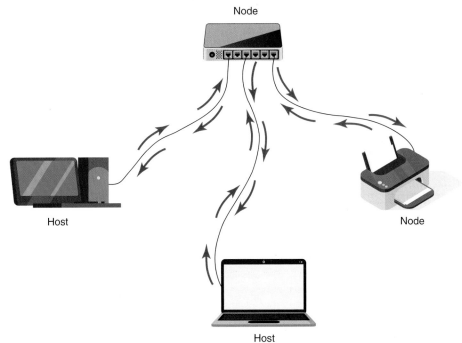

Node

Host

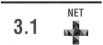

Node

Host

Clockwise from top: Vadim Ermak/Shutterstock.com; Vectors Bang/Shutterstock.com, Jemastock/Shutterstock.com; RedlineVector/Shutterstock.com; Goodheart-Willcox Publisher

Wireless technology is a popular form of linking networks. For these reasons, we will include wireless in our discussion of topologies.

It should be noted that topology can be physical or logical. *Physical topology* refers to the positioning of connectivity devices and cable. *Logical topology* refers to how the packets are routed through the network. In many cases, the physical and logical topologies will be the same. For example, a modern star physical topology will likely have a star logical topology, but in some cases, the physical and logical topology will differ. For example, in the older token ring technology, the physical topology was a star, but the logical topology was a ring.

As you read the following sections on each topology, note that each one is a re-sult of the type of media and network device used to form the network. The following sections briefly mention the type of media and network devices used in each topology. You will learn more about network media and devices later in this chapter and in the following chapters.

3.1 NET

Bus Topology

A **bus topology** uses a single cable or conductor to connect all nodes on the network. Look at Figure 1-3. Each node is connected to a common cable. A bus topology uses the least amount of cable when compared to other topologies. The bus topology is often used as a backbone to link other topologies. A *backbone* serves as a common path and often employs high-speed network cable such as fiber-optic. Backbones will be discussed in detail in Chapter 18.

A bus topology that uses coaxial cable requires a terminating resistor at each cable end. A terminating resistor absorbs the transmitted signals when they reach the end of the bus. Without the terminating resistor, the transmitted signals would deflect, causing the data to be distorted. Terminating resistors are covered in detail in Chapter 2.

Tech Tip

The term *backbone* may change somewhat when applied to specific types of network topology. In the bus topology, it is the common connecting cable. In a star topology, it describes the cable that connects different portions of the network, or different LANs.

Copyright Goodheart-Willcox Co., Inc.

Star Topology

A **star topology** involves running cables from each node to connect a single point, as shown in Figure 1-4. The center of the star is usually a device known as a hub. A *hub* provides a common electrical connection to all nodes in the star topology. Each network cable plugs into a hub connection called an **access port**. Hubs are discussed in detail in a later section of this chapter.

Figure 1-3 In a bus topology, all nodes connect to a common cable.

Bus Topology

Common cable

From left to right: RedlineVector/Shutterstock.com; Vectors Bang/Shutterstock.com; Goodheart-Willcox Publisher

Figure 1-4 In a star topology, all nodes connect to a central point.

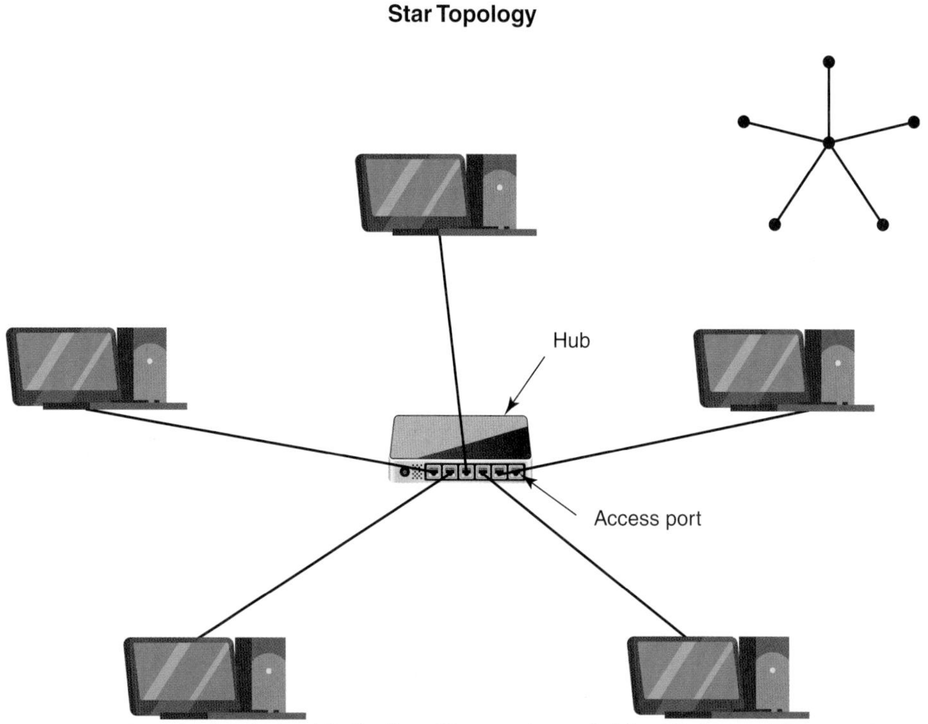

Star Topology

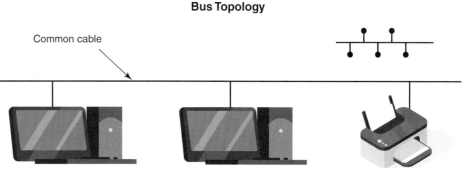

Hub

Access port

(workstation icon) RedlineVector/Shutterstock.com; (hub icon) Vadim Ermak/Shutterstock.com;
Goodheart-Willcox Publisher

Ring Topology

The **ring topology** consists of a single cable that runs continuously from node to node, as illustrated in Figure 1-5. The cable begins and ends at the first node in the network, and the ring must remain unbroken. A ring is essentially a bus with the ends connected.

Copyright Goodheart-Willcox Co., Inc.

Figure 1-5 In a ring topology, all nodes connect to a cable, forming a circle or ring.

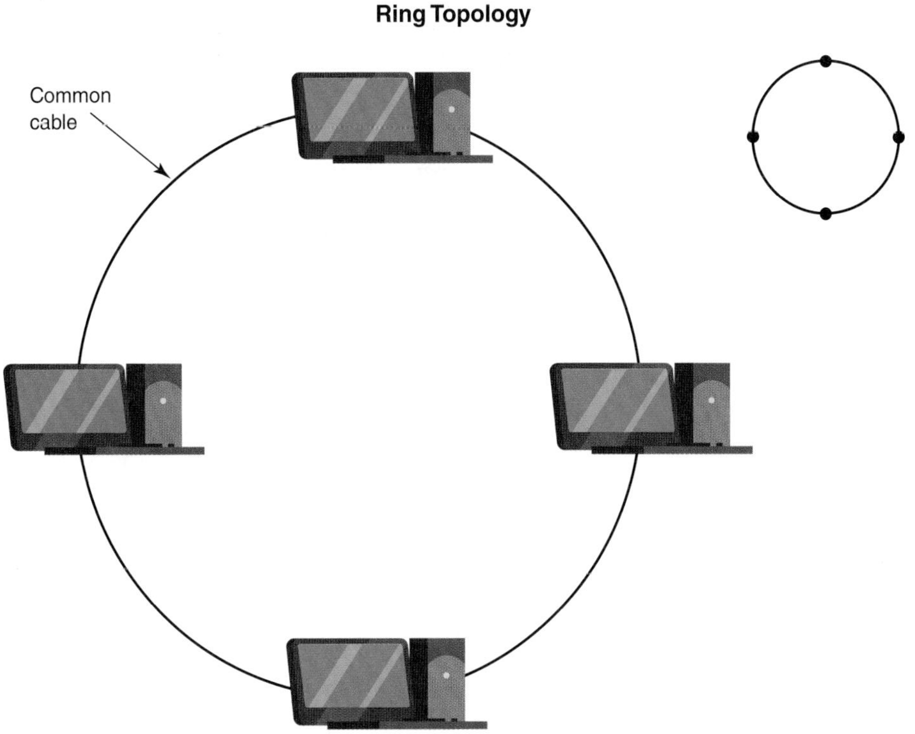

Ring Topology

Common cable

(workstation icon) RedlineVector/Shutterstock.com; Goodheart-Willcox Publisher

The classic example of ring topology is the token ring. With a *token ring*, each node is wired directly to a central location called a multistation access unit (MAU). A **multistation access unit (MAU)** allows for the quick connection and disconnection of token ring cables while maintaining the logic of the ring topology. In other words, the MAU keeps the circle intact when one of the token ring cables is removed. In a sense, an MAU functions similar to, but not exactly like, a hub.

Switches at the access ports maintain the ring, as illustrated in Figure 1-6. The unused ports act as closed switches, which maintain the logic of the ring topology. When a cable is plugged into the access port, the switch is opened. The pair of wires inside the cable run to and from the node and MAU. The integrity of the ring is maintained.

Tech Tip

MAU is also referred to as a *MSAU (multi station access unit).*

Mesh Topology

In a **mesh topology**, each node on the network connects to every other node on the network. This is the most reliable network topology and the most expensive because of the additional cost of cabling and equipment. A mesh is only practical when the network is essential to the day-to-day functioning of the client and cost is not a barrier. A network consisting of multiple servers may use a mesh topology to ensure the reliability of the servers. See Figure 1-7. In some cases, network administrators opt for a *partial mesh* rather than a *full mesh*. A partial mesh has only some of the nodes connected to multiple other nodes.

Wireless Topology

As the name implies, a **wireless topology** does not use cabling. It uses either infrared light or radio transmission to communicate between nodes. Infrared light requires line-of-sight for nodes. This means that the infrared light beam between the

Figure 1-6 A MAU maintains ring integrity while cables are connected to and disconnected from the network.

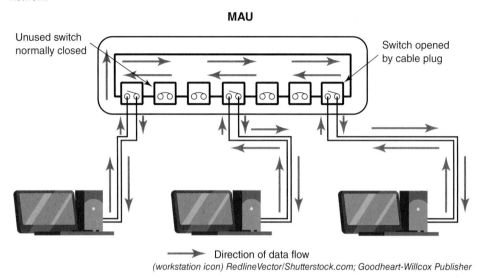

MAU

Unused switch
normally closed

Switch opened
by cable plug

→ Direction of data flow

(workstation icon) RedlineVector/Shutterstock.com; Goodheart-Willcox Publisher

Figure 1-7 In a mesh topology, each node is connected to each of the other nodes. The number of cable paths rapidly increases as more nodes are added to the mesh topology.

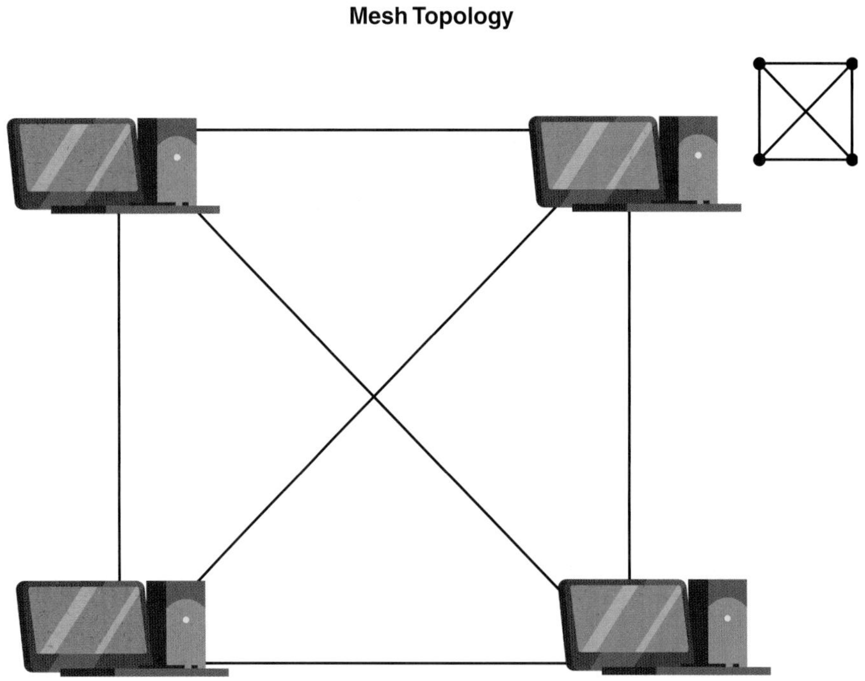

Mesh Topology

(workstation icon) RedlineVector/Shutterstock.com; Goodheart-Willcox Publisher

nodes cannot be interrupted in order for the nodes to communicate properly on the network. Radio transmission can experience difficulties caused by building structure and interference generated by other electrical equipment such as radios, motors, welders, and microwave ovens.

Despite these disadvantages, a wireless topology does have many advantages. For example, it is the only answer for communicating with vehicles. The transmission can originate from a building antenna or from a satellite, similar to the one shown

Copyright Goodheart-Willcox Co., Inc.

in Figure 1-8A. Using cable to connect two buildings could be very expensive and time-consuming when compared to installing a wireless network. Two buildings separated by a metropolitan street or a river or which need immediate connection can be connected through wireless technologyas shown in Figure 1-8B. A wireless topology provides a quick way to reconfigure a computer arrangement, whereas moving cables to rearrange computers may not be as easy.

Figure 1-8 A wireless topology allows nodes to connect to one another in areas where cabling would be impossible or difficult. A—A security vehicle receives a transmission from an antenna located on top of a building. B—Wireless technology connecting a network in one building with a network in another building.

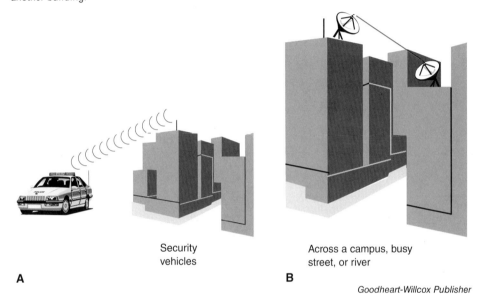

Security vehicles

Across a campus, busy street, or river

A

B

Goodheart-Willcox Publisher

Wireless communication also uses cell topology. A **cell** is an area that is served by a radio access tower. The towers are configured throughout an area and divide the area into zones known as *cells*. A similar technology is used for cellular telephone communication.

Hybrid Topology

As a network grows, it typically changes from a simple network topology, such as a bus or a star, into a hybrid topology. A **hybrid topology** is a mixture of topologies. Notice the different sections of the network in Figure 1-9. Two star topologies, a bus topology, and a ring topology are connected together.

Other Topologies

In addition to the four major topologies, plus wireless and hybrid, there are three others sometimes used in wide area networks. These topologies include tree, point-to-point, and point-to-multipoint. A *tree* is created when two or more star topologies are connected together by a common backbone, as shown in Figure 1-10. A point-to-point topology is simply two points, usually quite a distance from each other, that have a connection between them—for example, a company with offices in Chicago and Seattle that are connected on the same network. Point-to-multipoint topologies simply have one central point connected to many points.

Network+ Note ✚

Point-to-point and point-to-multipoint were first identified as topologies for the CompTIA Network+ Certification exam in 2009. *Point-to-point topology* generally refers to two nodes connected directly to each other either by cable or by wireless means. A *point-to-multipoint topology* is when one node is connected directly to two or more nodes. For example, when one computer broadcasts wireless signals to multiple computers.

Figure 1-9 This hybrid topology consists of a ring topology, bus topology, and two star topologies.

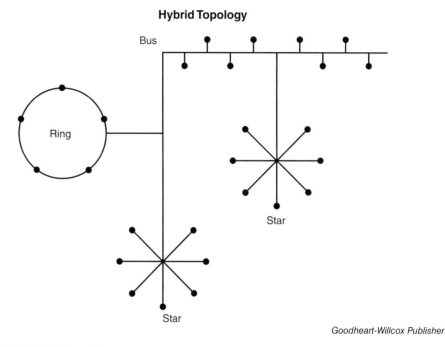

Hybrid Topology

Goodheart-Willcox Publisher

Figure 1-10 Example of a tree topology.

Tree Topology

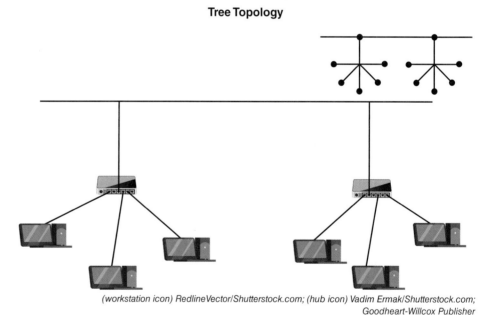

(workstation icon) RedlineVector/Shutterstock.com; (hub icon) Vadim Ermak/Shutterstock.com;
Goodheart-Willcox Publisher

Basic Network Administration Models

Once a network topology is established, an administration model must be selected and implemented. The phrase *network administration model* refers to how a network is designed and administered. The purpose and topology of a network often dictates which model is needed. In general, there are two basic network administration models: client/server and peer-to-peer.

Copyright Goodheart-Willcox Co., Inc.

Client/Server Network

A **client/server network** consists of computers connected via a network to one or more servers, as demonstrated in Figure 1-11. As its name implies, a **server** provides services to networked computers or *clients*. Typical services include security, database applications, data storage, Internet access, web page hosting, and e-mail.

Tech Tip

The term *server* can be used in two ways, which can be very confusing to a networking novice. The first and most obvious way is when identifying a physical server. The second is when a server is identified by a service such as a proxy server, web server, or gateway. In other words, a single network server may be referred to by many different names and be used for more than one purpose.

Figure 1-11 A client/server model has a central computer called a *server*, which controls network security and user access to hardware, software, and programs.

Client/Server Network

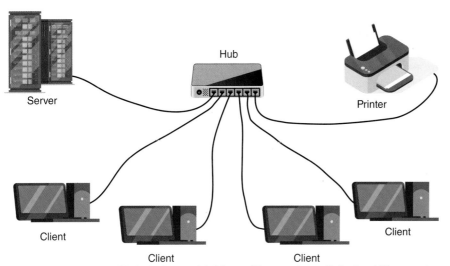

Clockwise from top-left: fullvector/Shutterstock.com; Vadim Ermak/Shutterstock.com; Vectors Bang/Shutterstock.com; RedlineVector/Shutterstock.com; Goodheart-Willcox Publisher

A client/server network has an overall administrator who controls access to the network and its shares. This person is called the **network administrator**. The methodology used to administer a client/server network is called centralized administration. **Centralized administration** is an administration model in which the administrator does not have to go to each server to perform administrative tasks. Rather, the administrator can view and access all resource and security information from a central location. Storing this information in a common database or directory makes this possible. It is the only practical solution for controlling a large number of computers. An administrator accesses this database to perform administrative tasks, such as adding a user or a share. Two examples of such databases are Microsoft's Active Directory Domain Services (AD DS) and Net IQ's eDirectory. AD DS is covered in Chapter 7.

A server may provide a multitude of services, such as access to files, the Internet, and mail services, or it may provide a single function. A server that provides a single function is referred to as a **dedicated server**. Some types of dedicated servers include:

- **file servers**, which are used to store data files that can be accessed by a client;

- **print servers**, which coordinate printing activities between clients and printers;

- **administrative servers**, which administer network security and activities; and

- **database servers**, which contain data files and software programs that query the data.

Copyright Goodheart-Willcox Co., Inc.

The design of a server is similar to that of a standard PC. In fact, many small networks use a standard PC as a server. For large networks, the server is an enhanced PC. It may contain two or more CPUs and ten times or more the normal amount of RAM found in a typical PC. The additional RAM and CPUs allow information to be processed faster, which is useful when the server has many client requests to service at one time. A server is usually equipped with several hard drives. The server may also have one or more duplicate sets of hard drives used to back up the data saved on the first set of hard drives. Backup systems are key to network success. They are covered, along with server hardware, in greater depth in Chapter 9.

Peer-to-Peer Network

All computers are considered peers or equals in a **peer-to-peer network**. As shown in Figure 1-12, there is no designated server in this model. A computer in a peer-to-peer network can serve as both a client and a server. Each computer is considered equal because each computer's user has equal authority to share his or her computer's resources with other users on the network. Peer-to-peer networks are often referred to as *workgroups*. Many small networks are constructed as a peer-to-peer network. This type of network is usually inexpensive and easy to install.

Tech Tip

Query is a term used to describe extracting data from a database system. Microsoft SQL Server is a typical database query software package.

Figure 1-12 In a simple peer-to-peer network, each computer has equal powers, or administration. Each computer controls the sharing of its data and hardware resources.

Peer-to-Peer Network

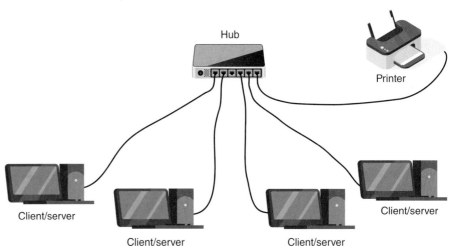

Clockwise from top-middle: Vadim Ermak/Shutterstock.com; Vectors Bang/Shutterstock.com; RedlineVector/Shutterstock.com; Goodheart-Willcox Publisher

In a peer-to-peer network, a computer's user may determine and control which files, drives, and printers will be shared. The computer's user may also determine and control access to the share and designate a password to use the share. Because administration is spread across the entire network, the methodology used to administer a peer-to-peer network is called **decentralized administration**. Administration of this type of network can be very difficult. Without a common database, it is often difficult to keep track of all the available users, resources, and access rights. This model is usually used on small networks of fewer than 25 computers.

The advantages of a peer-to-peer network, however, is that it is inexpensive to install and simple to administer as long as it remains small. No special, costly networking software is required for operation as it is with the client/server model. A simple Microsoft peer-to-peer network can be assembled using only Windows 95 or later.

Copyright Goodheart-Willcox Co., Inc.

Cloud Computing

Cloud computing is a very popular topic today. There are many services available through cloud computing. These services include Software as a Service (SaaS), Platform as a Service (PaaS), and Infrastructure as a Service (IaaS). **Software as a Service (SaaS)** delivers specific applications in a virtualized manner. The software is licensed to the end user on a subscription basis and is hosted centrally from the licensor. This type of software is often referred to as *on-demand software*. **Platform as a Service (PaaS)** provides access to operating systems in the same manner as SaaS. It allows the users to access a fully configured, patched and updated, version of the desired platform. PaaS can be delivered in two ways: through a public cloud-based service or as a private service inside the user's network and firewall. **Infrastructure as a Service (IaaS)** provides at least part of the network infrastructure, for example, servers, in a virtualized manner. IaaS is generally used in virtual environments

	NET
1.7	✚

Cloud Categories

Cloud computing uses geographically distributed servers. In some cases, the servers are in other countries. Cloud delivery is often categorized as private, public, or hybrid. *Private clouds* are those used specifically by a single organization without offering the services to an outside party. *Public clouds* are defined by the National Institute of Standards and Technology (NIST) as simply clouds that offer their infrastructure or services to either the general public or at least a large industry group.

Hybrid clouds combine the elements of a private and public cloud. These are essentially private clouds that have some limited public access. Hybrid clouds, or community clouds, are essentially a midway point between private and public clouds. These are systems wherein several organizations share a cloud for specific community needs. For example, several computer companies might join to create a cloud devoted to common security issues.

Cloud Connectivity

Connectivity to a cloud or other virtual resource is often accomplished over traditional network connections. This means users can use a computer on a network and access cloud-based resources through traditional network media. Given that clouds aggregate data, it is necessary to pay particular attention to security in a cloud. Two cloud-based security standards include ISO 27017, which is a cloud-security standard, and ISO 27018, which is a standard for privacy of customer data in a cloud.

Software-Defined Networking

A relatively new concept is software-defined networking (SDN). Virtualization, in one form or another, has become quite common. Using a virtual machine that hosts a different operating system is widespread, and various vendors allow users to have virtualized servers. A newer trend is for an entire network to be virtualized. This means the devices, servers, and everything associated with a network is virtual.

	NET
1.3	✚

Network Operating Systems (NOS)

A **network operating system (NOS)** provides a communication system between the computers, printers, and other intelligent hardware that exists on the network. Since a network can have machines running various operating systems, you may wonder which operating system is the network operating system. That is actually easy to

Copyright Goodheart-Willcox Co., Inc.

determine. The operating system running on the network's domain controller is the network operating system. Some common network operating systems in use are Windows Server 2016, Windows Server 2012, Unix, and Linux.

All networks provide communication between different operating systems, different brands of hardware, and various ages of equipment. A network operating system is also composed of software programs that provide for security, user identity, remote access, printer sharing, and other services. In reality, the network operating system *is* the network; everything else is hardware.

Network Communication

Network communication is the exchange of data and commands between network nodes. The data can range from simple text to an elaborate multimedia presentation containing sound and video. The network also communicates commands allowing users to log on, share hardware, and check conditions of the network system. Network communication can be very complicated and is based on network protocols. Network protocols determine how data is exchanged at the packet level.

Data is transmitted across a network in the form of digital signals, or pulses. Digital signals are rapidly changing levels of voltage often represented in binary terms as *1*s and *0*s. See Figure 1-13 for a visual representation of this comparison. For data to be sent across a network from node to node, a common scheme of packaging must be decided.

Figure 1-13 Data is transferred across a network as a series of digital signals, or pulses. These signals are sometimes expressed as binary numbers (1, 0) or as hexadecimal values (1B, F5, etc.). The way the data is presented is determined by the technology used.

12 3C 45 F5 BC 2E AD A2 78 91 9C 2A 34 53 5C FF D3 DC

Hexadecimal code

1010000111001001100101000010110110000110001111 1000100100

Binary code

Digital pulses

Goodheart-Willcox Publisher

Data is often divided into smaller segments. The data segments are given a sequence number and combined in a packet with other information, such as routing and error-checking code. The packet sequence number allows the receiving computer to reassemble the message in the order it was transmitted. An error-checking code ensures the data was not corrupted. Other information that may be coded into the packet is the packet's destination, the address of the node that originated the packet, and the time it was originated. The type of data and information contained in the packet varies depending on the protocol used. Protocols are discussed in the following section of this chapter and are revisited throughout the textbook.

Protocols

For intelligent hardware to communicate across a network, they must use the same protocol. A **protocol** is a group of computer programs that handle packet formatting and control data transmission. A protocol can also be defined as a set of rules

Tech Tip

The term *protocol* is often used as a label for a software program, a networking standard, or specification. Many times the exact definition depends on the context of the information to which it is applied.

Copyright Goodheart-Willcox Co., Inc.

governing communication between devices on a network. Some of the things a protocol is responsible for include the following:

- Determining how devices identify each other
- Determining the method of data exchange
- Determining the size of each packet
- Determining the timing for packet transmission
- Compressing data
- Determining the signal to be used to end a session
- Establishing the end of a session
- Providing and establishing error checking

A protocol determines how two computers will exchange data as well as how the data is packaged, sent, and processed. There are protocols for every type of network communication, including e-mail, web page, remote-connection, and many other types of protocols that will be examined throughout this text. For now, remember that a protocol is a set of communication rules between two or more devices.

Another function of a protocol can be to modify packets for the sake of the network. For example, a protocol may compress a packet's contents to allow for faster transmission rates. It also dictates when the communication session will end and what signal will denote this.

Protocols usually have some error-checking capabilities. Error checking ensures the information received is complete and is reassembled in the correct order. Some network systems, such as the Internet, are very complex. The packets may not be routed to their destination using the same route. Consequently, packets may arrive at different times and would be garbled when reassembled if not for error checking.

For now, understand that any activity you take on a network is governed by one or more protocols. There are protocols for e-mail, for web traffic, for connecting remotely, and any other network activity.

TCP/IP

Transmission Control Protocol/Internet Protocol (TCP/IP) was developed by the Defense Advanced Research Project Agency (DARPA) in the early 1970s and was designed to support communication over the Internet. TCP/IP has become the default protocol used to communicate across the Internet and on local area networks.

The name *TCP/IP* consists of two separate protocols: TCP and IP. TCP/IP is a comprehensive suite of protocols, each serving different functions. For example, TCP/IP network communication consists of mainly three protocols: IP, TCP, and UDP. *IP* routes information across a network by the use of IP addresses; *TCP* sends a packet to a destination and waits for a confirmation that the packet arrived intact; and *UDP* sends packets without confirmation of their arrival.

Another protocol in the TCP/IP suite is the *Network Time Protocol (NTP)*. NTP synchronizes time between network devices. All devices must have the same time reference to ensure security in the network. A time reference should be set in the domain controller as opposed to a hardware clock. This will help keep all devices in synchronization. Time can be examined to determine if a packet has been tampered with. The *File Transfer Protocol (FTP)* is used to upload and download files to web servers. *Simple Mail Transfer Protocol (SMTP)* is designed to send e-mail.

There are two versions of the TCP/IP protocol: TCP/IPv4 and TCP/IPv6. The lower case *v* represents *version*. TCP/IPv4 was adopted as a standard in 1981 and is still in use to support Internet communication. TCP/IPv6 was first introduced as

1.1 NET

1.1, 1.8, 5.5 NET

Copyright Goodheart-Willcox Co., Inc.

an official standard in 1995 but was slowly adopted and put into service by network operating software designers. TCP/IPv6 and TCP/IPv4 coexist today. For example, Windows 7, Windows 8, Windows 10, and Windows Server 2016 operating systems use TCP/IPv4 as the primary Internet communication protocol but use TCP/IPv6 as the primary protocol to communicate on a local area network, Figure 1-14. The main reason TCP/IPv4 is still in use is to ensure downward compatibility with older network devices that do not recognize the IPv6 protocol.

Figure 1-14 Windows 10 **Ethernet Properties** dialog box. Notice that both TCP/IPv4 and TCP/IPv6 are installed by default.

Goodheart-Willcox Publisher

ATM

NET
2.5

Asynchronous transfer mode (ATM) is a protocol designed especially for transmitting data, voice, and video. Data is segmented into packets containing 53 bytes each, which are switched between any two nodes in a system. ATM originally supported rates ranging from 1.5 Mbps to 622 Mbps, but later improvements increased these rates to over 2.0 Gbps. Transferring massive amounts of data between two points using existing technology such as copper-wire systems requires a protocol designed to accomplish this. Other existing protocols at the time would not meet this requirement. ATM is widely used in the backend network processes of large Internet service providers and media and cable television companies.

LLDP

The *Link-Layer Discovery Protocol (LLDP)* standard was released by the Institute of Electrical and Electronic Engineers (IEEE) in 2005 that allows network devices, such as computers, routers, and servers, to exchange information automatically. Microsoft first incorporated LLDP into Windows Vista and then later included it in Windows 10 and Windows Server 2016.

Tech Tip

Usually if you see the words "Discovery Protocol," the protocol is most likely a variation of LLDP. Many early implementations of LLDP were referred to as *Neighbor Discovery Protocol or Neighborhood Discovery Protocol.*

Copyright Goodheart-Willcox Co., Inc.

Microsoft refers to their implementation of LLDP as two separate protocols: *Link-Layer Topology Discovery Mapper I/O Driver* and *Link-Layer Topology Discovery Responder.* The LLTD Mapper I/O Driver sends out packets containing information about the computer. The LLTD Responder responds to inquiries. Together, the two versions of LLDP allow the computer to construct a network map. These maps were visible in Windows operating systems through Windows 7. As of the release of Windows 8, users must have third-party software to create such a visual representation of their networks. All network devices capable of using LLDP can exchange information, thus creating a map of logical locations of each device. A dashed line represents a wireless connection; a solid line represents a wired connection. The paths are not to scale but rather logically arranged to represent their location in the network. LLDP will be discussed in more detail in Chapter 6.

NetBEUI and NetBIOS

NetBEUI and NetBIOS were common protocols that were an integral part of the Microsoft network operating system. NetBIOS was an early Microsoft network standard and protocol. One of its specifications was limiting network device names to 15 characters. Even today, Microsoft limits computer names to 15 characters.

NetBEUI was installed by default on Microsoft operating systems earlier than Windows XP. Be aware that you can still encounter the term *NetBIOS* when configuring network adapters in Windows 7, Windows 8, Windows 10, and Windows Server 2008/2012/2016. You may also encounter references to NetBIOS and NetBEUI in other references and especially in practice questions and study guides found on the Internet.

Notice that in Figure 1-15, options are listed for the NetBIOS protocol in the **Windows Advanced TCP/IP Settings** dialog box. Windows 10 and Windows Server 2016 have the same advanced TCP/IP settings for NetBIOS over TCP/IP.

Some protocols can be a part of networking for many years after they are considered obsolete. Microsoft has always preserved options, even older, potentially obsolete ones, so that its operating system will retain downward compatibility with older Microsoft operating systems.

> **Network+ Note** ✚
>
> Protocols and network technology rapidly changes. NetBIOS and NetBEUI are no longer a valid CompTIA topic but still have influence on today's network and computer technology.

Network Addresses

A **network address** is a unique identifier for a node on a computer network. Think of the area code of your phone number or your street address. The primary function of each is to provide information about your location. A network address is similar. Specific information about a device on a network can be obtained solely by viewing a network address. There are two types of network addresses used today: *MAC addresses* and *IP addresses.*

A **media access control (MAC) address** is the physical identification number of a device on a network. This number is a six-byte, or 48-bit, hexadecimal number, such as 00 C0 12 2B 14 C5. It is a sublayer of layer two of the OSI model, which will be discussed later in this chapter. If you open your command prompt, enter ipconfig/ all on the command line, and press the **Enter** key, the *physical address* you see is the MAC address. The problem with MAC addresses is that they do not display what network to which the target computer is connected. In this regard, a MAC address is similar to an area code; it can provide general information but not a specific location. The MAC address has three bytes that provide information about the manufacturer who created that network card and three bytes identifying the card, but there is nothing to indicate the target computer's network. For this reason, MAC addresses are only used to direct traffic in an internal network.

Figure 1-15 The Windows 10 **Advanced TCP/IP Settings** dialog box includes settings for the NetBIOS protocol to ensure downward compatibility with older Windows operating systems.

Goodheart-Willcox Publisher

The second type of address is an Internet protocol (IP) address. An **Internet protocol (IP) address** uniquely identifies each node on a network. It is a 32-bit address with part of it designating the network and another part designating the node. This is comparable to a street address in that it provides a specific location. We will examine IP addresses in great detail later in this book. For now, just keep in mind that an IP address provides a network address as well as a node address, so it is routable across the Internet.

Network Media and Devices

A variety of media and devices are associated with networking. This section contains a brief description of each. Some of the network devices presented here may be difficult to distinguish because they are similar in function; however, their differences will become more apparent as protocols and the OSI model are further investigated. Also, each media type and network device is revisited in later chapters, and more detail regarding their use and operation is presented.

Media

Media is a general term that identifies the material used to transport packets and data streams between nodes. There are several broad classifications of media. Each type of media has advantages and disadvantages. The most common media is **copper-core cable**, which consists of a copper wire surrounded by plastic or synthetic insulation. There are many different types of copper-core cable used in networking. These types are discussed in depth in Chapter 2.

Copyright Goodheart-Willcox Co., Inc.

Another type of media, referred to as **fiber-optic cable**, uses a glass or clear, plastic core rather than copper. The core is thin and flexible. Under normal circumstances, it will not break. Fiber-optic cable carries pulses of light that represent commands and data.

In wireless networks, radio waves carry digital signals between various pieces of equipment in the network. Radio waves are the media, and transmission is similar to cell phone technology. Wireless technology is commonly used where cables are impractical, such as connecting a computer installed in a police car to a main network system.

Infrared light is another form of media in which an infrared beam is used to transport a digital signal. Infrared transmission uses a transmitter/receiver unit at each end of the transmission path. A transmitter converts the digital signal into a series of infrared light flashes and sends them to a receiver unit. The receiver unit decodes the signal. Infrared light transmission is similar to the remote control used for televisions.

Media Converter

A **media converter** changes one type of electrical signal into another or interfaces one cable type to another. For example, a media converter can connect an Ethernet 100-Mbps copper-core cable to an Ethernet 1-Gbps fiber-optic cable. The term *media converter* can also apply to other network equipment, such as a bridge or switch. This type of equipment often performs more than one function. Some media converters may even act as a repeater.

2.2   NET

Network Interface Card

A **network interface card (NIC)** contains the electronic components needed to send and receive a digital signal. A network card is known by many other names such as a *network host adapter*, *network expansion card*, and *network adapter card*. Look at Figure 1-16 to see what a typical network interface card looks like.

The network interface card fits into one of the motherboard slots inside a PC. This provides a way for the PC to connect to the network media. The network interface card must be equipped with the suitable connector for the type of network media used. Network connectors are discussed in Chapters 2 and 3.

A network interface card must first match the physical communication requirements of the network for which it is installed, such as Ethernet, Token Ring, wireless, or high speed FDDI. Next, a driver must be installed so that the computer can communicate with the network interface card. A **driver** is a software program that allows a PC to communicate with and transfer data to and from computer hardware, such as the network interface card. The network interface card must also be configured with a protocol, such as TCP/IP or ATM, to support network communication. The network interface card may be configured for a combination of more than one protocol. The exact requirements will become apparent as you progress through this course. Remember that a protocol is a set of rules for communication between two nodes. In general, all network interface cards in a LAN must be configured with the same protocol to communicate with each other.

After the network interface card driver and protocol are installed, the PC must be uniquely identified. There are two types of identification used on a typical network: a physical ID and a logical ID. The network card contains the physical ID, or MAC address. Recall that the first three bytes of a MAC address identify the manufacturer of the network interface card, and the second three bytes uniquely identify

Copyright Goodheart-Willcox Co., Inc.

Figure 1-16 A typical Ethernet network card equipped with an RJ-45 connector.

Courtesy of Cisco Systems, Inc.

the card. Together, these two sets of numbers give the network card its own unique, physical identification. The manufacturer stores the MAC address inside an electronic chip on the network interface card.

A **logical identification** is provided by the technician at the time of installation. It is usually a name that uniquely identifies the computer on the network. For example, the name *Station24* would be given to a computer that is the 24th computer to be added to a group of networked devices.

Repeater

As digital signals travel across copper wire, the signals lose strength and become distorted. The loss of signal strength is called **attenuation**. To reshape and regenerate the strength of the digital signal, a repeater is often used. A **repeater** amplifies or reshapes the weak signal into its original strength and form. See Figure 1-17. A repeater allows the network media to exceed its recommended maximum length.

Hub

NET
2.2

A **hub** is a central connection point where all network cables are concentrated, as shown in Figure 1-18. A hub is often called a *concentrator* and is classified as either passive or active. A **passive hub** simply acts as a central connection point for network cables. Packets transmitted from one node are passed to all nodes connected to the passive hub and through the hub to other sections of the network. Passive hubs are part of network history and no longer exist.

An **active hub**, sometimes called an *intelligent hub* or *switch*, is an enhanced passive hub. It is designed with a power supply. Active hubs not only act as central connection points for network cabling, they also regenerate digital signals similar to a repeater. An active hub can also determine whether a packet should remain in the isolated section of the network or pass through to another section of the network.

Copyright Goodheart-Willcox Co., Inc.

Figure 1-17 Digital signals lose their strength as they travel along a wire. A repeater is used to regenerate a signal so that it is returned to its original strength and form.

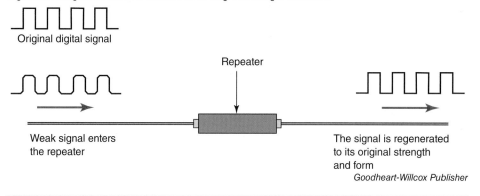

Original digital signal

Repeater

Weak signal enters
the repeater

The signal is regenerated
to its original strength
and form

Goodheart-Willcox Publisher

Figure 1-18 A hub is commonly used to connect computers on a network.

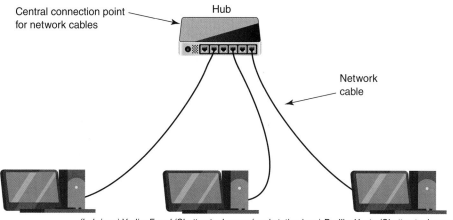

Central connection point
for network cables

Hub

Network
cable

(hub icon) Vadim Ermak/Shutterstock.com; (workstation icon) RedlineVector/Shutterstock.com;
Goodheart-Willcox Publisher

Look at Figure 1-19. *Station3* attempts to communicate with *Station1*. The intelligent hub does not allow the packets to be transmitted through the hub to the other areas of the network. The hub directs the packets to only those computers that are attached to it. Active hubs are used to reduce excessive data transmission on a network. A network with an excessive number of collisions can be broken into segments by using active hubs. This can reduce the number of packets transmitted over the entire network. However, this will only reduce the traffic if there are a significant number of transmissions to computers in the same area.

Gateway

Today, local area networks use the TCP/IP protocol like the Internet does, so the definition of gateway has changed. The accepted definition of **gateway** is a device that connects a local area network to the Internet.

In the early days of networking, the Internet used the TCP/IP protocol for communication, but local area networks used proprietary protocols such as NetBEUI and IPX/SPX. The local area network packets would need to be translated or encapsulated before they could be carried across the Internet to their destination. The network device that connected the local area network to the Internet was referred to as the *gateway* and the definition referred to translating or connecting two different

Network+ Note ✚

A server can be classified as a gateway if it provides gateway services to its clients.

Copyright Goodheart-Willcox Co., Inc.

Figure 1-19 In this example, *Station3* communicates with *Station1*. Rather than sending packets to other areas of the network, the active hub directs the packets to only those computers that are attached to it.

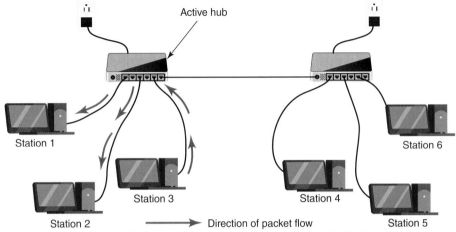

(hub icon) Vadim Ermak/Shutterstock.com; (workstation icon) RedlineVector/Shutterstock.com;
Goodheart-Willcox Publisher

networks that operate using different protocols. Most gateways today are part of a router, and the device is often called a *gateway router*.

Bridge

A **bridge** can be used to divide the network into smaller segments, reducing the chance of collisions. Networks, such as Ethernet, broadcast packets throughout the entire segment of the network. When two packets are sent across the network at the same time, a collision occurs, destroying each packet. As a network becomes larger and more and more packets are transmitted across the network, it is likely that the packets will collide and be destroyed. A bridge controls the flow of network traffic between two segments by reading the destination of a network packet. The bridge either allows a packet to pass through to the other segment or restricts the packet to the originating segment.

In Figure 1-20, a bridge is used to control network traffic. The network has been divided into two segments: one segment is for the business management department, and the other segment is for the engineering department. The engineering department is responsible for designing new products and for making drawings of the product's parts. The engineers often share the drawings with others in the engineering department. The business management segment contains executives and marketing personnel. By the nature of the arrangement, most of the packets broadcast in the engineering segment are between the engineers' computers. Most of the packets broadcast in the business management segment are between the executives' and marketing personnel's computers. Only when the business management and engineering departments wish to communicate do packets pass through the bridge.

Switch

A **switch** filters network traffic or creates subnetworks from a larger network. Some LANs can easily have hundreds, or even thousands, of nodes. A switch can be used to divide the transmission paths to improve data delivery. Switches direct traffic based on MAC addresses.

Tech Tip

The basic switch functions at layer 2 of the OSI model, whereas a multilayer switch functions at higher layers of the OSI model.

NET

2.2

Copyright Goodheart-Willcox Co., Inc.

A switch is a means for directing network traffic to the appropriate machine. In Figure 1-21, you can see that all the PCs are connected to one central point: the switch. The switch acts similar to a hub by providing a central connection point for the PCs. A switch also acts like a bridge by limiting traffic on the network. However, a bridge physically isolates segments of a network, while a switch isolates PCs into network segments, thus creating a virtual network. Virtual networks are

Figure 1-20 A bridge can be used to divide a network into segments. This reduces the amount of overall packet movement on the network media.

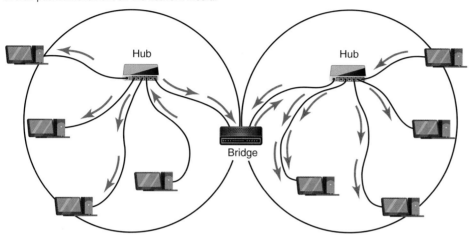

Business Management Segment   Engineering Segment
(hub and bridge icon) Vadim Ermak/Shutterstock.com; (workstation icon) RedlineVector/Shutterstock.com;
Goodheart-Willcox Publisher

Figure 1-21 A switch is similar to a bridge in that it can isolate packets. It is similar to a hub in that it acts as a central connection point. However, a switch can do more than a bridge or a hub. It can be used to create virtual networks.

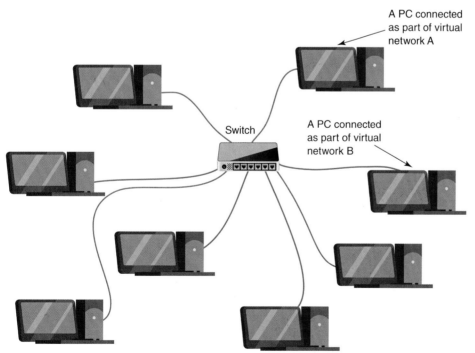

(switch icon) Vadim Ermak/Shutterstock.com; (workstation icon) RedlineVector/Shutterstock.com;
Goodheart-Willcox Publisher

Copyright Goodheart-Willcox Co., Inc.

configured by programming information into the switch, which permits the packets to only flow between designated nodes. By only allowing the packets to flow between the designated nodes, a virtual network within a network is created. The term *virtual*, when applied to networking, refers to a simulated network, as opposed to a physical one.

Multilayer Switch

NET

2.3, 5.2

A **multilayer switch** is an enhanced switch designed to perform more than basic switch functions. For example, a basic switch makes decisions about routing packets based on IP addresses. A multilayer switch can make decisions about routing a packet based on packet content. It can inspect the content of a packet to determine the type of material being downloaded. If a user is downloading a vast number of multimedia packets containing video or music content, the switch can limit the amount of network bandwidth allocated to that user. A bandwidth tester can be used to determine how much bandwidth a given user has available.

Router

NET

2.2, 3.4

A **router** navigates packets across large networks, such as the Internet, using the most efficient route, as demonstrated in Figure 1-22. A router maintains a table of information containing the location of other routers and their identification. Routers are typically installed between LANs, but may be installed inside a LAN if traffic conditions warrant their installation. Routers transfer data packets across WANs using the TCP/IP protocol-addressing scheme. TCP/IP is the standard protocol used for WANs and LANs. Routers direct traffic based in the destination IP address.

Figure 1-22 Routers are used to transfer packets across small and large networks. The Internet uses thousands of routers to route packets across the United States and the world.

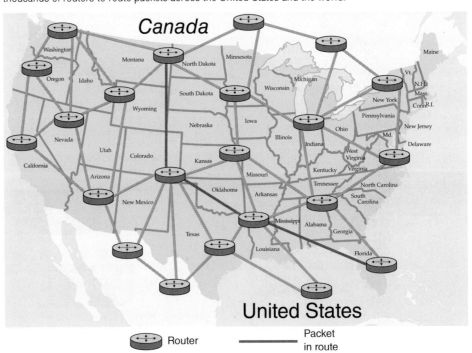

Goodheart-Willcox Publisher

Copyright Goodheart-Willcox Co., Inc.

Brouter

A **brouter** combines router and bridge functions. The brouter functions as a bridge by restricting or passing packets to other sections of a LAN based on the destination MAC address. It functions as a router by forwarding packets based on the destination IP address. The main difference between a router and a brouter is that a router typically provides many more functions than a brouter.

Standards and Organizations

A **standard** is a set of recommendations or practices presented by an organization that defines specific aspects about a technology. For example, an organization may design the specifications for a type of connector that connects to a given cable type. Every company that manufactures connectors for this type of cable must know the physical and electrical specifications of the connector to ensure compatibility with the cable. The physical qualities may be length, width, height, and the amount of weight the connector can support. The electrical qualities may specify the amount of voltage and current the connector can handle.

Many times, standards are adopted as law by local jurisdictions. For example, city, county, state, or country may adopt an organization's standards and make them the minimum standard to be followed by contractors or employees. In other words, a company might hire a contractor to install a network for its business. Since the company wants the network to be installed properly, it will write into the contract "all work shall follow the IEEE standards for networking." Those standards will also serve as the minimum standards for installing the cabling and network devices. The contract will usually specify that all cable and network devices used for the installation must be *UL approved*. UL stands for Underwriters Laboratories, which is an organization that tests products for safety purposes.

A number of organizations are referenced throughout this textbook. Membership of an organization is comprised of personnel who have an interest in the technology the organization represents. Aside from UL, some of the organizations that are referenced throughout this textbook are IEEE, ISO, ANSI, EIA, and TIA. The following is just a brief explanation of a few of the many organizations that exist. It is recommended that you visit these organizations' websites to gain better insight into the scope, membership, and function of each.

IEEE

The **Institute of Electrical and Electronics Engineers (IEEE)** (pronounced *I triple E*), founded in 1884, is a professional organization that continually develops standards for the networking and communication industry. This organization consists of scientists, students, commercial vendors, and other interested professionals from the industry. Network standards developed by the IEEE are identified with an 802 prefix, as shown in Figure 1-23.

The specifications outlined in the 802 standards are not laws but rather a set of recommended practices that ensure quality of work as well as the interoperability of equipment designed by different companies. The standards should only be thought of as a law if a contract to install a network requires that the network meet or exceed the IEEE standards. If a problem arises after the work is completed and the contractor did not follow the IEEE standards, the contractor can be held liable.

Copyright Goodheart-Willcox Co., Inc.

Figure 1-23 IEEE 802 standards. The standards in bold represent those that are still active.

IEEE Standard	Description
802.1	**High Layer LAN Protocols**
802.2	Logical Link Control (Inactive)
802.3	**Ethernet**
802.4	Token Bus (Disbanded)
802.5	Token Ring (Inactive)
802.6	Metropolitan Area Network (Disbanded)
802.7	Broadband (Disbanded)
802.8	Fiber Optic (Disbanded)
802.9	Integrated Services (Disbanded)
802.10	Security (Disbanded)
802.11	**Wireless Local Area Networking (WLAN)**
802.12	Demand Priority (Disbanded)
802.13	Not used
802.14	Cable Modem (Disbanded)
802.15	**Wireless Personal Area Network (WPAN), Bluetooth, and ZigBee**
802.16	**Wireless Metropolitan Area Network (WMAN), WiMAX, and Mobile Wireless**
802.17	**Resilient Packet Ring (RPR)**
802.18	**Radio Regulatory**
802.19	**Coexistence**
802.20	**Mobile Broadband Wireless Access (MBWA)**
802.21	**Media Independent Handover (MIH)**
802.22	**Wireless Regional Area Network (WRAN)**

Goodheart-Willcox Publisher

The 802 standards are referred to throughout your studies of networking, but be aware that the standards are constantly changing. The IEEE forms committees for each standard. Each committee is charged with creating, reviewing, and revising standards as needed. Over time, some of the standards become obsolete, which results in the disbanding of the committee or the committee becoming inactive.

Notice in Figure 1-23 that many of the standards that were once active are now disbanded or inactive. At times, the responsibility of a standard is absorbed by another entity, usually a communication organization or a newly formed professional organization that is interested in a particular aspect of the industry. For example, the cable-modem industry has its own organization known as Data-Over-Cable Service Interface Specification (DOCSIS) that ensures interoperability between cable television vendor hardware and software products. Soon after the forming of DOCSIS, the IEEE disbanded the IEEE 802.14 Cable Modem committee and discontinued writing specifications for cable modem hardware and software.

Many different trade magazines provide articles about changes in IEEE standards. Most networking professionals have at least a few periodicals or newsletters to which they subscribe to keep up-to-date with changes in the networking industry.

ISO

The **International Organization for Standardization (ISO)** is an organization interested in the standardization of computer equipment. The letters *ISO* are not an acronym. The term *iso* is derived from the Greek *isos*, meaning *equal*. The ISO

Copyright Goodheart-Willcox Co., Inc.

organization was founded in 1946 and comprises 46 different countries and other organizations, such as the ANSI (American National Standards Institute) organization. ISO developed the OSI model for networking technologies. The OSI model is discussed in more detail later in this chapter and referenced throughout the textbook.

W3C

Established in 1994, the **World Wide Web Consortium (W3C)** is an organization that provides recommendations for language standards of web pages. The organization focuses on the development of programming language standards used for displaying information in the form of web pages.

Some of the language standards developed and approved by W3C are hypertext markup language (HTML), extensible markup language (XML), eXtensible Hypertext Markup Language (XHTML), and Cascading Style Sheets (CSS). The Internet uses these programming languages to present text, graphics, and sound. A protocol known as *Hypertext Transfer Protocol (HTTP)* delivers web pages to a user's computer.

The Internet has become a standard tool for business. An entire chapter in this textbook is devoted to web servers. It includes an introduction to HTML and web-server communication.

TIA

The **Telecommunications Industry Association (TIA)** is a standards maintenance organization mainly concerned with fiber-optics, user equipment, network equipment, wireless communication, and satellite communication. TIA was founded in 1924. It was started by a small group of suppliers who wished to promote the independent telephone industry and to organize trade shows. Soon after, it evolved into the standards maintenance organization it is today.

ANSI

The **American National Standards Institute (ANSI)** is a private, nonprofit organization that does not develop standards, but rather prompts voluntary conformity and standardization. ANSI was founded by five engineering societies and three governmental organizations in 1918. It is the official representative of many international organizations such as ISO. ANSI is also one of the founders of the ISO organization. ANSI facilitates meetings and brings interested parties together to resolve issues and create a general census among its members to be presented to other standards committees.

OSI Model

The **Open Systems Interconnection (OSI) model** describes how hardware and software should work together to form a network communication system. It serves as a guide for troubleshooting and designing networks. The original design of TCP/IP communication over the Internet was first developed by the Department of Defense (DoD) in the 1970s. The DoD model is simpler in design than the OSI model. Differences between the two models can be seen in Figure 1-24. Notice that the DoD model has four layers and the OSI model has seven.

When the DoD model was designed, the structure of the Internet was new and concepts were much simpler. The communication protocol was TCP/IP. There was not an overwhelming number of applications used in the early days of the Internet.

Tech Tip

The OSI model is a joint effort of international members to standardize networking communication systems. Not all software companies follow the strict guidelines of the OSI model. Many systems were in place long before the OSI model was developed and adopted. Some models combine two or more layers into a single unit. It is important to remember that the OSI model simply serves as a guide for future development and illustrates the complexity of transmitting data between network devices.

1.2 NET

Copyright Goodheart-Willcox Co., Inc.

Figure 1-24 The original DoD model was much simpler in design than the OSI model. Note that there are two versions of the DoD model.

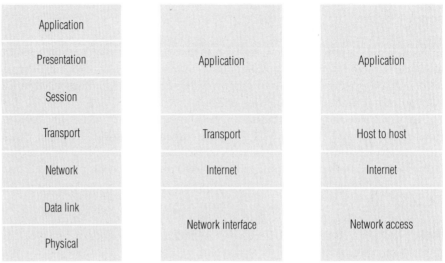

Goodheart-Willcox Publisher

Security was not considered a real problem, and encryption was not used. There was only one dominant operating system—Unix. As long as all hardware models adapted to the DoD model and used the TCP/IP protocol, compatibility was not an issue.

The original network media was existing telephone lines. Only plain ASCII text was exchanged, not graphics, sound, or animation. There was no exchange of e-mail as we know it today. The DoD model was based on the simple concept of exchanging text materials using TCP/IP over the Internet. As networking systems became more robust with full multimedia features, many more types of networking media and security features evolved along with a more complex model. The requirements of such advances led to the development of the OSI model as we know it today. Software developers and network equipment manufacturers use the OSI model as an outline when developing software and hardware devices.

The *Institute of Electrical and Electronic Engineers (IEEE)* is concerned with the electronic aspects of the OSI model. This organization is composed of engineers, students, scientists, and manufacturing representatives who form standards that promote interoperability of hardware devices. In other words, they set standards that ensure hardware, such as network adapter cards, cables, cable connectors, switches, and routers, will easily interconnect and support each other rather than be proprietary.

The IEEE organization is nonprofit and many members donate their time toward the development of the standards. Since the IEEE is concerned with the electrical aspects of network communication, they redesigned the OSI model to reflect their interests. The IEEE version of the OSI model splits the data link layer into two sublayers: logical link control (LLC) and media access control (MAC). This version became known as the IEEE 802 model, as shown in Figure 1-25.

NET
+ 1.2

One reason it is difficult for students to understand the OSI model is that much of it is intangible; the individual layers cannot be picked up and shown to another person. It helps to look at the OSI model from the point of view of hypothetical communication. Assume two people are using a chat program to talk. There are several complicated tasks that need to happen. First, the users must ensure the chat

Copyright Goodheart-Willcox Co., Inc.

Figure 1-25 The revised OSI model, referred to as the IEEE 802 model, divided the data link layer into two sublayers: logical link control (LLC) and media access control (MAC).

IEEE 802 Model

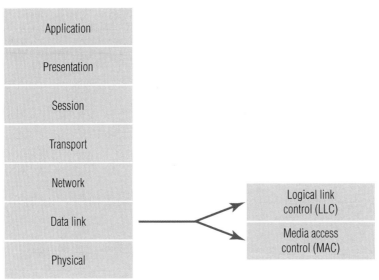

Goodheart-Willcox Publisher

messages go to the correct computer. Second, the session must stay open until the chat is completed. Finally, messages will need to be converted into 1s and 0s, put into packets, and transmitted as electrical or radio signals, based on the network connection. The OSI model handles all of these tasks.

Compare the characteristics of the various OSI layers in Figure 1-26. The top four layers are primarily descriptions of software functions and are hardware independent. The software in these upper layers include web browsers like Microsoft Edge, Google Chrome, and Mozilla Firefox; e-mail clients; instant messaging; FTP; and such. The lower three levels are directly related to specific hardware types. Notice that the gateway is assigned to the upper layers of the OSI model. This is because the gateway acts as a translator when two different operating systems attempt to communicate. Remember that an operating system is software. The term *gateway* is often confused to mean a specific piece of equipment; in reality, it is a software service typically installed on a router or server. The gateway translates the different file formats used to form packets.

All program-based interaction, such as a user sending messages in a chat program, occurs in the application and session layers. They are responsible for communication with user applications. The correct computer is determined at the network layer using IP addresses. The transport layer is responsible for ensuring transmissions are completed and nothing is lost. The session layer is responsible for maintaining a session. The data link layer organizes the 1s and 0s and transfers them to the physical layer to be sent out as either wireless or wired signals. This explanation is a bit of a simplification, but being able to first conceptually understand what the OSI model is doing will make studying the details of the layers easier.

Each layer in the OSI model is assigned a specific function. This section provides a brief description of each layer. It is intended as an overview of how networking components work together to send and receive information. The OSI model is referenced throughout the textbook.

Copyright Goodheart-Willcox Co., Inc.

Figure 1-26 OSI layer comparison table.

OSI Layer	Function	Hardware	Protocols	Keywords
Application	User interface	Gateways	HTTP, FTP, WWW, SNAP, SMB, SMTP, Telnet, POP, IMAP	Browser, e-mail, network applications
Presentation	Convert to common format such as ASCII, data encryption, and compression	Gateways	MPEG, WAV, MIDI, QuickTime	ASCII, Unicode, EBCDIC, CODEC, and bit order
Session	Establish and close communication between two nodes Coordinates communication	Gateways	NFS, DNS, SQL, RPC, NetBIOS, X.25, SMB	Establish and terminate a communication session, log on, user name, password, authentication, assign services through port numbers
Transport	Sequence packets Ensure error-free delivery Takes over after the session has been established	Gateways (layer 4 switches)	TCP, UDP, SPX	Segments, windowing, flow control, transport packets, error checking (if required), port numbers
Network	Navigates outside of the LAN	Routers (layer 3 switches)	IP, IPX, AppleTalk, ICMP, RIP, RIPv2, ARP, OSPF, IGRP, RARP, BGP, NLSP, IS-IS, EIRGP	IP address, routing, packets, datagrams, network address, packet switching, logical address, best and shortest route
Data link	Prepares data for media access Defines frame format	Bridges, switches, Wireless Access Points, network interface cards	CSMA/CD, CSMA/CA, LLDP	MAC address, hardware address, LLC, CRC, frame types, frames, topologies, contention
Physical	The physical aspect of the network	Copper-core cable, fiber-optic cable, wireless, hubs, repeaters, transceivers, amplifiers, transducers	NA	Bit, byte, cable, media, topology, transmission, voltage, digital signals

Goodheart-Willcox Publisher

Physical Layer

The **physical layer** is the lowest layer of the model. It is where a user sees something tangible, such as hardware, and consists of the cable and connectors used for constructing the network. It is important to note that, while not all hardware works at the physical layer, hubs, network interface cards, and cables do. This layer is only concerned with how digital signals, the binary 1s and 0s, are carried electrically from one

Copyright Goodheart-Willcox Co., Inc.

networked device to another. The physical layer is where actual raw bits are transmitted, regardless of transmission medium. When you think of the physical layer, think of cables, radio waves, or light pulses.

The physical layer is also called *layer one*. Recall that the OSI model has seven layers, beginning with the physical layer. Devices that do not perform any sort of traffic direction often operate at the physical layer. For example, traditional hubs and cabling are considered to operate at the physical layer.

Data Link Layer

The **data link layer** describes how raw data is packaged for transfer from one network interface card to another. The data link layer also contains information such as the address of the source and destination and the size of the packet, and it provides error checking. When you think of the data link layer, think of placing all the data in an orderly sequence of 1s and 0s with a definite beginning and end to each packet.

The data link layer, or *layer two*, is divided into two sublayers. Those layers are the logical link control (LLC) and media access control (MAC). The MAC sublayer should look familiar. This is where the MAC address comes from. Figure 1-27 demonstrates a summary of LLC and MAC sublayer functions.

Figure 1-27 LLC and MAC sublayer functions.

Data Link Layer

- Frames the content of the upper layers
- Frames the MAC address
- Ensures reliability of physical connection
- Performs CRC

- Converts frame into a series of digital pulses
- Performs collision avoidance
- Performs contention resolution
- Prepares for half-duplex or full-duplex transmission based on media type
- Negotiates transmission speed

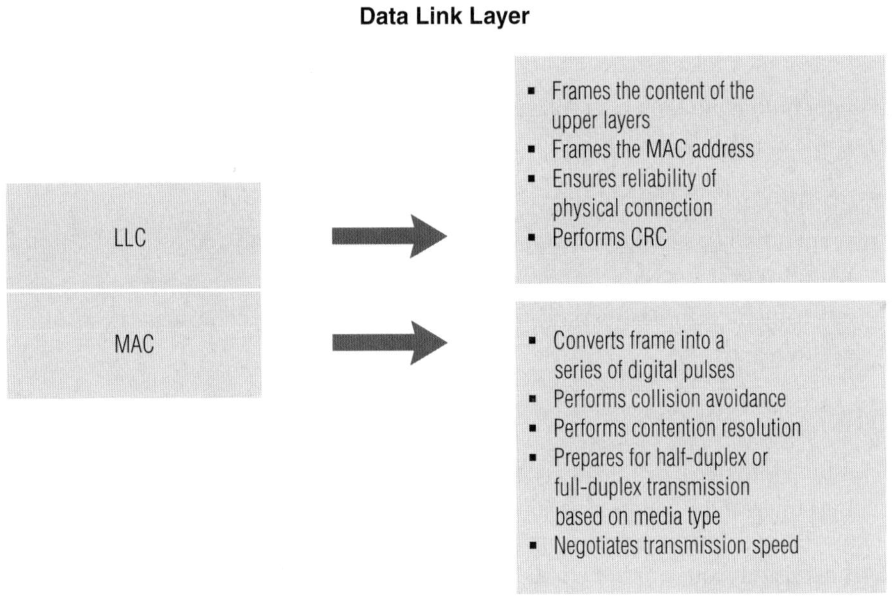

Goodheart-Willcox Publisher

Logical Link Control (LLC)

The LLC sublayer communicates with the upper-level protocols and is software by nature. It is responsible for framing the contents of the upper levels and includes the node address of the source as identified by the MAC address of the network interface card.

The LLC sublayer deals with physical addresses, as opposed to logical addresses. The LLC also ensures the reliability of the physical connection rather than the data contained within the frame. Frames will be discussed in Chapter 5. For now, think of a frame as a unit of transmission. The error check performed at the LLC sublayer is simple, consisting of a *cyclic redundancy check (CRC)*.

Copyright Goodheart-Willcox Co., Inc.

Media Access Control (MAC)

The MAC sublayer is concerned with accessing the network medium and converting the contents of a transmission into a serial stream of bits that will be carried by copper-core cable, fiber-optic cable, or wireless transmission. A general rule is that anything that directs traffic based on the MAC address operates at the data link layer. By that logic, a traditional switch (not an upper-layer switch) operates at the data link layer.

The MAC sublayer converts the transmission and its contents into a series of digital pulses to be carried on the media. According to IEEE, the primary functions performed by the MAC layer include:

- frame delimiting and recognition;
- addressing of destination stations;
- conveyance of source-station addressing information;
- transparent data transfer of LLC protocol data units (PDUs), or of equivalent information in the Ethernet sublayer;
- protection against errors; and
- control of access to the physical transmission medium.

In the case of Ethernet, the functions required the MAC sublayer include:

- receiving and transmitting normal frames;
- half-duplex retransmission and backoff functions;
- appending and checking frame check sequence (FCS);
- enforcing interframe gap;
- discarding malformed frames;
- prepending (tx) and removing (rx) preamble, start frame delimiter (SFD), and padding; and
- ensuring half-duplex compatibility: appending (tx) and removing (rx) MAC address.

Tech Tip

Packets may also be referred to as *datagrams*.

Network Layer

The **network layer** is primarily responsible for addressing and navigating networks by using generated IP addresses, as shown in Figure 1-28. Routing prevents or limits network congestion. It also can prioritize the transmission of packets. As packets are transmitted from one network to another, several different routes may be used. When you think of the network layer, think of navigating between networks.

The IP protocol works at this layer. That is one reason why IP addresses are also called *logical addresses*. Any device that directs traffic based on the IP address is operating at the network layer. Routers are a good example of devices operating at the network layer, also called *layer three*.

By itself, the IP protocol is *connectionless/unreliable*. Connectionless transmission will be covered in detail in Chapter 5. For now, understand that the IP

Copyright Goodheart-Willcox Co., Inc.

Figure 1-28 The network layer is concerned with navigating the network using IP addresses.

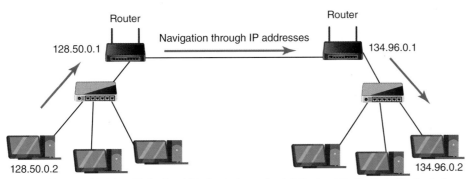

Network Layer

(router and hub icon)Vadim Ermak/Shutterstock.com; (workstation icon) RedlineVector/Shutterstock.com; Goodheart-Willcox Publisher

protocol simply designates an address to send packets to and does nothing to ensure the transmission is received. That responsibility is handled at the transport layer. Some protocols associated with the network layer include Address Resolution Protocol (ARP), Reverse Address Resolution Protocol (RARP), Internet Control Message Protocol (ICMP), Internet Group Management Protocol (IGMP), and Link Layer Discovery Protocol (LLDP).

Transport Layer

The main responsibility of the **transport layer** is to ensure reliable data by sequencing packets and reassembling them into their correct order. Packets are transmitted over many miles and may use different routes. The packets may not arrive in the same sequence in which they were transmitted and may require reassembly into their correct order. Reassembly into the correct order is especially important in transmitting digital images. When you think of the transport layer, think of packet quality.

Both TCP and UDP protocols operate at this layer. In the case of TCP, each packet is confirmed to have been received, or it is resent. With UDP, the packets are simply sent without confirmation they arrived. However, both protocols are responsible for packet delivery, and thus both are working at the transport layer, or *layer four*.

The integrity of the data is checked at the transport layer. This error check is more advanced than what is performed in the LLC sublayer. Here, the contents and proper sequence of frames are checked to ensure the data will be reassembled in the correct order at the destination. The transport layer is also where port numbers are inserted into segments. Port numbers are assigned in the session layer, and IP addresses are assigned in the network layer. Together, the port number and IP address form what is known as a *socket*.

Layer four is also concerned with the order of delivery. Since packets might take different paths through a network, it is important to see that they are assembled in the correct order at the destination. The transport layer also assists in avoiding congestion of network traffic.

Network+ Note ➕

It is very easy to confuse the transport layer and the data link layer when asked a question about error checking in the OSI model. You must carefully read any questions concerning the OSI model and error checking and concentrate on what type of error is being checked. The transport layer is concerned about the content of the protocol data unit (PDU) while the data link layer is concerned about the overall content of the frame, which includes the data content. Think of the transport layer as ensuring error-free data or contents of the PDU. The data link layer looks at the entire frame based on the CRC and then decides to either pass the frame along or drop it entirely. The corruption may be in the header rather than the data content.

Copyright Goodheart-Willcox Co., Inc.

Session Layer

The **session layer** establishes a connection between two different computers and provides a complete conversation context. It is responsible for ensuring that a communication session stays open until it is terminated by a user. Think about a phone call. You initiate the call, then you may spend some time speaking back and forth until the call is ended. That is a *session*.

The session layer, or *layer five*, determines what the correct virtual connection is by matching the port number of the service required to support the layers above it. For example, when connecting to a distant location, not only does the IP address need to be enclosed into the packet, but the port number that corresponds with the provided service must also be enclosed. If the requested port number is busy, the session layer determines if the connection can wait or if another port number can be assigned.

Communication between two hosts must be synchronized, meaning each host must recognize the other is ready to communicate or end the session. Properly ending a session is important because the connection must be released at both ends so the port addresses are freed for future communication. Therefore, each computer must be notified when the session is over. To do this, the session layer regularly checks if both hosts desire to continue communicating, thus resynchronizing them.

Layer five is also where differences in programming mechanics or code are worked out for communicating between two nodes in the same network or distant networks. The session layer solves problems, such as how to establish a connection between nodes on the same system architecture and diverse architecture.

The session layer can be involved in authentication and authorization. Authentication logically occurs here because parties need to be authenticated when establishing a session. A few protocols that operate at layer five include L2TP (used in VPNs), remote procedure call (RPC), session control protocol (SCP), and Telnet.

Presentation Layer

The **presentation layer**, or *layer six*, ensures character-code recognition. It is responsible for converting character codes into a code that is recognizable by a computer that uses a different character code. For example, Extended Binary Coded Decimal Interchange Code (EBCDIC) is widely used on mainframes, while most PCs use ASCII. EBCDIC uses numbers to represent characters similar to the way ASCII number codes represent character codes. When a PC communicates with a mainframe, the ASCII code must be converted to EBCDIC. When you think of the presentation layer, think of how the data must look for both parties to interpret or understand it.

The presentation layer works hand-in-hand with the application layer. Layer six is responsible for formatting and delivery of data to layer seven. Additionally, encryption is often done, at least in part, at this layer.

Copyright Goodheart-Willcox Co., Inc.

Application Layer

The application layer should not be confused with general software applications such as spreadsheet, word-processing, and database programs. The **application layer**, *layer seven*, interfaces directly to and performs common application services for the application processes. It works with specific networking applications such as web browser programs, file transfer programs, and e-mail. When you think of the application layer, think of establishing communication with the network.

Think of layer seven as the location of networking-specific applications. For example, a number of protocols operate at this layer, many of which will seem familiar. These protocols include Simple Mail Transfer Protocol (SMTP), Transport Layer Security (TLS), Lightweight Directory Access Protocol (LDAP), and others.

Network+ Note

The Network+ Certification Exam by CompTIA requires extensive knowledge of the OSI model and how it relates to network devices, protocols, and network technologies. If the OSI model seems confusing to you, you are not alone. You cannot have a complete understanding of the OSI model until you have a basic understanding of all the networking technologies and how they relate to each other.

OSI Model and Network Devices

It is important to understand how the OSI model and network devices correlate. In Figure 1-29, you will see the generally accepted classifications of network devices, such as hubs, switches, and routers, as compared to the OSI model. However, some alterations in the network device's technology may cause a network device to correlate to a different OSI layer.

Tech Tip

Some switches may be classified as a layer 2, layer 3, or layer 4 device. The generally accepted classification for a switch is layer 2. However, some companies advertise their switch as a layer 3 device if it has some router capabilities and as a layer 4 device if it is able to monitor a session.

Figure 1-29 A general correlation between network devices and the layers of the OSI model. This is only a general correlation. Some specific technologies may correlate a network device to a different OSI layer.

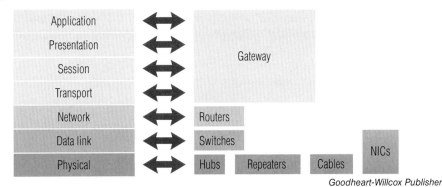

Goodheart-Willcox Publisher

Copyright Goodheart-Willcox Co., Inc.

Network devices are classified according to whether the device makes decisions about how a packet is sent. If the network device makes no decision about where a packet is sent but rather simply moves the packet along the network path such as through cabling, hubs, or repeaters, it is a **layer 1 device**. If decisions are made based on a MAC address or a logical name, it is a **layer 2 device**. If the network device makes a decision about where to move the data based on a protocol such as the Internet protocol, it is a **layer 3 device**.

A network device is often reclassified when its normal function is altered. For example, a switch, normally classified as a layer 2 device, may be reclassified as a layer 3 device if more intelligent decision-making is incorporated into it. The decision-making of a layer 3 switch is based on some similar information that routers use. A hub, which is normally a layer 1 device, may be reclassified as a layer 2 device when it acts as an intelligent hub. *Intelligent hubs* make decisions based on MAC addresses and behave more like a switch.

As you progress through the text and learn more about protocols and network communication, the exact placement of certain network devices on the OSI model will become clearer.

OSI Model and the Major Protocol Suites

The OSI model was developed after the majority of network protocols were already in use. As a result, not all network protocols match neatly to the OSI model design. For example, many protocols must span more than one layer to be properly represented when compared to the OSI model. Typically, higher-level protocols can perform multiple functions that span several layers of the OSI model.

TCP/IP Protocols

Notice in Figure 1-30 that the TCP/IP protocol suite is collected into three main areas: the top layers, which consist of the application, presentation, and session layer; the transport layer; and the network layer. The top layers are concerned with application protocols, such as HTTP, FTP, and Telnet. The transport layer packages the upper-level protocols into either TCP or UDP segments. The network layer encapsulates the TCP or UDP segments into packets. The protocols used at the network layer are IP, ICMP, and ARP. There is a TCP model that has only four layers. Each of these layers is analogous to one or more layers of the OSI model, as shown in Figure 1-31.

Copyright Goodheart-Willcox Co., Inc.

Figure 1-30 The TCP/IP protocol suite is collected into three main areas. The top layers are concerned with application protocols, such as HTTP, FTP, and Telnet. The transport layer packages the upper-level protocols into either TCP or UDP segments. The network layer encapsulates the TCP or UDP into IP packets.

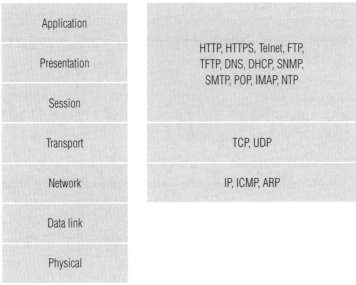

Application	HTTP, HTTPS, Telnet, FTP,
Presentation	TFTP, DNS, DHCP, SNMP,
Session	SMTP, POP, IMAP, NTP
Transport	TCP, UDP
Network	IP, ICMP, ARP
Data link	
Physical	

Goodheart-Willcox Publisher

Figure 1-31 Comparison between TCP and OSI layers.

TCP Layer	Corresponding OSI Layer
Network Interface	Physical and Data Link
Internet	Network
Transport	Transport
Application	Session, Presentation, and Application

Goodheart-Willcox Publisher

Copyright Goodheart-Willcox Co., Inc.

Summary

Definition of a Network

- Networks are interconnected collections of computers, computer-related equipment, and communication devices.
- Networks consist of nodes and hosts.
- Advantages of networking include providing a way to share equipment and data.
- Disadvantages of networks include personnel and cost increase as well as vulnerabilities to cyberattacks.

Network Classifications

- The three classifications of networks based on size, management, and use of private or public communication systems are local area network (LAN), metropolitan area network (MAN), and wide area network (WAN).
- Personal area network (PAN), campus area network (CAN), and global area network (GAN) are additional categories of networks.

Network Topologies

- The four common network topologies are star, ring, bus, and mesh.
- Hybrid topologies also exist, which blend more than one traditional topology.

Basic Network Administration Models

- The methodology used to administer a client/server network is centralized administration.
- The methodology used to administer a peer-to-peer network is decentralized administration.

Cloud Computing

- Cloud computing offers services to users, including Software as a Service (SaaS), Platform as a Service (PaaS), and Infrastructure as a Service (IaaS).
- Clouds can be private, public, or hybrid.
- Software-defined networking (SDN) is also available through cloud computing.

Network Operating System

- A network operating system (NOS) provides a communication system between nodes.
- Examples of a NOS include Windows Server 2008/2012/2016, Unix, and Linux.

Network Communication

- Data that is to be transmitted on a network is divided into segments.
- A typical packet contains a data segment, source and destination address, error checking, and sequence identification.

Copyright Goodheart-Willcox Co., Inc.

Protocols

- A protocol is a set of rules that controls communication between two nodes.
- In general, two computers need to use the same protocol to communicate with each other.
- Link-Layer Discovery Protocol (LLDP) is designed to exchange information between network devices in the same local area network.

Network Addresses

- A network address is a unique identifier for a node on a network.
- Two types of addresses are used: MAC addresses (physical addresses) and IP addresses (logical addresses).

Network Media and Devices

- A media converter is used to convert one type of electrical signal into another type of electrical signal.
- A repeater regenerates digital signals, allowing the network media to exceed its recommended length.
- A hub provides a central connection point for a network.
- A gateway device provides a connection between the local area network and the Internet.
- A bridge is used to segment a larger network to reduce the chance of collisions.
- A switch serves as a central connection point and can provide network segmentation.
- A router connects various networks together and provides a number of alternate routes for a data packet to travel.

Standards and Organizations

- Various organizations design specifications for network media.
- Organizations that develop standards include the Institute of Electrical and Electronic Engineers (IEEE), the International Organization for Standardization (ISO), World Wide Web Consortium (W3C), the Telecommunications Industry Association (TIA), and the American National Standards Institute (ANSI).

OSI Model

- The OSI model serves as a guide for troubleshooting and designing networks.
- The OSI model is based on a model first developed by the Department of Defense.
- The OSI model consists of seven layers: physical, data link, network, transport, session, presentation, and application.
- The data link layer is divided into two sublayers: logical link control (LLC) and media access control (MAC).

Copyright Goodheart-Willcox Co., Inc.

Review Questions

1. Define *node* and *host*.
2. Summarize the advantages and disadvantages of a network system.
3. List some things that might be shared on a network.
4. What are the three classifications of networks based on the size and complexity of the network system?
5. List four major network topologies.
6. The Internet would be best described as a _____.

   A. LAN   D. PAN
   B. MAN   E. CAN
   C. WAN   F. GAN

7. List the following network categories by size, starting with the smallest: MAN, LAN, and WAN.
8. Differentiate between a physical topology and logical topology.
9. Compare and contrast a client/server network with a peer-to-peer network.
10. Name four types of dedicated servers.
11. What does the term *client* mean in the context of a network?
12. List and describe three services offered through cloud computing.
13. How many categories of clouds exist?
14. Define network operating system and provide four examples.
15. Describe how devices communicate on a network.
16. List five common networking protocols.
17. What are the two types of network addresses and how are they different?
18. In the context of network, what is *media*?
19. List ten common networking devices.
20. Describe six organizations responsible for developing networking standards.
21. How does the OSI model compare to the DoD model?
22. What are the two sublayers of the data link layer called?
23. List the layers of the OSI model.

Copyright Goodheart-Willcox Co., Inc.

24. Match the following OSI layers with their corresponding responsibility.

i. Application

ii. Presentation

iii. Session

iv. Transport

v. Network

vi. Data link

vii. Physical

A. Cabling and connectors.

B. Converts frame codes to a serial stream of data.

C. Responsible for connecting across WAN systems.

D. Repackages long messages into smaller units.

E. Establishes rules for communication between two computers.

F. Translates data into a common compatible format.

G. File transfer service, e-mail, and web browser programs.

✚ Sample Network+ Questions

1. John is considering network topologies for his small office network. Which of the following is *not* a network topology he might choose?

   A. Ring

   B. Star

   C. Bus

   D. Square

2. Mary is describing network protocols to her colleague. She wants to explain what a protocol is. A protocol is best described as a _____.

   A. set of standards that serve as an installation guide for network media and devices

   B. set of rules and procedures that govern how two points on a network communicate

   C. special software utility that determines the amount of traffic on a network

   D. set of rules that assists personnel in using networks to communicate

Copyright Goodheart-Willcox Co., Inc.

3. Terrance is examining the OSI model and trying to decide what layer is responsible for which devices. Network cabling is assigned to the _____ layer of the OSI model.

   A. presentation

   B. physical

   C. network

   D. materials

4. Jane is considering standards to use when setting up her company network. Which standard organization is responsible for the 802 standards?

   A. ISO

   B. EIA

   C. ANSI

   D. IEEE

5. Which of the following statements is *true* about a peer-to-peer network? (Select all that apply.)

   A. It is controlled or administered from one central computer.

   B. Each user controls his or her personal resources.

   C. It is the best method for controlling a large number of networked PCs.

   D. There is no central file server.

6. Which protocol is responsible for delivering web page content to a user's computer?

   A. XTML

   B. XML

   C. HTTP

   D. HTML

7. Ramone is inventorying the various network devices on his network. Which piece of equipment would be used to connect his local area network to the Internet?

A. Hub

B. Bridge

C. Router

D. Repeater

8. Sheila is trying to find out the physical address of her computer, also called a MAC address. How large is the MAC address?

A. 6 bytes

B. 6 bits

C. 6 megabytes

D. 6 characters

9. Which item can be shared on a peer-to-peer network?

A. Hard disk drive

B. Floppy drive

C. Printer

D. Any of the above devices can be shared.

10. Emiliano is a network administrator for a large company. He is concerned about attenuation on his network. Which of the following is the best description for attenuation?

A. The loss of network digital signal strength along a cable.

B. Interference between two network cables.

C. Network cable resistance measured in ohms.

D. The term used to describe the procedure for calling attention to a particular node.

Network Media— Copper-Core Cable

Network+ Certification Exam Objectives

To prepare for the Network+ Certification exam, you must be very familiar with IEEE 802.3 network media such as copper-core cable characteristics. The characteristics include the following:

Objectives

1.3: Properties of Network Traffic—CSMA/CD, CSMA/CA

Properties of Network Traffic—MTU

PoE and PoE+ (802.3af, 802.3at)

1.8: DHCP Service—TTL

2.1: Media Types—Copper

Plenum vs. PVC

Connector Types—Copper

Copper Cable Standards

Copper Termination Standards

Ethernet Deployment Standards

2.4: Jumbo Frame

2.5: Service Type—Cable Broadband

Transmission Mediums—Copper

3.3: Bandwidth/Throughput

5.2: Crimper

5.3: Attenuation

Latency

Crosstalk

EMI

Open/Short

Incorrect Pin-Out

Learning Outcomes

- Define *network media*.
- Differentiate between analog and digital signals.
- Summarize the methods of data transmission.
- Recall the meaning of electronic terms.
- Differentiate and categorize copper-core cables.
- Recall the characteristics of the 802.3 classifications.
- Identify the various types of wiring faults.

Copyright Goodheart-Willcox Co., Inc.

Key Terms

10Base2
10Base5
10BaseT
alien crosstalk (AXT)
amplifier
analog signal
automatic medium-dependent interface crossover (Auto-MDIX)
AWG rating
bandwidth
baseband
broadband
carrier-sense multiple access with collision avoidance (CMSA/CA)
carrier-sense multiple access with collision detection (CSMA/CD)
coaxial cable
crossed pair

crossover cable
crosstalk
decibel (dB)
digital signal
equal level far-end crosstalk (ELFEXT)
far-end crosstalk (FEXT)
full-duplex
ground
half-duplex
impedance
interference
latency
magnetic induction
maximum transmission unit (MTU)
near-end crosstalk (NEXT)
noise
open

plenum-rated
Power over Ethernet (PoE)
reflected loss
resistance
reversed pair
RG-58
RG-6
RG-8
rollover cable
short
simplex
split pair
straight-through cable
terminating resistor
time to live (TTL)
twisted pair

Overview

Whether you are troubleshooting or designing a network, you must be familiar with the various types of network media. This chapter presents a general overview of network media and its electrical characteristics and covers copper-core cable in detail. In the following chapters, fiber-optic and wireless network media are covered, respectively. To understand the characteristics and limitations of copper-core cable, you will first be introduced to some electronics terminology. Later, the IEEE 802.3 and 802.5 standards are covered. You will see how these standards relate to network design and will understand the importance of knowing their specifications.

Network+ Note

In this chapter, 10Base2, 10Base5, and token ring have been presented as a historical reference to networking. You will see these particular technologies referenced on the Internet when you conduct networking-related searches. You will most likely *not* see any questions related to these technologies on the CompTIA Network+ exam.

Network Media

NET

2.1

Network media is a general term for the various ways to transmit data. There are two general classifications of network media: cable-based and wireless, as shown in Figure 2-1. Cable-based network media comprises copper-core cabling, such as coaxial and twisted pair, and glass or plastic core cabling, such as fiber-optic. Wireless network media comprises air, or the atmosphere.

All network communication originates from electronic signals. However, some media translates that into other types of signal. For example, fiber-optic uses light waves to transmit data. Wi-Fi uses radio waves to transmit data. Coaxial and twisted-pair cable use pulsating electrical energy to transmit data.

To understand the terminology related to network media and network communication, you must first learn some basics about electronic signals. In the following section, we will look at the characteristics of two general types of electronic signals: analog and digital.

Figure 2-1 Network media classifications and media types. At the bottom of the hierarchy are the types of electronic signals that each media type carries.

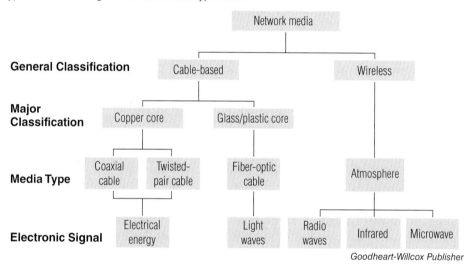

Goodheart-Willcox Publisher

Analog and Digital Signals

An **analog signal** is a signal that has a continuous range of values, much like a wave. Radio signals and light are common examples. A **digital signal** is a signal that has discrete values of *on* or *off*. Electrical transmissions often represent this by one voltage being a *1* and another voltage being a *0*.

However, analog signals must also contain digital information. You have probably used Wi-Fi, which depends on radio transmissions, which are analog. However, analog signals can be used to transmit digital information. This is done by using some aspect of the analog signal to represent a digital value. For example, the wavelength can be used. One range of wavelength represents a *1* and another represents a *0*.

Amplitude modulation is another method of encoding digital data into an analog signal. With this method, one specific amplitude represents a *1*, and another represents a *0*. The same thing can be accomplished with *frequency modulation*, with one frequency representing a *1*, and another representing a *0*.

Copyright Goodheart-Willcox Co., Inc.

Attenuation

All electronic signals degenerate, or lose amplitude, over long distances. Losing signal strength is referred to as *attenuation*. As an electronic signal travels across the media, the amplitude of the signal is lessened. The amplitude can be augmented to its original level with an amplifier. An **amplifier** is an electronic device designed to raise a signal's amplitude.

5.3 NET

Interference

In addition to attenuation, most electronic signals pick up interference from sources such as motors, fluorescent lights, transformers, radio transmitters, and other conductors carrying electronic signals. **Interference** is an undesired electromagnetic signal imposed on a desired signal that distorts or corrupts the desired signal. Electromagnetic interference is generally referred to as **noise**. Interference that comes from neighboring conductors inside a wire's insulating jacket is called **crosstalk**. Crosstalk is covered later in detail.

5.3 NET

Noise and crosstalk are unwanted signals that need to be removed from the desired signal, especially before it is amplified. When an analog or digital signal is amplified, the unwanted signals caused by interference are also amplified. To get rid of the unwanted signals, the signal must be filtered. *Filtering* electronic signals is the removal of unwanted signals.

Amplifiers often incorporate filters. The filter removes the unwanted signals before amplification so when the signal is amplified, it is an exact duplicate of the original signal. Networks use repeaters to amplify and filter signals. A repeater is not actually an amplifier. However, in a networking environment, a repeater is often referred to as an amplifier because it counters attenuation by reshaping the signal to its original form.

While both analog and digital signals can be used to express data in network communication, the digital signal is preferred. It is very difficult, and sometimes impossible, to filter all of the unwanted signals from an analog signal without changing the analog signal. Amplifying an analog signal not only amplifies the original signal, but also the unwanted signals, which results in a signal that no longer represents the original. However, when a digital signal is amplified, the unwanted signals are more easily filtered to restore the original look of the original signal.

Digital signals have a square or rectangular waveform and are produced at a fixed frequency. When digital signals are regenerated, they are regenerated by digital devices that also produce a square or rectangular waveform. A typical signal from a radio station is an analog signal composed of various amplitudes and a mixture of frequencies inside a set range of frequencies. Because the radio signal comprises various frequencies, the interference is sometimes impossible to separate or filter. This is a major drawback of using analog signals. Since interference can be easily removed from digital signals, the digital signal has become the norm for transmitting data over network cables.

Look at Figure 2-2. At the top is the original signal in digital and analog form. These signals represent transmitted data. Below each signal is a representation of the same signal after attenuation and added interference. The bottom drawings are a representation of the distorted signals after amplification and filtering. Notice the analog signal is distorted after amplification and is not an exact match of the original signal. The digital signal, however, looks exactly like the original signal after amplification. This is because the repeater is only capable of reproducing the original signal as 5-volt and 0-volt levels. Interference consists of many different levels of analog

Copyright Goodheart-Willcox Co., Inc.

Figure 2-2 The effects of filtering analog and digital signals. Top—Analog and digital signals in their original form. Middle—Analog and digital signals affected by interference and attenuation. Bottom—Analog and digital signals amplified and filtered. Note the fidelity of the digital signal in comparison to the analog signal after amplification and filtering.

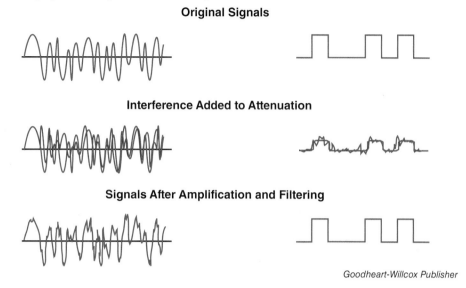

Original Signals

Interference Added to Attenuation

Signals After Amplification and Filtering

Goodheart-Willcox Publisher

voltage (amplitude) and cannot be reproduced by the repeater because the repeater only generates two levels of signal strength.

Excessively strong interference, however, can be impossible to filter from a digital signal. Interference strength is directly related to the distance from the digital signal and the power of the source producing the interference. For example, a portable telephone may interfere with a digital signal at a close proximity of five to 10 feet but not generate sufficient signal strength at 30 feet to interfere with the digital signal.

Latency

Latency is the amount of time it takes a signal to travel from its source to its destination. A general cause of latency is network equipment along the signal's path. Some networking devices regenerate, or reshape, a digital signal after it is received. For example, a repeater is used to extend the maximum distance that a signal can normally travel by reshaping the signal. A digital signal may travel through several repeaters before reaching its destination, thus slowing the time it takes the signal to reach its destination. Latency will be discussed in more detail in Chapter 12.

There is normally a maximum amount of time a packet is allowed to circulate through a network before it is destroyed. If the overall latency is too great, the packet is dropped from the network. However, this is not measured by time, but rather how many intermediate stops are between the source and the destination. This is defined as *hops*. The maximum number of hops allowed is referred to as the **time to live (TTL)**. If a particular network packet exceeds the allocated TTL, it is removed from the network to prevent it from circulating forever.

Data Transmission

Data transmission terminology and concepts are often referenced in network standards and equipment specifications. A good understanding of data transmission terminology will help you master some of the most difficult concepts of networking. Much of the original network terminology has its roots in the field of electronics.

Copyright Goodheart-Willcox Co., Inc.

Electronic terminology often requires an extensive background in electronics theory to fully grasp the concept being introduced. As networking has evolved over time, network technicians have coined their own terminology and have used electronics terms in some contexts that have slightly changed the original meaning of the term. Several of these terms and their influence on the data rate of data transmission are introduced in this section.

Bandwidth

Bandwidth is a measurement of the network media's ability to carry data. The definition of bandwidth varies according to the context to which it is applied. For example, when referring to a network cable, bandwidth refers to the amount of digital signal the cable can carry based on a given time. Network cable bandwidth is measured in bits per second (bps).

3.3 NET+

The term *bandwidth*, when applied to network cabling, can be confused with the term *frequency*. Technically speaking, frequency is a measurement of the network media's ability to carry an electronic signal. For example, a network cable can have a frequency rating of 250 MHz but a permissible bandwidth of 1000 MHz. The frequency rating is the rating of the individual wires inside the cable assembly; the bandwidth is the ability of the entire cable assembly (four pairs of conductors) to carry digital signals. In general, the higher the bandwidth, the more data that can be carried. Please take note of the fact that bandwidth does not always match data rates because data rates can be influenced by data compression techniques.

When referring to an analog signal, the term *bandwidth* means a measurement of the maximum frequency of a device or the total range of analog frequencies. Bandwidth in analog transmissions is measured in hertz (Hz). A range of frequencies would be all analog signal frequencies between two specific frequencies. An example would be television or radio analog signals transmitted and identified as channels. A typical television channel is assigned a 6-MHz bandwidth.

The bandwidth of analog transmission can support several different frequencies at once, whereas, the bandwidth of digital transmission usually supports only one frequency. In other words, when data is transmitted over a cable using a digital signal, the digital signal uses the entire bandwidth. When data is transmitted over a cable using analog signals, many different analog signals, or frequencies, representing data can be transmitted at once. See Figure 2-3.

Baseband

Baseband is a method of transmitting data in the form of a digital signal, using the entire bandwidth of a cable. Remember that the bandwidth of network media is its total capacity to transmit data, and a digital signal uses the entire bandwidth. The network media may be able to support more than one frequency, but in application, it is typically used to carry only one chosen frequency. For example, a copper-core cable may be used to transmit several analog signals, or frequencies, at once, but when used as part of an Ethernet network, will transmit digital signals at only one frequency. This frequency will consume the entire bandwidth of the cable.

You cannot send two digital signals on the same wire because they have matching frequencies and voltage levels. Figure 2-4 illustrates the effects of transmitting more than one digital signal on a wire. Each digital signal consists of a pattern of high and low voltage levels, which represent data such as letters and numbers. When both signals are placed on one wire, the two signals combine to form a new digital pattern. The new digital pattern of the combined signals cannot be separated into two individual signals; thus, all data is distorted and cannot be read at its destination.

Copyright Goodheart-Willcox Co., Inc.

Figure 2-3 Baseband transmission allows only one digital signal to be transmitted at a time. The digital signal uses the entire bandwidth of the network media. Broadband transmission allows multiple analog signals to be transmitted simultaneously, each of differing frequencies and amplitudes.

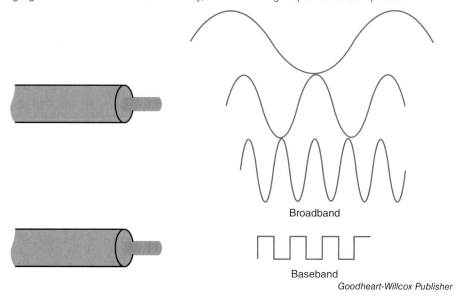

Broadband

Baseband
Goodheart-Willcox Publisher

Figure 2-4 Only one digital signal can be carried on the same wire. If two signals are sent on the same wire, the two would combine to form a new signal. The new signal cannot be filtered to restore the original signal.

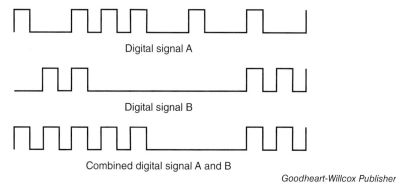

Digital signal A

Digital signal B

Combined digital signal A and B
Goodheart-Willcox Publisher

Broadband

NET

2.5

Broadband is a method of transmitting data in the form of several analog signals at the same time. Certain electronic techniques can be incorporated into communication systems that allow network media to carry more than one frequency at a time. In general, a network conductor that carries a single series of digital signals is baseband. A conductor that carries two or more analog signals is broadband.

Wireless media, such as radio, is an example of broadband transmission. In this case, the atmosphere is capable of carrying many different radio frequencies at the same time. For example, television signals range from 7 MHz to 1002 MHz. Inside this range of frequencies are individual channels specified in smaller ranges. For example, Channel 8 has a frequency range of 180 MHz to 186 MHz. Channel 9 has a frequency range of 186 MHz to 192 MHz. Each of the channels has a bandwidth of 6 MHz inside the allocated television bandwidth of 7 MHz to 1002 MHz. Wireless networks use radio waves as the network medium and use the terms *bandwidth* and *channel* when describing each radio signal path.

Copyright Goodheart-Willcox Co., Inc.

Simplex, Full-Duplex, and Half-Duplex Communication

Communication between two electronic devices can occur in one of three modes: simplex, full-duplex, and half-duplex, as shown in Figure 2-5. **Simplex** refers to communication that occurs in one direction only. An example of simplex communication is the transmission that occurs between a television station and a television. **Full-duplex** communication is bidirectional communication that occurs between two devices simultaneously. An example of full-duplex communication is communication via telephone. **Half-duplex** communication is also bidirectional communication; however, it can only occur in one direction at a time. Half-duplex communication is used with walkie-talkies. Most LANs use half-duplex communication. Ethernet is an excellent example. In an Ethernet network, only one computer or node can successfully transmit data over the network cable at a time. If two computers transmit data at the same time, a collision occurs and the data is destroyed.

Most modern communication is done with full-duplex communication. Simplex and half-duplex systems are very rare in modern computer networks, but were once common implementations.

Figure 2-5 Examples of simplex, half-duplex, and full-duplex communication.

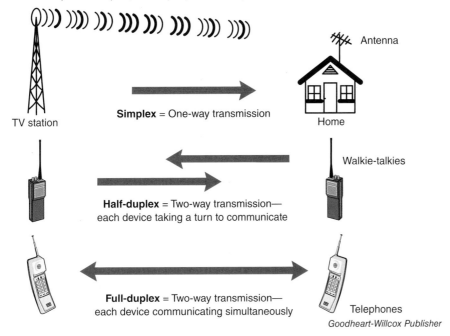

Goodheart-Willcox Publisher

Electronic Terms

Networks that incorporate copper cable have limits to the type of cable, length, number of segments, and the number of nodes that can be connected. These limits are based on certain electrical characteristics. As you read about the copper cable types and the IEEE 802 classifications, you will learn what these limitations are. However, there are several basic electronics terms you must first master to fully understand these limitations.

Direct Current and Alternating Current

The flow of electrical energy is described as either direct current (DC) or alternating current (AC). The term *current* describes the flow of electrons, which is the actual form of electrical energy. DC means that the current is in one steady direction. One of the most common sources of direct current is a battery. Electrical energy from a battery flows in a steady direction from the negative (–) terminal to the positive (+) terminal. AC does not flow in one direction. It alternates from a negative charge to a positive charge. The most common source of alternating current is the wall outlet.

Since the two forms of electrical energy flow differently, they produce different electrical characteristics. Because the two systems have different characteristics, different terminology is used to describe their characteristics. Two terms applied to these characteristics are *resistance* and *impedance*. These terms are inherited from the electronics industry and are applied to networking cable.

Resistance and Impedance

Resistance is the opposition to direct current (DC). Every conductor has a certain amount of resistance that affects current—the longer the conductor, the greater the resistance. *Resistance* is a DC term and should not be confused with **impedance**, which refers to the opposition in alternating current (AC). Impedance increases as frequency increases. In other words, the higher the frequency, the faster the speed of data transmission. However, the quality or integrity of the data will diminish because of impedance. This is why there are limitations to the speed at which data can be delivered across a conductor. The length of a conductor also influences impedance. As the length of a conductor increases, so does the total impedance.

Digital signals change current direction just as analog signals do. Digital signals consist of a series of square or rectangular waveforms, which sharply change current direction after a set time period. For this reason, digital signals are affected by impedance the same way analog signals are affected by impedance. See Figure 2-6 for a comparative summary of resistance and impedance.

Figure 2-6 Comparison of resistance and impedance.

Electrical Term	Definition	Symbol	Comments
Resistance	Opposition to direct current	Ω (ohm)	Current flow affected by cable length. Resistance is present in battery-powered circuits.
Impedance	Opposition to alternating current	Z	Current flow is affected by frequency, cable length, induction, and capacitance. Impedance is present in AC-powered circuits.

Goodheart-Willcox Publisher

Reflected Loss

In high-speed networks, data is transmitted in full-duplex mode. This means that data can flow in both directions at the same time. The original signal enters the cable and travels to the end. When it reaches the end, part of the signal is reflected. **Reflected loss** is the amount of signal reflected from the end of the cable. If it is of sufficient value, the reflected signal can disrupt communication.

Crosstalk

Crosstalk is a type of interference that occurs when one pair of conductors imposes a signal on another pair of parallel conductors, as shown in Figure 2-7. All energized conductors are surrounded by a magnetic field, as shown in Figure 2-7A. The magnetic field runs the length of the conductor. The strength of the magnetic field is

Copyright Goodheart-Willcox Co., Inc.

Figure 2-7 The occurrence of crosstalk. A—An energized conductor is surrounded by a magnetic field. B—Any conductor placed near the energized conductor and in the magnetic field will have electrical energy transferred to it. C—Twisting the pairs of conductors reduces the amount of electrical energy transferred between the pairs.

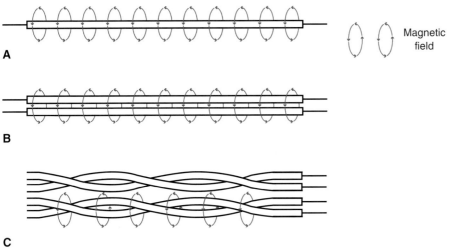

Magnetic field

A

B

C

Goodheart-Willcox Publisher

determined by the amount of current traveling through the conductor. Frequency also affects the strength of the magnetic field. When another conductor is placed in close proximity to a current-carrying conductor, the magnetic field encircles the other conductor and induces current, as demonstrated in Figure 2-7B. This electronic phenomenon is referred to as **magnetic induction**, or *mutual induction*. When a conductor in a cable assembly carries digital pulses, the digital pulses create a magnetic field pattern similar to the digital pulses. The magnetic field induces in a neighboring conductor an electrical current resembling the digital pulse pattern of the original conductor, thus creating crosstalk.

Analog telephone systems also suffer from crosstalk. In fact, the term *crosstalk* originated in telephone communication to describe the effect of hearing an additional telephone conversation from a neighboring telephone line while talking to someone else.

Network conductors, such as twisted pair, are designed to limit the effects of crosstalk by reducing the amount of contact between a pair of conductors, as shown in Figure 2-7C. This is why twisted pair must be used in place of the older style of telephone cable that has no twist. However, one place where crosstalk can be generated on twisted-pair cable is at the ends near the connectors. When cables are made by hand, the technician may leave too much untwisted conductor near the connector, leaving the cable vulnerable to crosstalk.

Figure 2-8 shows a twisted-pair cable properly connected to a connector and a twisted-pair cable improperly connected to a connector. Note that the improperly connected twisted-pair cable has too much wire exposed and that the pairs are not twisted. The improperly connected cable will produce crosstalk.

Twisted-pair cable segments are limited to 100 meters (328 ft.) maximum in length. Longer segment lengths produce crosstalk, as well as a reduction in signal strength. Cable shielding of wire mesh or foil also reduces crosstalk. The shielding absorbs and contains the magnetic field generated by a conductor and protects the pairs from electromagnetic interference generated by an outside source.

Four types of measurement can be taken on twisted-pair cable to measure the effects of crosstalk: near-end crosstalk (NEXT), far-end crosstalk (FEXT), equal level

Copyright Goodheart-Willcox Co., Inc.

Figure 2-8 Example of a twisted-pair cable properly connected to a connector and a twisted-pair cable improperly connected to a connector. Note the exposed, untwisted pairs of wire in the improper connection.

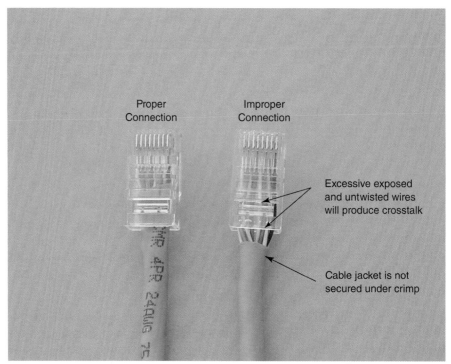

Goodheart-Willcox Publisher

far-end crosstalk (ELFEXT), and alien crosstalk (AXT). The first three measurements are taken by a manufacturer to determine cable specifications so that the cable can be correctly labeled. They are only taken in the field to see if an existing Category 5 cable could be used as a Category 5e cable. AXT was introduced as part of the Category 6a standard.

Near-End Crosstalk (NEXT)

Near-end crosstalk (NEXT) is a measurement of the reflected loss at the near end, or input end, of a cable, as illustrated in Figure 2-9. Losses are typically expressed in decibels. A **decibel (dB)** is a unit of measurement that expresses the relationship of power between two electrical forces. This measurement is often used to show the output-to-input ratio of a signal. For twisted-pair cable, it is used to compare the difference between the amount of power in the input signal and the amount of power generated by crosstalk. For networking fundamentals, it is the relationship of the input signal compared to the crosstalk signal.

Far-End Crosstalk (FEXT)

As the name implies, **far-end crosstalk (FEXT)** is a measurement of reflective loss at the far end, or output end, of the cable. Figure 2-10 provides an example of this loss. Far-end losses are also expressed in decibels.

Equal Level Far-End Crosstalk (ELFEXT)

Equal level far-end crosstalk (ELFEXT) is calculated by subtracting the effects of attenuation from the FEXT. Note that ELFEXT is a calculation, not a measurement. It is found by subtracting attenuation from the FEXT measurement. For example, if

Copyright Goodheart-Willcox Co., Inc.

Figure 2-9 Near-end crosstalk (NEXT) is a measurement of crosstalk taken at the near end, or input end, of a cable.

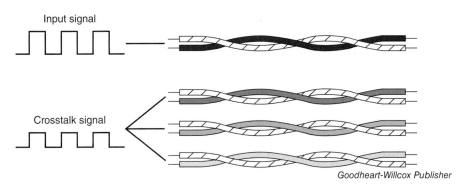

NEXT Measurement

Input signal

Crosstalk signal

Goodheart-Willcox Publisher

Figure 2-10 Far-end crosstalk (FEXT) is a measurement of crosstalk taken at the far end, or output end, of the cable.

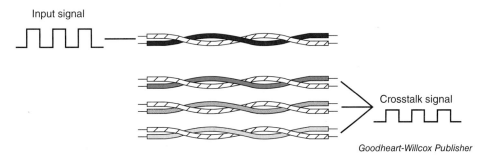

FEXT Measurement

Input signal

Crosstalk signal

Goodheart-Willcox Publisher

a 100-meter length of cable has a FEXT measurement of 45 dB with an attenuation measurement of 15 dB, the ELFEXT is calculated to be 30 dB. ELFEXT negates much of the attenuation by raising the attenuated signal by a value equal to the attenuation. This brings the attenuated signal back to the desired level. This is what the term *ELFEXT* implies by "equal level." It equalizes the loss with a gain.

Alien Crosstalk (AXT)

Alien crosstalk (AXT) is a measurement of noise introduced outside the cable jacket, typically caused by other network cables in close proximity. This measurement was first introduced in February 2008 as part of the Category 6a standard because of the high-frequency capabilities of this cable. Cables that carry high-frequency signals are susceptible to AXT. At lower frequencies, AXT is not a problem.

Copper-Core Cables

Copper-core cables are commonly constructed of a center core of copper surrounded by an insulating jacket. All copper-core cables have an AWG rating. An **AWG rating** describes the size of a conductor's diameter. The abbreviation AWG represents American Wire Gauge, which is the accepted standard for specifying the size of a conductor. The size of a conductor is expressed as a numeric value such as 22, 20, or 18. The smaller the number, the larger the diameter of the wire.

Figure 2-11 shows a wire gauge. A wire gauge is used to determine the AWG rating or the size of a conductor. Notice that the largest wire measurement on the gauge

2.1, 2.5 NET

Figure 2-11 Note the AWG ratings on this wire gauge. The AWG rating of 0 indicates the largest wire size on the gauge; whereas, the AWG rating of 36 indicates the smallest wire size on the gauge.

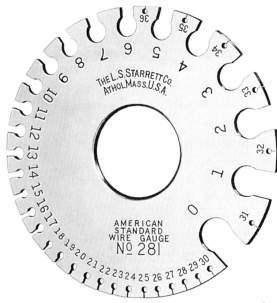

Goodheart-Willcox Publisher

is marked by the AWG rating 0, and the smallest wire measurement on the gauge is marked by AWG rating 36.

Cables are often identified as plenum-rated. **Plenum-rated** means that the cable has a special type of insulation that will not give off toxic gases should the cable be consumed by fire. The term *plenum-rated* is derived from the *plenum* in a building, which is the area above a drop ceiling and under a raised floor, as illustrated in Figure 2-12. Cables designed to pass through a building plenum must be plenum-rated.

Two types of copper-core cable are used in networking: coaxial and twisted pair. Twisted pair was derived from the telephone industry and was not originally designed for high frequencies. Voice signals are relatively low frequency when compared with other forms of electrical signals, such as radio, and did not require cable designed for high frequencies. Also, the original networks ran at only 1 Mbps to 4 Mbps. Early versions of telephone-communication cables worked fine for these applications.

Coaxial cable was designed to carry high-frequency signals and was first used in high-frequency radio communication to conduct a radio signal to and from an antenna. Coaxial cable was also used in early networks. It is used to some degree today because of its shielding effect. These two types of cables will be covered in the next section.

Coaxial Cable

Coaxial cable, or *coax*, consists of a copper-core conductor surrounded by an insulator referred to as a *dielectric*. Figure 2-13 shows a typical RG-58 coaxial cable assembly. The dielectric is covered with two shields: a foil shield and a braided copper shield. The shields protect the core from electromagnetic interference (EMI) and prevent the cable from transmitting EMI to other cables. The entire cable assembly is covered by an insulating outer jacket, which protects the shielding. Coaxial cable is very difficult to work with and relatively expensive when compared with some other cable-based media.

Tech Tip

Do *not* assume all types of coaxial cable can be used to extend a network. The electrical characteristics of each type of coaxial cable vary greatly, and some coaxial cable types can only be used for specific applications.

NET

2.1, 5.3

Copyright Goodheart-Willcox Co., Inc.

Figure 2-12 The plenum area of a building is located above a drop ceiling and under a raised floor.

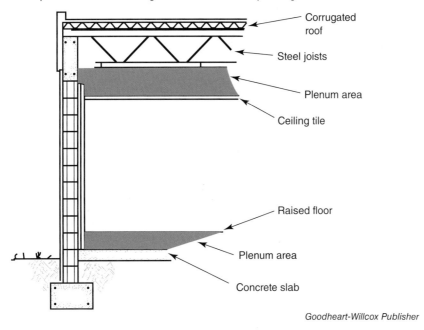

Corrugated roof

Steel joists

Plenum area

Ceiling tile

Raised floor

Plenum area

Concrete slab

Goodheart-Willcox Publisher

Figure 2-13 Coaxial cable layers.

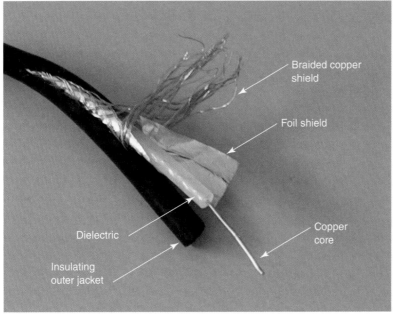

Braided copper shield

Foil shield

Dielectric

Insulating outer jacket

Copper core

Goodheart-Willcox Publisher

The core of a coaxial cable can be either solid or stranded. A solid core is stiffer and more difficult to work with than a stranded core. However, neither is as flexible as twisted pair and fiber-optic cable. Another interesting fact is a stranded core has the ability to carry more electrical energy (current) than a solid core of equal dimensions. Stranded-core coaxial cable, therefore, can contribute to a better quality of signal than solid-core coaxial cable.

Many times, the most important factor in determining which cable type to use is cost. Solid copper-core coaxial cable is less expensive than stranded copper-core coaxial cable. This is true for all copper cable types manufactured. The exact type

Copyright Goodheart-Willcox Co., Inc.

used typically varies according to installer preferences or the specifications of the installation.

Coaxial Connectors

Coaxial cable uses two main types of connectors: BNC and F-type. *BNC* makes a connection by pushing the connector onto the connection post and then twisting to the right, as shown in Figure 2-14. *F-type* connectors have threads and make a much better connection, as in Figure 2-15.

Figure 2-14 A BNC connector is pushed onto the BNC connection and twisted until it "locks" in place.

BNC connector

BNC connection

Goodheart-Willcox Publisher

Figure 2-15 An F-type connector is screwed onto an F-type connection.

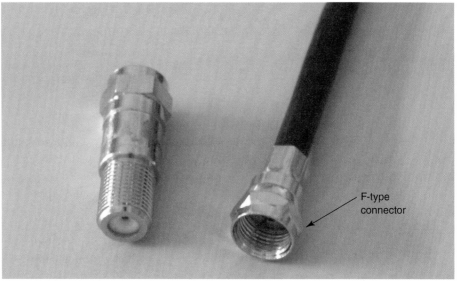

F-type connector

Goodheart-Willcox Publisher

Copyright Goodheart-Willcox Co., Inc.

Coaxial Applications

You may encounter coaxial cable being used from an antenna or satellite dish to a network system or as a network backbone. A media converter or bridge device is used to convert the signal from coaxial cable to a twisted-pair cable.

Video applications, such as cable and satellite TV, typically use coaxial cable "RG" as the medium to carry their high-frequency signals rather than twisted-pair cable. High-frequency signals are affected by twists in cables. When a video or audio signal is transmitted over a twisted conductor, the maximum length the signal can travel is drastically reduced. The twist in the cable causes an electronic characteristic known as *induction*, which will distort the high-frequency signal. The distorted signal results in a distorted image or audio at the destination.

Areas that are prewired with coaxial cable may be used as a part of a twisted-pair cabled network. D-Link, NETGEAR, and several other manufacturers have starter kits for using existing coax. The kit includes media bridges, or media converters, which have an F-type connection for the coaxial cable and an RJ-45 connection for twisted-pair cable.

Coaxial Cable Classifications

There are several classifications of network coaxial cable. Figure 2-16 lists some of the most common types of coaxial cable and their applications. The three most common coaxial cable types that have been used for networking are RG-6, RG-8 (thicknet), and RG-58 (thinnet).

2.1   NET   ⊹

Figure 2-16 Coaxial cable types and their applications.

Cable	Common Name	Impedance	Actual Size in Diameter	Description
RG-6	Broadband	75 Ω	0.332	Used for cable TV.
RG-8	Thicknet	50 Ω	0.405	Used for Ethernet networks.
RG-11	Thick coax	75 Ω	0.475	Used for cable TV trunk lines.
RG-58	Thinnet	50 Ω	0.195	Used for Ethernet networks.
RG-59	CATV	75 Ω	0.242	Used for cable TV and sometimes used for ARCnet.
RG-62	Baseband	93 Ω	0.249	Used for ARCnet.

Goodheart-Willcox Publisher

RG-6

RG-6 is the standard for cable television (CATV) systems and satellite systems, replacing other types of cable such as RG-59 for new installations. RG-6 in television applications typically use F-type connectors. RG-6 is often marked as RG-6/U and RG-6/UQ. The *U* represents *universal specification*, which is an old military grade standard. The *Q* in RG-6/UQ represents *Quad* for quad shielding. Quad shielding has four layers of shielding rather than the typical two layers like that in RG-6/U.

Coaxial cable used for television is not acceptable for use as a network cable. Its characteristics work well for television transmission but will cause problems if used for computer networks.

Tech Tip

The EIA/TIA 570 residential communication standard recommends RG-6 for new residential installations.

Copyright Goodheart-Willcox Co., Inc.

RG-8

> **Tech Tip**
>
> You may see references to 10Base2 and 10Base5 in outdated materials located on the Internet. 10base2 and 10base5 were early implementations of network media created from RG-58 and RG-8 cables, respectively.

RG-8, or *thicknet*, is a very rigid coaxial cable with a solid copper conductor in the center. The copper conductor adds to its rigidity and to its overall thickness. RG-8 allows for longer segments than other copper-core cables, but because of the difficulty in handling the cable and its wide diameter, it severely limits the number of cables that can be placed inside a conduit. Thicknet can be found in some network backbones because of its capability to carry a network signal as far as 500 meters.

RG-58

> **Network+ Note**
>
> The only RG type of cable listed in the CompTIA Network+ Exam objectives are RG-6 and RG-58.

RG-58, or *thinnet*, is smaller in diameter and easier to work with than thicknet coaxial cable. However, it does not carry a signal as far. RG-58 is still permitted but not recommended for use in new network installations.

Twisted Pair

Twisted pair is a type of cable that consists of four pairs of twisted conductors. Twisted-pair cable has been available for many years and was first used by telephone companies to carry voice transmissions. Today, twisted pair is the most common choice of network cable. AWG wire sizes range from 18 to 26. The AWG wire size 24 is used most often.

There are eight categories of twisted-pair cable: Category 1 through Category 8. The categories are based on the physical design, such as the number of pairs or twists per foot, and the capabilities of the cable, such as the maximum frequency rating and the data rate. The maximum frequency rating and data rate are only two of the measurements of a cable's capabilities. Other measurements to consider are crosstalk, NEXT, and impedance.

Twisted-pair cable can also be labeled as UTP (unshielded twisted pair) or STP (shielded twisted pair). Shielding can be applied over the entire cable assembly or over individual pairs of conductors. When shielding is applied to individual pairs of conductors, the shielding protects against crosstalk and outside sources of interference. The problem with shielding individual pairs of conductors is it makes the cable much harder to work with when applying connectors. This type of cable is also more expensive than unshielded twisted-pair cable.

Two different classifications of cable can have the same maximum frequency rating, but as a standard, they will support two different data rates. An example of a cable having the same frequency rating is Category 5 and Category 5e. Both have a frequency rating of 100 MHz, but because Category 5e has a better reflected loss rating based on NEXT and FEXT, it can be used in networks with a higher data rate standard. What makes this section so confusing is that information about cable

> **Tech Tip**
>
> When referring to a category of twisted-pair cable, it is common to use the term *Cat* for short. For example, it is common to use the term *Cat 5* instead of *Category 5*.

specifications can change between applications. The two main cable applications are voice (low-frequency analog) and data (high-frequency digital) signals. Also, different manufacturers sometimes post higher ratings for their cable than the minimum rating.

For a complete listing of twisted-pair categories, see the chart in Figure 2-17. Note that Category 5e is not a separate category but rather an addendum to the Category 5 specification.

Figure 2-17 Twisted-pair categories and their characteristics. There are eight twisted-pair categories. Category 5e is an addendum to Category 5, not a separate category.

	Type	Maximum Frequency Rating	Data Rate	Number of Pairs	Comments
Category 1	UTP	None	Less than 1 Mbps	2	Used for electrical signals representing voice transmission.
Category 2	UTP	1 MHz	4 Mbps	4	Used in earlier networks that were limited to 4 Mbps.
Category 3	UTP or STP	16 MHz	10 Mbps 16 Mbps	4	Can be found in existing networks rated at 10 Mbps and 16 Mbps and in some telephone installations.
Category 4	UTP or STP	20 MHz	16 Mbps	4	This cable type was only a slight improvement over Category 3.
Category 5	UTP or STP	100 MHz	100 Mbps 1000 Mbps (using 4 pairs)	4	Commonly used in 10BaseT and 100BaseTX network installations.
Category 5e	UTP or STP	100 MHz	100 Mbps 1000 Mbps (using 4 pairs)	4	This cable type is not a replacement for the Category 5 cable. It is an addendum to the cable classification.
Category 6	UTP or STP	250 MHz	1 Gbps	4	Has a plastic spine used to separate the conductors.
Category 6a	UTP or STP	500 MHz	10 Gbps	4	Introduced AXT.
Category 7	UTP or STP	600 MHz	10 Gbps	4	Each pair of twisted conductors is protected by foil shielding. Then, all four pairs are surrounded by foil or braided shielding.
Category 8	STP	1800–2000 MHz	40 Gbps	4	There is no unshielded version of this cable.

Goodheart-Willcox Publisher

Category 1

Category 1 cable is limited to low-frequency applications such as voice signals. It consists of two untwisted conductors. While this design is sufficient for electrical signals representing voice transmission, it is inadequate for computer networks.

Category 2

Category 2 cable consists of four pairs and has a maximum frequency rating of 1 MHz. It was once used in networks that were limited to 4 Mbps.

Category 3

Category 3 cable has a maximum frequency rating of 16 MHz. It consists of four twisted pairs and three twists per foot. This cable is rarely encountered today in network applications but may be found in many existing telephone installations.

Category 4

Category 4 cable has a maximum frequency rating of 20 MHz. It consists of four twisted pairs. This cable has a data rate of 16 Mbps. It is only a slight improvement over Category 3 cable.

Category 5

Category 5 cable has a maximum frequency rating of 100 MHz. It is capable of data rates of 100 Mbps (using two pairs) and 1000 Mbps (using four pairs). It is found commonly in 10BaseT and 100BaseTX networks.

Category 5e cable has a maximum frequency rating of 100 MHz. Category 5e is not a replacement for Category 5 cable but rather an addendum to the cable classification. With the growing need for cable that could support higher data rates, Category 5 standards were revised to Category 5e. Category 5e can support data rates up to 1000 Mbps using all four pairs of conductors. The improvements to Category 5 are based on Near-End Crosstalk (NEXT) and Equal Level Far-End Crosstalk (ELFEXT).

At the time of the introduction of Category 5e, any existing Category 5 cable was eligible to be reclassified as Category 5e if it met the requirements of the new standard. This would allow the use of Category 5 cable for newer network installations. Existing Category 5 cable could be tested to see if it met the Category 5e standard. If it met the standard, then it could be used. If not, it would require replacement. Some of the factors that determine the results of the tests include the AWG of the conductors and the insulation.

Category 6

Category 6 has a maximum frequency rating of 250 MHz and a data rate of 1 Gbps. It is similar in construction to Category 5 and 5e but does not require special shielding. Category 6 is similar to Category 5 in that it has four pairs of conductors. The main physical difference is that Category 6 has more twists per pair of conductors, and the pairs are separated by a plastic spacer in the core of the cable. Figure 2-18 compares Category 5 to Category 6 cable.

Notice that Category 6 has more twist per pair than Category 5 cable. The tighter twist is especially apparent when comparing the blue and blue/white pairs. Category 6 also has a plastic center cable core, which provides more space between the conductor pairs. The tight pair twist and the plastic center core are physical features which allow the Category 6 cable to support higher frequencies as well as higher data rates than Category 5e.

Enhanced Category 6 cable known as *Category 6e* is not a true standard but rather a marketing term used to identify Category 6 cable that exceeds the Category 6 standard. Category 6a, on the other hand, is a TIA-recognized standard. The *a* in Category 6a stands for *augmented*.

Category 6a is an excellent choice of network cable for noisy environments such as heavy industrial manufacturing. High-amperage industrial cables and equipment, such as welders, generate a great deal of EMI. It has a maximum frequency rating of 500 MHz and a data rate of 10 Gbps. Do *not* confuse Category 6e with Category 6a.

Copyright Goodheart-Willcox Co., Inc.

Figure 2-18 Category 5 and Category 6 cable.

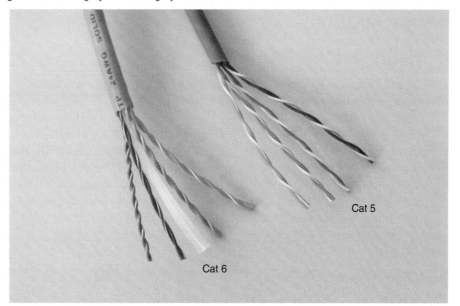

Cat 5

Cat 6

Goodheart-Willcox Publisher

Category 7

Category 7 cable has a maximum frequency rating of 600 MHz. It uses a different cable construction to achieve a high data rate. Category 7 is constructed of four pairs of twisted conductors with a protective foil or a conductive braid surrounding each pair. In addition to the individually covered pairs, there is an overall protective foil or conductive braid surrounding the complete assembly. In theory, it can achieve bandwidths of up to 10 Gbps.

Category 7a

Category 7a cable has a maximum frequency rating of 1000 MHz. In theory, it can achieve bandwidths of up to 10 Gbps.

Category 8

Category 8 cable was released in late 2016. It has a maximum frequency rating of 2 GHz and can achieve bandwidths of 1800–2000 MHz. This category of cable only comes in a shielded version.

Other Cable Types

These categories for unshielded twisted pair describe frequency and bandwidth. However, there are many variations. In addition to 100BaseTX, there is also 1000BaseLX and 1000BaseSX, among others. Like other deployment standards, the number indicated the bandwidth in megabits per second. The letters at the end describe cable type. For example, the *LX* in 1000BaseLX refers to laser, and the *SX* in 1000BaseSX refers to fiber.

IEEE 802 Standard

In Chapter 1, you learned that the Institute of Electrical and Electronic Engineers (IEEE) develops standards for the networking and communication industry. These standards begin with an 802 prefix, such as 802.1 for Internetworking and 802.2 for

Tech Tip

The IEEE specification for 802.3 is over 1000 pages long. You can download the complete specification from the IEEE website as an Adobe Acrobat file.

Copyright Goodheart-Willcox Co., Inc.

Logical Link Control. In this section, you will learn specifically about the 802.3 standard, which describes Ethernet network specifications and specifies the use of copper cabling.

IEEE 802.3 Classifications

NET
2.1, 2.4

The IEEE 802.3 standard comprises various Ethernet classifications. These classifications differ by data rate, topology, and media type and are named with short descriptions, such as 10BaseT and 10Base2. The chart in Figure 2-19 lists commonly encountered IEEE 802.3 classifications along with the maximum and minimum segment lengths in meters, data rate, cable type, and the topology of each. The 802.3 classifications are divided into four categories: 10 Mbps, Fast Ethernet, Gigabit Ethernet, and 10 Gigabit Ethernet. There is also *Jumbo Frame*, which is an Ethernet frame with a payload greater than the standard maximum transmission unit (MTU) of 1500 bytes. Frames will be discussed in detail in Chapter 5.

Figure 2-19 IEEE 802.3 categories and classifications.

Category	Classification	Data Rate	Maximum Segment Length	Minimum Segment Length	Cable Type	Topology
10 Mbps	10Base2	10 Mbps	185 m	0.5 m	RG-58 (thinnet)	Bus
	10Base5	10 Mbps	500 m	2.5 m	RG-8 (thicknet)	Bus
	10BaseT	10 Mbps	100 m	0.6 m	Category 3, 4, and 5	Star
Fast Ethernet	100BaseT4	100 Mbps	100 m	0.6 m	Category 3, 4, and 5	Star
	100BaseTX	100 Mbps	100 m	0.6 m	Category 5	Star
Gigabit Ethernet	1000BaseCX	1000 Mbps	25 m	0.6 m	Category 5	Star
	1000BaseT	1000 Mbps	100 m	0.6 m	Category 5e	Star
10 Gigabit Ethernet	10GBaseT	10 Gbps	55 m	0.6 m	Category 6	Star
	10GBaseT	10 Gbps	100 m	0.6 m	Category 6a	Star

Note: 1000BaseCX is obsolete and is no longer recognized.

Goodheart-Willcox Publisher

To help you decode the cryptic names of the classifications and to remember the specifications for each, look at Figure 2-20. In the first two examples, the *10* represents the data rate, which is 10 Mbps. In the third example, the 100 represents 100 Mbps. The *Base* in these examples stands for *Baseband*, which means that the digital signal is transmitted at one frequency, and this frequency consumes the entire bandwidth of the cable.

The last symbol in a cable classification is usually a number or a letter. A number indicates the approximate maximum segment length in hundreds of meters, and a letter indicates the media type. For example, in Figure 2-20A, the *2* represents the approximate maximum length of a segment in meters. A 10Base2 segment can therefore have a maximum length of approximately 200 meters (2×100). The actual maximum length, however, is 185 meters, but the *2* serves as an approximate. The 10Base5 classification specifies a maximum segment length of 500 meters (5×100). In this case, 500 meters is the actual maximum segment length.

Copyright Goodheart-Willcox Co., Inc.

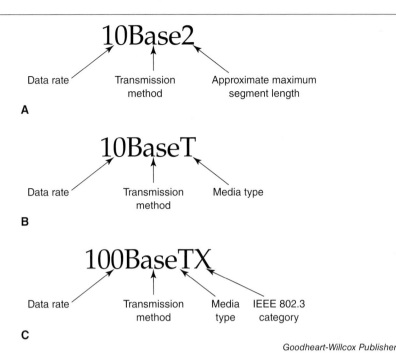

A

B

C

Goodheart-Willcox Publisher

Figure 2-20 Each IEEE 802.3 classification has an identifying name that reveals the classification's data rate, transmission method, and either the approximate maximum segment length or media type. A—10Base2 means 10 Mbps, Baseband, with a maximum segment length of 200 meters. B—10BaseT means 10 Mbps, Baseband, using twisted-pair cable. C—100BaseTX means 10 Mbps, Baseband, using twisted-pair cable and the Fast Ethernet specification.

In Figure 2-20B, the last character is a letter and represents the media type—in this case, twisted pair. Sometimes a classification will have two characters at the end, such as *VG* in 100BaseVG or *TX* in 100BaseTX. In the case of 100BaseVG, the *VG* represents *voice grade*. However, in 100BaseTX, the *T* represents *twisted pair* and the *X* represents *Fast Ethernet*, as demonstrated in Figure 2-20C.

The name of a given classification details quite a bit of information. The first number (in this case 10) is the bandwidth in Mbps. The *base* refers to baseband (as opposed to broadband). The *T* tells you it is twisted-pair cable. For example, Category 5 cable would be 100BaseT. This is not only used for twisted-pair cable, but for other types of cable, such as coax. Three specific types are discussed in this section.

10Base2

The **10Base2** classification specifies the use of RG-58 (thinnet) cable and a data rate of 10 Mbps. Figure 2-21 illustrates the physical characteristics of a 10Base2 network. Note that a 10Base2 network is configured in a bus topology and that the maximum segment length is 185 meters. This means that the segment length cannot exceed 185 meters. If it does, the signal strength will deteriorate due to attenuation and impedance. Also, note that the minimum segment length between nodes is 0.5 meters.

Terminating resistors are installed to absorb the electrical signals when they reach the end of the segment. If a terminating resistor is not installed, the signal will reflect, causing the other signals transmitted across the cable to distort. Also, one end of the segment must be electrically grounded. Remember, a fluctuating digital signal traveling along a cable's core produces an electromagnetic wave, which can be absorbed by a neighboring conductor. In the case of a copper-core cable, the cable's shielding absorbs the electromagnetic wave. Grounding one end of the cable helps to drain this interference so that the original signal is not affected.

Remember, if there is a break in the cabling or a problem with a BNC connector or a terminating resistor, no communication will take place. This is a major reason why coaxial cable is no longer used in networking.

Copyright Goodheart-Willcox Co., Inc.

Figure 2-21 Physical characteristics of a 10Base2 network.

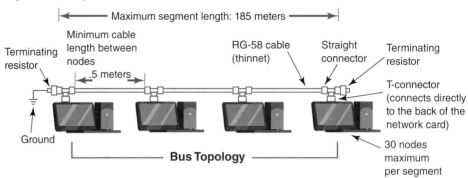

(workstation icons) RedlineVector/Shutterstock.com; Goodheart-Willcox Publisher

10Base5

The **10Base5** classification was the first IEEE 802.3 classification developed for Ethernet. The 10Base5 classification specifies the use of RG-8 (thicknet) and a 10 Mbps data rate. The 10Base5 network, like 10Base2, uses a bus topology. However, the maximum segment length for a 10Base5 network is 500 meters. Each of the three segments that can connect to computers can connect to a maximum of 100. This allows a 10Base5 network to have a total of 300 computers. A computer attaches to the thicknet coaxial cable through an AUI cable and AUI connectors. AUI is the acronym for *Attachment Unit Interface*. The AUI connector is a 15-pin D-shell connector that is used to attach a cable to a network interface card or network device. One end of the AUI connector connects to the network interface card and the other end connects to a transceiver unit, as illustrated in Figure 2-22. The transceiver unit has a pair of spikes that pierce the cable's insulating jacket, shield, and insulator and makes a connection with the center core conductor. The transceiver unit is often called a *vampire tap*.

Figure 2-22 10Base5 connections using a vampire tap, a transceiver unit, and an Attachment Unit Interface (AUI). Cable lengths and type are also indicated.

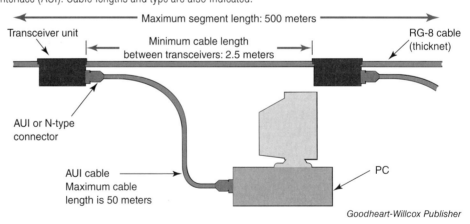

Goodheart-Willcox Publisher

Copyright Goodheart-Willcox Co., Inc.

10BaseT

The **10BaseT** classification specifies the use of the different categories of UTP cable. It is most often arranged in a star topology and follows the 100-meter rule, as seen in Figure 2-23. This rule specifies that any cable on the network should not exceed 100 meters. The 100-meter length ensures that the signal strength will be sufficient when reaching the final destination. At about 100 meters, signal attenuation begins. A repeater, however, may be used to extend the distance to an additional 100 meters. Most hubs encountered are active hubs, which means they also act as repeaters by regenerating electrical signals.

Figure 2-23 The 10BaseT network follows the 100-meter rule. This means that any cable used in a 10BaseT network should not exceed 100 meters in length.

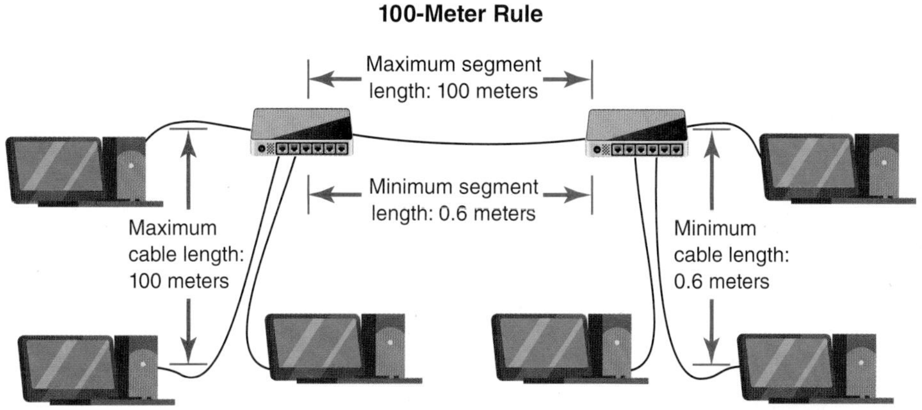

100-Meter Rule

(workstation icons) RedlineVector/Shutterstock.com; (hub icons) Vadim Ermak/Shutterstock.com; Goodheart-Willcox Publisher

A 10BaseT network can have two types of hub configurations: daisy chain and cascade. Study the hub configurations in Figure 2-24. Note that in the daisy-chain configuration, Figure 2-24A, an electronic signal from *Computer 1* must pass through four hubs before it reaches its destination, *Computer 8*. In the cascade configuration, Figure 2-24B, an electronic signal from *Computer 1* only has to pass through three hubs before it reaches its destination, *Computer 8*. This is a significant detail. Although both configurations have a similar number of hubs, an electronic signal does not have to pass through as many hubs in a cascade configuration as it does in a daisy-chain configuration.

If another hub were added to the daisy-chain configuration, an electronic signal from *Computer 1* would have to travel through five hubs before it reached a destination computer on the fifth hub, thus increasing the latency of the electronic signal. However, if another hub were added to the cascade configuration, an electronic signal from *Computer 1* would still only have to travel through three hubs before it reached a destination computer on the fifth hub. Adding another hub to the configuration would not increase the amount of hubs through which a signal has to travel.

As a general rule, no more than four hubs should be linked in a daisy-chain configuration. However, more than four hubs are allowed as long as an electronic signal does not need to travel through more than four hubs to arrive at its destination. If the signal passes through more than four hubs, the latency of the signal becomes excessive and causes the electronic signal to exceed its TTL setting. The electronic signal is then destroyed.

Copyright Goodheart-Willcox Co., Inc.

Figure 2-24 Daisy-chain and cascade hub configurations. A—When hubs are arranged in a daisy-chain configuration, an electronic signal must pass through all hubs to arrive at a computer on the last hub in the chain. B—When hubs are arranged in a cascade configuration, an electronic signal never has to pass through more than three hubs to arrive at its destination.

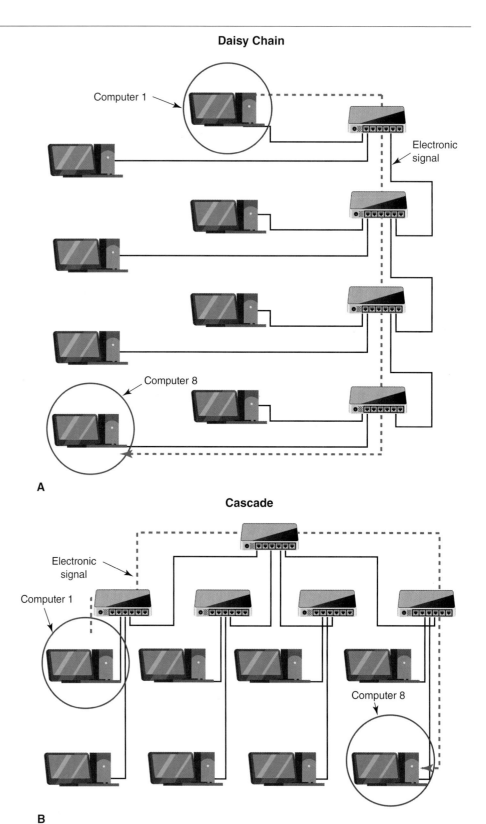

(workstation icons) RedlineVector/Shutterstock.com; (hub icons) Vadim Ermak/Shutterstock.com;
Goodheart-Willcox Publisher

Copyright Goodheart-Willcox Co., Inc.

IEEE 802.3 Media Access

Ethernet networks use a media access method called **carrier-sense multiple access with collision detection (CSMA/CD)** to control and ensure data delivery. CSMA/CD works by allowing a workstation to listen for data traffic on the network before transmitting data. When the network is silent, the workstation transmits data. However, if another workstation submits data at the same time, the data collides on the network. When this happens, the two workstations wait a random period before retransmitting the data. The random period is less than a fraction of a second. A typical network can transmit thousands of data packets in one second. Collisions usually remain unnoticed on a properly installed network. A poorly designed network may operate slowly as a result of too many collisions. Data collision is an inherent problem with Ethernet communication. When two data packets collide, they become corrupted and cannot be delivered.

Breaking down the acronym will help you better understand CSMA/CD as a standard for network communication. CSMA/CD can be separated into three distinct pairs of letters that correspond to words that explain the operation requirements that must be met to match the CSMA/CD standard. Carrier sense (CS) means that a network interface card can sense when data is transmitted on a network cable. Multiple access (MA) means that the network cable provides simultaneous access to all network interface cards connected to the cable. Collision detection (CD) means that the network interface card can detect when a collision has occurred and will automatically resend the damaged packet.

Today, however, what is most often used is **carrier-sense multiple access with collision avoidance (CSMA/CA)**, works much like CSMA/CD but tries to avoid collisions by waiting until there is a brief lull in network traffic before sending out a packet.

IEEE 802.3 Wiring and Connections

Wiring and connectors used for networking were first derived from the existing telephone communication industry. Even today, many of the cable standards apply not only to networking but also to other communication systems.

This section introduces the basics of twisted-pair network cable, connectors, and standards. The two main cable termination standards in use for twisted-pair cable are 568A and 568B as described by the TIA/EIA organization.

568A and 568B

When installing an RJ-45 connector, it is important that the conductors, which are color-coded, be inserted into the appropriate pin area. Two standard connections are recognized by industry: 568A and 568B. Long before standards existed, there were two common ways to make an RJ-45 connection. Since the industry was divided, both became standards but are denoted by the letters *A* and *B*. The only real difference in the connections is the color of the conductors inserted into the pin areas. Other than the color of the conductors, the electrical qualities are the same. Look at Figure 2-25. Compare the two standard connections, 568A and 568B, in Figure 2-25A. Notice that for the 10BaseT classification, Figure 2-25B, each connector uses only two pairs of conductors from the cable: the orange pair and the green pair. The other two pairs are not used for communication in a 10BaseT network.

UTP cables have two common classifications of assembly: *straight-through* and *crossover*. A **straight-through cable** is constructed with each numbered pin connecting to the matching numbered pin on the opposite end of the cable. Straight-through cables are used to connect computers with hubs. A **crossover cable** has

1.3 NET

2.1 NET

Copyright Goodheart-Willcox Co., Inc.

Figure 2-25 The 568A and 568B connection standards. A—The only difference between the two connection standards is the locations of pairs 2 and 3. B—The 10BaseT classification uses pairs 2 and 3. Either connection standard can be used.

Cable Pairs

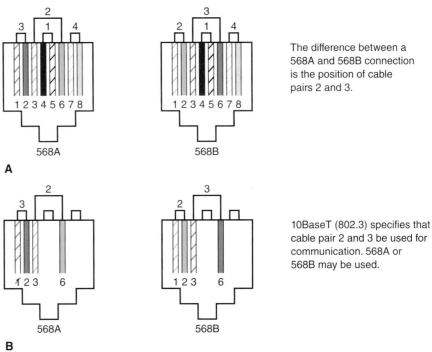

The difference between a 568A and 568B connection is the position of cable pairs 2 and 3.

10BaseT (802.3) specifies that cable pair 2 and 3 be used for communication. 568A or 568B may be used.

Goodheart-Willcox Publisher

Tech Tip

A *wire map* is an illustration of the correct circuit path of conductors from one end of a cable run to the opposite end. Wire maps are used to illustrate proper cable connections for a technician who makes cable assemblies.

two pairs (four individual conductors) that are cross-connected. Crossover cables are used to connect computers with other computers.

Look at the wire map in Figure 2-26. Notice that pin 1 connects to pin 1, pin 2 connects to pin 2, and so on. When a two-workstation 10BaseT network is configured, a crossover cable must be used for the network cards to communicate. Cross-connecting the pairs allows a transmit signal from one computer to be sent to the receive pins of a network card on the other computer. This allows the computers to communicate without a hub. A crossover cable is not needed when a hub is used because the circuitry at each access port crosses the connection internally. Therefore, a straight-through cable is used in this situation.

Look at the hub in Figure 2-27. Notice that each access port number on the hub has an *X* beside it. This indicates the access port's internal connection is crossed. Also, notice the uplink port. The uplink port serves a straight-through connection. It can be used to connect via a straight-through cable to an access port on another hub.

Some network devices, like switches and network adapters, are Auto-MDIX compliant. **Automatic medium-dependent interface crossover (Auto-MDIX)** is an electronic chip technology incorporated into Gigabit Ethernet devices to automatically reassign pin functions and eliminate the need for a crossover cable. To verify that the network device is Auto-MDIX compliant, look at the device specifications.

Devices such as switches have a **maximum transmission unit (MTU)**, which refers to the largest network-layer data unit that can be sent at one time, or the largest transmission unit. An MTU is adjustable, but it should only be adjusted by those with familiarity in doing so.

NET
1.3

Copyright Goodheart-Willcox Co., Inc.

Figure 2-26 Wire map of a straight-through cable and a crossover cable.

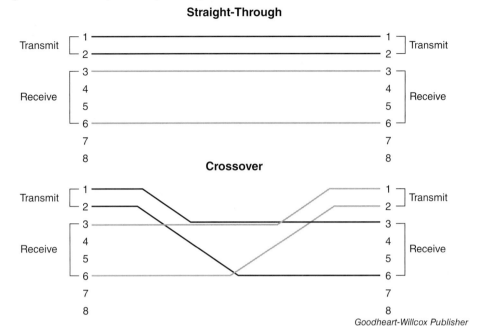

Goodheart-Willcox Publisher

Figure 2-27 A hub typically has many access ports and one uplink port. The circuitry inside the hub provides a crossed connection at each access port and allows for a straight-through connection at the uplink port.

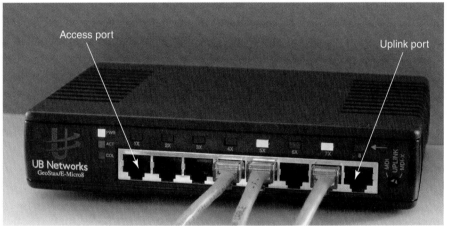

Goodheart-Willcox Publisher

Installing an RJ-45 Connector

The RJ-45 connector contains eight connection points, or pins, inside its plastic housing, as shown in Figure 2-28. To install an RJ-45 connector on a UTP cable, the insulating jacket of the UTP cable is first stripped from the cable, exposing the conductor pairs, as demonstrated in Figure 2-29. The pairs are untwisted so that each conductor can be inserted into one of the designated pin areas. A *crimp tool* is used to clamp an RJ-45 connector to the end of the cable, as shown in Figure 2-30. After a connector is inserted into the crimp tool with the wires in their appropriate positions, the handles of the tool are squeezed together. When the RJ-45 connector is crimped, each conductor makes contact with one of the eight pins and the connector is punctured to clamp down onto the cabling jacket.

> **Tech Tip**
>
> The RJ-45 is also known as the *8P8C connector*. The acronym 8P8C represents "8 pair 8 contacts."

2.1, 5.2 NET

Copyright Goodheart-Willcox Co., Inc.

Figure 2-28 Close-up of an RJ-45 connector.

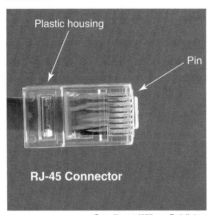

Goodheart-Willcox Publisher

Figure 2-29 The insulating jacket on this UTP cable has been stripped to reveal the conductor pairs.

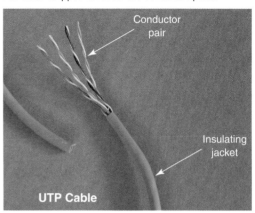

Goodheart-Willcox Publisher

Figure 2-30 An RJ-45 crimp tool is used to make the connection between the RJ-45 pins and the twisted-pair conductors.

Goodheart-Willcox Publisher

Rollover Cable

A **rollover cable** is a special cable in which the pin order is completely reversed on one end of the cable. Pin 1 connects to pin 8, pin 2 connects to pin 7, and so on. The Cisco console cable is wired like a rollover cable in that the pin numbers are reversed. However, a Cisco console cable uses an RJ-45 connector on one end and a DB-9 serial connector on the other, whereas, a rollover cable uses an RJ-45 connector on each end.

Bonding and Grounding

STP and coaxial cable requires equipment to be bonded and grounded before the shielding can be effective. All electrical systems have one centralized ground that is common for all electrical equipment. The centralized ground is typically located at the point in the building where the electrical company commercial power enters.

The ground path must be continuous from the equipment to which the cable is attached to the central ground in the electrical system. If the ground path is not continuous, the shielding will not effectively protect the network cables from electrical and radio interference. There will be more about grounding and bonding in Chapter 18.

Copyright Goodheart-Willcox Co., Inc.

Power over Ethernet (PoE)

The **Power over Ethernet (PoE)** IEEE standard 802.3af specifies the supply of small amounts of electrical power to network devices, such as cameras, IP phones, wireless access points, speakers, and phone or PDA chargers. The amount of power delivered is approximately 13 watts at 48 volts. The cable used for PoE must be rated as Category 5 or better. Two pairs of cables are used for network communication and one pair is used to supply the electrical power.

A more electronically sophisticated method of PoE is used for Gigabit networks in which all cable pairs are used to carry network communication. Electrical power is supplied via two of the existing cable pairs that provide communication.

A more technical explanation of how power is provided over a communication cable is beyond the purpose of this textbook. To learn more about the electronic aspect of PoE, visit www.poweroverethernet.com. For detailed electronic specifications, check the Texas Instruments web page focus.ti.com/docs/prod/folders/print/tps2370.html.

A common PoE application is building and area security when electrical power is not readily available. Using PoE is very cost-effective when compared to installing new electrical circuits to power devices such as cameras.

IEEE 802.5 Standard

The IEEE 802.5 standard describes the token ring network. The token ring network uses the token passing access method and is configured in a ring topology. Token ring networks operate at 4 Mbps, 16 Mbps, and 100 Mbps. Token ring can be used with proprietary cable, such as IBM design or UTP and STP. The maximum number of nodes allowed for a token ring network varies according to the network distance, speed, cable media, and equipment used. Always check with the manufacturer for the latest specifications. This is a very old technology and you are unlikely to discover it today. However, it was pivotal in the history of networking, so it still appears in many networking textbooks and certification tests, like the CompTIA Network+.

While a token ring network can be wired as a physical ring, as shown in Figure 2-31, most token ring networks use a multiple access unit (MAU) for a center

1.3 NET

Tech Tip

Some token ring networks do not use UTP as the network media. They use proprietary cable, but the electrical characteristics are similar.

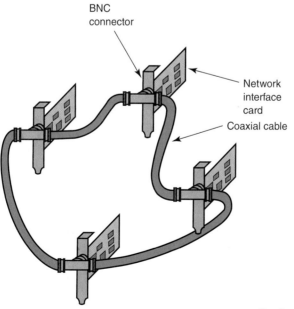

BNC connector

Network interface card

Coaxial cable

Figure 2-31 Token ring network using coaxial cable. When a token ring network uses coaxial cable, it resembles a physical ring.

Goodheart-Willcox Publisher

Copyright Goodheart-Willcox Co., Inc.

connection point. See Figure 2-32 for an example. When a MAU is used, the network arrangement resembles a star topology. However, because of the circuitry in the MAU, the network is physically connected as a ring. Each port on the MAU is designed to maintain an electrical ring. This can be seen on a close inspection of the MAU in Figure 2-33.

Each port located at the MAU is normally closed to ensure the integrity of the ring. When a computer is added by plugging in the network cable, the port opens the normally closed circuit, allowing the added computer to join the ring.

A token ring network commonly uses several MAUs. When two or more MAUs exist in the ring, integrity is maintained in the same way as with added computers. MAUs, however, connect through special ports called *ring in* and *ring out*.

Figure 2-32 Token ring network using twisted-pair cable. When a token ring network uses twisted-pair cabling, it resembles a physical star.

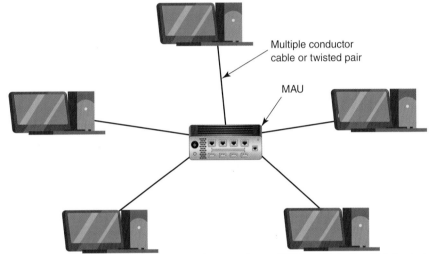

(workstation icons) RedlineVector/Shutterstock.com; (MAU icon) Vadim Ermak/Shutterstock.com; Goodheart-Willcox Publisher

Figure 2-33 Basic representation of the electronic circuitry inside a MAU. The MAU is designed to allow a continuous loop of data flow in the token ring topology. Look closely at the way the switches inside the unit are normally closed and then open when a cable plug is inserted.

MAU

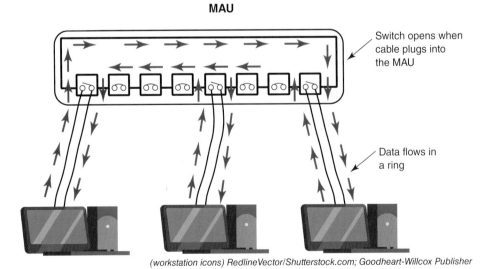

(workstation icons) RedlineVector/Shutterstock.com; Goodheart-Willcox Publisher

Copyright Goodheart-Willcox Co., Inc.

When a token ring network incorporates a MAU, twisted-pair cable is used. The twisted-pair cable attaches to an RJ-45 connector. Token ring only uses two pairs for communication and has one standard, 568A, as described in Figure 2-34.

Wiring Faults

When installing twisted-pair cabling, the pairs of conductors inside the cable jacket must be connected correctly at both ends or the network will not be able to communicate. The proper connection of individual conductors to pins is outlined in TIA standards T568A and T568B. The proper connection sequence must be maintained throughout the installation, from the network card to the server room. Incorrect wiring can result in shorts, opens, reversed pairs, crossed pairs, and split pairs.

Short

A **short** occurs in cabling when two conductors are improperly connected, resulting in a shorter circuit path. Look at the lamp circuit in Figure 2-35. The lamp circuit is connected with the splice point left open for viewing. Most short circuits and open circuits occur at splice points and connection points. In Figure 2-35A, the circuit is correctly wired. When the switch is closed, electrical energy flows through the lamp, and the bulb in the lamp is lit. In Figure 2-35B, the wires are touching at the splice point. The same can be applied to networking media. When the switch is closed, the electrical energy cannot reach the lamp because the electrical energy routes through the shortest path, the splice point. When a short occurs in a network cable, data takes a shorter route and does not reach its destination.

5.3   NET

Figure 2-34 The 802.5 standard specifies that only the 568A connection standard be used. Note that pairs 1 and 2 are used for communication.

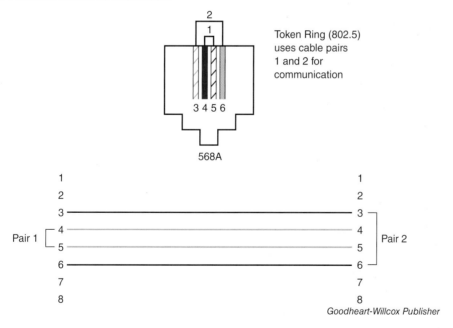

Goodheart-Willcox Publisher

Copyright Goodheart-Willcox Co., Inc.

Figure 2-35 A correctly wired circuit and a shorted circuit. A—This circuit is correctly wired. When the switch is closed, the current flows through the complete circuit, lighting the lamp. B—In this circuit, the wires are shorted (touching). When the switch is closed, the current takes the shortest path, and the lamp does not light.

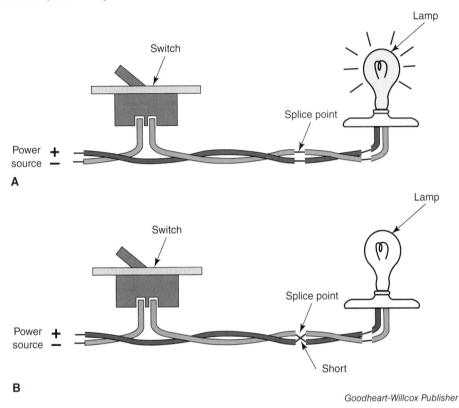

Goodheart-Willcox Publisher

Open

NET
5.3

An **open** is just as the name implies—a wiring fault that occurs when the circuit has an open spot along the length of the conductor. Look at Figure 2-36. In the illustration, you can see the open is at the splice point. When the switch is closed, no electrical energy can reach the lamp. The lamp will not light because the circuit is incomplete. When an open occurs in a network system, no data can travel past the point of the open.

Copyright Goodheart-Willcox Co., Inc.

Figure 2-36 In this circuit, there is a break in the wiring at the splice point. When the switch is closed, the lamp does light. This condition is called an open.

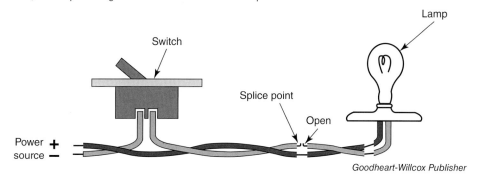

Goodheart-Willcox Publisher

Ground

A **ground** occurs when a conductor connects to the earth through a continuous path. Grounds typically occur where the conductor's insulating jacket is torn and the copper conductor makes contact with conduit or any other metal surface that is grounded. When a ground occurs in a network cable, all data is prevented from reaching its destination.

Reversed, Crossed, and Split Pairs

Reversed, crossed, and split pairs commonly occur when technicians install connectors on twisted-pair cables in the field. It is very easy to misconnect individual wires when installing an RJ-45 connector or when terminating a twisted-pair cable in a punch down block. The misconnection may go unnoticed until after the network system is installed and a computer has a problem accessing the network.

Study the examples in Figure 2-37 of reversed, crossed, and split pairs. A **reversed pair** occurs when two pairs of a cable assembly have reversed two connections, Figure 2-37B. For example, a blue pair has reversed pin connections with a green pair. A **crossed pair** occurs when one of each of the two cable pairs has become part of the other pair's connection. In Figure 2-37C, one conductor of the blue pair is connected as one conductor of the green pair. One conductor of the green pair is connected as one conductor of the blue pair. A **split pair** occurs when two pairs of conductors are reversed in connection with another pair. In Figure 37D, a complete pair of blue conductors has been reversed with connections intended for the green pair, and the green pair has taken the position intended for the blue pair.

Electronic cable testers are designed for testing a cable for the possibility of opens, crossed pairs, split pairs, and reversed pairs. You will use a cable tester often in the field when troubleshooting network communication problems. Figure 2-38 shows a cable tester.

Tech Tip

Remember, a short occurs between two conductors, a ground occurs between a conductor and the earth. The connection to the earth is usually provided by a metallic enclosure, such as the metal pipe used to carry network cables, or exposed metal building parts, such as I-beams or drop ceiling channels.

5.3   NET ⊹

Figure 2-37 Common wiring errors: reversed pair, crossed pairs, and split pair. The red numbers indicate the errors. A—Normal connection is made. Each conductor is wired to a corresponding connection number. B—Reversed pair. Conductors within the pair reverse their connection at the opposite end of the cable. C—Crossed pairs. Two pairs have switched positions at the opposite end of the cable. D—Split pair. One conductor from each of two pairs have switched positions at the opposite end of the cable.

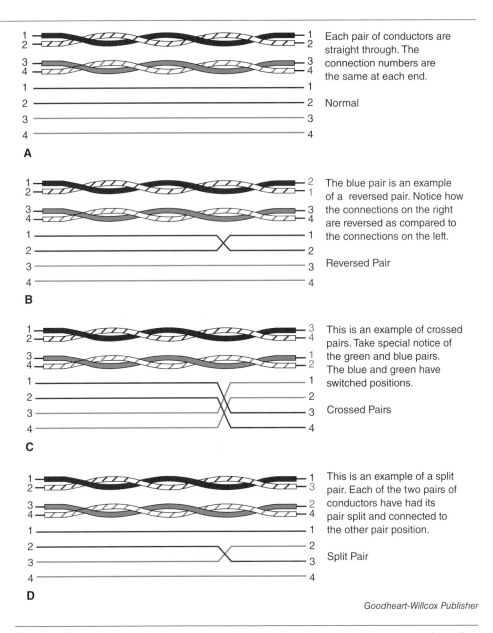

Each pair of conductors are straight through. The connection numbers are the same at each end.

Normal

The blue pair is an example of a reversed pair. Notice how the connections on the right are reversed as compared to the connections on the left.

Reversed Pair

This is an example of crossed pairs. Take special notice of the green and blue pairs. The blue and green have switched positions.

Crossed Pairs

This is an example of a split pair. Each of the two pairs of conductors have had its pair split and connected to the other pair position.

Split Pair

Goodheart-Willcox Publisher

Figure 2-38 An electronic cable tester is used to check for wiring faults such as crossed pairs, split pairs, and reversed pairs.

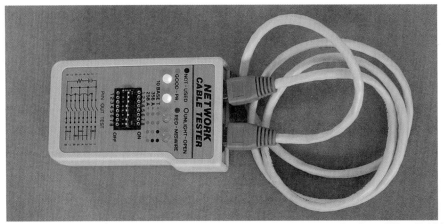

Goodheart-Willcox Publisher

Copyright Goodheart-Willcox Co., Inc.

Summary

Network Media

- The three major classifications of network media are copper cable, fiber-optic cable, and wireless radio waves.

Analog and Digital Signals

- Electronic signals are classified as analog and digital. Analog and digital signals differ by the shape of their waveforms.
- In the analog signal, time affects the degree of the slope. In the digital signal, time affects the duration of the voltage level.
- Both analog and digital waves have a frequency measurement.
- Bandwidth is a measurement of the ability of network media to carry data, whereas frequency is a measurement of the ability of network media to carry an electronic signal.

Data Transmission

- Baseband is a method of transmitting a single frequency using the entire bandwidth of a cable. Broadband is a method of transmitting multiple frequencies or data across a cable at once.
- Communication can occur in one of three modes: simplex, half-duplex, and full-duplex. Simplex communication occurs in one direction only. Half-duplex communication occurs in both directions, but not at the same time. Full-duplex communication occurs in both directions at the same time.

Electronic Terms

- Electrical energy that travels in only one direction is referred to as *direct current (DC)*.
- Electrical energy that constantly reverses its direction of flow is referred to as *alternating current (AC)*.
- Electrical resistance is the opposition to the flow of electrical energy. Resistance is generally used to describe this effect in DC circuits.
- Impedance is also the opposition to the flow of electrical energy, but it expresses the amount of resistance encountered in an AC circuit.
- Reflected loss is the amount of signal reflected from the far end, or receiving end, of a cable.
- The electrical phenomenon of a current-carrying conductor inducing current in a cable of close proximity is called *crosstalk*.
- Near-End Crosstalk is a measurement of crosstalk at the near end, or sending end, of a cable.
- Alien Crosstalk is crosstalk generated from network cables in close proximity to each other.
- The decibel (dB) is an electrical measurement that is used to express the amount of power or energy gained or lost.
- Far-End Crosstalk is a measurement of crosstalk at the far end, or receiving end, of a cable.

- Equal Level Far-End Crosstalk is a measurement of the negated effects of cable attenuation caused by crosstalk.

Copper-Core Cables

- Copper conductor wire size is based on its diameter and is expressed as a size according to the American Wire Gauge (AWG). The larger AWG the number, the smaller the wire size.

- Three common coaxial cable types that have been used for networking are RG-6, RG-8 (thicknet), and RG-58 (thinnet).

- Twisted-pair cable is divided into seven categories. The categories are based on the physical design and capabilities of the cable, such as the maximum frequency rating, the data rate that the cable is capable of, and number of twists per foot.

IEEE 802 Standard

- The IEEE 802.3 standard describes the characteristics of various Ethernet technologies, such as 10 Mbps, Fast Ethernet, Gigabit Ethernet, and 10 Gigabit Ethernet.

- An Auto-MDIX compliant device automatically reassigns the pin functions so that a crossover cable is not required for communication.

- Power over Ethernet (PoE) is a way of powering devices that consume small amounts of electrical energy, approximately 13 watts at 48 volts, over network cable.

Wiring Faults

- Wiring faults include shorts, opens, reversed pairs, crossed pairs, and split pairs.

Review Questions

1. What are two general classifications of network media?
2. Twisted-pair and coaxial cables both use pulsating _____ energy to transmit data.
3. _____ signals have discrete values, while _____ signals have continuous ranges of values.
4. What is attenuation?
5. What is latency?
6. Noise and crosstalk are types of _____.
7. Differentiate between baseband and broadband transmissions.
8. List the three modes in which communication can occur.
9. What is the difference between half-duplex and full-duplex communication?
10. Bandwidth in analog transmissions is measured in _____ and is represented by the abbreviation _____.

11. What is the difference between direct current (DC) and alternating current (AC)?

12. _____ is the opposition to direct current; _____ is the opposition to alternating current.

13. The amount of signal reflected from the end of the cable is called _____.

14. Describe *crosstalk*.

15. List four types of measurement that can be taken on twisted-pair cable to measure the effects of crosstalk.

16. List the four categories of the IEEE 802.3 classification.

17. RG-58 is also referred to as _____.

18. The size of a conductor's diameter is described by what rating?

19. Which conductor has a larger diameter, one that has a 22 AWG rating or one that has a 24 AWG rating?

20. What type of coaxial cable is recommended by the EIA/TIA 570 residential communication standard?

21. Which type of coaxial cable is referred to as *thicknet*?

22. How many categories of twisted-pair cables exist?

23. What is the maximum frequency rating of Category 6 UTP cable?

24. List the two main cable termination standards for twisted-pair cable.

25. What type of connector is used for UTP cable?

26. List and describe five wiring faults that can occur from incorrect wiring.

✚ Sample Network+ Exam Questions

1. Which type of cable is typically associated with a 10BaseT network?

    A. RG-58

    B. UTP

    C. Fiber-optic

    D. RG-8

2. Mary is a network technician and is installing cable. She needs to install several UTP connectors. Before starting installation, she is assembling all the equipment she will need. What connector is used with UTP cable?

    A. BNC

    B. RJ-45

    C. AUI

    D. ST

3. What is the maximum frequency rating for Category 7 cable?

   A. 250 MHz

   B. 500 MHz

   C. 600 MHz

   D. 10 Gbps

4. The loss of signal strength from one end of a cable to the opposite end is expressed as _____.

   A. attenuation

   B. crosstalk

   C. NEXT

   D. resistance

5. What is the purpose of twisted-pair shielding?

   A. To reduce the effects of environmental heat.

   B. To provide protection from EMI.

   C. To increase the rate of data flow.

   D. To identify which pair is used for transmitting data.

6. What is the difference in the 568B or 568A pinout sequence?

   A. The orange and green pairs are in reverse pin locations, and the blue and brown pairs remain in the same pin locations.

   B. The blue and brown pairs are in reverse pin locations, and the orange and green pairs remain in the same pin locations.

   C. The blue and red pairs are in opposite locations, and the gray and brown pairs remain in the same pin locations.

   D. All conductor pairs are in opposite locations.

7. Ferris is trying to measure signal loss in the cable used in his company's network. Which electrical characteristic is used to measure signal loss in cable?

   A. Decibel

   B. Resistance

   C. Amperage

   D. Wattage

Copyright Goodheart-Willcox Co., Inc.

8. Which type of cable reverses the pin connections of the transmit and receive pairs?

   A. Rollover

   B. Crossover

   C. Pitchover

   D. 1000BaseT

9. Georgia is working with an older network that has Category 5e cabling. She is concerned that it might not have enough bandwidth for the network requirements. What is the maximum data rate of a Category 5e cable if four cable pairs are used to transmit data?

   A. 10 Mbps

   B. 100 Mbps

   C. 1000 Mbps

   D. Only two cable pairs on a Category 5e cable can be used to transmit data.

10. You have been assigned to install cable in a new building. There is a great deal of concern about what would happen if a fire occurred. You want the safest cable possible. A cable with a special type of insulation that will not give off toxic gases should the cable be consumed by fire is _____.

    A. AWG-rated

    B. fireproof-rated

    C. plenum-rated

    D. safety-rated

Network+ Certification Exam Objectives

To prepare for the Network+ Certification exam, you must be able to do the following:

Objectives

2.1: Media Types—Fiber

Connector Types—Fiber

2.5: Transmission Mediums—Fiber

5.2: Hardware Tools—OTDR, Light Meter

5.3: Attenuation

5.4: Reflection, Refraction, Absorption

Learning Outcomes

- Describe the characteristics of fiber-optic cable and how it is used to transmit data.
- Explain the properties of light.
- Describe fiber-optic cable construction.
- Discuss fiber-optic cable specifications.
- Recall the characteristics and specifications of the IEEE 802.3 fiber-optic standards.
- Recall the characteristics and specifications of the FDDI standard.
- Differentiate between fiber-optic cable connectors.
- Describe the installation and troubleshooting of common fiber-optic cabling.

Copyright Goodheart-Willcox Co., Inc.

Key Terms

absorption
dispersion
electromagnetic wave
extrinsic losses
Fiber Distributed Data Interface
(FDDI)

Fresnel reflection loss
fusion splice
graded-index multimode fiber-optic
cable
multimode fiber-optic cable
optical time domain reflectometer
(OTDR)

scattering
single-mode fiber-optic cable
step-index multimode fiber-optic
cable

Overview

Fiber-optic cable supports transmission rates of well over 1 Gbps. It is primarily used for network backbones and long-distance cable runs. Fiber-optic cable has many advantages over copper-core cable and follows a different set of network standards such as FDDI and 802.3. This chapter explores the advantages of fiber-optic cable and its construction. It also covers the nature of light, transmission characteristics, the FDDI and 802.3 standards, and cable faults and testing.

Characteristics of Fiber-Optic Cable

Fiber-optic cable consists of a glass or plastic core that carries pulses of light. The pulses of light represent binary data, as shown in Figure 3-1. A transmitter is located at the source and a receiver is located at the destination. The transmitter and receiver are connected by fiber-optic cable. The transmitter at the source converts the binary data represented by electrical, digital pulses into light pulses. Binary values are encoded with different frequencies of light or different wavelengths. The light pulses travel the fiber-optic cable to the receiver at the destination. The receiver converts the light pulses back into an electrical signal consisting of a series of digital pulses.

2.1	**NET**
2.5	**NET**

It may seem like a lot of extra work to convert digital signals into light signals and then back to digital signals. One might question why it would not be more efficient to use copper-core cable. There are several reasons fiber-optic cable might be

Figure 3-1 Electrical energy representing digital signals is transferred from the source to the destination. The transmitter converts electrical digital signals to light pulses representing digital data. The light pulses are converted to digital signals at the receiver.

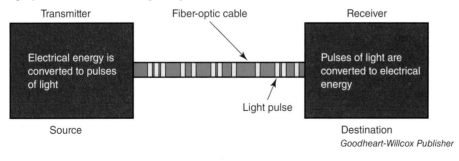

Goodheart-Willcox Publisher

Copyright Goodheart-Willcox Co., Inc.

chosen over copper-core cable. The following reasons are related to the following beneficial attributes of fiber-optic cable:

- Provides for data security
- Immune to electromagnetic interference
- Lightweight and small in diameter
- Wide bandwidth
- Resistant to corrosion and water
- Supports data transmission over longer distances than copper-core cable

Security

Information has become a profitable and, in some cases, priceless commodity. In business, industry, and military applications, it is important to protect this information from unethical people who would seek to gain from using it. Fiber-optic cable is much more difficult to tap into without being detected. Any cut made to the fiber-optic core disturbs the light signal and, by extension, data transmission. Removing the protective material around the fiber-optic core causes signal loss. For these reasons, fiber-optic cable is far more secure than copper-core cable.

Immunity to Electromagnetic Interference

Fiber-optic cable conducts light waves instead of electrical energy, which makes it immune to electromagnetic interference generated by motors, radio signals, fluorescent lighting, and other sources of electromagnetic energy. Conventional copper-core cable must be shielded to prevent electromagnetic interference. Shielding cable causes cable to be large in diameter and heavy.

The military began research in fiber optics many years ago. Nuclear weapons create a powerful electromagnetic field, which destroys communication systems that consist of copper-core cable. The destruction caused by an electromagnetic field could occur many miles from an actual nuclear explosion. Since fiber-optic cable is not affected by electromagnetic fields, military communications that use fiber-optic cable could remain intact.

Weight and Size

Fiber-optic cables are exceptionally lightweight compared with copper-core cable. This is unimportant in general wiring applications, but for applications where weight is a critical factor, it is very important. Some of the applications in which weight is a critical factor are aircrafts and ships. The lighter the aircraft or ship, the more cargo it can carry. Fiber-optic cables are approximately 1/10th the weight of comparable copper-core cables.

Fiber-optic cable has a smaller overall diameter than copper-core cable. This is extremely important when installing communication lines. Many more communication lines can be provided in the same conduit using fiber-optic cable rather than copper-core cable. In a telephone communication system, over 1,000 fiber-optic cables can easily fit in the same space as 100 copper-core cables.

Bandwidth

Fiber-optic cable has a much greater bandwidth than copper-core cable. Light can be transmitted at a much higher frequency through glass core than electronic digital signals through copper-core cable. Copper wire suffers from data rate limitations caused by impedance. Fiber-optic cable is not affected by impedance characteristics.

Copyright Goodheart-Willcox Co., Inc.

Since a higher signal frequency can be used, more data can be transmitted through fiber-optic cable per second than copper-core cable. Copper-core cable has limitations and losses due to inductive reactance. Copper-core cables lose their conduction capabilities at extremely high frequencies. Fiber-optic cable can handle high frequencies with little to no problem.

Corrosion and Water Resistance

The very nature of glass or plastic makes it resistant to most corrosives. Water does not affect the light conduction capabilities of a properly installed fiber-optic system. The fiber-optic cables that have been installed under the world's oceans are expected to last for many, many years.

Greater Distances

Fiber-optic cable can support data transmission over greater distances than copper-core cable. Copper-core cable used for network systems is typically limited to 100 meters, but fiber-optic cable can be used for long-distance applications spanning 20 kilometers or more. Fiber-optic cable is typically used for network backbones of 2000 meters and 3000 meters in a single segment length. For certain applications such as FDDI, distances of 200 kilometers or approximately 124 miles can be supported.

Nature of Light

Light is classified as electromagnetic energy and is identified in the electromagnetic wave spectrum chart along with radio waves, X-rays, and Gamma rays, as shown in Figure 3-2. An **electromagnetic wave** is a form of energy that behaves like a wave and can travel through a vacuum. It requires no other media for support. For example, sound is an energy that travels as a wave, but it must be carried by a gas (air), liquid (water), or solid (steel). Sound cannot travel through a vacuum like radio waves, X-rays, and light waves can. Hence, sound is not a form of electromagnetic energy. It should be noted that light behaves like both a wave and a particle. The details of that are beyond the scope of this book, but you should be able to find adequate information in many physics textbooks.

In Chapter 2, electrical energy wave patterns were described using the term *frequency*. Remember, frequency is based on the number of complete cycles of an

Note

The exact maximum distance for fiber-optic cable applications depends on many different factors, such as the type of fiber-optic cable (multimode or single-mode), the official standard being applied (IEEE, ISO, or EIA/TIA), and manufacturer specifications.

Figure 3-2 Visible light is only a small part of the total electromagnetic wave spectrum.

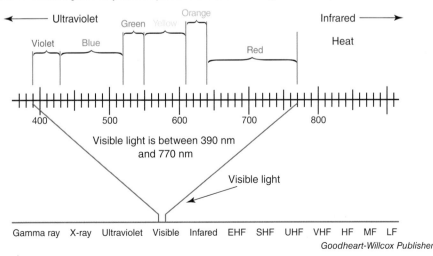

Goodheart-Willcox Publisher

Tech Tip

The term *wavelength* originated from the field of physics. Many of the terms first introduced in physics have been directly adopted and used to describe the phenomena of fiber-optic cable. It is interesting to note that early on the term *wavelength* was used to describe the fluctuating patterns of radio waves and is still used in the design of antenna systems.

electrical wave that occur in one second. Light energy can also be described using the term *frequency*, but the preferred term is *wavelength. Wavelength,* in relation to light waves, is the length of one complete cycle and is typically measured in nanometers. For example, visible light is composed of wavelengths between 390 nanometers and 770 nanometers. A *nanometer* is 1/1,000,000,000 of a meter. The nanometer is used to measure the distance of the repeating light wave pattern or the distance of one complete light wave cycle.

The three common wavelengths for fiber-optic communications are 850 nanometers, 1300 nanometers, and 1550 nanometers. Fiber-optic devices and cable, such as transmitters, receivers, and fiber-optic core diameters, are selected according to wavelength of the signal used. For example, a device such as a transmitter generates light at a specific wavelength. This requires that the receiver and fiber-optic core match the same wavelength to achieve the best performance.

Look again at Figure 3-2. Notice that the wavelength of visible light is between 390 nanometers and 770 nanometers. Below visible light are larger wavelengths, such as UHF and VHF television waves and radar waves. Above visible light are much shorter wavelengths, such as X-rays, Gamma rays, and cosmic rays. The actual spectrum of visible light is quite small compared with all other forms of electromagnetic wavelengths.

Most fiber-optic systems use infrared wavelengths between 850 nanometers to 1550 nanometers. At these wavelengths, there is less signal loss. A typical LED has a wavelength that is between 800 nanometers and 900 nanometers or 1250 nanometers and 1350 nanometers.

Fiber-Optic Cable Construction

Fiber-optic cable is composed of a glass or plastic core surrounded by a cladding, as shown in Figure 3-3. The glass or plastic core is the medium for transferring light waves. The cladding surrounds the core and causes the transmitted light to remain in the core. Without the cladding on the core, the light would be lost through the sides of the core material. A buffer area surrounds the cladding and core. The buffer is wrapped around the core and cladding to provide physical protection. In addition to the buffer area, waterproofing materials are sometimes inserted under the cable sheath. The sheath is similar to the insulating jacket on copper-core conductors. Its composition depends on the environment in which the fiber-optic cable will be installed. Some sheaths are designed to be oil- or water-resistant. Others may be installed in saltwater or buried directly in the earth. Some may be installed in a building plenum area. The size of fiber-optic cable is expressed in micrometers (mm).

Fiber-optic cable is generally classified as either loose tube or tight buffer. *Loose tube* is fiber-optic cable in which the core or cores are loosely fitted inside the sheath. The sheath is typically filled with gel to protect the core or cores, which are free to move inside the jacket. Loose tube is typically used for long cable runs where pulling the cable into conduit could result in breaking the core or cores. *Tight buffer* fiber-optic cable has a sheath that is tightly bound to the core or cores. This produces a smaller overall diameter of the cable assembly. The selection of cable type is left to the designer or installer.

When fiber-optic cable is installed in a plenum area, the installation usually falls under the jurisdiction of the National Electrical Code (NEC). The NEC is referred to for building specifications or standards. The standards describe minimal requirements for installing cables and conduits. Many electrical contractors are responsible for installing all of a building's cables, including data cables. Electrical contractors and building codes refer to the NEC as a guide.

Copyright Goodheart-Willcox Co., Inc.

Figure 3-3 A typical fiber-optic cable is constructed of a glass or plastic core surrounded by cladding, a buffer, and a sheath. The buffer provides strength for pulling the cable and serves as a soft padding to protect the core and cladding. The sheath protects the cable from physical elements.

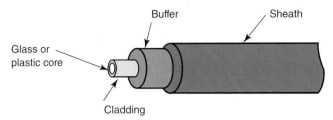

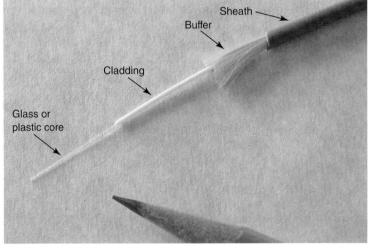

Goodheart-Willcox Publisher

The NEC has strict regulations about the composition of the sheath of fiber-optic cables installed in a plenum area. Fumes produced by this covering in a fire may be dangerous to people in the building. In many buildings, the plenum area also contains the air-conditioning system. Fumes and vapors present in the plenum area could be harmful to personnel throughout the building.

Two broad classifications of fiber-optic cable commonly used are single-mode and multimode. To understand the characteristics of these fiber-optic cable classifications, you must first be familiar with the characteristics of fiber-optic transmission.

Fiber-Optic Cable Transmission Characteristics

Since fiber-optic cable carries light and not electrical energy, a new set of terms is needed to describe the characteristics of light carried over fiber-optic cable. While some of the terms may be familiar from the last chapter, some new terminology that is unique to light is introduced. The first characteristic presented is attenuation. *Attenuation* was discussed in relation to copper-core media in the previous chapter. The causes for the loss of an electrical signal over copper-core cable, however, are different from the loss of a light signal over fiber-optic cable. The major causes of attenuation in fiber-optic cable can be characterized as scattering, dispersion, extrinsic losses (bends, splices, and connectors), and Fresnel reflection loss.

Attenuation

In Chapter 2, you learned that the loss in transmission of signal power from one end of the cable to the other is called *attenuation*. Attenuation is expressed in decibels

2.5 NET

5.3 NET

Copyright Goodheart-Willcox Co., Inc.

(dB), or decibels per kilometer (dB/km). The decibel is a relative measurement for signal strength. It is patterned after our sense of hearing.

Decibel measurement is nonlinear. It does not move in gradual increments, as does an analog speed gauge in an automobile. Look at the table in Figure 3-4A and compare the dB rating of 1, 3, 10, 20, and 50 to the power remaining and power loss values. Notice that a 50 percent power loss is represented by 3 dB. When the dB is doubled to 6, the power loss is only 75 percent, not the expected 100 percent. On close examination of the table, you will see that the relationship between power loss and dB is nonlinear. When decibel ratings are plotted as a chart, the result is a curve, not a straight line, as displayed in Figure 3-4B.

The most common use of the decibel chart in fiber-optic cable specifications is to express the attenuation over a given distance. Each cable manufacturer has a slightly different decibel rating of loss for its fiber-optic core. The variation is caused by the amount of impurities left in the core after the refining and manufacturing process is complete. Engineers use these decibel ratings to calculate the expected attenuation of an installation. For example, the engineering staff of many communication carriers calculate the loss of light over a given distance when running fiber-optic cable in long-haul installations. A *long-haul installation* is the installation of fiber-optic cable between two end points that are many miles apart. It is not unusual for a long-haul installation to span more than 40 miles. Long-distance telephone carriers are a prime example.

Scattering

Scattering is the loss of signal strength due to impurities in the core material. No core material can be made 100 percent pure. A microscopic amount of impurities will always remain. These impurities cause the light to scatter, as demonstrated in Figure 3-5. The total amount of impurities along the length of the cable is cumulative—the longer the cable, the greater the signal loss. Glass core is a better transmitter of light than plastic, but it is more expensive. To reduce attenuation, glass cores are used on very long runs of fiber-optic cable.

Dispersion

Light beams transmitted through fiber-optic cable do not travel in a straight line. This causes the light to reflect off the cladding. **Dispersion** is the distortion of a light wave pattern as it reflects off the core cladding. Dispersion is the main factor that limits the maximum length of a fiber-optic cable used as communications media.

Due to dispersion, digital light pulses transmitted into one end of a fiber-optic cable reach the opposite end of the cable at different times, as seen in Figure 3-6. This factor causes the light pulse to be distorted in shape. The light pulse appears flattened and elongated. However, a receiver can quickly reshape the signal into a square. On a short run of fiber-optic cable, there is no real problem with dispersion, but on a long run, not all of the light arrives at the end of the cable at the same time. The slight variation in time can be critical at high-frequency transmission rates.

Extrinsic Losses

Extrinsic losses are signal losses caused by physical factors outside the normal core. Physical factors can be splices, connectors, and bends in the fiber core. Splices in fiber-optic cable need special attention. Splices, couplings, and connectors are the main reasons for signal loss in normal runs of fiber-optic cable. Splices and connectors are covered in detail later in this chapter. Fiber-optic cables also have a minimum bend radius. Exceeding this radius causes attenuation.

Copyright Goodheart-Willcox Co., Inc.

Figure 3-4 The common unit of measure for power loss or gain is the decibel (dB). Light, sound, and electrical energy are often expressed in decibels. The decibel is based on a complicated mathematical formula. A—Notice that a 3-dB loss equals 50% power loss, but an additional 3-dB loss results in a total loss of 75%. B—The chart plots the power in decibels against power loss. As you can plainly see, the relationship is not linear, but rather curved.

dB	Power Remaining in Percent	Power Loss in Percent	Fraction of Power
1	79	21	
2	63	37	
3	50	50	1/2 power
4	40	60	
5	32	68	
6	25	75	1/4
7	20	80	
8	16	84	
9	12	88	
10	10	90	1/10
11	8	92	
12	6.3	93.7	
13	5	95	
14	4	96	
15	3.2	96.8	
16	2.5	97.5	
17	2	98	
18	1.6	98.4	
19	1.3	98.7	
20	1	99	1/100
30	0.1	99.9	
40	0.01	99.99	
50	0.001	99.999	1/1000

A

dB Power Loss

[Chart plotting Power (vertical axis, 0 to 120) against dB (horizontal axis, 0 to 60), showing a curved, decreasing relationship.]

B

Goodheart-Willcox Publisher

Figure 3-5 Impurities in the fiber-optic core cause the light signal to scatter and to decrease in strength.

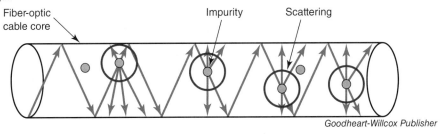

Fiber-optic cable core   Impurity   Scattering

Goodheart-Willcox Publisher

Copyright Goodheart-Willcox Co., Inc.

Figure 3-6 The original light pulse is a clean, concentrated pulse of light. As the light pulse travels through the fiber-optic core, optical dispersion distorts the light pulse.

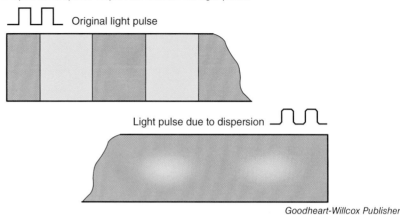

Goodheart-Willcox Publisher

Fresnel Reflection Loss

Fresnel reflection loss is typically due to the refraction property differences in the core material, the connector materials used for sealing the connector, and air. It commonly occurs at connection points in fiber-optic cabling. Light waves traveling from one type of core material to another causes signal loss. All glass- and plastic-core materials, sealing materials, and air have different refraction indices, or properties. Using a sealing material minimizes this type of loss. The sealing material uses a refraction index closely matching the index of the glass- or plastic-core material. A mismatch of sealing agent to core material can cause an excessive amount of signal loss. In addition to reflection and refraction loss, there can be loss due to absorption. **Absorption** occurs when intervening material absorbs some of the signal.

Fiber-Optic Cable Specifications

The two broad classifications of fiber-optic cable based on the diameter of the core are multimode and single-mode, as shown in Figure 3-7. In general, **multimode fiber-optic cable** has a larger core diameter than single-mode fiber-optic cable. A larger core diameter causes more light loss due to dispersion. **Single-mode fiber-optic cable** is much smaller in diameter than multimode cable. The diameter of single-mode fiber-optic cable is almost equal to the length of the light wave traveling through the cable. Because the core is designed to match the wavelength of the light wave closely, the light wave cannot readily disperse as it does in a large diameter core. The result is single-mode fiber-optic cable can carry light farther than multimode fiber-optic cable.

Look again at Figure 3-7. Note that the core dimensions are measured in micrometers (µ) or millionths of a meter. The size of a fiber-optic cable is expressed in two numerical values separated by a slash. The first number listed indicates the core diameter, and the second number lists the overall diameter, including the cladding. For example, a fiber-optic cable identified as 65.5/125 indicates that the core

Copyright Goodheart-Willcox Co., Inc.

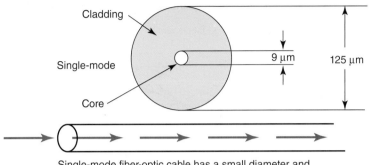

Single-mode fiber-optic cable has a small diameter and supports one light path.

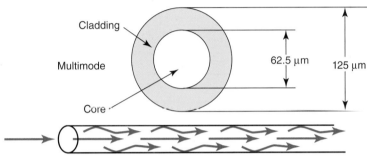

Multimode fiber-optic cable has a large diameter, causing multiple paths of light to be transmitted.

Goodheart-Willcox Publisher

Figure 3-7 Fiber-optic cable is classified as either single-mode or multimode. Multimode fiber-optic cable has a larger core diameter than single-mode. A large-diameter core contributes to dispersion. Single-mode fiber-optic cable is much smaller in diameter and has a more restrictive light path, which results in less dispersion. Single-mode fiber-optic cable is used for long-distance applications.

diameter is equal to 65.5 micrometers, and the overall core and cladding diameter is 125 micrometers. Typical multimode core dimensions are 50/125, 62.5/125, and 100/140. However, 100/140 is an older technology and is not encountered very often. A typical single-mode core is 8.3/125.

Multimode cable is divided into two classifications: step-index and graded-index. These classifications are based on the design of the multimode cable core. **Graded-index multimode fiber-optic cable** is designed with a varying grade of core material. Look at Figure 3-8. Note that the core of the graded-index fiber-optic cable is designed with maximum light conduction at the center of the core. The ability of the core to conduct light is gradually reduced toward the cladding. This lessens the light's tendency to disperse. Less dispersion causes less signal distortion and attenuation. The **step-index multimode fiber-optic cable** is a general multimode fiber-optic cable that does not counter dispersion.

IEEE 802.3 Standards

IEEE is mainly concerned with the lower levels of the OSI model and develops standards that serve as guidelines for hardware applications. The original IEEE 802.3 Ethernet standard has evolved as the demand for higher data rates, greater distances, and new technologies are introduced. In Figure 3-9, you can readily see that single-mode fiber-optic cable supports much greater distances than multimode fiber-optic cable.

Copyright Goodheart-Willcox Co., Inc.

Figure 3-8 There are two types of multimode fiber-optic cable: graded-index and step-index. Graded-index multimode cable is designed with maximum light conduction in the center of the core. Conduction gradually diminishes toward the cladding, which reduces dispersion. Less light dispersion produces less digital signal distortion. No special design is applied to step-index.

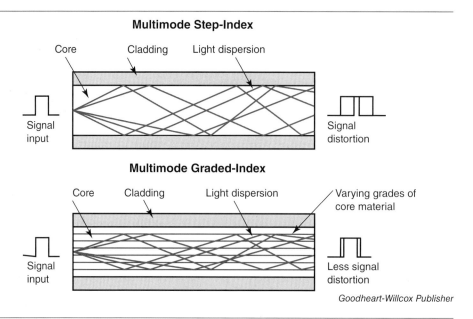

Goodheart-Willcox Publisher

Figure 3-9 Fiber-optic cable classifications.

Standard	Single-mode (S) or Multimode (M)	Core Diameter in Microns	Wavelength in Nanometers (nm)	Cable Distance in Meters	Remarks
10BaseFL	M	62.5 50	850	2000	Early generic fiber-optic standard.
100BaseFX	M	62.5 50	1300	2000	Known as Fast Ethernet.
1000BaseSX	M	62.5 50	850	300	Known as Gigabit Ethernet.
1000BaseLX	M	62.5 50	1300	550	Known as Gigabit Ethernet.
1000BaseLX	S	9	1300	5 k	Known as Gigabit Ethernet.
10GBaseSR	M	62.5 50	850	66–300	Known as 10 Gigabit Ethernet. Distance dependent on bandwidth.
10GBaseLR	S	9	1310	10 k	Known as 10 Gigabit Ethernet.
10GBaseER	S	9	1310	40 k	Known as 10 Gigabit Ethernet.
10GBaseSW	M	50 62.5	850	300 33	Commonly used inside commercial buildings.
10GBaseLW	S	9	1310	10 k	Has a long wavelength and is used for relatively long distances.
10GBaseEW	S	9	1550	40 k	Used for "long-haul" connections.

Note: Companies may calculate greater distances based on manufacturer cable specifications and equipment requirements. Such engineering is common in long-haul communication systems, such as long-distance telecommunications industries.

Goodheart-Willcox Publisher

Copyright Goodheart-Willcox Co., Inc.

At times, standards conflict with manufacturers' tables. Look at the ANSI/TIA/EIA 568-B 1 Standard table in Figure 3-10. You will see the recommended standard distances for network backbone distribution. This table is solely concerned with the maximum distance of backbone cabling without identifying specific IEEE cable standards. The chart simply categorizes backbone cable into one of three categories: UTP, multimode fiber-optic cable, and single-mode fiber-optic cable. The ANSI/TIA/EIA 568-B 1 standard makes no distinction for cable data rates. Data rates are specified in the IEEE standards.

Figure 3-10 The ANSI/TIA/EIA 568-B 1 standard for backbone distribution.

Media	Horizontal Cross Connect to Main Cross Connect in Meters	Horizontal Cross Connect to Intermediate Cross Connect in Meters	Main Cross Connect to Intermediate Cross Connect in Meters
UTP	800	300	500
62.5/125 and 50/125 Multimode Fiber-Optic Cable	2000	300	1700
Single-Mode Fiber-Optic Cable	3000	300	2700

Note: Single-mode fiber-optic cable can be installed to distances of 60 kilometers or greater based on engineering calculations and product manufacturers specifications.

Goodheart-Willcox Publisher

Gigabit Ethernet

In the 1990s, the IEEE amended the 802.3 Ethernet standard to include Gigabit Ethernet. The amended standard is known as *IEEE 802.3z*. When an IEEE standard is modified, it is identified with a lowercase letter, in this case, *z*. Gigabit Ethernet describes the 1000BaseSX, 1000BaseLX, and 1000BaseCX classifications. Take note that 1000BaseCX is a copper-core cable and not a fiber-optic cable. 1000BaseCX is limited to 25 meters and used to connect server room equipment. 1000BaseSX uses multimode fiber, and 1000BaseLX uses either single-mode or multimode fiber. Fiber-based Gigabit Ethernet uses GBIC connectors.

10 Gigabit Ethernet

In 2002, the IEEE amended the 802.3 Ethernet standard to include 10 Gigabit Ethernet. The amended standard is known as *IEEE 802.3ae*. The IEEE 802.3ae standard only recognizes fiber-optic cables; it does not recognize copper-core cables. The 802.3ae standard describes the 10GBaseSR (Short Range), 10GBaseLR (Long Range), and 10GBaseER (Extended Range) classifications. 10GBaseSR supports short distances using multimode fiber-optic cable, mainly 26 meters to 82 meters depending on the type of fiber-optic cable used. 10GBaseLR and 10GBaseER support 10 kilometers and 40 kilometers respectively. Long-distance communications use single-mode fiber-optic cable.

10GBaseW

10GBaseW is a collection of cable standards such as 10GBaseSW, 10GBaseLW, and 10GBaseEW. The *W* in the 10GBaseW standard represents *Wide Area Network*. When the *W* is used in reference to a specific standard such as 10GBaseSW, the *W* represents *wavelength*. For example, 10GBaseSW represents *10 Gigabit Short Wavelength*.

Network+ Note ✚

Be sure to read any test items carefully for reference to ANSI/TIA/EIA or IEEE.

10GBaseSW (short wavelength) can have two different core diameters: 50 micrometers and 62.5 micrometers. The 50 micrometers core diameter can support distances of up to 300 meters; while, the 62.5 micrometers core diameter can only support 33 meters. The wavelength for 10GBaseSW is 850 nanometers. You can commonly find 10GBaseSW used in commercial building backbones and server rooms.

10GBaseLW (long wavelength) is a single-mode fiber-optic cable capable of supporting distances of up to 10 kilometers. The wavelength for 10GBaseLW is 850 nanometers. While this is a "long-haul" type of cable, it is being replaced by 10GBaseEW. 10GBaseEW (extended wavelength) uses single-mode fiber-optic cable and is used for long-range applications. The wavelength for 10GBaseEW is 1550 nanometers. 10GBaseEW is similarly used in Synchronous optical networking (SONET) systems and supports cable length of up to 40,000 meters, or approximately 25 miles.

All 10GBase fiber-optic long-distance cable are used in SONET applications. SONET technology is commonly used for long-distance network systems. There will be more about SONET in Chapter 14.

Fiber Distributed Data Interface (FDDI)

Fiber Distributed Data Interface (FDDI) is a standard developed by ANSI that employs fiber-optic cable over great distances. The distances can reach as far as 200 kilometers (120 miles) and support data speeds of 100 Mbps or higher. FDDI is used mainly as a backbone for large network systems such as a MAN or WAN.

FDDI is structured as a pair of rings, as displayed in Figure 3-11. Two rings of fiber-optic cable connect to each node on the network system. One ring supports data flow in a clockwise rotation and the other ring supports data flow in a counterclockwise rotation.

Figure 3-11 A typical FDDI system uses two fiber-optic paths to provide continuous data communication. If one ring fails, the other provides a path for communication.

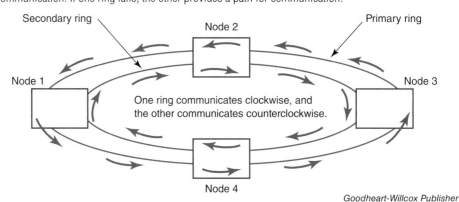

Goodheart-Willcox Publisher

Using FDDI guarantees continuous communication. If one ring fails, the other ring automatically takes over and provides the path for communication. One ring is considered the primary communication ring and the other the secondary communication ring. If a section fails in the primary ring, the secondary ring supports communication. If both the primary and secondary ring is cut or fails, the two rings join at the next node, forming a new ring and continuing communication, as shown in Figure 3-12.

FDDI uses a token passing method similar to IEEE 802.5. An enhanced version of FDDI called *FDDI Full Duplex Technology (FFDT)* supports speeds of 200 Mbps by allowing simultaneous communication in both directions. See Figure 3-13 for a summary of FDDI data rates and cable lengths. FDDI can also use UTP cable.

Copyright Goodheart-Willcox Co., Inc.

Figure 3-12 If the primary ring in an FDDI system fails, the secondary ring provides communication. When both rings break, the nodes closest to the break complete the circuit, allowing communication to continue.

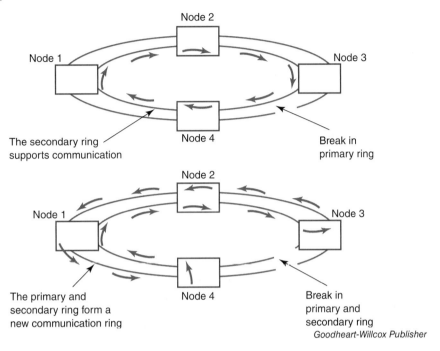

Goodheart-Willcox Publisher

Figure 3-13 FDDI specifications.

Media	Single-Mode (S) or Multimode (M)	Core Diameter in Microns	Wavelength in Nanometers (nm)	Cable Distance in Meters
FDDI	M	62.5/125	1300	2 k
FDDI	S	9	1300	40 k

Goodheart-Willcox Publisher

Fiber-Optic Cable Connectors

There are many different styles of fiber-optic cable connectors. Some are proprietary. It is best if you use connectors from the same manufacturer when installing a new fiber-optic network or extending an old one. The most common styles of fiber-optic cable connectors are SC, ST, FC, LC, and MTRJ.

Look at the close-up of ST and SC connectors in Figure 3-14A. Note that the ST connector is round and uses a push-and-twist connection similar to the BNC. The SC connector is square and uses retaining clips to hold its position. When two SC or ST connectors are fabricated into a single unit, they are generally referred to as *duplex connectors*. A single connector is referred to as a *simplex connector*.

FC connectors are designed to provide a maximum physical connection, as evidenced by Figure 3-14B. The FC connector is designed with screw threads as part of the physical design. They are very similar in design to coaxial-style screw-on connectors.

The LC connector is a style developed by Lucent Technologies. The LC is classified as a small form factor connector. Additional small form factor connectors are SFP, SFP+, and QSFP. The term *form factor* refers to the physical attributes of a connector. The LC connector is approximately half the diameter of an SC or ST connector. The LC connector can be converted into a duplex connector by the addition of a clip

2.1 NET

Network+ Note

Although there are many different types of fiber-optic cable connectors, CompTIA lists only five in the Network+ Certification Exam objectives: SC and ST, FC, LC, and MTRJ.

Figure 3-14 Fiber-optic cable connectors. A—ST and SC connectors. B—FC connector. C—LC connectors. D—MTRJ connector.

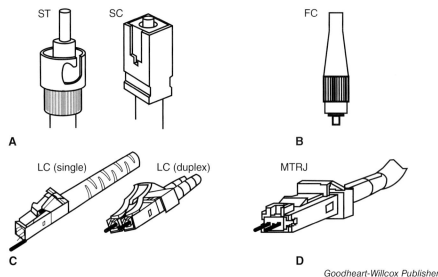

Goodheart-Willcox Publisher

designed to hold the two separate connectors together. See Figure 3-14C for an illustration of an LC connector.

The MTRJ connector is unique in design because it incorporates two fiber-optic cores into one assembly without the use of a clip, as seen in Figure 3-14D. It is always considered a duplex connector. The MTRJ is also a small form factor connector.

Fiber-Optic Cable Installation and Troubleshooting

Fiber-optic cables are typically not made in the field but are prepared prior to installation in a controlled setting. Installing a fiber-optic connector on a fiber-optic cable requires a great deal of expertise. Typically, a technician who installs fiber-optic cable connectors must be certified. *BICSI* is an organization that provides certification. Another such organization is the *Fiber Optic Association (FOA)*. Some companies, such as Ortronics, Corning Cable Systems, Nortel Networks, and Belden, oversee their own certification programs. Whether or not a technician requires certification is determined by the vendor or by installation specifications written for a new installation. Usually the purchasing company will prepare these.

Installing Connectors

A supplier may provide the necessary cable for a small fiber-optic network such as a LAN. This includes taking measurements and preparing cable splices and connections prior to installation. When fiber-optic cabling is obtained in this way, the highest quality-control standards are applied to cable preparation. However, this is not always possible. Cables may have to be installed in the field where factors such as dirt, dust, and chemicals can hamper the cable splicing, termination, and connector installation. Splices, couplings, and connections require special equipment and techniques. Fiber-optic cores must be in near-perfect alignment when splices are made. Misalignment or other improper splicing will cause attenuation. See Figure 3-15 for diagrams of misaligned splices.

Copyright Goodheart-Willcox Co., Inc.

Figure 3-15 Common causes of attenuation at splice points.

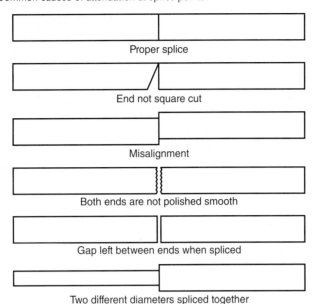

Proper splice

End not square cut

Misalignment

Both ends are not polished smooth

Gap left between ends when spliced

Two different diameters spliced together

Goodheart-Willcox Publisher

The fiber-optic cable is cleaved, not cut like copper-core cable. To cleave the fiber-optic cable core, it must be scribed with a sharp, cleaving tool. The edge of the cleaving tool is made of diamond or ceramic material. Once the core has been scribed, pressure is applied to the scribed area until the core breaks. This produces a clean, clear surface at the end of the core. Traditional cutting tools used for copper-core cable would badly scar the ends of the core. Marks or scratches on the ends of the core material cause attenuation due to reflection and refraction. The light scatters in many directions rather than transferring directly to the next cable or connector. Plastic-core cables do not have to be cleaved. An extremely sharp cutter must be used to obtain a clean, clear cut.

Figure 3-16 shows a high quality, fiber-optic cleaver and splicer. Note the eyepiece located at the top of the tool. Since the diameter of a fiber-optic core is small, a microscope with at least 30× magnification is needed to inspect the cut and splice. This tool is capable of cutting fiber-optic cable, polishing the ends, and fusing them together for a near-flawless splice.

Making a Fusion Splice

A **fusion splice** is the joining of two fiber-optic cores using heat to fuse, or melt, the materials together. Another, more expensive fusion splicer is shown in Figure 3-17. This fusion splicer performs all the functions of the splicer shown in Figure 3-16 and more. It is equipped with video cameras and a liquid crystal display (LCD) for close, simultaneous inspection of the splice at two different angles.

Before making a fusion splice, the outer, protective sheath and buffer must be removed from the fiber-optic cable end. The splice area of the core must be very clean. Dust and debris can contaminate the splice, resulting in a poor data rate through the finished splice. The cladding must be carefully handled. Damage to the cladding will cause signal loss. Once the fiber-optic cable is prepared, the end of the fiber-optic core is cleaved. A cleaver simply scores the core rather than cuts through it. The core can then be easily broken.

Copyright Goodheart-Willcox Co., Inc.

Figure 3-16 Fiber-optic cable splicer with cleaver.

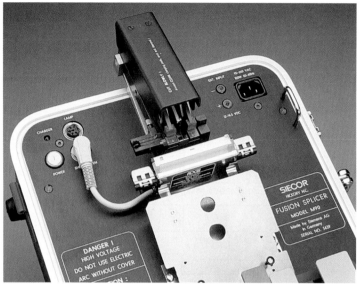

Siecor Corporation, Hickory, NC

Figure 3-17 A multiprocessor-controlled fusion splicer.

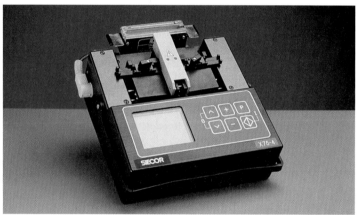

Siecor Corporation, Hickory, NC

Next, the two ends of the fiber core must be perfectly aligned. Because of the small diameters of the core, a magnifier is used to aid in the alignment. Some of the more expensive fusion splicing units combine the cleaver magnifier and fuser into one package.

When the two ends are aligned, they are melted together by an electrical arc. The two ends become permanently welded together, or fused. After fusing the cores, the splice must be protected so it will not be damaged through handling or installation. The splice is covered using material such as heat-shrink tubing, silicone gel, or mechanical crimps.

Copyright Goodheart-Willcox Co., Inc.

Mechanical splices are made in a similar way except for the fusing of the two cores. Mechanical splices do not use heat but rather a mechanical means of splicing the two cores. The two cores are aligned, and then a mechanical crimper clamps the two cores together. Between the two cores is a gel-like substance that maintains a consistent light path between the two ends by eliminating any air gap between the two cores. An air gap would cause the Fresnel effect, thus reducing the ability of the splice to carry light from one core to the other.

The main difference between the mechanical and the fusion splice is the cost of the equipment and the cost of each splice. The equipment for making a fusion splice is very expensive when compared with the equipment for making a mechanical splice. However, the cost of labor to make each splice is less expensive when using fusing equipment.

Using Fiber-Optic Cable Meters

Testing fiber-optic cable requires specialized instruments that employ the principles of light to obtain data. The most commonly used meter for testing short runs of fiber-optic cable consists of two items: a light meter and a light source. The light source is attached to one end of the fiber-optic cable, and the light meter is connected to the other end. The light source injects light into the fiber-optic cable, and the light meter measures the amount of light reaching the opposite end. Power loss is calculated and is typically expressed in decibels (dB) or microwatts (μW). The information gathered from the meter can be sent to and stored on a computer. For some new network installations, this test is more than adequate to assure a contractor that the fiber-optic cable installation is acceptable.

5.2 NET

Another type of meter is the optical time domain reflectometer (OTDR). An **optical time domain reflectometer (OTDR)** is a device for testing and troubleshooting long runs of fiber-optic cable. The OTDR accurately measures and records the effects of attenuation. It compares the amount of light injected into the fiber-optic cable core to the amount of light reflected to the meter. Figure 3-18 shows the Fluke OFTM-5612 OTDR, which is used to inspect and analyze fiber-optic cable installations.

5.2 NET

Figure 3-18 Fluke OFTM-5612 OTDR.

Reproduced with permission–Fluke Corp.

Copyright Goodheart-Willcox Co., Inc.

The OTDR can also accurately measure the total length of a cable run or locate breaks and faults in a cable and at its connections. The typical OTDR presents information in a graphical manner on an LCD. A slope is presented that represents the attenuation of the core. Major flaws in splices and such are presented as spikes, as seen in Figure 3-19. The distance to the fault and other pertinent information, such as signal loss in decibels (dB) or milliwatts (mW), is indicated along the bottom edge of the screen. Figure 3-20 illustrates how faults and distance are represented on a graph.

Figure 3-19 Attenuation and cable faults as indicated on an OTDR display. Note that faults are indicated by spikes.

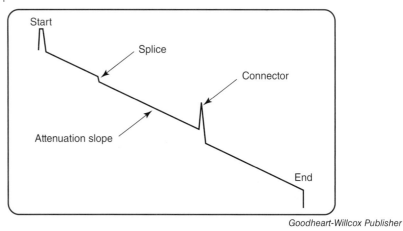

Goodheart-Willcox Publisher

Figure 3-20 An OTDR can indicate loss in decibels and the exact distance from the OTDR to the fault.

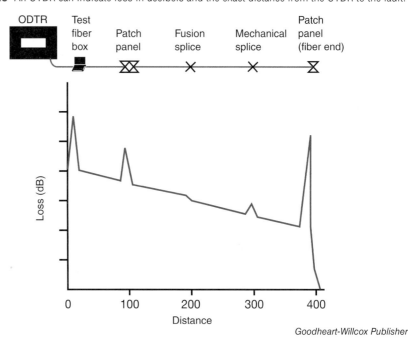

Goodheart-Willcox Publisher

Copyright Goodheart-Willcox Co., Inc.

Figure 3-21 shows an OTDR signal trace analysis indicating the attenuation of the cable and the location of a fault of 7.619 dB at approximately 53.481 kilometers from the meter. Using test equipment that can quickly identify the location of a fault can save many hours of testing by other means.

An OTDR is typically equipped with a port for connecting directly to a printer. Screen captures and a full report on the specifications of the fiber-optic cable can be printed. The OTDR is routinely used for the final inspection of a new fiber-optic cable installation. It not only provides information to prove a cable is flawless, but also provides a baseline of information for comparison at a later date when troubleshooting. The typical OTDR is an expensive piece of test equipment; however, it does not need to be purchased. To save money, contractors often rent an OTDR to test and certify a fiber-optic cable system they have installed. OTDR tests are not normally performed on short, fiber-optic cable runs associated with LANs. This type of installation is typically checked with a simple, handheld meter, not an OTDR. The OTDR is best suited for measuring cable runs spanning great distances like those found in network backbones.

Figure 3-21 A trace analysis is displayed on the LCD screen of an OTDR. Cable faults are indicated by the sharp spikes along the slope. Exact losses are also displayed in decibel units at the bottom of the display.

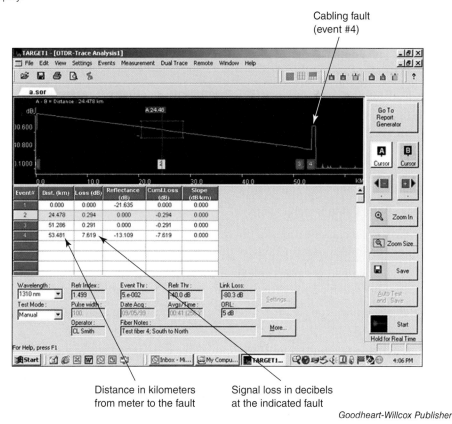

Cabling fault (event #4)

Distance in kilometers from meter to the fault

Signal loss in decibels at the indicated fault

Goodheart-Willcox Publisher

Copyright Goodheart-Willcox Co., Inc.

Summary

Characteristics of Fiber-Optic Cable

- Fiber-optic cable consists of a glass or plastic core that carries pulses of light that represent binary data.
- Fiber-optic cable has the following advantages: provides for data security, immune to electromagnetic interference, lightweight and small in diameter, safe from fire and explosion, wide bandwidth, corrosion- and water-resistant, supports data transmission over longer distances than copper-core cable.

Nature of Light

- Light is described in wavelengths.
- A wavelength is the total distance the electromagnetic wave or light wave travels during one full cycle.
- Wavelengths are measured in nanometers (nm), or one billionth of a meter.

Fiber-Optic Cable Construction

- Fiber-optic cable cores are composed of either glass or plastic.
- The glass or plastic core is surrounded by cladding, which restricts the light to the core area.
- Scattering is the loss of light due to impurities in the core material.
- Dispersion is the distortion of light waves caused by the light reflecting from the cladding material and arriving at different times at the far end of the cable.
- Extrinsic losses are caused by physical factors not normally found in the core material, such as at splices and connector locations.

Fiber-Optic Cable Specifications

- Two broad classifications of fiber-optic cable based on its ability to carry light are multimode and single-mode.
- Single-mode fiber-optic cable has a smaller core diameter than multimode fiber-optic cable and carries light farther and with less attenuation.
- Two classifications of multimode fiber-optic cable are graded-index and step-index.
- Graded-index multimode fiber-optic cable is designed with a varying grade of core material that allows for maximum light conduction at the center of the core. Step-index multimode fiber-optic cable does not have a special core design and is therefore greatly affected by dispersion.

IEEE 802.3 Standards

- The 802.3z standard describes the 1000BaseSX, 1000BaseLX, and 1000BaseCX Gigabit Ethernet classifications.

Copyright Goodheart-Willcox Co., Inc.

- The 802.3ae 10 Gigabit Ethernet standard describes the 10GBaseSR, 10GBaseLR, 10GBaseEW, and 10GBaseER classifications.
- 10GBaseW is a collection of cable standards such as 10GBaseSW, 10GBaseLW, and 10GBaseEW.

Fiber Distributed Data Interface (FDDI)

- FDDI is used mainly as a backbone for large network systems such as a MAN or a WAN.
- FDDI is structured as a pair of rings.

Fiber-Optic Cable Connectors

- Connector styles include SC, ST, FC, LC, and MTRJ.

Fiber-Optic Cable Installation and Troubleshooting

- Fiber-optic cabling is cleaved, not cut.
- A splice that is joined by heat is called a *fusion splice*.
- A light source and fiber-optic light meter is used to test short runs of fiber-optic cable by comparing the amount of light injected in one end of the cable to the light power at the other end of the cable.
- The OTDR is used to measure the effects of scattering and cabling faults in long fiber-optic cable runs. It can also measure the distance to a cable fault or break.

Review Questions

1. Describe how data is transferred across a fiber-optic cable.
2. List advantages of fiber-optic cable over copper-core cable.
3. Light is measured by its _____.
4. What is the wavelength range of visible light?
5. What are the three common wavelengths associated with fiber-optic cable?
6. What is *dispersion*?
7. Name three physical factors that contribute to extrinsic losses.
8. Describe Fresnel reflection loss.
9. What are the two classifications of fiber-optic cable based on the diameter of the core?
10. How does the diameter of the fiber-optic cable core affect the distance light can travel?
11. Fiber-optic cable core diameter is expressed in _____.
12. What are the two most common sizes of multimode fiber-optic cable?
13. What is the IEEE 802 standard for Gigabit Ethernet?
14. What is the IEEE 802 standard for 10 Gigabit Ethernet?

Copyright Goodheart-Willcox Co., Inc.

15. What do the following 10 Gigabit Ethernet acronyms represent: SW, LW, and EW?

16. What is the range of FDDI?

17. Why does FDDI use two rings of cable?

18. List the five most common types of fiber-optic cable connector.

19. What are some common causes of attenuation associated with fiber-optic cable splices?

20. Using heat to join two fiber-optic cores is called a(n) _____ splice.

21. What is required to test a short run of fiber-optic cable?

22. What device is commonly used to test long runs of fiber-optic cable?

23. What principle of fiber-optic cable loss does the OTDR use for measurements?

✚ Sample Network+ Exam Questions

1. Deepak is a network administrator for a defense contractor. He is deeply concerned about eavesdropping on the signal. Which of the following network media is typically the most secure from eavesdropping devices or security taps?
   A. Fiber-optic cable
   B. Copper-core cable
   C. Wireless
   D. Infrared

2. Identify the following connector.
   A. SC
   B. ST
   C. RJ-45
   D. BNC

3. Identify the following connector.
   A. SC
   B. ST
   C. RJ-45
   D. BNC
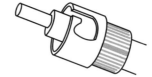

4. Where is fiber-optic cable typically found? (Select all that apply.)
   A. In network backbones.
   B. In network segments that are exposed to electromagnetic interference.
   C. Where security from wiretaps is of great concern.
   D. In network segments requiring slow data transmission rates.

Copyright Goodheart-Willcox Co., Inc.

5. Gerard is a network administrator for a large financial company. He is overseeing the implementation of new fiber optic cable. He is concerned about distortion of the light wave as it reflects off the core cladding. Which of the following best describes this?

   A. Scattering

   B. Attenuation

   C. Diffusion

   D. Reflection

6. The loss of signal strength in the core of a fiber-optic cable caused by impurities in the core is referred to as _____.

   A. scattering

   B. dispersion

   C. diffusion

   D. reflection

7. Juanita is trying to select cable for her companies CAN. She needs cable that supports a very long distance. Which of the following would be her best choice?

   A. 10GbaseER

   B. 10GBaseLX

   C. 1000BaseLX

   D. 100BaseCX

8. According to the ANSI/TIA/EIA standards for backbone distribution inside a premise, what is the maximum recommended distance for multimode fiber-optic cable?

   A. 100 meters

   B. 200 meters

   C. 500 meters

   D. 2000 meters

9. You are installing a new FDDI interface. You need to connect the appropriate media to that interface. What type of networking media is used in FDDI?

   A. Fiber-optic multimode

   B. Fiber-optic single-mode

   C. UTP

   D. All the above materials can be used for FDDI.

10. Which is a correct description of the FDDI topology?

    A. Star

    B. Bus

    C. Single ring

    D. Dual ring

Network+ Certification Exam Objectives

To prepare for the CompTIA Network+ exam, you must be able to specify the characteristics of the IEEE 802.11 standards. These characteristics include speed, bandwidth, and access method. You should also be able to define and identify an ad hoc wireless network and an infrastructure wireless network. There is heavy emphasis on wireless technology, so make certain you are quite familiar with it.

To better prepare yourself to answer questions on wireless technology, be sure to install and configure a wireless network card and view all of the configuration properties that are featured.

Objectives

1.5: Wireless Topologies

Types—WLAN

Technologies that Facilitate the Internet of Things (IoT)

1.6: Given a Scenario, Implement the Appropriate Wireless Technologies and Configurations

2.2: Wireless Access Point, Wireless Range Extender

2.3: Wireless Controller

2.5: Transmission Mediums—Wireless

4.3: WPA

WPA2

5.4: Incorrect Antenna Type, Interference, Incorrect Antenna Placement, Channel Overlap, Overcapacity, Distance Limitations, Frequency Mismatch, Wrong SSID, Wrong Passphrase

Learning Outcomes

- Explain the principles of electromagnetic waves.
- Identify the major antenna styles.
- Explain various transmission techniques used in radio-wave-based transmission.
- Recall characteristics of radio-wave-based networking.
- Compare types of microwave transmission and networks.
- Summarize the advantages and disadvantages of wireless networking.
- Give examples of how security is provided in wireless networks.

Copyright Goodheart-Willcox Co., Inc.

Key Terms

ad hoc mode
ANT+
basic service set (BSS)
Bluetooth
carrier wave
cellular technology
channel
channel bonding
demodulation
direct sequencing
directional
extended service set identifier (ESSID)
frequency hopping
geosynchronous orbit
independent basic service set (IBSS)
industrial, scientific, and medical (ISM) band
infrastructure mode
integrated circuit card identifier (ICCID)
modulation
multiple-input-multiple-output (MIMO)
near field communication (NFC)
omni-directional
orthogonal frequency-division multiplexing (OFDM)
personal area network (PAN)
personal unlocking key (PUK)
propagation delay
radio interference
radio waves
radio-frequency identification (RFID)
receiver
spatial multiplexing
spread spectrum
subscriber identity module (SIM)
transmitter
Wi-Fi
Wi-Fi Protected Access (WPA)
Wi-Fi Protected Access 2 (WPA2)
Wired Equivalent Privacy (WEP)
wireless access point (WAP)
wireless personal area network (WPAN)
Z-wave

Overview

Wireless media is often referred to as *unbounded media*, which means the path for network transmissions is unrestricted. When copper-core or fiber-optic cable is used, the transmitted network signals are bound to the medium. When the atmosphere is used, the transmission is spread throughout the atmosphere and is not limited to a single path.

Network signals transmitted through the atmosphere are electromagnetic waves. In Chapter 3, you learned that light waves are a part of the electromagnetic wave spectrum and are categorized as visible light. You learned specifically how light waves travel through fiber-optic cable to transmit data. In this chapter, you will learn about the three categories of electromagnetic waves that are used to transmit data across the atmosphere: radio waves, infrared, and microwaves. You will also learn about wireless transmission techniques and associated standards. To help you better understand wireless networking technologies, electromagnetic waves will be discussed in detail.

Copyright Goodheart-Willcox Co., Inc.

Electromagnetic Waves

The atmosphere is full of electromagnetic waves. Electromagnetic waves are categorized according to frequency ranges. For example, common radio waves used for communication on AM-band radio start at 0.5 MHz and span to 22 GHz for satellite communication. The frequency of an electromagnetic wave is based on the repeating pattern of its waveform just as it is with electrical energy. One complete waveform is called a *cycle*, as shown in Figure 4-1, and frequency is the number of times a cycle occurs in one second.

Electromagnetic waves are produced both intentionally and unintentionally as a by-product of electrical energy. Radio and television stations produce electromagnetic waves intentionally, while many household appliances produce electromagnetic waves unintentionally. Recall from Chapter 2 that unintentional electromagnetic waves are referred to as *interference* or, more specifically, *noise*.

Figure 4-1 Electromagnetic frequency is based on the repeating pattern of a waveform. One complete waveform is called a cycle. The frequency is how many cycles occur in one second.

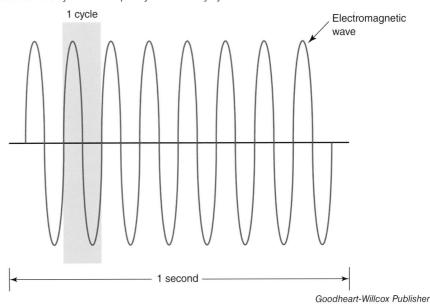

Goodheart-Willcox Publisher

Radio and Microwave Transmission

Radio and microwave transmission works on the principle of producing a carrier wave as the means of communication between two wireless devices. A **carrier wave** is an electromagnetic wave of a set frequency that is used to carry data. It is identified by a frequency number. For example, radio and television stations are assigned specific frequencies on which they must transmit. A radio identification such as 104.5 FM represents a carrier wave of 104.5 MHz. The carrier wave is how individual stations are identified on a radio or television, as shown in Figure 4-2.

A carrier wave is mixed with a data signal. The mixing of the carrier wave and data signal is known as **modulation**. The technique of modulation is how AM radio, FM radio, and television operate. A simple radio broadcast consists of a **transmitter**, which generates the carrier wave and modulates information into the carrier wave, and a **receiver**, which receives the modulated wave and demodulates it. The transceiver and receiver must both be at or very near the same carrier wave frequency for communication to occur.

Copyright Goodheart-Willcox Co., Inc.

Look at the example of a voice wave broadcast in Figure 4-3. In the example, a carrier wave of 104.5 MHz is shown. The human voice produces sound at a much lower frequency, typically in a range from 400 cycles per second to approximately 4,000 cycles per second. The human voice is converted into electrical energy using a microphone. The microphone produces a pattern of electrical energy in direct proportion to the human voice. Then, the electrical energy is mixed with the carrier wave. The carrier wave has a much higher frequency than the electromagnetic wave produced by the human voice. The two are combined so that the human voice can be transmitted.

The combined wave is transmitted across the atmosphere. When the combined wave reaches the receiver and is accepted, the electromagnetic energy is converted into electrical energy. The receiver separates the voice wave from the carrier wave. This process is known as **demodulation**. After the combined wave is demodulated,

Figure 4-2 A carrier wave is the means of communication between two wireless devices. In this example, a radio station assigned the 104.5-MHz frequency transmits data on a 104.5-MHz carrier wave. A radio with its dial set to 104.5 picks up the information broadcast from the radio station.

104.5-MHz carrier wave

Radio station

104.5

Goodheart-Willcox Publisher

Figure 4-3 Example of a voice wave broadcast.

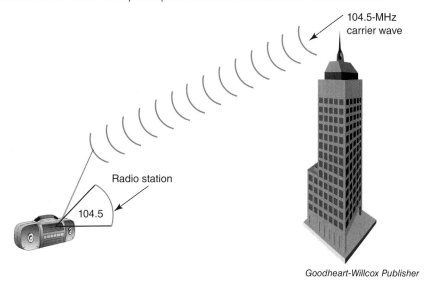

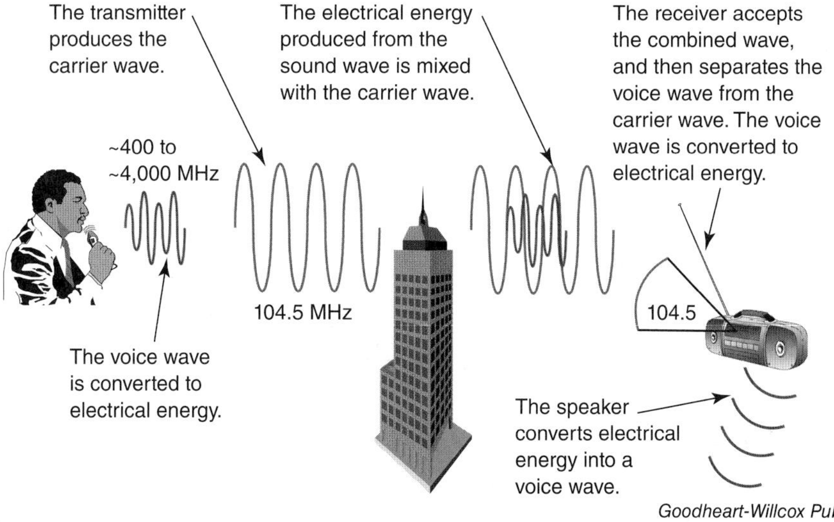

The transmitter produces the carrier wave.

The electrical energy produced from the sound wave is mixed with the carrier wave.

The receiver accepts the combined wave, and then separates the voice wave from the carrier wave. The voice wave is converted to electrical energy.

~400 to ~4,000 MHz

104.5 MHz

104.5

The voice wave is converted to electrical energy.

The speaker converts electrical energy into a voice wave.

Goodheart-Willcox Publisher

Copyright Goodheart-Willcox Co., Inc.

the transceiver discards the carrier wave, amplifies the voice wave, and sends it to a speaker. The speaker converts the electrical energy into a voice wave. While this is a simple, nontechnical explanation, it is important to remember that a carrier wave and a voice wave are combined, or modulated, before they are transmitted and are separated, or demodulated, after they are received. In this regard, a carrier wave is similar to an envelope in which a letter is mailed via the postal service. The envelope serves only as packaging to help the desired information reach its destination.

The same principle is used to transmit digital data signals. A carrier wave establishes the relationship between transmitter and receiver. The carrier wave is modulated with a wave pattern resembling the digital data signal. The two waves are combined before transmission and then separated at the receiver.

To modulate data, the carrier wave must be at a much higher frequency than the digital data. In the example of the voice wave and carrier wave frequency, the carrier wave is 104.5 MHz while the voice wave fluctuates between 400 Hz and 4,000 Hz. Based on an average voice frequency of 2,000 Hz, an approximate 500:1 ratio exists between the two frequencies. The carrier wave is only slightly distorted when combined with the voice wave. The same principle applies when a carrier wave is combined with a digital data signal. If the two signals do not have a high ratio, the digital data signal distorts the carrier wave to a point where the transmitter cannot recognize it.

A 104.5-MHz carrier wave is 200 kHz in width. Technically, a 104.5-MHz carrier wave has a bandwidth of 200 kHz. The bandwidth of a carrier wave is referred to as a **channel**. Technically, a channel is a small portion of the electromagnetic spectrum and is used to designate a set of frequencies for a particular electronic application. The FCC assigns channels and bandwidths for electromagnetic waves.

Infrared Transmission

Infrared was one of the early attempts to create wireless communication, but is not widely used today. It used light in the infrared spectrum just out of the range that humans can see. That made it an interesting method to transmit data. However, it suffered from line-of-sight issues. That means that if anything was between the sender and receiver, then the transmission was blocked. This proved to be a fatal flaw for infrared technology.

Radio Interference

Radio interference is interference that matches the frequency of a given carrier wave. The Federal Communications Commission (FCC) is responsible for dividing the entire electromagnetic spectrum to prevent electronic equipment from interfering with one another. However, this is not always possible. Think for a minute how many different devices use and produce electromagnetic waves—remote controls for remote-control cars, toys, garage-door openers, televisions, AM and FM radios, satellites, pagers, cellular phones, electrical power lines, radar equipment, motors, fluorescent lights, and such. The list is ever increasing. There are thousands of products that produce electromagnetic waves. The FCC regulates the electromagnetic spectrum and dictates the frequency that is to be used for each group of devices. Even with all these regulations, equipment fails and produces undesirable frequencies that can interfere with a regulated frequency. For example, if you were to move the tuner of an AM radio across the various stations, you would hear an excellent example of interference.

Virtually any type of electrical equipment can produce radio interference even if it is not assigned to the same radio frequency spectrum as wireless LAN communication. For example, some other sources of radio interference that could corrupt data

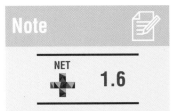

Note

NET
1.6

The phrase *channel bandwidth* is simply another term for *bandwidth*.

NET
1.5

NET
5.4

Tech Tip

AM radio is an old technology that was susceptible to radio interference. FM radio is an improvement over AM radio because it is less susceptible to radio interference.

Copyright Goodheart-Willcox Co., Inc.

packets are fluorescent lighting, electric motors, electrical control systems, welding equipment, portable radios, and such. While not intended to produce radio interference in the assigned wireless spectrum, a defective piece of equipment can produce electrical radio harmonics. The harmonic signal is a multiple of an original signal. For example, a radio frequency of 12,000 can also produce signals of 24,000, 36,000, 48,000, and so on. This means that harmonic frequencies produced by other areas of the electromagnetic spectrum can cause interference with the wireless network.

A less common, but still possible, issue is simply having the wrong antenna type. This is a very uncommon problem today. A more common issue is incorrect antenna placement. Antennae should be placed in a manner to ensure appropriate coverage. It is important to avoid channel overlap with neighboring WAPs and to ensure devices are broadcasting at the correct frequency. Frequency mismatch can cause a communication problem. Distance is the biggest problem. Every WAP will have a finite distance. The further away a user is, the more likely he or she is to have issues. One such issue is a decreasing signal to noise ratio.

Another major factor is proximity to the source of the signal. If radio interference is in close proximity to the wireless network system, it need not be at the same frequency. Close proximity and a powerful signal can disrupt the wireless communication. Radio signals can also reflect off surrounding materials, usually metallic surfaces, as seen in Figure 4-4. The reflected signal is an exact copy of the original signal. The reflected signal does not always disrupt the original signal. At times, the reflected signal actually increases the strength of the original signal by merging with it. A problem occurs if there is too much delay between the original signal and the reflected signal. When there is too much delay, the two signals overlap, causing the combined signal to be distorted. The difference in time it takes the two signals to travel from the source to the destination determines the level of distortion. The amount of time it takes to reach the destination depends on the angle and distance of the reflection.

There are many sources of radio interference that can affect communication on an IEEE 802.11 wireless LAN. Industrial, scientific, and medical devices occupy the frequency band allocated to the wireless network devices specified under the IEEE 802.11 standard. Wireless phones and microwave ovens are also included in the same frequency ranges. The band of radio frequencies associated with industrial, scientific, and medical devices is referred to as the **industrial, scientific, and medical (ISM) band**, as shown in Figure 4-5.

5.4 NET

Figure 4-4 A reflected radio signal can combine with the intended radio signal and either disrupt the intended signal or enhance it.

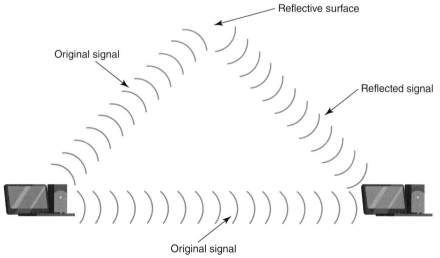

(workstation icons) RedlineVector/Shutterstock.com; Goodheart-Willcox Publisher

Copyright Goodheart-Willcox Co., Inc.

Figure 4-5 The industrial, scientific, and medical (ISM) band is often a source of wireless network interference.

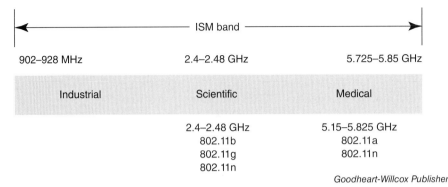

Goodheart-Willcox Publisher

Antenna Styles

NET
＋ 1.6

Two major classifications of antennae are associated with radio-wave- and microwave-based wireless networks: omni-directional and directional. These classifications are based on an antenna's ability to transmit electromagnetic signals. **Omni-directional** is the transmission of electromagnetic signals in all directions. **Directional** is the transmission of electromagnetic signals in a focused or aimed direction. Antennae can be further broken down by their individual style of construction, such as omni, dipole, flat panel, Yagi, and parabolic dish. Figure 4-6 shows each antenna style and the electromagnetic wave pattern it produces. Note that the electromagnetic wave patterns are viewed from overhead.

Omni

An omni antenna is a straight piece of wire. The wire is engineered to match the exact length or a fraction of the frequency's wavelength. For example, a frequency of 2.4 GHz produces a wavelength of approximately 2.19 inches. An antenna 2.19 inches in length would match the wavelength exactly. Matching the antenna length to the wavelength of the radio frequency ensures the best possible reception and reduces the possibility of picking up interference.

The omni antenna is typically used for a wireless transmitter to broadcast in a 360-degree pattern. This type of antenna is used for the source of a wireless transmission. For example, a wireless Internet service provider would use an omni antenna to facilitate broadcasting in all directions to better serve customers throughout the area.

Dipole

A dipole antenna is one of the most common radio antennae used. What makes it popular is its relatively inexpensive manufacturing costs when compared with many other antenna styles. The dipole is commonly used as a client or receiver antenna rather than as a broadcast antenna. The dipole antenna is bidirectional, as seen in Figure 4-6. Rotating the antenna until the dipole aligns with the source of the radio-wave transmission can enhance the received signal.

Yagi

A Yagi antenna is used for point-to-point links. It is a directional-type antenna. Yagi antennae are typically designed from many radio antenna elements (tubes). Each

Figure 4-6 Basic antenna styles and the electromagnetic wave patterns they produce.

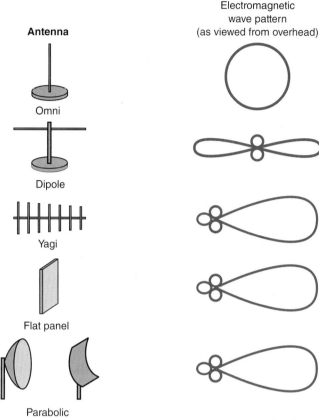

Goodheart-Willcox Publisher

element is progressively larger or smaller than the main element by approximately 5 percent. The way the Yagi antenna enhances the radiation of the electromagnetic wave is beyond the scope of this textbook. For now, just note and recognize the shape of the Yagi antenna and its electromagnetic wave pattern. Some Yagi antennae are constructed inside a metal tube, which further enhances the reception and transmission of electromagnetic waves. See Figure 4-7 for a photo of a Yagi antenna.

Flat Panel

Flat-panel antennae are directional-type antennae used for point-to-point links. The main advantage of a flat panel is the aesthetics. The antenna blends in well with building architecture, and many times it is unnoticeable. However, the disadvantage of a flat panel antenna is the consideration of wind load. High wind areas can catch the flat panel design like a sail on a ship. Flat panels must be rigidly supported to reduce the effects of wind.

Parabolic

A parabolic antenna is used for point-to-point links. It is a directional-type antenna typically constructed from a grid of rods or mesh wiring. The parabolic antenna enhances reception by reflecting incoming electromagnetic waves with its curved surface to a horn at its center. When the parabolic antenna transmits electromagnetic waves, the horn transmits the signal toward the curved surface of the antenna. The curved surface reflects the electromagnetic waves to produce a beam-like pattern in the same way light is reflected from the curved surface of a flashlight to produce a

Copyright Goodheart-Willcox Co., Inc.

Figure 4-7 Yagi antenna constructed inside a metal tube. The metal tube enhances reception and transmission.

Photo reprinted with the permission of PCTEL, Maxrad Product Group

beam of light. The parabolic antenna is constructed as a simple, curved surface or in the shape of a dish. When it is constructed in the shape of a dish, it is usually called a *parabolic dish* or simply *dish antenna*. The parabolic antenna greatly amplifies a weak radio-wave signal when compared with other antenna types.

Radio-Wave Transmission Techniques

NET

1.6, 2.5

Radio waves are electromagnetic waves with a frequency range of 10 kHz to 3,000,000 MHz. They have the longest wavelength when compared with microwave and infrared. Radio waves are used in LANs. Radio wave-based networks adhere to the IEEE 802.11 and Bluetooth standards and operate at 2.4 GHz.

To communicate between radio-based wireless network devices, several transmission techniques are used. Aside from a typical single-frequency transmission, which uses only one frequency to broadcast, transmission techniques include spread spectrum and orthogonal frequency-division multiplexing. You must become familiar with these techniques because most wireless network technologies are described using these terms. The techniques are based on the technology, the frequency band of operation, and the manufacturer's idea of the best way to achieve a high data rate. A high data rate not only relies on how quickly the data can move between two points, but also on how much data has to be retransmitted because of interference.

Transmission techniques divide an allocated frequency band into many separate frequency ranges, or channels. After the frequency band is divided, a carrier wave is generated for each of the channels.

Copyright Goodheart-Willcox Co., Inc.

Spread Spectrum

Spread spectrum is a transmission technique that uses multiple channels to transmit data either simultaneously or sequentially. The term *spread spectrum* refers to transmission channels *spread* across the *spectrum* of the available bandwidth.

Spread spectrum is essentially several radio wave paths designed to carry radio waves. Think of a spread spectrum transmission as a highway. A highway system consists of several separate lanes to carry vehicles. In the highway system, trucks carry supplies to a store. Each truck uses a separate lane. If one of the lanes is blocked, the other lanes can still carry the supplies to the store. This is the same method employed by spread spectrum. If one of the channels is blocked by radio interference, the other channels can still carry the radio-wave data.

In the spread spectrum technique, data can be transmitted on multiple channels simultaneously or sequentially. The spread spectrum technique that transmits data on multiple channels simultaneously is called **frequency hopping**. The spread spectrum technique that transmits data on multiple channels sequentially is called **direct sequencing**.

Spread spectrum is the chosen transmission method of most wireless technologies. Transmitting data on multiple channels decreases the likelihood of interference. Interference is typically limited to only one or two of the channels. The other channels in the frequency band are free to carry data undisturbed. Data that is lost can be easily retransmitted on a channel that is not affected by the interference.

Frequency Hopping

Frequency hopping is also referred to as *frequency-hopping spread spectrum (FHSS)*. Frequency hopping is named due to the transmission technique of data packets switching from channel to channel, or rather, frequency to frequency. Instead of transmitting the data packets over a single channel, the data packets hop from one channel to another in a set pattern determined by a software algorithm. None of the 79 channels is occupied for more than 0.4 seconds. This technique is used with wireless devices that use the 2.4-GHz radio band. The 2.4-GHz frequency has a bandwidth of 83.5 MHz. Rather than use the entire range as a single channel to carry radio data, the frequency band is divided into 79 different 1-MHz channels. See Figure 4-8 for an example of frequency hopping.

Many people assume that because data packets hop to various channels, this transmission technique was designed as a security measure. This assumption is false. The reason that the frequency-hopping technique is used is to avoid interference. If any interference matches the same frequency as the wireless networking devices, the data would be corrupted. If only one frequency were used and it encountered interference, the network would be useless. By using the frequency-hopping technique, interference can be tolerated. The interference would likely only affect one or two of the available frequencies in the entire 79 1-MHz channels. This allows more than an ample number of channels to ensure continuous transmission between wireless networking devices.

The frequency-hopping technique is limited to a maximum of a 2-Mbps data rate. A much higher data rate can be accomplished using direct sequencing.

Copyright Goodheart-Willcox Co., Inc.

Direct Sequencing

Direct sequencing divides the 2.4-GHz frequency band into 11 overlapping channels of 83 MHz each. Within the 11 channels are three channels with a 22-MHz bandwidth. The three channels do not overlap and can be used simultaneously. Using three channels at the same time results in higher data rates than frequency hopping. The data rates for direct sequencing are 11 Mbps and 33 Mbps. The 33 Mbps is a result of using all three 22-Mbps channels at the same time, as shown in Figure 4-9.

One disadvantage of direct sequencing is that a much larger portion of the transmitted data is affected by electromagnetic interference than with frequency hopping. The data rate of direct sequencing, therefore, is drastically affected by interference. Direct sequencing is also referred to as *direct sequencing spread spectrum (DSSS)*. Most vendors use DSSS technology at 11 Mbps for wireless network systems.

Figure 4-8 In frequency hopping, data is transmitted over 79 1-MHz channels. The data transmissions continuously use different channels in short increments of less than 0.4 seconds each.

Frequency Hopping Spread Spectrum (FHSS)

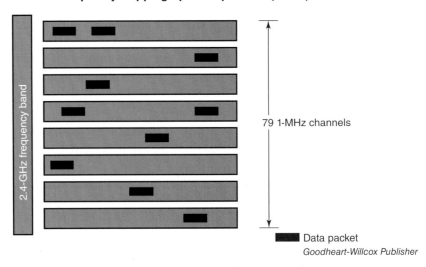

Goodheart-Willcox Publisher

Figure 4-9 In direct sequencing, a 2.4-GHz frequency band is divided into eleven overlapping 83-MHz channels. Each 83-MHz channel is further divided into three 22-MHz channels.

Direct Sequencing Spread Spectrum (DSSS)

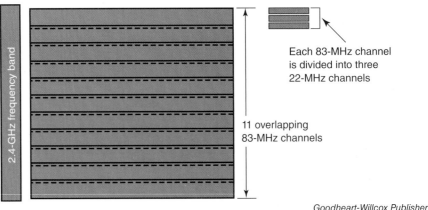

Goodheart-Willcox Publisher

Copyright Goodheart-Willcox Co., Inc.

Orthogonal Frequency-Division Multiplexing

The **orthogonal frequency-division multiplexing (OFDM)** transmission technique is used with wireless devices that use the 5-GHz radio band and can achieve a data rate as high as 54 Mbps. The OFDM transmission technique divides the allotted frequency into channels similar to frequency hopping and direct sequencing. *Orthogonal* means separate side by side over a range of values. In wireless application, the term *orthogonal* means there are multiple separate radio channels side by side within an assigned radio band. *Frequency division* means dividing the assigned frequency range into multiple, narrow subfrequencies. *Multiplexing* is an electronics term, which means to combine content from different sources and transmit them collectively over a single, common carrier. By combining the three terms, OFDM means to communicate wireless data over several different channels within an assigned frequency range. However, in OFDM, each channel is broadcast separately and is referred to as *multiplexed*.

OFDM is used in conjunction with the Unlicensed National Information Infrastructure (U-NII) frequency ranges. The FCC divided the 5-GHz radio frequency into three 20-MHz channels and classified them as the Unlicensed National Information Infrastructure (U-NII). The three classifications are U-NII-1, U-NII-2, and U-NII-3. See Figure 4-10 for an example. Each of the three U-NII classifications has a frequency range of 100 MHz. Using the OFDM transmission technique, each 100-MHz frequency range is broken into four separate 20-MHz channels. Each of the 20-MHz channels is further divided into 52 different 300-kHz subchannels. Of the 52 subchannels, 48 are used to transmit data, and the remaining four are used for error correction. It is the large number of channels that provides the high data rates. Additionally, communication is not affected as adversely by interference as it is with the other techniques mentioned. Even if one or two subchannels are affected, the overall data rate remains unaffected.

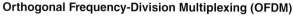

Orthogonal Frequency-Division Multiplexing (OFDM)

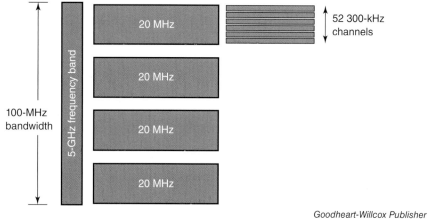

Figure 4-10 Orthogonal frequency-division multiplexing (OFDM) is used in conjunction with the U-NII frequency ranges to achieve a data rate as high as 54 Mbps. Each of the U-NII frequency ranges is 100 MHz wide. This bandwidth is divided into three 20-MHz channels, which are further divided into 52 300-kHz channels.

Goodheart-Willcox Publisher

The FCC U-NII classifications are based on the frequency range of the broadcast, the allowable maximum amount of power allotted to the broadcast, and the location of where the device may be used. There is no maximum distance measurement in feet or meters for the different classifications. The maximum distances are controlled by the maximum amount of output wattage generated by the devices. The actual range varies considerably due to influences such as building structures and materials, the electromagnetic environment, and atmospheric conditions. Use the chart in Figure 4-11 to get a relative idea of expected maximum distances.

Copyright Goodheart-Willcox Co., Inc.

Figure 4-11 U-NII classifications and their characteristics.

Classification	Frequency Range	Power	Application
U-NII 1	5.15 GHz–5.25 GHz	50 mW	Indoors
U-NII 2	5.25 GHz–5.35 GHz	250 mW	Indoors/outdoors
U-NII 3	5.725 GHz–5.825 GHz	1 W	Outdoors

Goodheart-Willcox Publisher

Distances vary by manufacturer and by location conditions such as placement of metal cabinets and building materials. The maximum power output of the device has a direct relationship to data throughput. Packet loss is generally caused by radio interference or excessive distance between two devices. When packet loss increases, the data rate decreases. The data rate is automatically adjusted to a lower rate when an excessive number of packets are lost. The data rate continues to be lowered until an acceptable packet loss is reached. The more powerful the signal, the less interference can disrupt the signal. This means that there will be fewer packets lost. Consequently, data rate is better when the signal is more powerful. The maximum transmission power rating for a wireless device is set by the FCC. Do not attempt to memorize distances because they are not standard.

Radio-Wave-Based Networking

NET

1.5, 2.5

Radio-wave-based networks are rapidly becoming the choice of many networking systems because of the fast and easy installation and convenience of no wires. A simple wireless network, such as one designed for home or business use, consists of two or more computers with wireless network adapters. Figure 4-12 shows a USB wireless network adapter.

Figure 4-12 USB wireless network adapter.

a_v_d/Shutterstock.com

Copyright Goodheart-Willcox Co., Inc.

Wireless Access Points

While not required, most wireless networks contain a wireless access point (WAP) also referred to as an *access point (AP)*. A **wireless access point (WAP)** provides a connection between a wireless network and a cable-based network. Wireless access points typically provide access from wireless network devices to needed hard-wired network devices such as printers, modems, and routers.

A typical WAP comes equipped with two omni antennae, as shown in Figure 4-13. One antenna is used for transmitting, and the other is used for receiving. This allows for full-duplex communication, which makes the WAP more efficient than if a single antenna were used.

Figure 4-13 A wireless access point (WAP) provides a connection between a wireless network and a cable-based network.

Wireless Access Point

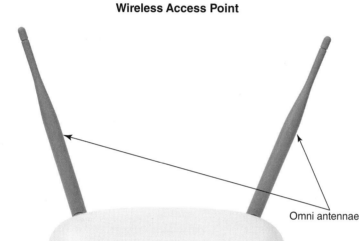

Omni antennae

Mkos83/Shutterstock.com

When a WAP is present in a wireless network, all communication must go through it. Think of a WAP as a traffic director for packets. The WAP controls the flow of all packets on the wireless network. When multiple wireless access points are used, the roaming device (laptop, smartphone, tablet, etc.) automatically detects and connects to the WAP with the strongest signal, which is typically the closest WAP.

All wireless access points in a wireless network use the same service set identifier (SSID). The SSID is similar in nature to a work group name or domain name. It is a name that identifies wireless access points within the same network. Multiple wireless access points within the same network should be configured with the same SSID to support network roaming. When separate network systems are within range of each other, the wireless access point for each separate network should use a different SSID to distinguish itself from each other. Most wireless access points and wireless network adapters come with a default SSID. If they are installed with minimal or no configuration at all, all wireless access points will have the same SSID. The SSID can be readily reconfigured. Devices must have the correct SSID and password or passphrase to connect to a network. If either is incorrect, the device will be unable to establish a connection.

Tech Tip

Service set identifier (SSID) names are case-sensitive.

Copyright Goodheart-Willcox Co., Inc.

When building a wireless network, it is a good idea to perform a *site survey*. This involves measuring the signal strength in various locations in order to determine the best location to put wireless access points. This can also require analysis of floor plans, inspection of building facilities, and interviews with people who will be using the network.

Wireless controllers are another topic important to WAPs. A WLAN controller uses Lightweight Access Point Protocol (LWAPP) to manage several lightweight access points. Simply put, several WAPs are controlled from a central location: the WLAN controller.

Keep in mind that with any technology, there is a limit to its capacity. This is true for wireless, regardless of the wireless connection method used. The connection of more devices than the wireless access point can handle is referred to as *overcapacity* and will degrade performance.

Wireless network adapters and wireless access points come with default settings to make configuration easy and, in some cases, automatic. However, easy or preconfigured settings make for weak security. Each device by the same manufacturer uses the same default SSID. The SSID should be changed to make the system more secure.

By default, most manufacturers do not enable encryption. The encryption process slows the overall data rate of the system. It takes time to encrypt and decrypt the packets. Encryption, however, should be enabled to make the network more secure.

Wireless Network Modes

NET

1.5, 2.2

A wireless network that contains one or more wireless access points is arranged in **infrastructure mode**, illustrated in Figure 4-14. When a WAP is not present in a wireless network, it is arranged in **ad hoc mode**, Figure 4-15. The phrase *ad hoc*, when translated from Latin, means *for that purpose*. The reference to the term *ad hoc* means that the system is put together rapidly and is usually intended to be a temporary installation rather than a permanent installation. An ad hoc network can contain a maximum of 20 computers. Typically, an ad hoc network consists of a laptop and a desktop computer. An ad hoc network can be compared to a peer-to-peer network where all devices are equal. All wireless networks are technically a logical mesh topology. This means any node can communicate with any other node.

The IEEE 802.11 wireless network standard does not use the terms *ad hoc*, *SSID*, or *ESSID* when describing the technical aspects of a wireless network. These terms

Figure 4-14 A wireless network in infrastructure mode.

Infrastructure Mode

(workstation icons) RedlineVector/Shutterstock.com; (laptop icon) Jemastock/Shutterstock.com; (router icon) Vadim Ermak/Shutterstock.com; Goodheart-Willcox Publisher

Copyright Goodheart-Willcox Co., Inc.

Figure 4-15 A wireless network in ad hoc mode.

Ad Hoc Mode

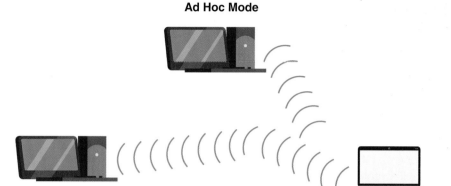

(workstation icons) RedlineVector/Shutterstock.com; (laptop icon) Jemastock/Shutterstock.com;
Goodheart-Willcox Publisher

are encountered when reviewing product information provided by wireless manu-facturers. The IEEE uses the terms *basic service set (BSS)* and *independent basic ser-vice set (IBSS)*. A **basic service set (BSS)** is a group of wireless devices connected as a network, which is described by manufacturers as an infrastructure network or an SSID. An **independent basic service set (IBSS)** is similar to an ad hoc network in that it does not use an access point and usually is a direct connection between two wireless devices. You will see the term *extended service set identifier (ESSID)* listed in the CompTIA Network+ objectives and acronyms list.

An **extended service set identifier (ESSID)** refers to two or more wireless ac-cess points or wireless devices using the same SSID. The subsequent devices are known as *wireless range extenders*. In other words, they "extended" the network by using the same SSID for more than one access point. When multiple access points use the same SSID, a portable wireless device can maintain a constant connection with the network as the user moves around the location.

IEEE 802.11 Standard

Radio-wave-based networks adhere to the 802.11 standard. The 802.11 standard consists of four classifications of wireless networks: 802.11a, 802.11b, 802.11g, and 802.11n. See Figure 4-16 for a chart of the 802.11 standards and their characteristics.

802.11a

The *802.11a* standard operates at the 5-GHz frequency and has a maximum data rate of 54 Mbps. An 802.11a device may use lower data rates of 48 Mbps, 36 Mbps, 24 Mbps, 18 Mbps, 12 Mbps, 9 Mbps, and 6 Mbps. At the 5-GHz frequency, 802.11a networking devices are not susceptible to interference from devices that cause in-terference at the 2.4-GHz frequency range. Devices compatible with the 802.11a standard are incompatible with 802.11b and 802.11g devices. Also, 802.11a devices use a higher frequency than 802.11b or 802.11g devices. The higher frequency can-not penetrate materials such as building walls like the lower frequency devices can. This results in 802.11a devices having a shorter range when compared with 802.11b, 802.11g, and 802.11n devices.

802.11b

Although the 802.11a and 802.11b standards were developed at the same time, *802.11b* was the first to be adopted by industry. The maximum data rate for 802.11b

Note

The exact meaning of net-working terminology can be confusing because device manufacturers often present the terminology at a novice level rather than at a technical level. For example, some manufac-turers use the term *enhanced* to indicate a feature that has been added by that particular manufacturer.

1.5, 1.6, 5.4 NET

Figure 4-16 IEEE 802.11 standards and their characteristics.

802.11 Standard	Radio Frequency	Frequency Range	Data Rate	Range (approximate)	Transmission Method
802.11a	5 GHz	5.15 GHz–5.825 GHz	6 Mbps 9 Mbps 12 Mbps 18 Mbps 24 Mbps 36 Mbps 54 Mbps	50 m	OFDM
802.11b	2.4 GHz	2.4 GHz–2.4835 GHz	1 Mbps 2 Mbps 5.5 Mbps 11 Mbps	100 m	DSSS
802.11g	2.4 GHz	2.4 GHz–2.4835 GHz	1 Mbps 2 Mbps 5.5 Mbps 11 Mbps	100 m	DSSS
	5 GHz	5.15 GHz–5.825 GHz	54 Mbps	50 m	OFDM
802.11n	2.4 GHz	2.4 GHz–2.4835 GHz	All previous data rates up to 300 Mbps and possibly as high as 600 Mbps	300 m	OFDM
	5 GHz	5.15 GHz–5.825 GHz			

Goodheart-Willcox Publisher

is 11 Mbps. When the highest rate cannot be achieved because of distance or radio interference, a lower rate is automatically selected. The lower rates are 5.5 Mbps, 2 Mbps, and 1 Mbps. An 802.11b device can operate over any of 11 channels within the assigned bandwidth. When communicating between wireless devices, all devices should use the same channel. When using devices from the same manufacturer, the same channel is automatically selected by default. Two wireless networks, one constructed of 802.11b devices and the other constructed of 802.11a devices, can coexist without interfering with each other because they use different assigned frequencies. This allows for two different wireless networks to operate within the same area without interfering with each other.

802.11 network devices are often referred to as **Wi-Fi**, which is a term coined by the Wi-Fi Alliance that refers to 802.11 wireless network products. *Wi-Fi* as a term is a play on the existing term *high fidelity (hi-fi)*, which describes high-quality reproduction of sound. The use of the term *Wi-Fi* was due to manufacturers forming the Wireless Ethernet Compatibility Alliance (WECA) in an effort to standardize wireless network devices. Devices approved as compatible with the 802.11 standards are given a "Wi-Fi Certified" seal, which means any device bearing the Wi-Fi seal is compatible with any other device bearing the seal, shown in Figure 4-17. This process led to competing, yet compatible, standards by both organizations. As a result, users are able to mix and match components from various manufacturers. There are many proprietary devices and software products on the market that may not be fully compatible with other devices.

Copyright Goodheart-Willcox Co., Inc.

Figure 4-17 Wireless router box showing the Wi-Fi Certified seal.

Wi-Fi Certified seal

Goodheart-Willcox Publisher

802.11g

The IEEE *802.11g* standard followed the 802.11a and 802.11b standards. The 802.11g standard operates in the 802.11b frequency range of 2.4 GHz. This makes it downward compatible with 802.11b devices. When communicating with 802.11b devices, the maximum data rate is reduced to 11 Mbps. The maximum throughput for the 802.11g standard is 54 Mbps, but the maximum distance is typically much shorter than an 802.11b device. An 802.11g device can use the lower data rates of 48 Mbps, 36 Mbps, 28 Mbps, 24 Mbps, 12 Mbps, 11 Mbps, 9 Mbps, 6 Mbps, 5.5 Mbps, 2 Mbps, and 1 Mbps. Since 802.11g is assigned to the same frequency range as 802.11b, it is susceptible to the same sources of radio interference.

802.11g and 802.11b devices are not compatible with 802.11a devices because they use different frequencies. It must be noted that while the standards are different, there are devices on the market that can communicate with any of the mentioned wireless standards. In other words, there are wireless devices that can communicate with 802.11a, 802.11b, and 802.11g devices.

802.11n

The *802.11n* standard operates at 5.0 GHz and is backward compatible with the 2.4-GHz frequency range. In 2009, the Wi-Fi Alliance organization ratified a standard based on a draft version of 802.11n. However, manufacturers developed 802.11n wireless network devices before the 802.11n classification was ratified in an effort to offer superior wireless devices. Therefore, these devices may not exactly match the 802.11n-ratified standard.

An 802.11n device is compatible with 802.11a, 802.11b, and 802.11g, but may not support MIMO technology when paired with these devices. **Multiple-input-multiple-output (MIMO)** is a wireless networking technology that uses two or more streams of data transmission to increase data throughput and the range of the wireless network. Transmitting two or more streams of data in the same frequency channel is referred to as **spatial multiplexing**.

> **Note**
>
> There cannot be a definitive range for individual IEEE wireless standards, only approximations. Range is determined by radio-wave power expressed in watts. There are many electronic factors that affect radio-wave ranges.

1.6 NET

1.6 NET

Copyright Goodheart-Willcox Co., Inc.

802.11n incorporates the multiple-input-multiple-output (MIMO) technology using 5-GHz and 2.4-GHz frequencies with an expected data rate of approximately 300 Mbps to 600 Mbps. The exact speed depends on the number of simultaneous data streams transmitted. Some 802.11n devices are advertised with data rates much higher than specified in the standard.

MIMO was designed as an integral part of the 802.11n standard. Some manufacturers have incorporated MIMO into the latest revisions of their 802.11g devices to take advantage of producing higher data rates.

Prior to MIMO, wireless access points and devices sent a single stream of data between the transmitter and receiver. MIMO uses two or more antennae, thus creating two or more streams of data simultaneously. For example, an 802.11n wireless device that transmits data at 150 Mbps can apply MIMO and raise the data rate to 300 Mbps. The latest 802.11n standard is 144.4 Mbps or rounded up to 150 Mbps. By using MIMO, 802.11n devices can raise the expected data rate to nearly 300 Mbps when using a 20-MHz channel and 600 Mbps when using a 40-MHz channel inside the assigned 2.4-GHz frequency range. The 40-MHz channel can carry twice the data as the 20-MHz channel.

The Wi-Fi Alliance uses a similar method in its standard and achieves a maximum throughput of 450 Mbps as posted on their website at the time of this writing. Visit the Wi-Fi Alliance website (http://www.wi-fi.org) for more information.

802.11n 2009

IEEE *802.11n 2009* describes technology that achieves bandwidth of up to 600 Mbit/s with the use of four spatial streams at a channel width of 40 MHz. It uses MIMO, which uses multiple antennas to coherently resolve more information than possible using a single antenna.

802.11ax

There have been several iterations of 802.11ax, each with its own advantages. These iterations include the following:

- *IEEE 802.11ac.* This standard was approved in January 2014 and has a throughput of up to 1 Gbps with at least 500 Mbps, and uses up to 8 MIMO.
- *IEEE 802.11ad.* This standard was developed by the Wireless Gigabyte Alliance and supports data transmission rates up to 7 Gbit/s—more than ten times faster than the highest 802.11n rate.
- *IEEE 802.11af.* Approved in February 2014, 802.11af allows WLAN operation in TV white-space spectrum in the VHF and UHF bands between 54 and 790 MHz. It is also referred to as *White-Fi* and *Super Wi-Fi.*
- *IEEE 802.11aj.* This is a rebranding of 802.11ad for use in the 45-GHz unlicensed spectrum available in some regions of the world, specifically China.

802.11 Channels

Today you are probably using some variation of 802.11ax. Regardless of what wireless standard you are using, when deploying wireless access points, the channel you use is also important. The 802.11 standard defines 14 channels. The channels that can be used are determined by the host nation. In the United States, a WAP can only use channels 1 through 11. Channels tend to overlap, so nearby WAPs should not use close channels. **Channel bonding** is a method whereby two or more links are combined. This is done either for redundancy, fault tolerance, or for increased throughput. Channel bonding can be used in wired or wireless networks.

Copyright Goodheart-Willcox Co., Inc.

802.11 Access Method

802.11 networks rely on carrier-sense multiple access with collision avoidance (CSMA/CA) as a media access protocol. Do *not* confuse this with CSMA/CD, which is used by IEEE 802.3 networks. The *carrier-sense multiple access* (CSMA) portion of the technology is the same for both the 802.11 and 802.3 networks. The difference is in the *collision detection* (CD) *versus collision avoidance* (CA). *Collision detection* (CD) detects a collision on the network after it occurs, while *collision avoidance* (CA) attempts to avoid a collision.

To understand the CSMA/CA process, look at Figure 4-18. The laptop equipped with a wireless card first listens for network traffic. If the airwaves are clear, it signals the WAP with a request to send (RTS) message. The WAP returns either a clear to send (CTS) or busy signal to the laptop. The process is repeated until the laptop is cleared to send data. After the data has been sent to the WAP, the WAP sends an acknowledgement message (ACK) to the laptop. Collision avoidance technology solves the problem of broadcast storms, which are associated with collision-detection technology. The collision-detection technology is designed to accept network collisions, wait, and then resend the complete transmission.

Figure 4-18 802.11 networks rely on carrier-sense multiple access with collision avoidance (CSMA/CA) as a media access protocol.

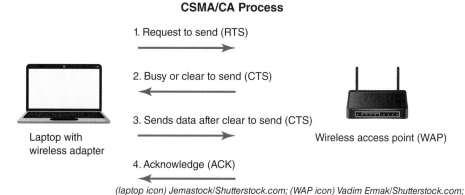

CSMA/CA Process

1. Request to send (RTS)

2. Busy or clear to send (CTS)

3. Sends data after clear to send (CTS)

Laptop with wireless adapter

4. Acknowledge (ACK)

Wireless access point (WAP)

(laptop icon) Jemastock/Shutterstock.com; (WAP icon) Vadim Ermak/Shutterstock.com; Goodheart-Willcox Publisher

The CSMA/CA access method was selected over CSMA/CD because of the nature of wireless media. In a typical Ethernet environment that uses cable, a collision can be detected anywhere on a segment by all nodes in that segment. The same is not true of a wireless network. Look at Figure 4-19 and compare the two networking technologies. In the cable-based network, all nodes are connected to the same segment via a hub. In fact, both wired and wireless networks have moved to CSMA/CA rather than CSMA/CD.

For nodes to communicate with each other on a wireless network, all nodes must be inside the same broadcast area, called an *overlap area*. See Figure 4-20 for a visual representation of overlap areas. This is not always possible, especially with mobile devices such as laptops, cell phones, automobiles, and such. It is not unusual to have a mobile computer outside of the normal overlap area. There is also the possibility of mobile users moving in and out of the overlap area, further complicating communication. The best logical choice of media access for a wireless network is CSMA/CA.

CSMA/CA is used because of the way wireless networks communicate as opposed to the way wired networks communicate. When communicating on a wired network, all devices in the same collision domain can hear each other when they

Copyright Goodheart-Willcox Co., Inc.

Figure 4-19 In an 802.3 network with CSMA/CD, all computers are wired to each other and each computer can hear traffic on the network. There is no need for a computer to send a signal notifying the other computers it is about to transmit data.

CSMA/CD Access Method

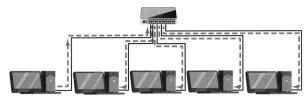

CSMA/CA Access Method

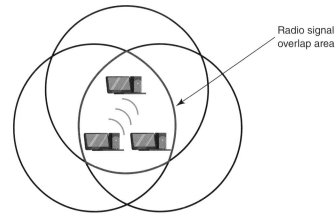

Radio signal overlap area

*(hub icon) Vadim Ermak/Shutterstock.com; (workstation icons) RedlineVector/Shutterstock.com;
Goodheart-Willcox Publisher*

Figure 4-20 Overlap area of an ad hoc and infrastructure wireless network. A—For computers in an ad hoc wireless network to communicate with each other, all computers must be in the same overlap area. B—In an infrastructure wireless network, the wireless access point (WAP) must be in the common overlap area of the wireless network computers. The WAP controls all communication.

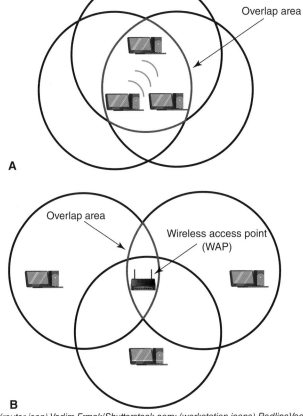

Overlap area

A

Overlap area

Wireless access point (WAP)

B

*(router icon) Vadim Ermak/Shutterstock.com; (workstation icons) RedlineVector/Shutterstock.com;
Goodheart-Willcox Publisher*

Copyright Goodheart-Willcox Co., Inc.

are communicating. The idea is that each device waits for when the cable is clear of communication before it communicates on the cable. When a collection of wireless devices is connected as a network, not all devices will always be within the range of all other devices. This causes a problem because a wireless device may not be aware when other devices are communicating. This is why a wireless network system requires CSMA/CA to access the network media, the wireless network area.

CSMA/CA is designed to make the WAP in charge of all communication. The WAP permits or denies wireless devices to communicate. The WAP is centrally located and can communicate with all the devices in the wireless network. The WAP hears all communication. A device sitting at the edge of the wireless network cannot hear the devices farthest from it, but the WAP can. If CSMA/CD were used as the access method, the devices would not take turns as permitted by the WAP and the result would be too many communication collisions on the network caused by two or more devices attempting to communicate at the same time.

Adding more wireless access points can expand the geographic area covered by a wireless network, as demonstrated in Figure 4-21. Connecting several WAPs with cable can also enlarge a wireless LAN. Figure 4-22 shows several WAPs joined by copper-core cable. This connection allows multiple WAPs to be spread over a large area without the need for overlapping radio signals. This type of arrangement is ideal for mobile users. As the user travels through the network system with a mobile device such as a laptop, he or she can access the network system from anywhere. For example, a college campus spanning hundreds of acres could incorporate a mesh arrangement of WAPs throughout the campus area. A professor or student could use his or her laptop equipped with a wireless network card to access the network system from anywhere on the campus, such as classrooms, the library, cafeteria, a dorm room, or even from outside on the lawn areas.

Figure 4-21 The range of a wireless network can be extended by adding additional wireless access points (WAPs).

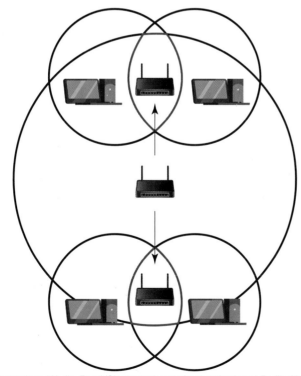

(router icons) Vadim Ermak/Shutterstock.com; (workstation icons) RedlineVector/Shutterstock.com;
Goodheart-Willcox Publisher

Copyright Goodheart-Willcox Co., Inc.

Figure 4-22 A wireless network can be greatly expanded by connecting multiple wireless access points (WAPs) to a cable-based Ethernet network such as 10BaseT.

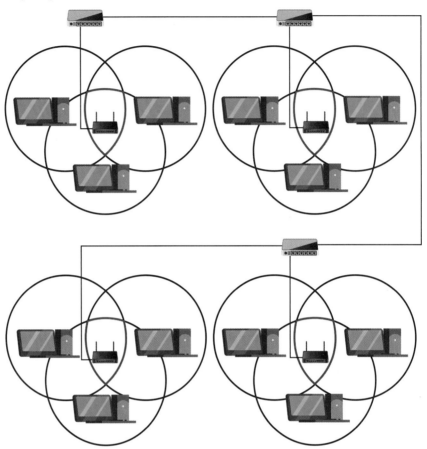

(router and hub icons) Vadim Ermak/Shutterstock.com; (workstation icons) RedlineVector/Shutterstock.com;
Goodheart-Willcox Publisher

Network+ Note ✚

Questions concerning the IEEE standards can be tricky on the Network+ Certification Exam because the standards are constantly changing. Before taking the certification exam, you should check the CompTIA website to see if any changes are reflected in the exam objectives.

802.15

The 802.15 Working Group for Wireless Personal Area Networks is better known as *personal area networks (PAN)* or *wireless personal area networks (WPAN)*. A **wireless personal area network (WPAN)** is typically a small Ethernet network consisting of personal wireless devices such as a cell phone, laptop, palmtop, wireless printer, wireless access point, iPod, Xbox 360, and similar items. Many of the standards developed here coexist with standards already developed and adopted by 802.11 wireless LANs. One of the concerns of 802.15 is the compatibility of Bluetooth standards with other mobile communication devices such as telephones, portable computers, and personal digital assistants.

The 802.15 standard breaks down into additional separate specifications. These are listed and defined in the following table. A complete copy of the IEEE 802.15 standard is located at http://standards.ieee.org/.

802.15 Standard	Description
802.15.1	Low-speed PAN based on the Bluetooth standard.
802.15.2	Allows 802.11 and 802.15 devices to coexist in the 2.4-GHz band.
802.15.3	High-speed PAN with a data rate of 10 Mbps–55 Mbps at a range of 10 meters or less.
802.15.4	Low-speed PAN with a data rate of 2 Kbps–200 Kbps using DSSS for 2.4 and 915 MHz.

Copyright Goodheart-Willcox Co., Inc.

ZigBee is a standard developed by a consortium of electronic manufacturers for mainly residential applications of wireless devices as related to appliances and security and such. It is based on the 802.15.4 standard, which creates personal area networks. These are used for very nearby purposes such as medical device data collection or home automation. ZigBee is low power and low bandwidth. What appears to be confusing is that the standard is represented by the name *ZigBee* rather than a number. The term *ZigBee* is used similar to the way the term *Wi-Fi* is used. Keep in mind that the IEEE standards will constantly change and be amended as manufacturers try to improve the network wireless technologies.

802.16

The IEEE 802.16 Working Group on Broadband Wireless Access Standards is better known as *broadband wireless access (BWA)* or *wireless metropolitan area network (WMAN)*. This project is concerned with connecting LANs to each other using wireless technologies. The working group is hoping to design data rates as high as 70 Mbps over distances of 30 miles or more. The working group is also attempting to expand the radio frequencies assigned by the FCC and the radio frequencies dedicated to only wireless mesh-type networks, such as wireless MANs. At the present time, private companies can achieve high data rates over many miles, but there is no single standard that allows devices manufactured by different companies to communicate with each other.

Bluetooth

Bluetooth is a short-range, wireless system that is designed for limited distances. Many texts and courses teach that Bluetooth has a maximum range of 10 meters. However, that is only partially true. In fact, it is only true for Bluetooth 3.0. The following table summarizes the ranges and bandwidth for the various versions of Bluetooth.

Version	Bandwidth/Range	
3.0	25 Mbit/s	10 meters (33 ft)
4.0	25 Mbit/s	60 meters (200 ft)
5.0	50 Mbit/s	240 meters (800 ft)

Bluetooth uses 79 channels that use the frequency-hopping spread spectrum transmission technique, starting at 2.4 GHz. The Bluetooth standard was developed separately from the IEEE network standards. It was never intended as a networking standard designed to carry massive amounts of information. Bluetooth was designed for appliances such as telephones, laptops, smartphones, digital cameras, tablets, headsets, printers, keyboards, and mice.

A Bluetooth network is referred to as a **personal area network (PAN)**, which is a very small network. Bluetooth became recognized by the IEEE organization and was incorporated into the IEEE 802.15 Working Group Wireless Personal Area Networks in July 2004. Bluetooth suffers from the same radio interference sources as other 802.11 devices, which are part of the ISM band. Bluetooth will not interfere with 802.11b devices when operated in the same area because they use different formats for configuring data. In other words, a wireless keyboard and mouse based on the Bluetooth standard will not interfere with the operation of an 802.11b wireless network.

Since Bluetooth has such a limited range, it is not used for actual wireless networks. However, it is used for wireless communication between devices that are

1.5 NET

Tech Tip

As always, when working with radio-wave devices, expect that practical data rates will be much lower than the data rate printed for the standard, except in ideal conditions.

Note

The phrase *wireless personal area network (WPAN)* is sometimes replaced with the word *piconet*.

Copyright Goodheart-Willcox Co., Inc.

typically located in close proximity. For example, you could have a Bluetooth headset for your smartphone. It is also quite common for modern automobiles to allow Bluetooth synchronization with smartphones.

For the very latest information about the Bluetooth standard, always check the Bluetooth organization website at www.Bluetooth.com.

Other Wireless Technology

NET
1.5

Several other wireless technologies have emerged in recent years. Each of these is suited for a particular purpose. One such technology is ANT. *ANT* is a proprietary wireless network technology that provides low power modes and is also used in Wi-Fi settings. It has been used in sports-related technologies, such as fitness trackers, and medical monitoring. **ANT+** (pronounced *ant plus*) is a function that can be added to base ANT protocols that allows for interoperability. Through this standardization, all ANT+ devices can be networked to allow for collection, analysis, and distribution of data. For example, ANT+ allows a person to link his or her fitness tracker with wireless or Bluetooth devices such as heart-rate monitors, pedometer, and scale. For more information, visit the ANT website at http://www.thisisant.com.

Radio-frequency identification (RFID) is the use of electromagnetic fields to identify and track objects equipped with active tags or chips. This technology has been in use for several years. For example, inventory in a warehouse or retail store is often tagged with an RFID chip to track individual products. The RFID chip broadcasts a radio frequency that is collected by a receiver to identify and track the chip. Recently, this technology has been implemented by businesses outside of networking. For example, amusement parks have begun using RFID tags to enhance their guests' experiences. In this instance, guests are given an RFID tag inside a bracelet or card, which is then linked to the credit card used to book the trip. The linked RFID tag can then be used to pay for tickets, merchandise, or food, and it can even be used as a hotel room key card.

Another technology is near field communication (NFC). **Near field communication (NFC)** is a set of communication protocols that allows mobile devices to exchange communication provided they are within a certain range of each other. NFC operates in very short ranges, often a matter of centimeters. Smart cards sometimes are equipped with a chip that can transmit data if it is very close to a receiver. This is used in some physical access situations and is usually done with an RFID chip.

Z-wave is a wireless communication protocol used for home automation. It operates in the 800 to 900 MHz range, and it allows users to control various residential devices such as lighting, security systems, thermostat data, and garage door openers, among others. Appliances can communicate with each other over relatively short distances using low-power technology.

Cellular Technology

NET
1.5, 1.6

Cellular technology is based on radio waves connecting to designated areas referred to as *cells*. Rather than communicate directly by radio wave from one cell to another, a remote device connects to a radio transmitter or receiver within its cell. The radio transmitter or receiver communicates to remote cells via microwave transmission or telephone lines. In the remote cell, the message is sent to a radio transceiver or receiver. The radio transceiver/receiver sends the message via radio waves to the remote device within its cell. See Figure 4-23 for a diagram of this communication.

Copyright Goodheart-Willcox Co., Inc.

Cellular technology is responsible for wireless telephone and telephone technology. The same technology connects mobile and stationary computer equipment. A text message can be transmitted to a pager by composing a message using a desktop computer. The message is sent over an Internet connection to a mobile-telephone-switching office. From there, radio microwaves transmit the encoded message to the distant pager system or paging app on a smartphone. See Figure 4-24 for an example of using cellular technology to send a message from a computer. Cellular technology supports duplex communication using a device such as a personal digital assistant or a palmtop configured for wireless radio services.

Figure 4-23 Cellular technology communication system.

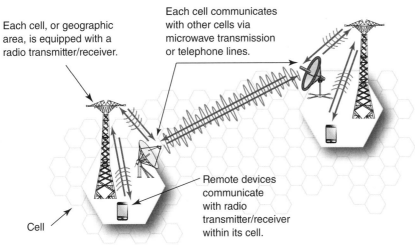

(smartphone icon) Tetiana Yurchenko/Shutterstock.com; Goodheart-Willcox Publisher

Figure 4-24 An example of using cellular technology to send a message from a computer to a mobile network device such as a paging service on a smartphone.

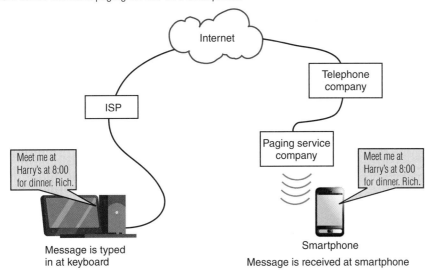

(smartphone icon) Tetiana Yurchenko/Shutterstock.com; (workstation icon) RedlineVector/Shutterstock.com;
Goodheart-Willcox Publisher

Copyright Goodheart-Willcox Co., Inc.

Cellular Networks

Cellular network technology has evolved. The most recent standard, 5g, exists, but it is not yet widely available. Available cellular networks include the following:

- *Global System for Mobile communications (GSM).* Developed by the European Telecommunications Standards Institute (ETSI), GSM is basically the 2G network.

- *Enhanced Data Rates for GSM Evolution (EDGE).* This standard does not fit neatly into the 2g, 3g, 4g spectrum. It is technically considered pre-3g but was an improvement on GSM (2g); one could consider it a bridge between 2g and 3g technology.

- *Universal Mobile Telecommunications Systems (UMTS).* This is a 3g standard based on GSM. It is essentially an improvement of GSM.

- *Long Term Evolution (LTE).* Commonly called *4g*, this is a standard for wireless communication of high-speed data for mobile devices.

- *Code-division multiple access (CDMA).* CDMA is a channel access method used in radio and cellular communication. It allows several transmitters to share bandwidth and is used in 3G phones.

- *Time-division multiple access (TDMA).* TDMA is a channel access method for networks that share a medium. It permits several users to communicate on the same channel by dividing the signal into time slots. TDMA is used in 2G cellular networks.

Cellular Advancements

Cellular technology does not exist in a vacuum by any means. Ancillary technologies have been developed and perfected to allow cellular devices to function with high levels of efficiency and security. From the storage of networking information to securing a device in the event of theft, advancements in cellular technology make it not only accessible, but more user-friendly as well. These advancements include a subscriber identity module (SIM), personal unlocking key (PUK), and integrated circuit card identification (ICCID).

Subscriber Identity Module (SIM)

Subscriber identity module (SIM) is a circuit that stores the international mobile subscriber identity (IMSI). Think of it as how you identify the phone. Many modern phones have a removable SIM, which means you could change out the SIM and essentially have a different phone with a different number. A SIM card contains its unique serial number, the IMSI, security authentication, and privacy information. This SIM will also usually have network information, services the user has access to, and two passwords. Those passwords are the personal identification number (PIN) and the personal unlocking key (PUK).

Personal Unlocking Key (PUK)

A **personal unlocking key (PUK)** is a code used to reset a forgotten PIN. When this code is used, the phone will return to its original state, losing most forensic data. If the code is entered incorrectly 10 consecutive times, the device becomes permanently blocked and unrecoverable.

Copyright Goodheart-Willcox Co., Inc.

Integrated Circuit Card Identifier (ICCID)

An **integrated circuit card identifier (ICCID)** is a unique serial number assigned to a SIM card for international identification. Every SIM card can be identified by this integrated number. These numbers are engraved on the SIM during manufacturing. This number has subsections that are very important for forensics. It starts with the *issuer identification number (IIN)*, which is a seven-digit number that identifies the country code and issuer. There is also a variable-length individual account identification number to identify the specific phone, and a *check digit*, which is a redundancy check for error detection.

Microwave Transmission and Networking

The term *microwave* is used to describe radio waves in the electromagnetic spectrum that have a wavelength from 1 millimeter (mm) to 30 centimeters (cm) and radio-wave frequencies between 1 GHz and 300 GHz. The amount of data carried by a radio wave is directly proportional to its frequency. In short, the higher the frequency, the more data that can be transmitted in a given period of time. The portion of the electromagnetic spectrum identified as microwave is the preferred technology used for wireless networking. Its application is described in the IEEE 802.11 standards. Microwave radio-wave transmission can be broadcast directly between wireless devices or routed through satellites orbiting Earth.

Satellites are often used as part of a WAN distribution. Satellites can offer the advantage of providing a wireless network connection to remote or mobile locations that cannot be achieved using conventional methods.

Look at Figure 4-25. The satellite in this illustration is positioned 22,300 miles (35,880 km) above Earth's surface and moves at a speed of approximately 68,000 mph. At this distance, it takes the satellite exactly 24 hours to make one revolution around Earth. This time is equal to the time of Earth's rotation. This equality causes the satellite to appear in a stationary position above Earth and is said to be in **geosynchronous orbit**, which means the satellite's speed is synchronized with Earth's rotational

1.5, 2.5   **NET**

Figure 4-25 A typical satellite in geosynchronous orbit is approximately 22,300 miles (35,860 km) above Earth's surface. At this distance, the satellite can maintain a fixed position above Earth.

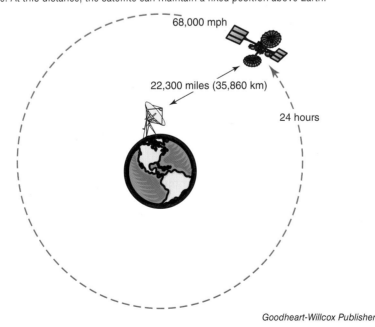

Goodheart-Willcox Publisher

Copyright Goodheart-Willcox Co., Inc.

speed. If the satellite were in a lower orbit, it would need to move at a much higher orbital speed. This would result in the need to track the satellite as it moves across the sky. Tracking a satellite in stationary position is easy when compared with tracking a constantly moving satellite.

One significant disadvantage to satellite communication is propagation delay. **Propagation delay** is the time it takes for data to be transmitted between Earth and satellite. It is caused by the great distance between the satellite and Earth and can be compared to latency. In the past, the Motorola Company attempted to send a large group of 66 satellites into orbit at approximately 460 miles (740 km) above Earth to eliminate much of the propagation delay. At this height, the propagation delay is significantly reduced and is relatively unnoticed by the users. Unfortunately, the project, called Iridium, proved too costly and was abandoned before it could be fully implemented.

While the propagation delay that normally occurs is generally short—only a fraction of a second—the effect of the delay depends on the type of data transmitted. For example, a delay of 250 milliseconds (ms) for a message consisting of several pages of text would go completely unnoticed by the end user. The same delay for data containing a telephone conversation would show slight pauses in the conversation. A series of frames containing millions of bits of picture or video data could show serious evidence of the delay. Picture or video data needs to be of relatively low resolution to limit the total amount of data transmitted. Transmitting high-resolution picture or video data would only be practical in half-duplex communication. Full-duplex communication for high-resolution picture or video data transmission is not yet practical. There are still very noticeable delays in high-resolution, two-way conference calls using satellite links in a network.

For one-way data transmission, buffering techniques similar to the buffering techniques used for downloading sound on a slow communication link, such as a 56k modem, could be used to prevent jitter in the transmission of the video. However, this can only be used in one direction. Two-way transmissions in real time could not take advantage of buffering to eliminate jitter. Delays of 250 milliseconds (ms) or less are tolerable for live telephone conversations and low-resolution graphics. Delays above 250 milliseconds (ms) are generally unacceptable.

Tech Tip

The term *propagation delay* is used in satellite transmission in much the same way that the term *latency* is used for data delay in network systems.

Advantages and Disadvantages of Wireless Technology

NET
1.5, 2.5

Wireless technology can be cost-effective as compared with cable-based network media when spanning long distances such as continents or oceans. Spanning across a city, a business district, or across a college campus can be difficult and expensive with copper-core cable or fiber-optic cable. The installation of landlines is not only expensive; it can cause major disruption while digging up streets and parking lots for installation. When installing a temporary network, wireless technology can be much more cost-effective than remodeling a building to accommodate wiring. Wireless technology is most appropriate for mobile devices such as smartphones, tablets, and laptops. Handheld scanners used to scan bar codes on product packages also use wireless technology to transmit data to a computer or cash register system.

However, some wireless technologies are affected to various degrees by atmospheric conditions such as lightning and sunspots. The greatest disadvantage or concern for wireless technology is security. Network signals are transmitted in the open air and are capable of being picked up by an unauthorized receiver.

Copyright Goodheart-Willcox Co., Inc.

Wireless Security

One major concern of wireless networks is security. Network infrastructures designed to use cable are inherently more secure than wireless networks. Cable can be installed so that it is physically secured. They can be installed inside walls, pipes, and locked server rooms. Because cables can be physically secured, cabled networks are considered more secure than wireless networks. Unauthorized persons cannot readily connect physically to a private, cabled network system. Wireless networks, on the other hand, transmit data through the air, making it possible for anyone with a standard wireless network card to intercept the radio waves.

Radio waves fill the building areas and areas outside the building. One of the most common building materials used today is glass, especially in commercial establishments. Windows do not limit radio-wave transmissions. Anyone near a building that uses wireless devices can easily intercept the wireless network signals with a laptop equipped with a wireless network adapter. However, security features can be implemented that will secure the transmission.

This section covers common wireless security features and provides a brief overview of wireless security. A more in-depth exploration of security features, such as encryption methods, authentication, and security standards are covered in Chapter 15.

802.1x Authentication

IEEE 802.1x is a standard for authentication methods for wireless networking. It provides a means for a client and server to authenticate with each other. Authentication is typically achieved through the exchange of a username and password based on the Extensible Authentication Protocol (EAP).

The Extensible Authentication Protocol (EAP) ensures authorized access to the network system and network resources. EAP is used for both wired and wireless network systems. The improved version of EAP is called PEAP, which represents Protected EAP.

Protected EAP (PEAP) allows the computer to be authenticated, not the person using it. A person who has his or her password compromised could have that password used to access a wireless network. However, when configured to authenticate the computer, an intruder would have to use the authenticated computer to access the wireless network. These authentication protocols will be discussed in more detail in Chapter 15.

802.1x Encryption

The second feature of the 802.1x standard is a way to hide the contents of network packets. Since packets are broadcast through the open air, anyone could capture the packets and inspect the contents using a *protocol analyzer* or *packet sniffer*. A wireless network encryption key is used as part of the mathematical equation (algorithm) to encrypt data that is to be transmitted over a wireless network. There will be more about encryption keys in Chapter 15.

The packets are encrypted using any one of a number of encryption software protocols. To make the encryption process unique to a particular network system, a key is used. You can think of a key as a string of alphanumeric characters that feed the random character generator used to encrypt the contents of each packet. The only way to crack the encryption would be to guess or steal the encryption key. The encryption key can be provided by a security service, manufactured into a hardware device, or created by the network administrator.

Copyright Goodheart-Willcox Co., Inc.

Wired Equivalent Privacy (WEP)

When establishing a wireless network, you may be prompted to select an encryption protocol. One of the first protocols to serve as wireless encryption was WEP. The acronym *WEP* represents *Wired Equivalent Privacy*. You can see by its name that the **Wired Equivalent Privacy (WEP)** protocol was intended to make a wireless network as secure as a wired network. However, it was flawed, and other protocols are recommended instead.

Wi-Fi Protected Access (WPA)

Wi-Fi Protected Access (WPA) is a protocol that combines authentication with encryption. It uses *Temporal Key Integrity Protocol (TKIP)*. TKIP is a 128-bit per-packet key, meaning that it dynamically generates a new key for each packet. WPA was introduced in Windows XP Service Pack 1 and combined the authentication method and encryption. An additional improvement to encryption is that it is more difficult to crack than WEP encryption. This is because WPA automatically changes the encryption key with each packet exchanged on the network.

Wi-Fi Protected Access 2 (WPA2) was developed by the Wi-Fi organization as an enhanced version of WPA. WPA2 is based on the IEEE 802.11i standard. It provides the following: The Advanced Encryption Standard (AES) using the Counter Mode-Cipher Block Chaining Message Authentication Code Protocol (CCMP). This provides data confidentiality, data origin authentication, and integrity for wireless frames.

For now, do not be overly concerned with the cryptographic details in the preceding paragraphs. They will be discussed thoroughly in later chapters. What you must know for now is that there are three different ways of security wireless: WEP, WPA, and WPA2. WEP should be avoided if possible, and if it is possible, always use WPA2.

Copyright Goodheart-Willcox Co., Inc.

Summary

Electromagnetic Waves

- Radio-wave and microwave transmissions work on the principle of producing a carrier wave as the means of communication between two network devices.

- Modulation is the mixing of two radio signals, typically a carrier wave with a data signal.

- Infrared is used in line-of-sight transmissions and is not susceptible to radio interference.

- The FCC regulates the use of the electromagnetic spectrum by assigning radio frequencies and maximum power ratings to devices.

- A common source of interference for wireless networks is industrial, scientific, and medical devices that use frequencies in the same range as wireless networks.

- Infrared is commonly used for point-to-point transmission between two devices such as a personal digital assistant and a PC.

Antenna Styles

- Two main classifications of antennae based on the shape of the electromagnetic wave pattern it produces are omni-directional and directional.

- Antennae are further categorized by their styles, which can be omni, dipole, flat panel, Yagi, or parabolic dish.

Radio-Wave Transmission Techniques

- Radio waves are electromagnetic waves that cover the 10 kHz to 3,000,000 MHz frequency range.

- Several transmission techniques are used to communicate between radio-wave-based network devices: single frequency, spread spectrum, and orthogonal frequency-division multiplexing.

- Spread spectrum is the radio transmission technique that subdivides the allocated frequency range into smaller units called channels. The two types of spread-spectrum transmission techniques are frequency hopping and direct sequencing.

- Frequency hopping avoids interference by changing channels while transmitting data.

- Another name for frequency hopping is *frequency-hopping spread spectrum (FHSS)*.

- Direct sequencing consists of 11 overlapping channels of 83 MHz each in a 2.4-GHz spectrum. Within the 11 channels are three channels with a 22-MHz bandwidth. The three channels do not overlap, and each can be used simultaneously.

- Another name for direct sequencing is *direct sequencing spread spectrum (DSSS)*.

- Orthogonal frequency-division multiplexing (OFDM) is similar to frequency hopping and direct sequencing and employs multiplexing.

Copyright Goodheart-Willcox Co., Inc.

Radio-Wave-Based Networking

- A wireless access point (WAP) provides a connection between a wireless network and a cable-based network. It also serves as the center of communication in a wireless network.

- A service set identifier (SSID) is similar in function to a workgroup name or domain name and must be assigned to a wireless access point (WAP).

- A wireless network that contains one or more wireless access points is arranged in *infrastructure mode*.

- A wireless network that does not contain a wireless access point (WAP) is arranged in *ad hoc mode*.

- IEEE 802.11a describes wireless networks operating at 5 GHz with a maximum data rate of 54 Mbps.

- IEEE 802.11b describes wireless networks operating at 2.4 GHz with a maximum data rate of 11 Mbps.

- IEEE 802.11g describes wireless networks operating at either 2.4 GHz or 5 GHz with a maximum data rate of 54 Mbps.

- IEEE 802.11n operates at 5 GHZ and 2.4 GHz with a maximum data rate of 300 Mbps to 600 Mbps.

- Multiple-input-multiple-output (MIMO) uses two or more streams of data transmission to increase data throughput and the range of the wireless network. MIMO is described in the IEEE 802.11n standard.

- Spatial multiplexing is the transmission of two or more streams of data simultaneously.

- IEEE 802.15 describes the use of wireless personal area networks (WPANs).

- Wireless networks specified under the IEEE 802.11 standard use carrier sense multiple access with collision avoidance (CSMA/CA) as the media access method.

- Bluetooth is a standard developed by a group of manufacturers to allow their devices to interoperate. Bluetooth is recognized by the 802.11 standard and is used for short-range data transfer applications using the 2.4-GHz radio band.

Microwave Transmission and Networking

- Satellite communication experience propagation delay because of the great distance a signal must travel.

Advantages and Disadvantages of Wireless Technology

- Wireless technology can be cost-effective when compared with cable-based network media.

- Disadvantages of wireless technology include vulnerability to atmospheric conditions and security.

Copyright Goodheart-Willcox Co., Inc.

Wireless Security

- Wireless networks are not secure when default settings are used for the configuration.
- Wireless encryption keys should be changed on a regular basis to maintain a high degree of security.

Review Questions

1. A(n) _____ is an electromagnetic wave of a set frequency that is used to carry data in radio-wave- and microwave-based networks.

2. What is an SSID?

3. What is modulation?

4. A simple radio broadcast consists of a(n) _____, which generates a carrier wave and a(n) _____, which receives a carrier wave.

5. What is a channel?

6. What is the main disadvantage to infrared?

7. What are the two major classifications of antennae?

8. Which of the following antenna types is *not* used in point-to-point links?

   A. Flat panel

   B. Omni

   C. Parabolic

   D. Yagi

9. Which antenna style was developed with aesthetics in mind?

10. What is spread spectrum?

11. The spread-spectrum technique that transmits data on multiple channels simultaneously is called _____.

12. Why is frequency hopping used?

13. The spread-spectrum technique that transmits data on multiple channels sequentially is called _____.

14. The _____ transmission technique uses the 5-GHz frequency and can achieve data rates as high as 54 Mbps.

15. List the frequency range for each of the three U-NII classifications.

16. What frequency does IEEE 802.11g specify?

17. What frequency does IEEE 802.11n specify?

18. What does the acronym MIMO represent?

19. What is MIMO wireless technology?

20. Describe the IEEE 802.11ac standard.

21. Which media access method does the 802.11 wireless standard specify?

Copyright Goodheart-Willcox Co., Inc.

22. What is the difference between CSMA/CA and CSMA/CD?

23. What is the maximum achievable distance of a Bluetooth device?

24. What is the data rate of the Bluetooth 3.0 standard?

25. _____ technology is based on radio waves connecting to designated areas referred to as *cells*.

26. Long Term Evolution (LTE) is also known as _____.

27. What is a geosynchronous orbit?

28. What is a disadvantage of satellite communication?

29. What is an advantage of wireless networking?

30. What is the one major disadvantage of wireless technology?

31. What does the acronym WEP represent?

32. What does the acronym TKIP stand for?

✚ Sample Network+ Exam Questions

1. Which IEEE 802.11 standard specifies a data rate of 300 Mbps?
   A. 802.11a
   B. 802.11b
   C. 802.11g
   D. 802.11n

2. Michelle is setting up wireless networks for her company. Which media access method is used by wireless networks?
   A. ARCnet
   B. CSMA/CA
   C. CSMA/CD
   D. Token Ring

3. Which of the following items is used to connect a wireless network to an Ethernet network?
   A. Wireless access point
   B. Ad hoc converter
   C. Ethernet converter
   D. Ethernet sequencing device

4. Gabriel has realized that the Wi-Fi he setup for his company is not getting the bandwidth it should. He thinks this is probably due to interference. What would most likely generate radio interference for an 802.11b network device?
   A. Microwave oven
   B. Another computer using an 802.11g network adapter card
   C. Wireless keyboard
   D. HP LaserJet printer

Copyright Goodheart-Willcox Co., Inc.

5. Who is responsible for regulating the electromagnetic spectrum and dictating the frequency that is to be used for each group of devices?

   A. IEEE

   B. The telephone company in the local area

   C. FCC

   D. WECA

6. Farris wants to get the most out of his wireless network. The maximum bandwidth is critical for his networking needs. Therefore, he is interested in eliminating devices that are likely to cause interference. Which item would *most likely* interfere with the operation of an 802.11ac wireless network?

   A. Hub

   B. Cordless phone

   C. Incandescent lights

   D. Copier

7. What is the function of an SSID?

   A. Replaces the network MAC address

   B. Encrypts all wireless communication

   C. Identifies the wireless network by name

   D. Increases the data throughput of a wireless network

8. Helena works as a network administrator for a bank. She has been instructed to ensure that all wireless access points are configured securely. Which protocol fully implements 802.11i requirements?

   A. WPA

   B. WPA2

   C. WAP

   D. WEP

9. Which IEEE standard is used to describe how to achieve secure authentication to a wireless network?

   A. 802.3

   B. 802.1x

   C. 802.5b

   D. 802.4a

10. Jerome has been tasked with setting up a WLAN that operates in the TV white-space spectrum in the VHF and UHF bands between 54 and 790 MHz. Which standard should he use?

    A. 802.11n-2009

    B. 802.11ac

    C. 802.11af

    D. 802.11ag

Digital Encoding and Data Transmission

Network+ Certification Exam Objectives

The Network+ Exam has been placing less and less direct emphasis on the topics in this chapter for the past few exam revisions. However, these topics are still foundational to understanding networking concepts. Furthermore, while there is less emphasis on these topics on the Network+ than in the past, that is not to say that there are no questions at all about these topics. With that in mind, this chapter is something you should study, but when preparing for the Network+ Exam, it may be slightly less important than some other chapters. There is one very important exception. That is the OSI model. The OSI Model will be very important on the Network+ Exam. Another item from this chapter that will be on the Network+ exam is the difference between connection-oriented and connectionless protocols.

Objectives

1.1: Connection-Oriented vs. Connectionless Protocol Types—UDP

1.2: Explain devices, applications, protocols, and services at their appropriate OSI layers.

1.3: Properties of Network Traffic—Protocol Data Units

Performance Concepts—Packet-Switched vs. Circuit-Switched Network

2.2: Modems

Learning Outcomes

- Give examples of digital signals and digital encoding.
- Explain the complete data packaging process.
- Identify the characteristics of the various data codes.
- Interpret the structure and contents of a UDP frame.
- Recall the function of each layer of the OSI model.

Copyright Goodheart-Willcox Co., Inc.

Key Terms

American Standard Code for Information Interchange (ASCII)
asynchronous transmission
bipolar digital signal
broadcast frame
circuit switching
cyclic redundancy check (CRC)

data encryption
digital encoding
encapsulation
frame
Manchester encoding
multicast frame
packet switching

parity check
port
segment
synchronous transmission
time period
Unicode
unipolar digital signal

Overview

In this chapter, basic terminology about data packaging and transmission is presented. Learning this terminology will be beneficial when more specific aspects of networking are covered in later chapters. Also, a sound understanding of the OSI model will help you when you further your networking education by studying security concepts, network infrastructure, and IEEE standards.

The chapter ends with a review of the OSI model and its relationship to digital encoding and data packaging. The OSI model is presented using some of the terminology you have learned thus far. The OSI model will be referenced throughout the textbook as you learn more network terminology and concepts. Presenting this material throughout the textbook will ensure you gain a solid understanding of the OSI model.

Digital Signals and Digital Encoding

Digital signals are used to transmit data and commands across network systems. In Chapter 2, you learned that all network communication originates from electronic signals. Electronic signals take many forms, such as electrical energy, light waves, radio waves, infrared light waves, and microwaves. All of these forms of electronic signals originate from digital signals.

Digital encoding takes place when a network interface card converts data into a digital pattern acceptable to the network media. After the data is encoded into a digital pattern, it is placed on the network media. So that you can better understand digital encoding and digital patterns, the digital signal will be reviewed.

As you have already learned, a digital signal is an electronic signal that has discrete values. Discrete values can be on or off, high or low. These can be represented in electricity by voltages. Often, five volts is used to represent *1*, and zero volts to represent *0*. This is not something that is required, but it is very common. The waveform of the digital signal is drawn at right angles, resembling a series of incomplete rectangles and squares, as shown in Figure 5-1. The height, or amplitude, of the digital signal represents the electrical voltage level. In Figure 5-1A, a positive voltage of five volts is illustrated. The digital signal, which is called a **unipolar digital signal**, fluctuates between a positive five-volt and zero-volt level. This pattern is similar to a light switch repeatedly turned on and off.

Copyright Goodheart-Willcox Co., Inc.

Figure 5-1 A digital signal has discrete voltage levels. Its waveform resembles a series of incomplete squares and rectangles. A—A unipolar digital signal fluctuates between 0 volts and +5 volts. B—A bipolar digital signal fluctuates between +5 volts and −5 volts.

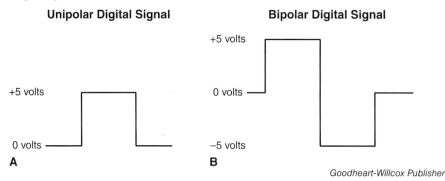

Goodheart-Willcox Publisher

Some digital electronic circuit designs fluctuate between a positive voltage level and a negative voltage level. In this approach, a positive value is a *1* and a negative value is a *0*. In Figure 5-1B, the digital signal fluctuates between a positive five-volt level and a negative five-volt level. This pattern is called a **bipolar digital signal**. The examples in Figure 5-1 are not meant to imply that all digital systems work at a standard five-volt level. Some systems work at lower voltage levels such as 3.3 volts.

Another important characteristic of the digital signal is the time period. The **time period** represents the rate of recurrence of an expected change in signal level. The time period used to encode digital data should not be confused with the term *time period* used when talking about frequency or cycles. In the context of encoding a digital signal, the time period represents the time period of an expected digital wave shape. A digital signal may or may not change within a given time period, but some form of change is expected. In some digital encoding schemes, the time at which the digital signal changes voltage levels is important. The transition of the digital signal's voltage level may occur at the beginning of the time period or at the midpoint of the time period, as illustrated in Figure 5-2.

One of the most popular encoding schemes is called **Manchester encoding**. This encoding scheme is characterized by the digital pulse transitioning during the midpoint of the time period. Look at Figure 5-3. Note that a binary one is represented by a transition from five volts to zero volts in the midpoint of the time period. A binary zero is represented by a transition from zero to five volts in the midpoint of the time period.

Digital signal characteristics vary from one encoding scheme to another. The selection of the encoding scheme varies according to the electronic characteristics designed into the network hardware. Further study into the encoding schemes would require more detailed electronics study than this textbook provides. The important point to remember is digital encoding happens at the data link layer of OSI model.

Two modes of transmitting data between two points are *synchronous* and *asynchronous*. In **synchronous transmission**, the digital signal is synchronized with a reference signal to ensure proper timing. The timing of the digital signal is extremely important for decoding some variations of digital encoding patterns. In **asynchronous transmission**, no reference signal is present.

You may be wondering how a digital signal can be decoded without a reference signal. A reference signal is not needed if there is a way to determine when a byte or stream of data begins or ends. Some data transmission schemes use a series of ones and zeros to identify the beginning and end of a byte or stream of data. A long period of no digital signal can also be used to signify the beginning. Again, there are many different ways the beginning and end can be acknowledged. There is no one universal

Copyright Goodheart-Willcox Co., Inc.

Figure 5-2 Some digital encoding schemes are marked by the voltage level changing during a time period. The voltage-level change can occur at the beginning of the time period or in the middle of the time period.

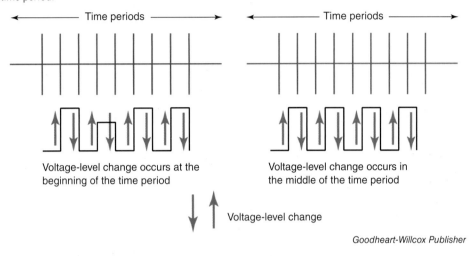

Voltage-level change occurs at the beginning of the time period

Voltage-level change occurs in the middle of the time period

↓ ↑ Voltage-level change

Goodheart-Willcox Publisher

Figure 5-3 The main characteristic of Manchester encoding is the direction of the voltage level during the midpoint of the time period, which is represented by a binary one or zero.

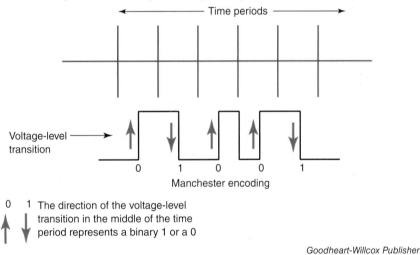

Manchester encoding

0 1 The direction of the voltage-level transition in the middle of the time period represents a binary 1 or a 0

Goodheart-Willcox Publisher

method. The methods with which data are encoded vary greatly between the computer bus system, network media, telephone signals, radio signals, and such.

Data Packaging and Transmission

To send data from one point to another across a network or the Internet, data is packaged with extra information to ensure its delivery and integrity. Often data is broken into smaller, deliverable pieces. Each piece of data is called a **segment** and contains information to aid in reassembly.

Sometimes, communication is established between a source and destination computer before data is sent. Other times, data is sent without establishing communication and without requiring a confirmation of delivery. Data routing can also differ among data transmissions. This section describes the components involved in data packaging, such as parity checks, segmentation, and encapsulation. It also covers communication and routing.

Tech Tip

Be aware that many references refer to data segments as *packets*.

Copyright Goodheart-Willcox Co., Inc.

Parity Checks

Digital signals can become corrupted for different reasons. In fact, it is actually quite common for a few data packets in any transmission to be somehow corrupted or damaged in transit. Some of the causes can be crosstalk, electromagnetic interference, loose connections, and faulty or improperly grounded equipment. Corruption can often be detected with a **parity check**, which is a method of verifying the integrity of transmitted data. Figure 5-4A shows an example of corrupted data displayed in a parity check.

In the example, one bit in the entire byte has changed from a binary one to a zero. The meaning of the byte has therefore been altered. Originally, the byte might have represented the letter *A*, but now it represents the letter *R* or a command such as "end of transmission." One way to ensure that data sent from the source to the destination is intact is to include a parity code with the data. For example, rather than all eight bits of a byte representing alphanumeric symbols, seven bits could represent alphanumeric symbols and the eighth bit could represent the parity code.

Look at Figure 5-4B. In this example, the total number of zeros in the data portion of the byte is used to validate data. An even number of zeros is represented by a parity code of a binary one. An odd number of zeros is represented by a parity code of a binary zero. When the destination receives the byte, it compares the parity code to the number of binary zeros to tell if the data has been corrupted. If the data is corrupted, the destination rejects the data and requests the data be resent.

Figure 5-4 Parity check. A—To perform parity checks, the last bit position in an 8-bit data transmission can be used for the parity code. B—A value of 1 or 0 in the parity bit may indicate odd or even parity.

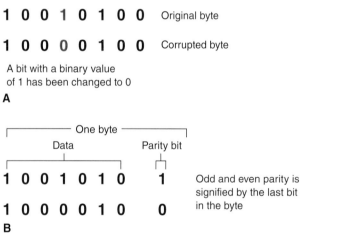

Goodheart-Willcox Publisher

Cyclic Redundancy Check (CRC)

A **cyclic redundancy check (CRC)** is based on the same principle for error detection as a parity check. However, a CRC is more sophisticated. The main problem with the parity check is if an even number of bits is corrupted, the corruption goes undetected. The CRC uses mathematical algorithms to determine if any bits are corrupt. After corruption has been detected, a CRC can correct it without requiring retransmission of data. The only drawback is a CRC requires more data to be sent in the form of a parity code. This slows the data transmission rate. Still, a CRC is a popular method of verifying data. It is incorporated into many different network protocols when data integrity is critical.

Copyright Goodheart-Willcox Co., Inc.

Segmentation and Encapsulation

Unless the amount of data transferred between two points is small, the data needs to be divided into smaller units, called *segments*. After the data is divided into segments, it is encapsulated. **Encapsulation** is the process of adding information to the segment that identifies such things as the source address and destination addresses, end of the segment, and size of the segment. This additional information is added in order to complete the transmission from one point to another. For example, if data is transferred across a vast distance using the Internet, the source and destination IP addresses must be added as well as a sequence number to ensure the segments are delivered to the appropriate location, rearranged in the proper order, and no segments are missing.

Figure 5-5 shows a generalization of the data packaging process, from raw data (text file, sound, or graphic) to digital signals. To transfer data between two locations, the source and destination must first establish a connection with each other. Assume the connection between the two points has been established and the data format, communication rules, encryption (if necessary), security, and any other communication details have been agreed upon. All these concerns are accomplished mainly at the top three layers of the OSI model: application, presentation, and session.

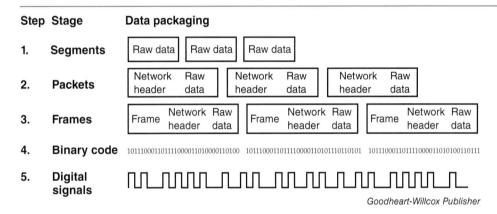

Goodheart-Willcox Publisher

Figure 5-5 Data packaging process. Raw data is broken into segments (step 1). The segments are encapsulated into packets (step 2). The packets contain extra information such as source and destination addresses and error-checking codes. Since the data in this example will travel the Internet, the packets are encapsulated into a frame (step 3). The frame contains extra information needed to navigate the Internet. The frame is converted into binary code (step 4). The binary code is converted to digital signals and placed on the network media (step 5).

Next, the data is divided into small units. This process is referred to as *data segmentation* or simply *segmenting*. A segment of data is simply a portion of the total amount of raw data broken into sizes that can be handled. The size of a segment is determined by the protocol selected to communicate between two points when the source and destination negotiate their connection and establish their rules for communication.

Each segment is placed into a packet. Packets of data contain additional information needed to deliver the segments. This additional information is called the *network header*, which contains the source and destination addresses. Other additional information that can be added to the packet is error-checking codes to ensure the packet is delivered without a distorted signal. First, the segment is typically enclosed in either a UDP or TCP envelope. If a large amount of data is to be transferred, TCP is used for constructing the envelope. Since TCP is used to carry the data segment, a port number must be assigned. The port number is necessary to set up a constant connection with the other workstation and to acknowledge if the data has arrived intact. If only a small amount of data, such as a command, were sent between the source and destination, UDP could be used. UDP does not require a port number because it does not require verification that the data was delivered.

After a segment has been enclosed in a TCP envelope, it is enclosed in a packet. The packet adds the IP address to the envelope carrying the data. An IP address for the source and destination is included in every packet.

Packets are limited to traversing only LANs. Therefore, the machine address is sufficient when delivering data on a LAN. However, if data will be sent across the Internet, it is further encapsulated, or framed. A packet that is encapsulated with information needed to travel the Internet is called a **frame**. The frame contains additional information such as an Internet address. An Internet address is different from a machine (MAC) address. A frame adds the MAC address for the destination and source to the packet. The frame is then converted first into a serial stream of data and then into digital pulses and placed on the network media. The type of media, such as Ethernet or wireless is also identified in the frame. The MAC address is used to move the frame through the LAN. The MAC address identifies the workstation and equipment along the LAN path until the frame reaches the outer edge of the LAN. When the frame encounters the first piece of Internet equipment, typically a router, the MAC address is stripped away, leaving the IP address of the source and destination. Remember, the Internet uses IP addresses to locate nodes, not MAC addresses. The frame can travel over thousands of miles using only an IP address to find the destination network.

When the frame reaches the destination LAN, the network operating system uses *Address Resolution Protocol (ARP)* to resolve the IP address to a MAC address. Inside the destination LAN, the MAC address identifies the final destination node or workstation. At the destination, the envelopes around the data are stripped away until the raw data is revealed. The segments of raw data are put back together in proper sequence to display the data at the destination. The data could be plain text or multimedia. Any missing segments invoke a request for retransmission.

This is the classic explanation of how data is transported across the Internet. At this point, it might seem that each level of the OSI model only takes one or two frames for communication to take place, but that is far from reality. Even a simple request takes many steps to perform. The OSI model functions, at best, as an abstract model of how network communication *should* work. In reality, an actual network communication sequence is more complex.

Figure 5-6 shows a screen capture of the Microsoft Network Monitor utility. A series of frames are captured as related to the network devices identified in the left pane. The frame details in the bottom pane of the utility reveal the encapsulated

Figure 5-6 The Microsoft Network Monitor utility can be used to capture and analyze frames.

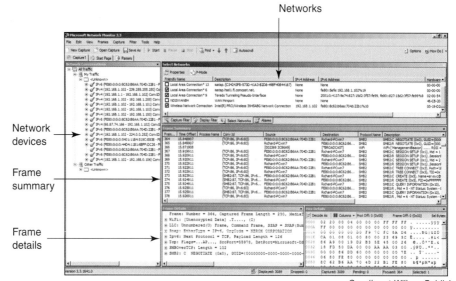

Networks

Network devices

Frame summary

Frame details

Goodheart-Willcox Publisher

protocols for each frame. In this particular set of frame captures, you can see the Microsoft SMB2 protocol, which is being used to negotiate a sharing transaction between two network devices. Additionally, the frame capture sequence involves both IPv4 and IPv6.

The terms *segment, frame, datagram, protocol data unit (PDU)*, and *packet* are often used interchangeably when discussing blocks of data. You can think of all of the terms as units of data transferred between two points. The ISO tends to use the term *PDU* when discussing data packaging. When discussing TCP/IP, the terms *packet* and *frame* are often used with packets described as fitting inside a frame. The term *PDU* is the most technically correct term, but it is awkward to use in conversation. Consequently, technicians tend to use the term *packet* to represent all types of data units collectively.

1.3 NET

Many times, it is acceptable to use any of the terms when discussing network data, but at other times, it is more important to be precise. Correct terminology is especially important when explaining protocols, OSI layers, and certain types of network equipment.

Network+ Note

Data packaging terminology can vary a great deal from one manufacturer to another. For example, one manufacturer may refer to the entire encapsulation process as *framing*, while another may break it down into different and distinct stages. When studying for the Network+ Certification Exam, remember that CompTIA certifications are vendor-neutral and use generally accepted terms like those used in this textbook to describe various technologies.

If you are planning to take a certification exam for a specific networking technology, such as Microsoft, it is best to become familiar with the specific vendor's terminology. Many provide a vocabulary listing on their websites.

Connection-Oriented and Connectionless Communication

1.1 NET

At one time, it was common to refer to connection-oriented or connectionless transmissions. These terms were a bit misleading. Obviously, one connects to a system before sending data to it, but the issue becomes whether packets should be sent to a destination address with or without any attempt to verify their completed transmission. The phrase *connection-oriented communication* stems from the fact that connection-oriented networking protocols establish a full session with the target of communication, including the verification of packet delivery. Thus, they are connection-oriented. *Connectionless communication* uses protocols that do not verify packet delivery; they simply start sending to the target, and if some packets do not make it, so be it. However, again, the terms were difficult to understand, so now the proper terminology is *reliable* or *unreliable* communication. A protocol that establishes a session and verifies that all packets were received is considered reliable.

One might question why anyone would ever use a connectionless/unreliable protocol. Consider for a moment, video. In the United States, standard broadcast television uses 30 frames per second. To send the same video over the Internet, many packets are required for a single frame. Frankly, if an entire frame per second were lost, the human eye would be unable to detect it. Furthermore, to verify every packet would dramatically increase the bandwidth needed for video. Therefore, video, as well as audio, is sent with connectionless/unreliable protocols.

Specifically, Session Initiation Protocol (SIP) is used to connect to the recipient, and then Real-Time Transport Protocol (RTP) is used to send the data. That can be modified with protocols like Secure Real-Time Transport Protocol (sRTP) and Compressed Real-Time Transport Protocol (cRTP).

Transmission Control Protocol (TCP) is connection-oriented/reliable. This means all TCP-based protocols, such as Simple Mail Transfer Protocol (SMTP), Hypertext Transfer Protocol (HTTP), File Transfer Protocol (FTP), are all connection-oriented/reliable. User Datagram Protocol (UDP) is connectionless/unreliable.

Network+ Note ✛

It is common to see a question on the Network+ Certification Exam that identifies connection and connectionless protocols. Try to remember that IP is a connectionless protocol and TCP is a connection-oriented protocol.

Circuit Switching and Packet Switching

NET
✛ 1.3

Two main categories describing the way data are routed between two points are circuit switching and packet switching. **Circuit switching** establishes a permanent connection between two points for the duration of the data transfer period. For example, a permanent connection is established when you connect to your Internet service provider using a cable modem or a DSL modem. This permanent connection is equivalent to circuit switching. Other types of telephone lines that use circuit switching are ISDN, ATM, and T1. When you think of circuit switching, think of a permanent or dedicated line. It is a set pathway between the two communicating ends.

Packet switching does not use a permanent connection. Instead, packet switching breaks the data transmission into smaller parts called *packets*. Each packet has a source and destination address and a sequence number attached to it. You could say each small unit of data is encapsulated into a packet that contains source and destination addresses and a sequence number. The Internet uses packet switching to send data between two points on the Internet such as a home user and a web server at a remote location. When a web page is downloaded from a remote site to a home computer, the web page is broken into smaller packets. The packets are sent out onto the Internet, and each may take a different route to their destination, as demonstrated in Figure 5-7.

Figure 5-7 The Internet is an excellent example of how data transfer is based on packet switching. The total amount of data is divided into packets that may take different routes to their destination.

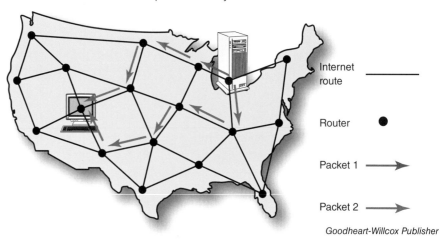

Internet route ——————

Router ●

Packet 1 ——→

Packet 2 ——→

Goodheart-Willcox Publisher

Copyright Goodheart-Willcox Co., Inc.

When packets travel across the maze of communication lines, many different factors can delay the packets, such as heavy traffic conditions in the different communication lines. The amount of traffic in each of the many communication lines constantly changes. Also, a communication line could be rendered unusable during transmission due to a lightning strike, maintenance, or equipment failure. The arrival time of the transmitted packets could be out of sequence due to the unforeseen circumstances. Sequence numbers included with the packets help to reconstruct the data. The sequence number also identifies missing packets that may have been destroyed en route to the destination. Some examples of packet switching technologies besides the Internet are FDDI, Frame Relay, and Ethernet.

Data Codes

There are many different coding standards, or data codes, for representing the written word. There are also many standards used for representing images, audio sound, and multimedia. Some you may be familiar with include JPEG, BMP, GIF, TIFF, and MPEG. Data codes must be converted for data exchange to take place. In the OSI model, this is addressed at the presentation layer. The most commonly encountered data codes are ASCII and Unicode. There are certainly other data codes, but these are by far the most common and the ones you will see on the Network+ Exam. Each of these data codes will be briefly introduced. Remember that in the OSI model, the presentation layer is responsible for putting the data into a format that is agreed on by the source and the destination.

ASCII

The **American Standard Code for Information Interchange (ASCII)** was an early attempt to standardize data codes. Look at the table of the ASCII character set in Figure 5-8. Note that 32 codes are command codes and 96 codes represent characters found on a standard keyboard. There are an additional 128 symbols not shown in Figure 5-8 that are operating-system dependent. *Operating-system dependent* means that the additional symbols are not standard but rather can only be interpreted by a specific software program. This results in ASCII codes ranging from 0 to 255 for a total of 256 codes. If the data file is opened by the wrong software application, the symbols are incorrectly interpreted and the result is unintelligible. The additional symbols represent such items as fractions, foreign letters, special symbols, lines, and more. The upper 128 characters are not standard. Also, note that an ASCII symbol does not indicate font attributes such as size, shape, color, or spacing. ASCII characters interpreted by a software application such as Microsoft Word can represent these additional attributes.

ASCII files are sometimes referred to as *plain-text files*. They contain no special alphanumeric enhancements such as bold, italic, or underline formatting. The ASCII file format is the most easily exchanged file format used by word-processing programs. ASCII uses eight bits to represent individual characters. The bit pattern represents the digital pulses used to encode data as alphanumeric characters.

In the early days of computing, there were many problems because of a lack of standard encoding patterns. Many times, an encoding pattern was proprietary. The hardware and software had to be purchased from the same vendor and may have been incompatible with other software programs or hardware devices. Today, some problems are still encountered when exchanging text files. For example, two different versions of the same word-processing software may not be compatible. Incompatibility may cause a file not to open when prompted. A good way to ensure a text

Copyright Goodheart-Willcox Co., Inc.

Figure 5-8 ASCII character set.

Standard ASCII Characters			(Continued)		(Continued)	
0	NUL	Null	43	+	86	V
1	SOH	Start of header	44	,	87	W
2	STX	Start of text	45	-	88	X
3	ETX	End of text	46	.	89	Y
4	EOT	End of transmission	47	/	90	Z
5	ENQ	Enquiry	48	0	91	[
6	ACK	Acknowledgment	49	1	92	\
7	BEL	Bell	50	2	93	]
8	BS	Backspace	51	3	94	^
9	HT	Horizontal tab	52	4	95	_
10	LF	Line feed	53	5	96	`
11	VT	Vertical tab	54	6	97	a
12	FF	Form feed	55	7	98	b
13	CR	Carriage return	56	8	99	c
14	SO	Shift out	57	9	100	d
15	SI	Shift in	58	:	101	e
16	DLE	Data link escape	59	;	102	f
17	DC1	Device control 1	60	<	103	g
18	DC2	Device control 2	61	=	104	h
19	DC3	Device control 3	62	>	105	i
20	DC4	Device control 4	63	?	106	j
21	NAK	Negative acknowledgment	64	@	107	k
22	SYN	Synchronous idle	65	A	108	l
23	ETB	End of transmit block	66	B	109	m
24	CAN	Cancel	67	C	110	n
25	EM	End of medium	68	D	111	o
26	SUB	Substitute	69	E	112	p
27	ESC	Escape	70	F	113	q
28	FS	File separator	71	G	114	r
29	GS	Group separator	72	H	115	s
30	RS	Record separator	73	I	116	t
31	US	Unit Separator	74	J	117	u
32	SP	Space	75	K	118	v
33	!		76	L	119	w
34	"		77	M	120	x
35	#		78	N	121	y
36	$		79	O	122	z
37	%		80	P	123	{
38	&		81	Q	124		
39	'		82	R	125	}
40	(		83	S	126	~
41	)		84	T	127	DEL
42	*		85	U		

Goodheart-Willcox Publisher

Copyright Goodheart-Willcox Co., Inc.

file can be exchanged between two different systems is by saving the file as an ASCII file or as a plain-text file. Figure 5-9 shows some of the options for saving the text file Networking Fundamentals.doc. Note that the **Plain Text** option is selected.

Unicode

Unicode is similar in principle to ASCII but uses 16 bits to represent individual characters. By using 16 bits for each character, over 65,000 possible characters can be represented. This may seem like an extreme number of possibilities when thinking in terms of the English alphabet, but languages that rely on symbols, for example Chinese, require many more possibilities than the typical 8-bit ASCII code pattern will produce. There are also many characters unique to the various languages around the world, such as Russian, Hebrew, Tibetan, Mongolian, and Cherokee, which require extra bits. Unicode is also used in bar codes for scanning merchandise and in Braille for the visually impaired.

HTML

Hypertext markup language (HTML) is an authoring language used to create documents that can be downloaded from the Internet and viewed by a web browser. Part of HTML is a standard set of color codes. The color codes are inserted into the coding of a web page. When a web browser interprets the page, the color code is translated into the color the code represents. Figure 5-10 shows a partial listing of color codes. Note the color codes are expressed in hexadecimal form, such as FFFFFF, FFFFCC,

Figure 5-9 Options in a word-processing program for saving a text file.

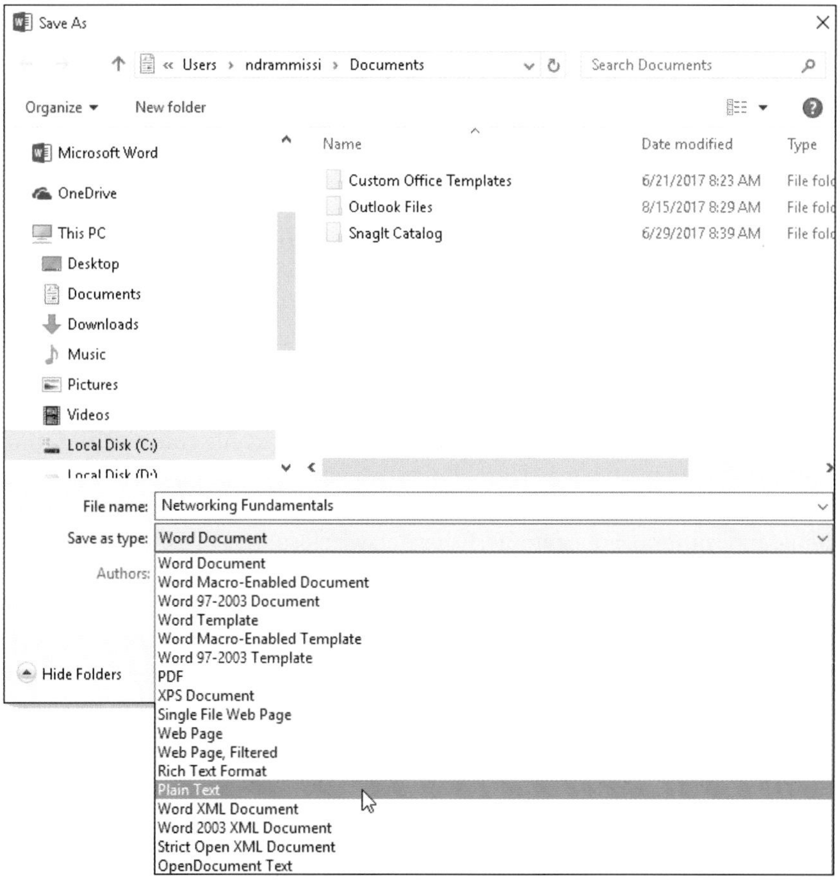

Goodheart-Willcox Publisher

Copyright Goodheart-Willcox Co., Inc.

Figure 5-10 HTML color codes are written in hexadecimal format and represent various colors.

Color code	Color		Color code	Color
#FFFFFF			#FFCC33	
#FFFFCC			#FFCC00	
#FFFF99			#FF99FF	
#FFFF66			#FF99CC	
#FFFF33			#FF9999	
#FFFF00			#FF9966	
#FFCCFF			#FF9933	
#FFCCCC			#FF9900	
#FFCC99			#FF66FF	
#FFCC66			#FF66CC	
#FFCC33			#FF6699	
#FFCC00			#FF6666	
#FF99FF			#FF6633	
#FF99CC			#FF6600	
#FF9999			#FF33FF	
#FF9966			#FF33CC	

Goodheart-Willcox Publisher

FFFF99, FFFF66, FFFF33, and FFFF00. Web browsers, such as Microsoft Edge, Firefox, Safari, or Google Chrome, interpret the color code and create the exact shade of color indicated. HTML will be discussed in more detail in Chapter 13.

Protocol Frame Structures

In Chapter 1, you learned that a *protocol* is a set of rules that determines how two nodes will communicate. One part of a protocol determines how data and commands are structured into packages, such as packets and frames. Many pieces of information, such as the source and destination address and the data field size, have to be built into each packet. Many different protocol data structures are used to communicate across networks. The exact protocol data structure is determined by the purpose of the communication (such as commands, text file transfer, and multimedia transfer), the type of network architecture (such as Ethernet or wireless), and the use of specialized equipment and media during the transfer (such as telephone lines, modems, and routers). For example, Ethernet, wireless, and FDDI use different frame formats to match the technology. The Point-to-Point Protocol (PPP) is designed to establish telephone modem connections. Network protocols such as Ethernet can transport other protocols. For example, a TCP or UDP protocol packet is typically carried inside an Ethernet protocol frame.

To help you better understand the concept of protocol data structures and how data is encoded into packets, we will first look at how a simple UDP packet is constructed. Afterward, a more complicated protocol will be presented as a comparison.

Copyright Goodheart-Willcox Co., Inc.

UDP Frame Structure

The User Datagram Protocol (UDP), introduced earlier in this chapter, is relatively compact and simple in design. It contains the data to be transferred, the destination and source information, the length of the packet, and a method to check for errors. Look at the illustration in Figure 5-11 for an example of a UDP frame.

1.1 NET

The first 16 bits (two bytes) of the packet identify the source port. The source port is the port from which the UDP originated. A **port** is a logical connection that matches a service with a computer. A computer uses many different port numbers when communicating. For example, the common port number for the HTTP service is port 80. There will be a much more detailed explanation about ports later in the textbook when discussing the TCP/IP protocol.

The second 16 bits contain the destination port number, which identifies the port to which the UDP is being delivered. The third 16 bits indicate the length of the entire UDP packet so that the destination can be sure the entire message or data package was delivered. Next, a 16-bit checksum block of information is included. The *checksum* is similar to the CRC discussed earlier.

Figure 5-11 UDP frame.

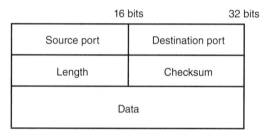

Goodheart-Willcox Publisher

Ethernet Frame Structure

Four types of Ethernet frames exist in networking technology: Ethernet II (DIX), IEEE 802.2, IEEE 802.3, and Ethernet SNAP. The Xerox Corporation developed the original Ethernet standard in the early 1970s. In 1982, companies such as Digital Equipment, Intel, and Xerox joined to develop another release of Ethernet known as DIX (Digital, Intel, Xerox). The DIX Ethernet frame format became better known as Ethernet II.

The Institute of Electrical and Electronics Engineers (IEEE) developed and released their first standard for Ethernet in 1985. The standard is called *IEEE 802.3: Carrier Sense Multiple Access with Collision Detection (CSMA/CD) Access Method and Physical Layer Specifications*. It is interesting to note that *IEEE 802.3 CSMA/CD* is the technically correct terminology for the type of media access described, and the terms *Ethernet* and *802.3* have become generally accepted to mean the same as CSMA/CD.

The Ethernet II frame type was developed before the release of the IEEE 802.3 CSMA/CD standard. Consequently, they are two different frame types. While the two frame types Ethernet II and 802.3 are generally compatible, there is no guarantee of full compatibility. Network interface cards are usually set to detect the frame type broadcast automatically, but network interface cards can be configured to accept a specific frame type to improve network performance. Ethernet SNAP is a modification of the original 802.3 and Ethernet II frame types.

Copyright Goodheart-Willcox Co., Inc.

A study of frame differences will help you better understand the compatibility issues that exist between different systems. Refer to Figure 5-12 for a comparison between the two frame types. You will notice the two frame types, Ethernet II and 802.3, are similar in construction. In fact, both frame types can coexist within the same network. However, there is no guarantee that the two frames can be used to exchange information compatibly. This is due to the slight variation in frame construction. This variation exists in the length of the preamble fields.

The *preamble* is used to identify and synchronize the start of the frame. It consists of a series of alternating ones and zeros and ends with a series of steady ones. The start frame delimiter (SFD) in the 802.3 frame follows directly behind the preamble. Prior to Ethernet frame version IEEE 802.3, the SFD and preamble were combined. In the IEEE 802.3 frame, the SFD indicates the actual start of the frame information by using a one-byte field consisting of the following binary pattern: 10101011.

The preamble is followed by the destination address. In the Ethernet II and 802.3 frame types, there is a slight variation of the initial bits in the destination field. The variations in the binary pattern are used to indicate if the intended destination is multicast (a group of computers) or unicast (only one computer). The remaining destination field identifies the MAC address of the computer or device.

It is important to remember that a frame containing only a MAC address can only be used for a LAN. To transmit the Ethernet frame to a distant network or across a WAN or GAN, additional destination information needs to encapsulate the frame. The Ethernet frame must contain both the source and destination IP addresses. The Internet is a GAN connected via routers. Routers are configured to recognize IP addresses, not MAC addresses. The router selects the proper route for the packet based on the IP address contained in the Ethernet frame. This is in contrast to NetBEUI, which does not use IP addresses to locate the destination. NetBEUI uses the name

Figure 5-12 Ethernet II and 802.3 frame comparison.

Ethernet II Frame

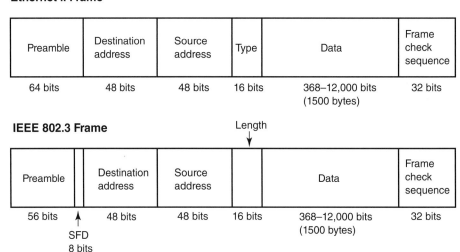

Preamble	Destination address	Source address	Type	Data	Frame check sequence
64 bits	48 bits	48 bits	16 bits	368–12,000 bits (1500 bytes)	32 bits

IEEE 802.3 Frame

Length

Preamble		Destination address	Source address		Data	Frame check sequence
56 bits		48 bits	48 bits	16 bits	368–12,000 bits (1500 bytes)	32 bits

SFD
8 bits

Preamble: Identifies and synchronizes the start of frame.
Start Frame Delimiter (SFD): Indicates the start of frame with a one-byte binary pattern in an 802.3 frame.
Destination address: Where the data is being sent.
Source address: Where the data is coming from.
Type: Which upper layer provides guaranteed delivery.
Length: The length of the data field.
Data: The data being transmitted.
Frame Check Sequence: Ensures data integrity.

Goodheart-Willcox Publisher

Copyright Goodheart-Willcox Co., Inc.

assigned to the destination and the MAC address. Since NetBEUI does not use IP addresses to identify the destination and source, a router cannot route NetBEUI transmissions.

Another point of interest is that when the destination address is filled with all ones, it becomes a **broadcast frame**. A broadcast frame is intended for every computer on the network, whereas a **multicast frame** is intended for a preselected number of computers, such as a specific workgroup. Ethernet is also described as broadcasting to every network interface card on a network with each frame it sends. This type of broadcasting is different from that described in the broadcast frame. When described as broadcasting, Ethernet frames are broadcast to every network interface card, but only a network card that matches the MAC address indicated in the destination field receives the frames. If the destination field does not match the MAC address of the network interface card, the frame will not pass through to the computer. The exception is when a broadcast frame is used.

Another difference between the two frame types is the type and length fields. The original Ethernet II frame was designed not to perform error checking at the data link layer. Since the original Ethernet II was not intended to perform data error correction at this level, the type field was used to indicate where error correction would occur. In other words, it identifies the upper layer of the OSI model that is responsible for checking damaged frames.

In the 802.3 frame, the length field exists in place of the type field. The length field indicates the total length of the frame not including the preamble. This information is used to perform error checking at the data link layer rather than pass the responsibility to upper-level layers of the OSI model. This is a fine example of how variations of network technology can occur because of developments in technology.

The data field contains the data, such as text, graphics, or sound, which is to be delivered to the destination. The two frames have identical data field maximum and minimum lengths.

The frame check sequence (FCS) field is used to determine a successful delivery of the frame. The data link layer does not perform the check. Rather, an upper-level layer in the OSI model uses the FCS to verify the frame's integrity.

The two Ethernet frames are very similar, but there are sufficient differences in the way the frames are constructed. The standard used today is Ethernet II, but most network adapters incorporate features to detect the frame type automatically. Many network adapter features are set to auto detect by default. These features can also be selected manually, usually through the **Network Connection Properties** dialog box under the **Advanced** tab.

Data Encoding, Transmission, and the OSI Model

The OSI model is used as a reference to determine how data can most effectively be transferred between networks. It is specifically designed for communication across WANs and MANs. LANs did not need a complex model when they were first developed. They were, in fact, proprietary in nature since communication was limited to nodes only on the local network. The network operating system could handle all that was required for identification, packet size, media access, security, and such. However, as the Internet grew, it became apparent that many different operating systems, networking devices, and media were going to be used to support communication. Some sort of standard or model was needed to help programmers and manufacturers design systems and computer programs to support the vast array of network technologies.

1.2 NET

The OSI model is sometimes referred to as the *protocol stack* because it is, in essence, a stack of protocols. Various protocols are associated and designed to work at different levels of the OSI model. Some protocols are designed to work with specific types of media, some are designed for security, and others are designed to encapsulate various types of data such as text, audio, or video. The exact protocol needed is determined by the type of media and networking devices used, the nature of communication, and the type of data sent.

For example, you may use the Internet to access information on a distant server. As the signal travels between your computer and the remote server, it may pass through a maze of telephone exchanges, fiber-optic cables, wireless satellite connections, microwave stations, and such. It may also pass through multiplexers, switches, and routers. As the data passes through various network media and devices, the data is packaged to match the technology it encounters. This is all done at remarkably high speeds.

When negotiating a connection, the protocol used for making the initial connection may be different from the protocol used to transfer the data. For example, the Point-to-Point Protocol (PPP) may be used initially to attach to an Internet service provider through a dial-up telephone modem. After the connection is established, IP and UDP are used to make a connection at the distant site. After the connection is established, IP and TCP may be used to transfer the data. As you see, no one protocol is used.

As data moves through the layers of the OSI model, each layer is responsible for a specific aspect of communication. In other words, each layer has a different set of responsibilities. The following sections present an overview of how communication takes place at each layer of the OSI model. Figure 5-13 provides a summary of each layer's function.

Application Layer

The application layer is not actually with the point of interaction for the user. Instead, it is the point of communication for applications installed on a device. Your e-mail client, web browser, and other programs all deal with the application layer of the OSI model. The application layer is at the top of the OSI model and is the start and the final destination of all data communication. When a user generates a request, such as to connect to a web page, the request is packaged, sent down the protocol stack to the physical layer, and sent across network media to the destination computer. At the destination computer, the request enters the physical layer and is sent up the

Figure 5-13 OSI layers and functions.

Layer	Function
Application	Interfaces to the network system.
Presentation	Packages data into a universally agreed on form, such as ASCII, BCD, BMP, JPG, and WAV.
Session	Establishes and coordinates communication between two points.
Transport	Ensures accurate delivery.
Network	Encapsulates packets for routing.
Data link	Converts frames or packets into electronic signals and places them on the network media.
Physical	The network media.

Goodheart-Willcox Publisher

Copyright Goodheart-Willcox Co., Inc.

protocol stack to the application layer. The data is finalized in the appropriate form, such as displaying the web page. The application layer is associated with applications, such as web browsers and e-mail. It also starts the file transfer mechanism associated with specific operating systems.

Presentation Layer

Data at the source computer leaves the application layer and enters the presentation layer where the raw data is packaged into a universally agreed-upon form. The data byte order must be agreed on and presented in the same manner. For example, most computer system CPUs were originally one of two types: Intel or Motorola. Mainframe computers were constructed from both, but the two different CPUs wrote data in opposite order. The presentation layer is responsible for making it possible for these two different types of data to function together. If all the hardware and software in the network were exactly the same, which is rarely, if ever, the case, there would be no need for a presentation layer outside of data encryption, which also takes place at the presentation layer. **Data encryption** is the encoding of data based on a mathematical formula, which converts the original data symbol into another symbol.

Session Layer

The session layer establishes a dialog between the source and destination computers. This dialog is called a *session*. In short, the session layer establishes and maintains the session between the two endpoints. When you connect to a server, perform operations during that connection, or end the connection, you are working within the session layer. Establishing, maintaining, and terminating the session are the responsibilities of the session layer.

Transport Layer

The transport layer is responsible for the flow of data to and from the destination computer. It is responsible for information reaching its destination free of error and in the correct order. The source and destination computers decide on an appropriate amount of data that can be sent at one time. This is where data is sent with either connection-oriented/reliable communication or connectionless/unreliable communication. TCP and UDP both work at the transport layer of the OSI model.

Network Layer

The network layer provides a means of routing data packets across a WAN, MAN, or GAN. For example, sending a data packet across a LAN only requires the destination computer's address. This means the name of the computer or the MAC address can be used to identify the destination. However, when sending a data packet across a WAN, MAN, or GAN, the packet must be encapsulated with an additional address. The MAC address and computer name is not a practical solution. A more precise address, specifically an IP address, is required to negotiate a route across the Internet. Each packet of data must be repackaged according to a protocol standard such as TCP/IP. The protocol used depends on the need for verification of the delivered package. The IP portion is the address portion and that operates at the network layer of the OSI model.

Look at Figure 5-14. Two virtual networks have been created with a router. The physical network consists of six computers; however, the router creates two separate virtual networks. The router constructs a database of the IP addresses of all connected devices. After all devices have been identified, the router can be programmed

Tech Tip

TCP/IP was designed to communicate over the Internet connecting millions of computers to each other. Originally, LANs used proprietary protocols to communicate. Today, TCP/IP is the default protocol used to communicate over LANs and the Internet. TCP/IP is covered in detail in Chapter 10.

Copyright Goodheart-Willcox Co., Inc.

Figure 5-14 A switch or router can be used to divide a physical network into two or more virtual networks. The router or switch maintains a table of addresses, which it uses as a reference.

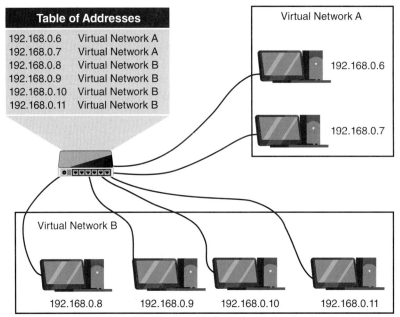

Table of Addresses	
192.168.0.6	Virtual Network A
192.168.0.7	Virtual Network A
192.168.0.8	Virtual Network B
192.168.0.9	Virtual Network B
192.168.0.10	Virtual Network B
192.168.0.11	Virtual Network B

(workstation icons) RedlineVector/Shutterstock.com; (hub icon) Vadim Ermak/Shutterstock.com;
Goodheart-Willcox Publisher

to limit packet broadcasts to only the devices identified or grouped together by IP addresses. In the example, two computers are grouped as *virtual network A* and four computers are grouped as *virtual network B*. Since broadcasts are limited to the designated virtual networks A and B, communication is limited to these networks. The two networks are not aware of each other. The router can also be programmed to allow communication beyond the virtual network.

Tech Tip

Network switches have become more complex as networking science has evolved. Switches are classified as layer 2 and layer 3. Some switch manufacturers claim layer 4 because of the enhanced features added to the switch.

Data Link Layer

The data link layer is where data is organized into frames or packets, and the packets are constructed, ready to go out onto the transmission media. The data link layer is subdivided into the media access control (MAC) sublayer and the logical link control (LLC) sublayer.

Copyright Goodheart-Willcox Co., Inc.

At the MAC sublayer, the data code is converted into electrical pulses. The MAC sublayer is not only concerned with how the data is encoded, but also with the type of topology and cable used. For example, it decides if the data frame needs to be converted for an 802.11 (wireless) network or an 802.3 10GBaseT network.

The LLC sublayer is only interested in getting the data to the destination on the LAN. The LLC sublayer uses the MAC address to address the packet. If data is to be sent across a WAN, the data link layer sends the data to the appropriate router. The router forwards the package based on the IP address inside the package. The router does not need the MAC address to deliver the data package.

The data link layer is responsible for error checking. However, at this level, the error checks are based on the binary-coded digital patterns. Checks such as parity are made to detect missing binary information. CRC checks are also performed at the data link layer.

Network+ Note

For the Network+ Certification Exam, remember that parity and CRC checks are performed at the data link layer. Checks at the transport layer ensure the entire data block was received intact. The transport layer also checks packet sequencing to ensure all data packets are reassembled in the proper order.

Physical Layer

The physical layer is concerned with the media, hardware, and topology of a network. The media may be infrared signals, copper wire, glass or plastic fiber, or electromagnetic radio waves. The choice of topology is typically a star, ring, mesh, or hybrid. The hardware is the connectors used for the media and unintelligible devices, such as hubs and repeaters. This is where data is sent out as a radio wave (Wi-Fi), an electrical signal (Ethernet), or other transmission type.

An unintelligent device makes no decision about where the data will go. It simply passes electrical pulses though the device. An example of an unintelligent device is a repeater or a hub. In Chapter 1, you learned that hubs could be either active or passive. A passive hub is an unintelligent device.

Network+ Note

For this textbook and for the Network+ Certification Exam, a hub is considered unintelligent. It simply provides a connection for the physical media and passes signals without making any choices.

Copyright Goodheart-Willcox Co., Inc.

Summary

Digital Signals and Digital Encoding

- Digital encoding is the conversion of data into a digital pattern acceptable to the network media.

- A digital signal that fluctuates between a positive voltage level and zero-volt level is called a *unipolar digital signal.*

- A digital signal that fluctuates between a positive voltage level and a negative voltage level is called a *bipolar digital signal.*

- Manchester encoding is a common digital-encoding scheme used on LANs. It is characterized by the digital pulse transitioning during the midpoint of the timing period.

- A synchronous signal is synchronized with a reference signal to ensure proper timing.

- An asynchronous signal is not synchronized with a reference signal and typically uses a binary pattern to determine the stop and start of the signal.

Data Packaging and Transmission

- A parity check is used to check the integrity of data.

- A cyclic redundancy check (CRC) is an enhanced parity check that not only identifies when an error occurs but also corrects the error.

- Data encapsulation is the process of surrounding the raw data with other information needed for delivery.

- The terms *segment, frame, datagram,* and *protocol data unit (PDU)* are used to describe blocks of data.

- The term *protocol data unit (PDU)* is the most technically correct term used to describe data packaging.

- A connection-oriented protocol establishes a connection with the destination, transfers the data, and then releases the connection after all communication has ended.

- A connectionless protocol simply sends data to the destination.

- A circuit-switching network establishes a physical connection between two points.

- A packet-switching network establishes a logical connection and may use many different, physical paths to send data from the source to the destination.

Data Codes

- ASCII, Unicode, and HTML are coding standards, or data codes, that represent the written word.

Protocol Frame Structures

- Various protocols are designed to package data in particular ways.

- The User Datagram Protocol (UDP) frame structure contains the data to be transferred, the destination and source information, the length of the packet, and a method to check for errors.

Copyright Goodheart-Willcox Co., Inc.

- Ethernet II and 802.3 frame structures are generally compatible, but there are differences that exist, which means full compatibility cannot be guaranteed.
- A broadcast frame is intended for every computer on the network, whereas a multicast frame is intended for a preselected number of computers, such as a specific workgroup.

Data Encoding, Transmission, and the OSI Model

- The OSI model is composed of seven layers that explain the process of encapsulating data for communication between two points on a network system.
- The OSI model is sometimes referred to as the *protocol stack* because it is, in essence, a stack of protocols.
- The application layer is the point of communication for applications installed on a device.
- Data at the source computer leaves the application layer and enters the presentation layer where the raw data is packaged into a universally agreed-upon form.
- Data encryption also occurs at the presentation layer.
- The session layer establishes a dialog between the source and destination computers.
- The transport layer is responsible for the flow of data to and from the destination computer.
- The network layer provides a means of routing data packets across a WAN, MAN, or GAN.
- The data link layer is where data is organized into frames or packets, and the packets are constructed, ready to go out onto the transmission media.
- The physical layer is concerned with the media, hardware, and topology of a network.

Review Questions

1. What layer of the OSI model is responsible for addressing?
2. Describe the Manchester digital encoding scheme and how it is related to binary signals.
3. The type of transmission in which the digital signal is synchronized with a reference signal to ensure proper timing is called _____ transmission.
4. The type of transmission in which no reference signal is present is called _____ transmission.
5. What is a parity check?
6. What is a cyclic redundancy check (CRC)?
7. A(n) _____ protocol first establishes a connection with the destination computer before transmitting data.
8. _____ communication uses protocols that do not verify packet delivery.

9. What types of transmission use connectionless/unreliable protocols?

10. What is the difference between packet switching and circuit switching?

11. What coding uses 256 codes to represent all the keys on an English language keyboard?

12. What does the acronym ASCII represent?

13. What code can be used to represent over 65,000 characters and is used for international codes?

14. Which standard was designed to represent plain-text files?

15. _____ is a data code used to create documents that can be downloaded from the Internet and viewed by a web browser.

16. What is a port?

17. Differentiate between a broadcast frame and a multicast frame.

18. What layer of the OSI model is responsible for information reaching its destination free of error and in the correct order?

19. At what layer does encapsulation occur?

20. What layer of the OSI model is divided into two sublayers?

✚ Sample Network+ Exam Questions

1. John is a network administrator for a mid-sized insurance company. He is concerned that all network packets have data integrity checking. Which of the following protocols would be most appropriate for this?

   A. Cyclic Redundancy Check (CRC)

   B. Data Parity Reference (DPR)

   C. Kerberos Security Check (KSC)

   D. Parity Data Unit (PDU)

2. Elizabeth is sending video conference signals to a remote office. Which of the following protocols would most likely be used to establish the connection?

   A. SIP

   B. RTP

   C. SMTP

   D. HTTP

3. Hector is connecting to a website that he likes to visit for networking study tips. Using a typical Internet connection, what type of connection is Hector most likely using?

   A. Packet switching

   B. Circuit switching

   C. Modular switching

   D. Enterprise switching

Copyright Goodheart-Willcox Co., Inc.

4. Which layer in the OSI model is responsible for converting data into electrical pulses?

   A. Physical

   B. Data link

   C. Application

   D. Presentation

5. The IEEE 802.3 standard is associated with which media access method?

   A. Carrier Sense Multiple Access with Collision Detection (CSMA/CD)

   B. Carrier Sense Multiple Access with Collision Avoidance (CSMA/CA)

   C. Asynchronous Transmission Mode (ATM)

   D. Wireless Ethernet Protocol (WEP)

6. You have been assigned to explain the OSI model to new network technicians. Which OSI layer has two sub layers and is responsible for the physical address of a NIC?

   A. Physical

   B. Data link

   C. Network

   D. Transport

7. Which of the following is an example of a connectionless protocol?

   A. UDP

   B. SMTP

   C. TCP

   D. HTTP

8. Roger is responsible for networking at a small bank. He is trying to set up addresses that will be used not just in his network, but on the Internet as well. What layer of the OSI model is used with routable addresses?

   A. Network

   B. Transport

   C. Session

9. Which items are responsible for identifying a destination computer? (Select all that apply.)

   A. IP number

   B. MAC address

   C. Port number

   D. Sequence number

10. What is the purpose of a multicast Ethernet frame?

    A. To broadcast a message to a specifically identified set of workstations.

    B. To broadcast a message to all workstations in the LAN.

    C. To broadcast a single frame to all servers in the WAN.

    D. There is no such thing as a multicast Ethernet frame.

Copyright Goodheart-Willcox Co., Inc.

Network Operating Systems and Network Communication

 ## Network+ Certification Exam Objectives

The CompTIA Network+ Certification exam emphasizes basic knowledge of the most common protocols encountered in networking. These protocols are used on all networks regardless of the network operating system.

Objectives

1.1: Protocol Types—TCP

1.3: Properties of Network Traffic—Collision domains

5.2: Software Tools—Command Line

Learning Outcomes

- Describe the evolution of networking protocols.
- Give examples of the common network operating system features.
- Explain how major operating systems use hardware protocols.
- Explain how major operating systems use networking protocols.

Copyright Goodheart-Willcox Co., Inc.

Key Terms

access method

Address Resolution Protocol (ARP)

broadcast storm

Cisco Discovery Protocol (CDP)

collision domain

command prompt

command syntax

graphical user interface (GUI)

Link-Layer Discovery Protocol (LLDP)

Link-Layer Discovery Protocol–Media Endpoint Discovery (LLDP-MED)

Link-Layer Topology Discovery (LLTD)

Link-Local Multicast Name Resolution (LLMNR)

segmenting

Overview

Network protocols are the basis for communicating between devices, regardless of the operating system the device is using. In this chapter, the relationship between networking technologies, protocols, and network operating systems is explained. You will learn about the features that are common to all major network operating systems and will further explore network protocols and network access methods that make network communication possible. This chapter lays the foundation for the next two chapters, which cover two major network operating systems: Windows and Unix/Linux, respectively.

Evolution of Network Protocols

In the very early days of networking, the Internet had very limited access and was used almost exclusively by the Department of Defense (DoD) and certain universities. The TCP/IP suite of protocols was developed many years before computers were common in homes and businesses and Internet access was available to the public. As the early computers used on the Internet were Unix computers, TCP/IP has always been the protocol used for Unix and Unix-based networks.

Later, as various companies developed networks, they each developed proprietary methods for networking. Thus, Novell, Microsoft, and Apple, were all using their own networking protocols, different from the TCP/IP being used on Unix systems and the Internet. These early proprietary network systems developed protocols to work on their particular network system. These protocols were not designed to work on the Internet because no one knew at the time that the Internet would be used by the general public and the private business sector. In the early days, networks were each self-contained, and there was no communication between them. Later, as the Internet grew, these proprietary networks were still used; they simply performed translation at the network gateway to translate between their proprietary protocols and the TCP/IP being used on the Internet.

Each network operating system developed its own network device naming system and protocols for logging on to the network, sharing files, and locating network devices and users. The proprietary systems did not use TCP/IP and thus did not use IP addresses for naming computers.

It has now been many years since these proprietary systems have been used, and the Network+ Exam no longer tests the details of any of them. Now the test focus is on TCP/IP. However, for historical purposes, a brief description of each would be useful.

Apple used *AppleTalk*. The system was very user friendly but not at all secure. When an Apple computer was connected to an AppleTalk network, the computer would generate a random 8-bit address and broadcast it to the network to see if any other device was already using it. If not, then it would use that address. If another device was using it, then AppleTalk would generate a different random number and try again.

Microsoft used *NetBIOS*. This system assigned names to various devices. You will still see the NetBIOS protocol used today alongside TCP/IP. NetBIOS is an acronym for *Network Basic Input/Output System*. It operates at the session layer of the OSI model. It was first created by IBM in 1983. Computers were given names that were limited to 16 ASCII characters. The Microsoft implementation limited this to 15 characters.

Novell used a system called *IPX/SPX*, which had similarities to TCP/IP. IPX/SPX is an acronym for *Internet Packet Exchange/Sequenced Packet Exchange*. The older Novell network operating system, NetWare, was written to work with DOS on workstations. A complete IPX address is a 12-byte number, usually represented in hexadecimal.

Common Network Operating System Traits

First, we should define what a network operating system is. You are aware that your computer has an operating system, which might be Linux, Windows, or Macintosh. However, your network also has an operating system. You are also probably aware that it is not at all uncommon for a network to have devices on it that use different operating systems. You may have a network with some servers that are Linux, others that are Windows, then a mixture of Windows and Macintosh workstations. So what determines the network operating system? It is the operating system of your domain controller.

Network operating systems share some common features, as seen in Figure 6-1. For example, they provide a means of sharing computer resources. Resource sharing, such as sharing files and hardware, is the main purpose of a network system. All network operating systems provide a way to store and manage files in an organized manner.

Network operating systems provide security through user authentication. Authentication is accomplished by entering a user name and password into a log-on dialog box on a networked computer. Then, the network authenticates that the username and password are correct using one of the authentication protocols we will discuss later in this book. Files, folders, and other resources are secured by setting *permissions*, which are levels of security assigned to a resource. Permissions work by

Figure 6-1 Common features of network operating systems.

Common Features of a Network Operating System	Examples
Internet communication	TCP/IP protocol
Resource sharing	Printer, scanner, storage devices, files
Security	Logon/ authentication and resource, file and directory permissions
Services	Web, e-mail, FTP
Storage and file management	File management utilities, backup utilities, encryption
Troubleshooting utilities	Network and server diagnostics
User interface	GUI and command line

Goodheart-Willcox Publisher

Copyright Goodheart-Willcox Co., Inc.

allowing only designated users to use the resource. Each user can also be assigned different access rights to the resource. You will learn more about permissions and access rights in Chapter 7.

While the network operating system is usually something the end user does not see or really think about, the individual operating systems on each workstation come in two forms, GUI-based and command-line based. A **graphical user interface (GUI)** is a pictorial representation of commands and computer hardware that allows a user to access resources and programs with a click of a mouse button. In Figure 6-2, a user has right-clicked the **Computer** icon to expose a shortcut menu. The menu contains commands, which the user can click to invoke. This is easier than typing commands at a command line. Windows was once simply a GUI shell on top of a command line operating system known as Disk Operating System (DOS). However, since Windows 95, the operating system is GUI-based with an optional command-line interface.

Figure 6-2 Windows 10 GUI. Right-clicking the mouse reveals a shortcut menu. The shortcut menu contains a list of commands.

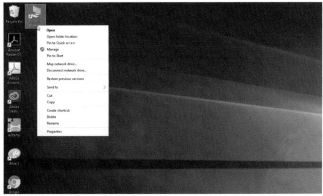

Goodheart-Willcox Publisher

In a command-line environment, commands are typed and entered at a text-based interface called a **command prompt**. Command prompts differ among operating systems and user settings. Compare the command prompts in Figures 6-3 and 6-4. The command prompt in Figure 6-3 is from Windows 10. It shows the default users directory on that computer. The command prompt in Figure 6-4 is from Kali Linux. Unix/Linux are based in a command line, called a *shell*. However, there are GUI environments you can use with Unix/Linux if you wish.

Commands are typed to the right of the command prompt. Many commands consist of several components. You will learn about these components in Chapter 8. The command and its components have to be typed correctly and in the correct arrangement or an error will occur. The correct manner and arrangement in which a command is to be typed is referred to as the **command syntax**.

As you will see in the next two chapters, there are similarities between the major network operating systems, and there are also many differences. As you become familiar with one of the operating systems, you will be simultaneously gaining knowledge that can be transferred to another operating system.

There are many opinions among network administrators and technicians about which network operating system is the best. There are also strong biases among administrators and technicians, usually based on their own personal training or experiences. Often, some network systems are better suited to some purposes than others, but in any particular situation, given many different variables, there may be another better-suited system. The best approach may be to know that the best system is the one you are working on at the time because it may be your job to move from system to system.

5.2   NET

Figure 6-3 Command prompt in Windows 10. A command prompt used in network operating systems is similar to the familiar DOS prompt. A command prompt appears on the screen and text commands are entered to the right of the prompt.

Goodheart-Willcox Publisher

Figure 6-4 Command prompt in the Kali Linux operating system.

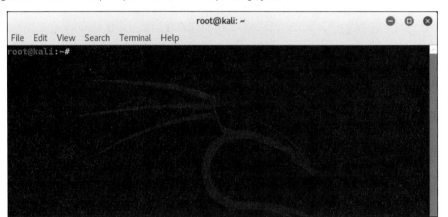

Goodheart-Willcox Publisher

Network Operating Systems and Hardware Protocols

As you have learned in previous chapters, networking technologies such as Ethernet, token ring, and wireless are tied to certain standards that define the hardware, topology, access method, and other specifications of that technology. Each technology uses a different frame type or way of packaging data and other information for accessing the network media. This type of access takes place at the data link layer of the OSI model.

The data link layer is responsible for accessing the network media and either placing the data on the network media or receiving the data and passing it up the OSI layers, as illustrated in Figure 6-5. Token ring and Ethernet are actually protocols that operate at the lower levels of the OSI model. The method of gaining access to the network media is called an **access method**. Examples of access methods are CSMA/CD, CSMA/CA, and token passing. The access method is designed into the network interface card electronics. This is the reason network interface cards are designed to match the network technology used, such as Ethernet, token ring, and wireless.

Fortunately, both Windows and Unix/Linux use the OSI model, thus each operating system can work with network protocols such as Ethernet. That also means that you can send packets from a Windows computer to a Linux computer and the

Tech Tip

The name of the network technology is often used interchangeably with the name of the access method. For example, the term *Ethernet* may be used in place of the term *CSMA/CD*.

Copyright Goodheart-Willcox Co., Inc.

two computers will understand each other.

Recall that layer two of the OSI model is subdivided into two distinct sublayers called the *logical link control (LLC) sublayer* and the *media access control (MAC) sublayer*, as shown in Figure 6-6. The LLC sublayer serves as an interface between the data link layer and network operating system. It is responsible for communicating with the upper layers of the OSI model regardless of the network operating system. The LLC sublayer is described in the IEEE 802.2 standard.

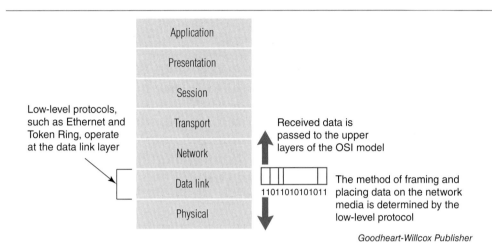

Figure 6-5 The data link layer is responsible for framing the data unit, acknowledging the reception of data, error detection, recovery, and data frame flow control.

Goodheart-Willcox Publisher

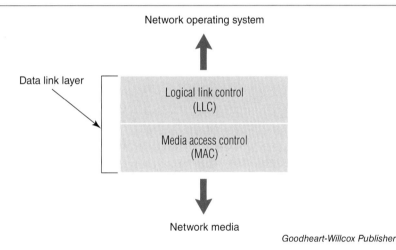

Figure 6-6 The data link layer is divided into two distinct sublayers: logical link control (LLC) and media access control (MAC). The LLC sublayer is responsible for interfacing with the network operating system. The MAC sublayer is responsible for formatting the data into frames and placing the data on the network media.

Goodheart-Willcox Publisher

The MAC sublayer is responsible for formatting the data into frames and placing the frames on the physical media. Examples of frame formats are Ethernet, token ring, and ATM. You can think of the MAC sublayer as the layer where raw data is converted into binary ones and zeros and packaged into frame formats according to the network architecture or network technology.

Ethernet

Since Ethernet is the most common networking protocol today, it bears a closer look. Ethernet networks originally used the CSMA/CD access method to control and ensure the delivery of data. Recall that CSMA/CD is a broadcast method of communication with collision detection. That simply means that a packet is sent out, and if there is a collision, it is resent. Now, Ethernet uses CSMA/CA. Recall that CSMA/CA, is much like CSMA/CD, except that it takes steps to avoid a collision before sending a packet.

Copyright Goodheart-Willcox Co., Inc.

Each computer in the network has a unique hex address, called a *MAC address*, programmed into the computer's network interface card. The MAC address is six bytes long. The MAC address is used at the MAC sublayer of layer 2 of the OSI model. The six-byte address is unique. The first three bytes identify the vendor that manufactured the network card; the next three identify that specific card.

Review the Ethernet 802.3 frame in Figure 6-7. Note the frame sections and the size in bytes of each. After the preamble and the start frame delimiter (SFD), the six bytes that represent the address of the destination computer are transmitted on the network. When the six bytes match the destination computer, the data packet is accepted. When the data packet is accepted, the next six bytes, which identify the source computer, are decoded and stored for a return message. Next, the data portion of the packet is decoded and checked for errors. If no errors are detected, a return message is transmitted to the source computer. If a return message is not transmitted to the source, the data packet will be retransmitted. The data will be retransmitted several more times until a message is received from the destination.

Figure 6-7 Ethernet 802.3 frame.

IEEE 802.3 Frame

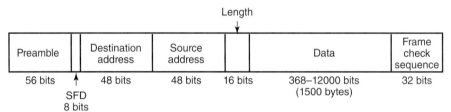

Goodheart-Willcox Publisher

Collisions

Ethernet is an excellent networking system until collisions become excessive. As collisions increase, so does the likelihood of more collisions. Each time a collision occurs, each computer involved in generating the collision ceases broadcasting for a random period of time. After that time, each computer rebroadcasts the packet. This increases the likelihood of another collision. If the number of collisions reaches a point that the network is flooded with a continuous number of collisions and rebroadcasts, a **broadcast storm** has occurred. When this happens, there are so many collisions and rebroadcasts that no significant amount of packets can be exchanged. The only solution to a broadcast storm is to either eliminate a significant number of network computers that are causing the problem, or shut down the entire network and then reboot it. Shutting down the network automatically disconnects the computers that have caused the broadcast storm.

Collision Domains

The section of a network where collisions occur is referred to as a **collision domain**. This is also sometimes called a *contention domain*. A collision domain consists of computers that can directly communicate with each other using broadcasts. The collision domain can be isolated by equipment that controls or limits the broadcasts. Equipment such as switches and routers control broadcasts by limiting the extent or physical boundary of a collision domain. Equipment such as hubs and repeaters do *not* limit broadcasts, and thus do *not* limit the physical size of the collision domain. Repeaters and hubs simply pass the packets and frames. Switches and routers sort packets and frames depending on the destination address. This helps to isolate the network into sections called *segments*. The act of dividing a network into smaller

Copyright Goodheart-Willcox Co., Inc.

sections to avoid collisions is called **segmenting**. Collision domains can be resized by strategically installing network devices such as switches and routers in a network topology.

Turn your attention to Figure 6-8. In the illustration, a LAN is segmented by replacing the hubs with switches. The switches isolate communication to a particular segment of the network, reducing the amount of collisions. The network is further segmented into three distinct departments: engineering, sales, and management. By limiting broadcasts to a particular department, the total number of broadcasts across the entire network is reduced. Each of these departments can still communicate with the entire network, but when communication is desired with a member of the department, the packets are limited to that particular segment of the network.

As more computers are added to a network segment, the likelihood of collision becomes greater. When the number of computers grows to the point of unacceptable collisions, the network segment needs to be segmented again to reduce the number of collisions further. It is important to note, however, that as more equipment is added to reduce the number of collisions, latency increases. Each piece of equipment that must analyze or repackage a packet increases the latency of the digital signal.

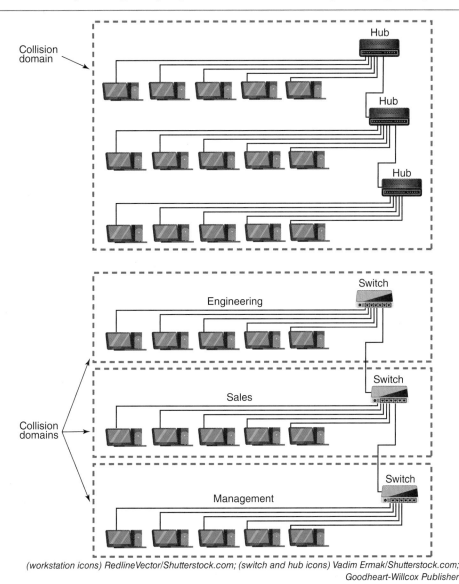

Figure 6-8 Replacing hubs with switches on an Ethernet network can reduce collisions. Switches limit broadcasts to specific areas of the network by creating virtual networks. In the illustration, the hubs are replaced with switches to create network segments, isolating some of the communication by departments, or workgroups.

(workstation icons) RedlineVector/Shutterstock.com; (switch and hub icons) Vadim Ermak/Shutterstock.com; Goodheart-Willcox Publisher

Copyright Goodheart-Willcox Co., Inc.

Token Ring

This is a very old technology, unlikely to be on the Network+ test still. It will be briefly discussed merely for historical reasons. A token ring worked by a token passing around a cable, which was arranged as a logical ring with a physical star topology. If a given device wished to use the network, it would grab the token and that device would then have control of the network transmission until it released the token. Keep in mind that token rings were popular before web pages and widespread use of e-mail. Network communication was limited.

ARCnet

ARCnet is no longer on the Network+ objectives. This is another older technology, simply provided for historical purposes. ARCnet was originally designed for LANs but has evolved into an industrial control-field bus technology. ARCnet is a popular industrial control technology because the protocol design is simple and compact and uses very short packet lengths, which is critical in industrial manufacturing timing systems.

The ARCnet technology is based on token passing for accessing the media. Token passing ensures equal access to all nodes on the network. This is critical to the design of an industrial manufacturing type application where sharing and timing of machine control is critical. Any one computer on the network cannot be forced to wait too long to transmit data to another computer on the network. CSMA/CD provides access to all nodes, but it is does *not* provide equal access.

The access method of ARCnet is similar to the access method of token ring. ARCnet, however, uses a deterministic method of cable access by passing the token to the next, highest-assigned node number, not necessarily the closest node like token ring.

ARCnet allows a maximum number of 255 nodes per network. Each node on the network must be uniquely identified by numbers ranging from *1* to *255*. No node is identified as zero because that digit is reserved for broadcast messages. Each node uses a network interface module (NIM) not a network interface card (NIC), and it is assigned a MAC address for identification rather than having one burned in at the factory. Assigning a MAC address is unique to ARCnet networks.

Network Operating Systems and Networking Protocols

There are numerous high-level network protocols in use today. Part of the reason is no one single protocol can adequately satisfy all possible network functions because network technology is constantly evolving. For example, network protocols were originally designed to exchange text documents. Before long, additional protocols were needed to support the exchange of media such as audio and video.

There is also the desire to maintain compatibility with older network devices that were not designed to handle the capabilities of the latest protocols. For example, the transition from IPv4 addresses to IPv6 addresses resulted in numerous new protocols that either replaced protocols designed exclusively for IPv4 or replaced protocols used to translate address information between IPv4 and IPv6 systems.

Also, as previously discussed, when networking was in its infancy there were many different network operating systems. Each operating system was developed

Tech Tip

Many times specific networking technologies use variations on acceptable terminology when identifying a particular type of equipment or technology. One such term associated with ARCnet is *network interface module (NIM)*. The term NIM is the equivalent to network interface card (NIC) when talking about the circuit board used to connect the network device to the network medium. ARCnet technology was among the first network systems ever used. Since the ARCnet standards use the acronym NIM not NIC, you should also use the preferred term NIM.

Copyright Goodheart-Willcox Co., Inc.

with its own way of communicating with network hardware. There were no standards, no OSI model, and no one set of protocols. Network companies were in direct competition with other companies and many treated the way they programmed their software and protocols as confidential trade secrets. As time went by, it became apparent that people purchasing network operating systems and hardware wanted to be able to communicate with other network systems and use the Internet.

Network operating systems had to provide software programs and protocols that would enable the exchange of data between different network operating systems. The exchange of data between different network operating systems was not easy to establish. One of the reasons for the difficulty was many network operating systems used different ways to identify the nodes on a LAN.

The common denominator for communicating between different network operating systems finally became apparent. Each of the various network operating systems would use the same method to identify individual nodes while maintaining compatibility with its own set of protocols. For example, while Mac OS and Microsoft Windows have different protocols, they all are capable of being encapsulated at the lower levels of the OSI model in protocols defined by the IEEE, such as Ethernet and token ring, as shown in Figure 6-9. The result was that numerous protocols were added to the various suites of vendor-specific protocols.

Network technology is never stagnant. It is constantly evolving, which results in new additional protocols or the replacement of existing protocols. As a student of networking technology, you will constantly experience new protocols. For example, if you connect a protocol analyzer to view the traffic on a network, you will see a wide variety of old and new protocols being transmitted across the network. Therefore, when studying protocols, you not only need to learn about the very latest protocols but also the legacy protocols.

This section presents TCP/IP and emphasizes how modern network operating systems use the TCP/IP suite of protocols, while using their own set of proprietary protocols to maintain backward compatibility with legacy systems and for file sharing and printer access. The network discovery protocols LLDP, LLTD, CDP, LLDP-MED, LLMNR, and ARP are also covered. Discovery protocols are used to detect devices on the network.

Figure 6-9 Different protocols such as those from Microsoft, SUSE, and Apple are capable of being encapsulated at the lower levels of the OSI model in the protocols defined by the IEEE.

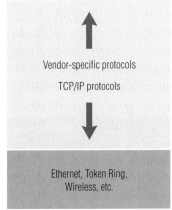

Goodheart-Willcox Publisher

Copyright Goodheart-Willcox Co., Inc.

TCP/IP

NET 1.1

TCP/IP is not a single protocol but rather an entire suite of protocols designed specifically to support communication between computers and network devices connected via the Internet. TCP/IP is native to Unix. Unix was the original operating system designed to communicate via the Internet. Other network operating systems were not originally designed to communicate via the Internet, but rather were designed to communicate over a LAN. In these operating systems, two or more LANs could be connected to form a MAN or WAN. These operating systems used their own address formats and naming conventions to identify nodes on the network. The following table compares the various address formats that were used.

Network OS	Original Network Address Format
NetWare	2b.0000.0e23.12ab
Mac	2.12
Linux/Unix	192.168.0.1
Windows	STATION1

Early Windows operating systems used 15-character NetBIOS names to identify network devices. They resolved the NetBIOS name to a corresponding MAC address. Today, all major network operating systems can communicate across the Internet and adhere to the naming rules of TCP/IP. Modern networks are all based on the TCP/IP protocol suite and use the IPv4 and IPv6 address format for network and node identification.

Even though modern network operating systems use the TCP/IP suite of protocols, some still use their own set of proprietary protocols to maintain backward compatibility with legacy systems and for file sharing and printer access, as shown in Figure 6-10. For example, Microsoft uses the Server Message Block (SMB) protocol for sharing files and NetBIOS for communicating with older Windows operating systems. Network adapters automatically configure NetBIOS over TCP/IP as a service for IPv4. Figure 6-11 shows the **Advanced TCP/IP Settings** dialog box from a Windows 10 computer. NetBIOS has a default setting that enables NetBIOS to be carried over TCP/IP if a static IPv4 address is used or when the DHCP server does not provide a NetBIOS setting.

SUSE Linux and other brands of Linux use the Network File Sharing (NFS) protocol to share files on the network. They also use SAMBA to share files with Windows operating systems. SAMBA supports sharing resources using the SMB protocol.

Mac OS X uses the Apple File Protocol (AFP), Network File Sharing (NFS), and Server Message Block (SMB) for file sharing. AFP is native to all versions of MAC OS. NFS allows MAC OS X to share files with Linux-based computers, and the SMB protocol allows MAC OS X to share files with Windows computers.

Figure 6-10 All major operating systems use the TCP/IP protocol as well as their own proprietary protocols to maintain backward compatibility with legacy operating systems and for file sharing and printer access.

OSI Model	TCP/IP	Microsoft	SUSE Linux	Apple Mac OS X
Application	HTTP FTP POP3 DNS SNMP SSL	SMB	NFS SAMBA	AFP NFS SMB
Presentation				
Session		NetBIOS		
Transport	TCP UDP			
Network	IPv4 IPv6			
Data link	LLC			
Physical	Ethernet 802.3			

Goodheart-Willcox Publisher

Copyright Goodheart-Willcox Co., Inc.

Figure 6-11 Network adapters still automatically configure NetBIOS over TCP/IP as a service for IPv4.

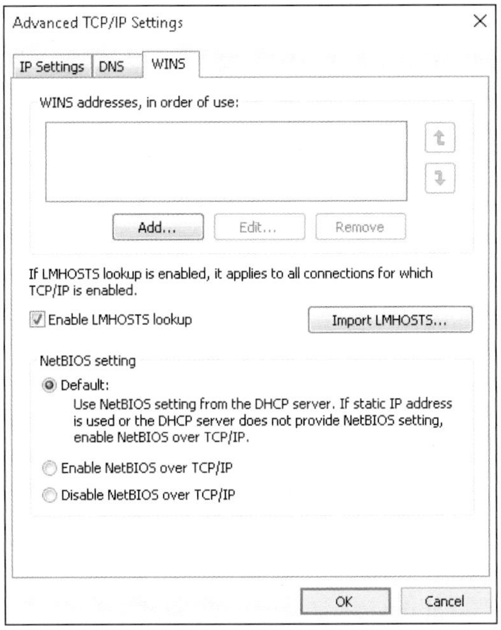

Goodheart-Willcox Publisher

There are many more protocols in use today than what is presented in Figure 6-10. For example, all major network and desktop operating systems support the TCP/IP suite of protocols, such as FTP, HTTP, POP3, and DNS.

Many new protocols will be introduced as they relate to network functions such as security, multimedia, and the Internet. While this was only a brief introduction to TCP/IP, Chapter 10 covers TCP/IP in detail.

Discovery Protocols

The development of IPv6 introduced a new array of protocols that dynamically discover network devices located in the network. These new protocols, LLDP, LLTD, CDP, LLDP-MED, and LLMNR, are covered in this section as well as the legacy protocol ARP. When there is a full implementation of IPv6, legacy discovery protocols such as ARP will no longer be required for name resolution. However, until then, they are still part of network systems.

LLDP

The **Link-Layer Discovery Protocol (LLDP)** was developed as an IEEE specification designed to identify devices connected on the local area network. The protocol can be found in section 802.1ab and is referred to as "Station and Media Access Control Connectivity Discovery." It allows network devices to exchange information automatically. As its name indicates, LLDP works at the data link layer of the OSI model. Since it works at the data link layer, it is designed to work in isolation on a small section of a network bound by a router or gateway.

LLDP is the basis of many proprietary protocols introduced by router manufacturers, such as Cisco Systems, Juniper, and 3COM as well as telephone device manufacturers that rely on Ethernet network systems, to support the Voice over Internet Protocol (VoIP). Many new protocol designs are based on LLDP, resulting in enhanced versions of LLDP. When LLDP is enhanced by a private company, the enhanced version changes the acronym but generally retains the terms *link* and *layer*. The enhanced versions are proprietary while the original LLDP is an open-source protocol developed by IEEE and can be used by anyone.

LLTD

Link-Layer Topology Discovery (LLTD) protocol is the core protocol behind the Microsoft Network and Sharing Center map function in older Microsoft operating systems. In Windows 7, if the user opens the **Microsoft Network and Sharing Center** and selects the **View Full Map** option, a series of inquiry packets are sent out to devices on the local network. The devices reply with information such as their MAC address, device name, and function. A map of the local area network is then constructed and presented to the user.

Microsoft implements two versions of the LLTD protocol: *Link-Layer Topology Discovery Mapper I/O Driver* and *Link-Layer Topology Discovery Responder*. Figure 6-12 shows the two protocols listed in the **Wireless Network Connection Properties** dialog box.

Link-Layer Topology Discovery Mapper I/O Driver broadcasts information about the host computer to neighboring devices in the LAN. Link-Layer Topology Discovery Responder, as its name implies, responds to broadcasts sent by the Link-Layer Topology Discovery Mapper I/O Driver. Together, the two protocols work to produce a map of local devices. Both wired and wireless devices are displayed. Devices that are not running LLTD and not configured for IPv6 can still be identified, but cannot be shown as a logical connection in the network map.

Windows XP operating systems can be discovered after downloading and installing a special hot fix called "Link-Layer Topology Discovery (LLTD) Responder." To learn more about this hot fix, conduct a search online using the phrase Microsoft KB922120.

Figure 6-12 The two versions of the LLTD protocol, Link-Layer Topology Discovery Mapper I/O Driver and Link-Layer Topology Discovery Responder, are listed in the **Ethernet Properties** dialog box.

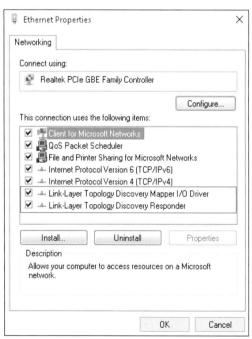

Goodheart-Willcox Publisher

CDP

Cisco Discovery Protocol (CDP) is a variation of LLDP designed to support equipment such as Cisco routers, switches, and telephones. It is an enhanced version of LLDP, which can be routed and is not restricted to a single section of a network bounded by a gateway or router.

LLDP-MED

Link-Layer Discovery Protocol–Media Endpoint Discovery (LLDP-MED) is an enhanced version of LLDP used for routers, switches, Voice over Internet Protocol (VoIP) devices, and Power over Ethernet (PoE) devices. There are many different proprietary versions of LLDP-MED available. VoIP systems do not perform well when competing with other network activity such as workstations downloading or transferring large volumes of data. One way to provide better support for VoIP devices is to incorporate advanced switches into the local area network. Advanced switches will not only automatically locate and configure VoIP devices, they will provide better bandwidth by creating logical networks for the devices. The logical network, called a *Virtual LAN (VLAN)*, provides a dedicated bandwidth to VoIP devices, and does not share the bandwidth with workstations.

LLMNR

Link-Local Multicast Name Resolution (LLMNR) protocol serves the same function as a DNS server when a DNS server cannot be reached. LLMNR resolves names of devices connected collectively on a local network.

Modern network operating systems are using a more sophisticated naming solution for devices rather than simple NetBIOS names. As a result, new protocols are needed to resolve names on a local area network when a DNS server cannot be reached. Early Microsoft network systems used Windows Internet Name Service (WINS) to resolve devices based on NetBIOS names. With the introduction of advanced networking technologies such as Lightweight Directory Name Service (LDNS), a better method to resolve names was needed. The method to resolve names needed to be based on the Domain Name Service (DNS). LLMNR serves the same purpose as a DNS server, but is not meant to replace the function of a DNS server.

LLMNR is limited to a LAN link because it is not routable at this time. LLMNR cannot be used for resolving Internet names to IP addresses, because resolving Internet names is under the jurisdiction of the Internet Assigned Numbers Authority (IANA) and is handled by DNS servers.

ARP

Address Resolution Protocol (ARP) is a communication protocol that resolves an assigned IPv4 network address to a physical address (MAC address). ARP is one of the oldest protocols associated with networking. You can think of ARP as a protocol that can merge layer two (data link-layer) information with layer three (network layer) information. When a computer or network device is first booted, it sends out a series of ARP broadcasts to build the ARP table. There will be more about ARP in Chapter 10.

Copyright Goodheart-Willcox Co., Inc.

Summary

The Evolution of Network Protocols

- In the very early days of networking, the Internet had very limited access and was used almost exclusively by the Department of Defense (DoD) and certain universities.

- As various companies developed networks, they each developed proprietary methods for networking.

- These protocols were not designed to work on the Internet because no one knew at the time that the Internet would be used by the general public and the private business sector.

Common Network Operating System Traits

- Some common features that a network operating system provides are shared resources, file storage, file management, security, troubleshooting utilities, services, and a user interface.

- A graphical user interface (GUI) is a pictorial representation of commands and computer hardware that allows a user to access resources and programs with a click of a mouse button.

- In a command-line environment, commands are typed and entered at a text-based interface called a command prompt.

Network Operating Systems and Hardware Protocols

- The data link layer is responsible for placing data on the network media or receiving data and passing it up the OSI layers.

- The data link layer is defined by the IEEE 802.2 standard.

- Ethernet uses CSMA/CA to access the network media.

- A broadcast storm occurs when there is continuous activity on an Ethernet network.

- The CSMA/CA access method attempts to avoid collisions through detecting communication on the network media.

- A collision domain is an area where collisions occur in an Ethernet network.

- Segmenting an Ethernet network can reduce collisions.

Network Operating Systems and Networking Protocols

- TCP/IP is not a single protocol but rather an entire suite of protocols designed specifically to support communication between computers and network devices connected via the Internet.

- The Link-Layer Discovery Protocol (LLDP) identifies devices connected on a local area network.

- The Microsoft Link-Layer Topology Discovery Mapper I/O Driver and Link-Layer Topology Discovery Responder protocols are both based on LLDP.

- Cisco Discovery Protocol (CDP) is based on LLDP.

Copyright Goodheart-Willcox Co., Inc.

- Link-Layer Discovery Protocol–Media Endpoint Discovery (LLDP-MED) is an enhanced version of LLDP used for switches, Voice over Internet Protocol (VoIP) devices, and Power over Ethernet (PoE) devices.

- Link-Local Multicast Name Resolution (LLMNR) serves the same function as a DNS server when a DNS server cannot be reached.

- Address Resolution Protocol (ARP) is one of the oldest protocols associated with networking.

Review Questions

1. Briefly describe why companies designed proprietary protocols originally not designed to function with the Internet.

2. How long was a Microsoft NetBIOS address?

3. How long is an IPX address?

4. List some common features of network operating systems.

5. List two forms in which an individual operating system interface can take.

6. What was the first Windows operating system to have a graphical user interface?

7. What is the purpose of the data link layer?

8. The Ethernet protocol uses the _____ access method.

9. When too many packets on a network collide, a(n) _____ storm has occurred.

10. On which type of network do broadcast storms typically occur?

11. Describe a *contention domain*.

12. What is the purpose of LLDP?

13. What two Microsoft protocols are based on LLDP and can be viewed in the **Network Connection Properties** dialog box?

14. Why would a network device such as a computer running Windows XP not appear in Network Map?

15. What is the name of the Cisco version of LLDP?

16. Which link layer protocol design is similar to DNS?

17. What is the purpose of ARP?

✚ Sample Network+ Exam Questions

1. Which of the following is the UNC format for a shared directory called MyFiles on a server called *Server1*?

   A. //Server1/MyFiles

   B. //MyFiles /Server1

   C. \\Server1\MyFiles

   D. \Server1\MyFiles

Copyright Goodheart-Willcox Co., Inc.

2. John is trying to match physical (MAC) addresses to IP addresses on his network. Which protocol would be most useful in accomplishing this?

A. IP

B. ARP

C. DNS

D. TCP

3. Carol is concerned about congestion on her network. She is trying to reduce the number of network collisions. Which of the following would be most helpful in accomplishing this goal?

A. Assign static IP addresses to all devices.

B. Replace network switches with hubs.

C. Segment the network using switches.

D. Add additional network servers.

4. Which protocol serves the same purpose as DNS but is limited in scope to a local network?

A. FTP

B. ARP

C. HTML

D. LLMNR

5. Broadcasting data to a few select workstations is referred to as _____.

A. beaconing

B. multicasting

C. conferencing

D. multiplexing

6. The IEEE 802.3 standard is associated with which access method?

A. Carrier Sense Multiple Access with Collision Detection (CSMA/CD)

B. Carrier Sense Multiple Access with Collision Avoidance (CSMA/CA)

C. Asynchronous Transmission Mode (ATM)

D. Wireless Ethernet Protocol (WEP)

Copyright Goodheart-Willcox Co., Inc.

7. Albert is responsible for a small network. The network has 15 computers connected to two hubs. He is noticing a great deal of collisions on the network. Which device could he add that would be most helpful in reducing collisions?

   A. Switch

   B. Hub

   C. Gateway

   D. Repeater

8. Elizabeth is looking for a protocol that will aid in discovery and works well with routers, switches, Voice over Internet Protocol (VoIP) devices, and Power over Ethernet (PoE) devices. Which of the following would be most helpful for her in accomplishing this goal?

   A. LLDP-MED

   B. CDP

   C. LLTD

   D. LLDP

9. Which network operating system can communicate over Ethernet?

   A. Microsoft Windows

   B. OS X

   C. Unix

   D. All of the above.

10. Which answer is a correct example of a MAC address?

   A. AB C3 D4 23 54 F2

   B. 192.168.000.123

   C. A12.34E.676.FF2

   D. 1926867721

Copyright Goodheart-Willcox Co., Inc.

CHAPTER 7

Microsoft Network Operating Systems

Network+ Certification Exam Objectives

The CompTIA Network+ Certification is not a certification for Windows Server or any other network operating system. It measures general knowledge, not specific systems. However, Microsoft Windows is a ubiquitous operating system, thus there is some emphasis on Microsoft operating systems on all CompTIA exams. The A+ Exam has Windows-specific questions, and the Network+ Exam also has Windows-specific questions. This chapter does not address specific Network+ objectives, but it is important for you to study order to be an effective network administrator.

Learning Outcomes

- Differentiate between a Microsoft peer-to-peer network and a Microsoft client/server network.
- Describe the features and use of Windows Server 2016.
- List common Windows Server administrative components.
- Explain the Active Directory structure.
- Discuss the use of Windows Server administration utilities.
- Describe the POSIX standard.
- Recount the evolution of network interoperability.

Copyright Goodheart-Willcox Co., Inc.

Key Terms

Active Directory (AD)
auditing
basic disk
complex trust relationship
contiguous namespace
disjointed namespace
disk quota
distinguished name
domain
dynamic disk
EFI partition
extended partition
external trust
forest
forest trust
free space
global security policy
globally unique identifier (GUID)
group account

interactive logon
local security policy
Logical Disk Manager (LDM) partition
logical drive
logon right
Microsoft Reserved (MSR) partition
multimaster replication
namespace
network authentication
Network File System (NFS)
network share
New Technology File System (NTFS)
NTFS permissions
object
one-way trust relationship
organizational unit
partition
permission

physical drive
primary partition
realm trust
security policy
server cluster
Server Message Block (SMB)
share-level security
simple volume
snap-in
spanned volume
striped volume
tree
trust relationship
two-way trust relationship
user-level security
volume
volume set
workgroup

Overview

This chapter and the next introduce the dominant Microsoft and Unix/Linux network operating systems. As you read the content of these chapters, you will see the similarities and differences among network operating systems. The material presented is limited to an introductory level. Knowledge of these network operating systems fills volumes of textbooks. In fact, a typical resource book for any of these operating systems typically contains over 1000 pages.

Network+ Note

The Network+ Certification Exam only requires introductory-level knowledge of the Microsoft network operating system. After finishing this course on networking fundamentals, you may wish to expand your knowledge in this area.

Brief History of Microsoft Network Operating Systems

Microsoft began developing network operating systems in 1993 when it introduced Windows for Workgroups and Windows NT 3.1. Windows for Workgroups was designed as a peer-to-peer technology, while Windows NT 3.1 was designed as a client/server technology. Both network operating systems became popular because of the GUI.

Windows for Workgroups was one of the first peer-to-peer network models developed. At the time, most networks were the client/server type requiring expensive server software and hardware or a system to access mainframes through dumb terminals. The peer-to-peer model allows a collection of computers to communicate in similar fashion as the client/server model and also allows the computers to function as stand-alone computers.

Computers in a Windows for Workgroups peer-to-peer network are grouped as workgroups. A **workgroup** is a group of computers that share resources such as files and hardware, as shown in Figure 7-1. This type of network structure is limited in scope and is not used for large networks. In the peer-to-peer workgroup model, each computer contains its own database of users. Each user must have a separate account on each computer to use the computer's shared resources. As a peer-to-peer network grows in size, it becomes impractical to manage.

Figure 7-1 A workgroup is a group of computers that share resources. Some examples of resources are files, directories, databases, and printers.

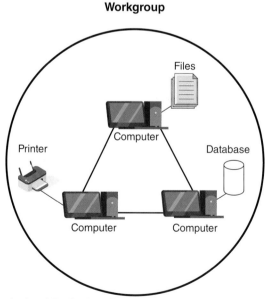

(workstation icons) RedlineVector/Shutterstock.com; (printer icon) Vectors Bang/Shutterstock.com; Goodheart-Willcox Publisher

Copyright Goodheart-Willcox Co., Inc.

Windows NT 3.1 based its network administration on the client/server model. A client/server model stores user and resource information in one location called a *security database*. In a client/server network, the security database is stored on a server. The user logs on to the server and is then cleared to access the network resources.

Computers in a Windows client/server network are grouped together in a domain. A **domain** is a logical grouping of users and equipment as defined by the network administrator, as demonstrated in Figure 7-2. Domain members share a common security database. It is much easier to manage a large number of users when the network is configured as a client/server. The key element in a domain is a server designated as a domain controller. To be a Windows domain, the domain controller must be a Windows server (Windows Server 2008, 2012, 2016, etc.)

Tech Tip

Workgroups can also be implemented on a client/server network. However, the ability of a Microsoft client/server model to organize users into groups makes workgroups obsolete.

Figure 7-2 A domain consists of a collection of users and equipment under one administration.

Domain

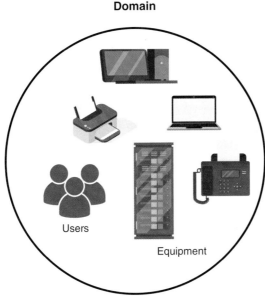

Users

Equipment

Clockwise from top: RedlineVector/Shutterstock.com, Jemastock/Shutterstock.com, KittyVector/Shutterstock.com, fullvector/Shutterstock.com, musmellow/Shutterstock.com, Vectors Bang/Shutterstock.com; Goodheart-Willcox Publisher

Windows NT

It is interesting to note that the first release of Windows NT was called Windows NT 3.1. Typically, the first release number of software is labeled as 1.0. Major releases follow in whole numbers such as 2.0, 3.0, and 4.0. Revisions increment in tenths, such as 2.1 and 2.2, and minor revisions generally increment in one hundredths, such as 2.11 and 2.22. The first version of Windows NT, however, was labeled 3.1 to match the version of DOS that was available at the time.

In 1996, Microsoft introduced Windows NT Workstation 4.0 and Windows NT Server 4.0. The workstation version could function as a stand-alone computer or support up to ten computers in a peer-to-peer environment.

Copyright Goodheart-Willcox Co., Inc.

Two of the major differences between Windows NT 3.1 and Windows NT 4.0 are the interface and plug-and-play capabilities. Windows NT 4.0 was designed to look like Windows 95. The operating system was capable of recognizing and installing plug-and-play devices, a feature that NT 3.1 lacked.

Windows 2000 Professional

In February of 2000, Microsoft introduced Windows 2000 Professional to replace Windows NT Workstation 4.0 and Windows 2000 Server to replace Windows NT Server 4.0. In addition, Microsoft introduced Windows 2000 Advanced Server, which was designed to replace Windows NT 5.0 Server Enterprise Edition and Windows 2000 Datacenter Server.

Windows Server 2003

In 2003, Microsoft released Windows Server 2003. Windows Server 2003 came in four versions: Standard Edition, Enterprise Edition, Datacenter Edition, and Web Edition. The names reflect the design and administrative tool collection of each. For example, the Standard Edition functions as a network server for controlling a simple network. The Enterprise Edition is designed especially for a large-scale network. The Datacenter Edition is designed to serve as a storage server for a central database. The Web Edition is designed to serve as a web server with limited capabilities.

Windows Server 2008

Windows Server 2008 was officially released on February 4, 2008. Later, Windows Server 2008 R2 was released in June 2009. Server 2008 included BitLocker encryption as well as an improved Windows Firewall. Server 2008 also introduced the server core version. This is a version of Windows Server that uses only a command line without any GUI. A Windows Server Core can be used as a domain controller, DNS server, DHCP, server, or other role. To learn more about Windows Server 2008 not printed here, conduct a search on the Internet using the phrase Microsoft Server 2008 or Microsoft TechNet Server 2008.

Small Business Server (SBS) was designed specifically for the small-office environment, usually consisting of 50 to 75 computers. It was introduced in Windows Server 2008, but as of the release of Windows Server 2016, it is no longer available. However, many people still use older server releases, so it is worth discussing. It was designed to automatically set up in a typical installation configuration and provide features such as e-mail, collaboration and messaging software, security features, automatic updating, and website support. SBS comes in two editions: Standard and Premium. The main difference between the Standard and Premium editions is Premium includes database server support using SQL. *Structured Query Language (SQL)* is the standard language for database-management systems. An SQL database provides services such as retrieval information for accounting, marketing, and other various business purposes.

Windows Server 2012

In September 2012, Microsoft released Windows Server 2012. This included a new version of the Task Manager, as well as a new file system named ReFS. Server 102 R2 was released in October 2013. Server 2012 had the option of switching between Server Core and GUI. The GUI interface was much more optimized for managing multiple servers from one location. Windows Server 2012 was replaced by Windows Server 2016 in September of 2016. The newest server software includes improved

Copyright Goodheart-Willcox Co., Inc.

active directory federation servers, a new version of IIS, a new version of PowerShell, as well as failover clustering. A detailed discussion of Windows Server 2016 is forthcoming in this chapter.

Common Features

Each edition supports IPv6, Remote Desktop, Active Directory, IIS (Internet Information Services), Microsoft's web server, .NET Application Services, and the Encrypting File System (EFS). The interfaces of the server edition is usually similar to the current client. For example, Windows Server 2003 had a similar interface to Windows XP, whereas Windows Server 2016 has an interface that is more like Windows 10. This means that if you are comfortable with the Windows client operating system, you would likely be able to navigate the relevant server version, provided you have received the specific training to do so. The major differences are the technical features, such as how much RAM and how many processors each can support and whether it supports hot-swappable hard drive storage and cluster services.

One issue to keep in mind is that while older versions of Windows Server still function, Microsoft eventually ceases support for those systems. That means that even if a vulnerability is found, there will be no patch released for it. While you do not necessarily need the very latest version of Microsoft Windows Server, you may want to avoid using particularly old versions. A good rule of thumb is that you never wish to be more than two versions behind the latest version.

Windows Server 2016

As of this writing, Windows Server 2016 is Microsoft's latest server operating system. There are many variations of Windows Server 2016. The variations range from a modest version known as Server Core, which does not use a GUI, to Server Enterprise, which is a GUI-based system designed to support thousands of workstations and devices worldwide. In this section, you will learn about the various Windows Server 2016 editions and their available features. To learn more about Windows Server 2016 aside from what is discussed here, you can visit https://docs.microsoft.com/en-us/windows-server/get-started/whats-new-in-windows-server-2016.

Windows Server 2016 Editions

There are three different editions of Windows Server 2016: Standard, Datacenter, and Essentials. Windows Server 2016 Standard is an entry-level server operating system. Datacenter is designed specifically for use in virtualized or software-defined datacenter environments. Essentials is cloud-based specialty server software.

Windows Server Features

Figure 7-3 lists some of the major features introduced first in Windows Server 2008 that still exist in Windows 2016. Note that most features are not available in all of the editions. This section details some of the features listed in Figure 7-3.

BranchCache

BranchCache was new for Windows Server 2008 and Windows 7. The BranchCache feature is designed to improve network performance by storing information downloaded from the Internet or a web server onto a local area network client. In a peer-to-peer network such as a home office, one of the Windows 7 computers stores the downloaded content and has it available for other clients in the network.

Copyright Goodheart-Willcox Co., Inc.

Figure 7-3 Windows Server 2016 editions and features comparison chart.

Feature	Enterprise	Datacenter	Standard	Web Server	Itanium-Based Systems	Foundation	HPC Server
64-bit RAM	2 TB	2 TB	32 GB	32 GB	NA	8 GB	128 GB
AD Rights Management Services	Yes	Yes	Yes	No	No	Yes	No
BranchCache Content Server	Yes	Yes	Yes	Yes	Yes	Yes	
DirectAccess	Yes	Yes	Yes	No	No	No	No
Failover Cluster	Yes	Yes	No	No	Yes	No	No
Hot Swap CPU	No	Yes	No	No	Yes	No	No
Hot Swap Memory	No	Yes	No	No	Yes	No	No
Hyper-V	Yes	Yes	Yes	No	No	No	Yes
Internet Information Services 7.5	Yes	Yes	Yes	Yes	Yes	Yes	Yes
Network Access Protection	Yes	Yes	Yes	No	No	Yes	No
Remote Access using VPN	Unlimited	Unlimited	250	NA	NA	50	250
Remote Access using RADIUS	Unlimited	Unlimited	50	NA	2	10	NA
Remote Desktop Services	Yes	Yes	Yes	No	No	Yes	Yes
Server Core	Yes	Yes	Yes	Yes	No	No	No

Goodheart-Willcox Publisher

In a client/server network, a copy of the downloaded content is stored on the server and made available to network clients. BranchCache greatly improves LAN performance by providing an alternate location of the requested information to reduce network traffic.

DirectAccess

DirectAccess is a new feature in Windows Server 2008. Prior to DirectAccess, users typically connected to a remote server using a *virtual private network (VPN)*. A VPN connection requires manual user authentication each time the connection is made. DirectAccess only requires user authentication the first time the connection is established. After that, connections are made automatically. Another important feature of DirectAccess is if a network remote connection is temporarily lost, the computer will automatically reconnect when the network remote connection is re-established. For example, mobile users use wireless connections while out of the office. A wireless connection can easily be disrupted by radio interference or loss of signal strength. When the wireless connection returns, the DirectAccess feature resumes the remote connection to the office.

Network Access Protection (NAP) is incorporated into the DirectAccess feature. NAP automatically checks if the system is healthy. Being "healthy" means the computer has the latest critical updates and anti-malware definitions installed.

Copyright Goodheart-Willcox Co., Inc.

Failover Cluster

Failover cluster is the name Microsoft uses to refer to what other vendors generally call a server cluster. A **server cluster** is a group of individual servers connected both physically and logically to ensure constant service to clients. An example of the function of a server cluster is when two or more servers provide file sharing, printer services, and mail service. When one server fails, the other server automatically begins servicing clients connected to the failed server. Failover clustering is a way to provide near perfect service, even during routine server maintenance or server failure. Failover cluster is only available in the more advanced editions.

Load balancing is typically included with failover cluster. The client load is distributed evenly through all servers participating in the load-balancing service. Load-balancing software constantly checks the performance of each server and makes decisions based on client/server demand. When the demand is too high on one server, some of the client connections can be automatically switched to a different server that provides the same service. Load balancing is a key factor for server farms.

Hyper-V

Hyper-V is the Microsoft version of server virtualization software. The computer running Hyper-V is referred to as the "host." When Hyper-V is installed, the host can run other server operating systems. Virtualization is a very economical way to run two or more servers simultaneously using only one computer. The host shares physical resources such as the CPU, RAM, and hard disk drive storage with the other installed operating systems.

Virtualization allows a network administrator to phase in a new server system such as Windows Server 2016 and run an earlier version such as Windows Server 2008 at the same time. After a test period, the administrator can migrate the entire network system to the new server operating system while both servers are running. There is no service interruption or network downtime during the migration. Network clients can continue to use network resources such as shared files during the migration. Hyper-V also allows the network administrator to host operating systems other than Microsoft, such as Linux. Many organizations prefer to use a Linux server as a web server. Again, a separate computer is not required to host the Linux web server.

Another advantage is redundancy of servers, which provides services while a network server is taken off-line. For example, if a company is using two physical servers, one as a system file server and the other as a web server, client service could be denied if one of the two servers were to fail. However, with each of the two servers running Hyper-V and each server hosting a file server and a web server, if one of the two physical servers fail, the other could still provide services to network clients.

Internet Information Services

Internet Information Services (IIS) is the Microsoft version of web-service hosting software. Once installed, a server with IIS can host web-page applications and web services. Microsoft has a proprietary website development suite called Microsoft Expression Studio. The suite consists of web page and website design tools as well as programming tools for constructing database web pages. The suite is quite elaborate.

Copyright Goodheart-Willcox Co., Inc.

Network Access Protection

Network Access Protection (NAP) was a new feature introduced in Windows Server 2008 R2. NAP inspects the "health" of the computer before it completes a connection to the domain, which means it checks if the latest software patches and updates and the latest antimalware definitions are installed. If not, the user is denied access to the domain. This feature helps prevent the spread of malware through the network. It is especially useful for preventing infection through wireless connections, such as when using a laptop in a public environment.

Remote Access

Remote access to the server is typically performed in one of two ways. One way is by using a server that is running RADIUS. RADIUS is a security feature that requires clients connecting from remote locations to the network server to authenticate with a user name and password. In addition, the RADIUS server keeps track of user activity.

The other way is through a virtual private network (VPN) connection, which does not require a server to be running RADIUS but does require a password. There will be much more about VPN connections and RADIUS in Chapter 15.

Server Core and Nano Server

Server Core is a minimal server configuration that provides specialized or limited services. For example, Server Core can be configured to function as only a DHCP, DNS, or web server. Server Core is available in all of the Windows Server 2016 editions except for Essentials. The most drastic difference between Server Core and a full server version is Server Core does not use a GUI interface. Server Core only provides a command prompt interface for configuring the server and viewing server information. By providing a limited number of services or a single service without the enhancements of a typical server, Server Core is less vulnerable to network attacks. For example, Server Core does not use Windows Explorer, thus any malicious attack based on Windows Explorer will not affect it.

With the release of Windows Server 2016, users now have the option of installing Nano Server, which is a server operating system administered remotely. Nano Server is optimized for cloud-based server administration. It is similar to previous versions of Server Core, but it has no local logon abilities or remote desktop support, and it only supports 64-bit applications.

Common Windows Server Administrative Components

This section provides an overview of the common administrative components and basic terminology of all Microsoft network operating systems. A basic understanding of Microsoft network operating systems will serve as a foundation when studying the specific Microsoft network operating systems.

Domain, Workgroup, and HomeGroup Membership

Students new to networking find it difficult to tell the difference between the terms *domain*, *workgroup*, and *HomeGroup*. A HomeGroup is a group of computers on a residential network that can share files and printers. The main differences are found by comparing security, administration features, and general limitations. See Figure 7-4 for a brief comparison.

Copyright Goodheart-Willcox Co., Inc.

Figure 7-4 Workgroup, domain, and HomeGroup comparison.

Workgroup	Domain	HomeGroup
A computer must be a member of either workgroup or domain.	A computer must be a member of either workgroup or domain.	Membership is optional.
Peer-to-peer configuration.	Client/server configuration.	Peer-to-peer configuration.
Each computer has a set of user accounts.	User accounts are stored in a single location called a security database.	Each computer has a set of user accounts.
Passwords are optional.	Passwords are required.	Passwords are required.
All workgroup computers must be on the same LAN or subnet.	Domain membership is not limited to a subnet or local area network.	Must be a Windows 7 computer with the network location set to Home.
A workgroup typically contains 10–20 computers.	A domain can contain thousands of computers.	Same as the workgroup limit.

Goodheart-Willcox Publisher

Note that HomeGroup membership is optional, whereas membership to a workgroup or domain is not. A computer must be a member of either workgroup or domain in order to communicate with other devices on a network. By default, Microsoft operating systems are configured as a member of a workgroup unless otherwise specified.

HomeGroup was first introduced in Windows 7 and was designed to provide an easy way for users to share resources on a home network. It is configured automatically in addition to workgroup membership during the operating system installation process. HomeGroup membership is designed to share common folders such as Pictures, Music, Documents, and Videos, which are referred to as *Libraries*. Some hardware devices such as printers and media players can also be shared.

Note

HomeGroup was first made available in Windows 7.

In a workgroup, all computers are equal or peers. Each computer has a collection of user accounts. You must have a user account configured on a specific computer to access the computer. Each workstation controls access to its own resources. In a domain, there are one or more servers. The server designated as the domain controller controls access to the network and to the network's resources. A single user account can allow a user to log on to any computer in the entire domain. A domain provides for centralized network control, typically by one person called the *administrator*.

Domain membership and HomeGroup membership require a password; workgroup membership does not. All computers in a workgroup must be on the same local area network or subnet. Domain membership is not limited to a subnet or local area network. A domain can span across the globe and comprise individual networks and computers. A domain can contain thousands of computers, whereas a workgroup typically contains 10 to 20 computers.

User Account

Each person who needs to access a Microsoft server and its resources must have a user account. The basic requirement for a user account is a username and password. A user account can be assigned properties such as rights and restrictions. Rights

Copyright Goodheart-Willcox Co., Inc.

include logon rights and permissions. A **logon right** is the ability to log on to the network. This ability may be restricted by disabling a user's account or by limiting the time the user is allowed to access the network. A **permission** is the ability to access a network share. Permissions may be limited. For example, a user can be given permission to read a file on the server, but not given permission to write to the file. A user can also be given permission to store personal files on the server's hard drive, yet restricted to using a limited amount of hard drive space.

When a computer running a Windows server operating system boots, a dialog box appears prompting the user to press [Ctrl] [Alt] [Del] to begin. After the user presses [Ctrl] [Alt] [Del], a logon dialog box displays, prompting the user for a username and password. After the username and password are authenticated, the user's default desktop appears.

One of the most common errors made by users is to type their usernames or passwords incorrectly or to forget their passwords incorrectly. The following is an example of a typical Windows Server message that is displayed when a user incorrectly enters his or her name or password:

> The system could not log you on. Make sure your username and domain are correct, and then type your password again. Letters in passwords must be typed using correct case. Make sure that CAPS LOCK is not accidentally on.

Network+ Note

Logon failures are a common question topic on the Network+ Certification Exam. Practice logon procedures and create logon failures to observe error messages firsthand.

Group Account

To simplify user and resource administration, a network administrator can create a group account and then add users to that account. A **group account** is a collection of users who typically share a common job-oriented goal or similar function. Think of a group as a container or a collection of users who share the same responsibilities, duties, or interest. The group account may also consist of equipment. A group account can be assigned rights and restrictions like a user. Assigning rights and restrictions to the group level rather than to the user level makes administration simpler. For example, if users of a group need to access a new folder, the administrator can simply change the rights of the group account rather than change each user account.

Some groups are created by default when a network operating system is installed. The following is a list of some typical default groups found in Windows Server:

- Administrators
- Account Operators
- Backup Operators
- Guests
- Server Operators
- Remote Desktop Users
- Event Log Readers

Copyright Goodheart-Willcox Co., Inc.

- Network Configuration Operators
- Performance Operators
- Pre-Windows 2000 Compatibility Access
- Print Operators
- Replicator
- Users

The system administrator may create additional groups to match the network environment better. For example, typical groups that may be created for a school setting would be *Teachers, Students, Science, English, Math, Counseling,* and *Administration.* Once the groups are established with permissions and restrictions, users can be assigned to the groups. Users may be assigned to more than one group. For example, a teacher may be assigned to the *Teacher* group, the *Math* group, and the default *Backup Operators* group.

Security Policy

A **security policy** is a blanket policy that secures resources on the network. This policy is set before users are added to the network. Users added to the network are automatically affected by these policies unless specific properties are assigned to the users that override the policy's settings. Two types of security policies exist: local security policies and global security policies. A **local security policy** affects local users. A **global security policy** affects users throughout the domain.

Security policies can define password requirements such as whether a user should be allowed to reuse an old password when a password change is required. This is conducted in the **Local Security Policy** menu, as shown in Figure 7-5. Security policies can also be set that affect auditing. **Auditing** is a service that tracks the events, use, and access of network resources and writes these actions to a log. In Figure 7-6, a file server error is displayed in the Server Manager utility. Error logs for server versions of Windows are very similar to the error logs generated in desktop versions of Windows.

Figure 7-5 Security policies are created and modified using the **Local Security Policy** menu.

Goodheart-Willcox Publisher

Copyright Goodheart-Willcox Co., Inc.

Figure 7-6 Server Manager provides a set of Event Viewer logs that contain information and error messages.

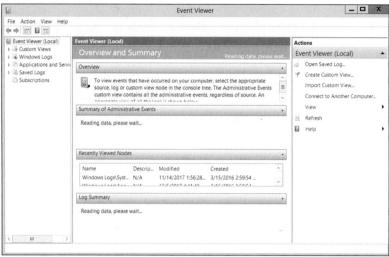

Goodheart-Willcox Publisher

Network Share

A **network share**, or *shared resource*, is a resource on the network that is shared among assigned users. Examples of resources include files, directories, hard drives, CD drives, and printers. A network share as viewed from a computer workstation looks similar as that in Figure 7-7. Earlier systems used an open hand icon to indicate a shared object. An open hand beneath an object is still used by Windows 7 through Windows 10 and Windows Server 2008–2016 to indicate a shared object as a local share for access by local users, not a network share. A network share is indicated by a cable connected to the shared object. Originally, a public folder share was typically named *Public* in a Windows Server environment. Today, Windows 7, 8, and 10 use the term *Public* to indicate shared resources on a local computer.

Two administrative shares automatically created in the Windows Server 2008 environment are "netlogon" and "sysvol." They can only be accessed by the system administrator or a user with equal to system administrator privileges. The share labeled "Test Folder1" in Figure 7-7 was created for demonstration purposes. This shared folder can be accessed by anyone with the proper permissions.

Permissions granted to shares delegate who can use the share and in what way. Permissions to a share can be granted at the user or group level. Examples of permissions are Full Control, Modify, Read, and Write.

Tech Tip

The permissions available for selection will vary according to partition file type (NTFS, FAT, etc.), the type of user account (local or domain), and the operating system version or edition.

Figure 7-8 shows the permissions assigned to the group *Everyone* for the shared folder, test share. The group *Everyone* is assigned the Full Control permission over the contents of the folder. When a user is assigned to the group *Everyone*, the user will be able to have full control over the shared folder, test share.

Copyright Goodheart-Willcox Co., Inc.

Figure 7-7 Shares are indicated by the object's icon with a cable connection. This indicates that the share is network accessible.

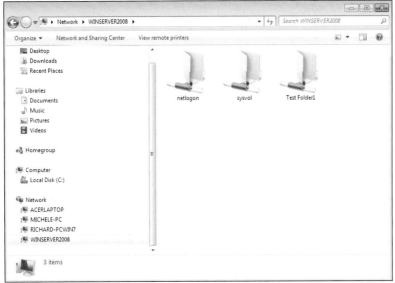

Goodheart-Willcox Publisher

Figure 7-8 Permissions granted to the group **Everyone** for the **test share** folder.

Goodheart-Willcox Publisher

File-Sharing Protocols

Microsoft Windows Server uses the **Server Message Block (SMB)** protocol to support file sharing from a Windows operating system. SMB is also referred to as

Common Internet File System (CIFS), which is technically incorrect. CIFS was an attempt by Microsoft to standardize a universal file-sharing protocol for the Internet to be used by all operating systems. Today, CIFS is considered a dialect of SMB. SMB is not limited to file sharing. SMB is also used to support network printing, network browsing, and locating other SMB servers on the network.

The other major file-sharing protocol is **Network File System (NFS)**, which is used by Unix and Linux operating systems. There will be more about NFS in Chapter 8.

Disk Management

The disk management tool that comes with Windows Server as well as desktop operating systems is graphical. Figure 7-9 shows the hard drive volumes of a Windows machine displayed with a disk management tool. Notice that the system has two hard disk drives, Disk 0 and Disk 1. Disk 0 is formatted with NTFS. If there were any area of the disk not yet formatted, the label Unallocated would appear. The size of each partition and its location in the directory structure is displayed. Note the color code used to indicate the primary partition, extended partition, and logical drives. Disk management tools and disk terminology are discussed in more detail later in this chapter.

Figure 7-9 The Disk Management tool provides a graphical display of disks, volumes, partitions, the type of file system, and more.

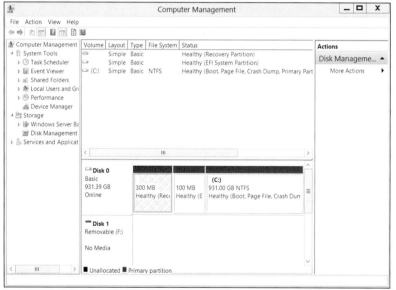

Goodheart-Willcox Publisher

New Technology File System

The **New Technology File System (NTFS)** is the native file format for Windows NT and Windows Server operating systems. NTFS was introduced with Windows NT 3.1. The original file system, known as *File Allocation Table (FAT)* or *FAT16* has several limitations. It is limited to a 2-GB partition, which has made it obsolete by

Copyright Goodheart-Willcox Co., Inc.

today's standards. This is a severe limitation for a server that needs to provide a large amount of storage space. FAT32 overcame the FAT16 size limitation. FAT32 can create a partition size of up to 32 GB. FAT16 is also limited to eight-character file names and a three-character extension. FAT32 can use file names with a maximum length of 255 characters. NTFS, on the other hand, can create partition sizes as large as 16 exabytes (EB). NTFS file names can be as long as 255 characters and have multiple extensions. See Figure 7-10 for a comparison of FAT16, FAT32, and NTFS.

Note

One exabyte (EB) is equal to one quintillion bytes, or one billion GB.

Figure 7-10 File system comparison chart.

File System	Partition Size (Maximum)	File Name (Maximum characters)	File Extension (Maximum characters)
FAT16	2 GB	8	3
FAT32	32 GB	255	*
NTFS	16 EB	255	*

*For FAT32 and NTFS, the file extension is optional.

Goodheart-Willcox Publisher

Note that for FAT32 and NTFS, the file extension is optional. Commonly used extensions have three characters to maintain backward compatibility, but this is less of an issue today. Some Microsoft Office documents are saved with four-letter extensions, such as DOCx. The main difference between the original DOS file extension and those used today is for the original DOS file you can only use the period symbol once to identify the file extension. Today, file names can contain more than one period, for example MyFile.one.two.three.four.doc. The period is an accepted special symbol that can be used in the file path and file name.

When Windows 2000 was released, the NTFS file system was further improved and was introduced by Microsoft as dynamic disk. Since the release of dynamic disk, it has been renamed NTFS5.0. The original NT file system was renamed NTFS4.0 so the two could be easily distinguished. NTFS4.0 and NTFS5.0 are covered in detail later in this chapter.

An excellent feature of the NTFS file system is disk quota. **Disk quota** is the amount of disk space assigned to specific users. A common problem with networks that have shared hard disk drive space is users filling disk space with graphics and audio files. Graphics and audio files take a tremendous amount of storage space when compared with database files and document files.

NTFS allows the administrator to allot a specific amount of disk space to a user and a warning level in the **Quota Settings** menu, shown in Figure 7-11. As the user approaches the limit (warning level) of his or her assigned disk space, a warning message appears on the screen. The message is displayed before the user runs out of space. This is so the user may purge some of his or her files or request additional space from the system administrator.

Networking Fundamentals

Figure 7-11 Disk storage space can be controlled using the Quota Settings option.

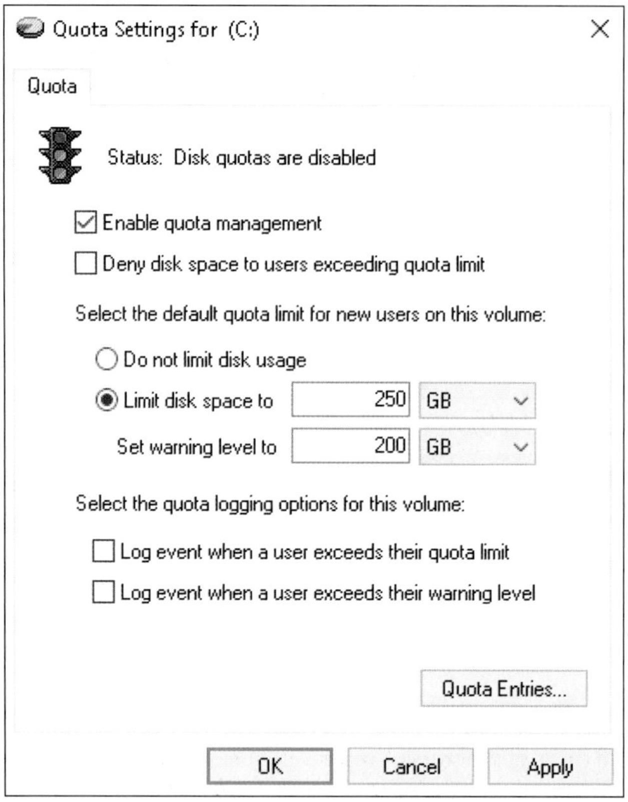

Quota Settings for (C:)   ✕

Quota

🚦 Status: Disk quotas are disabled

☑ Enable quota management
☐ Deny disk space to users exceeding quota limit

Select the default quota limit for new users on this volume:

○ Do not limit disk usage
⦿ Limit disk space to   250 | GB ⌄
    Set warning level to   200 | GB ⌄

Select the quota logging options for this volume:

☐ Log event when a user exceeds their quota limit
☐ Log event when a user exceeds their warning level

                              Quota Entries...

        OK   Cancel   Apply

Goodheart-Willcox Publisher

Tech Tip

Be aware that many resources refer to any Microsoft Server product and network system as simply Microsoft NT even though the Microsoft Server product is a later technology belonging to Windows 2000 Server, Windows Server 2003, and Windows Server 2008–2016.

Share- and User-Level Permissions

Not only does NTFS offer larger disk capacity, it also offers many security features that were not available directly for FAT16 and FAT32. NTFS can be configured to share directories and control access to files. FAT16 and FAT32 allow only for share-level security. **Share-level security** provides password protection for a share and minimal share permissions. Share-level permissions are commonly called *share permissions*, as seen in Figure 7-12. Share-level security applies only to shares that are accessed over the network. It does not secure shares that are accessed locally. For example, a user who accesses a shared directory over the network may be asked to provide a password or may be limited to only **Read** access. If the same user accesses the shared directory locally, no security would be enforced. The user would be able to make changes to the file.

An object which is to be shared, such as a folder, can be directly configured by simply right-clicking the desired folder and selecting **Share** from the shortcut menu. This applies to all Microsoft operating systems, both desktop and server versions. Once accessed, you are provided with two buttons: **Share Permissions** and **NTFS Permissions**. The **Share Permissions** option is provided for configuring folders

Copyright Goodheart-Willcox Co., Inc.

Figure 7-12 Share-level permissions, or share permissions, dictate how much access and authority a user has for a given file.

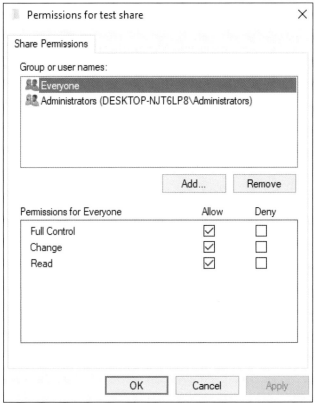

Goodheart-Willcox Publisher

based on FAT file system permissions. The **NTFS Permissions** option is used to configure folder access based on NTFS permissions. You may use either system to configure permissions for an object. When both share permissions and NTFS permissions are applied to the same share, there can be a conflict. When a conflict with permissions occurs, the most restrictive permission is always applied to the object. The following is a list of NTFS and share permissions for the Windows operating systems:

NTFS Permissions

- Full Control
- Modify
- Read & Execute
- List Folder Contents
- Read
- Write
- Special Permissions

Share Permissions

- Full Control
- Change
- Read

NTFS allows for user-level security. **User-level security** requires a user to authenticate through a security database to access a share. During authentication, user permissions are checked and access to the share is given accordingly. User-level security provides security to shares accessed over the network and locally. User-level security permissions are commonly called *NTFS permissions* or just *permissions*. **NTFS permissions** can be applied to both the directory level and file level. Starting with Microsoft Server 2008, the Share and Storage Management tool was added to allow you to set up shares and permissions for the network. This tool is accessed directly off the **Administrative Tools** menu as shown in Figure 7-13. After selecting the **Share and Storage Management** menu item, a screen appears similar to the one in Figure 7-14. **Share and Storage Management** provides a centralized location for share and storage configuration and modification.

Figure 7-13 Shares and disk storage can be managed through Computer Management.

Goodheart-Willcox Publisher

Figure 7-14 Share and Storage Management displays all shares and all storage areas available for the network.

Goodheart-Willcox Publisher

Copyright Goodheart-Willcox Co., Inc.

All shares and storage areas available for the network are displayed in Share and Storage Management. The dollar sign symbol indicates shares and storage controlled solely by the system administrator. You can create a new share by selecting the **New Share** button located in the **Action** menu, as demonstrated in Figure 7-14. Once **New Share** is selected, a wizard will open with a dialog box similar to the one in Figure 7-15.

Figure 7-15 The server provides a wizard to assist with creating a share.

Goodheart-Willcox Publisher

The **Create a Shared Folder Wizard** will guide the administrator through a series of dialog boxes that will automatically configure a new folder share or modify an existing share. You will be able to select features such as who can access the folder and what permissions to assign to the folder. You can also limit the number of users who can access the folder at one time. The wizard provides a foolproof method of creating a shared folder so that no aspect of a proper share creation is left out. It can create shares not only on the server but also anywhere in the entire network domain.

Tech Tip

Although both Share and NTFS permissions can be applied to a share, it is best to set only the NTFS permissions and to leave the Share permissions set to their default. Working with both types of permissions is unnecessary and complicates administration.

Administrative Tools

Administrative tools are designed to make network administration easy and convenient. Some of the administrative tools allow the administrator to view logs, manage the domain, manage users and groups, configure the server, set security policies, and add and manage services. Windows provides a wide variety of administrative tools located directly from the **Control Panel** menu, as displayed in

Figure 7-16. Some of the most commonly used administrative tools are Active Directory User and Computers, Computer Management, Event Viewer, and Share and Storage Management.

Note

The Active Directory tools will only appear as a menu item after the server is configured for Active Directory.

The Microsoft Management Console (MMC) is accessed by selecting **Computer Management** or running **MMC** in the **Start Search** box located at the bottom of the **Start** menu. MMC is an early version of an administrative tool that can be used to complete some of the most common administrative tasks in a centralized location. The MMC is covered in detail later in this chapter. You will find that the features of many of these administrative tools are very similar to administrative tools found in a typical Windows desktop operating systems such as Windows 7, 8, or 10.

Figure 7-16 Windows provides a wide variety of Administrative Tools located directly off the **Control Panel** menu.

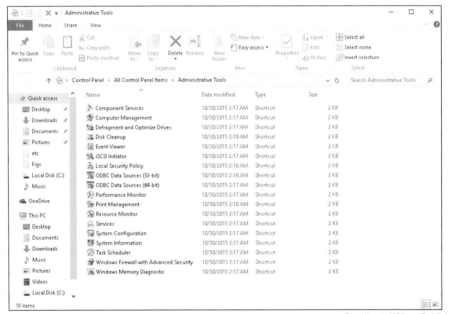

Goodheart-Willcox Publisher

Active Directory Domain Services

Microsoft introduced Active Directory with the introduction of Windows Server 2000. Active Directory features vastly improved the way network systems shared information. Today, **Active Directory (AD)** is the Windows Server standard used to manage large and small network systems. It uses a hierarchical directory structure that is designed as a database containing information about objects belonging to the entire network. In the Active Directory environment, an **object** is any physical or logical unit that is defined as part of the network. Some examples of objects are users, groups, printers, volumes, directories, and services. Active Directory stores information about each object in its database, including usernames, passwords, permissions,

Copyright Goodheart-Willcox Co., Inc.

and restrictions. AD is not installed by default when installing the server operating system. It is configured as a server role after the server operating system is installed.

Note

Starting with Windows Server 2008, Active Directory is referred to as *Active Directory Domain Services (AD DS)*.

Active Directory uses Lightweight Directory Access Protocol (LDAP) as well as Hypertext Transfer Protocol (HTTP) to transmit directory information between domain controllers. Both LDAP and HTTP are Internet standard protocols. LDAP allows the exchange of directory information between different computer platforms. For example, a server running Windows Server can freely exchange directory information with a Unix/Linux server as long as both use LDAP. HTTP is the protocol used on the Internet that determines how web pages are displayed. HTTP is used to display directory information across the network in a form of a web page. Later in the textbook, you will see the striking similarity of the Active Directory structure and the Novell SUSE Linux directory structure. This is because both are based on LDAP technology.

Tech Tip

Do not confuse HTTP with HTML. HTML is an authoring language used to create documents that appear as web pages. It is not a protocol.

Active Directory Structure

Active Directory is a hierarchical structure that consists of forests, trees, domains, and organizational units (OUs), as seen in Figure 7-17. The definition and an introduction to each are presented briefly in this section. An in-depth knowledge of the Active Directory structure requires in-depth study and more information than can be presented here.

Figure 7-17 An Active Directory hierarchical structure consists of a forest, trees, domains, and organizational units.

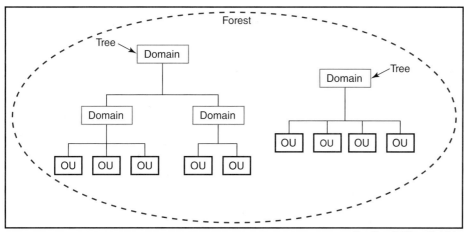

Goodheart-Willcox Publisher

The hierarchical structure is designed like the Internet structure. Look at Figure 7-18. Objects inside a hierarchical structure can be traced to a root, or root domain. Each object in the hierarchical structure is a part of the object above it.

Domains

As previously discussed, a domain is a logical grouping of users and equipment as defined by the network administrator. Users and equipment, such as computers, are assigned to a domain for administrative purposes and security. A small company may use a single domain name for the entire business. A large company may divide the company into several distinct domains. For example, a company spanning the United States may divide the company into regions, such as San Francisco, New York, and Orlando. Look at the example in Figure 7-19. This example consists of three distant locations connected via the Internet or a private line. Although each region is represented as a separate domain, it is set up to allow the free flow of data and communication between them. The flow of data and communication can also be restricted.

Tech Tip

The term *domain* as it is used here should not be confused with the term *domain* used in Internet terminology. The term *domain* when used in Internet terminology describes a collection of computers sharing an Internet name or address. A better understanding of the differences will become evident after reading Chapter 10.

Another scenario is the company illustrated in Figure 7-20. The company spans several distant locations yet is configured into a single domain. Typically, multiple domains are used to organize a large company into logical working units such as re-

Figure 7-18 Internet domain structure. A—In an Internet domain structure, objects can be traced back to a root domain. The root domain in this example is com. B—The domain structure in this example has been broken into sections to illustrate how each object in the hierarchy belongs to the object above it.

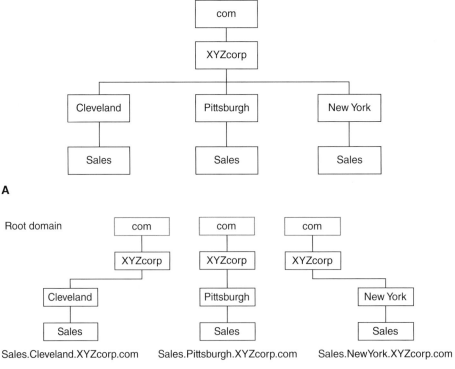

Goodheart-Willcox Publisher

Copyright Goodheart-Willcox Co., Inc.

Figure 7-19 The XYZcorp company has assigned each of its locations to a separate domain. The domains have been configured to allow the free flow of data between them.

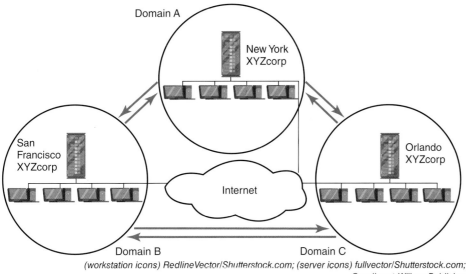

(workstation icons) RedlineVector/Shutterstock.com; (server icons) fullvector/Shutterstock.com;
Goodheart-Willcox Publisher

Figure 7-20 A company may span several distant locations yet be configured as a single domain.

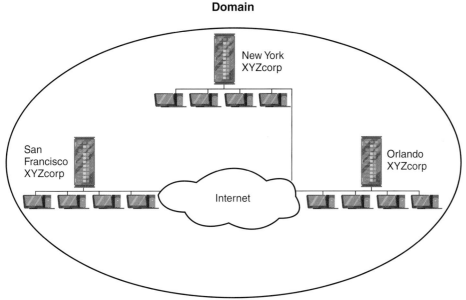

(workstation icons) RedlineVector/Shutterstock.com; (server icons) fullvector/Shutterstock.com;
Goodheart-Willcox Publisher

search, sales, accounting, executive administration, and human resources. There is no one set method to arrange a domain structure. The size and arrangement of a domain structure design is left to the network engineer or administrator.

The members of the domain need not be physically located together. They are joined by using the same root domain name and having an account established in the domain.

Typically, each domain in the Active Directory structure must conform to the naming convention used by the Domain Name System (DNS). The term *root domain* can be confusing because it is also used when describing the Internet structure. In the Internet, the root domain is the highest level of the organizational structure and is composed of a period and a name such as .edu and .com. In Active Directory, the

Copyright Goodheart-Willcox Co., Inc.

root domain is the highest level of the organizational structure but consists of a name followed by a dot and a name such as XYZ.com.

Trees and Forests

In the simplest of terms, a **tree** is a collection of domains that share a common root domain name and Active Directory database. A **forest** is a collection of domain trees that share a common Active Directory database. The definitions are very similar, but the most important trait that distinguishes whether a domain is part of a tree or forest is the domain name. For a domain to belong to a tree, it must share a contiguous namespace. A forest is a collection of domain trees that have disjointed namespaces. To understand these definitions better, definitions for the terms *namespace, contiguous namespace*, and *disjointed namespace* must first be established.

A **namespace** is a label that identifies a unique location in a structure such as the Internet. The uniform resource locator (URL) standard uses a namespace to identify locations on the Internet. For an object or location to conform to a **contiguous namespace** standard, it must use the root domain name as part of its URL or as its complete name. For example, the root domain name in an Active Directory structure is G-W.com. For a domain in the Active Directory to have a contiguous namespace with G-W.com, the G-W.com must be part of its domain name, for example, Chicago.G-W.com. Any domain name that is a part of the Active Directory, but does not follow the contiguous namespace requirement is considered a **disjointed namespace**. A disjointed namespace occurs commonly when two networks are merged or an existing network is upgraded using Windows 2000 Active Directory. When two organizations or companies merge, it is unlikely that they will have a contiguous namespace. Look at Figure 7-21 for an example.

Figure 7-21 Example of a contiguous namespace and a disjointed namespace. Domains that share a contiguous namespace have a common root domain name. A disjointed namespace does not share a common root domain with the other domains in the Active Directory. A disjointed namespace in an Active Directory indicates that the domains within it are a part of a forest.

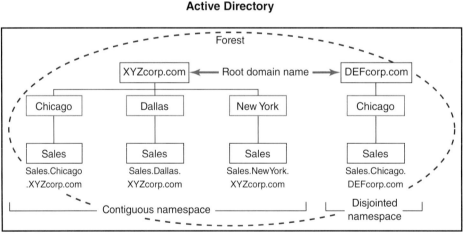

Goodheart-Willcox Publisher

In the illustration, you can see three domains with a contiguous namespace: Chicago.XYZcorp.com, Dallas.XYZcorp.com, and NewYork.XYZcorp.com. These three are in contrast to the other domain name, Chicago.DEFcorp.com, which has a different root domain name. The root domain name is the determining factor that distinguishes whether a domain is part of a tree or forest. The URL Chicago.DEFcorp.com is a disjointed namespace and is therefore part of a forest.

Copyright Goodheart-Willcox Co., Inc.

Tech Tip

Forest and tree definitions came after the original NT domain structure. Because of the radical changes, an existing NT domain may not meet the criteria to belong to a tree.

Organizational Unit

An **organizational unit** is a container that holds objects or other organizational units. Organizational units serve to organize a network into manageable units and often model a company's business structure. Look at Figure 7-22. A tree with a root domain name of XYZcorp.com has a domain named Chicago. This domain has an organizational unit for each department in the Chicago office. The Chicago.XYZcorp.com domain has *Accounting*, *Administration*, and *Warehouse* organizational units. Each organizational unit contains objects that belong to each department. An object in Active Directory can be any component that is part of the network, such as users, groups, computers, and printers.

Figure 7-22 Organizational units are used to organize a network into manageable units. An organizational unit can contain organizational units and objects. Examples of objects are users, groups, computers, and printers.

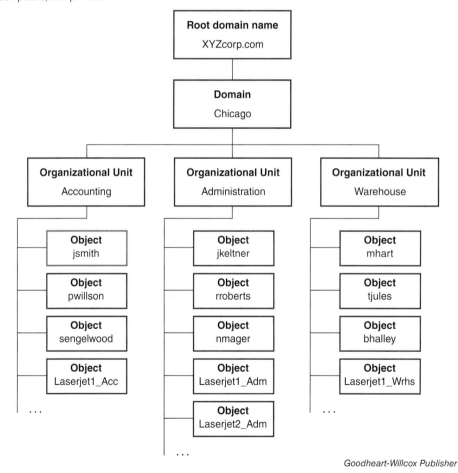

Goodheart-Willcox Publisher

Copyright Goodheart-Willcox Co., Inc.

Common Name

When an administrator creates a new object in the directory, the administrator also assigns a name to identify it. This name is called a *common name (CN)*. The object also receives a number called a *globally unique identifier (GUID)*. The GUID links to the distinguished name. A **distinguished name** uniquely identifies the location of the object in the Active Directory structure. An example of a distinguished name for an object named *jsmith* located in the Accounting organizational unit in the Chicago.XYZcorp.com domain would be CN=*jsmith*, OU=*Accounting*, DC=Chicago.XYZcorp.com.

The letters in front of the names are referred to as *attributes*. The following list defines each attribute:

- DC=Domain component
- OU=Organizational unit
- CN=Common name

The distinguished name is an LDAP requirement. The attributes are used to decode distinguished names when transferring directory information between two dissimilar network operating system directories. You will see a similar naming structure in SUSE Linux.

Network+ Note

Be careful when answering a question that contains the term *domain*. Look at the context in which the term *domain* is used. The term *domain* in a Windows NT network content refers to the network, not to the Internet domain. In a Windows network, the term *domain* means the network name and Internet domain name.

Authentication

In a Windows network, authentication occurs during two types of processes: when a user logs on to the network and when the user requests access to a resource. The first process is called *interactive logon*, and the second process is called *network authentication*.

During the **interactive logon**, the user is verified and given access to the Active Directory. When the user accesses a resource, the network authentication process occurs. During **network authentication**, the security descriptor of the resource the user wishes to access is verified. The security descriptor contains information regarding users and groups, permissions, auditing, and ownership. The security descriptor applies to objects in the Active Directory, such as resources, users, and groups. The interactive logon and the network authentication processes use the *Kerberos v5* authentication protocol. Kerberos is covered in detail in Chapter 15.

Windows 2016 uses a single sign-on method. This means that once the user is authenticated and given access to the Active Directory, the user can access any computer in the Active Directory to which he or she has permission. The user does not have to log on again. Authentication occurs behind the scenes and is handled through the network authentication process.

AD Replication

Active Directory allows the use of more than one domain controller within a domain. The Active Directory database is replicated on all domain controllers within the

Copyright Goodheart-Willcox Co., Inc.

domain so that each has the current status of all objects in the network. For example, if an administrator disables a user account, the information is instantly transmitted to all domain controllers in the domain.

Windows NT servers use a *primary domain controller (PDC)* and a *backup domain controller (BDC)*. Microsoft servers today configured with Active Directory no longer use the earlier design of a PDC and BDC. Servers in a Microsoft Windows network can perform one of three roles: domain controller (DC), member server, and stand-alone server. The Windows Server environment uses a process called **multimaster replication**. In this model, all DCs are equal. Each DC stores a copy of the Active Directory database, as demonstrated in Figure 7-23. Changes to the database can be made at any DC in the domain. When changes to the database are made, the changes are replicated to the other DCs.

Figure 7-23 A Windows 2000/2003/2008/2016 Active Directory can have multiple domain controllers. An administrator may make changes to the Active Directory at any of the domain controllers. Changes are replicated to every domain controller in the domain.

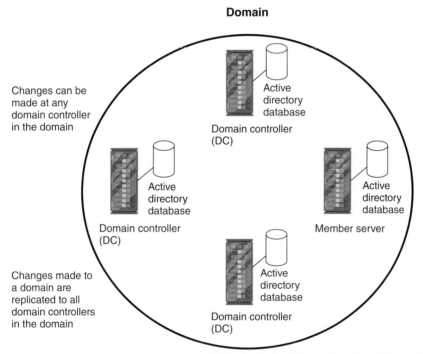

(server icons) fullvector/Shutterstock.com; Goodheart-Willcox Publisher

The Read Only Domain Controller (RODC) was introduced in Windows Server 2008 as an optional configuration. RODC is designed to be used in locations that are hard to secure or locations such as branch offices that do not have IT support administrators assigned on-site. The intention of RODC is to prevent personnel from tinkering with the server, which could result in disabling the system or creating a security problem. The RODC has a read-only Active Directory structure, and the DNS portion of the server cannot be modified. As an option, a person at the RODC location can be given very limited administrative privileges, such as capabilities to install hardware drivers. User accounts at the RODC site cannot access other domain controllers at other locations. Also, users are not authenticated at the RODC. User authentication is performed through a regular domain controller at another site.

Windows Server 2008 and 2016 use a Primary Domain Controller Emulator to ensure backward compatibility with Windows NT, 2000, and 2003. The Primary Domain Controller Emulator provides the same function as the earlier PDC. When

Copyright Goodheart-Willcox Co., Inc.

there are multiple servers in a domain providing similar services such as user log-on service, there is still only one PDC Emulator, which is the ultimate authority for user account security. For example, when a user password is updated on one of the servers, it is automatically sent to the designated master PDC Emulator server. The master PDC Emulator is responsible for distributing up-to-date and accurate information to the other servers.

Trust Relationships

To allow the free flow of data and communication between domains, a trust relationship between the domains must be established. A **trust relationship** is a relationship between domains that allows users from one domain to access resources on another domain in which they do not have a user account. The user can then access resources on another domain without having to log on to that domain. The user, however, must have permissions to access the resources.

A trust relationship can be set up to allow domains to have a two-way trust relationship or a one-way trust relationship. In a **two-way trust relationship,** both domains are designated as a *trusted domain* and a *trusting domain.* A two-way trust relationship allows both domains in the trust relationship to share its resources with the other. A two-way trust relationship is sometimes referred to as a *full-trust relationship.* Figure 7-24 shows an example of a two-way trust relationship. *Domain A* trusts *Domain B* and allows *Domain B* to access its resources. *Domain B* trusts *Domain A* and allows *Domain A* to access its resources.

In a **one-way trust relationship**, one domain is the trusted domain and the other is the trusting domain. The trusting domain allows the trusted domain to access its resources. Look at the one-way trust relationship established in Figure 7-25. *Domain B* has been designated the trusting domain and *Domain A* has been designated the trusted domain. In other words, *Domain B* trusts *Domain A* to access its resources. However, since a one-way trust has been established, *Domain A* does not trust *Domain B* to access its resources.

Two-way trust relationships can be implemented to develop a complex trust relationship. A **complex trust relationship** is a trust relationship in which more than two domains have a full-trust relationship. Notice that a two-way trust relationship is established between all three domains in Figure 7-26. Trust relationships can also be formed between forests in addition to domains.

Figure 7-24 This is an example of a two-way trust relationship established between two domains. Each domain can access resources on the other domain.

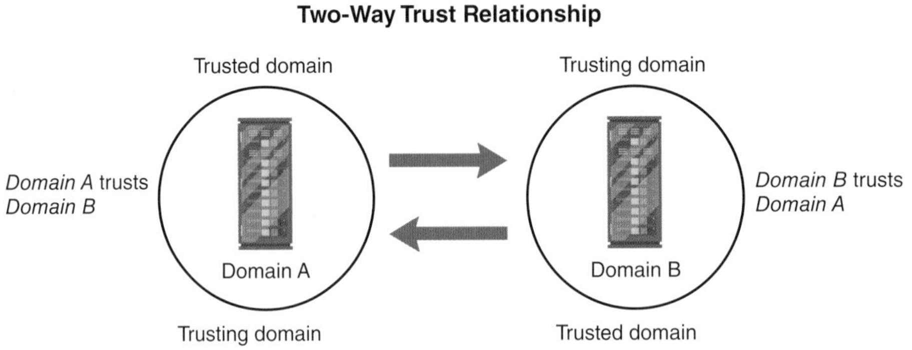

Two-Way Trust Relationship

Trusted domain

Trusting domain

Domain A trusts *Domain B*

Domain B trusts *Domain A*

Domain A

Domain B

Trusting domain

Trusted domain

(server icons) fullvector/Shutterstock.com; Goodheart-Willcox Publisher

Copyright Goodheart-Willcox Co., Inc.

Figure 7-25 In a one-way trust relationship, a domain may access resources on another domain even though there is no user account established on the other domain. The trust honors the logon authentication of the domain the user is in.

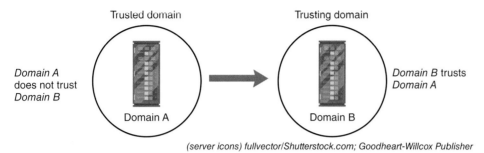

One-Way Trust Relationship

Trusted domain   Trusting domain

Domain A does not trust Domain B

Domain A

Domain B trusts *Domain A*

Domain B

(server icons) fullvector/Shutterstock.com; Goodheart-Willcox Publisher

Figure 7-26 An example of a complex trust relationship. You can think of a complex trust relationship as two-way trusts established between all domains in the configuration.

Complex Trust Relationship

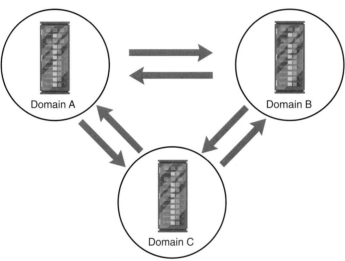

Domain A

Domain B

Domain C

(server icons) fullvector/Shutterstock.com; Goodheart-Willcox Publisher

Forest Trusts

When you create a new domain in the same forest, you automatically create a two-way trust. A **forest trust** is a two-way trust and is designed to share resources between the two forests. In a forest trust, users can be authenticated in either forest.

External Trusts

An **external trust** is created when Windows Server 2016 configures a trust relationship with an older Windows Server operating system or with another Windows Server 2016 computer or when the other domain is located in an entirely separate forest. The two forests are not joined in an external trust relationship.

Copyright Goodheart-Willcox Co., Inc.

Realm Trusts

A **realm trust** is formed when you create a trust relationship between a Windows Server 2016 domain and a non-Windows domain, for example, when you wish to establish a trust relationship between Windows Server 2016 and a Unix/Linux network system. A realm trust also applies to creating a trust relationship between Windows Server 2016 and any network that does not use Kerberos 5 to implement the authentication of user accounts.

Windows Server Administration

Windows Server administration includes utilities for managing objects in the Active Directory and setting security policies. The following is a table of the utilities covered in this section and a description of each:

Utility	Description
Computer Management	Allows an administrator to add local users to a Windows server.
Active Directory Users and Computers	Allows an administrator to manage users, groups, computers, and OUs in the Active Directory.
Local Security Policy	Allows an administrator to set global security policies for a single computer.
Domain Security Policy	Allows an administrator to set global security policies for the entire domain.
Disk Management	Allows an administrator to manage a server's hard disk drives.

These utilities can be accessed individually or through the Microsoft Management Console (MMC). The MMC was first introduced with Windows 2000.

Note

Beginning with Windows Server 2008, the Domain Security Policy utility was modified and renamed *Group Policy Management Console.*

Microsoft Management Console

Microsoft Management Console (MMC) is used as an interface to commonly used utilities in Windows 2000 and later operating systems. The MMC can be used on any Microsoft system including Windows 95, 98, and NT. The MMC is not a utility itself, but rather a container that holds commonly used utilities. It is set up as a customized Windows interface. It is empty by default and allows the user to select utilities from one convenient location.

A tool or utility that is added to the MMC is referred to as a **snap-in**. Figure 7-27 shows some of the many snap-ins that can be added to the MMC. When the snap-ins are selected, they are automatically sent to the MMC. Figure 7-28 shows a customized MMC.

Copyright Goodheart-Willcox Co., Inc.

Figure 7-27 List of snap-ins that can be added to the Microsoft Management Console (MMC).

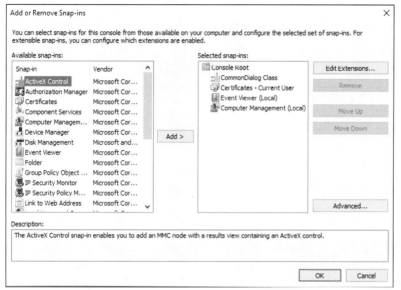

Goodheart-Willcox Publisher

Figure 7-28 Example of a customized MMC.

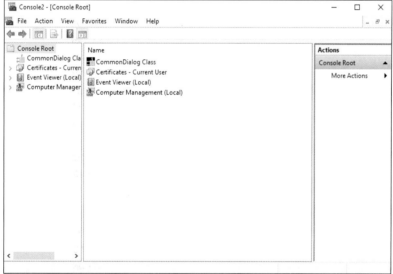

Goodheart-Willcox Publisher

Managing Local Users and Groups

Local users and groups are managed on the server by using the **Computer Management** utility or the MMC Computer Management snap-in. To add a new user, right-click the **Users** folder in the left-hand pane of the Computer Management window or the MMC. Select **New User** from the shortcut menu. The **New User** dialog box displays, as in Figure 7-29. Complete the requested information.

Tech Tip

You cannot create a local user account on a domain controller or view local user accounts on a server that has been promoted to domain controller status.

Figure 7-29 The Windows 10 **New User** dialog box for adding local users.

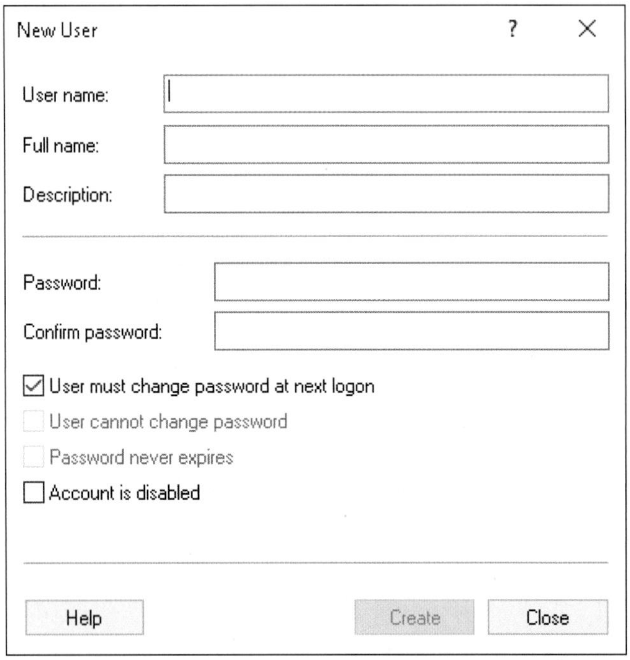

New User dialog box with the following fields:
- User name:
- Full name:
- Description:
- Password:
- Confirm password:
- ☑ User must change password at next logon
- ☐ User cannot change password
- ☐ Password never expires
- ☐ Account is disabled

Buttons: Help, Create, Close

Goodheart-Willcox Publisher

You may select a password option from the options beneath the **Confirm Password** text box or leave it set to the default. The default is set to the **User Must Change Password at Next Logon** option. This option means that the user needs to change his or her password when he or she logs on to the system the first time. When the user completes the logon, he or she will be prompted to change the password. The administrator will not know the user's password after the user changes it. As you can see, security starts with the user password and can be very strict.

Adding more restrictions to passwords can further enhance security. This can be accomplished in the **Local Security Policy** utility. Various policies can be set to increase password security, such as keeping a history of the user's password to prevent reuse, specifying a minimum and maximum password length, and forcing the user to select a password that meets complexity requirements.

Account lockout policies can be set that cause the user account to be locked if the user incorrectly enters the password a number of times, as demonstrated in Figure 7-30. This prevents unauthorized persons from attempting to guess a user's password. Lockout times can be set to last a few minutes to an indefinite period of time. A lockout time that is set for an indefinite period requires that the system administrator unlock the account. This explanation is a brief overview of how a user account can be configured and some of the security policies that can be established.

Groups can be added by right-clicking the **Groups** folder and selecting **New Group** from the shortcut menu. When the **New Group** dialog box displays, enter a group name and a description. To add members to the group, click **Add**. The **Select Users** dialog box displays. Click **Advanced** and then **Find Now**. You can select mul-

Copyright Goodheart-Willcox Co., Inc.

Figure 7-30 Account lockout policy settings.

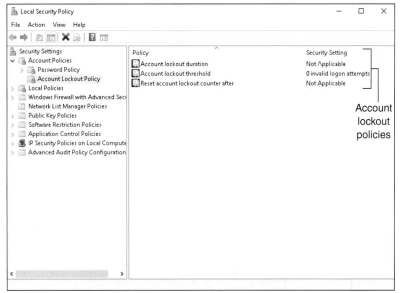

Goodheart-Willcox Publisher

tiple users by holding down the [Ctrl] key as you click each user's name. After you have selected the desired users, click **OK**. Click **OK** again to close the **Select Users** dialog box. In the **New Group** dialog box, click **Create** and then click **Close**.

Tech Tip

Network security has become such an issue in networking and e-commerce that it has created the demand for highly trained specialists. If you wish to become a certified network administrator, you must learn everything there is about a particular network operating system's security.

Managing Domain Users and Groups

Domain users and groups are accounts that are members of a domain. Domain user and group accounts can only be created at a server that is a domain controller. The Active Directory Users and Computers utility is used to add user accounts and group accounts to the domain.

To add a user to the domain, open the Active Directory Users and Computers utility. Right-click the container you wish to add the user to and select **New**>**User** from the shortcut menu. The **New Object—User** dialog box displays, as referenced in Figure 7-31. Enter the user's first, middle, and last name in the appropriate text boxes, shown in Figure 7-31A. The **Full name** text box is automatically completed as you enter this information. Enter a logon name and then click **Next**. Enter a password in the **Password** and **Confirm Password** text boxes, as in Figure 7-31B. Change the password options to reflect the security policies set for the network. Click **Next** and review the account settings, similar to Figure 7-31C. Click **Finish** if the settings are correct. Otherwise, click **Back** to review and change the settings in the previous screens.

To add a group to the domain, open the Active Directory Users and Computers utility. Right-click the container you wish to add the group to and select **New**>**Group** from the shortcut menu. The **New Object—Group** dialog box will display. Enter the name of the group in the **Group name** text box. The **Group name (pre-Windows**

Copyright Goodheart-Willcox Co., Inc.

Figure 7-31 The **New Object—User** dialog box in the Active Directory Users and Computers utility. A—The user's full name is automatically entered when the first and last name and middle initial are entered. B—Enter and confirm the user account password and select password options. C—Review the new user account settings and click **Finish** if the settings are correct.

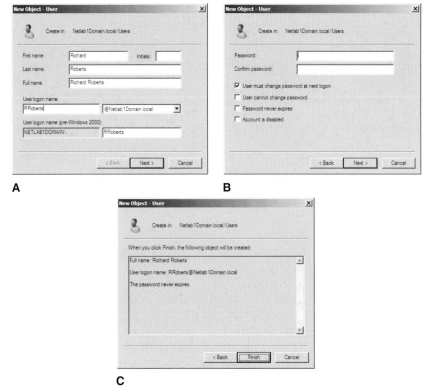

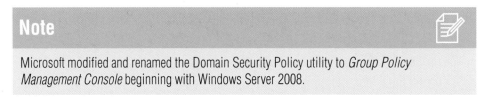

Goodheart-Willcox Publisher

2000) text box will be completed automatically with this name. Leave the **Group scope** and **Group type** options at their default settings. To learn more about these options, see **Help and Support** located in the server's **Start** menu.

> ## Note
>
> Microsoft modified and renamed the Domain Security Policy utility to *Group Policy Management Console* beginning with Windows Server 2008.

Password restrictions and account policies for a domain can be further enhanced through the Domain Security Policy utility. This utility provides the same policies as the Local Security Policy utility.

To modify the password and account lockout-policy settings for the domain, open the Domain Security Policy utility. In the left-hand pane of the Domain Security Policy window, expand the **Account Policy** folder. Select **Password Policy**. In the right-hand pane, right-click the policy you wish to modify. Select **Properties** from the shortcut menu. The **Properties** dialog box for the selected policy displays, as shown in Figure 7-32. Make the desired changes, and then click **OK**.

Windows Disk Management

The Disk Management utility is used to create partitions and volumes, format volumes, and to add fault tolerance. Windows Server is installed on an NTFS partition. It also supports older file systems such as FAT16 and FAT32; however, these file systems are no longer options for installing a modern Windows server operating system.

Figure 7-32 Password policies are modified by right-clicking the password policy, selecting Properties from the shortcut menu, and entering the changes.

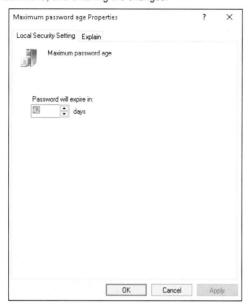

Maximum password age Properties   ?   ✕

Local Security Setting   Explain

Maximum password age

Password will expire in:

42   days

OK   Cancel   Apply

Goodheart-Willcox Publisher

Tech Tip

Windows 2000 Server and Windows Server 2003–2016 can be installed on a FAT16, FAT32, and NTFS partition. An NTFS partition offers the highest level of security.

Disk Management Terminology

Some terminology you should be familiar with when working with the Disk Management utility is *physical drive, free space, partition, primary partition, extended partition, logical drive, volume,* and *volume set.* The **physical drive** is the hard disk drive inside the computer. The computer BIOS assigns a number to each physical drive in the computer. This number is displayed in Disk Management as *Disk 0, Disk 1,* and so on. See Figure 7-33. Displaying the disk number aids the administrator in properly identifying the hard disk drive before making changes to it.

Free space is the space on a hard disk drive that has not been partitioned. A **partition** is an area of the hard disk drive that is to be allocated to an operating system. When a hard disk drive is partitioned, it is assigned a drive letter and becomes a **logical drive**. This term makes sense when you think that a hard disk drive can be divided into multiple partitions and assigned a separate drive letter.

A hard disk drive may contain up to four primary partitions, as in Figure 7-34. A **primary partition** is a partition that stores a bootable copy of an operating system. Although four primary partitions, or bootable partitions, may exist on a single hard disk drive, only one primary partition can be active at a time, Figure 7-34A.

An administrator may want to store an operating system's boot files and system files on the primary partition and create an extended partition with logical drives on which to store data. An **extended partition** is a partition that can contain one or more logical drives. Only one extended partition can exist on a hard disk drive, Figure 7-34B.

Figure 7-33 The Disk Management utility. Notice that colors are used to identify unallocated space, primary partition, extended partition, free space, and the logical drive.

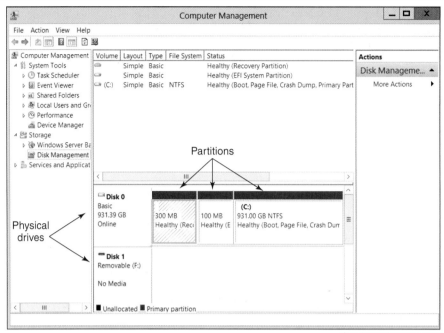

Goodheart-Willcox Publisher

Figure 7-34 Hard disk drive partition configurations. A—A hard disk drive may contain up to four primary partitions. A primary partition contains an operating system's boot files. Only one primary partition on a hard disk drive may be marked active. B—A hard disk drive may contain only one extended partition. An extended partition is not assigned a drive letter. It is instead divided into logical drives, which are assigned drive letters.

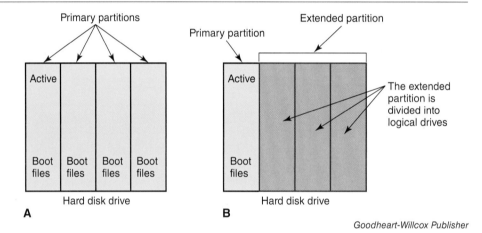

Goodheart-Willcox Publisher

Once the hard disk drive is partitioned, it can be formatted. When a hard disk drive is formatted, it is physically prepared to receive an operating system. This preparation includes dividing the surface of the hard disk drive's platters into tracks and sectors and writing pertinent information to the drive, such as a file allocation table (FAT).

A **volume** is an accessible unit of hard disk drive space as seen through the Windows interface, such as in Windows Explorer. A volume may be assigned a single drive letter yet contain multiple partitions. A volume that consists of partitions from two or more hard disk drives is called a **volume set**. An example of a volume set is shown in Figure 7-35.

Basic Disk and Dynamic Disk

Windows 2000 introduced two new disk management terms: *basic disk* and *dynamic disk*. **Basic disk** is the term applied to the old system of hard disk drive configuration. This includes creating primary and extended partitions.

Copyright Goodheart-Willcox Co., Inc.

Figure 7-35 A volume set is assigned a single drive letter and consists of partitions from multiple hard disk drives.

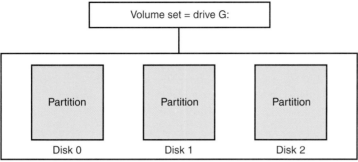

Goodheart-Willcox Publisher

In Windows Server 2016, a basic disk cannot contain volumes, volume sets, or any of the fault tolerance levels. These features are reserved for drives configured as dynamic disk. **Dynamic disk** is a new system of disk configuration and management introduced with NTFS 5.0. Dynamic Disks are managed by the system as a group. Dynamic Disk is a requirement for Active Directory. The previous versions of disk formats (FAT16, FAT32, and NTFS 4) do not meet the requirements of Active Directory. Dynamic disk allows the creation of five different volume types. These types include the following:

- simple
- spanned
- mirrored
- RAID 5
- striped

A **simple volume** exists on a single drive. A simple volume is similar to a volume in Windows NT. It is an accessible unit of hard disk drive space as seen through the Windows interface, such as in Windows Explorer. A **spanned volume** is similar to a Windows NT volume set in that it is a single volume that combines two or more physical drives. Mirrored and RAID 5 volumes incorporate fault tolerance. Fault tolerance is discussed in detail in Chapter 9. A **striped volume** increases the read/write access speed by spreading data across multiple hard disk drives. The disadvantage to this is if one of the hard disk drives in the striped set fails, the data will no longer be accessible from any of the hard disk drives in the striped volume. A striped volume, therefore, does not provide fault tolerance.

Globally Unique Identifier

Starting with the introduction of 64-bit processors and operating systems, a new partitioning style was developed. The new partitioning style is called **globally unique identifier (GUID)**, which uses a partition table called GUID partition table (GPT).

The GPT partition table is required for a 64-bit operating system to boot. It can support up to 18 (EB) and 128 partitions per disk. Both MBR and GPT disks can exist on the same computer. The GPT disk contains three new partitions in addition to any volumes created on the disk: EFI, Logical Disk Manager (LDM), and Microsoft Reserved (MSR). The EFI partition was developed as a replacement for BIOS functions. The **EFI partition** contains all programs required to boot the computer in the same way the BIOS boots the computer. The EFI is not a required partition. It can be created on a basic disk or on a GPT disk. At the time of this writing, EFI is an unproven technology and is only available for 64-bit operating systems.

The **Logical Disk Manager (LDM) partition** contains information about dynamic volumes and is created during the conversion from NTFS 4.0 to dynamic disk. There can be more than one LDM partition in a system. The **Microsoft Reserved (MSR) partition** is a required partition on every GPT disk. The MSR reserves disk space for use by system components. On a dynamic GPT disk, the first partition is the EFI if it is present, the second is the LDM, and the third is the MSR partition. Other partitions would be any additional LDM partitions.

The Disk Management utility provides tools for applying fault tolerance. The two levels of fault tolerance that can be applied to hard disk drives in a Windows Server system are RAID 1 and RAID 5. Fault tolerance is discussed in detail in Chapter 9.

POSIX

Windows Server supports the POSIX standard as defined by the IEEE. The acronym POSIX represents Portable Operating System Interface. The term *portable* is a programming term, which means that the program can be installed and run on various computer hardware systems. The C programming language by nature is very portable. A program written in C language can be run on most hardware systems despite the hardware system's manufacturer.

The POSIX standard covers areas such as file name structure, file access, and file sharing. The POSIX standard was originally designed to ensure compatibility between applications and the Unix operating system. POSIX had originally stood for Portable Operating System Interface for Unix. The term has come to mean portability with all operating systems, not just Unix.

Microsoft Windows Services for Unix introduced with Windows Server 2003 far exceed the original POSIX standards. Windows operating systems can run some Linux programs, such as scripts designed for the C Shell and Korn Shell. Linux shells are covered in Chapter 8.

Network Interoperability

Interoperability was once a major problem between different proprietary network operating systems. For example, it was often difficult and complex to configure communication between a Microsoft network and a Novell NetWare network because they both used different communication standards and protocols. Today, the default protocol for network systems is TCP/IP. Part of the TCP/IP suite of protocols is HTTP which is the protocol used to communicate across the Internet. The HTTP protocol is used to establish communication between two network systems using different operating systems, such as Linux and Microsoft or Mac OS X.

Originally, for networks of different operating systems to communicate, a gateway service was typically required. A gateway service provides translation between the different operating systems. The term *gateway* is also used to represent the network device that connects the local area network to the Internet.

Because all the major networking systems were redesigned for Internet communications and since the introduction of IPv6, networks of different design operating systems are now much easier to integrate.

Copyright Goodheart-Willcox Co., Inc.

Summary

Brief History of Microsoft Network Operating Systems

- The first network operating system from Microsoft was Windows for Workgroups and Windows NT 3.1, released in 1993.

- Computers in a Microsoft peer-to-peer network are grouped as workgroups.

- A workgroup is a group of computers that share resources.

- Computers in a Microsoft client/server network are grouped together in a domain.

- A domain is a logical grouping of users and equipment as defined by the network administrator.

Windows Server 2016

- Windows Server 2016 is Microsoft's latest server operating system.

- Three different editions of Windows Server 2016 include Standard, Datacenter, and Essentials.

- Features included in Windows Server 2016 are BranchCache, DirectAccess, Failover Cluster, Hyper-V, Internet Information Service, Network Access Protection, Remote Access, Server Core, and Nano Server.

- *Failover cluster* is the name Microsoft uses to refer to what other vendors generally call a server cluster, which is a group of individual servers connected both physically and logically to ensure constant service to clients.

Common Windows Server Administrative Components

- A domain is a logical grouping of users and equipment as defined by the network administrator; a workgroup is a group of computers that share resources such as files and hardware; and a HomeGroup is a group of computers on a residential network that can share files and printers. HomeGroup membership is optional, whereas membership to a workgroup or domain is not.

- Group accounts are collections of users that typically share a common job-oriented goal or similar function.

- Security policies are set before users are added to the network. Two types of security policies are local and global policies.

- Windows native file-sharing protocol is Server Message Block (SMB).

- The New Technology File System (NTFS) is the native file format for Windows NT and Windows Server operating systems.

- The NTFS file system is an improvement over FAT16 and FAT32.

- NTFS can create partition sizes as large as 16 EB. NTFS file names can be as long as 255 characters and have multiple extensions.

- FAT16 is limited to a 2-GB partition and to an eight-character file name with a three-character extension.

- FAT32 is limited to a 32-GB partition.

- Dynamic disk is an improved version of NTFS and is referred to as *NTFS 5.0*.

Copyright Goodheart-Willcox Co., Inc.

- Network shares have assigned permissions, such as Full Control, Modify, Read, and Write.
- Administrative shares are indicated by a dollar sign symbol.

Active Directory Domain Services

- Active Directory uses LDAP and HTTP to transfer information between domain controllers.
- The Active Directory structure consists of trees, forests, organizational units, and objects.
- A tree is a collection of domains that have a contiguous namespace and share a common Active Directory database.
- A forest is a collection of domains that have a disjointed namespace and share a common Active Directory database.
- An organizational unit is a container that holds objects or other organizational units and serves to organize a network into manageable units.
- The two processes that handle authentication in a Windows network are interactive logon and network authentication.
- Windows Server networks use the Kerberos protocol for authentication.
- A Windows 2000–2016 server can support one of three roles: domain controller (DC), member server, and stand-alone server.
- Windows Server 2000–2016 supports multimaster replication.
- A trust relationship between Windows domains allows the free flow of data and communication between domains. Forests can also form trust relationships with other forests.

Windows Server Administration

- The Microsoft Management Console (MMC) is a utility used to organize commonly used utilities.
- The Active Directory Users and Computers utility is used to add user and group accounts to a Windows domain.

POSIX

- A POSIX-compliant operating system can run on numerous hardware platforms.

Network Interoperability

- A gateway service provides communication between dissimilar network systems.
- A gateway is also the device used to provide a connection between the local area network and the Internet.

Copyright Goodheart-Willcox Co., Inc.

Review Questions

1. A(n) _____ is a group of computers that share resources such as files and hardware.

2. A(n) _____ is a logical grouping of users and equipment as defined by the network administrator.

3. List and differentiate between the editions of Windows Server 2016.

4. What phrase does Windows use to refer to a server cluster?

5. What is the purpose of a server cluster?

6. What is the purpose of load balancing?

7. What is a HomeGroup?

8. In a(n) _____ network model, each computer contains its own database of users.

9. A(n) _____ network stores user and resource information in one location.

10. What protocol is native to Windows file sharing?

11. What other protocol is often identified as SMB?

12. What protocol is commonly associated with sharing on a Unix/Linux system?

13. What does the dollar sign symbol indicate when located beside a share?

14. What two Internet protocols are used by Active Directory to exchange directory information with other servers?

15. The Active Directory is a hierarchical structure that consists of _____, _____ _____, and _____.

16. What namespace feature determines if a domain is part of a tree or forest?

17. What is the difference between a disjointed and a contiguous namespace?

18. What two processes handle authentication in a Windows Server network?

19. List and describe four types of trust relationships.

20. The _____ file system is limited to a 32-GB partition.

21. The _____ file system is limited to a 2-GB partition.

22. The _____ file system can create partition sizes as large as 16 EB.

23. _____ can be set up to share directories and control access to files.

24. The _____ and _____ file systems allow only for share-level security.

25. What is the Microsoft Management Console (MMC)?

26. What utility would an administrator use to add users and groups to an Active Directory?

Copyright Goodheart-Willcox Co., Inc.

27. Define *basic disk* and *dynamic disk*.

28. What does the acronym POSIX represent?

29. What was the original purpose of the POSIX standard?

30. Today, the default protocol for network systems is _____.

31. What is a gateway service?

✚ Sample Network+ Exam Questions

1. What will happen on Windows Server if a user presses the [Ctrl] [Alt] [Del] keys simultaneously after the server boots?

   A. The system will reboot.

   B. The **Windows Security** dialog box will display.

   C. The **Logon** dialog box will appear.

   D. Nothing will happen. Only the system administrator can invoke [Ctrl] [Alt] [Del].

2. Which device is used to translate protocols when two different networks are connected together?

   A. Switch

   B. Router

   C. Hub

   D. Gateway

3. Which file system supports the largest disk partition?

   A. FAT16

   B. FAT32

   C. NTFS

   D. OS/2

4. What can RAID do for a network server?

   A. Provide a secure network connection.

   B. Provide data storage redundancy.

   C. Provide protection from malware.

   D. Provide a secure method of user authentication.

5. Which of the following is not a classification associated with LDAP?

   A. Forest

   B. Tree

   C. Branch

   D. Domain

Copyright Goodheart-Willcox Co., Inc.

6. Which of the following is an authentication protocol?

   A. FTP

   B. HTML

   C. Kerberos

   D. ARP

7. A client can log on to a network and see a network folder. She can read the contents of all documents located inside the network folder but cannot make changes to the documents. What is the most likely reason she cannot make changes to the documents in the folder?

   A. The client is configured with the wrong protocol.

   B. The folder is located on a different subnet.

   C. The client does not have the correct permission to change the contents of the folder.

   D. The client is using the wrong software application when attempting to make changes to the shared documents.

8. Which device is used to store user accounts in a client/server network?

   A. Each workstation stores user-account security information and permissions.

   B. The server stores user-account security information and permissions.

   C. Both the user workstation and the server store user security information and permissions.

   D. Security account information and permissions are stored at Microsoft headquarters, not on the actual network system.

9. Which three are typical characteristics of a peer-to-peer network? (Select three.)

   A. A centralized server to control user accounts.

   B. Each computer requires individual user accounts.

   C. There is no limit to number of workstations.

   D. Total clients are limited to 20.

   E. Each computer must be configured with LDAP.

   F. LDAP is not required.

10. What is the minimal requirement for a client/server network user account?

    A. User logon name and no password

    B. User logon name and password

    C. User logon name and a password shared folder

    D. No user logon name, just a password

Network+ Certification Exam Objectives

Starting with the CompTIA Network+ objectives, system interoperability is no longer a certification objective. You will most likely see nothing about Unix or Linux on the examination. If Unix/Linux is reinstated for the certification exam, it will most likely cover only the basics of Unix/Linux.

Currently, the only reference to Unix/Linux in the Network+ objectives are the **ifconfig**, **dig**, and **traceroute** commands listed in Domain 5.2.

Objectives

1.1: Protocols and Ports—FTP

Protocols and Ports—TFTP

Protocols and Ports—Telnet

Protocols and Ports—SMB

3.4: Telnet

Remote File Access—FTP/FTPS, TFTP

5.2: Software Tools— traceroute, iptables, netstat, pathping, nmap, route, arp, dig

Learning Outcomes

- Outline the history of Unix operating systems.
- Summarize the advantages and disadvantages of using the Linux operating system.
- Compare and contrast Unix/Linux operating systems to other operating systems.
- Describe an X Windows system.
- Summarize how Unix/Linux can establish communication with Windows operating systems.
- Discuss Mac OS X Server.

Copyright Goodheart-Willcox Co., Inc.

Key Terms

boot loader
Common Unix Printing System
    (CUPS)
daemon
device file
inode

journal file
journaling file system
kernel
module
mount point
session

shell
tarball
windows manager
X client
X server
X Windows

Overview

Unix is the fountainhead of modern network operating systems. After its inception, it served as a model of how network operating systems should operate. There have been many variations of Unix, though none of these variations produced a large-scale change in networking or desktop operating systems. Many software companies have adopted the open-source technology of Linux in their networking operating systems.

While Microsoft Windows dominates the desktop computer world in the United States, Linux is the preferred desktop for most C and C++ programmers and computer-science majors. Linux allows programmers complete control over the operating system and the kernel. In fact, a programmer can write a new kernel if he or she has sufficient skills. This is why Linux is popular with serious programmers.

This chapter presents a basic foundation of Unix/Linux operating systems. The Unix and Linux information in this chapter is combined because talking about one operating system is like talking about the other.

Unix

Unix was developed at the AT&T Bell Laboratories in the 1960s. It was the first major operating system for networking. Scientific communities, academic communities, and governmental agencies readily accepted Unix. The original version of Unix has spawned countless variations, such as Berkeley Software Distribution (BSD), Sun Solaris, HP, and IBM.

Many networking concepts originated from the early versions of Unix. While Unix was still in its early development, the TCP/IP protocol was developed to support communication between universities, governmental sites, and scientific research companies. Unix adopted TCP/IP as its native communication protocol.

What makes Unix and Linux unique when compared with Windows operating systems is the source code used for the components is readily available to anyone. Windows is a proprietary operating system; however, Microsoft has made some aspects of its Windows code available in a similar manner as open source. The availability of the source code has made the Unix/Linux system a favorite among programmers and programming enthusiasts. If a program needs to be modified or to have a new procedure developed, the administrator can simply write the code for the change. The most common programming language used for writing Unix/Linux code is the C programming language. If you cannot program, you can usually find the code you need through an Internet search. There are many organizations devoted to developing and sharing program code.

Unix/Linux consists of the system kernel surrounded by modules, as shown in Figure 8-1. A **kernel** is the core of an operating system. A **module** is a small program, such as a hardware driver or a kernel enhancement. Modules are used to expand the

Figure 8-1 The Unix/Linux kernel is surrounded by modules. A module is typically a hardware driver, file-system driver, or other kernel enhancement.

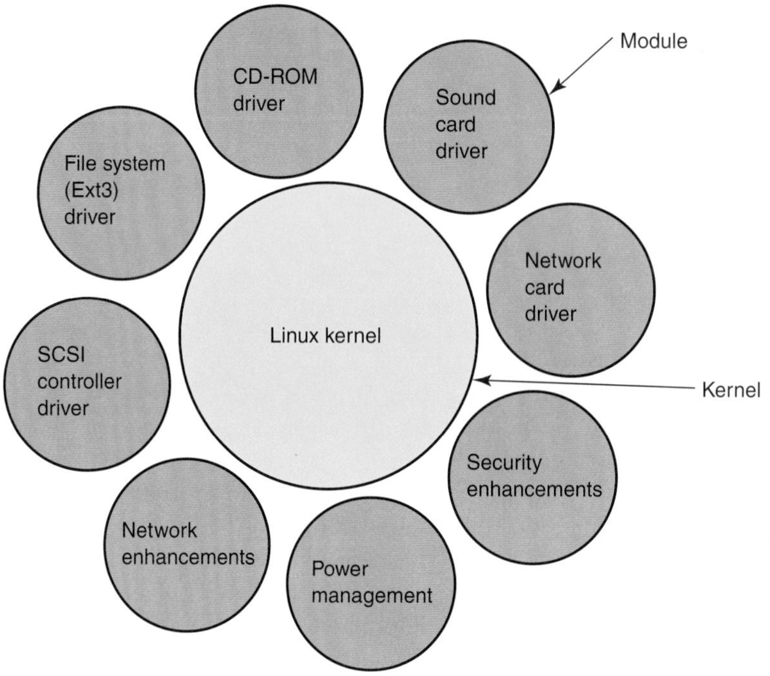

Goodheart-Willcox Publisher

kernel and to allow for flexibility. An administrator can load and unload modules as needed or configure the kernel to load them automatically during the system boot.

The Unix/Linux system also consists of daemons. A **daemon** is a program that runs in the background and waits for a client to request its services. It is much like a service in Windows operating systems. An example of a daemon is the Simple Mail Transfer Protocol (SMTP). SMTP waits for e-mail to arrive. When e-mail does arrive, SMTP either transfers the e-mail to another server or delivers the e-mail to the recipient's mailbox. This all occurs in the background without the user's knowledge until a notification appears on the screen alerting the user to a new message. Figure 8-2 shows a list of currently running programs on a Linux computer.

The kernel combined with modules and daemons defines the total operating system and its capabilities, as illustrated in Figure 8-3. An administrator can customize the operating system and load only the modules and services desired. By building a custom operating system, overall performance is improved. The operating system is more efficient than when loading an operating system with all of its possible components. The administrator can also unload modules and services no longer needed. The ability to load or unload separate modules to support the kernel results in efficient use of system resources such as RAM. As each module is loaded, valuable RAM is used. There are also more demands on the CPU. Processor time is required for each running module.

Linux

In 1991, a University of Helsinki student, Linus Torvalds, developed the Linux kernel and freely distributed the source code rather than retaining proprietary rights. What makes this operating system unique is that the code is a collaboration through the years of countless numbers of developers, programmers, students, and engineers. Linux is distributed for free or for a relatively small cost. It is licensed under the *GNU General Public License (GPL)*, which allows users to freely modify, copy, and distribute

Copyright Goodheart-Willcox Co., Inc.

Figure 8-2 In this example, a utility called **top** has been run to reveal currently running programs and daemons. Files on a Unix/Linux system that are daemons, typically end with the letter *d*.

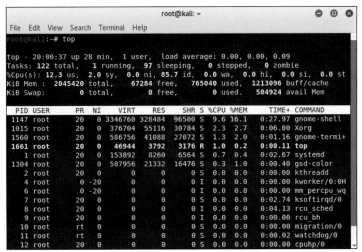

Goodheart-Willcox Publisher

Figure 8-3 The kernel, modules, and daemons make up the Unix/Linux operating system.

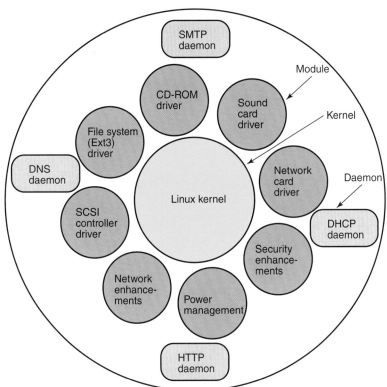

Goodheart-Willcox Publisher

the Linux software system. This subject will be discussed in further detail later in this chapter.

While Linux has been presented as an open-source operating system, this can be misleading. The kernel and many other Linux components are free to download, but many versions are a mix of open-source and proprietary programs and components. For example, Xandros Linux includes a proprietary file management system, proprietary applications, and proprietary utilities. It also contains several third-party applications, such as Netscape Communicator and Adobe Acrobat Reader.

Since Linux was designed to emulate Unix, most of its features are the same as Unix. You can think of Linux as another version in the evolution of Unix. There are many variations of Linux available, such as Red Hat, Caldera, Mandrake, SUSE, Turbo, and Corel. You will see many similarities between the different versions of Linux. These similarities are due to all of the Linux operating systems using the most common, available programs to enhance the kernel, such as Gimp, KDE, GNOME, Mozilla, XFree86, Apache Web Server, Evolution, and Samba.

Linux has evolved rapidly and has been incorporated into other operating systems. Linux was once difficult to install, mainly because of the lack of hardware driver support by manufacturers. Since companies such as IBM have endorsed Linux, hardware manufacturers have increased their driver support.

There are various Linux certifications available. They range from vendor-specific, such as Red Hat certification, to vender-neutral, such as Linux certification offered by CompTIA and IBM. IBM uses a vender-neutral approach because they endorse Red Hat, SUSE Linux, and TurboLinux versions.

Linux will continue to grow because it has incorporated all of the common protocols associated with other operating systems. Protocols such as SMB, LDAP, and SNMP make the operating system more compatible with Microsoft Windows operating systems. The expansion of operating system interoperability has helped to develop the popularity of Linux.

Tech Tip

After completing this course, you may wish to pursue a Linux certification, such as CompTIA's Linux+, especially since Linux servers are becoming more common in the network industry.

Linux Advantages

The features that have made the versions of Linux popular are its flexibility and price. Linux is flexible because it can be easily modified or customized. Since the program code is open source, an experienced programmer can customize the operating system and security to meet their needs. Generally, Linux is priced reasonably when compared to other network operating systems. In fact, an entire system can be downloaded for free. Prices for network operating systems that allow only a limited number of users to access the server typically start at several thousands of dollars. As the number of users increases, so does the cost of the network operating system.

Linux Disadvantages

Commercial versions of Linux are tested on various systems and have somewhat of a guarantee they will not harm your computer. Downloaded versions of Linux and associated files are not guaranteed. The user has no recourse, no one to blame, and no cost-recovery source if the software destroys or loses data or crashes the system.

Many Linux companies do not have a highly structured support system. Commercial versions of Linux, however, do provide support, either for free or for a low cost. Commercial versions of Linux also have the broadest range of hardware compatibility when compared to the free download versions. Remember the old saying, "You get what you pay for." If the operating system is free, the support is typically less than desirable. Also, since Linux is an open-source operating system, the code is not secret. It can be hacked or cracked more easily than some other operating systems.

Copyright Goodheart-Willcox Co., Inc.

Another concern is independent-vendor support. There are not as many venders that provide driver support for Unix/Linux in the same way as they do for Microsoft products. Also, not all versions of Unix/Linux services or programs are interchangeable and compatible. You must be very careful when adding a free service or utility. It may not be compatible with the version of Linux you are running. Other operating systems may have problems too, but not to the extent as the Linux operating system. It is best to stick with a well-established Linux operating system, such as Red Hat or SUSE.

Copyright and Copyleft

One of the most interesting and often misunderstood aspects of Linux is the copyright. Linux is copyrighted under the *GNU General Public License (GPL)*, often referred to as *copyleft*, which is shown in Figure 8-4. Many people are under the impression that you cannot sell Linux software. This is not true. The intent of the GNU GPL is to make the Linux kernel source code freely available. This allows anyone to modify the code to suit his or her needs. In short, the GNU GPL allows anyone the right to copy, modify, and distribute software without the permission of the original copyright holder, as long as he or she passes the same rights on to the next user. In other words, all users who receive a copy of the source code may freely modify the programs and freely distribute the programs.

This may lead to the question of how companies have the right to sell Linux. Commercial companies extend all the rights associated with the GNU GPL. The commercial companies distribute the source code and allow copies to be made and distributed under the same guidelines as stated above. What the companies are charging for is a neat package with manuals and support via the Internet and telephone for the consumer. The consumer actually pays for the enhancements while not being charged for the software. In fact, you can go to the commercial sites and download an image of the software to use on a computer. The fact that you can download and install the software from the commercial site and access the source code is what keeps the commercial sites in compliance with the GNU general public license. For more information on the GNU GPL, visit www.gnu.org/licenses/copyleft.html.

Figure 8-4 An explanation of copyleft can be viewed on the www.gnu.org/licenses/copyleft.html web page.

Goodheart-Willcox Publisher

Copyright Goodheart-Willcox Co., Inc.

The Free Software Foundation (FSF), a nonprofit organization founded in 1983, develops many different software packages that complement Linux systems. The FSF promotes the free distribution of software and source code similar to the GNU GPL. See Figure 8-5. The FSF develops utilities and programs that interface with GNU/Linux operating systems. For more information on the FSF, visit www.gnu.org/fsf/fsf.html.

You should note that not all versions of Linux are under the free distribution plan. Many commercial versions are independent of the GNU GPL license and are very expensive.

Figure 8-5 The www.fsf.org web page provides information about the Free Software Foundation (FSF) and its purpose.

Goodheart-Willcox Publisher

Unix/Linux Basics

This section introduces the basics of the Unix/Linux operating system. It is not comprehensive in its coverage. It would take a full textbook to cover the basics in detail. The intention of this section is to introduce you to some Unix/Linux terminology and to the basic differences and likenesses between Unix/Linux and other operating systems.

LILO and GRUB

The acronym LILO represents Linux Loader. GRUB represents Grand Unified Boot Loader. LILO is an older version of the boot loader; GRUB has been used for many years now. LILO and GRUB are both boot loaders. A **boot loader** is a program that starts the operating system load process. Linux boot loaders are used in much the same way as ntldr is used in Windows NT-based operating systems. LILO or GRUB installs in the master boot record (MBR) of a Linux partition. After the power-on self-test (POST), the system looks for and transfers control to the boot loader. The boot loader loads the kernel. When the kernel loads, it loads the operating system.

LILO or GRUB can be used to load other operating systems. When LILO or GRUB is configured on a computer with multiple operating systems, the LILO or

Copyright Goodheart-Willcox Co., Inc.

GRUB boot loader takes control after the system POST but before the operating system is selected. It allows the user to choose between two or more operating systems and then boots directly into the selected operating system. Modern Linux systems like SUSE Linux incorporate the boot loader into the Yet another Setup Tool (YaST) utility, which is a central installation and configuration tool.

Shells

A **shell** is a user interface that interprets and carries out commands from the user similarly to the way the command interpreter (cmd.exe) interprets and carries out commands. The shell directly interfaces with the operating system kernel. There are numerous shells available. Some are freeware and others are proprietary. Some of the more common shells are the Bourne Again Shell, Korn Shell, and Turbo C Shell. See Figure 8-6 for a list of common Unix/Linux shells.

Figure 8-7 shows the **set** command issued at the Bourne Again Shell in Kali Linux. The Unix/Linux **set** command is similar to the DOS **set** command. Entered without options, the **set** command displays a list of a user's shell variables, including the name of the current shell. In the example, you can see that the user's shell is set to bash, which is the Bourne Again Shell.

Figure 8-6 Common Unix/Linux shells.

Shell	Full Name
bash	Bourne Again Shell
bs	Bourne Shell
csh	C Shell
ksh	Korn Shell
tcsh	Turbo C Shell

Goodheart-Willcox Publisher

Figure 8-7 The **set** command lists the current shell's variables.

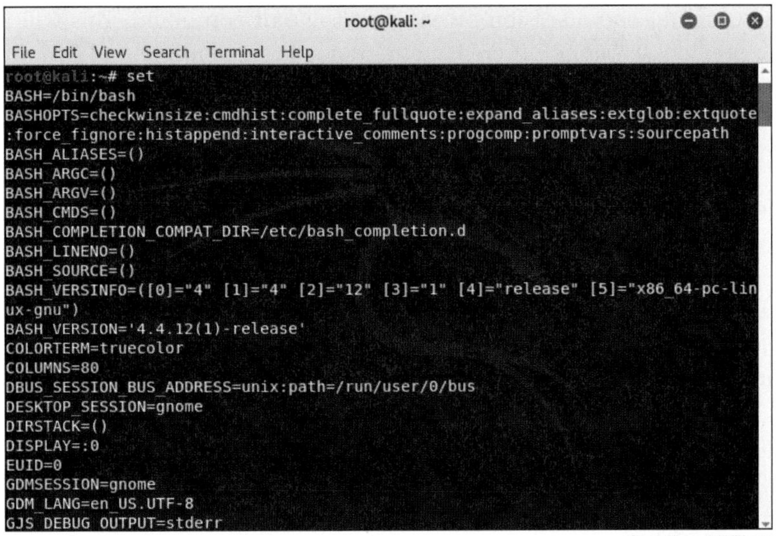

Goodheart-Willcox Publisher

A user can change to a different shell by typing the desired shell name at the prompt. For example, to activate and use the Turbo C Shell, you would simply type tcsh at the prompt. In Figure 8-8, the user has issued the **tcsh** command and then entered set at the shell prompt. Since each shell has its own set of variables, the SHELL

Copyright Goodheart-Willcox Co., Inc.

Figure 8-8 The user has entered **tcsh** at the shell prompt to start a new shell (Turbo C Shell). The SHELL variable, as indicated by the **set** command now reads /bin/tcsh.

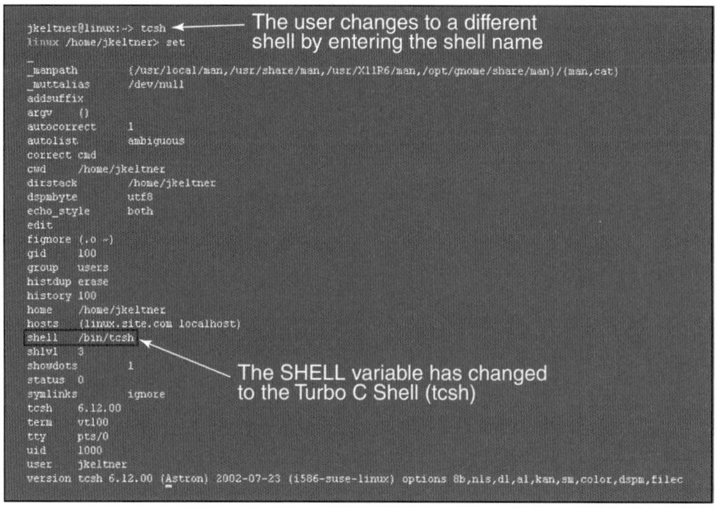

Goodheart-Willcox Publisher

variable now reads /bin/tcsh. It should be noted that this command does not exist in all versions of Linux, however. A user can also run another session of the current shell by entering the shell name. For example, to run another session of the bash shell, the user would enter bash at the prompt.

Note that each time a user enters the name of a new shell or the name of the current shell being used, a new session is invoked. One of the greatest advantages of the Unix/Linux operating system is the ability to run multiple sessions on a single computer. A **session** is a logical connection with the Linux computer. Each session provides its own set of variables as shown in Figures 8-7 and 8-8. A session will allow remote users to log on to a Linux computer and use the computer at the same time as the user sitting at the computer workstation. It also allows a user to run a lengthy batch process in one session and perform other tasks in another session concurrently.

The user can end a session by entering the **exit** command. This will return a user to a previous session. If there is not a previous session, the **exit** command will log the user off the system.

Commands

Linux commands are similar among the various versions of Linux, but they do not match perfectly. This lack of standardization can be frustrating. You can usually enter a command followed by --help at the shell prompt to obtain help about a particular command. You can also access the manual pages for a particular command by typing man followed by the command. However, even these commands are not universal.

The command syntax of DOS commands is similar to that of Unix/Linux commands. The command may stand alone or be followed by options, an argument, or both. The following shows the complete syntax of a Linux command:

    command <options> <arguments>

An *option* alters the output of a command. Some options must be preceded with one or two hyphens, and some options do not need a hyphen at all. In any case, a space must exist between the command and the option. Options, like commands and file names, are case-sensitive.

An *argument* is the target for the command. It can be a file name, a directory name, wildcard characters, or other piece of information designated as an argument for a particular command.

Copyright Goodheart-Willcox Co., Inc.

Figure 8-9 shows an example of using a command without options and an argument. The **ls** command is used to list the contents of the current directory. Now look at Figure 8-10. In this example, entering **ls** with the **l** option displays the directory listing in a long form. The long form lists details about each file and directory, such as permissions and file size. The **ls** command can also be used with an argument.

Note

The **ls** command and the **-l** option are both conducted using a lowercase **l** (el).

Figure 8-9 Example of issuing the **ls** command.

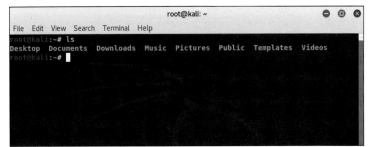

Goodheart-Willcox Publisher

Figure 8-10 Issuing the **ls -l** command displays a long directory listing. Items listed include permissions, file or directory owner, file size, and date and time last modified.

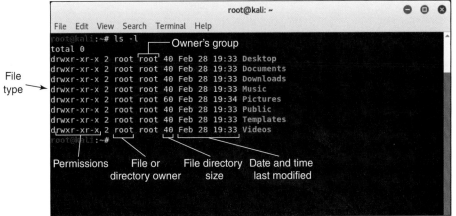

Goodheart-Willcox Publisher

The argument can be a path name to list the contents of a directory other than the working directory. The argument can also be a file name or part of a file name with wildcard characters. Look at Figure 8-11. In this example, the **ls** command is used with an argument that contains a wildcard character. This argument tells the **ls** command to list only files and directories that begin with the letter *S*. The **-l** option tells the **ls** command to list the results in long form. See Figure 8-12 for a list of other common Linux commands and their functions.

File Systems

Several choices of Linux file systems are available. Among these file systems are Ext2, Ext3, Ext4, ReiserFS, JFS1, and JFS. Ext2 is the original Linux file system. It supports long file names (255 characters) and stores information in blocks much like the DOS and Windows file systems. Information about each file is stored in an inode. An **inode** is a table entry that contains information such as permissions; file size; name of the owner; the time stamps of the file's creation, modification, and last access; and a pointer to where the file is stored.

The Ext3 file system is basically the Ext2 file system with the journaling feature added. In fact, each of the Linux file systems, except for Ext2, is a journaling file

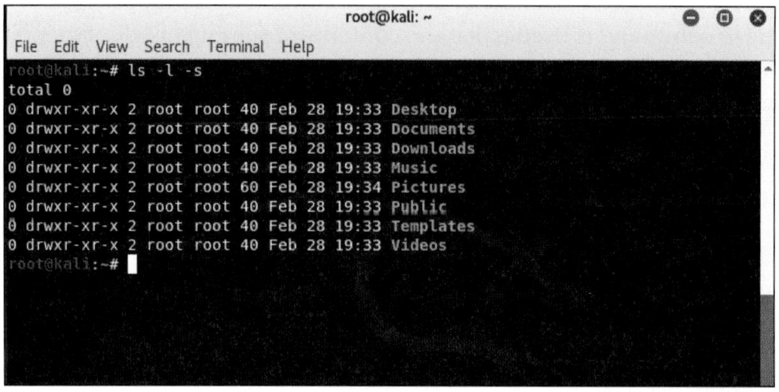

Figure 8-11 The **ls** command has been listed here with an argument. The argument in this example includes a wildcard character, the asterisk (*). Together with the letter *S*, it tells the **ls** command to list only those files and directories that begin with the letter *S*. The **-l** options tells the **ls** command to output the result of the argument in a long listing format.

Goodheart-Willcox Publisher

Figure 8-12 Common Unix/Linux commands.

Linux Command	Description
cd	Changes the directory to the user's home directory.
cd ..	Changes to the parent directory of the current working directory.
cd <directory>	Changes the directory to the specified directory.
cp <filename> <directory>	Copies a file to a specified directory.
ls	Lists the contents of the current working directory.
ls <directory>	Lists the contents of the specified directory.
ls -l ls -l <directory>	Lists the contents of a directory, including file and subdirectory details.
mkdir <new directory>	Makes (creates) a directory.
mv <filename> <directory>	Moves a file to a new directory.
mv <filename> <new filename>	Renames a file.
pwd	Displays the path of the current working directory.
rm <filename>	Removes (deletes) a file.
rmdir <directory>	Removes (deletes) a directory.

Goodheart-Willcox Publisher

system. A **journaling file system** ensures file integrity whenever an unexpected system shutdown occurs, such as a power outage. The journaling file system maintains a log of all file activity. This log is called the **journal file**. Three time stamps that contain information about the creation of the file, the last date the file was modified, and the last date the file was accessed are added to the journal file. The journaling file system uses the journal file to restore a file to its most usable state. This can be accomplished even if the file is corrupted or incomplete. A journaling file system also allows for faster boot time and consumes less memory than other file systems. The Ext4 file system is a continuation of Ext2 and Ext3 and provides the largest storage capacity to date. Ext4 is backward compatible with Ext3 and Ext2.

The *journaling file system (JFS)* was originally developed by IBM for the OS/2 Warp operating system. JFS is similar to Ext3 in that information is stored in blocks and metadata is stored in inodes. However, JFS is a 64-bit file system, which allows for a larger file system and larger file sizes.

File Structure

The Unix/Linux file structure looks similar to the DOS file structure. However, the most noticeable difference between the Unix/Linux file structure and the DOS file

Copyright Goodheart-Willcox Co., Inc.

structure is the lack of drive letters. This means that your system does not have a storage limit based on the number of drive letters.

The root (/) directory is the top of the directory structure, as demonstrated in Figure 8-13. All files and directories are under the root directory. The root directory can be subdivided into additional directories and files like it can with the DOS file structure. Unlike DOS, Unix/Linux has the ability to append file structures from external devices such as hard disk, CD-ROM, DVD, and flash drives and to append the file structures from remote computers. This ability makes the file structures appear to be part of the root file structure. To append a file structure to the root, the file structure or device that holds the file structure must be mounted.

Tech Tip

Do not confuse the root of the directory (/) with the **/root** directory. The **/root** directory belongs to the root user, also known as the *superuser*. It is the superuser's home directory.

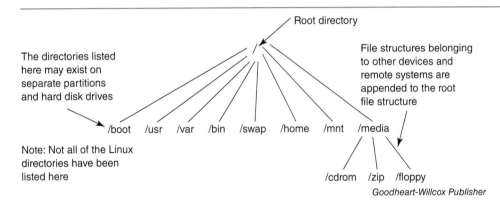

Goodheart-Willcox Publisher

Figure 8-13 The root directory is the top of the directory structure. File structures belonging to other devices, such as hard disk drives, CD-ROMs, and remote systems, are appended to the root directory when they are mounted.

Mounting a device makes it appear as part of the directory structure. Figure 8-14 shows the contents of the /etc/fstab file. This file indicates the drives and partitions that are to be mounted during the system boot. The first entry represents the device file associated with the device. In Unix/Linux, each device on the local system has an associated device file in the /dev directory. The **device file** serves as a means of communication between the driver and the device. Devices are referred to by the device file name. For example, a primary drive designated as the master drive is called hda. The device file for this drive is /dev/hda. Figure 8-15 shows the storage device naming scheme and related device files. Partitions are indicated by numbers, starting with the number one for the first partition. For example, the first partition on /dev/hda would be indicated as hda1.

Look again at Figure 8-14. The second entry in the /etc/fstab file is the mount point. The **mount point** is the location in the directory structure where a device is mounted or inserted. For example, a mount point of /media/cdrom mounts the file structure of the /dev/hdc device in the /media/cdrom directory.

The third entry indicates the type of file system on the device. Note that various file systems can exist on the devices and still be a part of the complete file structure.

The fourth entry lists the options that should be used by the mount command to configure the device. For example, the **ro** option indicates that the device is to be mounted as read only. The **users** option indicates that all users should be allowed to mount and unmount the device. Finally, the fifth and sixth entries set administrative parameters. These will not be discussed because the details about these parameters are beyond the scope of this chapter.

Note

Historically, Linux users were able to mount media devices using the **/mnt** command. Now, the **/media** command is used for removable media, such as CD-ROMs, and **/mnt** is used as a temporary mount point.

Copyright Goodheart-Willcox Co., Inc.

Figure 8-14 Contents of the **/etc/fstab** file.

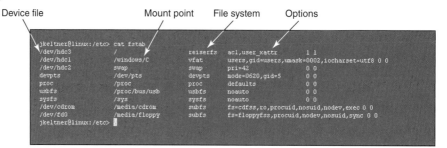

Goodheart-Willcox Publisher

Figure 8-15 Storage device naming scheme.

Hard Drives	Type	Description
hda	IDE	Master or single hard drive on primary controller.
hdb	IDE	Slave hard drive on primary controller.
hdc	IDE	Master or single hard drive on secondary controller.
hdd	IDE	Slave hard drive on secondary controller.
sda	SCSI	First SCSI drive in chain.
sdb	SCSI	Second SCSI drive in chain, and so on.

Goodheart-Willcox Publisher

Typical PC devices such as a keyboard, mouse, and most common file systems are mounted during the system boot process. Before you can save a file to a device such as hard disk drive, CD, or flash drive, the device must be mounted. Before removing a CD disc or flash drive, the device should be unmounted. This will ensure that the file can be read by other systems. If the device is not unmounted, the file may be unreadable.

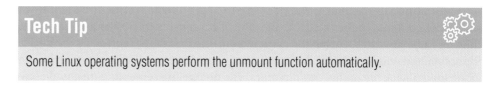

Tech Tip

Some Linux operating systems perform the unmount function automatically.

Common Files and Directories

There are many directories commonly associated with Unix/Linux systems. This is not to say that all Unix/Linux file system structures are identical. They do vary among operating systems and versions. Figure 8-16 lists the most universal directories associated with Unix/Linux systems.

While it is not necessary for the common user to navigate the directory structure, it is required for the system administrator who commonly modifies software packages designed for Linux. Typically, a common user has access to only part of the directory structure and can only modify his or her directories and files.

Unix/Linux file and directory names are case-sensitive. This means that two files can be spelled the same but be recognized by the operating system as two separate files. For example, Myfile and myfile are two separate files. Also, be aware that Unix/Linux files typically do not use file extensions. For example, when looking for an executable file, you will not see the familiar **.exe** extension appended to the file name. An executable file is identifiable by the file's permissions accessed through one of the utilities that display the file name, directory, and permissions or by using the **ls -l** (el) command.

Copyright Goodheart-Willcox Co., Inc.

File and Directory Security

Like other network operating systems, the Unix/Linux operating system has the ability to assign permissions to files and directories. Look at the long directory listing in Figure 8-17. Note the first entry for each file and directory. This entry lists the file or directory type followed by permissions. There are ten spaces available for this

Figure 8-16 Common Unix/Linux directories.

Directory	Description
/dev	Contains system device files.
/bin	Contains system commands.
/etc	Contains system configuration files.
/tmp	Used as a temporary storage area for files created by utilities and executables. It is emptied when the system is rebooted.
/var	Contains variable data associated with administrative, logging, and temporary files.
/home	Contains user directories and files. The startup files are located here by user.

Goodheart-Willcox Publisher

Figure 8-17 Note the permissions for the files and directories in this long directory listing.

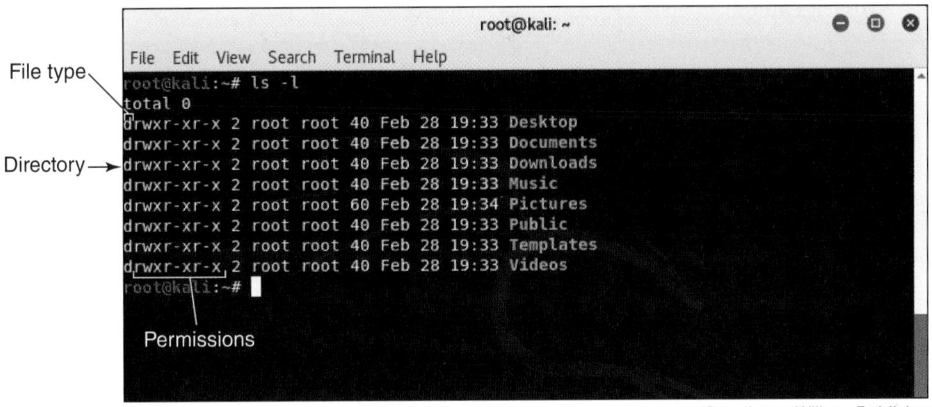

Goodheart-Willcox Publisher

information. The file or directory type occupies the first space. Some of the characters that may fill this space are *d*, *l*, or a hyphen (-). The following list shows the meaning of each:

- d = directory
- l = link
- - = normal file

The file and directory permissions occupy the other nine spaces. The permissions represent the file and directory permissions assigned to user, group, and other. The user is typically the owner of the file or directory. The group is typically the user's default group. Other is anyone else who is not the file's owner or a member of the group.

Note the letters *r*, *w*, and *x* as well as a hyphen (-). A hyphen within any of the file and directory permissions spaces indicates that no permission for that entry has been set. The permissions associated with the letters are as follows:

- r = read
- w = write
- x = execute

Copyright Goodheart-Willcox Co., Inc.

These permissions vary in meaning, depending on whether they are set for a file or for a directory. See Figure 8-18 for descriptions about these meanings.

Each of the nine permission spaces is a placeholder for the read, write, and execute permissions for user, group, and other. If any of these values are not set, then a hyphen displays in its place. To understand how to interpret permissions better, look at Figure 8-19. Note that *user, group*, and *other* is each assigned three placeholders. Each of these placeholders can be filled with the read, write, or execute permission. In the example, the user and group have permission to read and write to the file. All other users are only able to read the file.

The administrator or user with equal administrative powers can set file and directory permissions. They can even change the owner of the file or of the default group. The owner of a file or a directory can also change permissions or the owner and group.

Figure 8-18 Files and directory permissions and their meanings.

File Permissions	Description
read	Open a file and view its contents.
write	Change a file's contents.
execute	Run a file. This attribute is assigned to executable files.
Directory Permissions	**Description**
read	Display the contents of a directory.
write	Create, modify, or delete files in the directory that you own.
execute	Change to that directory.

Goodheart-Willcox Publisher

Figure 8-19 In this example, the user and default group are granted the read and write permissions to a file. All other users can only read the file name.

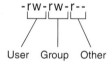

Goodheart-Willcox Publisher

Network Authentication

Procedures for logging on and off Unix/Linux systems are similar to other network operating systems. Logging on to the system can take place through a command-line prompt or a GUI-based prompt, depending on how Linux is configured. In either case, the user must supply a username followed by a password. The username and password is compared to that in the /etc/passwd file. The /etc/passwd file stores user account information. After the user is authenticated, the user may use the services for which he or she is authorized.

The highest level of administration is the superuser, which has the default user account name of *root*. The initial password for *root* is set during the installation of the operating system. The system administrator uses the root account to make changes in the system configuration. Changes in the system configuration or file structure can render the entire system inaccessible. When the administrator is using the system for normal tasks, the administrator logs on under a common username and password similar to any typical user. Mistakes made by a common user can be fixed, and typically, the common user cannot access critical areas of the system.

Copyright Goodheart-Willcox Co., Inc.

File and Print Sharing

File sharing is made possible through the Network File System (NFS) protocol. NFS was originally developed by Sun Microsystems and later released to the public as an open standard. NFS allows a Unix/Linux system to share its files with users from remote locations. The system that shares its files is called the *NFS server*, which runs the NFS service. The NFS service consists of several daemons. These daemons handle services such as authentication and client mount requests. NFS also relies on support from the kernel. The system that accesses files on the NFS server is called the *client*. It relies on support from the kernel and from several NFS client daemons.

An administrator makes an NFS server's files available to remote users by listing in the /etc/exports file the directories to be shared, associated permissions, and the systems that are allowed to access each directory. The administrator then runs the **exportfs** command to export the directories. To view the exported directories, a user at the client computer must mount the directory. Mounting the directory makes the directory appear as if it were part of the client's file structure.

The line printer daemon (lpd) handles remote and local printing services. It listens for incoming print jobs and sends the jobs to the printer. Security is set through the /etc/host.equiv or /etc/host.lpd file. Remote access can be denied through the /etc/printcap file. Denying remote access allows only local users to send print jobs. The **lpr** command is used to send print jobs to the line printer daemon (lpd). For example, to print a file named ch08unix located in the /home/networking directory, the user would enter lpr /home/networking/ch08unix at the command prompt.

The **Common Unix Printing System (CUPS)** daemon has been designed to support network printing using the Internet Printing Protocol (IPP). CUPS is used in many Linux operating systems as well as Mac OS X. Since CUPS is based on IPP, it is designed to locate and configure printers located on the LAN and WAN through the use of a browser. Linux systems typically provide the user with a choice of using the traditional lpd printing system or CUPS.

Remote Access Features

Unix/Linux is designed to share resources but not in the same way that other networking systems share resources. For example, when you create and configure a share on a Windows network, the share is run on the client's computer. In Unix/Linux, when a share is set up on the Unix/Linux computer and is then accessed by the client, the program runs on the Unix/Linux computer. This means that the client only needs minimal resources, but the resources of the Unix/Linux computer must be increased as the number of clients increases.

Any operating system can access a Unix/Linux system by using remote access protocols and services. There are several remote access protocols and services with which you are probably familiar, including FTP, TFTP, Telnet, and Apache. These various protocols and services provide remote access to clients anywhere in the world. Linux also provides the SFTP service as a way to secure the remote connection. The SFTP protocol differs from FTP and TFTP in that it encrypts the user password and data.

FTP

The *File Transfer Protocol (FTP)* is designed to transfer files between a server and a client. Using FTP, you cannot run a program or manipulate a file on the server. FTP transfers files rather than running or manipulating them. In other words, using FTP,

1.1, 3.4 **NET**

Copyright Goodheart-Willcox Co., Inc.

you can only download or upload files. If you need to edit a file on the server while using FTP, you can download the file, modify it, and then upload it to the server.

FTP can require a username and password, or it can permit anonymous access. Most often, however, anonymous access requires some form of authentication, such as the client's e-mail address.

TFTP

Like FTP, the *Trivial File Transfer Protocol (TFTP)* is designed to transfer or copy files to and from a remote system. The main difference between FTP and TFTP is the protocol it uses to transfer the information. FTP uses the Transmission Control Protocol (TCP) to transfer data, while TFTP uses the User Datagram Protocol (UDP) to transfer data. TFTP does not require a user name or password and does not guarantee data delivery. It is a connectionless protocol.

Telnet

Telnet is designed to access remotely any computer running as a Telnet server. The Telnet service allows a user to log on using a username and password. After the connection is made, the client communicates with the Telnet server using text-based commands. The Telnet session allows a user to manipulate a file on the remote computer. However, the amount of manipulation is limited to the set of Telnet commands. Telnet is often referred to as a *terminal emulation program* because it emulates a terminal connected to a mainframe. Telnet is commonly used to control WAN servers and routers remotely. See Figure 8-20 for a comparison of FTP, TFTP, and Telnet.

Figure 8-20 FTP, TFTP, and Telnet comparison. A—FTP and TFTP allow a client to transfer files to and from an FTP or TFTP server. FTP uses the TCP protocol and TFTP uses the UDP protocol. B—Telnet allows a client to manipulate files while they reside on the server.

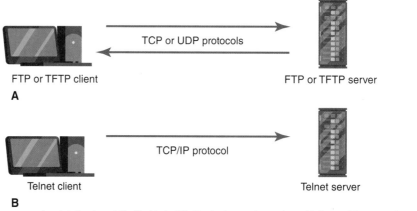

(workstation icons) RedlineVector/Shutterstock.com; (server icons) fullvector/Shutterstock.com;
Goodheart-Willcox Publisher

Linux Shell Tools

Linux and Unix have a number of utilities from the shell that are quite useful. Some of these are similar to the ones you have seen in Windows. In fact, Windows borrowed the idea from Unix. For example, **traceroute** is simply the Unix/Linux way of doing **tracert**. The utility **pathping** also exists in both Windows and Unix/Linux. It combines **traceroute** with **ping** functions. However, the **dig** tool is strictly associated with Unix/Linux. The **dig** utility retrieves DNS information.

The **arp** command also exists in Windows and Unix/Linux. It looks up address resolution tables, and it can be used to determine the relationship between an IP address and a MAC address for a network card. The command **route** is another utility that is common to both Windows and Unix/Linux. It provides information on a specific computer's routing table.

Copyright Goodheart-Willcox Co., Inc.

The **netstat** command provides the status of all current connections on a given computer. It is found in both Windows and Unix/Linux. When troubleshooting connectivity issues, the **netstat** command is quite useful.

The **nmap** command, short for Network Mapper, is another utility common to both Windows and Unix/Linux. It is used to find hosts and services available to users on a network. In essence, it builds a map of the network, hence its name. The map is created by sending specialty packets to host machines and analyzing the responses.

IPTables

The **iptables** command is the built-in firewall for Linux. The first firewall for Linux was **ipchains**. That firewall was literally a chain of rules. Each rule either allowed or blocked traffic. That utility was expanded to tables, each with multiple chains of rules. Thus, it is now called **iptables**.

Apache

Apache is web server software developed in the public domain to run on Unix/Linux. Many web servers use the Apache web-server software. It is popular because not only is it a robust and stable system, it is free. The Apache web-server software was designed as a free distribution by a group of approximately 20 developers. Apache derives its name from the fact that it consists of a series of software patches for the original NCSA web server software. Hence, the name Apache. Apache is the default web-server package in most commercial Linux operating systems.

X Windows System

The **X Windows** system provides a GUI for Unix and Linux systems. Other operating systems integrate the GUI into the operating system, which cannot be separated from the GUI to function as a single unit. The X Windows system is separate from the operating system. A user can operate a Unix/Linux computer without ever installing the GUI.

The X Windows system consists of an X server and an X client. **X server** is a program that communicates with the computer hardware, such as a keyboard, mouse, and monitor. The **X client** is an application, such as a word-processing program. The X client can also be a windows manager. A **windows manager** controls the display. In other words, it provides the GUI such as the icons, boxes, and buttons. Figure 8-21 shows the relationship between the hardware, X server, and X client applications and windows manager.

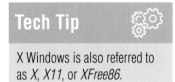

Tech Tip

X Windows is also referred to as *X*, *X11*, or *XFree86*.

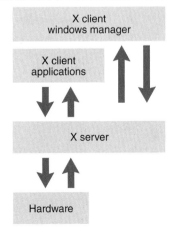

Figure 8-21 Relationship between hardware, X server and X client applications and windows manager.

Goodheart-Willcox Publisher

Copyright Goodheart-Willcox Co., Inc.

The X Windows system has a client/server architecture. The X server and the X client can run on the same computer, as in Figure 8-22, or on separate computers, as seen in Figure 8-23. However, in contrast to a typical client/server architecture in which the client receives resources from the server, the X Windows system works in the opposite manner. The X client provides the processing power and display, and the X server communicates with the hardware. The X server component serves as an interface between the system hardware and X clients. It allows the windows manager and X clients to operate independently of the hardware.

When X server is installed, it is configured for the system hardware. Typical configuration settings include mouse, keyboard, and video card type and monitor settings, such as the refresh rate and resolution.

The X Windows system is an open-source program for which many X clients or applications have been written. The various applications differ in appearance. To provide a common look among the various X clients, a desktop environment is often installed. A desktop environment is a software package that includes many applications and a windows manager. The desktop environment provides a common look among X clients.

Tech Tip

The term *X client* can refer to an application, windows manager, or the computer running the X client software. The term *X server* can refer to the X server program or to the computer running the X server program.

Figure 8-22 The X server and X client are typically installed on the same computer.

X server

X client

(workstation icon) RedlineVector/Shutterstock.com; Goodheart-Willcox Publisher

Tech Tip

When the X client and the X server are installed on separate computers, the computer that runs the X clients is typically the more powerful of the two computers.

Figure 8-23 The client/server architecture of the X Windows system allows the X server and X client to be installed on different computers on the network. Unlike the typical client/server design, the X client acts as the server in that it provides the processing power. The X client also sends display information to the X server.

The X server sends display information to the hardware

X server

The hardware displays the information on the monitor

The hardware also sends user input to the X server

An X client processes information and sends the display to the X server

X server sends user input received from the hardware to the X client

X client

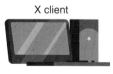

(workstation icons) RedlineVector/Shutterstock.com; Goodheart-Willcox Publisher

Two of the most commonly used desktop environments are K Desktop Environment (KDE) and GNU Network Object Model Environment (GNOME). Figure 8-24 shows the KDE GUI. Notice that it is similar to the Windows GUI in that it contains a desktop area, icons, and a menu.

Copyright Goodheart-Willcox Co., Inc.

Figure 8-24 The K Desktop Environment (KDE) with a view of the Applications Launcher.

Goodheart-Willcox Publisher

Tech Tip

An incorrect configuration of the monitor identification or frequency can permanently damage your monitor.

Desktop environments offer a large assortment of software packages included as part of the installation or available for download. Many popular software packages are designed for both KDE and GNOME desktop environments. Software packages that are not included in the installation can be downloaded from the Internet, typically in a file format called a tarball.

A **tarball** is a compressed file containing one or more software programs. Once downloaded, it must be decompressed. Additional configuration may be required before the programs are installed. Always read the documentation that is included in the tarball. You will typically find a readme file, which contains an overview of the package, and an install file, which includes instructions for installing the software.

The X Windows system is started by entering **startx** at the command prompt. Most Linux systems can be configured to load and run the X Windows system automatically. When loaded automatically, a logon dialog box prompts for a username and password. Many of the tasks an administrator performs at the command line, such as adding users or configuring services, can also be performed in the GUI.

Interoperability

Interoperability is supported between Microsoft and Unix/Linux systems using protocols such as *Service Message Block (SMB* and *SMB2)* and *Network File System (NFS)*. SMB is the Microsoft Windows protocol designed for sharing system resources. SMB is used with IPv4, and SMB2 is designed for use with IPv6 communication. SMB2 requires fewer packet exchanges than SMB. This reduces network latency when accessing resources. SMB2 was first introduced in Windows Vista. The SMB protocol has been the traditional way to support file access and sharing between Unix/Linux and Microsoft systems. NFS is the default file sharing protocol for Unix/Linux systems.

There are also many third-party software and open-source software applications designed to support file access and sharing between Unix/Linux systems and Microsoft systems.

1.1   NET

Samba

Samba is a free, open-source software package included in most Unix/Linux systems. Samba is designed to share files on a Unix/Linux computer with Windows computers using the SMB protocol. It is configured on a Unix/Linux computer. Figure 8-25 shows the option for **Samba Server** in the YaST Control Center. This option will allow you to configure the Linux computer as a Samba server.

The Linux computer and the Windows computer should be in the same workgroup, and both computers should have a user account with a matching user name and password. You will also need to configure the shared resource with the proper sharing permissions for the user account.

After Samba is configured, a Windows computer can access the shared directory structure of a Unix/Linux computer, provided the Windows user has the proper permissions. Figure 8-26 shows the devices available on the network as viewed

Figure 8-25 **Samba Server** option in the YaST Control Center.

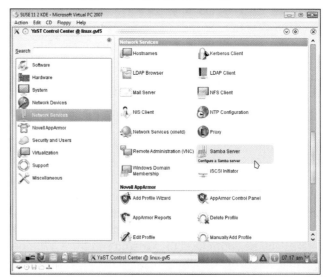

Goodheart-Willcox Publisher

Figure 8-26 When Samba is installed on a Unix/Linux system, Unix/Linux resources can be viewed through Network Neighborhood, My Network Places, or Network on a Windows workstation.

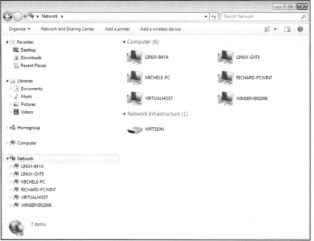

Goodheart-Willcox Publisher

Copyright Goodheart-Willcox Co., Inc.

from a Windows 7 computer. Notice the two Linux computers: LINUX-84YA and LINUX-GVFS. The Linux computers appear with the same icon as the Windows computers. You can see that the Linux SUSE computers use "Linux" as part of the default computer name. Some Linux versions use "Tux" as part of the default computer name. The term *Tux* refers to the traditional Linux mascot—a penguin that looks like it is wearing a tuxedo.

Tech Tip

Firewall settings are the most common reason for failure to access shares between a Windows system and a Linux system.

Unix/Linux computers can be configured to require a username and password when a Windows computer attaches to the Unix/Linux shared folder. Shares can also be accessed anonymously, but this is not recommended because of obvious security problems.

Sharing resources from a Windows 10 and Windows Server 2016 computer with a SUSE Linux computer is very easy. Simply use the **Windows Domain Membership** option in the YaST Control Center on the SUSE Linux computer to join SUSE Linux users to the Windows workgroup or domain, as shown in Figure 8-27.

Figure 8-27 Windows Domain Membership option in the YaST Control Center.

Goodheart-Willcox Publisher

Shared resources from the Windows computer can be viewed from the SUSE Linux computer using the smb-Dolphin application. See Figure 8-28 for an example.

One of the most commonly encountered problems is Windows Firewall blocking access from the Linux computer. Windows Firewall needs to be configured to allow the Linux computer to access the Windows computer.

NFS

NFS is the default protocol used by Unix/Linux systems to access and share files between Unix/Linux computers. NFS can also be used to share files with Microsoft computers. Originally, Microsoft used a "gateway service" to translate the NFS protocol for interoperability between Unix/Linux systems and Microsoft Windows

Copyright Goodheart-Willcox Co., Inc.

systems. Microsoft also used Client for NFS as a way to support file sharing and access using the NFS protocol. The NFS translation occurs on the Microsoft gateway service server, thus supporting all Microsoft Windows clients. The other option for earlier Microsoft systems was to install Client for NFS on each Microsoft workstation. When Client for NFS is installed, a server running the gateway service is not required.

Windows Server 2016 supports NFS through the Services for Network File System server role. Once this server role is installed, you can use Server Manager to configure an NFS share. Through Server Manager, the **Provision a Shared Folder Wizard** can be used to configure a shared folder for NFS. To start this wizard, click the **Provision Share** option located in the right-hand pane, as demonstrated in Figure 8-29. The **Provision a Shared Folder Wizard** is shown in Figure 8-30. After configuring NFS permissions on a Windows Server, Unix/Linux computers will be able to access shared resources on the Windows Server.

There are options in Server Manager to configure NTFS share permissions for an NFS share. This provides access control for local users accessing the NFS share.

Figure 8-28 Windows 7 shares viewed from a SUSE Linux computer using the smb-Dolphin utility.

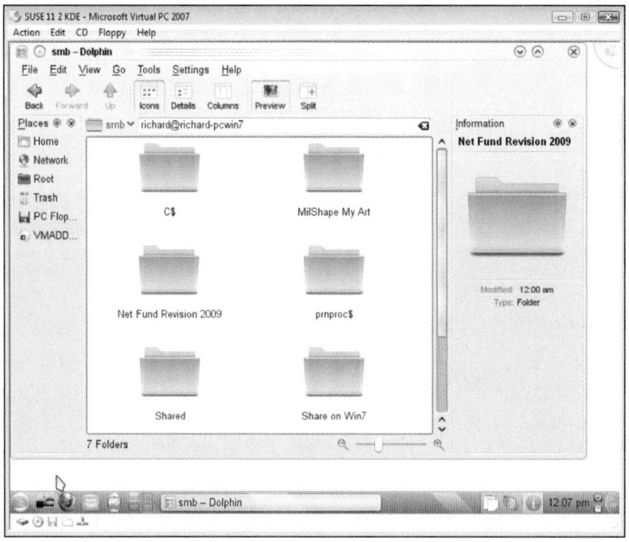

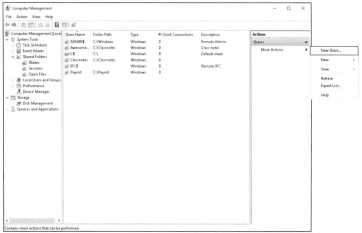

Goodheart-Willcox Publisher

Figure 8-29 To start the New Shared Folder Wizard, click the **New Share** option.

Goodheart-Willcox Publisher

Copyright Goodheart-Willcox Co., Inc.

NFS permissions used in Unix/Linux systems are somewhat similar to NTFS permissions but are not an exact match. By clicking the **NTFS Permissions** button in the **Properties** dialog box for the NFS shared folder, you can configure the share permissions to react as NTFS permissions rather than as NFS permissions. The **Permissions** dialog box is shown in Figure 8-31.

Network+ Note

When taking the Network+ Certification Exam and you see a question referring to NFS, you can generally bet the right answer involves Unix.

Figure 8-30 Selecting NFS permissions when provisioning a share in Windows.

Goodheart-Willcox Publisher

Figure 8-31 **Properties** dialog box for an NFS shared folder.

Goodheart-Willcox Publisher

Troubleshooting Interoperability

A successful ping between computers of different operating systems confirms that the computers are correctly connected physically by network media and devices operating at OSI layers 2 and 3, such as hubs, bridges, switches, wireless access

Copyright Goodheart-Willcox Co., Inc.

points, network adapter cards, and routers. If you can successfully ping computers of different operating systems but cannot view them or their shares, check the following:

- Is the firewall configured to block packets from the other operating systems? To check this, temporarily disable the firewall and attempt to view the computers and shares.

- Are the computers assigned to the same workgroup/domain? Correct if necessary.

- Are the IP assignment, subnet mask, and DNS server assignment to the network adapter all properly configured?

- Is the Samba or NFS configuration correct?

- Is the user attempting to access the share from a local user account with the proper permissions to access the share when configured as a peer-to-peer network?

- Is the user and the user's computer a member of the domain when configured as a client/server network?

- Are there any typographical errors, or *typos*, in the user account name or computer name in share permissions and domain members? Typos are very common when setting up a new system.

Always check the operating system FAQ for known issues involving interoperability. Check the Microsoft and the appropriate Unix/Linux system support websites.

Note

At the time of this writing, the Network+ Exam does not cover competencies associated with system interoperability and Unix/Linux systems. This may change in the future because system interoperability is crucial for the technician. For example, many Internet service providers, web-host providers, and network backup and storage sites use Unix and Linux servers.

Mac OS X Server

Mac OS X Server is the latest in the series of Apple server network operating systems. It is included in this chapter because it is basically a Linux system designed from open-source software. The Mac OS X Server operating system contains all the features found in a typical Linux system, such as Samba, Apache, X Windows, CUPS, and LDAP.

The Mac OS X Server can be configured as a primary domain controller to control user authentication. When configured as a primary domain controller, Windows workstations can log on directly to the network using the Mac OS X Server for authentication. You can connect workstations running Mac OS X, Microsoft Windows, or Unix/Linux. A Mac OS X Server can also be integrated into a network that is managed by Microsoft servers.

Copyright Goodheart-Willcox Co., Inc.

Summary

Unix

- Unix was developed at the AT&T Bell Laboratories in the 1960s.
- The source code used for components is readily available to anyone.
- Unix/Linux consists of the system kernel surrounded by modules.
- A *daemon* is a program that runs in the background and waits for a client to request its services.

Linux

- Linux is a variation of the Unix operating system.
- The term *Linux* refers to the operating system kernel.
- The Linux kernel was created in 1991 at the University of Helsinki by Linus Torvalds.
- Linux uses a *General Public License (GPL)*, known as a *copyleft*, to allow Linux users to copy, modify, and distribute Linux software.
- The Linux kernel is further enhanced by many software packages, such as GNOME, KDE, Apache, and Samba, which have become the de facto standard for distribution with Linux.
- Advantages to Linux include flexibility and price. Disadvantages include a lack of support and vulnerability to hacking or cracking.

Unix/Linux Basics

- LILO and GRUB are boot loader programs that start the Linux operating system load process and can be used to load other operating systems.
- A *shell* is a user interface that interprets and carries out commands.
- Unix/Linux file and directory names are case-sensitive.
- Several choices of Linux file systems are available, such as Ext2, Ext3, Ext4, ReiserFS, JFS1, and JFS.
- ReiserFS, JFS, JFS1, Ext3, and Ext4 are journaling file systems.
- A journaling file system ensures file integrity by maintaining a log of all file activity whenever an unexpected system shutdown occurs.
- The Unix/Linux file structure looks similar to the Microsoft file structure; however, Unix/Linux does not use drive letters.
- The top of the Unix/Linux directory structure is called the *root directory* and is indicated by the forward slash (*/*) symbol.
- All file structures from storage devices, such as CD-ROM drives and shared resources from remote systems, are appended to the root through the mounting process.
- Hardware such as the DVD device must be mounted before it can be used.
- The read, write, and execute permission can be set for a file or directory's owner, default group, and other users.
- The highest level of administration is the superuser and has the default user account name of *root*.

Copyright Goodheart-Willcox Co., Inc.

- The Network File System (NFS) was developed by Sun Microsystems for exchanging files on a network.
- NFS works in conjunction with TCP/IP to transfer files across a network system.
- Local and remote printing services are handled by the line printer daemon (lpd).
- Various protocols and services, such as FTP, TFTP, Telnet, and Apache, provide remote access to clients anywhere in the world.
- Apache is the default Web server software package used with Unix/Linux.

X Windows System

- The X Windows system provides a GUI for Unix and Linux systems.
- The X Windows system consists of an X server and an X client and has a client/server architecture.
- When X server is installed, it is configured for the system hardware.
- Two of the most commonly used desktop environments used with Unix/Linux are GNOME and KDE.
- A tarball is a compressed file containing one or more software programs.

Interoperability

- Samba is a free software package that allows Unix/Linux systems to share files and printers with Windows-based clients.
- Originally, Microsoft used gateway services to support interoperability between Unix/Linux systems.
- Windows Server 2016 provides support for NFS through the Services for Network File System server role.

Mac OS X Server

- Mac OS X Server is designed from open-source software and contains all the features found in a typical Linux system, such as Samba, Apache, X Windows, CUPS, and LDAP.
- Workstations running Mac OS X, Windows, or Unix/Linux can be connected.

Review Questions

1. What is the native communication protocol used for Unix?
2. Why are Unix and Linux a favorite among programmers and programming enthusiasts?
3. What is a daemon?
4. What are some advantages and disadvantages of Linux?
5. Describe the purpose of a GNU General Public License.
6. What is the purpose of LILO and GRUB?
7. What is the function of a shell?

Copyright Goodheart-Willcox Co., Inc.

8. List three common shells used with Unix/Linux.

9. What is Ext2?

10. What is Ext3?

11. What is JFS?

12. What is a journaling file system?

13. Using the DOS file system as a comparison, describe the Unix/Linux file system.

14. All files and all directories on a Unix/Linux system are located under the _____ directory.

15. What does mounting a device do?

16. What is a mount point?

17. What are the three Linux file and directory permissions and how are they indicated?

18. What is the difference between FTP and TFTP?

19. What is Telnet used for?

20. What does X Windows do?

21. What are the two most common desktop environments associated with X Windows?

22. What is the purpose of the Samba program?

23. What does the acronym NFS represent?

24. What is the purpose of NFS?

25. _____ is basically a Linux system designed from open-source software.

✚ Sample Network+ Exam Questions

1. What program is most commonly used on Unix/Linux systems to provide web services?

   A. Samba

   B. TFTP

   C. Telnet

   D. Apache

2. In a Linux system, how is the second partition on the first hard disk drive identified?

   A. /dev/hda1

   B. /dev/hda2

   C. /hda/dev2

   D. /dev0/part2

Copyright Goodheart-Willcox Co., Inc.

3. What program is used to allow Windows workstations to access files on a Linux server?

    A. Samba

    B. Network File System

    C. TCP/IP

    D. Microsoft Client

4. Which file system is *not* typically associated with a Linux system?

    A. Ext2

    B. Ext3

    C. ReiserFS

    D. NTFS

5. What protocol is used for communication between a Unix and a Microsoft domain?

    A. SMB

    B. NetBEUI

    C. RIP

    D. DHCP

6. Which of the following server operating systems is based on Unix design and open-source software?

    A. Mac OS X

    B. Microsoft Enterprise Server 2016

    C. Microsoft NT 4.0

    D. Novell Netware 5.0

7. What is the default name of the server administrator in Unix?

    A. Admin

    B. Administrator

    C. Root

    D. Man

8. Which of the following protocols is used by Windows to support communication with a Unix system?

    A. IPX/SPX

    B. SMB

    C. NetBEUI

    D. AppleShare

9. Where is the C partition located in a Linux directory structure?

    A. Directly under the root.

    B. Between the B and D partition.

    C. Users have their own C partition created when their user account is created.

    D. There is never a C partition in the Linux directory structure.

10. What is required to run a graphical user interface on a Linux server?

    A. Samba

    B. Apache

    C. X Windows

    D. Inode

Introduction to Servers

Network+ Certification Exam Objectives

The Network+ Certification exam specifically references fault tolerance and network storage. Pay particular attention to the characteristics of RAID 0, RAID 1, RAID 5, and RAID 6 and to network storage, such as storage area network (SAN) and network-attached storage (NAS). RAID is no longer directly listed as a Network+ objective, but questions will come up that involve RAID.

Objectives

2.4: Virtual Networking Components
Network Storage Types
Connection Type

Learning Outcomes

- Provide examples of server types and services.
- Recall the characteristics of a Small Computer Systems Interface (SCSI).
- Describe the ACPI and ACPICA standards.
- List examples of system resources.
- Compare RAID systems.
- Explain the purpose of external storage systems.
- Differentiate between Fibre Channel applications and topologies.
- Interpret an iSCSI IQN address.
- Describe uses of virtualization in networking environments.
- Describe the purpose of a hypervisor.
- List resources for furthering study of servers.

Copyright Goodheart-Willcox Co., Inc.

Key Terms

ACPI Component Architecture (ACPICA)

Automatic Configuration and Power Interface (ACPI)

backplane

blade server

direct memory access (DMA) channel

disk mirroring

disk striping

duplexing

error correction

fabric switch

fault tolerance

Fibre Channel

firmware

hot swapping

hot-swap technology

input/output (I/O) port

Internet Small Computer Systems Interface (iSCSI)

interrupt request (IRQ)

logical unit number (LUN)

memory address assignment

Network Address Authority (NAA)

network-attached storage (NAS)

parallel processing

power-on self-test (POST)

Redundant Array of Independent Disks (RAID)

Serial Attached SCSI (SAS)

Small Computer Systems Interface (SCSI)

storage area network (SAN)

thin server

virtualization

Overview

A complete understanding of server hardware can take a great deal of study. This chapter provides an overview of a server and identifies different server types and their roles. You will be introduced to some of the hardware that makes the server unique from an ordinary PC, and you will learn about RAID and other storage systems.

Essentially, a server is simply a computer that responds to request for some service using some protocol (HTTP, FTP, SMTP, etc.). However, because servers are generally intended to have a larger volume of connections and workflow than a typical PC, there are special hardware improvements designed to facilitate stability and fault tolerance.

Server Types and Services

As the name implies, servers provide a variety of services. Some of the services a server can provide are authentication and security, web access, mail, and printing. A server can be called by many names. For example, it can be called an *authentication and security database server*, *web server*, *mail server*, and *print server*, as demonstrated in Figure 9-1. A network may have a single server that provides a variety of services, or it may have a group of servers, each providing a specific service.

A small network usually has one server equipped to handle many different services. A large network usually has several servers, each providing a different service or set of services. For example, a large corporation may use one server to handle e-mail requests and web hosting; another server to serve as a domain controller to provide security for the entire network; and a third server to provide application software, a database for its clients, and support for print operations.

Each network system is uniquely designed, even though each network has many similarities. Some network equipment providers have software programs to help design a network. Information, such as the number of clients, offices, cities, countries, and the type of software and services to be provided is entered by an administrator. After all the information is collected, the software program provides an estimate of the size and number of servers required. This topic will be discussed in further detail in Chapter 18.

Figure 9-1 Servers provide a variety of services, such as authentication and security, web, mail, and print.

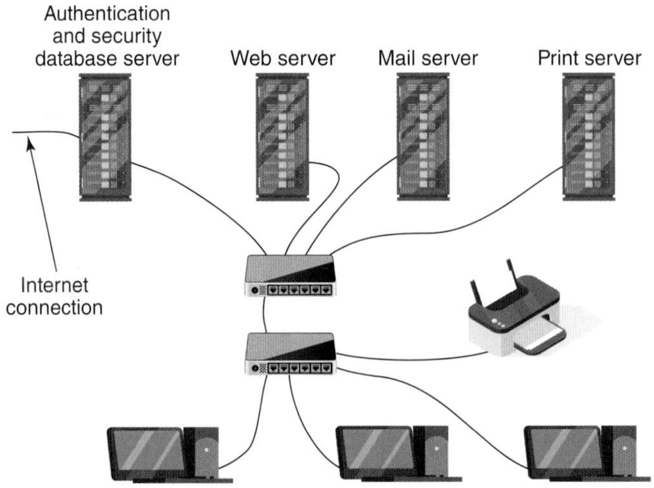

Top row: fullvector/Shutterstock.com; Middle row: Vadim Ermak/Shutterstock.com, Vectors Bang/Shutterstock.com; Bottom row: RedlineVector/Shutterstock.com; Goodheart-Willcox Publisher

Thin Servers

A **thin server** is a server that has only the hardware and software needed to support and run a specific function, such as web services, print services, or file services. This term is not widely used in industry anymore, but it may be encountered in day-to-day activities. The primary feature of a thin server is limited hardware. Therefore, thin servers tend to be less expensive. It is more economical to use a thin server as a print server than to tie up a more expensive server simply to handle printing on a network. IBM markets a thin server, which consists of a sealed box that contains only the essential hardware and software required for supporting the server's dedicated function.

Server Classification by Number of CPUs

Servers vary a great deal by size and power. The number of processors they contain usually classifies them. For example, Sun Microsystems has three classifications of servers: entry-level, midrange, and high-end. Sun Microsystems defines these classifications by the number of processors they contain. A Sun Microsystems entry-level server has up to eight processors. A midrange server has up to 30 processors, and a high-end server has up to 106 processors. Other vendor's definitions vary somewhat, but this is a general idea. In this chapter, the HP ProLiant DL740 server is the main focus. The HP ProLiant DL740 is one of the most powerful entry-level servers manufactured.

Major Server Components

It is assumed you have some PC hardware background from completing a course on PC service and repair or have a CompTIA A+ Certification. If not, it is strongly advised that you take a course in PC repair or, at the very least, complete a home-study program. A good background in PC hardware proves to be beneficial to anyone working with network servers. As a matter of fact, IBM and other companies require the CompTIA A+ Certification as part of its progression toward certification as a server technician.

Copyright Goodheart-Willcox Co., Inc.

When handling electronic components, it is standard practice to use electrostatic discharge (ESD) safety practices. Electronic components based on complementary metal-oxide semiconductor (CMOS) technology can be easily damaged by static electricity. The human body and clothing can build up a tremendous static electricity charge. When touching a static-sensitive electronic component, the static electricity can discharge and cause the component to be destroyed. To avoid damaging electronic components, use an antistatic wrist strap, which is designed to drain static charges safely.

The major components of a server are similar to a typical PC. In fact, a typical PC can be used as a server for a small network. A network server can be as simple as a typical PC or as complex as a piece of equipment designed exclusively for networks. Some server models with multiple CPUs, large amounts of RAM, and vast amounts of storage space can be thought of as a "small" mainframe rather than as a PC. There are many server designs available. As part of your study of network servers, it is highly advisable to check the IBM, Sun Microsystems, HP, and Cisco websites to see the available designs. This section looks at the following components: case, hot-swap components, power supply, motherboard, BIOS, and CPU.

Server Case

Server case styles vary greatly. Some are similar to desktop models. Some are designed to be mounted into a rack similar to the server depicted in Figure 9-2. Large enterprise servers are actually a group of individual servers mounted in a rack system or cabinet, as shown in Figure 9-3. The group of servers acts as one unit that has multiple CPUs and a large amount of system resources, such as hard disk drive storage and RAM.

Caution

Do *not* use an antistatic wrist strap when servicing any component with live voltage present.

Caution

Do *not* open a CRT monitor while wearing an antistatic wrist strap, even if the CRT is unplugged. CRT screens can hold a high voltage charge for long periods of time after they have been disconnected from electrical power.

Figure 9-2 The ProLiant DL740 can be mounted into a rack.

Hewlett-Packard Company

Figure 9-3 This cabinet can store many servers, allowing them to act as a single unit.

Hewlett-Packard Company

A **blade server** is an extremely thin server designed to allow a large number of servers to be mounted in a small space. Its name is derived from its size and shape, as illustrated in Figure 9-4. A blade server can contain more than one processor and be quite powerful. They are often selected for applications where there is a requirement for many servers to perform the same or similar function. For example, they may be used in a large web service facility or a file-server farm.

Hot-Swap Components

Servers are generally designed to provide continuous service with minimal interruptions and data loss. The main feature that most servers use to provide this continuous service is hot-swap technology. **Hot-swap technology** allows a component to be removed or installed while the system is running. There is no need to power down the system while replacing or adding major components. The most common hot-swappable component is a hard drive. This only works if there is redundancy in the drives, such as a RAID array, which will be discussed later in this chapter. Never assume a component is hot-swappable. Always check the system manual before removing any component while the system is powered on.

Copyright Goodheart-Willcox Co., Inc.

Figure 9-4 A blade server is thin, yet powerful. It is designed to allow many blade servers to be installed in a small area. A—A single blade server. B—Many blade servers installed in a single rack.

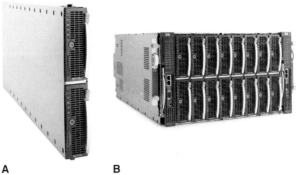

A   B

Hewlett-Packard Company

Power Supply

The power supply converts standard 120-volt or 240-volt AC power into lower DC voltage levels that can be used by the motherboard and other devices inside the computer case. A typical power supply provides an assortment of output plugs. The plug style matches the intended piece of equipment. For example, a standard ATA drive uses a Molex plug, which supplies 5 volts DC and 12 volts DC to the ATA drive. An ATX-style motherboard plug supplies 3.3 volts, 5 volts, and 12 volts as well as a ground connection to the motherboard. It is also designed to plug into the motherboard correctly. Older style connections could be incorrectly plugged into the motherboard if you did not pay attention to the color-coding.

Entry-level servers are typically equipped with two power supplies, similar to the one shown in Figure 9-5. The two power supplies balance the load. If one power supply fails, the other power supply carries the full load. Some servers are designed with "hot-swappable" power supplies, which permit the defective power supply to be changed while the server is running.

To prevent the loss of data, most server manufacturers recommend disconnecting the server from the network while replacing hot-swappable power supplies.

Motherboard

Servers generally use a backplane. A **backplane** is a simple motherboard designed with minimal components. It typically serves as the interface of all the major components. It is designed to allow major components to be added or removed without powering down the system. Removing components without shutting down the system is called **hot swapping**.

Figure 9-6 shows the general backplane layout of the HP ProLiant DL740 server with and without the added modules. An I/O board attaches to the backplane. It contains six PCI hot-swappable slots. The processor boards each contain four CPUs, for a total of eight CPUs. Each memory module in the system is hot-swappable and contains eight DIMMS. The HP ProLiant DL740 can contain up to 40 GB of RAM. The multiple CPUs and vast amount of RAM are required to provide the many different services to numerous network clients with minimal delay. The CPUs need not be the latest, high-speed processors available because there are numerous processors in the server.

BIOS

The *basic input/output system (BIOS)* contains a small software program that starts the server boot operation when power is applied to the server. The combination BIOS

Figure 9-5 Back view of the ProLiant ML350. This system comes with two power supplies that evenly distribute power throughout the system. When one power supply fails, the other carries the full load.

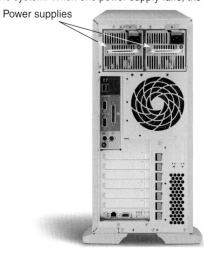

Power supplies

Hewlett-Packard Company

Figure 9-6 The backplane layout of the ProLiant DL740.

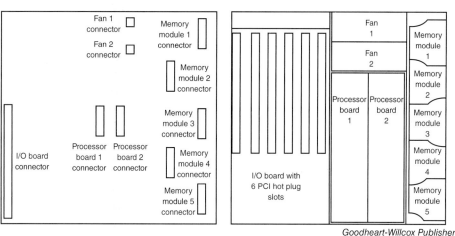

Backplane

Backplane with modules and I/O board

Goodheart-Willcox Publisher

chip and the software program are usually referred to as **firmware**. The BIOS is responsible for the **power-on self-test (POST)**, which is a quick, initial check of the major components, such as memory, disk drives, keyboard, mouse, and monitor, performed at startup to be sure that a minimum working system is available. After a general check is made of the major hardware components is completed, the BIOS turns control over to the operating system software. The operating system completes the boot process by loading more advanced hardware drivers than the BIOS did. It also performs a more sophisticated check of hardware and software systems. If all the software and hardware components appear to be in working order, the final screen, which serves as a user interface, appears.

Most modern computers use the Unified Extensible Firmware Interface (UEFI) instead of BIOS. It accomplishes the same purpose, and many people still refer to the BIOS, even though it is UEFI. Version 1 of UEFI was released in 2005. Version 2.5 was released in 2015. UEFI has a few features that are superior to BIOS. First, UEFI supports very large disks, over two terabytes using a GUID partition table (GTP). UEFI is also CPU-independent and has a flexible pre-operating system environment that can even support networking.

Copyright Goodheart-Willcox Co., Inc.

Central Processing Unit (CPU)

One major difference between a server and a typical PC is that many servers have multiple CPUs installed rather than just one. When multiple CPUs are installed, the server can perform **parallel processing**, which is when a program can be processed through more than one CPU simultaneously. Another advantage of multiple CPUs is several clients may be serviced at the same time rather than waiting their turn to access a single CPU. Supercomputers and enterprise servers may contain over 1,000 CPUs.

A small-office server can function efficiently with one processor, especially if demand on the server is low. A large enterprise system requires multiple processors to meet the demands of the server's clients.

Small Computer Systems Interface (SCSI)

Small Computer Systems Interface (SCSI), pronounced *skuzzy*, is a computer bus technology that allows for the connection of multiple devices to a single controller. The benefits of SCSI technology can be readily observed in the chart in Figure 9-7. SCSI technology not only allows multiple devices to connect to a single controller, it also supports high data transfer rates. This is quite a performance improvement when compared to the traditional IDE or ATA attachment. SCSI is ideal for servers that must hold large amounts of data that is accessed by numerous clients.

Figure 9-7 SCSI technology specifications.

Common Name	Class	Devices	Bus Width in Bits	Speed	MBps
SCSI-1	SCSI-1	8	8	5 MHz	4-5 MBps
Wide SCSI	SCSI-2	16	8	5 MHz	10 MBps
Fast SCSI	SCSI-2	8	8	10 MHz	10 MBps
Fast/Wide SCSI	SCSI-2	16	16	10 MHz	20 MBps
Ultra SCSI	SCSI-3	8	8	20 MHz	20 MBps
Ultra/Wide	SCSI-3	8	16	20 MHz	20 MBps
Ultra2	SCSI-3	8	8	40 MHz	40 MBps
Ultra2/Wide SCSI	SCSI-3	16	16	40 MHz	80 MBps
Ultra3 SCSI	SCSI-3	16	16	40 MHz	160 MBps
Ultra Wide 320	SCSI-3	16	16	80 MHz	320 MBps
Ultra Wide 640	SCSI-3	16	16	160 MHz	640 MBps

Goodheart-Willcox Publisher

Many SCSI drives are hot-swappable devices. Often, SCSI drives are arranged in the server with hot-swap bays open to the outside of the case to provide easy access. This allows you to connect or disconnect a drive without opening the server case. See Figure 9-8 for an image of these hot-swappable SCSI drives.

SCSI technology has evolved over the years. With this evolution, new names have emerged to describe the improved technology. The term *Wide* is used to indicate 16-bit data transfers in place of 8-bit data transfers. To reflect the increase in frequency, the term *Fast* was used and then the term *Ultra*. Combination of the words, such as *Ultra/Wide*, are also used to express the newer technologies. Ultra/Wide means the SCSI device is faster and supports 16-bit transfers. A close study of the table in Figure 9-7 will help you understand the evolution of the SCSI technology.

A SCSI hardware system consists of a host adapter or controller card, a flat ribbon cable to connect SCSI devices, and SCSI devices such as disk drives, CD-ROMs,

Copyright Goodheart-Willcox Co., Inc.

and tape drives. SCSI cables come in a variety to match the many different classifications of SCSI. The cables come as DB-25, 50-pin, 68-pin, and 80-pin styles.

Look at Figure 9-9 to see the way a typical SCSI host adapter, cable, and devices might appear. The host adapter and devices can connect to any part of the chain. The chain of SCSI devices must be terminated. Termination is typically completed at the last device with a termination block.

Figure 9-8 Hot-swap drives are typically accessible from the front of the server for easy access.

Hewlett-Packard Company

Figure 9-9 Typical SCSI drive arrangement.

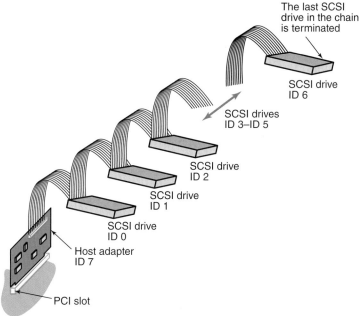

Goodheart-Willcox Publisher

SCSI ID Numbers

Each device, including the host adapter card, must have a unique ID number. The numbers start at zero and end at either seven for an eight-device SCSI chain or at 15 for a 16-device SCSI chain. The host adapter typically is assigned the highest number.

SCSI ID numbers are assigned through pins and jumpers on the SCSI drive. The pins are arranged in pairs. When a jumper is applied across the pins, an electrical

Copyright Goodheart-Willcox Co., Inc.

connection is made. The pairs of pins represent the binary number system. The jumpers are applied in a binary pattern that represents the SCSI ID number. Figure 9-10 illustrates each of the binary patterns and the related SCSI ID number.

Logical Unit Number (LUN)

SCSI devices are not limited to internal devices. The SCSI chain can extend outside the case by adding an extender card to the SCSI chain. The extender card allows more devices to be attached to existing SCSI systems. The extender card is an integrated circuit card connected to the SCSI chain as a SCSI device. Figure 9-11 diagrams the use of extender cards.

Figure 9-10 SCSI binary patterns.

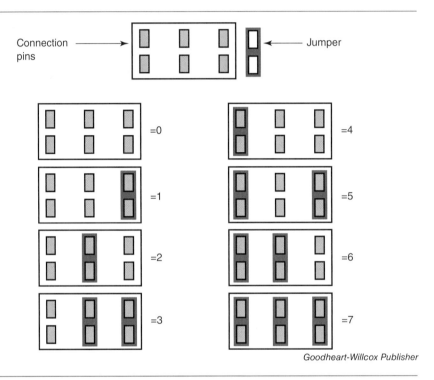

Goodheart-Willcox Publisher

Figure 9-11 The SCSI limit of seven devices can be expanded by using extender cards. Each extender card allows an additional seven devices to be connected to the SCSI system. LUN numbers are assigned to the additional SCSI devices so they can be identified by the system software and BIOS.

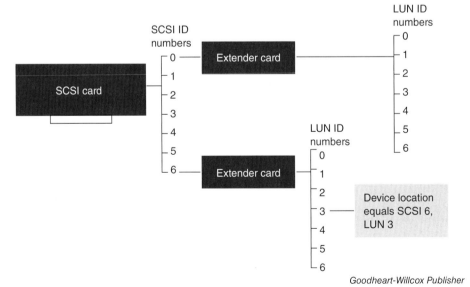

Goodheart-Willcox Publisher

Copyright Goodheart-Willcox Co., Inc.

When additional devices are attached, they are identified separately from the original chain of devices. Each additional device connected to the SCSI extender is identified with a **logical unit number (LUN)**. SCSI bus extenders are also referred to as *SCSI expanders*, *repeaters*, and *regenerators*. External SCSI device chains are commonly used in Redundant Array of Independent Disk (RAID) systems. RAID systems are covered later in this chapter.

Serial Attached SCSI

Serial Attached SCSI (SAS) is the next generation of SCSI. It uses a serial port similar to the SATA serial drive port, as shown in Figure 9-12. This eliminates the need of the wide SCSI cable and produces faster data transfer rates. First-generation SAS devices can achieve data rates as high as 3 Gbps. Second-generation SAS devices can achieve rates of 6 Gbps. Note that these speeds are expressed in bits per second (bps), not bytes per second (Bps). This is because SAS transfers data in a serial fashion. The SAS design allows 128 devices to be attached directly. Through the use of edge expander devices, a maximum of 65,000 SAS devices can be connected. That is of course hypothetical. No one would really want to connect 65,000 devices.

Figure 9-12 SAS and SATA disk drive connectors. Notice the two connector types are similar.

SAS

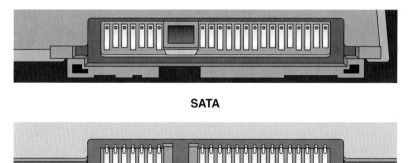

SATA

Goodheart-Willcox Publisher

ACPI and ACPICA

Automatic Configuration and Power Interface (ACPI) is a standard for controlling the power options for computer hardware devices. The first implementation of the ACPI standard gave users the ability to select how they wanted their computers to behave to conserve power. For example, a user could configure a computer or individual devices to go into a state of hibernation after a period of inactivity.

Figure 9-13 shows the power options available for a wireless network adapter. These options allow the computer to turn off the adapter to save power and allow the adapter to wake the computer when network activity occurs.

ACPI Component Architecture (ACPICA) is an extension to the original ACPI standard. The goal of ACPICA is to create a nonproprietary software package for configuring hardware. An ACPICA-compliant device is independent of an operating system. ACPICA is written in the C language and is an open standard, allowing any computer software or hardware manufacturer to share power-saving features rather than developing proprietary power-saving features. ACPICA is compatible with both 32-bit and 64-bit systems.

Copyright Goodheart-Willcox Co., Inc.

Figure 9-13 Power options for a wireless network adapter.

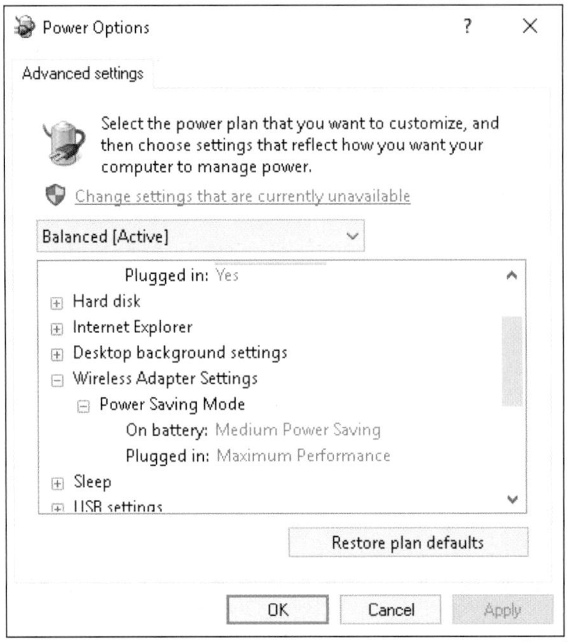

Goodheart-Willcox Publisher

Some of the companies that participate with the goals of ACPICA are Microsoft, HP, Intel, and several Linux organizations. To learn more about ACPICA, navigate to the ACPICA website at www.acpica.org.

System Resources

System resources refer to resources such as interrupt requests, direct memory access (DMA) channels, input/output ports, and memory. System resources are assigned to components installed in the computer system, such as hard disk drives, keyboards, and mice. In a Windows-based server, you can view system resource assignments in Device Manager.

Not all devices have all four types of resources assigned to them. For example, some devices do not require a DMA channel assignment. System resources typically cannot be shared between two devices. Sharing the same system resource causes a system resource conflict, referred to simply as a *conflict*. Conflicts must be resolved before the system can operate properly. An exception to this rule is motherboard chips used to bridge different bus systems. A motherboard chip can share an interrupt request (IRQ) with a hardware device.

Interrupt Request (IRQ)

An **interrupt request (IRQ)** is a circuit that communicates with the CPU. Hardware devices send an electrical signal to the CPU using an assigned IRQ circuit. Historically, there were originally 16 IRQ assignments numbered from 0 to 15. Having only 16 IRQs harkens back to 16-bit operating systems. Today, there are IRQ numbers over 16 (namely up to 32) that are used in computers today, as shown in Figure 9-14. IRQ numbers start from 0 and go to 31. Many of the assignments cannot be changed, but some can. When plug-and-play devices are used, the IRQ is automatically assigned. Typically, each hardware device must use a separate IRQ to communicate with the CPU. If two hardware devices are assigned the same IRQ, an IRQ conflict occurs.

Copyright Goodheart-Willcox Co., Inc.

Figure 9-14 IRQ assignments.

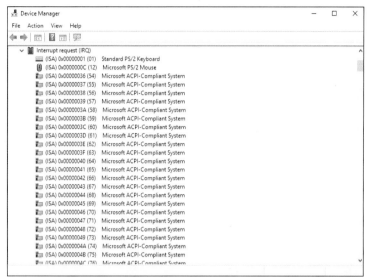

Goodheart-Willcox Publisher

Tech Tip

Yellow question marks next to devices in Device Manager indicate there is a problem with the device or assignment.

Once the first device contacts the CPU using the IRQ assignment, the other device cannot communicate with the CPU. An IRQ conflict can lead to problems such as an inoperable device, system crash, or system lockup. An IRQ can typically be assigned manually by first entering the BIOS setup program and disabling plug-and-play detection. Changes to the IRQ can then be made through Device Manager. After the problem device has been assigned the proper IRQ, plug-and-play detection can be activated without a problem.

Direct Memory Access (DMA) Channel

A **direct memory access (DMA) channel** is a circuit that allows devices to communicate and transfer data to and from RAM without the need of CPU intervention. Computer systems were first designed with the CPU handling all communication. Every bit of data had to travel through the CPU. DMA technology was introduced to save valuable processor time.

DMA works in conjunction with motherboard chipsets, BIOS software, and the CPU. Large blocks of data that need to be transferred between hardware devices and memory are transferred through a DMA channel that is assigned to the device. Figure 9-15 shows the DMA controller identified by Device Manager.

One of the devices controlled by the DMA memory access controller is the computer ATA drive. Figure 9-16 shows what the **Advanced Settings** tab for the IDE channel used to look like. In this figure, the IDE channel has been assigned to a DMA channel to take advantage of fast data transfer. Since most drives are now SATA, IDE is not commonly encountered, if at all. It is included here for historical purposes.

Input/Output (I/O) Port

The **input/output (I/O) port** is a small amount of memory assigned to a device that temporarily holds small amounts of data. It is used to transfer data between two locations. The data remains in the I/O port assignment until it can be moved.

The system has many hardware devices and software programs that depend on transferring data between hardware and memory locations. When a device or software program wants to transfer data, it may need to wait until the CPU is finished with its current process. In fact, it may need to wait until several processes are com-

Figure 9-15 DMA assignment.

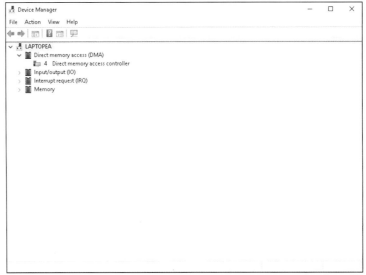

Goodheart-Willcox Publisher

Figure 9-16 IDE Channel Properties dialog box **Advanced Settings** tab. The IDE channel is assigned to a DMA channel by enabling DMA.

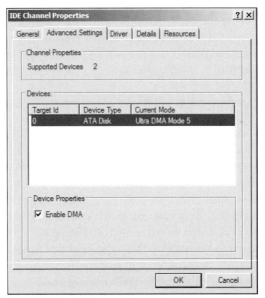

Goodheart-Willcox Publisher

pleted before the CPU can handle the data. The I/O port stores this data until the CPU is free. Figure 9-17 shows the I/O port assignments associated with a system's hardware devices.

Memory Address Assignment

A **memory address assignment** is a large block of memory assigned to a device and is used to transfer data between two locations. A device is assigned a range of memory addresses. Some devices, such as video and sound cards, require a great deal of memory. The blocks of RAM assigned to a device cannot be used by any other device. Figure 9-18 shows the memory assignments associated with a system's hardware devices.

Copyright Goodheart-Willcox Co., Inc.

Figure 9-17 I/O port assignments.

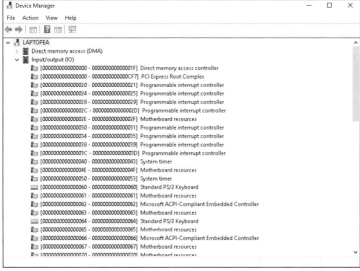

Goodheart-Willcox Publisher

Figure 9-18 Memory assignments.

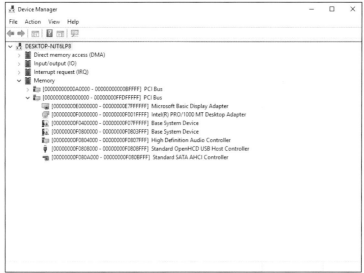

Goodheart-Willcox Publisher

RAID Systems

Redundant Array of Independent Disks (RAID) is a system of disks arranged for speed, fault tolerance, or both. **Fault tolerance** as applied to RAID systems means the ability to recover from a hard disk or hard disk controller failure without the loss of stored data. *Fault tolerance* as applied to a network infrastructure means the ability to continue operation during a system hardware or software error. To achieve a high data transfer rate, a technique known as *disk striping* is used. **Disk striping** involves dividing the data into separate sections and writing the data across several hard disk drives at the same time. This reduces the total amount of time it takes to store large amounts of data.

Another RAID technique is **error correction**, which can use traditional error-checking code (ECC) or parity. ECC is obsolete as a method for RAID because

Tech Tip

Another accepted representation of the RAID acronym is Redundant Array of Inexpensive Disks.

most hard disk drive systems use ECC as a standard way to protect data. Incorporating ECC into a RAID system would be redundant.

Parity is a technique that allows data to be recovered if one of the hard disk drives fails in a multiple disk drive system. A minimum of three hard disk drives must be used for this technique. If three hard disk drives are used, one hard disk drive is used to store parity and the other two are used to store data. Data is spread evenly between the two data storage drives, and the parity code for the sum of the two data storage drives is stored on the parity drive.

Parity is also a binary code that represents the total data pattern shared between the data storage drives. If any data storage drive fails, the system can use the parity bit to rebuild the missing data.

RAID systems are referred to as *RAID levels*. There are many RAID levels, each incorporating a different technique to increase speed, provide data redundancy, or both. Things to consider when selecting a RAID level are cost, reliability, and speed. There is no single best RAID level. The appropriate level depends on the value of the data being protected and the amount of budget available. If a bank were protecting financial data, cost would most likely be of little concern. A RAID 5 with an optical, tape, or other suitable backup would be quite appropriate. If you were protecting a personal computer, you would not likely need a RAID system. See Figure 9-19 for a list of RAID levels and a short description of each. RAID levels will be discussed in detail in the next section of text.

Figure 9-19 RAID levels.

RAID Level	Description
RAID 0	Striping.
RAID 1	Mirroring or duplexing.
RAID 2	Error checking code (ECC).
RAID 3	Byte-level striping with parity.
RAID 4	Block-level striping with parity.
RAID 5	Block-level striping with distributed parity.
RAID 6	Dual parity.
RAID 0/1 or 10	Disk mirroring with striping.
RAID 0/5 or 50	Block striping with parity and striping.

Goodheart-Willcox Publisher

In the event of a failed RAID array, the physical drive must be replaced and then the data reconstructed. In a Microsoft Windows operating system, the Disk Management utility is used to reconstruct data. If using proprietary SCSI drives, data is reconstructed by the data-array manufacturer software package.

RAID 0

RAID 0 uses disk striping across a group of independent hard disk drives, as illustrated in Figure 9-20. This technique increases data flow but provides no fault tolerance. If one hard disk drive fails, all data is lost and cannot be reconstructed. This RAID level is most useful when speed is important, not fault tolerance.

RAID 1

RAID 1 uses the technique of disk mirroring. **Disk mirroring** is the act of writing the same information to two hard disk drives at the same time, as in Figure 9-21. Each of the two hard disk drives contains the same data. If one hard disk drive fails, a copy exists on the other hard disk drive.

Tech Tip

When implementing a RAID system in a Microsoft Windows operating system, all drives must be dynamic disk.

Copyright Goodheart-Willcox Co., Inc.

Figure 9-20 RAID 0 divides data and writes it to multiple drives. It provides excellent data transfer rates but no data loss protection.

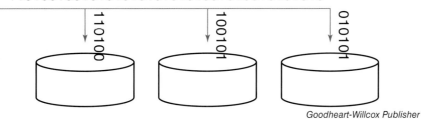

Goodheart-Willcox Publisher

Figure 9-21 RAID 1, or disk mirroring, provides a copy of data on two disk drives.

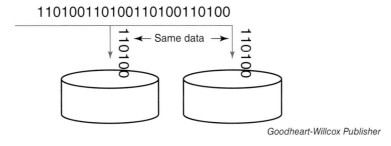

Goodheart-Willcox Publisher

Another form of RAID 1 is duplexing. **Duplexing** is the technique of placing each mirrored hard drive on a separate hard disk drive controller. Duplexing adds another level of fault tolerance. If one hard disk drive controller fails, the other is still operable. Mirroring contains the risk of the hard disk drive controller failing and causing both hard disk drives to fail. RAID 1 provides data protection at the cost of speed when compared to RAID 0. When there is a small demand for disk read/writes, RAID 1 is an appropriate technique. RAID 1 is very common in less-expensive servers.

RAID 2

RAID 2 uses common ECC error-correction code to provide fault tolerance. All drives provide some sort of ECC, so this form of RAID is obsolete and unlikely to be encountered in today's networking environments.

RAID 3

RAID 3 stripes data across multiple drives and stores parity on a separate drive. Data striping is performed at the byte level. See Figure 9-22 for an illustration of RAID 3 striping.

RAID 4

RAID 4 stripes data across several drives and stores parity on a separate drive. The main difference between RAID 3 and RAID 4 is RAID 4 stores data in blocks. The size of the block can vary.

RAID 5

RAID 5 is also called *block striping with distributed parity*. RAID 5 distributes parity across all drives rather than writing parity to one drive, as illustrated in in Figure 9-23. It provides fault tolerance and some increase in read-write data transfer. RAID 5 is very common for high-end servers.

Copyright Goodheart-Willcox Co., Inc.

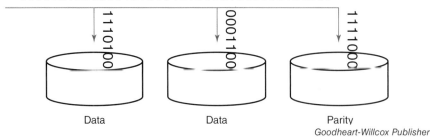

Figure 9-22 RAID 3 writes across multiple drives with parity stored on a separate drive.

Data Data Parity

Goodheart-Willcox Publisher

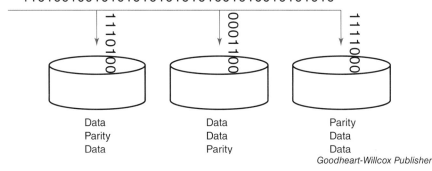

Figure 9-23 RAID 5 provides both disk striping and parity. Parity and data is distributed across all drives.

Data / Parity / Data   Data / Data / Parity   Parity / Data / Data

Goodheart-Willcox Publisher

RAID 6

RAID 6 is similar to RAID 5 in that it distributes parity across all drives, except RAID 6 uses a second set of parity. This technique is referred to as *dual parity*. The additional parity set allows for protection from simultaneous two-disk failure. Since two simultaneous disk failures are rarely encountered, RAID 6 is not commonly used.

RAID 1+0

RAID 1+0 first stripes a set of disks, then mirrors that striped set. It combines the speed advantage of striping with the fault tolerance of mirroring.

Network+ Note

Pay particular attention to RAID 0, 1, and 5. These systems are the most commonly used and are the ones most likely to be covered on the Network+ Certification Exam.

NET 2.4

External Storage Systems

Data is often stored separately from a server. There are network devices that serve specifically as storage containers for network data. These devices are typically called *network-attached storage (NAS)*. There are also facilities external to the local area network that provide data storage. These devices are typically called a *storage area network (SAN)*. This section discusses both types of storage systems.

Copyright Goodheart-Willcox Co., Inc.

Network-Attached Storage (NAS)

Network-attached storage (NAS) is a device or collection of devices that provides storage for network data. Network-attached storage units are typically composed of disk arrays or tape arrays. The file systems used on a disk array and tape array do not typically match the file system used by network clients or servers. The file systems are proprietary and are made to facilitate access speed and data integrity.

Data can be accessed on a NAS device through a client submitting a request for data from the file server. The file server then makes a request to the NAS device. The NAS device retrieves the data and sends it to the file server. The file server, in turn, sends the data to the client. See Figure 9-24 for an illustration of NAS.

Figure 9-24 In a network-attached storage (NAS) design, clients make requests for data through the network file server. The file server then makes a request to the NAS device. The NAS device retrieves the data and sends it to the file server. The file server forwards the data to the client.

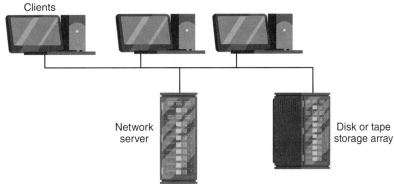

Top row: RedlineVector/Shutterstock.com; Bottom row: fullvector/Shutterstock.com; Goodheart-Willcox Publisher

Storage Area Network (SAN)

A **storage area network (SAN)** is a separate, high-speed network that provides a storage facility for one or more networks. Typically, a SAN uses a high-speed access media such as Fibre Channel. Figure 9-25 provides a visual overview of SAN. Fibre Channel is discussed in the next section of the chapter.

Tech Tip

Exact definitions of storage area network vary according to different manufacturers. Often, the differences are blurred.

Fibre Channel

Fibre Channel is a high-speed access method that typically uses fiber-optic cable as network media. It may also use copper-core cable and wireless. The term *Fibre Channel* also refers to a set of standards and a protocol. The Fibre Channel standard provides a relatively high data transmission rate between supercomputers, mainframes, servers, and desktops. Fibre Channel is often used for storage area network (SAN) access. Fiber technology can also be combined with other technology. For example, Fibre Channel over Ethernet (FCoE) uses Ethernet frames sent over fiber cable.

2.4 NET

Copyright Goodheart-Willcox Co., Inc.

A Fibre Channel device uses a **Network Address Authority (NAA)**, which is a naming standard developed by the International Committee for Information Technology Standards (ICITS). The NAA address consists of the *naa.* prefix followed by a string of hexadecimal characters, for example, naa.02034D12B12124. There are three common Fibre Channel topologies: point-to-point, arbitrated loop, and fabric-switched as shown in Figure 9-26.

Figure 9-25 The storage area network (SAN) is a separate, high-speed network that provides a storage facility for other networks.

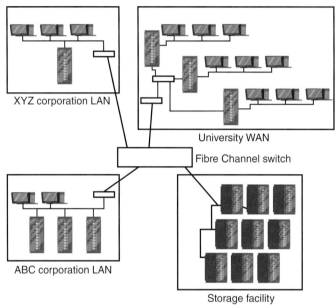

(workstation icon) RedlineVector/Shutterstock.com; (server and storage icons) fullvector/Shutterstock.com;
Goodheart-Willcox Publisher

Figure 9-26 Three major topologies associated with Fibre Channel systems are point-to-point, arbitrated loop, and fabric-switched.

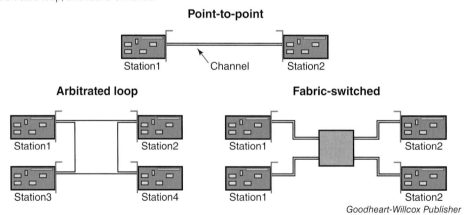

Goodheart-Willcox Publisher

Fibre Channel Point-to-Point Topology

A *Fibre Channel point-to-point topology* is simply a straight connection or channel between two points, such as a mainframe and a server. The channel is isolated from other channels or media, and the total bandwidth is dedicated to the channel between the two devices.

Copyright Goodheart-Willcox Co., Inc.

Fibre Channel Arbitrated Loop Topology

The *Fibre Channel arbitrated loop* is a common Fibre Channel topology. It looks similar to the token ring topology. The arbitrated loop differs from token ring in that two devices in the loop set up a direct communication link, or channel, for the duration of the data transfer. In a token ring network, a token is passed around the ring while one device on the ring controls communication. Token ring has a maximum control time of approximately eight milliseconds in contrast to the arbitrated loop standard, which allows two devices to communicate until all the data requested has been transferred.

The arbitrated loop is limited to 127 connections. It is used to move large volumes of data between two devices such as a disk-storage array and a server. It is not used for sporadic communication between multiple nodes as it is on a token ring network.

Fibre Channel Fabric-Switched Topology

The fabric-switched topology uses a device known as a *fabric switch*. A **fabric switch** is a switch designed specifically for Fibre Channel networking. The fabric switch provides a direct or switched connection between two points. When two points wish to communicate, a private link, or channel, is set up between the two devices. This method is best used when numerous nodes wish to access the same disk-storage array. For example, a university consisting of many buildings can connect each building's server to a common disk-storage array using the fabric-switched topology. This way, departments in each building can have access to research documents stored in the disk-storage array. They can also access servers in other buildings through a high-speed connection.

InfiniBand

InfiniBand is a network communication standard that has very high throughput with very low latency. It is a competing technology to Fibre Channel. There are several variations of InfiniBand, some achieving rates as high as 50 Gbit/s. This technology usually uses a fabric-switched technology.

2.4 NET

Internet Small Computer Systems Interface

2.4 NET

Internet Small Computer Systems Interface (iSCSI) is a network storage standard developed by the Internet Engineering Task Force (IETF). It is used to access a wide variety of storage devices such as tapes, disks, and storage arrays. The iSCSI (pronounced *eye-scuzzy*) standard is referred to as *IP-based storage* because it is designed to work on a LAN, MAN, or WAN using IPv4 and IPv6 network addresses to identify the storage device. iSCSI operates by sending SCSI commands over Ethernet using NFS or SMB/CIFS protocols. The advantages of iSCSI include the following:

- Storage devices can be located at great distances from the client, overcoming the limitations of systems such as Fibre Channel.

- It is less expensive than Fibre Channel SANs.

Windows 10 and Windows Server 2016 have a GUI interface called *iSCSI Initiator* for configuring iSCSI. It can be accessed from the **Administrative Tools** menu, as shown in Figure 9-27.

Copyright Goodheart-Willcox Co., Inc.

The iSCSI initiator is the workstation or server making the requests to the storage device. It is called the *target* and can be located either on the local area network or at some distant location across the Internet.

The iSCSI properties can be configured manually or automatically through the Network Discovery feature. Look at Figure 9-28 to see how the Network Discovery feature can automatically locate an iSCSI device on the local area network. In this

Figure 9-27 The iSCSI Initiator, located under the **Administrative Tools** menu, is a GUI used for configuring an iSCSI system.

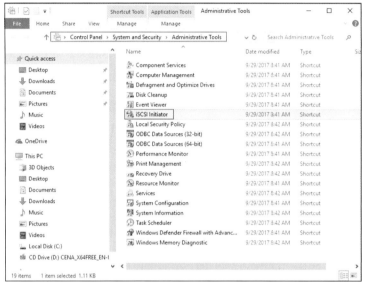

Goodheart-Willcox Publisher

Figure 9-28 Discovery tab of the **iSCSI Initiator Properties** dialog box.

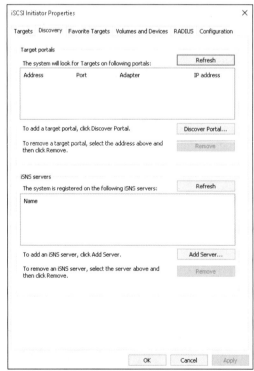

Goodheart-Willcox Publisher

Copyright Goodheart-Willcox Co., Inc.

example, the iSCSI storage device is located on a Windows Server 2016 computer using the private IP address 192.168.1.103.

iSCSI devices can be located across the Internet by using an iSCSI-qualified name (IQN) or an Enterprise Unique Name (EUI). The name can be automatically generated based on information provided by the Network Discovery feature. Figure 9-29 shows an example of an IQN address. The IQN address in the example is iqn.1991-05.com.microsoft:richar7.netlab1domain.local. The IQN name format is <type>–<date>–<authority>–<string defined by naming authority>: where

Type = iqn

Date = month and year domain was acquired

Authority = domain name

String defined by naming authority = String of characters identifying the iSCSI object

The string of characters consists of letters *A–Z*, numbers *0–9*, and special symbols hyphen (-), period (.), and colon (:). The string of characters typically provides a general description, but this is not a requirement. The string of characters can represent anything. Everything before the colon is a mandatory standard. Everything after the colon is entirely up to the naming authority.

The IQN address in the example is first identified by *iqn*. Following this are the date of origination of the address *1991-05*, the reverse domain name of the authority *com.microsoft*, and the computer name and domain.

The IEEE has developed another naming format known as the *Extended Unique Identifier* or the *IEU-64* format. The IEU format consists of the prefix *ieu* followed by a period and then by a string of hexadecimal numbers. For example,

Figure 9-29 **Configuration** tab of the **iSCSI Initiator Properties** dialog box.

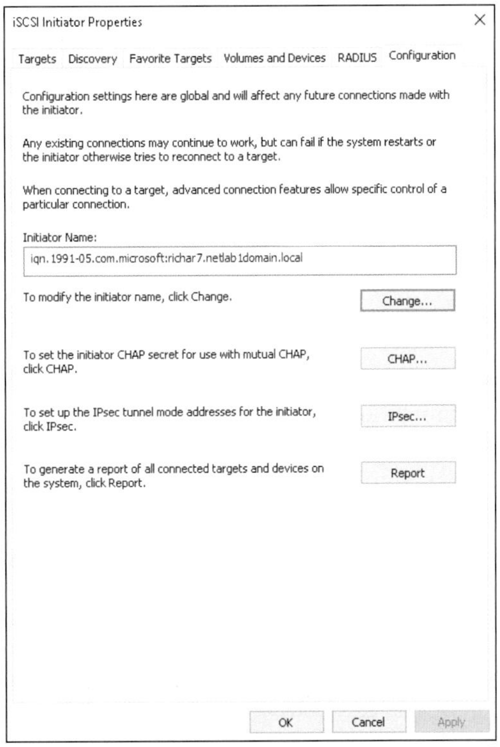

Goodheart-Willcox Publisher

Copyright Goodheart-Willcox Co., Inc.

ieu.0123D0123F0A. This type of address is issued by IEEE and is used by equipment manufacturers to identify its network storage devices.

Virtualization

Virtualization is the act of creating a software-based, or *virtual*, environment. The concept of virtualization is not new, but is certainly expanding. The idea is to have at least some of your components as virtual devices or systems. Usually, a server or cluster of servers is used as the hardware base, and then the resources are allocated to virtual systems as needed.

Virtual operating systems are something with which you may be familiar. For example, Oracle Virtual Box is a free download and allows you to host another operating system on your computer. For example, you might have a Windows 10 computer but use Virtual Box to host a virtualized Linux system. Virtualization, however, has grown beyond this.

It is not uncommon today to find large components of a network virtualized. This includes devices such as virtual switches, virtual firewalls, virtual network cards (NICs), virtual routers, virtual servers, virtual IDS, etc. Some advantages of virtualization include the following:

- cost reduction
- server consolidation
- utilization of resources
- security
- disaster recovery
- server provisioning
- application isolation
- support for legacy applications

Hypervisor

The *hypervisor mechanism*, also called *Virtual Machine Monitor (VMM)*, is the process that provides the virtual servers with access to resources. There is usually an audit monitor that monitors usage of the resource pool. This monitor will also ensure that one virtual server does not or cannot access data of another virtual server.

Furthering Your Study

You may be interested in further study and possible certification as a server technician. The CompTIA organization has a certification called *Server+*, which is designed to verify your competence for installing, repairing, and maintaining servers. You can download a complete description of the exam objectives from the CompTIA website.

Many of the areas in the Server+ Certification Exam overlap those on the A+ Certification Exam. However, even if you have scored high on the A+ Certification Exams, there are sufficient differences between the certifications that will prevent you from passing the Server+ Certification Exam without specialized study.

For additional study materials and more detailed information about server hardware, access the IBM and the Sun Microsystems websites. For detailed information on SCSI technology, access the Adaptec website.

Copyright Goodheart-Willcox Co., Inc.

Summary

Server Types and Services

- Servers play many roles in a network, such as print server, file server, database server, application server, backup server, web server, and mail server.

- A thin server has only the hardware and software needed to support and run a specific function, or role.

- Typically, entry-level servers contain 1 to 8 processors; mid-range servers contain 9 to 30 processors; and high-end servers contain 31 to 106 processors.

- Servers typically incorporate hot-swap technology to allow components to be removed or installed while the system is running.

Small Computer Systems Interface (SCSI)

- Small Computer Systems Interface (SCSI) is a computer bus technology that allows for the connection of multiple devices to a single controller.

- The term *Wide* is used to indicate 16-bit data transfers in place of 8-bit data transfers. To reflect the increase in frequency, the term *Fast* was used and then the term *Ultra*. Combination of the words, such as *Ultra/Wide*, are also used to express the newer technologies. *Ultra/Wide* means the SCSI device is faster and supports 16-bit transfers.

- Each SCSI device must have a unique ID number.

- SCSI devices can extend outside the server case through an extender card.

- Serial-attached SCSI uses a serial port similar to a SATA serial drive port.

ACPI and ACPICA

- Automatic Configuration and Power Interface (ACPI) is a standard for controlling the power options for computer hardware devices.

- ACPI gave users the ability to select how they wanted their computers to behave to conserve power.

- ACPI Component Architecture (ACPICA) is an extension to the original ACPI standard with the goal of creating a nonproprietary software package for configuring hardware.

System Resources

- System resources associated with hardware are direct memory access (DMA), interrupt request (IRQ), input/output (I/O) port address, and memory address assignment.

- When two hardware devices share the same resource assignment, a system conflict occurs.

RAID Systems

- Redundant Array of Independent Disks (RAID) is a system of disks arranged for speed, fault tolerance, or both.

- The most common RAID levels are RAID 0, RAID 1, and RAID 5.

- RAID 0 is known as striping. Striping increases data read/write speed but does not provide fault tolerance.

Copyright Goodheart-Willcox Co., Inc.

- RAID 1 is mirroring or duplexing two hard disk drives.

- RAID 5 is known as striping with parity, which combines data read/write speed with fault tolerance.

External Storage Systems

- Network-attached storage (NAS) is a device or collection of devices used to provide storage for a local area network. The NAS shares the bandwidth of the local network.

- Storage area network (SAN) is a separate network dedicated to data storage. It does not affect the bandwidth of the other connected networks.

Fibre Channel

- Fibre Channel is a high-speed access method that typically uses fiber-optic cable as network media.

- A Fibre Channel devices uses a Network Address Authority (NAA), which is a naming standard developed by the International Committee for Information Technology Standards (ICITS). An NAA address consists of the *naa.* prefix followed by the string of hexadecimal characters.

- A *Fibre Channel point-to-point topology* is simply a straight connection or channel between two points, such as a mainframe and a server.

- The *Fibre Channel arbitrated loop* is a common Fibre Channel topology that looks similar to the token ring topology.

- InfiniBand is a network communication standard that has a very high throughput with very low latency.

Internet Small Computer Systems Interface

- The iSCSI standard is an IP-based storage technology that uses IPv4 and IPv6 network addresses to identify storage devices on a LAN, MAN, or WAN.

- Advantages to iSCSI include allowance of storage devices to be a great distance from the client and it is less expensive than Fibre Channel SANs.

- iSCSI devices can be located across the Internet by using an iSCSI-qualified name (IQN) or an Enterprise Unique Name (EUI).

- The IQN address in the example is first identified by *iqn* followed by the date of origination for the address, the reverse domain name of the authority, and the computer name and domain.

Virtualization

- Virtualization is the act of creating a software-based environment.

- Large components of a network can be virtualized, resulting in cost reduction, server consolidation, utilization of resources, security, disaster recovery, server provisioning, application isolation, and support for legacy applications.

Hypervisor

- The hypervisor mechanism is the process that provides the virtual servers with access to resources.

Copyright Goodheart-Willcox Co., Inc.

Furthering Your Study

- The CompTIA Server+ Certification Exam is designed to verify a person's competence for installing, repairing, and maintaining servers.

Review Questions

1. What are some typical services that servers provide?
2. What is a thin server and what applications can it be used for?
3. What type of motherboard is commonly used for servers?
4. What does the term *hot-swapping* mean?
5. Differentiate between the BIOS and the POST.
6. Differentiate between the SCSI terms *Wide*, *Fast*, and *Ultra*.
7. What must be done to the last device on a SCSI chain?
8. Describe a SCSI ID number.
9. What does the acronym LUN represent?
10. What does the acronym ACPI represent?
11. What is the purpose of ACPI?
12. What does the acronym ACPICA represent?
13. What is the goal of ACPICA?
14. List the four system resources that may be assigned to a hardware device.
15. How many IRQ settings are there in a typical computer?
16. What is a DMA channel?
17. What does the acronym RAID represent?
18. How is parity used to replace data lost on a damaged disk?
19. Which RAID level(s) provide no fault tolerance?
20. Which RAID levels provide disk mirroring?
21. What is the difference between disk mirroring and duplexing?
22. Which RAID level provides both striping and parity?
23. Your system storage is accessed many times throughout the day by many users. The data is not critical. Rather, it is a collection of application software. A tape backup system is used to restore data from a system failure. Which RAID level would most likely be appropriate and why?
24. Which RAID level is denoted by the use of two hard disk drives, each containing identical data?
25. What does the acronym NAS represent?
26. What does the acronym SAN represent?
27. What is the difference between NAS and SAN?
28. What type of media is used for Fibre Channel?
29. What does the acronym NAA represent, and what is it used for?

Copyright Goodheart-Willcox Co., Inc.

30. What are the three common Fibre Channel topologies?

31. What does the acronym iSCSI represent?

32. What are the two main advantages to iSCSI storage?

33. What two protocols are used to send SCSI commands across the network?

34. What two naming formats are used to identify iSCSI targets?

35. Identify the following address type:
    iqn.2008-06.com.rmroberts:myiSCSIstorage.

36. What are some advantages of server virtualization?

37. What is a hypervisor mechanism?

✦ Sample Network+ Exam Questions

1. Cherie is looking for a solution that will increase the speed of her server's response time. Which RAID level provides the fastest reading and writing data transfer time?

   A. RAID 0

   B. RAID 1

   C. RAID 5

   D. RAID 0 and RAID 1

2. Tom is working as a network administrator for a small financial company. He is looking for a fault-tolerant solution for the server. Which network RAID level provides a duplicate copy of one hard disk drive on another hard disk drive?

   A. RAID 0

   B. RAID 1

   C. RAID 5

   D. RAID 4

3. How does SAN differ from NAS?

   A. SAN provides access to a SCSI disk exclusively, while NAS provides access to SCSI, ATA, and EIDE drives.

   B. SAN offers encryption; NAS does not.

   C. SAN does not increase local network traffic; NAS does.

   D. SAN is connected to the local network system, while NAS is accessed remotely via a WAN link.

4. Sofia is responsible for the servers at her company. Her servers utilize RAID 5 for fault tolerance. What is the minimum number of drives required for implementing a RAID 5 installation?

   A. 1

   B. 2

   C. 3

   D. 4

Copyright Goodheart-Willcox Co., Inc.

5. What does the term *fault tolerance* mean?

    A. The ability to find faults in data before it is backed up.

    B. The ability of the network administrator to tolerate system policy breeches by users.

    C. The ability to recover from a system failure.

    D. The ability to continue normal operation despite a system failure.

6. Which of the following describes the ability to change a module such as hard disk drive or power supply on a server without the need to shut down the server?

    A. System substitution

    B. On the fly changes

    C. Hot-swap

    D. Infinite run ability

7. What is the function of disk striping?

    A. Reduces the total amount of time it takes to store large amounts of data.

    B. Stores duplicate data across two or more drives.

    C. Ensures data integrity.

    D. Aids in disaster recovery.

8. How does a client access files on a NAS device?

    A. Through NAS client software.

    B. Through a server that is attached to the NAS device.

    C. Directly through Category 5e cable.

    D. Directly through high-speed, fiber-optic cable.

9. An investment broker is installing a network system for his employees and to provide customer access. Money transactions will occur on a continuous basis. Which RAID level would you recommend for this business?

    A. RAID 0

    B. RAID 1

    C. RAID 1 (with duplexed drives)

    D. RAID 5

10. Multiple CPUs in a server can perform which of the following?

    A. Unilateral processing

    B. Multiplexed processing

    C. Synchronous processing

    D. Parallel processing

TCP/IP Fundamentals

Network+ Certification Exam Objectives

The Network+ Certification Exam requires extensive knowledge of how IP addresses function in a network. You need to have a solid grasp of the relationship of IP addresses and subnet masks as well as the common TCP/IP troubleshooting command line utilities: **ping**, **tracert**, **nbstat**, and **ipconfig**. In fact, you may get questions that show one or more commands (with flags), and you will need to know what command produced the output. Be able to explain how WINS, DNS, DHCP, and APIPA services operate in a network. You cannot study this chapter too much! Be sure to perform laboratory activities relating to the topics in this chapter.

Objectives

1.1: Protocols and Ports

1.3: Segmentation and Interface Properties—ARP Table

IPv6 concepts—Addressing, Tunneling, Dual Stack, Neighbor Discovery

NAT/PAT, Port Forwarding, Distributed Switching

1.4: Private vs. Public, Loopback and Reserved, Default Gateway, Subnet Mask, Subnetting

Address Assignments

1.8: DNS Service, DHCP Service, IPAM

4.2: LDAP

5.2: Software tools—ping, tracert, traceroute, nslookup, ipconfig, ifconfig, netstat, tcpdump

5.5: Incorrect netmask

Learning Outcomes

- Summarize IPv4 addressing.
- Explain the operation of the Domain Name System (DNS).
- Differentiate between IP, TCP, and UDP.
- Describe methods of assigning IP addresses.
- Explain the difference between TCP/IP ports and sockets.
- Differentiate between IPv4 and IPv6 addresses.
- Describe various IPv6 transition technologies.
- Summarize broadcast and multicast addresses.
- Define IPv6 lifetimes.
- Discuss IPv6 DHCP.
- Summarize usage of IPv6 in Windows 7, 8, and 10.
- List TCP/IP troubleshooting utilities.

Copyright Goodheart-Willcox Co., Inc.

Key Terms

6to4

Address Resolution Protocol (ARP)

anycast address

Automatic Private IP Addressing (APIPA)

Class A network

Class B network

Class C network

default gateway address

Domain Name System (DNS)

dynamic addressing

Dynamic Host Configuration Protocol (DHCP)

dynamic IP assignment

EUI-64 identifier

Fully Qualified Domain Name (FQDN)

global address

Integrated Network Information Center (InterNIC)

Internet Corporation for Assigned Names and Numbers (ICANN)

Intra-Site Automatic Tunneling Address Protocol (ISATAP)

IPv6

link-local

loopback address

multicast address

Neighbor Discovery

Network Address Translation (NAT)

octet

port number

registrar

resolver

Reverse Address Resolution Protocol (RARP)

socket

static addressing

static IP assignment

subdomain

subnet mask

subnetwork

Teredo

unicast address

unique-local

Windows Internet Naming Service (WINS)

Overview

The TCP/IP protocol is used for network communication by all major network operating systems. It was especially designed for the Internet. Entire textbooks have been written on the subject of TCP/IP, and it accounts for a large portion of the Network+ Certification Exam. Other certifications from Micro Focus, Nortel, Microsoft, Linux, and IBM also rely heavily on TCP/IP principles for their certification exams.

As a network administrator, you need to be able to configure a host to use the TCP/IP protocol and to troubleshoot network connection problems in a TCP/IP environment. To be able to do this, you need to understand the Domain Name Service (DNS) structure, TCP/IP addressing, and how services such as Dynamic Host Connection Protocol (DHCP) work. You also need to be able to use TCP/IP troubleshooting utilities and interpret their output to solve communication problems.

This chapter introduces TCP/IP addressing and the Domain Name Service (DNS), which provide functionality and structure to the Internet. It takes a detailed look at how TCP/IP hosts are identified and relates TCP/IP communication to the OSI model. Lastly, a brief overview of some of the many TCP/IP troubleshooting utilities is presented.

NET 1.4

Tech Tip

The term *IP address* could mean either IPv4 or IPv6.

IPv4 Addressing

Earlier in the text, IPv4 was discussed in very basic and general terms. Now, it will be discussed with a much deeper level of understanding. The TCP/IP protocol was developed by the Department of Defense (DoD). It was specifically designed for communication over the Internet. As the Internet evolved, it became evident that a means of identifying network nodes was needed. The IP address was the solution and was approved in 1980.

There are two types of IP addressing schemes: IPv4 and IPv6. IPv6 addressing is covered later in this chapter. An IPv4 address consists of four octets, as shown in Figure 10-1. An **octet** is an eight-bit (or one-byte) value. Each octet in an IPv4 address is composed of eight digits of 0s and 1s. Periods separate each octet from neighboring octets. This method of displaying IP addresses is called *dotted decimal notation*. IP addresses are displayed in base 10, but the computer actually generates them in binary format, thus 8 bits.

Although IPv4 numbers are computed in the binary form, they are interpreted and used in the decimal form. When an octet is interpreted as a decimal number, the values range from 0 through 255. This range is based on the maximum possibilities of an eight-position binary number. Figure 10-2 shows an IPv4 address specified in binary and decimal. The decimal expression of an IPv4 address is much shorter than the binary expression of the same address. It is also much easier to read and interpret.

Figure 10-1 An IPv4 address consists of four octets (eight-bit units).

IP Address in Binary Form

Four octets

0011110.00111100.00010111.10011010

Octet

Goodheart-Willcox Publisher

Figure 10-2 An IPv4 address is typically written in decimal form. Each octet in decimal form can range from 0 through 255. This figure is based on the maximum number of binary positions in a binary octet.

IP Address in Decimal Form

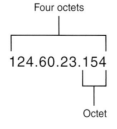

Four octets

124.60.23.154

Octet

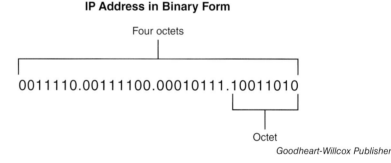

Binary range = decimal range

00000000 = 0
00000001 = 1
00000010 = 2
00000011 = 3
00000100 = 4

11111110 = 254
11111111 = 255

Goodheart-Willcox Publisher

Copyright Goodheart-Willcox Co., Inc.

IPv4 addressing is a method of identifying every node or host on a network. Recall from Chapter 1 the terms *host* and *node* are used to describe computers on a network and any device that can be attached to a network, respectively.

A near perfect analogy of IPv4 addressing is a telephone system. A telephone system is hierarchical in that it uses area codes to identify areas outside a local area. The first three digits identify the area code, and the last seven digits identify the telephone inside the area code, as illustrated in Figure 10-3.

Figure 10-3 The IPv4 addressing scheme can be compared to the telephone system. In a telephone system, a three-digit number indicated the area the telephone is in, and the telephone number indicates the telephone. In an IPv4 address, part of the address indicated the network the host is in and the other part indicated the host.

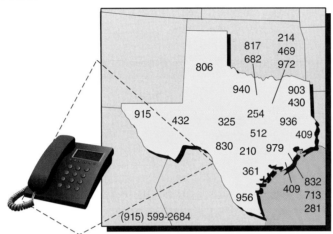

(telephone icons) Tetiana Yurchenko/Shutterstock.com; Goodheart-Willcox Publisher

IPv4 addresses work in much the same way. An IPv4 address has two parts: the network number and the host number. The network number identifies the network to which you are trying to connect and the host number identifies the host or network node. The relationship of IPv4 addresses to a network system is the same as telephone numbers to a telephone system. Each telephone is identified with a unique telephone number, and each device on a network is identified by a unique IPv4 number.

Network Class

While modern networking technology has moved beyond distinct network classes, this is how network addresses were originally grouped. If you take the Network+ Exam, you may get a few questions regarding classes of IP addresses. Classes are often still discussed on various networking certification exams, so it is important to understand the concept, even if it is unlikely to be encountered in the workforce. For the purpose of assigning IPv4 addresses, networks are divided into three major classifications: Class A, Class B, and Class C. Large networks are assigned a Class A classification. A **Class A network** can support up to 16 million hosts on each of 127 networks. Medium-sized networks are assigned a Class B classification. A **Class B network** supports up to 65,000 hosts on each of 16,000 networks. Small networks are assigned a Class C classification. A **Class C network** supports 254 hosts on each of two million networks. *Class D* addresses are used for multi-cast messages and has nothing to do with typical IP addresses. *Class E* addresses are strictly for experimental purposes.

1.4 NET

Copyright Goodheart-Willcox Co., Inc.

Networks are assigned an IPv4 address based on their network classification. Look at Figure 10-4. In the table, you can see that the class of the network determines the numeric value of the first octet in its IPv4 address. The range for a Class A network is from 1 to 127, for a Class B network it is from 128 to 191, and for a Class C network it is from 192 to 223.

IPv4 addresses for Class A networks use only the first octet as the network address. The remaining three octets define nodes on the network. The first two octets of a Class B network identify the network. The remaining two octets identify nodes on the network. A Class C network uses the first three octets to identify the network and the last octet to identify the nodes. For example, a typical Class C network might have an IPv4 address of 201.100.100.12. The network is identified by the 201.100.100, and the node is identified as 12. Refer to Figure 10-5 to help illustrate the different uses of octets by network class.

Figure 10-4 IPv4 address classifications.

Class	Range	Number of Networks	Number of Hosts
Class A	1–127	127	16,000,000
Class B	128–191	16,000	65,000
Class C	192–223	2,000,000	254

Goodheart-Willcox Publisher

Figure 10-5 The octets that make up an IPv4 address are used differently according to the network class.

Network Class	First Octet	Second Octet	Third Octet	Fourth Octet
Class A	Network address	Defines node	Defines node	Defines node
Class B	Network address	Network address	Defines node	Defines node
Class C	Network address	Network address	Network address	Defines node

Goodheart-Willcox Publisher

Network+ Note

For the Network+ Certification Exam, be sure you can identify IPv4 addresses by their class.

Subnet Mask

A company may divide their network into several smaller networks. A network within a network is known as a **subnetwork**. A **subnet mask** is a number similar to an IP address used to determine in which subnetwork a particular IPv4 address belongs. The subnet mask can also be used to identify the class of network, but it is really intended to allow the network address to be broken down into subnetworks. Two nodes must share the same subnet mask in order to be on the same subnetwork.

When a subnet mask is encountered, it is usually viewed in dot-decimal form—a series of four three-digit numbers separated by periods. At first glance, a subnet mask may appear identical to an IPv4 address. However, a subnet mask is distinguishable from an IP address because it begins with one or more octets of 255. An IPv4 address cannot begin with 255.

The octets of a subnet mask correspond to octets in the IPv4 address. The numbers found in a subnet mask depend on the class of the network and the number of subnetworks into which the network is divided. The subnet mask is combined with the IPv4 address using the bitwise **AND** operation, the details of which are beyond

Copyright Goodheart-Willcox Co., Inc.

the scope of this textbook. The resulting address is the subnet address. Put simply, a subnet mask literally masks its IP address. The part that is masked is the portion of the address used for the network. The part that is unmasked is the part for individual hosts. The subnet masks for all three network classes are as follows:

- Class A subnet mask: 255.0.0.0
- Class B subnet mask: 255.255.0.0
- Class C subnet mask: 255.255.255.0

Chapter 11 will cover subnetting in more detail. For now, remember that the subnet mask is used to identify any subnetwork at the network address.

Reserved IPv4 Addresses

A number of IPv4 addresses are reserved for private networks. They are often used for offices sharing an Internet address or for experimentation. They are not valid for use as a direct connection to the Internet. Pay close attention to the following list of private IPv4 addresses:

- 10.0.0.0 to 10.255.255.255
- 172.16.0.0 to 172.31.255.255
- 192.168.0.0 to 192.168.255.255

At times, a computer may connect to the Internet through another host. Microsoft refers to this type of connection as Internet Connection Sharing (ICS). ICS uses the Network Address Translation (NAT) protocol to translate private network addresses into an assigned Internet address, and vice versa. **Network Address Translation (NAT)** was specifically designed for implementing private network configurations by allowing an unregistered private network addresses to communicate with a legally registered IP addresses. For example, a client that wishes to access the Internet sends a request to the host. The host, in turn, uses the IP address assigned by the ISP to connect to the Internet. See Figure 10-6. Some advantages to using NAT include the following:

- Hides internal IP addresses behind a firewall-type service
- Allows computers on a network to share one common IP address to access the Internet without the need of multiple IP addresses to be assigned to the subnetwork

Network+ Note ✚

For the Network+ Certification Exam, be sure you can identify a private IPv4 address.

1.4 NET ✚

1.3 NET ✚

Network+ Note ✚

For the Network+ Certification Exam, be sure to know the purpose of the Network Address Translation (NAT) protocol.

Figure 10-6 Internet Connection Sharing (ICS) uses the Network Address Translation (NAT) protocol to translate unregistered IP addresses to a registered IP address. In this example, an ICS client sends an Internet request to the IP address of the ICS host, **192.168.0.1**. The ICS host uses the ISP assigned address to access the Internet.

The ICS Model

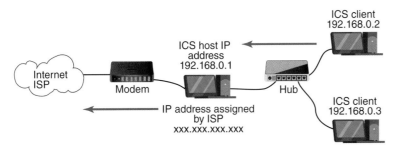

(modem and hub icons) Vadim Ermak/Shutterstock.com; (workstation icons) RedlineVector/Shutterstock.com;
Goodheart-Willcox Publisher

Port Address Translation (PAT) is essentially an extension of NAT. PAT does for ports what NAT does for IP addresses. Multiple ports can exist inside a given network that are private. Port address translation represents these with a single port at your gateway. This is related to, but not the same as, port forwarding. Port forwarding takes inbound traffic for a particular port and forwards it to a different internal port.

It is important to note that a private network such as an intranet may use any possible IP address as long as it does not connect to the Internet. Using a number that is assigned to a URL would not only confuse the network system, it is illegal. The reserved private addresses can be used even when the network connects to the Internet. The Internet does not recognize private network addresses, so they do not affect the system. This is why private network addresses are ideal for creating a subnetwork.

The NAT protocol is commonly installed automatically in Microsoft Windows 2000 and later versions when the Network Setup Wizard is used. For example, when installing the Internet Connection Service (ICS) through the Network Setup Wizard, the user is asked a series of questions. Based on the responses that are entered by the user, the operating system automatically sets up a connection share for a single Internet connection.

Figure 10-7 shows the **Ethernet Properties** dialog box from Windows 10, which provides an option to allow other network computers to access the Internet through its Internet connection. This option will automatically create an ICS configuration.

Note

With the development of the NAT protocol, the numbers of IPv4 addresses are lasting longer than expected. By using the NAT protocol to translate private IPv4 addresses on a home or office network, thousands, if not millions, of IPv4 addresses are saved.

Figure 10-7 The **Ethernet Properties** dialog box for a Windows 10 computer provides an option to allow networked computers to access the Internet through the computer's Internet connection.

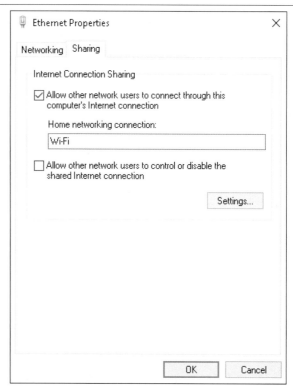

Goodheart-Willcox Publisher

Copyright Goodheart-Willcox Co., Inc.

Viewing IP Configuration Settings

The IPv4 configuration is a group of settings made on a host that allows it to communicate in a TCP/IP environment. The IPv4 configuration consists of the host's IPv4 address, the subnet mask, and the default gateway. The **default gateway address** is the address of the computer that provides a connection to the Internet. The Internet service provider's software or the network DHCP server usually determines these settings automatically. Occasionally, you may have to adjust the settings manually or verify the information while working with an ISP to troubleshoot a connection. On a Windows-based computer, you can use the IP Configuration utility to verify the settings.

Beginning with Windows 2000, all versions of Windows use the **ipconfig** command issued from the command prompt to run the IP Configuration utility, which is shown in Figure 10-8. The assigned IPv4 address, subnet mask, and default gateway addresses are displayed. To reveal more information about the connection, the **ipconfig /all** command can be used, as demonstrated in Figure 10-9. Notice that the MAC address (physical address), DHCP server address, and DNS server are revealed as well as other information. The additional information provided, such as the IPv4 address of the DHCP server and the DNS server, will become more relevant to you later in the chapter. If you need to renew your IP address from the DHCP server, use the command **ipconfig /renew**. The command **ipconfig /?** will reveal all the options available with ipconfig.

1.4 NET

5.2 NET

Note

NET **5.2**

Unix/Linux systems use the ifconfig command to produce similar results as ipconfig.

Figure 10-8 IP Configuration display when the **ipconfig** command is issued.

Goodheart-Willcox Publisher

Figure 10-9 The IP Configuration display when the **ipconfig /all** command is issued.

Goodheart-Willcox Publisher

Copyright Goodheart-Willcox Co., Inc.

Tech Tip

The terms *physical* and *logical* are often used to describe network systems and devices. It is important to be able to determine the difference between a physical and a logical component. For example, the IP address is a logical address assigned to a network host. It is logical because it is assigned and can be changed at any time. In contrast, the MAC address is a physical address electrically etched into the network interface card associated with each host.

Domain Name System (DNS)

NET
1.1

Since IP addresses are difficult to remember, the Internet uses a Domain Name System (DNS), also called *Domain Name Service*, to make it easier for people to identify and find networks on the Internet. **Domain Name System (DNS)** allows a name, called a *domain name*, to be associated with a network address. You can communicate on the Internet by using a domain name or an IP address. For example, when you use a web browser, you can enter the domain name for the URL or an IP address. The IP address connects faster to a distant location than a domain name. When a domain name is entered, it must be converted to an IP address before communication can begin. The amount of time to do this varies according to conditions. Many of these conditions are discussed throughout this chapter.

Internet Corporation for Assigned Names and Numbers (ICANN)

The **Internet Corporation for Assigned Names and Numbers (ICANN)** is a private, not-for-profit organization that coordinates the assignment of domain names and IP addresses. It does so by allocating domain name registration to select private companies. Each private company to which domain-name registration privileges is given is called a **registrar**. To obtain a domain name and an IP address, a business or organization places an application through a registrar. Once the registrar processes the application, the business or organization receives an official second-level domain name and an IP address that is registered to the domain name they have been issued.

IP addresses were once regulated and assigned through the governmental organization known as the **Integrated Network Information Center (InterNIC)**. InterNIC was a branch of the United States government under the direction of the Department of Commerce. It was responsible for regulating the Internet, overseeing the issue of domain names, and assigning IP addresses to them. InterNIC managed the domain root for .com, .net, .org, .edu, and .gov top-level domains.

The *Internet Assigned Numbers Authority (IANA)* was the original authority that the US contracted in the early 1990s. IANA established the Internet Network Information Center (InterNIC) funded by the National Science Foundation. Late in the 1990s, the government felt that the assigned numbers and names should be somewhat privatized, so they subcontracted the responsibilities to ICANN. ICANN assumed many of the responsibilities of IANA, but the ultimate authority for assigned numbers and names rests with the US government.

Currently, InterNIC is a website that provides services and information about Internet-assigned names and numbers and is a registered service mark of the US Department of Commerce. The Department of Commerce licensed InterNIC to ICANN, which operates the InterNIC website. The US Department of Commerce is responsible for the overall assignment of the assigned numbers and names in the United States. To find out more about ICANN, visit their website at www.icann.org.

Fully Qualified Domain Name (FQDN)

To locate a host on a large network, you need to use the complete name of the host, which includes a combination of the host name and domain name. The complete name of the host is referred to as the **Fully Qualified Domain Name (FQDN)**. For example, a host called *Station12* in the domain xyzcorp.com would have an FQDN of station12.xyzcorp.com. *Station12* is the host name, and xyzcorp.com is the domain name.

As you have seen in previous chapters, network operating systems follow the domain name structure for naming servers, workstations, and other network devices. This was not always the case. Earlier systems using NetBIOS and NetBEUI had their own naming schemes. These naming schemes are not consistent with naming rules used for Fully Qualified Domain Names.

Network operating systems such as Linux and Windows 2000 and later follow the rules of Fully Qualified Domain Names when creating their network structure. However, these operating systems can still communicate with older networking technologies.

Realizing the difference between a host name and a NetBIOS name can help you understand how communication can occur between systems that use Fully Qualified Domain Names and those that use NetBIOS names. A NetBIOS name is a computer name limited to a maximum of 15 characters. A host name can be a Fully Qualified Domain Name or the first part of the Fully Qualified Domain Name. A host name is limited to 63 characters. Many of the symbols allowed in NetBIOS names cannot be used in Fully Qualified Domain Names. These symbols include the following: ; : " < > * + = \ / ? ,

To allow for communication between a system that uses NetBIOS names and one that uses host names, computer names are converted automatically for compatibility. For example, consider a network that contains computers with legacy operating systems. Many legacy operating systems use NetBIOS names to identify computers on a Microsoft network. Modern operating systems use the Fully Qualified Domain Name to communicate. However, to communicate with the legacy computers, the Fully Qualified Domain Name is shortened automatically to match the NetBIOS maximum length of 15 characters. Windows computers can use NetBIOS names to communicate with other Windows computers on the network. However, when communicating with Windows 2000 computers, any symbols in the NetBIOS name need to be replaced with hyphens. Figure 10-10 shows the System menu, which lists important information about a computer. Notice in the Full computer name field, the computer name is DESKTOP-NJT6LP8, which is compliant with the 15-character NetBIOS name requirement.

DNS Structure and Operation

DNS is hierarchical, similar to a typical file system structure comprising directories and files. This hierarchical structure is depicted in Figure 10-11. At the top of DNS is the root. Directly under the root are the top-level domains. The top-level domains start the process of dividing the organizational structure into specialized areas. The most common top-level domains are .com, .edu, .gov, .int, .mil, .net, and .org.

The next level of the structure is composed of second-level domains. Second-level domains represent the domain names as assigned by ICANN. Second-level domains identify various companies and organizations. For example, the Massachusetts Institute of Technology domain name is known as mit.edu. The structure is further divided into subdomains controlled by the second-level domains. A **subdomain** is any level domain located beneath the secondary domain. For example,

Copyright Goodheart-Willcox Co., Inc.

Figure 10-10 Notice that the computer name **DESKTOP-NJT6LP8** is compliant with the 15-character NetBIOS name requirement.

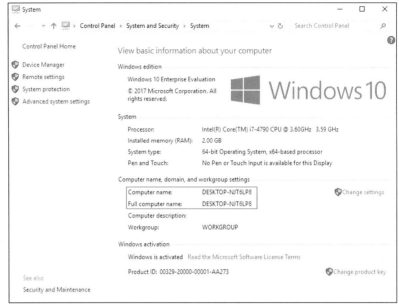

Goodheart-Willcox Publisher

Figure 10-11 The Domain Name System structure.

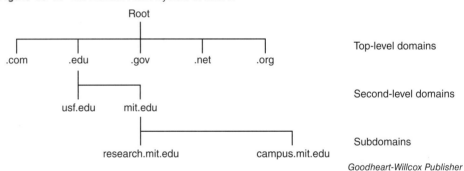

Goodheart-Willcox Publisher

the mit.edu, second-level domain can be divided into subdomains such as faculty.mit.edu, research.mit.edu, and students.mit.edu. A subdomain can also be called a *lower-level domain.*

DNS root servers are located at the top of the domain-name hierarchy structure. The root domain server stores the ultimate database for resolving an Internet domain name to a specific IP address. Currently, there are 13 DNS root servers. A top-level domain server stores DNS information of all top-level domains. A second-level domain server stores DNS information of all second-level domains.

DNS operation begins when a resolver requests that a domain name be resolved to an IP address. The **resolver** is a software program located on a host that queries a DNS server to resolve a host name to an IP address. The first DNS server the resolver contacts is a subdomain server, as depicted in Figure 10-12. For example, when the resolver attempts to connect to research.mit.edu, it queries the first subdomain server it encounters. This could be the domain server the host is connected to as part of a workgroup or domain, or it could be the Internet service provider (ISP) for a home PC.

A subdomain server may be queried for the same information many times. Because the request is likely to occur again from a different host, domain names are

Copyright Goodheart-Willcox Co., Inc.

Figure 10-12 The resolver queries the closest DNS server for IP information. If the DNS server does not have this information, the DNS server passes the request to a higher-level DNS server.

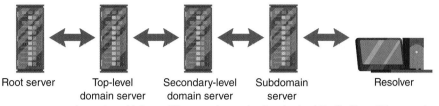

Root server

Top-level domain server

Secondary-level domain server

Subdomain server

Resolver

(server icons) fullvector/Shutterstock.com; (workstation icon) RedlineVector/Shutterstock.com;
Goodheart-Willcox Publisher

placed in a cache on the domain server for future requests. This method speeds up the process of supplying IP address information when the request is repeated. If the IP address for the domain name is not in the cache, the domain server queries higher-level domain servers until reaching the root. When the information is found, it is returned to the resolver. The resolver then connects to the intended host.

The domain name service is dynamically changing all the time. It is like a living entity that continues to grow and update with new information and changes. During the update period, errors can be encountered while trying to resolve a domain name to an IP address. Most servers will cache domain name information for approximately three days. The network administrator controls the time period. If a domain changes its IP address during the three-day period, an error can be generated attempting to connect to the domain site. This is because the old information about the IP address is still in the server cache and has not been updated.

A closer inspection can help provide information as to how DNS is used to acquire information about a domain name and its associated IP address. The following are the possible steps that occur when a resolver requests the IP address of a domain name. Refer to Figure 10-13 when reviewing these steps.

1. The user types in www.g-w.com in the browser.

2. The browser checks if the domain name g-w.com exists in its own browser cache.

3. If not, the browser sends a DNS query to the network's domain name server. The domain server checks its own cache for the requested domain IP address. If this information is in the cache, it connects the host to the destination IP address.

4. If the IP address is not in the domain server cache, it is then requested from a higher-level domain server. The highest level is the top-level domain server located beneath the root.

5. If the domain name is an authorized domain name, the top-level domain server returns the IP address information. This information is added to the domain server and workstation cache.

6. The computer that originally attempted to connect to www.g-w.com now uses the IP address to connect to the web server located at www.g-w.com.

DNS servers have several types of records. An *A record* (or *AAAA records*) are simply links from a domain name to an IP address. These records may also be referred to as *forward records*. They are the most basic type of DNS record. A *PTR record* is the opposite; it links an IP address to a domain name. These types of records may also be called *reverse records*. Additional DNS record types include *SRV records*, which identify services; *MX records*, which identify e-mail servers; and *CNAME records*, which provide easy names for resources. Sender Policy Framework (SPF) records indicate e-mail servers that are authorized to send e-mail for a particular domain. The original standard for SPF records was RFC 4408, which was revised by RFC 7208.

1.8

NET

Figure 10-13 This example shows the possible steps that can occur while resolving a domain name to an IP address.

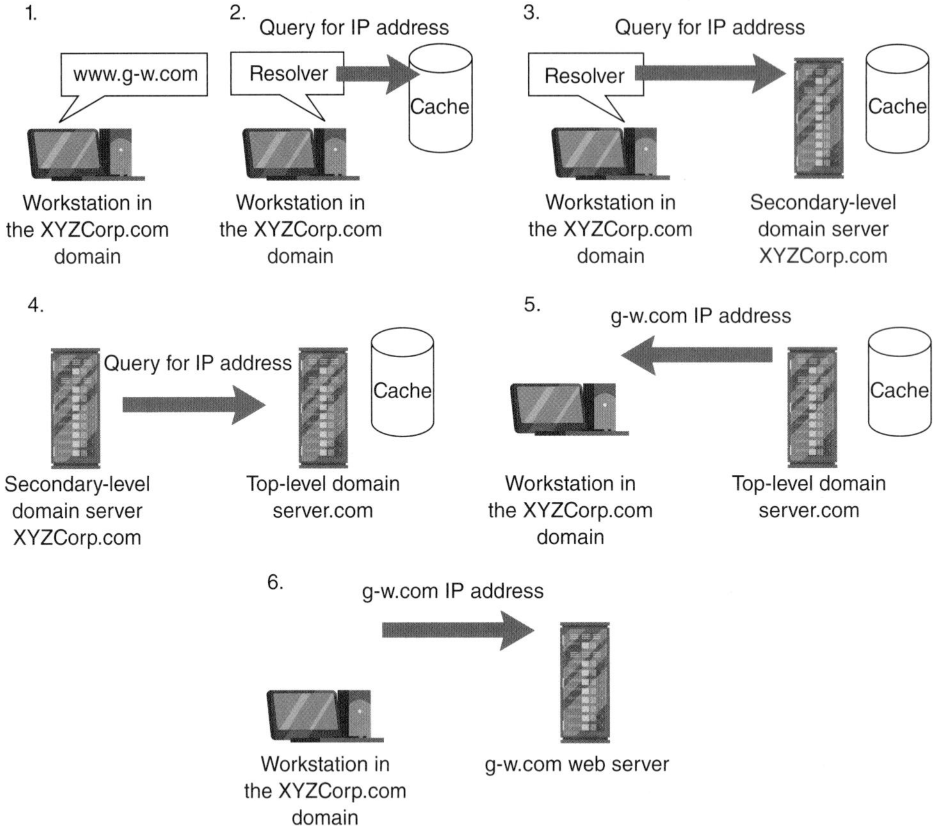

(server icons) fullvector/Shutterstock.com; (workstation icons) RedlineVector/Shutterstock.com;
Goodheart-Willcox Publisher

There are technologies related to DNS that do not provide direct access to resources but rather support such communication. For example, DomainKeys Identified Mail (DKIM) is used to authenticate e-mail. It uses digital signatures to identify the e-mail origin, and the public keys are in the DNS record.

Domain Name System Security Extensions (DNSSEC) is a suite of specifications from the Internet Engineering Task Force (IETF). These specifications are used to add some level of security to DNS. This helps to prevent applications from using forged DNS data.

The DNS server itself can be internal or external. Most sizable networks have their own DNS servers, while home users and small business tend to rely on an external DNS hosted by the Internet service provider (ISP). Additionally, cloud-based DNS servers are becoming increasingly popular as more and more services are designated to the cloud.

Hosts and Lmhosts Text Files

Originally, all computer names were resolved using a text database. A text database is simply a text file that contains IP addresses and related information. The two text files used to resolve host and NetBIOS names to IP addresses are hosts and lmhosts. These files can still be used as a backup in case other means of resolving computer names to IP addresses fail.

The text file hosts was the original method used by Unix systems to match computer names to corresponding IP addresses. The following is an example of the contents of a hosts file.

Copyright Goodheart-Willcox Co., Inc.

127.0.0.1	Localhost
192.168.0.25	PcsAreUs.com
65.100.50.25	Station23.XYZcorp.com
182.63.10.24	USF.edu

Note that Fully Qualified Domain Names are considered host names and can appear in a hosts file. A list of IP addresses and corresponding host names are created using a simple, plain-text editor and saved as a hosts file. The hosts file is referenced automatically to assist in locating computers, printers, and servers on a network. The hosts file is used when the automatic functions provided by a DNS server fails.

The lmhosts file is similar to the hosts file but is designed for use with NetBIOS name resolution to IP addresses. Look at the following example of the contents of an lmhosts file.

192.168.23.104	Station12
10.23.105.21.1	Sales4
173.76.22.231	Computer25

Note that the file contains NetBIOS names of computers matched to IP addresses. The lmhosts file is read when the Windows Internet Naming Service (WINS) server fails. A **Windows Internet Naming Service (WINS)** server resolves NetBIOS names to IP addresses.

The hosts and lmhosts files must be edited with a plain-text editor such as Notepad. A more sophisticated editor uses many different fonts that make the file unreadable by the network client software. The hosts and lmhosts file must be in plain, ASCII text to be read. The key point to remember is that the hosts file resolves host names to IP addresses related to DNS, and the lmhosts file resolves NetBIOS names to IP addresses related to WINS.

IP, TCP, and UDP

TCP/IP is the default protocol for communication across the Internet. It is actually a suite of protocols. The three most commonly used protocols in the TCP/IP suite are Internet Protocol (IP), Transmission Control Protocol (TCP), and User Datagram Protocol (UDP). The function of the Internet Protocol (IP) is logical addressing. IP does not care if the packet is delivered correctly; it simply transmits the data. This makes IP a connectionless/unreliable protocol. UDP functions similar to IP. It establishes a link but does not ensure that data is delivered correctly. It is also a connectionless/unreliable protocol.

TCP regulates connections and provides flow control. TCP is a connection-oriented/reliable protocol. The main difference between TCP and UDP is that TCP can break large amounts of data into smaller packets and UDP cannot. UDP sends a single packet to transmit control information and data. This section looks at how the IP, TCP, and UDP move data from source to destination.

1.1 NET ✚

Relationship to the OSI Model

Figure 10-14 shows the relationship of some TCP/IP protocols to the OSI model and typical data formats. In the illustration, you can see that the three upper layers—application, presentation, and session—take raw data and send it down to the transport layer. Each layer builds a protocol data unit (PDU) by adding control information from the previous layer to the header. At the transport layer, large blocks of raw data are broken into smaller units referred to as *segments* for TCP or *datagrams* for UDP.

Copyright Goodheart-Willcox Co., Inc.

Figure 10-14 The relationship of TCP/IP protocols and data formats to the OSI model.

 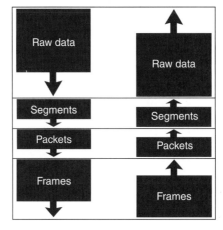 

Goodheart-Willcox Publisher

The segments are placed into the data portion of the TCP or UDP header. The selection of TCP or UDP depends on:

- the software used in the upper layers of the OSI model;
- the amount of data to be sent; and
- whether a connectionless/unreliable or connection-oriented/reliable transport of data is desired.

Both the TCP and UDP formats provide the port number of the source and destination. For UDP, the port number is optional, but for TCP, the port number is required. There will be more about port numbers later in the chapter.

The content of the TCP or UDP protocol is then moved to the network layer. At the network layer, the TCP or UDP data unit is encapsulated in an IP packet with addressing information added. The entire unit is referred to as a *packet*. The IP packet contains a source and destination IP address and is sent to the data link layer.

The data link layer performs the final encapsulation of the combined formats (TCP or UDP and IP). The data link layer supplies the physical address of the destination and source. The physical address is the MAC address associated with the network card of the source and destination computer. The collective unit of frame formats is referred to as a *frame*.

The frame is placed on the physical media as a series of digital pulses. If the network is Ethernet, the frame is broadcast to all nodes in the segment of the network. When the frame arrives at the destination, the process is reversed. As the data moves up the OSI model, each of the protocol frame formats is removed until the raw data is received at the highest level of the OSI model, the application layer.

Frame Formats

Taking a closer look at the frame formats of IP, TCP, UDP, and Ethernet will help to get a better understanding of the mechanics of the process. Look at Figure 10-15. In the illustration, a UDP frame is inserted into the data portion of an IP frame.

The UDP frame format is simple in construction. The header information contains only four significant items: source port, destination port, message length, and checksum. The frame's structure reveals that only port addresses are used to identify the source and destination. There is no way to identify the source or destination by IP address or MAC address. UDP and TCP rely on the IP frame format for the IP address of the destination and source. The IP frame relies on the Ethernet frame for the source and destination MAC address.

Now look at Figure 10-16. Notice that the TCP header contains more information than the UDP header. The TCP header contains additional information such as a sequence number, which is used to reassemble data in a correct order. UDP does not need a sequence number. It is used to transfer small blocks of data or commands.

Figure 10-15 UDP is framed in an IP packet, and then the IP packet is framed in an Ethernet frame.

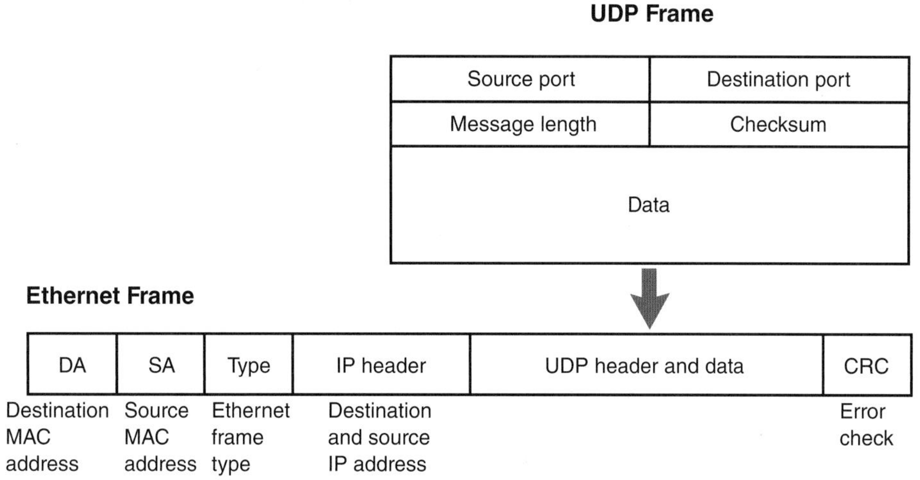

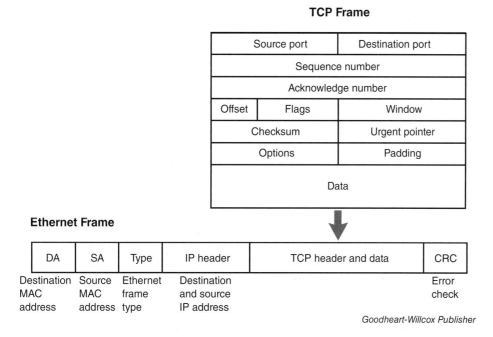

Goodheart-Willcox Publisher

Figure 10-16 TCP is framed in an IP packet, and then the IP packet is framed in an Ethernet frame.

As the protocol frames reach the data link layer of the OSI model, the final step is to encapsulate the entire set of protocol frames into a frame matching the network standard used, such as Ethernet, token ring, or FDDI. Look at Figure 10-17. In the example, Ethernet has been chosen. The Ethernet frame relies on the MAC addresses for transmitting between workstations. Remember that a unique MAC address is embedded into each network interface card. The Ethernet frame is broadcast to all the network interface cards on the LAN. When the destination network interface card

Copyright Goodheart-Willcox Co., Inc.

Figure 10-17 IP is framed in an Ethernet frame. The Ethernet frame is then placed on the network media.

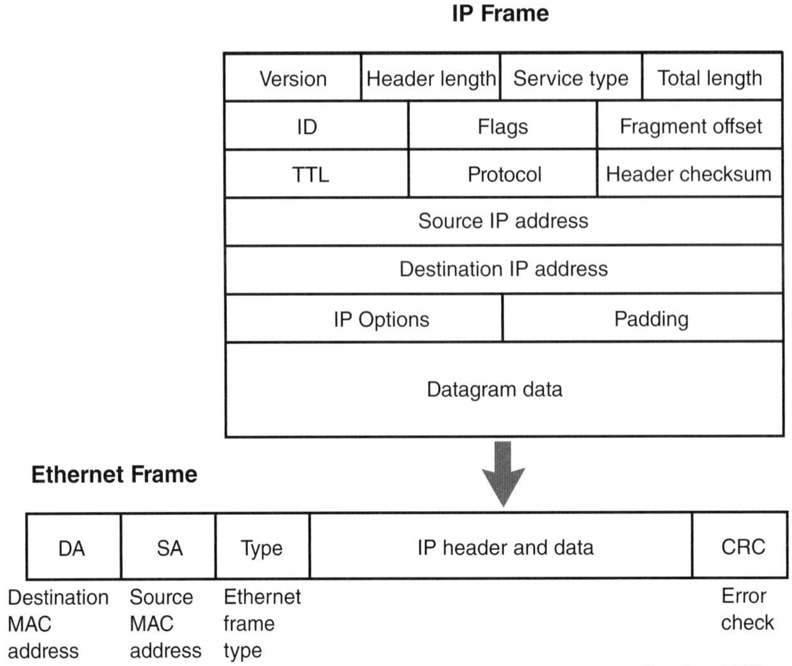

IP Frame

Version	Header length	Service type	Total length
ID		Flags	Fragment offset
TTL		Protocol	Header checksum
Source IP address			
Destination IP address			
IP Options		Padding	
Datagram data			

Ethernet Frame

DA	SA	Type	IP header and data	CRC
Destination MAC address	Source MAC address	Ethernet frame type		Error check

Goodheart-Willcox Publisher

receives the entire frame of protocol formats and data, it removes the Ethernet frame and passes the remaining protocol frame formats to the OSI model at the destination. If the destination is on the same LAN as the source, then the remaining formats are removed until the data reaches the application layer.

If the destination is at a distant location that requires navigation across the Internet or a WAN link, a network device such as a router removes the Ethernet frame. The IP address is used to deliver the entire contents to the distant location. At the distant location, the remaining protocol formats are removed until the raw data is revealed.

This is a simplified explanation of the role of the various protocol frame formats. You will rely on these basic concepts to understand how bridges, switches, routers, and gateways operate. Other protocols classified as application protocols, such as FTP, TFTP, Telnet, and SNMP, fit inside a TCP or UDP frame.

Conduct a search on the Internet to learn more about various protocol formats associated with TCP/IP. Supplementing your understanding with hot links, acronyms, and technical papers available will assist you in furthering your network expertise.

Other Protocols

Dynamic Host Configuration Protocol (DHCP) is an important and common protocol. It allows you to have IP addresses dynamically assigned to a machine when the machine connects to the network. This is commonly used for network workstations. Servers and printers usually have a static IP address. DHCP typically works on ports 67 and 68.

Copyright Goodheart-Willcox Co., Inc.

Lightweight Directory Access Protocol (LDAP) is the protocol used for keeping a record of everything on a network. Think of it as a phone book for your network. It works in port 389. LDAP that is encrypted with Transport Layer Security (TLS) is called *LDAPS* (the *S* is for *secure*) and works on port 636.

As Voice over IP (VoIP) and video conferencing become more widely used, the protocols for establishing communication are more important. *Session Initiation Protocol (SIP)* is the most common protocol for establishing a voice or video over IP connection. It typically works on ports 5060 and 5061. *H.323* is an older protocol for establishing video or voice connections; it works on port 1719 and 1720.

As Windows is so widely used, it is important to know how Windows machines communicate on a network. Typically, they use *Server Message Block (SMB)* that works on port 445. You may recall in early 2017 the WannaCry virus attacked a flaw in SMB.

Assigning IP Addresses

There are several methods for assigning IP addresses. The assignment of IP addresses falls into two broad categories: static and dynamic. A **static IP assignment** means that an IP address is entered manually for each host on the network. This is typically done when a network interface card is configured. A **dynamic IP assignment** means that the IP address is issued automatically, typically when the computer boots and joins the network.

Windows Internet Naming Service (WINS)

WINS is an older technology. Windows has used DNS since the release of Windows 2000. However, a brief description of WINS is helpful for historical reasons. Windows Internet Naming Service (WINS) is used to resolve computer NetBIOS names to IP addresses. WINS is unique to Microsoft networks. WINS maintains a dynamic database of computer names and IP addresses. The computer names and IP addresses are automatically updated as computers log on and off the network, as shown in Figure 10-18.

Figure 10-18 The Windows Internet Naming Service (WINS) resolves NetBIOS computer names to IP addresses.

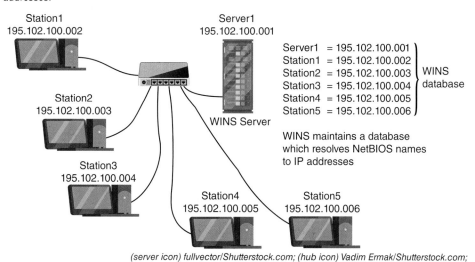

Station1
195.102.100.002

Server1
195.102.100.001

Server1 = 195.102.100.001
Station1 = 195.102.100.002
Station2 = 195.102.100.003
Station3 = 195.102.100.004
Station4 = 195.102.100.005
Station5 = 195.102.100.006

WINS database

WINS Server

Station2
195.102.100.003

Station3
195.102.100.004

Station4
195.102.100.005

Station5
195.102.100.006

WINS maintains a database which resolves NetBIOS names to IP addresses

(server icon) fullvector/Shutterstock.com; (hub icon) Vadim Ermak/Shutterstock.com; (workstation icons) RedlineVector/Shutterstock.com; Goodheart-Willcox Publisher

Network+ Note

WINS and DNS are often confused. For the Network+ Certification Exam, be sure you can distinguish between DNS and WINS.

Dynamic Host Configuration Protocol (DHCP)

Originally, computers on a network had to have their IP addresses assigned manually. This method was called **static addressing**. Static addressing was a time-consuming operation if a large number of PCs were on a network. A log of computer names, locations, MAC addresses, and the assigned IP addresses had to be recorded manually. An administrator or network technician had to be careful not to use the same IP address on another computer. Each IP address has to be unique. Using the same IP address for two different computers causes communication conflicts, resulting in erratic behavior.

Dynamic Host Configuration Protocol (DHCP) is designed to replace the manual setup of IP addresses on a network. When a server runs DHCP, the IP addresses are assigned automatically. The act of automatically assigning IP addresses is known as **dynamic addressing**. This is how dynamic addresses are generated.

The DHCP server has a *pool*, or list, of IP addresses to draw from, as illustrated in Figure 10-19. Each computer that logs on to the network is assigned an address from the pool. The IP address assignment is temporary. The address is released after a period of time and may be reissued to another computer.

Figure 10-19 The Dynamic Host Configuration Protocol (DHCP) on a DHCP server automatically assigns a temporary IP address to a host. The IP address is randomly selected from a pool of addresses. The temporary IP address is returned to the pool when the lease expires. Certain types of equipment, such as servers, must maintain the same address all of the time. They are assigned an IP address manually. When an IP address is manually assigned, it is said to be a static IP address.

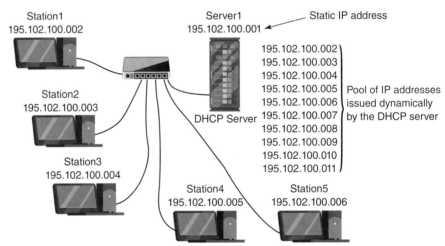

Each workstation receives a temporary IP address from the DHCP server

(server icon) fullvector/Shutterstock.com; (hub icon) Vadim Ermak/Shutterstock.com; (workstation icons) RedlineVector/Shutterstock.com; Goodheart-Willcox Publisher

This is how a client is assigned an IP address from a DHCP server. First, when a workstation is booted, it automatically requests an IP address assignment from the DHCP server. The workstation does not know where the DHCP server is, so it sends out the request for an IP address as a broadcast to all nodes on the network segment. The protocol used for the request is UDP, which is especially designed for broadcast communication.

Second, the DHCP server receives the request and returns an unassigned IP address from its pool of IP addresses. This is also done in the form of a broadcast. The server returns the information as a UDP broadcast so that any other device connected to the same network as the workstation will have the IP address information.

Copyright Goodheart-Willcox Co., Inc.

Third, the workstation accepts the assigned IP address and acknowledges this with a UDP broadcast to all nodes on the network. This allows any other device, like a backup DHCP server, to update its database of IP address assignments.

Fourth, the DHCP server acknowledges that the workstation has accepted the assigned IP address. This completes the four-step process.

The temporary assignment of the IP address to the workstation requires four broadcast packets. This is not a lot of network traffic, especially when compared to several hundred or even thousands of computers logging on to the network at the beginning of the workday. Each computer generates four broadcasts to acquire an IP address from a DHCP server. In addition, each computer generates traffic when downloading e-mail. The traffic on a network in this scenario is heavy, and the number of collisions can greatly increase.

During the IP address negotiation between the DHCP server and a workstation, other information is transmitted, such as the lease period for the assigned IP address, the subnet mask, and the location of the default gateway. The IP address assignment can be easily confirmed by using **ipconfig**.

It is important to note that when setting up a network using a DHCP server, static IP addressees must be assigned to all servers and printers and any other equipment required to have a static IP address. When the DHCP server assigns an IP address to a host, it does not necessarily assign the same IP address to the same piece of equipment each time. The IP address is randomly assigned. For computers to be able to find devices such as servers and printers consistently, the devices must have static IP addresses assigned to them.

DHCP Lease

The DHCP server sets a lease period for IP address assignments. The default lease period is eight days, but the network administrator can modify the lease period. The length of the lease period depends on factors such as the type of network, number of users, typical user profiles, and available number of IP addresses assigned to the network. A large corporate network would need a longer lease period. It is up to the professional judgment of the network administrator to determine the lease period. If the network belongs to an ISP, the ISP administrator would issue a shorter lease period.

1.4, 1.8 NET

If the lease period spans 30 days, for example, the client would not need to request an IP address from the DHCP server, each subsequent log on as long as the logon occurs during the 30-day time period. If the lease period expires, the computer must request a new temporary IP address from the DHCP server.

However, when a lease has expired, it is important that a user properly log off or shut down his or her computer when ending a session. The IP address is only released when a user logs off or properly shuts down the computer. If a person simply shuts down the computer using the power switch, the computer cannot properly release the IP address. The IP address will still be in use and will not be available to other clients.

When configuring DHCP, one must organize the range, or scope, of DHCP addresses. For example, you may want to issue IP addresses in the range of 192.168.1.100 to 192.168.1.200. If there are any static IP addresses in that range, these will be implemented as *IP exclusions*. IP exclusions are exactly as the name implies—addresses that are excluded from being assigned by DHCP and removed from the address pool. Since DHCP is used to assign IP addresses to network cards, it is, in effect, mapping an IP to a specific MAC. You may need to reserve certain ranges of IP addresses for particular MAC addresses.

Keep in mind that DHCP depends on the Bootstrap Protocol (BOOTP). BOOTP is not routable. Therefore, one common tactic is to have a DHCP relay at each router to relay the DHCP communication from workstations to the DHCP server.

Copyright Goodheart-Willcox Co., Inc.

IPAM

IP Address Management (IPAM) was introduced in Windows Server 2012. It is a set of tools for deploying IP addresses and management of IP addresses. IPAM includes support for virtual IP addresses.

Automatic Private IP Addressing (APIPA)

A special set of IP addresses have been set aside by IANA to use when a DHCP server cannot be reached. The range is 169.254.0.0 through 169.254.255.255. If a network interface card fails to connect to a DHCP server and the card has not been set up with a static IP address, the workstation automatically generates an IP address in the range from 169.254.0.1 to 169.254.255.254. It uses this IP address to communicate with other workstations on the same segment. Once the DHCP server comes back online and can resume issuing IP addresses from its pool of available addresses, the workstation releases the 169.254.xxx.xxx IP address and takes one from the DHCP server. This type of addressing is called **Automatic Private IP Addressing (APIPA)** and is compatible with all Microsoft products starting with Windows 98.

This process was not necessary in prior versions of Windows because the Net-BEUI protocol was automatically configured when a network interface card was installed. If the TCP/IP protocol failed because the DHCP server did not issue an IP address to the workstation, the workstation used the NetBEUI protocol. The NetBEUI protocol uses the MAC address to communicate with workstations on the local segment. On Windows 98 and later workstations, NetBEUI is not installed by default. When the DHCP server fails, there is no way for the computers to communicate on the local segment.

APIPA is configured in the **Internet Protocol (TCP/IP) Properties** dialog box, which is shown in Figure 10-20. At the top of the dialog box is the **Automatic private IP address** option. Notice that the other option, **User configured**, allows the

Figure 10-20 The **Internet Protocol Version 4 (TCP/IPv4) Properties** dialog box allows a workstation to be assigned alternate TCP/IP settings.

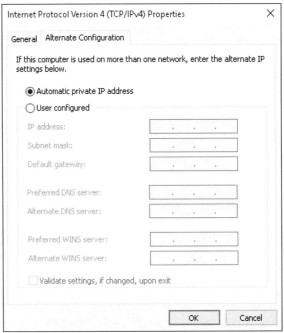

Goodheart-Willcox Publisher

workstation to be installed on more than one network by assigning an alternate set of IP settings and preferred DNS and WINS server settings. The **User configured** option is an excellent feature for laptop computers that may be moved to more than one location.

Duplicate IPv4 Addresses

A static IP address is configured manually rather than using a DHCP server to issue an IPv4 address to a workstation automatically. You cannot manually configure a duplicate IPv4 address. Windows Vista and Windows XP will generate a warning message and will not allow you to complete the task of configuring a duplicate IPv4 address. Windows 7 and beyond will not generate a warning but will automatically assign an APIPA.

TCP/IP Ports and Sockets

A **port number** is associated with the TCP/IP protocol and is used to create a virtual connection between two computers running TCP/IP. A computer, especially a server, runs many services at the same time. For example, a server could coordinate many e-mail requests, directory lookups, file transfers, Internet search requests, and web-page requests. If it were not for port numbers, communication would be confused and errors would occur.

Port numbers are assigned to network services. When the port number is combined with an IP address, it is referred to as a **socket**. The following is an example of a socket: 192.168.20.45:80. Notice that the IP address 192.168.20.45 is connected with a colon (:) to port 80.

To understand how port numbers work, think of an old telephone switchboard. A human operator plugs a connection cord into specific, physical sockets to complete a connection between two telephone lines. The connection is maintained for the duration of the call. The switchboard has many simultaneous conversations occurring at the same time. Like an old telephone switchboard, socket technology allows multiple, simultaneous services to run between a server and a workstation.

Look at Figure 10-21. You can see how the server uses port numbers combined with an IP address to sort the various communication taking place. Note that two sockets are created between the workstation and the server for file transfer and another socket is created for web-page browsing. Port number assignments are not limited to client/server communication. They are used to communicate between any two devices on a network.

Tech Tip

A duplicate IPv4 address is not a concern when IPv6 is configured by default because all exchanges of packets are performed in isolated local area network (link-local) by using IPv6 addresses.

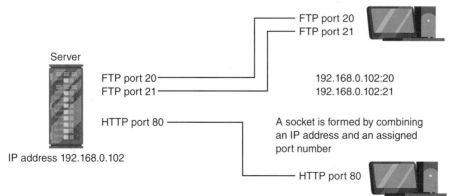

Figure 10-21 Communication can be sorted by the creation of a virtual circuit between a server and a workstation or between a workstation and a workstation. The virtual circuit is a combination of an IP address and a port number. This combination is called a socket. The socket creates and maintains a logical communication channel between two points on a network.

(server icon) fullvector/Shutterstock.com; (workstation icons) RedlineVector/Shutterstock.com;
Goodheart-Willcox Publisher

Copyright Goodheart-Willcox Co., Inc.

Network+ Note

To be prepared for the Network+ Certification Exam, memorize the common port numbers associated with TCP/IP and their functions. The most common port numbers encountered on the exam are 20, 21, 23, 80, and 110.

Figure 10-22 lists some typical port number assignments. Looking at the chart you can see some familiar port assignments such as port 80, which is associated with a web server; port 20, which is assigned to data transfers using FTP; and port 21, which is used for FTP control commands. For a complete list of assigned ports, visit www.iana.org/assignments/port-numbers.

Figure 10-22 Typical port assignments.

Port Number	Service	Description
7	ECHO	Echo a reply
20	FTP	File Transfer Protocol data
21	FTP	File Transfer Protocol control commands
22	SSH	Secure Shell
23	TELNET	Terminal emulation connection
25	SMTP	Simple Mail Transfer Protocol
43	NICNAME	Who Is
49	LOGIN	Login Host Protocol
53	DNS	Domain Name Server
67	DHCP	Dynamic Host Configuration Protocol data
69	TFTP	Trivia File Transfer Protocol
80	HTTP	Hypertext Transfer Protocol
110	POP	Post Office Protocol
119	NNTP	Network News Transfer Protocol
123	NTP	Network Time Protocol
137	NETBIOS	NetBIOS name service
143	IMAP4	Internet Message Access Protocol version 4
161	SNMP	Simple Network Management Protocol
389	LDAP	Lightweight Directory Access Protocol
443	HTTPS	HTTP Security
445	SMB	Server Message Block protocol data
500	IPSEC	IP Security
636	LDAPS	Lightweight Directory Access Protocol encrypted with TLS
1719	H.323	Establishes video or voice connections
1720	H.323	Establishes video or voice connections
1723	PPTP	Point-to-Point Tunneling Protocol
3389	Windows Remote Desktop	Remote access to desktops
5060	SIP	Session Initiation Protocol
5061	SIP	Session Initiation Protocol
5631	pcAnywhere data	pcAnywhere data
5632	pcAnywhere status	pcAnywhere status

Goodheart-Willcox Publisher

The port number is derived from a sixteen-bit binary field, which means there are over 65,000 different possible port numbers available for use. Ports 0 through 1023 are assigned by IANA and are called *well-known port numbers* because they have typical assignments. Port numbers higher than 1023 are referred to as *upper-level port numbers*. They do not have typical assignments. Private companies commonly use the numbers from 1023 through 49151 to support their software utilities. The remaining numbers, 49152 through 65535, can be used by anyone.

Copyright Goodheart-Willcox Co., Inc.

IPv6 Addressing

The newest Internet addressing scheme is called **IPv6**. It is referred to as a "classless IP addressing scheme" because there is no need for a subnet mask based on network class. Windows Vista, 7, 8, and 10, as well as Microsoft Server 2008, 2012, and 2016, automatically configure an IPv6 address in addition to an IPv4 address. While IPv6 is still not fully implemented, it is now incorporated into all modern operating systems and is here to stay. Many networks now use IPv6 alongside IPv4 as they prepare to eventually fully transition.

The original reason for developing a new IP address system was the rapid development of the Internet and the almost immediate shortage of available IP addresses. Today, almost all electronic communication equipment uses the Internet and some form of an Internet address. The development of the IPv6 standard has led to other network addressing improvements.

1.3 NET

Advantages of IPv6

The IPv4 standard is still primarily the same as it was when it was finalized in 1980. IPv6 provides many advantages and improvements when compared with the limitations of IPv4 such as a larger pool of Internet and network addresses, reduced broadcast traffic, better security, and improved quality of service.

Number of Possible IPv6 Addresses

The main reason IPv6 was developed was to increase the number of available Internet addresses. The IPv4 address is equal to 32-bits, i.e. 2^{32} addresses, or approximately 4,000,000,000 possible addresses. IPv6 uses 128-bit addresses, so there are 2^{128}, or over 340,000,000,000,000,000,000,000,000,000,000,000,000 possible addresses. As you can see, the possible number of unique addresses seems inexhaustible.

Reduced Broadcast Traffic

IPv4 uses Address Resolution Protocol (ARP) to resolve IPv4 addresses to Media Access Control (MAC) addresses. IPv6 uses the Neighbor Discovery (ND) protocol, which is carried inside a series of Internet Control Message Protocol (ICMP) packets on the local area network. ND will eventually replace ARP broadcasts, which will significantly reduce network traffic on the local area network. At this time, the implementation of both IPv6 and IPv4 by default does not result in total reduced local area network traffic.

The ARP protocol produces bursts of three UDP packets every few minutes containing the ARP request. This is followed by UDP packets returning from the destinations. Each destination typically produces a series of three UDP packets. UDP packets do not guarantee delivery. They are connectionless/unreliable, thus they can create more traffic than IPv6. The IPv6 address contains the MAC address identifier of the network device, so it does not require ARP to resolve the MAC to IPv4 assigned address.

Improved Security

IPv6 incorporates IPSec to provide better security than IPv4. IPSec is not a single protocol but rather a collection of protocols used to encrypt and authenticate each packet that uses an IP address over the Internet. The reason IPv6 has improved security is the use of IPSec is mandatory for IPv6 and optional for IPv4. There will be much more about IPSec in Chapter 15.

> **Note**
>
> The IPv6 standard is still evolving and not fully implemented at this time. While all information is accurate at the time of this writing, IPv6 standards may be modified in the future. You should check reliable references for the latest changes concerning IPv6.

Better Quality of Service

Quality of service refers to a protocol's ability to deliver certain packets in a timely fashion. For example, a long text document can have delays between packets that do not affect the content of the document. However, packets containing video or audio, such as a telephone conversation, must not have delays between the packets. A long delay between packets can cause a choppy conversation with parts of speech missing. IPv4 does have a quality of service feature, but when using security such as IPSec, packet delivery is slowed. The IPv6 standard significantly improves quality of service and does not let IPSec security cause long delays between packets.

IPv6 uses fewer packets to achieve the same results as IPv4. IPv4 uses the Type of Services (TOS) field in the header in conjunction with UDP and TCP packet port numbers to deliver time-sensitive data. IPv6 contains header information that allows routers to identify packet priority immediately and allows the router to act on the packet without the need for more information. The IPv6 packet allows the router to maintain direct flow of packets with an assigned priority. In short, the IPv6 format allows the router to process a priority packet faster than the IPv4 format, thus improving quality of service.

Support for Neighbor Discovery

Neighbor Discovery is an IPv6 data link layer mechanism used to identify network devices automatically, without the need of user intervention. IPv6 encapsulates ICMPv6 packets to exchange information with other devices connected in the same section (subnet) of a local area network. ICMPv6 supports two new message types that are not offered in ICMPv4. The two new message types that support discovery are Neighbor Solicitation and Neighbor Advertisement.

Proprietary discovery protocols are based on the Neighbor Discovery protocol standard. For example, Cisco Discovery Protocol (CDP) and Microsoft Link Layer Topology Discovery Mapper/Responder are both examples of the Neighbor Discovery mechanism.

Internet Control Message Protocol Version 6 (ICMPv6) is designed to exchange messages between neighboring nodes on the same link. This is the basis of Network Discovery, which allows a computer to identify other devices connected in the local link. Network Discovery also allows for automatic configuration of network devices and the discovery of router devices attached to the local area network.

IPv6 Address Format

Modern computer equipment and software readily accepts IPv6 addresses and uses them to communicate across a network. The IPv6 standard uses a total address length of 128 bits. The 128 bits are divided into eight units of 16 bits. These units can be represented as a 4-digit hexadecimal number separated by colons, as shown in Figure 10-23. The IPv6 address is assigned to network interface cards and equipment in a similar fashion as IPv4 addresses.

IPv6 EUI-64 Identifier

The original IEEE 802 MAC address consists of a 24-bit manufacturer's ID and a 24-bit unique ID associated with each network interface card. The IPv6 standard uses a 24-bit manufacturer's ID and a 40-bit unique ID to identify each network interface card. See Figure 10-24. Together, the 24-bit manufacturer's ID and 40-bit unique ID make up the last 64 bits of an IPv6 address known as the **EUI-64 identifier**.

Copyright Goodheart-Willcox Co., Inc.

Figure 10-23 The IPv6 addressing scheme.

The 128-bit IPv6 address is divided into eight 16-bit blocks each separated by a colon.

FE80:0000:0000:0000:4DE1:F01B:80FA:CCA3

A single 16-bit block containing all zeros can be expressed as a single zero.

FE80:0:0:0:4DE1:F01B:80FA:CCA3

A series of 16-bit blocks containing only zeros can be expressed as a simple double colon.

FE80::4DE1:F01B:80FA:CCA3

Only one double colon can be used in an IPv6 address.

FE80::0:0:0:A23D:0:0:CCA3

Using a double colon more than once is illegal!

FE80::A23D::CCA3

Goodheart-Willcox Publisher

Figure 10-24 IPv4 MAC address compared with an IPv6 EUI-64 identifier.

MAC Address

|← 24 bits →|← 24 bits →|
|Manufacturer's ID|Unique ID|

EUI-64 Identifier

|← 24 bits →|← 40 bits →|
|Manufacturer's ID|Unique ID|

MAC Address   00-19-D2-B3-5E-4F

EUI-64 Identifier   00-19-D2-FF-FE-B3-5E-4F

FF-FE

Goodheart-Willcox Publisher

The EUI-64 identifier serves the same function as the IPv4 MAC address. Since the original MAC address is 48-bits and the EUI-64 identifier is 64-bits, the original MAC address is modified to fit inside the 64-bit frame. The hexadecimal values "FF" and "FE" are inserted in the middle of the original 48-bit MAC address, which results in a 64-bit EUI-64 identifier. For example, an original MAC address of 00-19-D2-B3-5E-4F would be expressed as 00-19-D2-FF-FE-B3-5E-4F after being converted to a EUI-64 identifier.

Look at Figure 10-25, which compares the results of the **ipconfig /all** command issued at a Windows 10 computer. This is very similar regardless of the version of Windows; the view has remained largely unchanged from Windows 2000 through Windows 10.

Copyright Goodheart-Willcox Co., Inc.

Figure 10-25 EUI-64 identifier in Windows 7 and Windows 10.

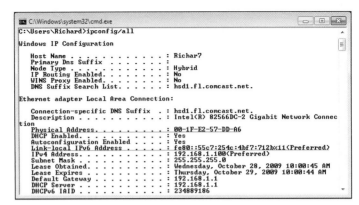

Goodheart-Willcox Publisher

IPv6 Topography Terminology

IPv6 introduced new terminology to redefine the network topography. The new terms are used to classify portions of an organization's network. When using IPv4 addressing, an organization can subdivide the network into subsections using subnet masks or subnets. IPv6 does not use a subnet mask but rather incorporates a similar function into the complete IPv6 address. IPv6 classifies the scope or range of an IPv6 address by its prefix, such as FE80 and FEC0.

Three terms used to describe the scope of the network are *global*, *link-local*, and *unique-local*, as shown in Figure 10-26. IPv6 addresses can divide the entire network of an organization into separate parts in much the same way as a separate subnet mask does for IPv4 addressing. This limits communication to portions of the entire network.

The term *site-local* was originally used in the series of RFCs that specified the IPv6 address standard. Later in October of 2005, the term *Unique Local IPv6 Unicast Address* was defined in RFC 4193 and used to clarify and replace the term *site-local*. In September 2004, RFC3879 deprecated the term *Site Local Address*. The term *deprecated* means that it is no longer being developed. Also, the terms are not hyphenated in the RFCs.

Global address is the public address used to identify the local network, and it is administered by IANA. It is equivalent to the IPv4 public address and can be routed.

Link-local is a portion of the organization's network. For example, the entire network might be the whole network within the XYZ Corporation. Within the XYZ

NET
✚ 1.4

Copyright Goodheart-Willcox Co., Inc.

Figure 10-26 IPv6 network classifications. The global IPv6 address is routable and serves as the Internet address. It is used to communicate outside the confines of the corporation network. The link-local IPv6 address identifies a portion of the corporation's network and is not routable. The unique-local IPv6 address spans portions of a corporation's network or the entire network.

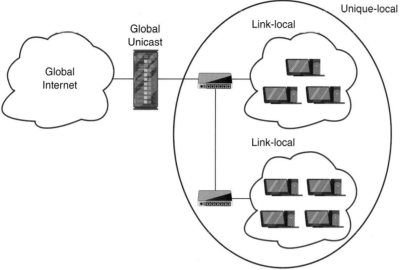

(server icon) fullvector/Shutterstock.com; (hub icons) Vadim Ermak/Shutterstock.com; (workstation icons) RedlineVector/Shutterstock.com; Goodheart-Willcox Publisher

Corporation are three smaller units such as payroll, sales, and management. Each of these three subunits is referred to as *link-local* or portions of the XYZ Corporation network. Routers will not forward packets that have a link-local address.

Unique-local is the entire organization's network or a portion of it. A router can forward packets to any portion of the organization's network but not outside the organization's network.

Network+ Note

The IEEE uses the term *interface* when describing the assignment of an IPv6 address to a device rather than the term *node*, which is commonly used to identify connections on a network. The main difference between these terms is a node can only have one IP address assigned to it. In contrast, an interface can have more than one IPv6 address assigned to it. This might seem like a trivial difference, but look for the term as it will most likely appear on the CompTIA Network+ exam.

Types of IPv6 Addresses

There are three broad classifications of IPv6 addresses: unicast, multicast, and anycast. A **unicast address** delivers packets to a single network address. A **multicast address** delivers packets to multiple addresses and is also referred to as *many-to-one*. An **anycast address** delivers packets to the nearest interface and is used mainly for supporting router functions.

1.3 NET

Unicast Address

A unicast address is organized by the scope of the address such as global unicast, link-local, site-local, unique-local, and special. Global is used for the IPv6 portion of the Internet and is similar in function as an IPv4 public address. Link-local is used on a local area network when there is no router or gateway available. Site-local serves

Copyright Goodheart-Willcox Co., Inc.

the same function as local area network. The site-local can encompass part of the local area network or the entire local area network to include remote locations. Other special unicast addresses covered in this section are loopback address, unspecified address, and zone IDs.

Global Unicast IPv6 Address

A global unicast IPv6 address is similar to an IPv4 public address. The global unicast address is unique and used for Internet addresses. A global unicast address can broadcast to all IPv6 addresses in the IPv6 portion of the local area network as well as to other global IPv6 addresses across the IPv6 portion of the Internet. The scope of the IPv6 global unicast address is the entire Internet as well as the local area network. A global unicast address starts with 2000: or is written as 2000:/3. The first three bits are set to 001, like the example shown in Figure 10-27. This is how a global address is identified and distinguished from other IPv6 addresses. The subnet ID is used to identify subnets or sections of an organization's network. The interface ID is used to identify a specific interface or device on the subnet.

Figure 10-27 Global unicast address format.

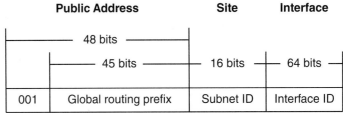

Goodheart-Willcox Publisher

Link-Local Unicast IPv6 Address

A link-local IPv6 address is used to communicate on a local area network and will not be forwarded by a router. The link-local address serves the same function as an IPv4 APIPA address (169.254.xxx.xxx). The IPv6 link-local address always starts with FE80 or FE80::/64. A link-local IPv6 is never forwarded beyond the local-link by an IPv6-capable router.

Link-local IPv6 addresses are automatically assigned by the operating system. Link-local IPv6 addresses are required for the Network Discovery feature. Without a link-local IPv6 address, Network Discovery will not function. This is why Microsoft operating systems configure a link-local address automatically for network devices.

Look at Figure 10-28 and compare the link-local, site-local, and unique-local address format. You will notice immediately that the link-local address does not have a subnet ID. This part of the IPv6 is usually filled with zeros or simply ::. Link-local addresses can be easily identified because they always start with the prefix FE80.

Global, site-local, and unique-local addresses use a subnet ID, which makes them different from link-local addresses. The subnet ID serves same function as a subnet mask.

Unique-Local Unicast IPv6 Address

The unique-local unicast IPv6 address is a replacement for site-local address. Site-local is still valid but is now considered deprecated. This means site-local addresses will be replaced by unique-local addresses.

A unique-local address serves the same function as a site-local address. A unique-local address can represent an entire local area network or just a portion. Unique-local addresses can also represent multiple locations such as New York and

Copyright Goodheart-Willcox Co., Inc.

Figure 10-28 Global unicast, link-local, site-local, and unique-local IPv6 address comparison.

Global Unicast

48 bits	16 bits	64 bits
001 Global routing prefix	Subnet ID	Interface ID

Local-link FE80::/64

10 bits	54 bits	64 bits
1111 1110 10		Interface ID

Site-local FEC0::/10

10 bits	54 bits	64 bits
1111 1110 11	Subnet ID	Interface ID

Unique-local FC00::/7

7 bits	40 bits	16 bits	64 bits
1111	Global ID	Subnet ID	Interface ID

Goodheart-Willcox Publisher

Chicago as long as the two locations are members of the same network. Look at Figure 10-28 and compare the site-local address to the unique-local address. Notice that a global ID and a subnet ID is assigned to the address. The unique-local address is easily identified by the prefix FC00.

Note

You will see the unique-local address expressed as **FC00::/7** or **FC00::/8**. The correct version is **FC00::/7**. The difference is the result of a single bit that follows the first seven bits of the unique-local address. This single bit is always set to binary *1*, which results in the address being expressed as **FC00::/8**.

Site-Local Unicast IPv6 Address

A site-local unicast IPv6 address serves the same function as IPv4 private addresses (10.0.0.0, 172.16.0.0, and 192.168.0.0). Site-local addresses always start with FEC0 or FEC0::/10. They are designed not to be routable beyond the local area network but are routable among the local-link sections of the local area network. Site-local IPv6 addresses are used for an organization with a defined geographic area, such as a business, school, campus, local area network, or a portion of an organization's local area network. In contrast to link-local addresses, site-local must be assigned manually.

IPv6 Loopback Address

The IPv6 **loopback address** is the reserved IP address of the network interface card. It is used to test if an IP address is configured for the network interface card and if the network interface card is functioning normally. The loopback address for IPv4 is 127.0.0.1. The loopback address for IPv6 is 0:0:0:0:0:0:0:1 or ::1. Note that the double colon eliminates fields containing only zeros.

1.4 NET

IPv6 Unspecified Address

An IPv6 unspecified address is 0:0:0:0:0:0:0:0: or simply a double colon :: to represent a string of zeros. It is the equivalent of the IPv4 address 0.0.0.0. An unspecified address is used when an interface is checking for its own duplicate address during the initial connection to the network. Because the identifier is randomly generated, there is a possibility that two devices could have the same identifier. When a device first comes on the network, it identifies itself with all zeros in its address and checks if its random address has already been assigned to another device. If no other device is using an address that matches the random address, then the randomly generated address will be used.

Local-Use Address Zone IDs

Zone IDs are used for local-use addresses to indicate which zone on a local area network a site-local address is used. The geographical area of the network is a section of the network that spans one or more link-local sections or a lesser part of a site-local section. Local-use IPv6 addresses can be used more than once to identify computers connected on different zones within the same geographic local area network (LAN or WAN). A zone ID is represented at the end of an IPv6 address as a percent sign followed by a number. For example, in Figure 10-29 the zone ID is %10.

A zone ID may also be referred to as a *scope ID*. Numeric values used for the zone ID are selected by the sending network device, not the receiving network device. It is possible for a single computer to be identified by more than one zone ID.

IPv6 Prefixes

An IPv6 prefix is the portion of the address with a fixed value that informs network devices of what action to take. For example, **FF00::/8** is a prefix indicating a multicast address.

Figure 10-29 Network Connection Details dialog box displaying the link-local IPv6 address with the zone ID "%10."

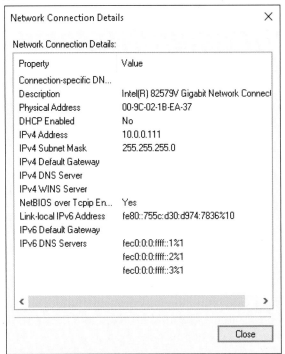

Goodheart-Willcox Publisher

Copyright Goodheart-Willcox Co., Inc.

Prefixes for IP addresses may be expressed using Classless Inter-Domain Routing (CIDR), which indicates what portion of the network IP address represents the subnet or network address. CIDR is covered in much more detail in Chapter 11.

IPv6 has been designed not to use a separate subnet mask, but it does use a prefix which serves the same purpose as the IPv4 subnet mask. The IPv6 prefix is expressed as address/prefix. For example, FE80::/64 means that the first 64 bits represent the network address. You will see IPv6 addresses expressed in both forms: the entire IPv6 address or the CIDR. See Figure 10-30 for a list of common IPv6 address prefixes.

To see a more complete list of multicast IPv6 address prefixes, visit the IANA website at www.iana.org/assignments/ipv6-multicast-addresses. For more information on IANA IPv6 addresses, visit www.iana.org/assignments/ipv6-address-space.

Figure 10-30 Common IPv6 address prefixes.

Prefix	Address Type
2000::/3	Global unicast
FE80::/10	Link-local unicast
FC08::/10	Site-local unicast
FD08::/8	Unique-local unicast
FF00::/8	Multicast
FF01::1	Interface multicast local all nodes
FF02::1	Link-local multicast all nodes
FF01::2	Interface-local multicast all routers
FF02::2	Link-local multicast all routers
FF05::2	Site-local multicast all routers

Goodheart-Willcox Publisher

IPv6 Transition Technologies

There are several technologies used to help in the transition from IPv4 to IPv6. Three of these technologies are 6to4, ISATAP, and Teredo. These technologies are intended to be used until IPv6 is fully implemented and IPv4 is fully deprecated. Aside from the protocols discussed in this section, there are also *dual-stack network cards* that can be used. These cards include both IPv4 and IPv6 addresses.

1.3 NET

6to4

6to4 is a mechanism that provides a means of communicating across the IPv4 Internet while preserving the original IPv6 assigned address of the network device. The 6to4 address technology supports network-to-network communication between routers. It is designed for router-to-router communication. A router must be designed to support 6to4 to be able to forward 6to4 packets. 6to4 solves compatibility issues between IPv6 and IPv4 addresses. For example, the IPv4 address 134.175.27.10 displayed as a 6to4 IPv6 address is 2002::86AF:1B0A. Each set of IPv4 decimal numbers are converted to IPv6 hexadecimal pairs, where

Decimal 134 = Hex 86

Decimal 175 = Hex AF

Decimal 27 = Hex 1B

Decimal 10 = Hex 0A

Copyright Goodheart-Willcox Co., Inc.

The IPv6 unicast 6to4 address always starts with 2002 or is represented by 2002::/16. A global unicast address is followed by a subnet ID and finally an interface ID. For example, Global site prefix:Subnet ID:Interface ID or 2002::WWXX:YYZZ, where WWXX:YYZZ corresponds to the original IPv4 address:

Octet 1 = WW

Octet 2 = XX

Octet 3 = YY

Octet 4 = ZZ

Thus,

2002::86AF:1B0A = 134.175.27.10

ISATAP

Intra-Site Automatic Tunneling Address Protocol (ISATAP) was developed jointly by Microsoft and Cisco Systems. ISATAP is designed to tunnel IPv6 addresses inside IPv4 packets at the data link layer. ISATAP is a node-to-node and node-to-router technology used for IPv4-based network devices to eliminate the need to upgrade these devices.

ISATAP supports Neighbor Discovery, which identifies computers and network devices such as local routers. The main advantage of ISATAP over 6to4 is ISATAP is used to discover routers using the ICMPv6 protocol. ISATAP has been implemented in all versions of Windows since Windows XP and Windows Server 2003, including the more recent Windows 10 and Windows Server 2016.

Teredo

Teredo is configured by default in Windows Vista, 7, 8, and 10 and is considered a last-resort technology when ISATAP cannot be used. Teredo functions as a network address translator similar to the NAT protocol. NAT devices are used to convert an IPv4 public address to one or more private addresses. 6to4 requires a 6to4-enabled router at the edge of the network system that connects to the Internet. Teredo does not. Teredo creates a tunnel in similar fashion to 6to4 and allows incoming IPv6 traffic through a firewall designed for IPv4. This is especially important for small-office systems and homes that use a router/gateway firewall system.

Teredo was first implemented by Microsoft Windows XP SP2 and later and has been continually refined. You will see a reference to "automatic tunneling pseudo interface" or to "tunneling" when you issue the **ipconfig /all** command on a Windows Vista or later computer.

Broadcast and Multicast Addresses

A broadcast address sends packets to all network addresses while a multicast address sends packets to a specific set of addresses. IPv4 uses broadcast and multicast addresses to distribute packets. IPv6 uses only multicast addresses.

Multicast addressing is used for topology discovery, gateway discovery, and group discovery. A computer or network device can announce its presence to other computers and devices on the local link using a multicast address. For example, an IPv6 address with the prefix of FF02 is used to distribute a packet to all computers on a link-local.

The Link-Layer Multicast Name Resolution (LLMNR) protocol uses both IPv4 and IPv6 for name resolution through multicast. The IPv4 multicast destination

Copyright Goodheart-Willcox Co., Inc.

address is 224.0.0.252. The IPv6 multicast destination address is ff02::1:3. These two multicast addresses will not be forwarded by a router, thus limiting the broadcast to the local-link. These two multicast destination addresses are used by the LLMNR protocol. The LLMNR protocol is used by Windows Vista, 7, 8, and 10, as well as Windows Server 2008 and 2016 for name resolution using the multicast addresses and the NetBIOS Name Service (NBNS) protocol.

IPv6 Lifetimes

IPv4 addresses are leased for a definite period of time. IPv6 addresses are configured with two lifetime values: valid lifetime and preferred lifetime. *Valid lifetime* is typically a week, and a *preferred lifetime* is a day. A valid lifetime value has been validated by a router. An IPv6 address with a valid lifetime value can send and receive unicast messages. A preferred lifetime value is the period of time that an interface can start new communication sessions.

IPv6 DHCP

IPv6 uses DHCP just as IPv4. However, there are some differences. With IPv6, there are two flags that are set on the computer to determine what that computer will get from the DHCP server: the M flag and the O flag. The *M flag* determines whether a computer will get an IP address from the DHCP server or if it has a static IP address. The *O flag* determines if a computer will get other data, such as the gateway IP address and DNS server IP address, from the DHCP server. A typical workstation likely has M =1 and O =1 and receives all the information from the DHCP server. A web server, however, would use a static IP address. It would likely have M = 0 but O=1.

NET
1.4

IPv6 in Windows 7, 8, and 10

As far back as Windows XP, Windows came with support for IPv6. However, IPv6 was not the default version in XP. To install IPv6, users would have to enter **ipv6 install** at the command prompt. To remove IPv6, the command was **ipv6 uninstall**. Windows XP uses the **ping6** and **tracert6** commands to ping and trace the route of an IPv6 address. Starting with Windows 7, on through 8, and now with Windows 10, IPv6 is supported by default in Windows. In fact, if a user runs the utility **ipconfig /all** in command prompt, the computer's IPv6 address, as well as the IPv4 address can be seen.

TCP/IP Troubleshooting Utilities

There can be many types of problems associated with TCP/IP technology. Fortunately, there are a number of useful utilities that can identify the problem. These utilities are **netstat, nbtstat, ping, tracert, arp, nslookup,** and **tcpdump**. This section only introduces these tools. Further experience can be gained by using these tools in the lab and in the field.

Netstat

The **netstat** command displays current TCP/IP and port statistics. It can be used to determine network problems such as excessive broadcasts on the network. It also allows the user to monitor network connections.

NET
5.2

Figure 10-31 shows the results of the **netstat -a** command issued at the command prompt. Notice that the **netstat -a** command has returned a list of services,

Copyright Goodheart-Willcox Co., Inc.

port addresses, and type of packet sent (TCP or UDP). The **-a** switch is just one of the many switches available to use with the **netstat** command.

Nbtstat

The **nbtstat** command is used to display NetBIOS over TCP statistics. In Figure 10-32, you can see a list of NetBIOS names of equipment connected to the local area network and workgroup names.

Figure 10-31 The **netstat -a** command displays a list of services, port addresses, and type of packet sent (TCP or UDP).

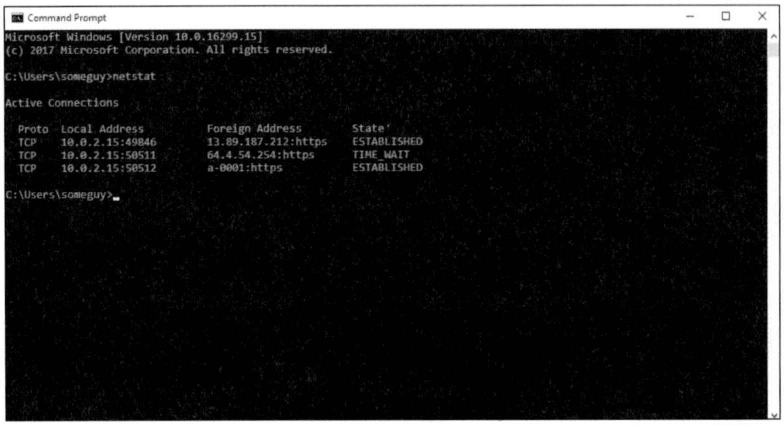

Goodheart-Willcox Publisher

Figure 10-32 The **nbstat -n** command displays NetBIOS over TCP statistics including computer and workgroup names.

Goodheart-Willcox Publisher

Remember, NetBIOS does not use IP addresses to identify computers on a network. Windows-based networks use the Server Message Block (SMB) protocol and NetBIOS names to identify computers on a network. For TCP/IP to resolve NetBIOS names, the WINS utility must be running or the lmhosts file must be manually configured.

The **nbtstat** command can be issued from the command prompt with various switches that affect the outcome of the command. Remember, switches for commands issued from the command prompt can be revealed by using the **/?** or **/help** switch after typing the command at the command prompt. Be sure to leave a space between the switch and the end of the command.

Copyright Goodheart-Willcox Co., Inc.

Tech Tip

SMB, CIFS, and SMB2 are the Microsoft network protocols designed to support print and file sharing on a Microsoft network.

Ping

The **ping** command is used to send a packet from one host to another on a network and then echo a return reply. It is commonly used to check the connection state of network media between two hosts on a network quickly. The **ping** command can be used on LANs and WANs. To run the **ping** utility, you simply issue the **ping** command at the command prompt followed by the IP address or the host name with which you wish to test communication. Users can also ping URLs by entering the ping command followed by the domain, for example **ping www.g-w.com**.

Figure 10-33 shows a simple way to issue the **ping** command. In the top portion of the screen, the command is issued using the destination domain name *Google* (**ping www.google.com**). When a domain name is used, the reply displays the destination IP address. In this example, it is 173.194.70.105. Note that each reply from the destination indicates the number or bytes, lapse time in microseconds, and the Time to Live (TTL) of the packet sent. The **ping** command can also be issued using the destination IP address instead of a domain name. In this scenario, the same results as in the previous command would be displayed.

Figure 10-33 The **ping** command sends a packet from one host to another on a network and then echoes a return reply.

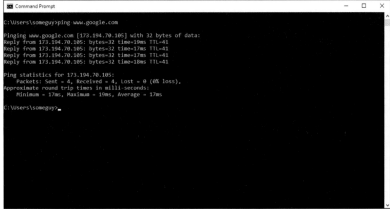

Goodheart-Willcox Publisher

The **ping** command uses the Internet Control Message Protocol (ICMP) to carry troubleshooting data across the network. The *Internet Control Message Protocol (ICMP)* is a part of the TCP/IP suite of protocols and provides the ability to remotely troubleshoot and monitor devices on network systems.

The command **ping6** was the equivalent of the IPv4 **ping** command. However, beginning with Windows Vista, none of the Windows operating systems recognize the **ping6** command. Instead, **ping -6** is used. The **-6** switch forces the command to use the IPv6 address. Figure 10-34 displays **ping -6** results as viewed in Windows 8. When the **ping -6** command is entered followed by the name of a local network computer, the echo response will display the IPv6 address of the destination computer. Using the **-4** switch with the **ping** command forces the command to use the IPv4 address.

Tech Tip

The **ping -6** command is carried inside the ICMPv6 packet.

Figure 10-34 Windows uses the **-6** switch to force the **ping** command to use the IPv6 address.

```
                    Administrator: Command Prompt                    _  □  X

Microsoft Windows [Version 6.2.9200]
(c) 2012 Microsoft Corporation. All rights reserved.

C:\Users\Administrator>ping -6 www.google.com

Pinging www.google.com [2607:f8b0:4003:c05::63] with 32 bytes of data:
Reply from 2607:f8b0:4003:c05::63: time=17ms
Reply from 2607:f8b0:4003:c05::63: time=30ms
Reply from 2607:f8b0:4003:c05::63: time=16ms
Reply from 2607:f8b0:4003:c05::63: time=16ms

Ping statistics for 2607:f8b0:4003:c05::63:
    Packets: Sent = 4, Received = 4, Lost = 0 (0% loss),
Approximate round trip times in milli-seconds:
    Minimum = 16ms, Maximum = 30ms, Average = 19ms

C:\Users\Administrator>_
```

Goodheart-Willcox Publisher

Tracert or Traceroute

NET
5.2

Think of the trace route utility, **tracert** or **traceroute**, as an advanced **ping** utility. Unix/Linux systems use the **traceroute** command, while Microsoft systems use the **tracert** command. In this section, examples of the trace route utility use the **tracert** command.

The trace route utility sends a packet to a destination host, gathers statistics and information along the way, and displays the information on the monitor of the originator. The final destination point echoes information such as who owns the site's domain name, the IP address, and geographic location. Also displayed is each connection point along the route of the trace with information about its location. Most of the connection points displayed are routers.

The trace route utility also displays the approximate hop lapse times between points along the route. The amount of time delay can help analyze network failure or problems caused by excessive time delays.

Figure 10-35 shows the information revealed when a **tracert** command has been issued from the local host to the www.google.com website. A series of hops, or router connections, are revealed along with the amount of time between each hop. Trace route is a good utility for troubleshooting a path to a distant destination.

ARP

Address Resolution Protocol (ARP) is used to map the host MAC address to the logical host IP address. For a computer to be able to run ARP, ARP must know the computer's IP address. ARP is a protocol in the TCP/IP suite of protocols. Since it is dependent on TCP/IP, it needs to have an IP address assigned before it can reveal any information. ARP also caches information about contacts on the network.

Reverse Address Resolution Protocol (RARP) is used to find the MAC address of the host when the IP address is known. It serves the opposite function of ARP. RARP was originally developed to support the BOOTP protocol. Remember that BOOTP is used to obtain an IP address automatically from the BOOTP server.

In Figure 10-36, the **arp -a** command lists IP addresses resolved to MAC addresses. The information displayed comes from the ARP cache, sometimes called

NET
1.3

Figure 10-35 The **tracert** utility is used to gather and display statistics and information about the route to a destination host.

```
Command Prompt - tracert www.google.com                                    —   □   ×

C:\Users\someguy>tracert www.google.com

Tracing route to www.google.com [173.194.70.105]
over a maximum of 30 hops:

  1    <1 ms    <1 ms    <1 ms   10.0.2.2
  2     1 ms     1 ms     1 ms   Tardis [192.168.1.1]
  3     2 ms     1 ms     1 ms   192.168.0.1
  4    32 ms    10 ms    11 ms   142.254.141.53
  5   128 ms    30 ms   116 ms   tge0-0-4.plaotxso01h.texas.rr.com [24.28.90.1]
  6    13 ms    13 ms    13 ms   agg21.plantxmp01r.texas.rr.com [24.175.49.221]
  7   107 ms    14 ms    13 ms   agg27.crtntxjt01r.texas.rr.com [24.175.36.177]
  8    19 ms    14 ms    14 ms   agg21.dllatxl301r.texas.rr.com [24.175.49.0]
  9    21 ms    13 ms    14 ms   bu-ether14.dllstx976iw-bcr00.tbone.rr.com [66.109.6.88]
 10    18 ms    11 ms    13 ms   0.ae0.pr1.dfw10.tbone.rr.com [107.14.17.232]
 11    13 ms    14 ms    14 ms   ix-ae-23-0.tcore2.DT8-Dallas.as6453.net [66.110.57.97]
 12    12 ms    13 ms    11 ms   74.125.50.214
 13     *
```

Goodheart-Willcox Publisher

Figure 10-36 The **arp -a** command reveals information found in the ARP cache. The ARP cache stores the IP and MAC addresses the host has communicated within the last two minutes.

```
Command Prompt                                                             —   □   ×

Microsoft Windows [Version 10.0.16299.15]
(c) 2017 Microsoft Corporation. All rights reserved.

C:\Users\someguy>arp -a

Interface: 10.0.2.15 --- 0x3
  Internet Address      Physical Address      Type
  10.0.2.2              52-54-00-12-35-02     dynamic
  10.0.2.255            ff-ff-ff-ff-ff-ff     static
  224.0.0.22            01-00-5e-00-00-16     static
  224.0.0.252           01-00-5e-00-00-fc     static
  224.0.0.253           01-00-5e-00-00-fd     static
  239.255.255.250       01-00-5e-7f-ff-fa     static
  255.255.255.255       ff-ff-ff-ff-ff-ff     static

C:\Users\someguy>
```

Goodheart-Willcox Publisher

the *ARP table*, on the 192.168.0.3 host. The ARP cache contains the IP and MAC addresses the 192.168.0.3 host has communicated within the last two minutes. The information presented is displayed in a database format. The **arp** command can be used to verify IP address and MAC address assignments.

Nslookup

The **nslookup** command is a Unix/Linux utility used to query domain servers when seeking information about domain names and IP addresses. The **nslookup** command maps, or resolves, domain names to IP addresses. This is a convenient tool when looking for information about a particular domain or IP addresses. **Nslookup** is very similar to the **whois** command found at many web server providers.

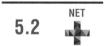

Tcpdump

The **tcpdump** utility comes with Linux and can be downloaded for Windows. This utility reads the network packets that are being seen by your network card. This means it can provide rather detailed information about network traffic. It is essentially a packet sniffer.

Summary

IPv4 Addressing

- There are two types of IP addressing schemes: IPv4 and IPv6.

- IPv4 uses four octets separated by periods to identify each host uniquely.

- The decimal number located in the first octet of an IP number can identify its class: Class A network is identified by the 1–127 range, a Class B network by the 128–191 range, and a Class C network by the 192–223 range.

- The three reserved, or private, IP address ranges are 10.0.0.0 to 10.255.255.255, 172.16.0.0 to 172.31.255.255, and 192.168.0.0 to 192.168.255.255.

- The Network Address Translation (NAT) protocol provides the technology to allow multiple workstations to share one common Internet connection.

Domain Name System (DNS)

- The Domain Name System (DNS) matches host and domain names to IP addresses.

- A Fully Qualified Domain Name (FQDN) consists of a host name and a domain name.

- DNS is a hierarchical system composed of top-level domains, second-level domains, and subdomains.

- A hosts file is used to resolve computer names to IP addresses when a DNS server is unavailable.

- WINS matches IP addresses to NetBIOS names.

IP, TCP, and UDP

- The three most commonly used protocols in the TCP/IP suite are Internet Protocol (IP), Transmission Control Protocol (TCP), and User Datagram Protocol (UDP).

- A UDP frame format is simple in construction. The header information contains only four significant items: source port, destination port, message length, and checksum.

- A TCP header contains additional information such as a sequence number, which is used to reassemble data in a correct order.

Assigning IP Addresses

- A static IP assignment means that an IP address is entered manually for each host on the network; a dynamic IP assignment means that the IP address is issued automatically, typically when the computer boots and joins the network.

- The Dynamic Host Configuration Protocol (DHCP) is used to dynamically, or automatically, assign IP addresses to workstations.

- The DHCP server sets a lease period for IP address assignments.

- Automatic Private IP Addressing (APIPA) is a technique that temporarily issues an IP address in the range of 169.254.0.1 to 169.254.255.255 in case of a DHCP server failure.

Copyright Goodheart-Willcox Co., Inc.

TCP/IP Ports and Sockets

- A port number is associated with the TCP/IP protocol and is used to create a virtual connection between two computers running TCP/IP.
- When the port number is combined with an IP address, it is referred to as a *socket.*

IPv6 Addressing

- IPv6 is referred to as a "classless IP addressing scheme" because there is no need for a subnet mask based on network class.
- Four advantages of IPv6 are larger pool of Internet addresses, better security through mandatory IPSec, better quality of service, and reduced number of network broadcasts.
- IPv6 uses eight sets of 16-bit hexadecimal numbers to identify each host uniquely; it does not require a subnet mask.
- An EUI-64 identifier serves the same purpose as a MAC address.
- Global address is the public address used to identify the local network, and it is administered by IANA.
- Link-local IPv6 addresses always start with FE80 and are not routable.
- Unique-local IPv6 addresses begin with FD00 and are routable only within the private network.
- A single network adapter can have more than one IPv6 addresses assigned.

Types of IPv6 Addresses

- A unicast address delivers packets to a single network address.
- A multicast address delivers packets to multiple addresses and is also referred to as many-to-one.
- An anycast address delivers packets to the nearest interface and is used mainly for supporting router functions.
- The loopback address for an IPv4 address is 127.0.0.1.
- The loopback address for an IPv6 address is ::1.

IPv6 Transition Technologies

- 6to4 addresses always start with 2002: and are used to support communication between IPv6 and IPv4 addresses on an IPv4 network system.
- ISATAP is designed as a node-to-node and node-to-router technology supporting IPv6 tunneling over an IPv4 network.
- Teredo creates a tunnel to allow incoming IPv6 traffic through a firewall designed for IPv4.

Broadcast and Multicast Addresses

- Link-Layer Multicast Name Resolution (LLMNR) protocol uses both IPv4 and IPv6 for name resolution through multicast.

IPv6 Lifetimes

- An IPv6 *valid lifetime* is typically a week.
- An IPv6 *preferred lifetime* is a day.

IPv6 DHCP

- There are two flags that are set on the computer to determine what that computer will get from the DHCP server: the M flag and the O flag.
- The *M flag* determines whether the computer will get an IP address from the DHCP server or if it has a static IP address.
- The *O flag* determines if the computer will get other data, such as the gateway IP address and DNS server IP address, from the DHCP server.

IPv6 in Windows 7, 8, and 10

- To install IPv6 in Windows XP, users would have to enter **ipv6 install** at the command prompt. To remove IPv6, the command was **ipv6 uninstall**.
- Starting with Windows 7, on through 8, and now with Windows 10, IPv6 is supported by default in Windows.

TCP/IP Troubleshooting Utilities

- The trace route utility is essentially an advanced ping.
- The **netstat** command displays current TCP/IP and port statistics.
- The **nbtstat** command is used to display NetBIOS over TCP statistics.
- The **ping** command is used to send a packet from one host to another on a network and then echo a return reply.
- The trace route utility sends a packet to a destination host, gathers statistics and information along the way, and displays the information on the monitor of the originator.
- Unix/Linux systems use the **traceroute** command, while Microsoft systems use the **tracert** command.

Review Questions

1. How many bytes are in an IPv4 address?
2. How many bits are in an IPv4 address?
3. How many octets are in an IPv4 address?
4. What is the range of numbers in an IPv4 octet?
5. How many hosts can a Class A network support?
6. How many hosts can a Class B network support?
7. How many hosts can a Class C network support?
8. List the IP addresses commonly assigned as private networks.
9. The _____ protocol allows an unregistered private network address to communicate with a legally registered IP address.
10. Briefly explain how NAT protocol works.
11. What command can a technician use to find the subnet mask information of a network?
12. What two parts make up an FQDN?

Copyright Goodheart-Willcox Co., Inc.

13. What is contained in a typical lmhosts file?

14. What is contained in a typical hosts file?

15. Compare and contrast DNS and WINS.

16. What is the default protocol for communication across the Internet?

17. Identify each of the following protocols as either connectionless or connection-oriented.

    A. TCP

    B. IP

    C. UDP

18. Explain how TCP, UDP, and IP relate to the OSI model.

19. On what does a TCP frame rely to identify source and destination IP addresses?

20. On what does a UDP frame rely to identify source and destination IP addresses?

21. On what does a IP frame rely to identify the source and destination MAC addresses?

22. What is the function of DHCP?

23. What two methods are used to assign an IP address to a host?

24. What type of addressing automatically generates an IP address in the range of 169.254.0.1 to 169.254.255.255 if a network interface card fails to connect to a DHCP server?

25. What port is indicated by the following address: 192.168.23.45:80?

26. IPv6 is referred to as a _____ IP addressing scheme because there is no need for a subnet mask based on network class.

27. What are some advantages of IPv6?

28. How is an EUI-64 identifier created?

29. List three terms used to describe the scope of a network.

30. What are the three broad classifications of IPv6 addresses?

31. Which IPv6 address type is similar in function as the IPv4 public addresses?

32. Which IPv6 address type serves the same function as IPv4 APIPA?

33. What are the three transition technologies used to implement IPv6?

34. Briefly describe the function of a broadcast address.

35. Briefly describe the function of a multicast address.

36. Differentiate between a valid lifetime and a preferred lifetime.

37. What does an *M flag* determine?

38. What does an *O flag* determine?

39. What command was used to install IPv6 on Windows XP computers?

40. Starting with Windows 7, what command can be entered in command prompt to view IPv6 and IPv4 addresses?

41. What utility is most likely used to verify a connection between two network points quickly?

42. What TCP/IP utility can reveal the number of hops between the source and destination host?

43. What TCP/IP utility displays current network protocol statistics, such as the number of packets sent?

44. What TCP/IP utility displays a current listing of NetBIOS names and their associated IP addresses?

✚ Sample Network+ Exam Questions

1. Jared is working with IPv6 on his network. If he sets the client M flag to 1 and O flag to 0, which of the following outcomes is most likely to happen?
   A. The workstation will receive an IP and MAC address from the DHCP server.
   B. The workstation will obtain a gateway IP address and DNS server IP address from the DHCP server, but it will *not* receive an IP address from the DHCP server.
   C. The workstation will obtain an IP address from the DHCP server, but it will *not* get other data from the DHCP server.
   D. The workstation will obtain an IP address, gateway IP address, and DNS server IP address from the DHCP server.

2. Which technology supports the automatic assignment of IP addresses to network hosts?
   A. WINS
   B. DHCP
   C. ARP
   D. DNS

3. You have issues with the IP address on your computer. Your computer is configured to use dynamic IP addresses. Which command will help you obtain a new address?
   A. **ipcfg /renew**
   B. **ifconfig /retrieve**
   C. **ipconfig /renew**
   D. **winipcfg /renew**

4. Lucy is reviewing network traffic logs for her network. She has noticed a private IP address in the log. Which of the following is a private IP address?
   A. 123.244.12.0
   B. 192.168.0.0
   C. 255.255.255.255
   D. 1.1.1.0

5. Identify the subnet mask of a Class B network.

    A. 255.0.0.0

    B. 255.255.0.0

    C. 0.0.255.255

    D. 255.255.255.0

6. What is the IPv4 loopback address?

    A. 127.0.0.1

    B. 255.255.255.255

    C. 0.0.0.0

    D. 255.0.0.0

7. What function does a WINS server perform?

    A. Automatically assigns a MAC address to a network adapter.

    B. Resolves IP addresses to MAC addresses.

    C. Resolves NetBIOS names to IP addresses.

    D. Resolves domain names to IP addresses.

8. Gabriel is examining logs for his network firewall log. He is trying to track down all the FQDN's that were visited from his network. Which is an example of a Fully Qualified Domain Name?

    A. 3F 2B 12 CC D2 1F

    B. //workstation1/server

    C. //server1/client23

    D. workstation1.auditing.abc.com

9. A technician enters **ipconfig** at the command prompt of a Windows workstation and sees the assigned IP address for the workstation is 169.254.1.12. What can the technician surmise from the assigned address?

    A. The workstation is using a static IP address.

    B. The DHCP server is down.

    C. The WINS server is not online.

    D. The network is functioning normally.

10. What type of information is stored in the ARP cache?

    A. IP and MAC addresses.

    B. IP addresses only.

    C. IP addresses and domain names of workstations.

    D. MAC addresses only.

CHAPTER 11 Subnetting

Network+ Certification Exam Objectives

The Network+ Certification Exam requires only a basic understanding of TCP/IP addressing and its relationship to the subnet mask. You should know how to identify a network class by looking at the first octet of an IPv4 address. The numeric value of the first octet will identify the network class. Questions concerning the network class can be quite difficult unless you memorize the decimal values associated with each class. You should be familiar with switches and VLANs. Questions concerning subnetting, bridges, switches, routers, and VLANs will typically make up 10 to 15 percent of the test, so be prepared. Also, should you choose to take any Cisco certifications, subnetting is tested quite prominently. Beyond certification testing, subnetting is a very common task for network administrators. Therefore, it should be studied carefully.

Objectives

1.3: Properties of Network Traffic—Broadcast Domains

Segmentation and Interface Properties— VLAN, Trunking (802.1Q), Tagging and Untagging Ports, Port Mirroring, Switching Loops/Spanning Tree

Routing

IPv6 Concepts—Router Advertisement

Performance Concepts—Distributed Switching

1.4: Virtual IP, Subnetting

2.2: Bridge

4.2: Access Control—MAC Filtering

4.6: Switch Port Protection—Spanning Tree, BPDU Guard, Root Guard

Network Segmentation—VLAN

Learning Outcomes

- Interpret the binary number system.
- Summarize dotted decimal notation.
- Describe the purpose, advantages, and disadvantages of subnetting.
- Identify and differentiate between network segmenting devices.
- Summarize the characteristics and purpose of a Virtual LAN.
- Interpret CIDR notation.
- Summarize link aggregation.

Copyright Goodheart-Willcox Co., Inc.

Key Terms

adaptive cut-through

Border Gateway Protocol (BGP)

Classless Inter-Domain Routing (CIDR)

convergence

cut-through

distance vector protocol

dotted decimal notation

dynamic IP address table

dynamic VLAN

Enhanced Interior Gateway Routing Protocol (EIGRP)

Exterior Gateway Protocol (EGP)

filtering

fixed-length subnet mask (FLSM)

fragment-free

hop

Interior Gateway Protocol (IGP)

Interior Gateway Routing Protocol (IGRP)

Intermediate System to Intermediate System (IS-IS)

link aggregation

link-state protocol

Open Shortest Path First (OSPF)

RIP next generation (RIPng)

Router Information Protocol (RIP)

router metric

routing

Spanning Tree Protocol (STP)

static IP address table

static VLAN

store-and-forward

subnetting

trunking

variable-length subnet mask (VLSM)

virtual local area network (VLAN)

Virtual Trunking Protocol (VTP)

Overview

This chapter covers a concept that some students find difficult to master. However, the concepts are simple enough. Subnetting means taking a single IP address issued from a registrar or an ISP and creating two or more subnetworks from it. For example, if a small business is issued only one IP address, it can increase security or subdivide the network by creating two different networks from the issued IP address. It can do this by using the subnet mask technique explained in this chapter. Put another way, a subnet mask is simply the part of the IP address that is masked for the network. The part that is masked represents the network address, and the unmasked part can be used to assign addresses to nodes on that network.

To learn how to subnet, pay close attention to the information presented in this chapter and practice the calculations. Before going any further in this topic, you must master binary-to-decimal conversion and decimal-to-binary conversion. The term *mastery* means a complete understanding and ability to use and apply a concept, not simply becoming familiar with it. A simple familiarity is not sufficient. Without fully understanding binary counting and conversion to decimal, the following information is difficult to understand and impossible to apply in the field.

For this chapter, you may be able to use a calculator for making binary to decimal conversions. One such calculator is available in Microsoft Windows 98 or later in the **Start** menu. However, some certification exams require subnet masks to be calculated manually. If you plan to take one of the other various certification exams, it would be wise to verify if calculating subnet masks by hand is required. If so, be sure to get plenty of practice making binary to decimal conversions without a calculator or reference table.

Binary Number System

The binary number system is a perfect match for digital electronic systems, such as computer systems. Digital electronics consists of circuits that have only two electrical states: on and off. The binary number system consists entirely of ones (1s) and zeros (0s). The ones typically represent electrical energy, and the zeros represent the absence of electrical energy.

Digital circuit patterns can be represented by binary bit patterns. The major problem with the binary number system is reading and interpreting the numeric values of the binary bit patterns. We are used to the decimal number system, and our minds are trained to interpret and perform calculations based on decimal numbers. In addition, decimal numbers require much less space than binary numbers when written out.

The fact that large numeric expressions written in binary can be quite lengthy adds to the difficulty of using the binary number system and quickly interpreting their numeric value. For this chapter, you will need to be able to convert binary numbers to their decimal equivalents. You may use the tables provided as you progress through this chapter, but you should be able to convert an eight-digit binary number to its decimal equivalent without a table to understand the technology fully. Think of the exercises in this chapter as learning an entirely new numbering system, such as roman numerals.

Following this paragraph is a simple table that can help you convert binary numbers to their decimal equivalents. The table is limited to eight positions. This is equal to one byte—the most common unit you will encounter. It is also equal to one octet of an IPv4 IP address.

1	1	1	1	1	1	1	1
128	64	32	16	8	4	2	1

To convert a binary bit pattern to a decimal value, simply insert the decimal value for each individual bit position represented by a one, and then add the decimal values together. Study the following example.

1	0	0	1	0	1	0	1
128	0	0	16	0	4	0	1
128 + 16 + 4 + 1 = 149							
10010101 = 149							

Dotted Decimal Notation

Typically, the numeric values of an IPv4 address encountered in computer technology are displayed in decimal form, not binary. This form is referred to as dotted decimal notation. **Dotted decimal notation** consists of each octet of an IP address separated by a period. Look at Figure 11-1 to see an example of a Class B IPv4 address and subnet mask expressed as both binary and dotted decimal notation.

The figure shows a network IPv4 address of 130.50.125.25 with a subnet mask of 255.255.0.0. The subnet mask, like the IP address, is divided into two parts: the network address and the host address. In the example, the subnet mask network address is 255.255.0.0 and the host address is 0.0. All IPv4 addresses indicate a host address and a network address.

Copyright Goodheart-Willcox Co., Inc.

Subnetting

1.4 NET

Recall from Chapter 10 that a subnet mask serves to identify the portion of the IP address that represents the network. In the past, when network classes were used, the subnet determined the class. Dividing a network into subnetworks, or subnets, is called **subnetting**. Router technology also relies on subnetting for creating large sections of network communication paths.

A subnet is a network created by borrowing bits from the host portion of an assigned network IP address. Look at Figure 11-2. In this example, a Class B network subnet mask has been extended into the first host octet. The first three bits borrowed from the host portion of the address are used to identify the subnets created from the original IP address. By borrowing the first three bits from the host portion, six subnets may be formed. Take particular notice of the new dotted decimal notation of the subnet mask. It is now 255.255.224.0. The original subnet mask was 255.255.0.0.

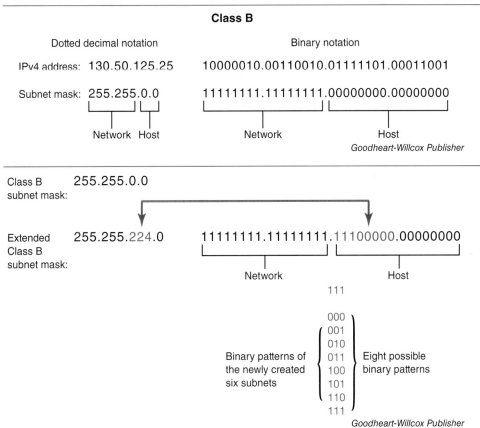

Figure 11-1 A Class B IPv4 address and subnet mask in binary and decimal form. Notice that in the subnet mask, all ones indicate the network and all zeros indicate the host.

Figure 11-2 Look carefully at the extended subnet mask. Notice that the third octet is equal to 224, which generates a binary bit pattern matching the binary example on the right. The value, 224, indicates a subnet that can be used to create eight possible binary bit patterns. Only six of the binary bit patterns can be used because 000 and 111 cannot be used.

The three bits borrowed from the host can create a total of eight binary patterns. Refer to Figure 11-2. Notice that only six of the eight possible binary patterns can be used to identify the subnets. The binary pattern containing all zeros and the binary pattern of all ones are reserved values. The fact that they are reserved means they cannot be used to identify a particular network.

When messages are broadcast to all network nodes, a pattern of all ones is used in the destination address. This indicates that the message is intended for all network addresses. A bit pattern of all zeros is normally used for special functions such as a temporary address of a network card when it is set up for an automatic IP address assignment from a DHCP server. The all zero pattern indicates to the DHCP server that an IP address needs to be issued to the network card.

Copyright Goodheart-Willcox Co., Inc.

When looking at binary bit patterns for subnet masks, be sure to subtract all zeros and all ones from the total possible number of patterns. When a binary bit pattern is converted directly to a decimal equivalent, subtract one from the total. For example, an extended portion of a subnet mask consisting of three binary ones equals 4 + 2 + 1 = 7. Subtract one from the total to derive the total number of subnets, as shown in Figure 11-3.

A subnet reduces broadcasts and provides additional security. Broadcasts on Ethernet networks are typically limited to their immediate network, which is identified by the network portion of an IPv4 address. When traffic becomes too heavy, creating subnets reduces the number of broadcasts. Users with similar duties can be placed into the subnet areas to reduce the number of broadcasts affecting the immediate network. Subnets also increase security because they do not normally appear when viewed by intruders from outside the network area.

Class B and Class C are the most common networks to be used to create subnets. Take a close look at the Class C IP address and subnet mask shown in Figure 11-4. When a Class C network is used to create subnets, bits are borrowed from the fourth octet, which is the host portion of the address.

Figure 11-3 To calculate the total number of subnets, simply add the value of the three bits together and then subtract one from the total.

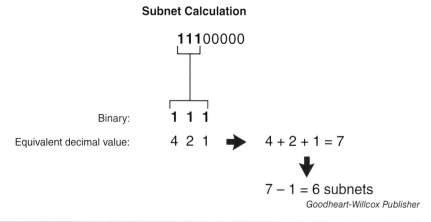

Goodheart-Willcox Publisher

Figure 11-4 A Class C network uses a subnet mask consisting of three octets of 11111111 followed by one octet of 00000000.

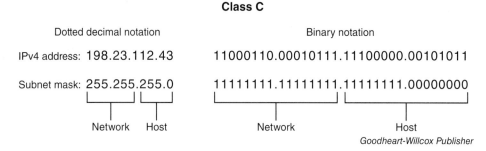

Goodheart-Willcox Publisher

In addition to determining the number of subnetworks that can be created, as demonstrated in Figure 11-5, the number of actual hosts on each subnetwork are determined. The number of zeros in the address determines the number of hosts. To calculate the number of hosts available for each subnet, simply convert the bit pattern to decimal numbers and then add them together as shown in Figure 11-6. Subtract one from the total to find the number of hosts per subnet.

A typical point of confusion for students is the difference between total possible binary bit patterns and total decimal equivalent value. The total number of binary

Copyright Goodheart-Willcox Co., Inc.

Figure 11-5 In this example, three bits have been borrowed from the host of a Class C network.

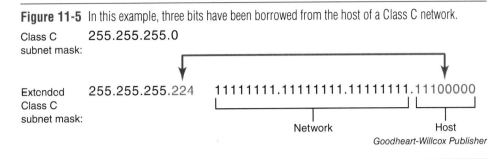

Class C
subnet mask: 255.255.255.0

Extended
Class C
subnet mask: 255.255.255.224   11111111.11111111.11111111.11100000

Network   Host

Goodheart-Willcox Publisher

Figure 11-6 To calculate the total number of hosts per subnetwork, convert the binary value to decimal and then subtract one from the total.

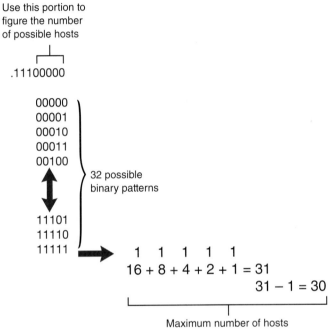

Use this portion to
figure the number
of possible hosts

.11100000

00000
00001
00010
00011
00100

} 32 possible
binary patterns

11101
11110
11111

1 1 1 1 1
16 + 8 + 4 + 2 + 1 = 31
31 − 1 = 30

Maximum number of hosts

Goodheart-Willcox Publisher

bit patterns always includes a bit pattern consisting of all zeros. When completing a conversion of binary to decimal, a pattern of all zeros is not considered. Just remember to subtract one from the total number of hosts when converting from binary to decimal. Also, you can use the tables in Figures 11-7, 11-8, and 11-9 to assist you. The first table, Figure 11-7, is designed for determining the dotted decimal value based on the subnet mask bit pattern. The last column of the table lists the decimal values that correspond to the binary bit patterns displayed in the table. This is valuable for determining the subnet mask in dotted decimal format.

The second table, Figure 11-8, will help you determine the number of subnets and the number of hosts based on the subnet mask of a Class B network. The table has fourteen entries. This is because a Class B network has two host octets. When creating subnets, it is possible to borrow bits from both host octets to create the subnet mask.

The third table, Figure 11-9, is used to determine the number of subnets and hosts corresponding to a Class C network. Notice that there are only six possibilities for a Class C subnet mask. Also, pay attention to the fact that a Class C and a Class B network have several matching subnet masks in dotted decimal form, but the quantity of subnets differs.

Figure 11-7 Binary bit pattern to decimal conversion table. This table can be used to convert decimal values to subnet mask bit patterns.

128	64	32	16	8	4	2	1	
1	0	0	0	0	0	0	0	128
1	1	0	0	0	0	0	0	192
1	1	1	0	0	0	0	0	224
1	1	1	1	0	0	0	0	240
1	1	1	1	1	0	0	0	248
1	1	1	1	1	1	0	0	252
1	1	1	1	1	1	1	0	254
1	1	1	1	1	1	1	1	255

Goodheart-Willcox Publisher

Figure 11-8 Common values used for Class B subnetting. Notice that a Class B subnet mask can span across two octets.

Number of Bits	Subnet Mask	Number of Subnets	Number of Hosts
2	255.255.192.0	2	16,382
3	255.255.224.0	6	8190
4	255.255.240.0	14	4094
5	255.255.248.0	30	2046
6	255.255.252.0	62	1022
7	255.255.254.0	126	510
8	255.255.255.0	254	254
9	255.255.255.128	510	126
10	255.255.255.192	1,022	62
11	255.255.255.224	2,046	30
12	255.255.255.240	4,094	14
13	255.255.255.248	8,190	6
14	255.255.255.252	16,382	2

Note: Values for all binary patterns of all ones and all zeros in the network portion of the subnet mask have been eliminated from the table.

Goodheart-Willcox Publisher

Figure 11-9 Common values used for Class C subnetting. Notice that the Class C subnet mask values match many of the Class B subnet mask values and host values. However, for the same network subnet masks, the quantities of subnets generated do not match.

Number of Bits	Subnet Mask	Number of Subnets	Number of Hosts
2	255.255.255.192	2	62
3	255.255.255.224	6	30
4	255.255.255.240	14	14
5	255.255.255.248	30	6
6	255.255.255.252	62	2

Note: Values for all binary patterns of all ones and all zeros in the network portion of the subnet mask have been eliminated from the table.

Goodheart-Willcox Publisher

NET 1.4

Closer Look at Subnets

In Figure 11-10, a subnet mask of 255.255.255.192 has been applied to a Class C IP address of 202.130.46.125. When applied, two subnets containing 62 hosts each

Copyright Goodheart-Willcox Co., Inc.

Figure 11-10 Subnetting two subnets.

Original IP address: 202.130.46.125
Original subnet mask: 255.255.255.0

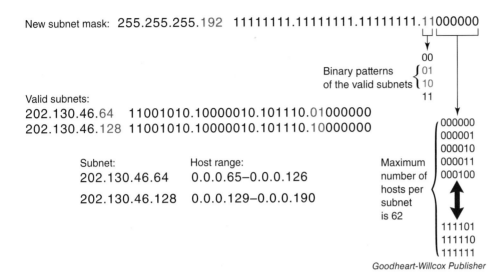

New subnet mask: 255.255.255.192   11111111.11111111.11111111.11000000

Binary patterns { 00
of the valid subnets { 01
                        10
                        11

Valid subnets:
202.130.46.64   11001010.10000010.101110.01000000
202.130.46.128 11001010.10000010.101110.10000000

Subnet:	Host range:
202.130.46.64	0.0.0.65–0.0.0.126
202.130.46.128	0.0.0.129–0.0.0.190

Maximum
number of
hosts per
subnet
is 62

{ 000000
000001
000010
000011
000100

111101
111110
111111 }

Goodheart-Willcox Publisher

are created. Note that the only two valid network addresses are 202.130.046.64 and 202.130.046.128. The other two calculated network addresses 202.130.046.0 and 202.130.046.192 cannot be used. The first address is based on a network binary bit pattern of all zeros, and the other is based on a binary pattern of all ones. Remember that you cannot use those two binary bit patterns while subnetting.

Certain software-hardware combination equipment is able to use a network address consisting of all zeros or ones, which increases the total possible number of subnets and hosts. You will encounter both systems until one becomes the dominant system. For now, consider the subnet mask system that does not allow the use of consecutive ones or zeros in the network portion of the subnet mask as the legacy system. The system that accepts the use of ones and zeros is the preferred system because it allows for more possible combinations of IP addresses. RFC 1874 allows the use of all ones and all zeros in the extended portion of the subnet mask.

A subnet mask that is not expressed in standard eight-bit or one-byte values is often referred to as a **variable-length subnet mask (VLSM)**. The term *variable-length subnet mask* is derived from the fact that by subnetting, the total length of the binary one-bit pattern can vary in length rather than be held to the traditional series of eight-bit or one-byte patterns. Look at Figure 11-11. Notice how two additional subnets have been created out of two subnets. This makes a total of four subnets—two original subnets plus two smaller subnets created from the originals. The original subnets are referred to as *fixed length* because each subnet is of equal length.

A **fixed-length subnet mask (FLSM)**, therefore, has subnets that are equal in length and have an equal number of hosts. With the additional subnets, however, there is more than one length of subnet mask. The term *variable-length subnet mask* applies because multiple subnets with more than one length of subnet mask have been created. The length refers to the binary ones used to identify the network and the host.

Subnetting can cause confusion, which has led to IP addresses being presented in a different written manner at times. For example, you may see an IP address that contains a variable-length subnet mask written as 202.130.046.125/26. The /26 indicates that a mask with a total length of 26 bits is used for the mask. Do not confuse the slash symbol with the colon symbol, which follows an IP address to iden-

Copyright Goodheart-Willcox Co., Inc.

Figure 11-11 A variable-length subnet mask (VLSM) is formed when a subnet is used to create an additional subnet, which is not equal to the original subnet in length or in the number of hosts.

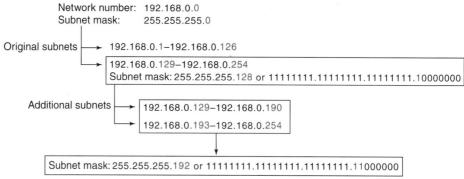

Goodheart-Willcox Publisher

tify a port number. Variable-length subnet mask notation, also known as *classless inter-domain routing (CIDR)*, is covered in detail later in this chapter.

There are many software programs available that can automatically calculate the number of subnets, hosts, subnet mask, and all addresses for a given IP address. Unfortunately, you cannot use software or a calculator on any actual certification exams at the time of this writing. This procedure may change in the future. For now, you must learn to calculate these values manually to pass most certification exams that involve IP addressing and TCP/IP protocol. Many certification authorities feel that when students can successfully perform the necessary calculations, they prove they have mastered the basic concept of subnetting networks.

Advantages of Subnetting

As stated previously, subnetting creates a more secure network by placing hosts on separate networks. Network users cannot readily access resources on a host of a different subnet unless the system administrator creates the necessary user profile to allow it. Subnetting creates two or more segments out of the original network. When the original network is divided into two or more segments, broadcast packets from one network are not forwarded to the other network. If broadcast packets are not forwarded, the amount of data traffic is reduced. When the amount of data traffic is reduced, fewer collisions occur. As the number of collisions is reduced, the network appears faster to users. Subnetting, therefore, also reduces the amount of collisions on a network segment by dividing the original segment into two or more segments.

Disadvantages of Subnetting

Subnetting by using calculated subnet mask assignments could be difficult to manage because of the inherent confusion of the IP address assignments. There is also confusion because some equipment is designed to use subnets based on all one and all zero bit patterns to increase the total number of possible subnets and hosts.

Network Segmenting Devices

Another way to segment a network is to use a physical device such as a bridge, switch, or router. A bridge or switch segments a network at the data link layer or layer 2 level. A router segments a network at the network layer or layer 3 level. Bridges, switches, and routers were covered previously in the textbook. In this chapter, these devices are covered in more depth since you have a better understanding of networking principles involving physical and logical addresses.

Copyright Goodheart-Willcox Co., Inc.

Bridge

A *bridge* is a device that segments a network by filtering network traffic based on MAC addresses. Because the bridge filters MAC addresses, it is considered a layer 2 or data link layer device. Bridges are not associated with a particular protocol. As frames pass through the bridge, the bridge automatically creates a bridging table. The bridge refers to the table when determining whether to pass or block a frame based on its MAC address. The selective passing and blocking of frames is referred to as **filtering**. Bridges only pass frames that reside on the other side of the bridge. Bridges also forward broadcast frames. All devices connected to the bridge must have the same subnet when using a bridge.

Bridges are seldom encountered because electronic network devices are becoming more reasonably priced. Therefore, network designers are opting to use more sophisticated devices, such as switches. They do not cost much more than a bridge. The most commonly encountered bridges are wireless bridges or wireless access points, which incorporate the bridge function. Switches are often referred to as *multiport bridges*.

2.2, 4.2 NET

Tech Tip

Technically, switches and bridges filter frames and operate at layer 2. Routers filter packets and operate at layer 3. Frames are associated with the data link layer while packets are associated with the network layer. However, you will often see the terms *packet* and *frame* used interchangeably from a variety of sources.

Tech Tip

The IEEE standard still uses the term *bridge* when describing devices that filter frames by MAC address. You will also see the term *bridge* used to describe individual ports of a switch.

Switch

Switches are the most commonly used device for segmenting a wired network. Subnetting is based on the principle of using an IP address subnet mask to isolate sections of a network, thus creating small broadcast zones. Subnetting by subnet mask requires no special hardware and is considered a logical, not a physical, way to create a subnet. Switches use MAC addresses to create isolated segments of a network, but they do not create a subnet. Switches do not prevent broadcasts because they do not filter frames by IP address. All network broadcasts are still forwarded through a switch.

Switches filter network activity by the physical address of the destination device without broadcasting every frame to all devices. For example, a network could be organized by corporate workgroups such as accounting, engineering, administration, or by physical locations such as *Building 1* and *Building 2*. A switch could be used to create network segments for each corporate workgroup or location so that overall network traffic is reduced. Only broadcasts would be forwarded to all devices through the switch.

Switches can be programmed or can operate in automatic mode to learn about adjacent devices. In many ways, a switch is like a multiple-port bridge. Each port on the switch can be programmed to act independently of the other ports.

One common technique in switches is *port mirroring*. This is a process by which the network packets that are seen on one switch port are sent to another switch port. This is sometimes done to get a copy of all traffic to an intrusion detection system for analysis.

Switches also have MAC address tables. A MAC address table is a table used by the Address Resolution Protocol (ARP) to map IP addresses to the MAC address of the network card to which a packet is being delivered.

Distributed switching is an architectural approach that uses a centralized switch coupled to one or more remote switches. This is actually rather common and

1.3, 2.2 NET

Network+ Note

When taking the Network+ Certification Exam, be careful not to confuse the term *port* used for the switch physical port with the term *port* used to describe the port address, such as port 80 for HTTP used with TCP and UDP packets.

is how telephone networks function. In the case of telephone networks, this is done with devices other than a typical layer 2 switch.

Switches are a great way to segment a network or create a *virtual local area network (VLAN)*. A VLAN creates a group of network devices that operate in a single broadcast domain even when the devices are located on physically separated networks. VLANs are covered later in this chapter.

A switch is often used to correct network conditions such as reduced bandwidth caused by too many devices in the same broadcast domain. Since the devices share the same bandwidth, network performance is reduced as more and more devices are added to the network.

Switch vs. Hub

A *hub* is an inexpensive common connection point used for multiple Ethernet network connections. However, the hub passes all broadcasts. The hub can be replaced with a switch to correct this problem. Each port on a switch can support the same bandwidth as the network. For example, a 1-Gb switch can support 1 Gb through each of its ports. The bandwidth does not need to be shared with other devices connected to the switch. A 100-Mb hub shares the 100-Mb bandwidth with other devices connected to the hub, thus reducing the amount of bandwidth for each device. For example, if five devices are connected to a 100-Mb hub, each would use approximately 1/5, or 20 Mb, of the total bandwidth. If the same five devices were connected to a 100-Mb switch, each device would have 100 Mb of bandwidth. Therefore, there is no reduction of bandwidth when connecting with a switch.

Look at Figures 11-12 and 11-13 to compare the actions of a hub and switch. Notice that the hub in Figure 11-12 forwards the frame sent to the server from PC-1 to all nodes, including the Internet gateway. In other words, the hub forwards all frames and does nothing to limit broadcasts or correct collisions. The hub shares the bandwidth with all devices connected to it. Each device can send an Ethernet frame onto the network. Frames from each device can collide with other frames causing frames to become corrupted. When an Ethernet frame is corrupted, it is sent again, thus reducing bandwidth.

In Figure 11-13, the hub is replaced with a switch. A switch reads the destination MAC address and then forwards the frame to only that address. The switch limits the number of frame collisions and provides full bandwidth for each device. The exception is for a broadcast frame with an address such as 255.255.255.255. Broadcast frames are sent to all devices.

Figure 11-12 Each network device must share the 100-Mb bandwidth of the local network segment.

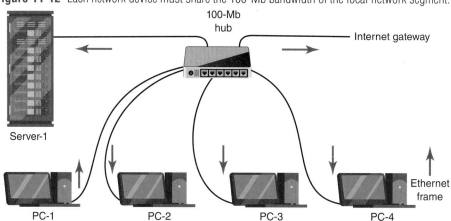

(server icon) fullvector/Shutterstock.com; (hub icon) Vadim Ermak/Shutterstock.com;
(workstation icons) RedlineVector/Shutterstock.com; Goodheart-Willcox Publisher

Copyright Goodheart-Willcox Co., Inc.

Consider the fact that this discussion includes only the local area network and connections between two devices. When connections are shared through another device, such as an Internet gateway or a server with Internet connection sharing, then bandwidth will be reduced.

Look at Figure 11-14. The switch in this example only provides the maximum bandwidth within the local segment of the network. If most of the workstations are constantly accessing resources on the Internet or a centralized shared device such as a file server, then the switch will not provide significant benefit, except for reducing collisions. To increase network bandwidth to the gateway, install higher bandwidth cable, network cards, routers, gateways, or modems. For example, replace all the 100-Mb devices and cable with 1-Gb devices and cable.

Figure 11-13 Each PC can use the full 100-Mb bandwidth between it and other devices connected to the switch.

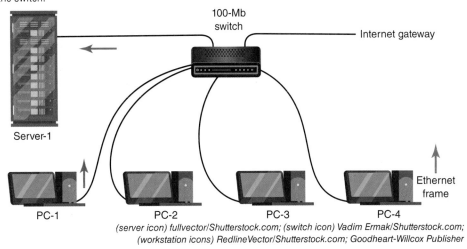

(server icon) fullvector/Shutterstock.com; (switch icon) Vadim Ermak/Shutterstock.com;
(workstation icons) RedlineVector/Shutterstock.com; Goodheart-Willcox Publisher

Figure 11-14 Devices on a switch share bandwidth when accessing server resources or the Internet gateway.

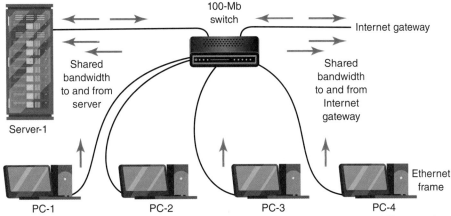

(server icon) fullvector/Shutterstock.com; (switch icon) Vadim Ermak/Shutterstock.com;
(workstation icons) RedlineVector/Shutterstock.com; Goodheart-Willcox Publisher

Switch vs. Bridge

To understand better how a switch is superior to a bridge, one must first look at how a switch operates. A switch automatically learns the location of hardware devices by reading a frame's source MAC address as the frames are transmitted to the switch. This is similar to the way a bridge learns the location of a device. The switch then maps the MAC address to the switch port, thus creating a switch port table.

Note

Cisco refers to a switch port table as *content-address memory (CAM)*.

A bridge simply passes or blocks a frame based on the MAC address. Switches are designed with forwarding modes. The forwarding mode determines how packets are passed through the switch. The common forwarding modes are *cut-through*, *store-and-forward*, *fragment-free*, and *adaptive cut-through*. All but cut-through mode are used to detect packet errors and then react according to design.

The **cut-through** method forwards the frame immediately after receiving it. Cut-through, also known as a *low latency*, is the quickest method of switching. *Latency* refers to the delay created by networking devices receiving and transmitting frames.

Store-and-forward reads the entire contents of the frame before forwarding the frame to its destination. The store-and-forward method drops corrupt frames. The cut-through method does not drop corrupt frames. Store-and-forward has a much higher latency than cut-through because each frame is inspected.

Fragment-free is a mixture of the store-and-forward and cut-through methods. This method inspects the first 64 bytes of an Ethernet frame. Since most errors are detected in the first 64 bytes, there is no need to check the entire frame. This means the latency is less than that with the store-and-forward method but not quite as good as that with the cut-through method.

The last method, **adaptive cut-through**, is unique in the way it operates as cut-through until an unacceptable number of corrupt frames are detected. After a certain number of corrupt frames are detected, the switch operates in a store-and-forward mode or fragment-free mode until the number of corrupt frames is reduced to an acceptable number. Then, the switch once more operates as a cut-through switch.

Router

NET 1.3, 2.2

The main function of a router is to route packets to their proper destination within an IP-based network or across the Internet. **Routing** is the process of selecting the "best route" through which to send packets. Networks, especially large networks covering great distances, can comprise a variety of media and network devices. There may be several different paths from the source to the destination using a variety of network media such as copper core, fiber, and wireless as well as network systems managed by different communication companies and ISPs. The router determines the best network and Internet path on which to forward packets. Routers interface with other routers and exchange routing table information. The routing tables contain information about the other routers and networks. This information is processed by the router and then used to determine the best route to send the packet to its final destination.

The router is the most diverse network device because it can be programmed to perform a much wider amount of functions than a switch. For example, routers can be programmed to filter network traffic and can be used to create more networks. Routers can be used to create logical networks and subnets, but it is more practical and less expensive to use a switch for these purposes. Routers can limit broadcast domains and create new broadcast domains. Unlike hubs, bridges, and switches, routers do not forward broadcasts. This reduces collision domains.

One major disadvantage of routers is they can be slower than switches and bridges because they analyze the data in the routing table. A router operates at layer 3 of the OSI model and makes decisions based on the IP address of the destination and source, which is contained inside the packet header. The IP address is also known as the *logical address*. Switches and bridges need only to examine the physical (MAC) address and do not need to analyze logical addresses to determine the best path.

Copyright Goodheart-Willcox Co., Inc.

Router advertisement is a multicast message sent out announcing the IP addresses of its interfaces. This lets other routers know how to find those IP addresses. This is one way each router knows what router to send a packet to in order to reach a particular destination.

Routers can be programmed to operate from static IP address tables or dynamic IP address tables. A **static IP address table** is a table in which IP addresses are entered manually. A **dynamic IP address table** is a table in which IP addresses are generated automatically by a software program that communicates with nearby routers. The software program allows a router to exchange IP address information with other routers and build a reference table based on this information.

Convergence is a routing table term that applies to dynamic routing. With static routing, all routing tables are always the same. With dynamic routing, tables are constantly changing. When all dynamic routing tables contain the same information, a state of **convergence** is said to exist. Convergence is also referred to as *steady state*.

1.3 NET

Router Metric

A **router metric** is a mechanism used to determine or measure the best route. Some of the various elements of a router metric are throughput, reliability, packet loss, latency, and number of hops. A **hop** is a measure of how many network devices such as routers and gateways a packet must pass through until the packet reaches its destination. Hops are the oldest and most basic metric used for determining the best route. When a **tracert** command is issued, the number of hops that the **tracert** packet has passed through to reach the final destination is displayed.

Routing protocol metrics vary according to the routing protocol design. For example, the *Router Information Protocol (RIP)* simply uses the number of hops to determine the best route. More sophisticated routing protocols take into account other factors such as throughput, reliability, and latency.

Routing Protocol Classifications

1.3 NET

Two basic routing protocol classifications are *Interior Gateway Protocol (IGP)* and *Exterior Gateway Protocol (EGP)*. **Interior Gateway Protocol (IGP)** is confined to an autonomous network. The term *autonomous* is used by the IEEE organization to describe the confines of the network system protocol. Autonomous means that the network is under one authority or is a single domain. For example, a campus network with a domain name of USF.edu would be under one authority. Examples of IGP are RIP, IGRP, OSPF, and IS-IS. **Exterior Gateway Protocol (EGP)** is designed to exchange information between different autonomous networks. For example, the exchange of information between a campus network and some other network location across the Internet would require the use of EGP. Examples of Exterior Gateway Protocol are BGP and EGP. Exterior Gateway Protocol is both a type of protocol and a protocol itself. Pay close attention to the table in Figure 11-15, which lists various routing protocols and identifies them as IGP, EGP, link state, or distance vector.

Two additional classifications of routing protocols are *link state* and *distance vector*. A **link-state protocol** performs its own calculations of the best route. It only transfers information about connections and does not pass its routing table to other devices. Examples of link-state protocols are IS-IS and OSPF. A **distance vector protocol** shares its routing table with other routers. Eventually, the routers will be in a state of convergence when all of the routers contain the same routing table information. Convergence rarely occurs with link-state systems. Examples of distance vector are RIP, IGRP, EIGRP. The following sections will briefly introduce some of the most common router protocols.

Copyright Goodheart-Willcox Co., Inc.

Figure 11-15 Routing protocols.

Routing Protocol	Internet Gateway Protocol (IGP)	Exterior Gateway Protocol (EGP)	Link State Protocol	Distance Vector Protocol	Comment
BGP		×			Exchanges routing information between different autonomous networks.
EGP		×			Exchanges routing information between different autonomous networks.
EIGRP	×		×	×	Guarantees loop-free operation. Cisco advertises EIGRP as a link-state protocol and a distance vector protocol.
IGRP	×			×	Allows a maximum hop count of 255 and uses a metric based on bandwidth, latency, route traffic, and reliability.
IS-IS	×		×		Detects router types as level 1 or level 2 when determining shortest route.
OSPF	×		×		Can detect network link failures and then automatically determine next best path.
RIP	×			×	Supports a maximum of 15 hops.
RIPng	×			×	IPv6 version of RIP.

Goodheart-Willcox Publisher

RIP and RIP2

The **Router Information Protocol (RIP)** is one of the oldest protocols ever developed for routers. RIP periodically exchanges an entire table of routing information with nearby routers. Each router maintains a database containing information about the devices connected to the network. RIP sends the information to other routers so they can update their own routing table.

Each router location in the network structure is referred to as a *hop*. RIP supports a maximum of 15 hops, which means it will forward a message update for a total of 15 locations. The router hop is also referred to as the *metric*. Maximum metric or hop is the distance the packet can travel before being dropped.

Each frame sent contains a time stamp. The time stamp is used to determine the time-out or time to live (TTL) for each frame. RIP and RIP2 are examples of interior gateway protocols. RIP and RIP2 can forward information to other devices located on the network domain but cannot forward information outside the domain, which makes it an example of IGP. RIP also uses distance vector algorithms that allow it only to exchange routing table information with its neighboring devices and not the entire domain. RIP2 has a simple authentication feature not supported in RIP.

RIPng

RIP next generation (RIPng) is an IPv6 version of RIP. RIP was designed for IPv4 networks and has certain limitations associated with IPv4. RIPng is designed for IPv6 type devices and does not need the intervention of translation protocols as long as the routing devices used support RIPng. Also, RIP provides authentication as part of

Copyright Goodheart-Willcox Co., Inc.

the protocol. RIPng does not provide authentication as part of the protocol because IPv6 provides authentication.

OSPF

Open Shortest Path First (OSPF) is a routing protocol that only exchanges the most recently changed information in the table. OSPF saves bandwidth because it does not transfer the large amounts of data associated with RIP. It is a Cisco proprietary, IGP, and link-state protocol. It is a dynamic protocol in that it uses link state to update its routing table. OSPF, in contrast to RIP, uses more than just hop count to determine the best path. OSPF can detect network link failures and then automatically determine the next best path if one exists. OSPF also contains an authentication mechanism to ensure that the exchange of data is only from trusted routers. Router data tables can be corrupted by unethical hackers, causing network security to be compromised.

Tech Tip

All routing protocols are designed as dynamic. The classification of static refers to changes to a router table made manually which override dynamic entries.

IS-IS

Intermediate System to Intermediate System (IS-IS) is an IGP link-state protocol. IS-IS is used in similar applications as OSPF but has a different approach to router communication and the exchange of data. IS-IS determines router type as level 1 or level 2. Level 1 routers are typically inside the autonomous network. Level 2 routers are outside the autonomous network. Level 1 routers can communicate with level 1 or level 2 routers. Level 2 routers can only communicate with other level 2 routers.

IGRP

Interior Gateway Routing Protocol (IGRP) is a Cisco proprietary, distance-vector protocol. Cisco developed IGRP as an improved version of RIP. For example, RIP is limited to a 15-hop count, but IGRP has a maximum hop count of 255 and a default value of 100 hops. IGRP has a more complex metric calculation than RIP. RIP uses hops for the metric. IGRP metric is based on items such as bandwidth, latency, route traffic, and reliability. To learn more about the various routing protocols, visit the Cisco website.

EIGRP

Enhanced Interior Gateway Routing Protocol (EIGRP) is another Cisco proprietary distance-vector protocol and an improved version of IGRP. EIGRP is a sophisticated routing protocol that guarantees loop-free operation. Router loops can occur with older dynamic protocol versions and corrupt routing table data. The corrupt data can cause packets to circulate endlessly in the network. Cisco has advertised EIGRP as a hybrid routing protocol that combines both distance-vector and link-state characteristics.

BGP

Border Gateway Protocol (BGP) is an Internet routing protocol that supports the exchange of routing information between autonomous networks. BGP is a type of

Copyright Goodheart-Willcox Co., Inc.

gateway protocol and has replaced EGP. BGP routers contain typically over 90,000 route entries. They are assigned a unique IP address and domain name by IANA, the same authority that assigns IP addresses to corresponding domain names for websites. IANA assigns each authorized BGP router an Autonomous System (AS) number in the range from 1 to 64511. One AS number can be assigned to more than one router. For example, a collection of routers under the same administrative authority can be represented by one AS number. The AS number is embedded into the BGP packet in much the same way the IP address is embedded into a packet.

Figure 11-16 shows the results of a **tracert** command issued as **tracert www. google.com**. The path to the Google network is traced starting with the client computer with IP address 10.0.2.2. Each hop or router is identified by a unique domain name and IP address. The AS number is not apparent because it is embedded into the packet when BGR exchanges information about the best route to use. To learn more about assigning Internet numbers, visit the IANA website at www.iana.org.

Figure 11-16 The **tracert** command reveals the names of the routers along the Internet path.

```
Command Prompt - tracert www.google.com                                    —    □    ×

C:\Users\someguy>tracert www.google.com

Tracing route to www.google.com [64.233.180.105]
over a maximum of 30 hops:

  1    <1 ms    <1 ms    <1 ms  10.0.2.2
  2     1 ms     1 ms     1 ms  Tardis [192.168.1.1]
  3     2 ms     1 ms     1 ms  192.168.0.1
  4    10 ms    11 ms    10 ms  142.254.141.53
  5    24 ms    37 ms    31 ms  tge0-0-4.plaotxso01h.texas.rr.com [24.28.90.1]
  6    12 ms     9 ms    10 ms  agg21.plantxmp01r.texas.rr.com [24.175.49.221]
  7    17 ms    14 ms    14 ms  agg27.crtntxjt01r.texas.rr.com [24.175.36.177]
  8    14 ms    14 ms    11 ms  agg21.dllatxl301r.texas.rr.com [24.175.49.0]
  9    16 ms    13 ms    13 ms  bu-ether14.dllstx976iw-bcr00.tbone.rr.com [66.109.6.88]
 10    11 ms    11 ms    11 ms  0.ae1.pr1.dfw10.tbone.rr.com [107.14.17.234]
 11    12 ms    11 ms    11 ms  ix-ae-23-0.tcore2.DT8-Dallas.as6453.net [66.110.57.97]
 12    12 ms    11 ms    11 ms  74.125.50.214
 13     *
```

Goodheart-Willcox Publisher

Router vs. Multilayer Switch

The main difference between a router and a multilayer switch is their physical construction and intended use. A router is constructed around a programmable microprocessor. The microprocessor is very similar to the microprocessor used in a computer referred to as the *CPU*. You can think of a router as a computer with multiple network adapters installed, one adapter for each port. The router can be programmed and reprogrammed numerous times and is designed to specifically route frames based on IP addresses. A basic switch cannot communicate directly across the Internet. The basic switch needs to be assisted by a router to reach a distant Internet address.

A multilayer switch typically has much simpler electronic components than a router. An additional electronic chip known as *Application-Specific Integrated Circuit (ASIC)* is incorporated into the switch. The addition of the ASIC gives a layer 2 switch additional capabilities typically found at upper levels of the OSI model. Hence the name *multilayer switch*. Multilayer switches are generally limited to a specific task and have limited programmable functions. For example, a layer 2 switch with an ASIC can perform specific layer 3 functions necessary to pass frames associated with IP phone addresses to their appropriate location and to block all others. Multilayer switches are referred to by many different ways such as *4-7 switch*, *layer 7 switch*, *URL switch*, and *web-content switch*.

A layer 3 switch has a dedicated function and can use IP information in addition to MAC information to route frames/packets. Since it uses the layer 3 IP address, it is commonly referred to as a *layer 3 switch*.

Copyright Goodheart-Willcox Co., Inc.

A content switch routes frames based on the content of the packet. For example, a content switch can be used for load balancing a cluster of web servers. Another application might be to provide support for voice over IP (VoIP) applications, providing dedicated ports, and ensuring maximum bandwidth for the VoIP application.

Other names for content switches are *4-7 switch* and *layer 7 switch* because they route frames based on applications that align with the upper layers of the OSI model, such as mail services, printing services, HTTPS, and video streaming.

Router communication can be quite complex and require several semesters of study. This section was simply a short introduction of routers so that you might obtain a general understanding of their role in networking. Cisco Systems has a complete curriculum devoted to router studies and router programming. Visit the Cisco Networking Academy online to look at the contents of their complete certification program. Navigate to the Cisco Networking Academy using the URL www.cisco.com/c/en/us/training-events/resources/networking-academy.html, or conduct an online search using the phrase Cisco Academy.

Virtual LAN

A **virtual local area network (VLAN)** is a broadcast domain created by one or more switches based on logical (IP) addresses. VLANs are typically used to improve network performance by reducing the size of collision domains. VLANs can also be used to create secure subnets on shared network media.

Switches are the most-common choice for the creation of a VLAN on a wired network. A VLAN is based on the layer 2 physical address (MAC). A switch automatically creates a VLAN for each physical port because each port isolates the transfer of frames. Each port sends frames to the attached devices by filtering the frame based on physical addresses contained inside the frame. Broadcasts are sent to all devices based on the IP address.

A *broadcast domain* is a segment of a network that forwards all broadcasts to all devices on that segment. In Figure 11-17, the switches forward broadcasts based on IP addresses. The typical broadcast IP address is 255.255.255.255. Notice how the router segments the network into two separate broadcast domains.

Note

The CompTIA Network+ Certification Exam uses the term *multilayer switch* in place of *content switch*. Read exam questions carefully and look for specific terms, such as *basic switch, layer 3 switch*, and *content switch*, as a clue to the correct answer. For example, a basic switch is limited to layer 2 functions while a content switch is related to higher level functions.

1.3, 1.4, 4.6 NET

1.3 NET

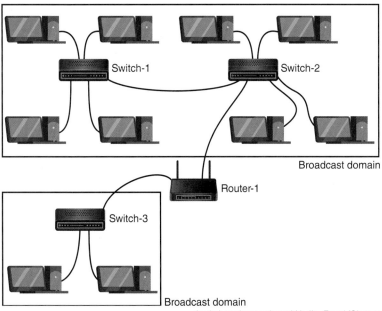

Figure 11-17 A VLAN is created for each physical port on each switch shown. Each port sends frames to the attached device by filtering the frame based on the MAC address. Broadcasts are sent to all devices in a broadcast domain based on the IP addresses.

(switch and router icons) Vadim Ermak/Shutterstock.com; (workstation icons) RedlineVector/Shutterstock.com; Goodheart-Willcox Publisher

A switch can create virtual LANs based on the physical (MAC) address. Notice how, in Figure 11-18, multiple VLANs have been created by the switches. Each port on a switch is assigned to a specific VLAN such as VLAN1 and VLAN2. You can connect to a programmable switch using the Telnet service. Once connected, you can assign ports to a specific VLAN. When a hub is connected to a specific port, the hub becomes part of that particular VLAN. All devices connected to the hub become part of the assigned VLAN.

Figure 11-18 Multiple VLANs are created with switches based on MAC addresses. Each port on a switch is assigned to a specific VLAN such as VLAN1 or VLAN2.

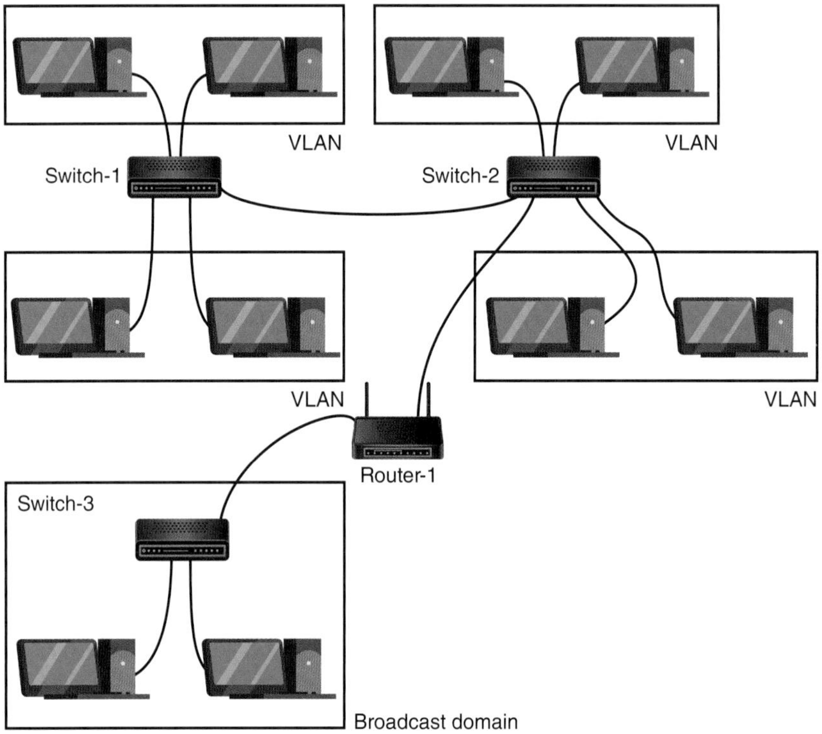

(switch and router icons) Vadim Ermak/Shutterstock.com; (workstation icons) RedlineVector/Shutterstock.com; Goodheart-Willcox Publisher

Switches cannot connect to other switches in separate broadcast domains directly. A router is used to connect two or more switches that are in separate networks or separate domains. After connecting the switches together with a router, the switches can extend a VLAN connection to include devices in the other network. Figure 11-19 shows how a VLAN can be extended to a separate network switch.

This is a key difference between routers and switches. Routers can create networks and separate networks. Switches are confined to a single network. Remember that routers operate at layer 3 and communicate through IP addresses. Switches operate at layer 2 and communicate through MAC addresses. They are thus confined to a network and cannot route frames directly through the Internet.

Associated with VLANs is port tagging. When a port is tagged, it will send a packet with a header with a tag number matching that of the VLAN. This practice identifies which VLAN to which a packet belongs and allows the acceptance of traffic from multiple VLANs. Tagged ports can belong to multiple VLANs, but untagged ports can only belong to one. Untagged ports are often referred to as *access ports*. Tagging a port is similar to trunking a port. Trunking will be discussed in detail later in the chapter.

Copyright Goodheart-Willcox Co., Inc.

Figure 11-19 A router must be used to connect two or more switches that are in separate networks or separate domains. After connecting the switches together with a router, the switches can extend a VLAN connection to include devices in the other network.

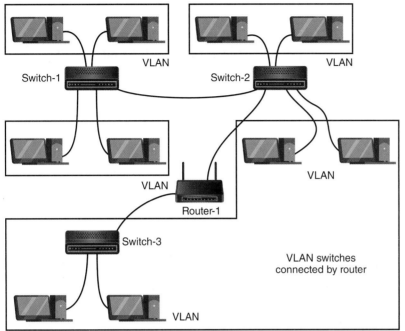

(switch and router icons) Vadim Ermak/Shutterstock.com;
(workstation icons) RedlineVector/Shutterstock.com; Goodheart-Willcox Publisher

Static vs. Dynamic VLAN

VLANs can be created statically or dynamically. A **static VLAN** is created when physical ports on a switch are assigned manually to a particular VLAN. A **dynamic VLAN** is created through software without the need of manual intervention. A dynamic VLAN will assign the device MAC address and the user name automatically to a VLAN. For example, when two devices are connected to two different ports on a switch and they exchange packets, the switch automatically assigns a default VLAN to these ports.

VLAN Trunking

VLAN technology is described in the IEEE 802.1Q standard and is referred to as *VLAN Trunking*. The standard describes the use of VLAN tags to identify individual network sections or broadcast zones. **Trunking** is the technique of connecting different VLANs together using a single network link. Switches are connected to each other through a router or routers. The router can then be used to exchange information between switches using the Spanning Tree Protocol (STP), which is discussed in the following section. The cable that is used for trunking is referred to as the *trunk*. The ports used for trunking are referred to as the *trunk ports*.

    Virtual Trunking Protocol (VTP) is a proprietary protocol developed by Cisco Systems that automatically reconfigures multiple switches across an entire network. This drastically reduces administration time when changes need to be made. A technician can make configuration changes to one switch. The switch will then automatically forward message packets to the other switches throughout the network to update its configurations.

1.3 NET

Copyright Goodheart-Willcox Co., Inc.

Note

The IEEE 802.1Q standard treats switches as multiport bridges. You will see the term *bridge* used throughout the document. When you encounter the term *bridge* in the IEEE standard, you can think of a port on a switch.

Cisco VTP does not conform to the IEEE 802.1Q standard but rather exceeds it. Cisco switches typically can be configured to run in two different modes to ensure compatibility between legacy switches: IEEE 802.1Q mode and Cisco VTP mode. The 802.1Q mode restricts switches to communicating with MAC addresses and does not allow switches to communicate with other switches. Switches need to be connected together by routers to communicate. Cisco VTP controls the exchange of information such as switch tables between all switches without the need of a router to be directly connected to each switch. Cisco VTP mode allows for the direct connection of switches with or without the use of routers. Look at Figure 11-20. Notice that the router connects directly to the switch and then the switch connects directly to the next switch. This is an example of *trunking*.

Figure 11-20 Cisco VTP mode allows for the direct connection of switches with or without the use of routers.

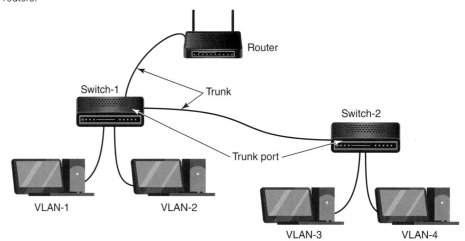

(server icon) fullvector/Shutterstock.com; (switch and router icons) Vadim Ermak/Shutterstock.com; (workstation icons) RedlineVector/Shutterstock.com; Goodheart-Willcox Publisher

For very detailed information about the IEEE 802.1Q standard, visit http://standards.ieee.org/getieee802/download/802.1Q-2005.pdf. An account must first be established, but the website does not require any information other than selecting a user type and entering an e-mail address. Select Academic/Student from the list of user types, and enter a preferred e-mail address. A link to the PDF will be sent to that address.

Spanning Tree Protocol

NET
1.3, 4.6

The **Spanning Tree Protocol (STP)** is a layer 2 protocol designed to manage networks based on MAC addresses. STP was originally designed to prevent broadcast storms created from improperly configured bridges or switches. Bridges can be accidentally wired incorrectly, resulting in a physical network loop. When a network loop is created, frames are continually circulated in the loop causing a broadcast storm that renders the network inoperable.

Switches that act as multiport bridges are often intentionally configured with redundant connections to provide a backup link in case one of the links fails. These connections are referred to as *switch loops* or *switching loops*. Switch loops occur when packets are routed back to a switch they have already traversed. If the redundant links are misconfigured, the switch will send a continuous stream of packets, caus- ing a bridge loop, also known as a *broadcast storm*. The spanning tree protocol uses a special method to detect misconfigured backup links and prevent the creation of broadcast storms. Most misconfigurations occur when routers are added to a network with multiple switches. A misconfigured (incorrectly programmed) router will cause a broadcast storm.

The Spanning Tree Protocol prevents broadcast storms caused by network loops. The combination of the STP and the discovery protocol(s) allows switches and routers to discover other network devices and to be self-programmed for the most appropriate configuration.

STP uses the spanning tree algorithm to determine and eliminate the presence of a physical or logical network loop. The algorithm calculates and compares MAC address locations to identify bridge and switch ports. The protocol then automatically assigns specific MAC address to specific ports and eliminates any existing loop. A table of addresses and ports is maintained and exchanged with other switches.

There are other methods to prevent loops, for example a BPDU guard. Bridge Protocol Data Units (BPDUs) are frames containing information about the Spanning Tree Protocol that are sent from the switch using a multicast address. BPDU guards prevent the accidental connection of switching devices, thus preventing loops from occurring. This method is sometimes referred to as *BPDU filtering*. Another method is the use of a root guard. Root guards can prevent certain switching devices from becoming the top-level bridge in the Spanning Tree.

Classless Inter-Domain Routing

1.4   NET

Classless Inter-Domain Routing (CIDR) uses a special notation to identify which part of an IP address is the network portion. It does not use specific classes. Rath- er there is a variable-length subnet mask (VLSM) that determines what part of the address is the network, and what part is the node. The network portion is identified by a slash (/) symbol followed by a numeric value that represents the length of the network prefix, for example, XXX.XXX.XXX.XXX/N where N represents the network prefix length and is a number from 0 to 32.

The CIDR expression 192.168.123.106/24 means that the first 24 bits of the ad- dress represent the network address or 192.168.123 and the last 8 bits, 106, repre- sent the host.

The CIDR correlates to the IPv4 address by assuming each portion (octet) of the IPv4 address represents a maximum value of eight bits. To calculate the CIDR, simply think of each part of the IPv4 address of having a value of eight bits. For example, to figure out the CIDR for the network address 192.168.123 you would add together three values of eight:

$$8 + 8 + 8 = 24$$

Figure 11-21 shows examples of how the subnet mask is derived based on the CIDR. Notice that as each of the binary patterns are reduced by one, the final octet representing the subnet mask also changes. For example, look at the subnet mask and binary pattern for 255.255.254.0. The complete binary form of the network por- tion of 255.255.254.0 is 11111111.11111111.11111110. Adding the bits together octet by octet, we have the following:

$$8 + 8 + 7 = 23$$

Copyright Goodheart-Willcox Co., Inc.

Figure 11-21 Deriving the CIDR from a subnet mask

Subnet Mask	Binary Pattern		CIDR
255.255.255.0	11111111.11111111.11111111.00000000	8+8+8	**/24**
255.255.254.0	11111111.11111111.11111110.00000000	8+8+7	**/23**
255.255.252.0	111111111.11111111.11111100.00000000	8+8+6	**/22**
255.255.248.0	111111111.11111111.11111000.00000000	8+8+5	**/21**
255.255.240.0	11111111.11111111.11110000.00000000	8+8+4	**/20**
255.255.224.0	11111111.11111111.11100000.00000000	8+8+3	**/19**
255.255.192.0	11111111.111111111.11000000.00000000	8+8+2	**/18**
255.255.128.0	11111111.11111111.10000000.00000000	8+8+1	**/17**

Goodheart-Willcox Publisher

Thus, the CIDR notation will be /23 for the IPv4 address represented by the subnet mask of 255.255.254.0. See Figure 11-22 for a table of CIDR lengths and related subnet masks.

Link Aggregation

Link aggregation is when two or more network cables are paralleled to increase bandwidth and provide redundancy. For example, a server can be configured with two network adapters and then the two cables can be run to two ports on a switch. This configuration results in twice as much bandwidth available to the devices connected through the switch.

Link aggregation is a great way to increase bandwidth for network backbones. The redundancy ensures availability when one of the cables or connections fails. A switch can be placed on each end of the backbone and multiple cables can be connected to each switch.

Tech Tip

You should always completely configure both ends of a link aggregation before physically connecting the switches together. If you physically connect the two switches first and then configure the link aggregation, a network loop could be created, causing a broadcast storm and packet loss.

Figure 11-22 CIDR table for IPv4 networks.

CIDR Length	Subnet Mask	# of Networks	Class	# of Hosts
/1	128.0.0.0	128	A	2,147,483,392
/2	192.0.0.0	64	A	1,073,741,696
/3	224.0.0.0	32	A	536,870,848
/4	240.0.0.0	16	A	268,435,424
/5	248.0.0.0	8	A	134,217,712
/6	252.0.0.0	4	A	67,108,856
/7	254.0.0.0	2	A	33,554,428
/8	255.0.0.0	1	A	16,777,214
/9	255.128.0.0	128	B	8,388,352
/10	255.192.0.0	64	B	4,194,176
/11	255.224.0.0	32	B	2,097,088
/12	255.240.0.0	16	B	1,048,544
/13	255.248.0.0	8	B	524,272
/14	255.252.0.0	4	B	262,136
/15	255.254.0.0	2	B	131,068
/16	255.255.0.0	1	B	65,024
/17	255.255.128.0	128	C	32,512
/18	255.255.192.0	64	C	16,256
/19	255.255.224.0	32	C	8,128
/20	255.255.240.0	16	C	4,064
/21	255.255.248.0	8	C	2,032
/22	255.255.252.0	4	C	1,016
/23	255.255.254.0	2	C	508
/24	255.255.255.0	1	C	254
/25	255.255.255.128	2	C subnets	124
/26	255.255.255.192	4	C subnets	62
/27	255.255.255.224	8	C subnets	30
/28	255.255.255.240	16	C subnets	14
/29	255.255.255.248	32	C subnets	6
/30	255.255.255.252	64	C subnets	2
/31	255.255.255.254*	NA	NA	NA
/32	255.255.255.255*	NA	NA	NA

*255.255.255.255 and 255.255.255.254 reserved for broadcast.

Goodheart-Willcox Publisher

Summary

The Binary Number System

- The binary number system consists entirely of ones (1s) and zeros (0s). The ones typically represent electrical energy, and the zero represents the absence of electrical energy.
- To convert a binary bit pattern to a decimal value, simply insert the decimal value for each individual bit position represented by a one, and then add the decimal values together.

Dotted Decimal Notation

- Numeric values of an IPv4 address encountered in computer technology are displayed in decimal form, not binary.
- Dotted decimal notation consists of each octet of an IP address separated by a period.

Subnetting

- Dividing a network into subnetworks, or subnets, is called subnetting.
- To create a subnet, bits are borrowed from the host portion of an IP address to expand the network portion of the IP address.
- A subnet mask uses a series of ones to identify the network portion of an IP address and a series of zeros to identify the host portion.
- An IP address with all zeros or ones in the host portion cannot be assigned to any network device.
- A variable-length subnet mask (VLSM) occurs when you create additional subnets from a subnet.
- A fixed-length subnet mask (FLSM) has two or more equal-sized subnets.
- Subnetting provides security because subnetworks cannot be seen from outside the subnetwork.
- Subnetting reduces network traffic by isolating broadcasts to each subnet.

Network Segmenting Devices

- Bridges and switches are layer 2 devices that filter frames based on physical (MAC) addresses.
- Switches are the most commonly used device for segmenting a wired network.
- Switches can be programmed or can operate in automatic mode to learn about adjacent devices.
- Switches are a great way to segment a network or create a virtual local area network (VLAN).
- Routers are layer 3 devices and filter frames based on logical addresses (IP addresses).
- A router is used to connect switches that are located in a separate network.
- Routers make decisions based on source and destination IP addresses.

Copyright Goodheart-Willcox Co., Inc.

- Routers do not forward broadcasts and, therefore, reduce collision domains.
- A router metric is the mechanism used to determine or measure the best route.
- A metric calculation may be based on but not limited to throughput, reliability, packet loss, latency, and number of hops.
- A hop is a device such as a router located in the network path between the destination and the source.
- Two basic routing protocol classifications are Interior Gateway Protocol (IGP) and Exterior Gateway Protocol (EGP).
- An autonomous network is a network under one authority.
- RIP is one of the oldest router protocols and determines the best path based on number of hops.
- EIGRP is a sophisticated routing protocol that guarantees loop-free operation.
- A multilayer switch is a dedicated switch that uses IP information and packet contents to route frames or packets.
- An Application-Specific Integrated Circuit (ASIC) is incorporated into a switch to expand its function.

Virtual LAN

- A Virtual LAN (VLAN) is a communication path between workstations on separate or the same network segment.
- VLANs can be created statically or dynamically.
- VLAN technology is described in the IEEE 802.1Q standard and is referred to as VLAN Trunking.
- Spanning Tree Protocol detects and corrects switch loops.
- Switch loops are generally caused by misconfigured routers and switches or corrupt data. A switch loop occurs when packets actually get switched back to a switch they have already traversed.

Classless Inter-Domain Routing

- Classless Inter-Domain Routing (CIDR) uses a special notation to identify which part of an IP address is the network portion.
- The network portion is identified by a slash (/) symbol followed by a numeric value that represents the length of the network prefix, for example, XXX. XXX.XXX.XXX/N where N represents the network prefix length and is a number from 0 to 32.
- The CIDR correlates to the IPv4 address by assuming each portion (octet) of the IPv4 address represents a maximum value of eight bits.

Link Aggregation

- Link aggregation is when two or more network cables are paralleled to increase bandwidth and provide redundancy.

Copyright Goodheart-Willcox Co., Inc.

Review Questions

1. Convert the following binary bit patterns to decimal number values. Do not use a calculator for this activity. You may use the following tables for support.

1	1	1	1	1	1	1	1
128	64	32	16	8	4	2	1

1	0	0	1	0	1	0	1
128	0	0	16	0	4	0	1

A.

0	0	0	0	1	1	0	0

B.

0	0	0	0	1	1	1	1

C.

1	1	0	0	0	0	0	0

D.

0	0	0	1	0	1	0	1

E.

1	1	0	1	1	1	1	1

2. A subnet mask can be divided into two descriptive sections. What are the two sections called?

3. Why would a network administrator create subnets?

4. What do the binary ones in a subnet mask indicate?

5. What do the binary zeros in a subnet mask indicate?

6. Using the information provided, identify which part of the IP address 190.134.124.112 with a subnet mask of 255.255.255.0 is the network address and which part is the host address?

7. How many bits are borrowed from a Class B host address to create 30 new subnets?

8. How many bits are borrowed from a Class C host address to create six new subnets?

9. How many subnets can be formed using a subnet mask of 255.255.255.224 for a Class C network and using hardware that allows the use of all zeros and all ones in the network portion of the subnet mask?

Copyright Goodheart-Willcox Co., Inc.

10. How many hosts are created from the following Class C subnet mask: 255.255.255.240?

11. A network administrator decides to partition an existing Class C network into six equal parts. Each part of the network must hold at least 22 computers. What subnet mask must be used to satisfy the requirement?

12. How many subnets can be created from the following Class C subnet mask: 255.255.255.224?

13. How many subnets can be created from the following Class C subnet mask: 255.255.255.248?

14. What is the difference between a router and a layer 3 switch?

15. A bridge filters frames based on which type of address?

16. A switch filters frames based on which type of address?

17. A router filters frames based on which type of address?

18. At which layer of the OSI model do bridges operate?

19. At which layer of the OSI model do routers operate?

20. Name three devices that will forward a broadcast.

21. Name one device that will not forward a broadcast.

22. What is a broadcast domain?

23. What is the difference between an Interior Gateway Protocol and an Exterior Gateway Protocol?

24. What is an autonomous network?

25. Which IGP router protocol uses only hop count to determine the best path?

26. List four IGP protocols.

27. What is a VLAN?

28. What is the difference between a static and dynamic VLAN?

29. What is STP?

30. What network class is represented by the following CIDR: XXX.XXX.XXX.XXX/16?

31. What is the network portion of 179.124.244.2/16?

32. What is the host portion of 179.124.244.2/16?

33. How does link aggregation increase bandwidth for network backbones?

✚ Sample Network+ Exam Questions

1. John works for a large bank. He is attempting to create a Class A network. What subnet mask is used to identify a typical Class A network and host?

   A. 255.255.255.255

   B. 255.255.255.0

   C. 255.255.0.0

   D. 255.0.0.0

2. Maria is a network administrator for a small financial company. She is planning to expand the network and add several devices to the network. Which devices can filter network frames? (Select two.)

   A. Server

   B. Repeater

   C. Bridge

   D. Switch

   E. Router

3. Gregory is responsible for network administration at a large e-commerce company. He is trying to create a map of his network, and all the network IP addresses. What is the network class most likely associated with the IP address 150.150.23.34?

   A. Class A

   B. Class B

   C. Class C

   D. Class D

4. Which of the following IP addresses is a reserved address and cannot be used when connecting to the Internet?

   A. 123.001.001.21

   B. 192.168.0.23

   C. 154.23.168.32

   D. 200.200.200.200

5. Mary is trying to master the concepts of subnetting. She is trying to recall what portion of the IP address represents the network, and what part represents the node. What is the host address for an IP address of 199.200.12.45 with a subnet mask of 255.255.255.0?

   A. 199.200.12

   B. 45

   C. 255.255.255

   D. .0

Copyright Goodheart-Willcox Co., Inc.

6. You have been assigned the task of creating subnets for your company's network. You have to select the appropriate subnet masks. What subnet mask is used to identify a typical Class B network and host?

    A. 255.255.255.255

    B. 255.255.255.0

    C. 255.255.0.0

    D. 255.0.0.0

7. What is the network class most likely associated with the IP address 198.150.25.10? (Hint: The network class can be identified by the first octet.)

    A. Class A

    B. Class B

    C. Class C

    D. Class D

8. Juan is very concerned about switch loops. He wants to use a protocol that will mitigate this concern. Which protocol is designed to prevent switch loops?

    A. ICMP

    B. STP

    C. FTP

    D. SSL

9. What does a router use to determine the best route?

    A. Metric

    B. Vector

    C. MAC address

    D. TTL

10. Which two are link-state router protocols?

    A. RIP

    B. OSPF

    C. IS-IS

    D. RIPng

CHAPTER 12

Additional Transmission Modalities

Network+ Certification Exam Objectives

The Network+ Exam does not emphasize transmission modalities as heavily as it does topics such as subnetting or RAID. However, there will likely be some questions regarding diverse transmission protocols on the Network+ Exam. Additionally, protocols most closely associated with Voice over IP (VoIP) are likely to be on the exam.

Objectives

1.1: Protocols and Ports—SIP, H.323

1.3: Performance Concepts—Traffic Shaping, QoS, DiffServ, CoS

2.2: VoIP endpoint

2.3: VoIP PBX

2.5: Characteristics of Service—ATM, Frame Relay

5.2: Software Tools—Protocol Analyzer

5.3: Jitter, Latency

5.4: Jitter, Latency

Learning Outcomes

- Explain the basics of voice and audio signal transmission.
- Explain how video data is compressed and decompressed.
- Recall the purpose and characteristics of transmission protocols.
- Apply proper troubleshooting methods to identify and fix VoIP issues.

Copyright Goodheart-Willcox Co., Inc.

Key Terms

acoustical echo
analog-to-digital converter (ADC)
available bit rate (ABR)
bandwidth shaper
bit rate
codec
committed information rate (CIR)
constant bit rate (CBR)
digital-to-analog converter (DAC)
Frame Relay
H.323

hard phone
impedance mismatch
jitter
Moving Picture Experts Group (MPEG)
permanent virtual circuit (PVC)
public switched telephone network (PSTN)
Quality of Service (QoS)
Real-time Transport Protocol (RTP)
sampling frequency

sampling rate
Session Initiation Protocol (SIP)
soft phone
telephone gateway
unspecified bit rate (UBR)
variable bit rate (VBR)
variable bit rate non-real-time (VBR-nrt)
variable bit rate real-time (VBR-rt)
Voice over IP (VoIP)
X.25

Overview

This chapter introduces a wide range of transmission protocols. Some of these network technologies were originally designed to support the transfer of audio, video, and multimedia (a mixture of audio, video, text, and images) data. When transferring these types of data, there are some concerns that are not found in typical file-transfer situations consisting of text-only documents. The beginning of the chapter introduces basic concepts about audio and video that will help you better understand the technologies used to transport multimedia. Later in the chapter, protocols such as X.25, Frame Relay, ATM, and VoIP and the technologies that support them are introduced. Today, Ethernet can be used to transmit multimedia, but the other transmission protocols are still widely used.

Voice and Audio Signals

Of the various transmission methods, voice and video transmission over Internet or network connections is perhaps the most widely used. It is also a focus on the Network+ Certification Exam. Anyone reading this sentence has most likely transmitted his or her voice over a section of network owned by a long-distance telephone company. Digitizing a voice and transporting it over existing telephone lines began in the early 1970s. It was brought on in part by the rapid development of digital electronics.

The human voice and other audio signals are analog signals. Remember from earlier chapters how an analog signal fluctuates in amplitude. For an audio signal to be transported across a network system, it must be converted into a series of digital pulses that represent the analog waveform. After the digital pulses reach their destination, they must be converted back into an analog signal so that the human ear can detect and understand it.

Converting digital pulses to an analog waveform is called *digital-to-analog conversion*. Converting an analog waveform to digital pulses is called *analog-to-digital conversion*. The following section takes a closer look at both of these processes.

Copyright Goodheart-Willcox Co., Inc.

Signal Conversion

Audio signals must be converted into digital signals and placed in packets before being transmitted across a network. When packets of digital signals reach their destinations, they are reassembled and converted into analog signals. The quality of the analog signals depends on the detail of the digital coding.

An analog signal is converted into a digital code by taking samples of the analog signal's amplitude at specific times. The number of times the sample is taken during a specific period is referred to as the **sampling rate**. The number of bits used to represent the amplitude of the analog signal is referred to as **bit rate**. Bit rate is also referred to as *bit resolution*, or *bit depth*. The quality of the sound conversion is directly related to the sampling rate and the bit resolution. In other words, the higher the sampling rate and the greater the bit resolution, the better the sound.

The rate at which amplitude is measured per second is called **sampling frequency**. Sampling frequency varies significantly. A typical voice sampling frequency is approximately 11 kHz, or 11,000 times per second. The sampling frequency of quality sound applications, such as professionally recorded music, is approximately 44 kHz.

A typical human voice or any other audio signal fluctuates over a period of time. Figure 12-1A shows how an audio signal's amplitude is plotted against time. Amplitude is plotted vertically on the graph, and the time period is plotted horizontally on the graph. The quality of the analog-to-digital conversion depends on the sampling frequency, which is based on the number of bits available to store the sampling.

Compare the two sampling rates in Figure 12-1B and Figure 12-1C. Notice that the low sampling rate has fewer sampling points than the high sampling rate. The high sampling rate contains more sampling points to represent the original analog signal. As the sampling rate increases, a better representation of the original signal is made.

Figure 12-1 The sampling rate of the human voice. A—In this graph, the amplitude of the human voice is plotted on the vertical axis. The time period represents the frequency of the human voice and is plotted on the horizontal axis. B—This graph depicts a low sampling rate. Each point on the graph represents the point at which a sample is taken. C—This graph depicts a high sampling rate. In a high sampling rate, more data about the original signal is collected.

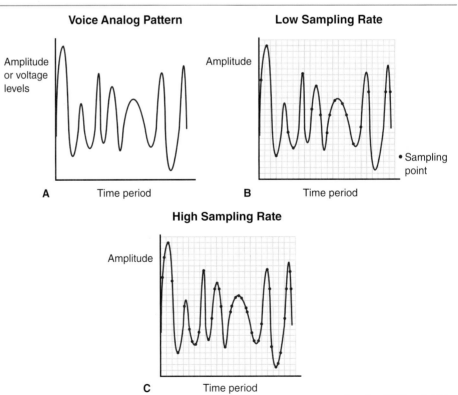

Goodheart-Willcox Publisher

Copyright Goodheart-Willcox Co., Inc.

The maximum number of sampling points represented in digital form depends on the number of bits used to represent the analog signal at any given point of time. The maximum number of possible bits per sample represents the bit rate. The higher the number of bits used, the better the digital description of the analog signal. For example, if only four bits are used to represent the voltage level, a total of 16 distinct voltage levels are represented. Four bits can have a maximum of 16 binary patterns. Notice in Figure 12-2 that 16 voltage levels (0 through 15 volts) are represented by 16 different four-bit binary patterns. A distinct binary pattern represents each voltage level. Now look at Figure 12-3. In this example, eight bits are used to represent the voltage levels 0 volts through 15 volts. A maximum of 256 distinct voltage levels are represented. Notice the intervals at which the voltage increases. In Figure 12-2, the voltage increases by one volt with each increment. In Figure 12-3, the voltage increases by 0.05859 volts with each increment. If 16 bits are used, a total of 65,536 levels can be used to represent voltage levels 0 volts through 15 volts. With each increment, the voltage level would increase by 0.000229 volts. Therefore, the greater the number of bits used, the more levels of voltage can be sampled, resulting in a better representation of a given analog signal.

The human analog voice can be converted to a digital signal using a relatively low sampling rate. Originally, speech was recorded using an eight-bit, or one-byte, voltage level at a low frequency such as 11 kHz. This resulted in a poor, but acceptable, quality of recorded voice.

Figure 12-2 Voltage levels, 0 volts through 15 volts, represented by 4-bit binary patterns.

Voltage Level	Binary Code
0 volts	0000
1 volts	0001
2 volts	0010
3 volts	0011
4 volts	0100
5 volts	0101
6 volts	0110
7 volts	0111
8 volts	1000
9 volts	1001
10 volts	1010
11 volts	1011
12 volts	1100
13 volts	1101
14 volts	1110
15 volts	1111

Goodheart-Willcox Publisher

Figure 12-3 Voltage levels, 0 volts through 15 volts, represented by 8-bit binary patterns.

Voltage Level	Binary Code
0 volts	0000 0000
0.05859 volts	0000 0001
0.11718 volts	0000 0010
0.17577 volts	0000 0011
0.23436 volts	0000 0100
0.29295 volts	0000 0101
0.35154 volts	0000 0110
0.41013 volts	0000 0111
0.46872 volts	0000 1000
0.52731 volts	0000 1001
0.58594 volts	0000 1010
0.64449 volts	0000 1011
0.70308 volts	0000 1100
0.05859 volts	0000 1101
0.82026 volts	0000 1110
0.87885 volts	0000 1111
0.93744 volts	0001 0000
0.99603 volts	0001 0001
1.05462 volts	0001 0010
⬇	⬇
14.94141 volts	1111 1110
15 volts	1111 1111

Goodheart-Willcox Publisher

Copyright Goodheart-Willcox Co., Inc.

Today, higher sampling rates are used to achieve higher sound quality. As shown in Figure 12-4, quality sound equal to recording studio levels can be achieved through sampling rates and bit depth, such as **2 channel, 24-bit, 48000 Hz**.

When working with sounds that require a high degree of quality, such as music and singing voices, a high sampling rate is needed. Musical instruments have a much wider range of fluctuating sound patterns compared with human speech. Look at Figure 12-5. You can see high rates for speakers, which improve the quality of sound for the listener. A 24-bit, 48-kHz output is constructed from a sampling rate as high as 1.5 Mbps.

Figure 12-4 The sound level of a microphone can achieve studio quality.

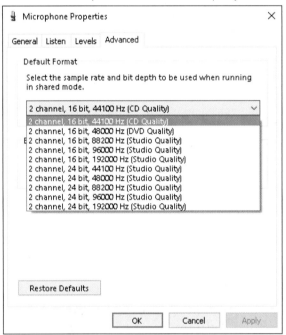

Goodheart-Willcox Publisher

Figure 12-5 Speaker output can also achieve studio quality.

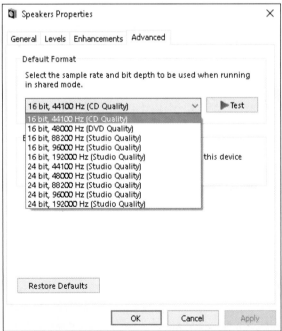

Goodheart-Willcox Publisher

Copyright Goodheart-Willcox Co., Inc.

Jitter

5.3, 5.4 NET

A high sampling rate requires high bandwidth, or *throughput*. A practical compromise between the maximum obtainable bandwidth of the network media and the sampling rate of the audio signal must be reached. If the sampling rate is too high, there will be too much data to transmit across the network, and some of the packets will be dropped to accommodate the inefficient bandwidth. This results in jitter. **Jitter** consists of small staggers or hesitations in the delivery sequence of audio or video data caused by latency or missing packets. A good example of jitter can be seen at times during a television news broadcast. A reporter located in some distant country is talking in real time to a news correspondent in the United States over a videophone or a similar device. You will often see a disrupted picture and time delay of responses to questions while the broadcast takes place. If the sampling rate is too low, the quality of the sound suffers, resulting in an artificial sound produced at the destination point.

Multimedia data transmitted across a large network requires network media such as T1 or fiber-optic. Low-quality data such as voice can be transmitted over traditional copper cabling. The distance traveled by the data and the type of data (voice, music, video, and multimedia) determine the cabling requirements.

Latency

5.3, 5.4 NET

The term *latency* refers to the delay of data as it travels to its destination. Latency may not be a problem for text-file transfers or e-mail exchanges. Even the common practice of downloading music has an acceptable latency period. Audio files contain a tremendous amount of data. When music is downloaded, it is buffered before it is played. *Buffering* means data is stored in memory until a sufficient amount of data is stored. When a sufficient amount is stored, the music begins to play. If buffering did not occur, there would be many momentary interruptions in the music.

A music file contains a large amount of data. This data must be processed at a very high data rate. If something acts as a bottleneck, the flow of data could slow. For example, if a music file required a data rate of 1 Mb per minute to produce a steady stream of music and there were a restriction between the origin and destination, such as a modem, the music would start and stop every time the data-transfer rate fell lower than the required data rate to produce a steady sound. When buffering takes place, a large volume of data is stored in memory before the music begins to play. This reserve ensures a steady flow of music data is provided while the music is playing. This same technique is used for video.

When a real-time application such as a telephone conversation occurs, only a minimal latency period can be tolerated. The human ear can tolerate small breaks in the flow of audio data. If the breaks are small, they will go completely unnoticed. For example, a break in the data flow of fewer than 150 milliseconds (150/1000 or 0.15) can be tolerated. The human ear likely will not detect any break in the conversation. When a latency period of approximately 250 milliseconds is present, the listener will notice it but will probably be able to tolerate it. However, a period of 500 milliseconds is most likely unacceptable to the listener.

Latency occurs due to several factors. One factor can be equipment, for example, gateways that change the data frame from one format to another while connecting two dissimilar network systems. Satellite transmission can generate delays from 50 to 500 milliseconds. The time it takes a software-compression program to compress data can increase latency, and can result in lost or destroyed frames.

The total amount of latency between data packets produces jitter. Remember, jitter is the effect on the quality of sound or images when they arrive at their destination in other than regularly spaced, minimum intervals. As the data packets

Copyright Goodheart-Willcox Co., Inc.

enter the Internet system, latency periods between the packets may increase to an undesirable level, as shown in Figure 12-6. In the figure, notice that each packet leaves the source in regularly spaced intervals, but after navigating long distances, irregular spacing develops. If the spaces are too large (250 milliseconds), jitter is produced at the destination.

Figure 12-6 Packets leaving the source are evenly spaced with minimal delay. After they traverse the Internet, latency increases, causing packets to arrive at their destination in other than regularly spaced, minimum intervals. The total amount of latency between data packets produces jitter.

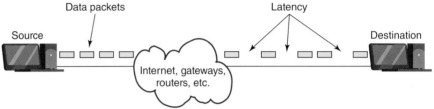

(workstation icons) RedlineVector/Shutterstock.com; Goodheart-Willcox Publisher

Acoustical Echo

Acoustical echo is a condition that takes place when a microphone and a speaker are in close proximity or the audio is improperly adjusted, causing feedback. The sound coming from the speaker is so loud that it is received by the microphone, thus generating an echo effect. The electronic sound components convert the sound wave sent to the microphone to digital and then back to analog for output on the speaker(s). The echo effect occurs because the conversion of analog to digital to analog is not instantaneous. The echo effect can be prevented by decreasing the level of amplification.

Acoustical echo is commonly encountered in VoIP when using laptop computers and computer audio headsets equipped with microphones. Acoustical echo can be easily corrected by reconfiguring the sound level of the equipment.

Some audio devices are equipped with echo-cancellation components. These components detect an echo condition and then automatically change circuit conditions to eliminate the echo. Echo-cancellation components are just one of the reasons for the difference in prices between audio devices.

Other conditions that contribute to echo conditions for VoIP are packet latency and packet loss. Latency problems are typically increased by long distances and mixing media, such as telephone lines and satellite signals, to carry audio packets. Latency is the main reason for packet loss. Since audio requires a constant stream of packets in a timely fashion, corrupt packets are dropped and not retransmitted. They are not retransmitted because it would not serve any useful purpose. By the time a missing or corrupt packet is discovered and retransmitted, it would no longer fit correctly into the sequence of packets without increasing the delay of the packet stream.

A whole field of electronics is referred to as *digital signal processing (DSP)*. DSP is dedicated to processing digital signals through all types of electronic equipment and signal-carrying media. At times, the DSP equipment and components can cause problems rather than correct them. For example, some systems insert a "best guess" of the missing packet contents to fill in audio gaps so the listener does not experience gaps in sound. At times, this technique can result in echo.

Also, be aware that there is a direct correlation between the number of participants in a conference call and the generation of echo. It only takes one participant to experience echo to produce additional echo affecting all participants in the conference call.

Copyright Goodheart-Willcox Co., Inc.

When experiencing echo, one must consider the following factors: impedance mismatch, acoustical echo, latency, and packet loss. For more detailed information about acoustical echo, visit www.adaptivedigital.com/product/echo_cancel/echo_explain.htm. To find this website, you can also conduct a search using the phrase impedance mismatch echo. Some search results can be very technical and therefore require an understanding of basic electronics.

Video

Video is a result of flashing still images in front of a viewer at a rate faster than the human eye can detect. For example, a typical movie consists of a series of still images running through a projector at a rate of 24 frames per second. In other words, 24 images flash in front of the viewer every second. A frequency lower than this would cause the picture to be choppy and a jitter effect would be detected.

Figure 12-7 shows a set of still images taken from a digital movie of a dog returning a ball in a game of catch. Look closely at the dog's front legs to see the gradual change in position. When the series of frames are displayed on a monitor at 24 frames per second, a smooth video motion is displayed. Full motion video for Internet and intranet require the same number of frames per second. However, there are more variables than frame rate that need to be considered, such as picture resolution, color depth, processing speed of the computer, amount of video RAM available, and the type of network medium used to transfer the video.

Figure 12-7 A typical strip of movie film must change at a rate of 24 frames per second. The film consists of a string of still prints. Each frame contains a slight change in position of the object in motion.

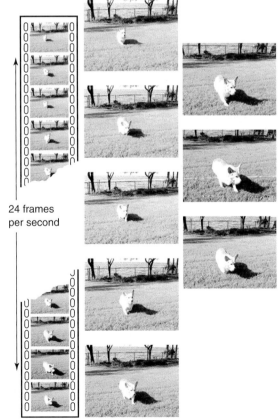

24 frames per second

Goodheart-Willcox Publisher

Copyright Goodheart-Willcox Co., Inc.

Video Resolution

Video resolution is described in pixels and is measured horizontally and vertically across a display. For example, a typical VGA resolution is 640 × 480, or 640 pixels on each of the 480 lines of the display, as referenced in Figure 12-8.

Assuming that an image was at a VGA resolution in full color (32-bit), the amount of RAM required to contain the image would be approximately 1 MB (480 × 640 × 32) per second. If 24 frames were required for full-motion video, approximately 24 MB of data would need to be delivered across the network every second. A three-minute video sequence would require approximately a 4320-MB (180 seconds × 24 MB) data stream.

Video requires many computer resources and a lot of network media bandwidth. While most computers will support video as well as audio, many network systems will not. Full-motion video with audio requires a network medium with high bandwidth, or the color resolution and frame rate will need to be significantly reduced. Think of the actual bandwidth of a telephone modem rated for 56 kbps. It would be impossible to produce a live videoconference using a 56 kbps modem. This is one reason that video conferencing did not become such a widely used technology until most people had moved to higher bandwidth communication, such as cable modems and T1 lines. High-definition video makes the bandwidth issue even more significant.

Figure 12-8 The image in the display represents a VGA resolution of 640 × 480 pixels, or a total of 307,200 pixels. Each pixel location may require as many as 3 bytes to represent a color depth of 256 possible colors. This means that one frame of an image would require approximately 1 MB of memory or storage.

A closeup of the hand area reveals the pixel pattern

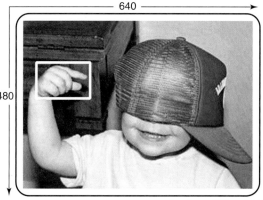

Goodheart-Willcox Publisher

Compression

All video systems use a form of compression and decompression to reduce the total number of bytes required for each image. The term **codec** is used to represent software, hardware, or combination of software and hardware that compress and decompress video and audio information. The name *codec* stems from *compressor/decompressor*. Some common codecs are MPEG, Indeo, and Cinepak.

One of the most common codecs in use is MPEG. **Moving Picture Experts Group (MPEG)** is an industry standard that ensures compatibility between different cameras, displays, and other multimedia equipment.

The compression technique that MPEG uses is simple to understand. Look again at Figure 12-7 of the dog playing ball. Notice how much of the image is redundant; most of the background image does not change. MPEG capitalizes on this typical video feature. The MPEG compression software is written to predict which areas

Copyright Goodheart-Willcox Co., Inc.

of the next frame will change and which areas will not. The prediction is based on the likelihood that if an area has not changed from one frame to the next, it is unlikely to change in the next frame. The areas that do not change do not need to be transmitted or stored. The result is a reduction of the total amount of data that needs to be stored or broadcast.

There are various MPEG standards, such as MPEG-1 and MPEG-2. *MPEG-1* produces a relatively low-resolution image of approximately 320 × 240 pixels with a data rate of approximately 1.5 megabits. This is an excellent standard for applications such as e-mail, where high resolution is not required. MPEG is also used to compress audio files. *MPEG-2* produces a resolution of 720 × 480 pixels with a data rate of approximately six megabytes. These levels are comparable to quality CD audio. The development of MPEG-3 was canceled and never fully developed. It was to support high-definition television (HDTV). The MPEG-2 standard, however, is adequate to support HDTV.

MPEG-4 is a new standard used on multimedia applications for the Internet. It is designed to meet the requirements to support broadcast quality audio and video. For full-motion video, MPEG-4 supports data rates higher than 1 Gb per second. This is a vast improvement over MPEG-2 data compression.

Other Transmission Protocols

Audio and video broadcasts are transmitted over networks as data. The following section looks at some of the protocols designed to transmit various types of data aside from traditional network data. These protocols include X.25, Frame Relay, ATM, VoIP, telephone gateway, H.323, QoS, SIP, and RTP.

X.25

The **X.25** protocol is a transport protocol that uses analog signals to transmit data across long distances. The use of analog signals may seem strange, but X.25 was developed in the early years of the telecommunication industry, prior to the widespread use of digital signals. An analog transport design for data was natural. What makes X.25 unusual when compared with other analog technologies is that it uses packet switching rather than permanent, electrical connections. Analog signals are routed around the world in packets that often follow different routes to reach their destination. X.25 laid the foundation for packet-switching technology. X.25 is not commonly used in the United States, but many locations overseas are still committed to X.25. The X.25 protocol is limited to a maximum data rate of 56 kbps.

Frame Relay

Designed to replace X.25, **Frame Relay** is a packet-switching protocol that typically uses leased lines such as T1 to carry data over long distances. Think of Frame Relay as an upgraded digital version of the analog X.25 protocol. Frame Relay allows for a data rate as high as 1.544 Mbps. Whereas, X.25 is limited to 56 kbps.

Both X.25 and Frame Relay can be configured as a permanent virtual circuit (PVC). A **permanent virtual circuit (PVC)** behaves like a hard-wired connection between a destination and source. It can follow many different paths during transmission. A PVC is not committed to following a single path, such as a T1 line.

This may sound confusing because Frame Relay is generally transmitted over T1 lines to ensure a minimum data rate known as a committed information rate (CIR). A **committed information rate (CIR)** is guaranteed bandwidth a commercial carrier will provide to a subscriber. Many times, a T1 line is shared with other users.

2.5 NET +

When the T1 line is shared, the data rate can fluctuate because of the variations in traffic, which includes the number of users and the type of data on the line. Frame Relay data transfer speeds are limited to the media used. A T1 line has a bandwidth of 1.544 Mbps. T-3 is limited to 45 Mbps.

ATM

Recall from Chapter 1 that *asynchronous transfer mode (ATM)* is a widely used protocol that is especially designed for carrying audio, video, and multimedia. The original ATM protocol could support a bandwidth of 622 Mbps. More recent improvements can get in excess of 2 Gbps bandwidth. ATM technology was designed in the 1970s at Bell Labs for use as a telephone technology. At that time, digital electronics was rapidly expanding and replacing electronic analog devices. Bell Labs was experimenting with a way to transmit analog voice signals as digital signals across telephone lines and networks. ATM technology was developed very early during the evolution of network communication and did not come into common use for WAN applications until the 1990s.

ATM is used in the backbones of some cable companies. It is a good choice for transmitting high bandwidth video signals. ATM maintains a constant stream of voice or video from the source to the destination and avoids jitter. Traditionally, audio and video were transferred over analog media, such as telephone lines and radio and television frequencies. An analog signal can be converted into a digital signal through the use of specialized electronic chips referred to as **analog-to-digital converter (ADC)** and **digital-to-analog converter (DAC)**. As the names imply, the chips are designed to change an analog signal into a digital signal and vice versa.

Figure 12-9 shows a simplification of ATM technology. The sound of a person's voice is converted into electrical energy. The electrical energy is a series of voltage fluctuation patterns known as an *analog signal*. The voltage fluctuation patterns are converted into a series of digital signals. At the destination, the digital signal is converted into an analog signal. The analog signal is amplified and applied to a speaker, which converts the analog signal into the sound of the voice.

Figure 12-9 An example of analog-to-digital and digital-to-analog conversion.

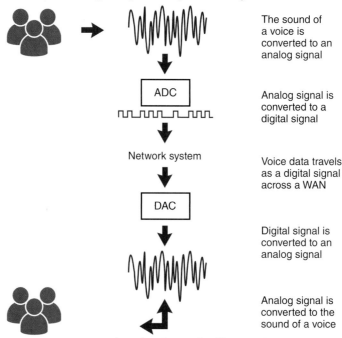

The sound of a voice is converted to an analog signal

Analog signal is converted to a digital signal

Voice data travels as a digital signal across a WAN

Digital signal is converted to an analog signal

Analog signal is converted to the sound of a voice

(users icons) musmellow/Shutterstock.com; Goodheart-Willcox Publisher

Copyright Goodheart-Willcox Co., Inc.

ATM Data Transmission Model

ATM is designed to divide text and audio/video into cells of 53 bytes each. Figure 12-10 illustrates how ATM technology works. Notice that the cells are placed in sequence giving higher priority to the audio/video cells. Remember that the audio/video packets cannot tolerate excessive latency. Any delay in transporting the cells disrupts the audio and video during a live transmission, resulting in jitter.

Figure 12-10 In this example, two forms of data, text and audio/video, are separated into cells and multiplexed. All cells are placed on a single line as a series of packets. Priority is given to the time-sensitive audio/video cells. At the destination, a demultiplexer separates the two forms of data.

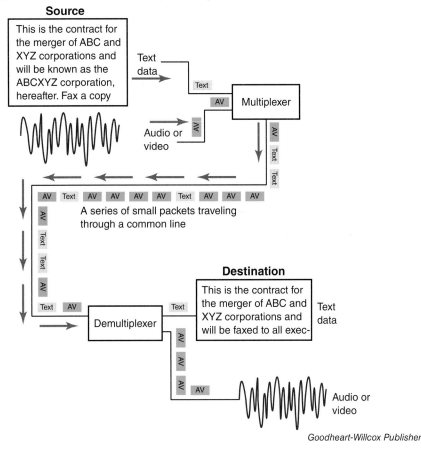

Goodheart-Willcox Publisher

ATM can be transmitted at a *constant bit rate (CBR)* or as a *variable bit rate (VBR)*. A **constant bit rate (CBR)** is a steady stream of ATM cells moving at a predictable rate. CBR is best used for video conferencing, telephone conversations, television broadcasts, or anywhere real-time data transfer is required. When a CBR is desired, a dedicated circuit or a virtual circuit must be established between two points. By establishing a constant connection between the two points, the data rate can be guaranteed, which is required for a live or real-time exchange of data.

A **variable bit rate (VBR)** is an ATM cell rate that automatically adjusts to support time-sensitive data. It uses multiplexing techniques to provide a minimum CBR for time-sensitive audio and video transmissions while controlling the data rate of non-time-sensitive data, such as text or plain e-mail. A VBR may be used when cost prohibits a CBR system. For example, a high-bandwidth system equipped with a multiplexer at one end and a demultiplexer at the other end can transfer telephone conversations, e-mail messages, and files across a single carrier. The most important thing is to maintain a minimum data transfer rate for the telephone conversation

Copyright Goodheart-Willcox Co., Inc.

and video, both of which are time-sensitive, while allowing delay to occur in the e-mail and file transfer. The ATM cells carrying audio and video are given the highest priority so a constant flow of the time-sensitive data can be maintained. The cells carrying e-mail and file transfers can be delayed.

Before ATM, separate systems were required to accommodate the various types of data. ATM allows text, voice, and video to be carried on the same network system. This can prove to be cost-effective in certain instances. For example, a corporation spanning the globe generates a large number of long-distance telephone calls. It is less expensive to use the corporate WAN for voice transmission than separate telephone lines. ATM communication may also prove to be an effective way of holding corporate meetings, which would otherwise require employees from various locations to converge and meet at a central location. Conferencing over a network is more economical than traveling, and in many instances, it is a more effective use of employee time.

ATM Switch

An ATM switch provides virtual circuits between various points on the network system and is used with the ATM protocol. This can provide a separate virtual circuit between several computers at the same time.

Look at Figure 12-11. In the illustration, the ATM switch provides virtual circuit connections between *Computer A*, *Computer B*, and *Computer C* and at the same time provides a connection between *Computer D* and *Computer E*. The computers are connected as virtual circuits, not permanent circuits. During a communication period between two or more computers, the ATM switch makes the connection appear as a permanent connection. When the transfer of text, audio, or video is complete, the circuits disconnect. A computer can then connect to a different computer.

Figure 12-11 *Computer A* provides video to *Computer B* and *Computer C* while *Computer D* exchanges a file with *Computer E*. The ATM switch creates a separate virtual circuit between these computers, which behave as though they were wired directly to each other.

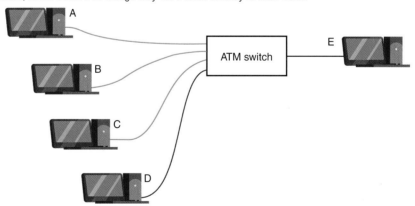

(workstation icons) RedlineVector/Shutterstock.com; Goodheart-Willcox Publisher

In the illustration, the ATM switch is used to provide a temporary connection between designated computers. The switch can also be set up to provide a permanent, virtual connection that provides a guaranteed bandwidth between two or more computers.

ATM Data Transfer Classifications

There are five ATM classifications: CBR, VBR-nrt, VBR-rt, ABR, and UBR. Each classification describes the degree to which the virtual circuit is dedicated to ATM cell transmission.

Copyright Goodheart-Willcox Co., Inc.

Recall that constant bit rate (CBR) is a steady stream of ATM cells moving at a predictable rate. CBR is used for applications such as video conferencing and telephone communication. Variable bit rate (VBR) has the ability to change the rate of flow in contrast to CBR. VBR is divided into two major classes: *VBR real-time (VBR-rt)* and *VBR non-real-time (VBR-nrt)*.

Variable bit rate non-real-time (VBR-nrt) allows ATM cells to move at a variable rate. The rate of movement depends on the type of data contained in each cell. For example, an e-mail that contains a text and multimedia attachment contains two types of data. Each type of data needs to be handled with a different priority. The multimedia data would have the highest priority. However, there is no need for the cells that contain multimedia data to be transferred in real time because the communication is strictly in one direction, not two-way as in a telephone conversation.

Variable bit rate real-time (VBR-rt) is similar to VBR-nrt in that it moves cells at a variable rate, depending on the cell's contents. The main difference between the two bit rates is VBR-RT adjusts the bit rate to support real-time audio and video transfers. For example, when transferring text files and telephone conversation at the same time, the telephone conversation is transferred in real time while the text file is sent at a lower rate.

Available bit rate (ABR) is most appropriate for file transfer. It uses the available bit rate associated with the networking medium. The speed of a file transfer using the ABR classification is affected by the amount of traffic on the network.

Unspecified bit rate (UBR) does not guarantee any speed or meet requirements of any special application such as multimedia or telephony. This classification is typically applied inside TCP/IP frames. A good example is a webcam that updates the image every 30 seconds or so, rather than providing full-motion video.

The ATM data transfer classifications reflect a matching cost factor. The highest quality is CBR, and it is the most expensive to use. The least expensive is UBR, which is minimal to no cost when used across the Internet as part of a TCP/IP frame. The minimal cost is the cost of the ISP.

ATM Cell Design

The Network+ Exam likely will not ask about the details of the ATM cell. However, briefly covering this topic will help to deepen one's understanding of the ATM protocol. The ATM cell is simple in design. The maximum size of the cell is 53 bytes, consisting of a 5-byte header and a 48-byte payload, as illustrated in Figure 12-12.

The most significant characteristic of the ATM cell is it carries only a 48-byte payload. While this may seem small, you must consider that the idea behind the design is to be able to mix many different cells on the same network medium. Remember, it is important not to cause too much latency or destroy a multimedia cell. Any cells that are destroyed or do not reach the destination are not retransmitted over the media. There is no time to retransmit a cell or to reorder cells if they become out of order when traveling across a network.

Tech Tip

The ATM cell is at times referred to as a *packet* or *frame*. This is incorrect according to the ATM forum organization.

Figure 12-12 The ATM protocol is designed for efficiency. Compared with other protocols, such as IP, the ATM protocol is quite small.

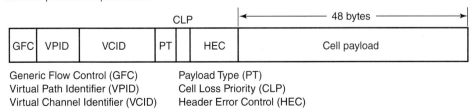

Generic Flow Control (GFC)
Virtual Path Identifier (VPID)
Virtual Channel Identifier (VCID)
Payload Type (PT)
Cell Loss Priority (CLP)
Header Error Control (HEC)

Goodheart-Willcox Publisher

Copyright Goodheart-Willcox Co., Inc.

The four bits in the Generic Flow Control (GFC) field were originally designed to contain information about the function of the cell. It is not used at the time of this writing. The exact specifications for this field have not yet been standardized, so it is normally set to all zeros. The eight bits in the Virtual Path Identifier (VPI) field and the 16 bits in the Virtual Channel Identifier (VCI) field identify the path from the source to the destination using a series of ATM switches. The three bits in the Payload Type (PT) field indicate the type of payload carried in the cell, such as data or control instructions. The one bit in the Cell Loss Priority (CLP) field indicates whether the cell should be dropped should it encounter severe congestion on the network. The CLP field keeps time-sensitive transmissions up-to-date and prevents latency issues. The eight-bit Header Error Control (HEC) field detects errors in the header portion of the cell, not in the payload.

ATM is a connection-oriented protocol. This means that it establishes a logical connection between the source and destination. Logical connections are also referred to as *virtual connections*. Remember that a virtual connection is not a permanent, physical connection, but rather a connection that behaves as a physical connection. A virtual connection is set up and controlled by a software program. There are two types of virtual connections associated with ATM, and they are identified in the header of the ATM cell. The two types of connections are *virtual path connections (VPC)* and *virtual channel connections (VCC)*.

Figure 12-13 shows a backbone running between two ATM switches. The backbone is considered a virtual path. The virtual path contains the individual virtual circuits, or *virtual channels*, between specific computers or network equipment. In the illustration, there are two virtual channels, *A* and *B*. The virtual channels merge into the virtual path when traveling between the switches and then split into separate virtual channels when serving the computers identified as *A* and *B*.

To understand virtual path connections and virtual channel connections better, a complete highway system can be used as an analogy. A complete highway system includes state highways and an interstate highway. The state highways can be compared to virtual channels, and an interstate highway can be compared to a virtual path. State highways connect at different points along the interstate highway. A car travels from its home (source) across a state highway, merges onto the interstate highway where it travels with other cars from various state highways, and then exits onto a state highway to reach its destination.

Figure 12-13 The ATM backbone contains paths, which consist of two or more virtual channels. The backbone is referred to as the *virtual path*.

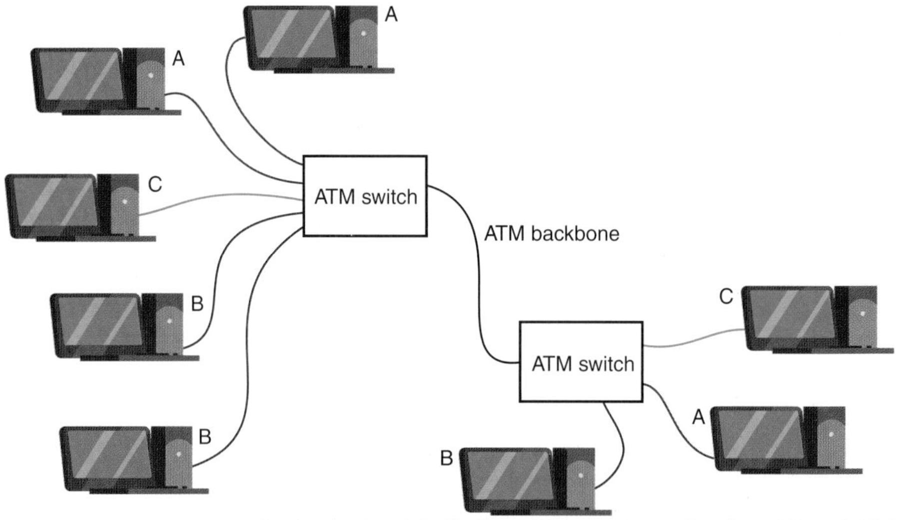

(workstation icons) RedlineVector/Shutterstock.com; Goodheart-Willcox Publisher

In reality, there can be many virtual path connections between ATM switches. The virtual path connections can be configured as permanent virtual circuits (PVCs) or switched virtual circuits (SVC). For example, a corporation may have a PVC established between its Chicago and St. Louis offices to maintain a constant update of a critical database. Other connections can be set up as SVCs. The SVCs would be used only as needed by individuals who only connect to resources at the other locations on a temporary basis. Remember that connections across long-distance lines are very expensive, even virtual ones. A dedicated, physical connection between two locations is more expensive than a switched circuit that is only connected temporarily. ATM and other cell-switching technologies are designed with flexibility in mind. However, because of the flexibility, much confusion can arise.

ATM switches are designed to support ATM protocol functions. The ATM switch processes millions of cells per second and provides multiplexing, which is required to deliver each cell in a timely fashion while sharing a common media. Each ATM switch maintains routing tables based on information contained in the ATM cell header. A routing table for the ATM switch is similar in design and purpose to the routing table used for a router. Remember that the virtual path identifier and the virtual channel identifier are used to locate and maintain the connection between two devices. Based on the information contained in the header, the ATM switch sets up the virtual channels and paths between end users.

The ATM switch controls the bandwidth allocated to each virtual circuit and controls the cells by priorities set in the Cell Loss Priority (CLP) field in the ATM cell header. The switch also drops some of the cells if cell traffic exceeds the capacity of the switch, media attached to the switch, or both.

A typical ATM switch is designed with multiple ports. The switch is used to make a physical connection to various network media such as fiber-optic cable, twisted-pair cable, and coaxial cable. Because of costs, ATM switches are mostly found on long-haul communication portions of a WAN rather than on a LAN.

VoIP

Voice over IP (VoIP), also known as *Internet telephony*, is similar in concept to ATM in that it is designed for high-performance data delivery and quality of service. VoIP, however, relies on existing TCP/IP technology and existing TCP/IP networking equipment. ATM is a protocol separate from the TCP/IP stack and uses special equipment designed for the protocol, such as ATM switches and dedicated communication lines. ATM requires expensive equipment for support, while support for VoIP is inexpensive.

2.2   NET

VoIP is less expensive for long-distance calls when compared with existing telephone technologies. This is why it is appealing to so many people, especially to corporations communicating over long-distance lines with overseas corporations. The specific protocols used for VoIP will be discussed in some detail later in this chapter.

VoIP Transmission Model

VoIP typically uses a series of UDP packets to send voice data across a network. The construction of the UDP packet is similar to that of ATM. Remember that ATM designed its packet for efficiency. The ATM packet is a short packet with little overhead like the UDP packet. UDP provides a best-effort delivery of data with no mechanism to check if the data arrived in sequence or intact. The UDP packet does not generate high latency because it does not attempt to resend lost packets. This works for both video and voice because the loss of a small number of packets will not change the message. For example, if one packet per 100 were lost from a VoIP call, it would go unnoticed. However, if TCP rather than UDP were used, and each packet had to be

Copyright Goodheart-Willcox Co., Inc.

confirmed to have been delivered, it would dramatically increase the bandwidth consumed by VoIP and video.

VoIP Infrastructure

For TCP/IP to be an excellent means of carrying multimedia, a media carrier from source to destination with high bandwidth is required, such as Gigabyte Ethernet or fiber-optic cable.

One of the major technical problems with Internet communication has been the location of the last few hundred feet of cabling to the home computer, known as the *local loop*. The local loop is typically designed for low-bandwidth analog voice communication. Since the bandwidth is low, it is the bottleneck for the entire system, even if the rest of the communication link uses the very latest technology. The last few hundred feet of the system can affect the overall latency of packet transmission, which negates the latest technology. Traditional telephone lines cannot adequately carry audio and video in real time. For VoIP to work successfully, there must be adequate bandwidth. Without adequate bandwidth, latency becomes a problem. DSL and cable Internet access provide adequate bandwidth for VoIP to run without latency. DSL and cable are not connected to the local loop.

There are several ways VoIP can be used, including the following:

- Communicating from PC to PC using TCP/IP

- Mixing TCP/IP telephone technology with existing and modern telephone technologies

- Communicating from a PC to a cell phone via traditional LAN cabling network, a public switched telephone network (PSTN), and wireless technology

VoIP can communicate from PC to PC using only the TCP/IP protocol. This is easy to set up and is similar to using Windows XP **NetMeeting**, Windows Vista **Meeting Space**, Windows 7 **People Near Me**, or the Windows 10 **My People** app. All of these programs are collaboration programs that support the exchange of text messages and documents and remote desktop access. NetMeeting supports audio and video and is therefore a VoIP application. This feature is not included in Meeting Space and People Near Me. Microsoft claimed that support for video and audio used too much bandwidth which caused latency problems in the peer-to-peer network. As an alternative, Microsoft offers a subscription collaboration software package called Microsoft Office Live Meeting. Also, Windows 7 through 10 can be incorporated with Skype to provide video and audio during a meeting session. Both the Windows Vista and Windows 7 collaboration require IPv6 for support.

VoIP can be used by mixing TCP/IP with modern telephone technologies. For example, a PC can connect to a standard telephone via a TCP/IP network, Public switched telephone network (PSTN), and the more modern ISDN or FDDI technologies. **Public switched telephone network (PSTN)**, or *plain-old telephone service (POTS)*, usually refers to the older telephone technology that uses twisted-pair cable and analog signals.

Mixing TCP/IP with telephone technologies is very complex. It requires translating TCP/IP into traditional telephone protocols and vice versa. There can be substantial delays or latency using a hybrid protocol system required for communication over the variety of media encountered.

VoIP can also be used to communicate from a PC to a cell phone via traditional LAN cabling, a PSTN, and then wireless technology. This type of communication is even more complicated than the last scenario and can create even longer delays.

Copyright Goodheart-Willcox Co., Inc.

A PC can communicate with a wide variety of communication devices, as shown in Figure 12-14. There are many communication scenarios that mix PC communication with conventional telephone, wireless cell phones, and personal digital assistants. Each of these communication technologies requires special protocols and protocol conversions. Each set of protocols varies according to the communication path. The path can be over public analog or digital telephone lines, private company lines, fiber-optic cable, infrared, satellite, and wireless.

Figure 12-14 Computers can communicate with a wide variety of communication devices such as cell phones, pagers, palmtops, personal digital assistants, and landline telephones. The wide variety of equipment and devices requires a wide variety of communication lines and equipment.

(workstation icon) RedlineVector/Shutterstock.com; (phone icons) Tetiana Yurchenko/Shutterstock.com; Goodheart-Willcox Publisher

Bandwidth-Shaping Techniques

VoIP often relies on bandwidth-shaping techniques to ensure quality of service. A **bandwidth shaper**, or *traffic shaper*, is used to prioritize network packets to ensure quality of service for time-sensitive applications such as VoIP. A bandwidth shaper prioritizes network traffic by protocol or assigned switch port or port number.

The bandwidth shaper can delay the delivery of low-priority packets, thus allowing high-priority packets the maximum throughput. For example, to ensure the delivery of VoIP packets, web pages requested for download to a workstation are throttled back, ensuring the highest quality of service to the VoIP packets. The phrase *throttled back* means that the number of packets to be downloaded during a given period of time is limited to reduce bandwidth consumption. Bandwidth shapers are commonly employed by Internet service providers and other large providers of Internet access such as corporations and educational institutions.

Bandwidth shaping can be accomplished with hardware or software and is used to control the bandwidth through a particular device such as a gateway, shared Internet connection, network switch, or router. When a switch is used, the bandwidth rate for a switch port can be manually set. For example, you could configure the switch port for 10 Mb, 100 Mb, or 1 Gb maximum throughput. When bandwidth- or traffic-shaping software is used, the bandwidth can be limited for a particular set of IP addresses, type of protocol such as HTTP, or a particular application. To learn more about bandwidth-shaper equipment and applications, visit the NetEqualizer website at www.netequalizer.com.

Telephone Gateway and H.323

A **telephone gateway** is a specialized piece of equipment that connects a packet-style network communication system to a telephone system using the H.323 protocol. The **H.323** standard is an older telecommunication standard for audio, video, and data communication using IP or packet-type networks defined by the International Telecommunication Union (ITU). On one side of the telephone gateway

Copyright Goodheart-Willcox Co., Inc.

is the telephone system, and on the other side is the network system. The telephone system side is the H.323 side. You can think of the gateway as the H.323 server and the computers on the network side as the H.323 clients, as illustrated in Figure 12-15.

H.323 is not one specific protocol but rather an entire suite of protocols similar to the TCP/IP suite of protocols. There are over 20 different protocols designed to work with H.323. The protocols are systems that control processes such as name-to-telephone number conversion, call forwarding, caller ID, call blocking, conversion from TCP/IP to wireless, and conversion to European telephone systems. H.323 has been largely supplanted by SIP and RTP, both of which will be discussed in detail later in this chapter.

Figure 12-15 The H.323 client is installed on the workstations, while the H.323 gateway service is part of the telephone system.

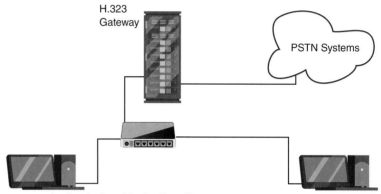

(workstation icons) RedlineVector/Shutterstock.com; (server icon) fullvector/Shutterstock.com; (hub icon) Vadim Ermak/Shutterstock.com; Goodheart-Willcox Publisher

Quality of Service (QoS)

The biggest problem in using packet-based networking systems is latency. The **Quality of Service (QoS)** protocol was developed to minimize latency. It should be noted that QoS is more often used to denote that concept of Quality of Service rather than the actual protocol. This is closely related to Cost of Service (CoS). *Cost of Service* refers to the cost, in resources, it will take to deliver a given service, packet, or message. The QoS protocol gives time-sensitive packets, such as those carrying telephone conversations, a higher priority than data packets. The QoS Packet Scheduler, shown in Figure 12-16, is available in Windows XP and later.

Windows operating systems later than Windows XP install QoS by default during installation if the computer supports a network connection. The QoS feature works for both wired and wireless networks.

Frame Relay and ATM are sometimes carried over typical Internet backbones packaged inside the IP protocol. These technologies are referred to as *ATM over IP (ATMoIP)* and *Frame Relay over IP (FRoIP)*. Chapter 14 takes a closer look at how these systems work.

DiffServ, or differentiated services, is a network architecture that classifies and manages network traffic. This provides QoS by sending the most important traffic at a higher priority. DiffServ works by using a six-bit code in the Differentiated Services files of the IP header. This code is used to classify network traffic.

Copyright Goodheart-Willcox Co., Inc.

Tech Tip

Nortel Networks specializes in integrating telecommunication and networking. You may want to visit the Nortel website at www.nortelnetworks.com to learn more about the telecommunication industry as a possible source of employment. Nortel also offers a variety of certifications. Many of these certifications involve a detailed understanding of networking.

Figure 12-16 Quality of Service (QoS) is an optional protocol available in Windows XP and installed by default in later Windows operating systems. The QoS protocol gives time-sensitive packets a higher priority than data packets.

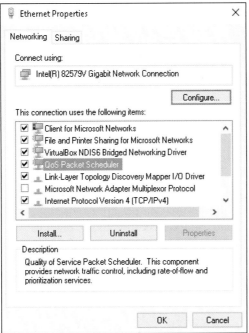

Goodheart-Willcox Publisher

Session Initiation Protocol (SIP)

Session Initiation Protocol (SIP) is a standard and a protocol. The SIP standard was specified by the Internet Engineering Task Force (IETF). SIP is used for initiating, maintaining, and terminating the exchange of voice, multimedia, gaming, chat, and more. SIP does not carry the data but rather establishes and maintains the session until the session is terminated. The control of a VoIP session is referred to as *call signaling*. SIP is used for both VoIP and video transmissions.

An example of a SIP application is Skype, a software program that supports telephone communication across the Internet using hard or soft phones. A **hard phone** is a physical telephonic device. A **soft phone** is a virtual telephonic device. An example of a soft phone is shown in Figure 12-17. Notice the keypad for entering telephone numbers. The software takes care of establishing a connection with the entered phone number. A user would simply need a headset connected to the computer to serve as an input/output device for the conversation.

Copyright Goodheart-Willcox Co., Inc.

Figure 12-17 The Skype software application provides "soft phone" local and long-distance service for a PC and also incorporates video as an option.

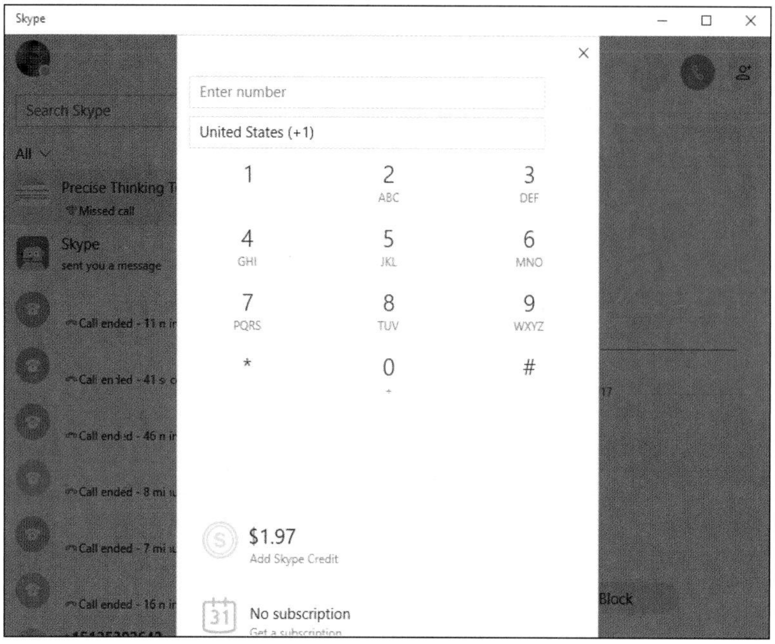

Goodheart-Willcox Publisher

SIP usually does not generate any charges when using the Internet for conversations between two soft phones. Charges are typically incurred when a soft phone connects to a hard phone using the Internet as the medium.

The typical default port for SIP is 5060 for UDP and 5061 for TCP. SIP is an application layer protocol for connecting network end points. You can think of network end points as configured in a point-to-point topology. The entire SIP RFC can be viewed at www.ietf.org/rfc/rfc3261.txt.

Real-time Transport Protocol (RTP)

Real-time Transport Protocol (RTP) is a standard as well as a protocol developed by IETF. The term *real time* means delivering the packets as fast as possible without any delay. To achieve this, RTP uses UDP; hence, it does not guarantee packet delivery. RTP is used to stream voice and video as used in video conferencing and gaming. RTP is typically used in conjunction with *Real-time Transport Control Protocol (RTCP)*. RTP is a packet design that carries the streaming data. RTCP is used to ensure quality of service and to monitor performance.

RTP may also use other protocols, such as SIP, H.225, and H.245, to accomplish its task. For example, a session may use SIP to establish a multimedia link, RTP to carry the multimedia, and SIP to terminate the session. RTP is an open standard that can be used by anyone when designing a communication system. It is up to the designer as to which protocols it uses with RTP to accomplish the task.

There are variations of RTP. Examples of these variations include Secure Real-time Transport Protocol (sRTP), which encrypts the RTP transmissions, thus securing them, and Compressed Real-time Transport Protocol (cRTP), which compresses the RTP packets, thus conserving bandwidth. Of the two, sRTP is probably more important. By itself, RTP is not encrypted, so all transmissions are sent in the open and could be intercepted with a common packet sniffer.

Copyright Goodheart-Willcox Co., Inc.

Basic VoIP Troubleshooting

The exact procedure for troubleshooting VoIP applications depends on the type of system installed, topology, and symptoms of the problem. First, you must determine if the problem is performance-related or a complete failure of the system. A performance issue is generally related to the quality of the VoIP service—in other words, how well a person can hear the conversation. Is the conversation clear, or is it garbled or broken up? Performance issues are typically caused by latency and jitter. A complete failure of the VoIP system generally relates to a connection failure between the destination and source. Both performance and complete failure can be verified in many cases by the use of a protocol analyzer. The protocol analyzer will prove to be of vital importance when troubleshooting VoIP systems.

Using a Protocol Analyzer to Verify Packet Exchange

2.3, 5.2   NET

A protocol analyzer can be used to verify the exchange of packets needed to support a VoIP service. Figure 12-18 shows a collection of packet exchanges between a VoIP destination and source captured with the Microsoft Network Monitor protocol analyzer. The packets were captured while a telephone call was made using a PC to a cell phone. As you can see, there are several IP addresses associated with the Skype VoIP call. The IP addresses are associated with the Skype Luxembourg office, Comcast Internet service provider, and IP address of the final destination.

Figure 12-18 The Microsoft Network Monitor protocol analyzer can be used to verify the packet exchange of a VoIP system such as Skype.

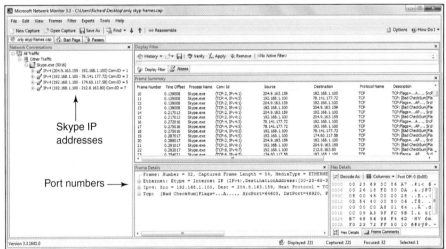

Goodheart-Willcox Publisher

In the figure, packet exchanges to and from the destination are verified. This is an indication that there is a complete network path and that the Skype VoIP system is in fact configured properly.

The use of a protocol analyzer can also be used to view the time it takes to exchange packets. In the figure, the time is listed in the **Time Offset** column. A latency of 250 microseconds will be very noticeable by the user.

A protocol analyzer can also be used to verify jitter by performing a TCP/IP trace. When a trace is performed, the protocol analyzer will automatically verify the stream of packets and indicate if any are missing from the stream. Missing packets result in jitter.

Copyright Goodheart-Willcox Co., Inc.

VoIP Jitter

Jitter, as associated with VoIP, will cause sound quality problems. It is caused by dropped or lost packets and results in a choppy voice transmission. If the jitter is severe enough, the conversation can be unintelligible. Many devices such as routers, switches, and gateways allow for the configuration of QoS, which improves VoIP quality and may eliminate jitter completely. For example, in Figure 12-19, a Linksys router is configured to enable the voice device "Skype" to have a high priority. This will allow Skype-related packets to be passed through the router before other types of packets associated with other software application.

QoS can also be configured for other software applications, such as online gaming, Google Hangouts, and Yahoo! Messenger. When the specific software application is not an identified option in the selection box, you can simply assign a priority to the port numbers directly related to the application.

Figure 12-19 The Cisco Linksys router provides support for QoS. You can configure priority for specific applications, which means the packets associated with the application will be sent through the router before other packets.

Goodheart-Willcox Publisher

Firewall Blocking VoIP Packets

One of the most common sources of VoIP problems is the computer's firewall blocking the packets. The firewall should be configured automatically during the VoIP software installation process to allow the exchange of VoIP packets. If the VoIP software application is newer than the existing computer operating system, then the computer's firewall may need to be configured manually to allow the packets to pass, as demonstrated in Figure 12-20. The port numbers associated with the VoIP software application can be found in the VoIP manufacturer's website, typically listed under Support or Frequently Asked Questions (FAQs). The PC may be connected to a switch or router before the modem in a small office or home office. When a router or switch is used to share the Internet connection, that device may need to be configured

Figure 12-20 Windows Firewall configured to allow packets associated with Skype to pass when the computer is in the Private or Public setting.

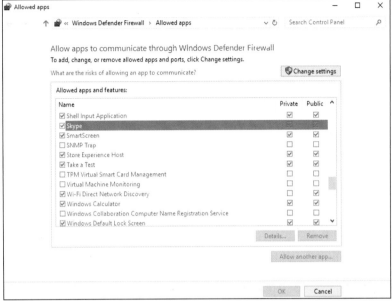

Goodheart-Willcox Publisher

to allow the VoIP application to pass through. Again, the device should be configured to accommodate specific port assignments associated with the VoIP software application.

If the VoIP system has never worked, then you have most likely made an error in the system configuration. You will need to check the installation instructions carefully and follow each step closely.

Audio Device Configuration

Another reason for complete failure could be due to the microphone, speaker, or headset. Sometimes, a user cannot get his or her VoIP system to work properly because he or she did not turn on the headset speaker switch or the microphone. Speaker and microphone configuration and testing can be completed through Windows Control Panel. Look at Figure 12-21, which shows the **Hardware and Sound** menu in Windows 7 Control Panel. This menu is very similar to that in Windows Vista Control Panel. By selecting the **Manage audio devices** option, you can verify the configuration of sound devices such as the microphone and speakers. You can also test these items to ensure they are working properly.

Troubleshooting a simple VoIP system is not very difficult—most of the time. A much more complex system that involves traditional telephone equipment merged into an Ethernet network system is far more difficult to troubleshoot. The manufacturer's resource guides must be referenced when troubleshooting the system. Manufacturers supply complete step-by-step guides to assist the network technician in correctly performing the troubleshooting task. The basic concepts presented in this section will most likely also be present in the manufacturer's materials.

Copyright Goodheart-Willcox Co., Inc.

Figure 12-21 You can configure and verify an audio device, such as if the speakers and microphone are working correctly, by accessing the **Manage audio devices** option in the Windows 10 Control Panel **Hardware and Sound** menu.

Goodheart-Willcox Publisher

Impedance Mismatch

Impedance mismatch is an electronics term, which refers to the effect of connecting two different electronic audio systems that have different electronic characteristics. When the two systems have different electronic characteristics, you will have an impedance mismatch. A common example of impedance mismatch is connecting a two-wire, local-loop telephone circuit to a four-wire telephone circuit. The two-wire circuit uses half-duplex communication because only one person can talk at a time. The same two wires carry the conversation to and from the source and destination. The four-wire circuit uses hybrid duplex communication, which means it can carry source and destination audio signals separately and simultaneously. This mismatch of two-wire and four-wire circuits is the most common cause of telephone audio echo. Impedance mismatch also occurs when VoIP technology uses telephone transmission cables for part of the circuit. Impedance mismatch is one of the most common causes of VoIP echo.

Copyright Goodheart-Willcox Co., Inc.

Summary

Voice and Audio Signals

- An analog signal is converted into a digital code by taking samples of the analog signal's amplitude at specific times.

- Sampling rate is the number of times a signal is sampled during a specific period.

- Sampling frequency is the number of times a signal is sampled per second.

- Jitter is the small staggers or hesitations in the delivery sequence of audio or video data and is caused by latency or missing packets.

- The term *latency* means the delay of data as it travels to its destination.

- While latency with a delay of approximately 250 milliseconds will be noticed by a user, it is acceptable.

- Acoustical echo is a condition that takes place when a microphone and a speaker are in close proximity or the audio is improperly adjusted, causing feedback.

Video

- Video images typically occur at a minimum rate of 24 frames per second.

- The term *codec* represents software, hardware, or combination of software and hardware that compresses and decompresses video and audio information.

Other Transmission Protocols

- X.25 is one of the early protocols used to transfer data over telephone lines.

- Frame Relay is a packet switching protocol that typically uses leased lines, such as T1, to carry data over long distances.

- The asynchronous transfer mode (ATM) protocol is designed to carry audio, video, and multimedia.

- The five ATM classifications are CBR, VBR-nrt, VBR-rt, ABR, and UBR.

- The maximum size of an ATM cell is 53 bytes, consisting of a 5-byte header and a 48-byte payload.

- Voice over IP (VoIP) is a technique that relies on the TCP/IP protocol suite to carry audio and video data.

- VoIP uses the UDP protocol when sending time-sensitive data, such as a telephone conversation.

- VoIP uses the TCP protocol when sending audio and video streaming data.

- A bandwidth shaper prioritizes network packets to ensure quality of service for time-sensitive applications.

- The H.323 protocol is used by telecommunication and telephone equipment.

- A gateway is used to convert the TCP/IP protocol to the H.323 protocol.

- The Session Initiation Protocol (SIP) is used for initiating, maintaining, and terminating the exchange of data.

Copyright Goodheart-Willcox Co., Inc.

- QoS was developed to minimize latency.
- The Real-time Transport Protocol (RTP) is used to stream voice and video as used in video conferencing and gaming.

Basic VoIP Troubleshooting

- A protocol analyzer is an excellent tool for identifying VoIP-related problems.
- Impedance mismatch refers to the effect of connecting two different electronic audio systems that have different electronic characteristics.

Review Questions

1. Converting digital pulses to an analog waveform is called _____ conversion.

2. Converting an analog waveform to digital pulses is called _____ conversion.

3. What is the number of times a sample is taken during a specific period referred to as?

4. What is jitter?

5. The delay of data from its origin to the final destination is called _____.

6. What is the principle use for MPEG compression?

7. What communication protocol is characterized by analog packets rather than digital packets for communication?

8. What is the maximum data rate of X.25?

9. What protocol could be called an upgrade of the X.25 protocol?

10. What is the maximum data rate of Frame Relay?

11. Which of the following scenarios requires the constant bit rate (CBR) classification of ATM communication?

    A. Live telephone conversation

    B. FAX

    C. Real-time broadcast of a movie

    D. Business conference call

    E. Cell phone conversation

    F. Transfer of an image from an archive

12. Which ATM classification provides the best support for video conferencing?

13. What does the phrase *variable bit rate* mean in reference to ATM classifications?

14. What is the total length of a typical ATM cell including the header?

15. What happens when one of the ATM cells is destroyed or does not reach the destination?

Copyright Goodheart-Willcox Co., Inc.

16. Why is the ATM cell payload so small (48 bytes)?

17. An ATM virtual path may contain two or more _____.

18. A switched virtual circuit (SVC) is a (temporary, permanent) _____ connection between two devices on a network.

19. Based on what two factors will an ATM switch drop a cell?

20. Which VoIP protocol is used to establish and terminate a VoIP session?

21. Which VoIP protocol is used to stream multimedia in real time between two network nodes?

22. What is another name for a *bandwidth shaper*?

23. What is the purpose of a bandwidth shaper?

24. What is the purpose of the QoS protocol?

25. What is the most common source of VoIP echo?

26. Name four factors that contribute to echo.

✚ Sample Network+ Exam Questions

1. Kelli is setting up VoIP and video conferencing for her company. She is concerned about any delay in video or audio packets. The delay of video/audio data packets is referred to as _____ in networking terminology.

   A. Packet Loss Ratio

   B. latency

   C. Variable Rate Overflow

   D. heading

2. You are working for a large telecommunication company. You are setting up ATM services for various customers. One particular customer is deeply concerned with quality of service. Which ATM data transfer classification provides the highest quality of ATM service?

   A. VBR

   B. CBR

   C. UBR

   D. ABR

3. Which upper-layer protocol is typically used to package voice data that is to be transferred using Voice over IP (VoIP) technology?

   A. PPP

   B. SLIP

   C. UDP

   D. CHAP

4. Which definition best describes multiplexing as it applies to ATM?

   A. Combining multiple signals or sequencing different data packet streams over a single medium.

   B. Combining several different protocols to use as a single protocol.

   C. Combining several different types of networking media to form one cohesive media.

   D. Combining separate data packets into one large data packet before transmitting across a single network line.

5. Which of the following statements are true concerning ATM? (Select all that apply.)

   A. The ATM protocol allows voice, video, and text data to be carried on the same media.

   B. The maximum cell size for ATM is 1500 bytes.

   C. ATM is a connection-oriented protocol.

   D. ATM is a connectionless protocol.

6. Horace works for a telecommunication company. He has to configure a variety of protocols. Right now, he is working with an older protocol that transmits data in the form of an analog signal. Which protocol transmits data in the form of an analog signal?

   A. IP

   B. IPX

   C. X.25

   D. ATM

7. Franklin has been asked to set up multimedia conferencing for a client. The client is concerned about achieving the highest data transmission rates possible. Franklin wants to use compression to help improve bandwidth utilization. Which compression method is used to achieve the highest data rates for multimedia over a network?

   A. MPEG-1

   B. X.25

   C. SLIP

   D. MPEG-4

8. Which protocol is used to support Internet telephony?

   A. CHAP

   B. VoIP

   C. SLIP

   D. AppleTalk

9. Which protocol is designed specifically to ensure the delivery of time-sensitive packets and reduce latency?

   A. QoS

   B. TCP

   C. X.25

   D. MPEG

10. Which telephone protocol suite is designed to support audio, video, and data communication?

    A. SLIP

    B. RADIUS

    C. RAS

    D. H.323

Copyright Goodheart-Willcox Co., Inc.

CHAPTER
13 Web Servers and Services

 ## Network+ Certification Exam Objectives

The Network+ Certification Exam presents questions about web server basics. It does not contain in-depth questions in this area. Rather, it tests your knowledge of protocols such as HTTP, HTML, POP3, IMAP4, SMTP, and FTP commonly used in conjunction with web servers and e-mail servers. You need a basic understanding of how these protocols are used. Also, be sure you can configure a workstation for e-mail. However, these are common tasks that any network administrator will need to perform frequently.

Objectives

1.1: Protocols and Ports—SMTP, FTP, TFTP, HTTP, HTTPS, POP, IMAP

3.4: HTTP/management URL

Remote File Access—FTP/FTPS, SFTP, TFTP

Learning Outcomes

- Differentiate between Internet, intranet, and extranet.
- Identify the parts and function of a URL.
- Describe the purpose of a web server.
- Explain how search engines retrieve search results.
- Differentiate between markup languages.
- Understand the function of File Transfer Protocol (FTP).
- Restate the purpose of Network News Transfer Protocol (NNTP).
- Summarize how e-mails are transferred from one device to another.

Copyright Goodheart-Willcox Co., Inc.

Key Terms

anonymous FTP site
cascading style sheets (CSS)
extensible markup language (XML)
extranet
File Transfer Protocol (FTP)
HTML tag
hyperlink
hypertext markup language (HTML)
Hypertext Transfer Protocol (HTTP)
Internet
Internet Message Access Protocol (IMAP)
intranet

JavaScript
mail filter
mail gateway
Multipurpose Internet Mail Extensions (MIME)
Network News Transfer Protocol (NNTP)
newsgroup
Post Office Protocol (POP)
search engine
Secure File Transfer Protocol (SFTP)
Simple Mail Transfer Protocol (SMTP)

Simple Object Access Protocol (SOAP)
spam
spammer
spamming
standard generalized markup language (SGML)
Trivial File Transfer Protocol (TFTP)
uniform resource locator (URL)
web browser
web server
website

Overview

The need for web servers has greatly increased over the years. Web servers provide a means to display informational pages to viewers across the World Wide Web or a local area network. E-mail has rapidly grown to become one of the most common forms of communication.

In this chapter, you will learn the differences between the three types of networks that provide web-page distribution. You will also be introduced to two of the most popular web-server software packages and to the basic operation of an e-mail system.

Internet, Intranet, and Extranet

Over the last few decades, the ability to navigate web pages for information and communication has become an ordinary occurrence. Most people know how to navigate and use the Internet to obtain information, but it is not the only source of web-page distribution. There are three types of networks that provide web-page distribution: Internet, intranet, and extranet. The type of access allowed to a network's web pages determines each classification.

Internet

An **Internet** is a collection of interconnected networks from all around the world. Put simply, it is all the various networks around the world communicating with each other. Therefore, when a person installs a web server for the Internet, he or she is establishing a computer to be accessed by anyone in the world. The Internet relies on the TCP/IP suite of protocols to transport web pages. The Internet is also referred to as the *World Wide Web* because when the various network cable connections that make up the Internet are diagrammed, it resembles a spider's web.

There are other types of networks that function similar to the Internet but on a limited or restricted basis. These networks are called *intranet* and *extranet* and are commonly found in business environments.

Tech Tip

An intranet has almost all of the characteristics of a website, but it is not a true website by strict definition.

Intranet

A web server need not be connected to the Internet to serve as a way for companies to communicate and to distribute information. A web server can be connected to an intranet. An **intranet** is a private network that serves a specific group of users within a LAN. For example, a corporation or an educational institution may set up a private web server to be accessed only by a designated group of users from within its local area network. In a corporation, an intranet is designed for only the employees to access. In an educational setting, it may be accessed only by school employees and students. Normally, an intranet cannot be freely accessed by anyone. If the intranet is accessible from the World Wide Web, the intranet uses a firewall to isolate it from the outside world. The main reason for access limitations is security.

An intranet can be used to post forms, explanations and examples of forms, policy books, maps, address books, and other important information. The advantage of using an intranet is users already know how to surf the Internet and can start using the system immediately. In a traditional network, a new user often needs training in how to access network shares and navigate directory structures. This is very common for human resources departments. They frequently place information on a company intranet for employees to access.

Extranet

An **extranet** allows internal access to web pages while simultaneously allowing authorized personnel from outside the network to access the network's web pages. An extranet is often designed to allow employees, business partners (other businesses), and customers access to the intranet from outside the network, through the Internet. Access to the extranet is available only if the user has a valid username and password. The username and password determines what areas of the extranet are accessible. For example, members of partner companies may have only limited access to the website, while employees may have full access to the website.

Look at Figure 13-1 for a comparison of an intranet and an extranet. Remember that an extranet does not let the general public access the website—only partner companies, employees, and authorized customers.

Domain Name and URL Resolution

Since the TCP/IP protocols use IP addresses to transfer data, the Internet must use the Domain Name Service (DNS) to translate domain names and uniform resource locators (URLs) to IP addresses. A **uniform resource locator (URL)** is a user-friendly name associated with an IP address. An example of a URL is http://support.microsoft.com. When a URL is typed into a web browser, the web browser uses a DNS server to translate or resolve the URL name to its IP address.

A user can directly access a web page by typing in the IP address of the web server that hosts the web page. This eliminates the need to use a DNS server to resolve the URL name to an IP address and may expedite access. However, people do not generally communicate by IP addresses. They use domain names.

A complete URL can be seen in Figure 13-2. Note the way the URL is expressed. The first item in the URL is the protocol. Typical choices are HTTP or FTP. The next part of the URL is the domain name of the web server hosting the site followed closely by the path to the resource or page desired. The path is actually a single directory or a directory with subdirectories on the web server that lead to the web-page file. In the example, the contact.aspx web page is located in the /contact directory. The port number at the end of the URL is optional and is not generally used. The default port number of a web-page TCP/IP connection is 80.

Copyright Goodheart-Willcox Co., Inc.

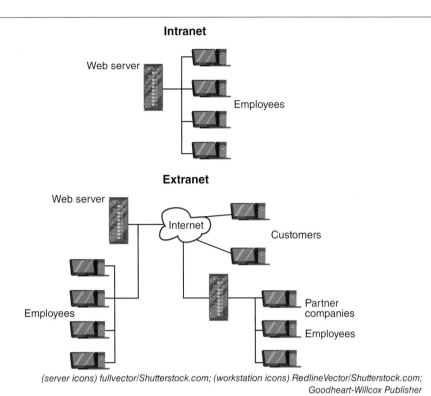

Intranet

Web server

Employees

Extranet

Web server

Internet

Customers

Employees

Partner companies

Employees

*(server icons) fullvector/Shutterstock.com; (workstation icons) RedlineVector/Shutterstock.com;
Goodheart-Willcox Publisher*

Figure 13-1 An intranet allows employees limited access to a company web server. The web server is accessible only through the company LAN. It is not accessible through the Internet. An extranet provides limited access to the company web server to both employees within the LAN and to customers, partner companies, and employees through the Internet.

URL

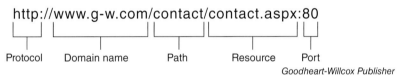

http://www.g-w.com/contact/contact.aspx:80

Protocol   Domain name   Path   Resource   Port

Goodheart-Willcox Publisher

Figure 13-2 Structure of a URL.

Tech Tip

Network proxy servers store IP and URL addresses in their cache to expedite the connection process. A proxy server intercepts all requests for websites and then provides the requested web page without the need to connect to the website. If the proxy server does not contain a copy of the requested page, it forwards the request to the website.

DNS is organized as a hierarchical structure with the root at the top. As discussed in Chapter 7, Microsoft Active Directory (AD) has a similar structure to DNS. NetBIOS domain names of earlier systems have come to look like a URL. Lightweight Directory Access Protocol (LDAP) has made it possible for Microsoft AD and DNS to look and function similarly. In each structure, the entire directory appears as though it is one structure on one computer; in reality, it can comprise many computers spread across the world. You may wish to review the DNS structure in Chapter 10.

Web Servers

A **web server** is, as the name implies, a server configured to provide web services. Essentially, any computer with software that is configured to respond to the HTTP protocol is a web server. To create a web server, a software package, such as Apache HTTP Server or Microsoft Internet Information Services (IIS), is installed on a computer. The computer can be a server or a PC. Typically, web-server software is installed on a server that is running a network operating system, such as Windows Server 2016. However, IIS can be installed on a PC running a workstation version of the Microsoft operating system, such as Windows 10. The only requirement is the computer should provide sufficient resources such as memory, CPU speed, and hard disk drive space to accommodate the software package.

A **website** is traditionally defined as a location on the World Wide Web. Each website on the World Wide Web contains a collection of web pages and files, which can be accessed through the Internet. A website is owned and managed by an individual, company, or organization.

For a web server to operate while connected to the Internet, it must be assigned a domain name and IP address. A domain name can be acquired through a domain name provider or a web-hosting service. A domain name must be registered before an IP address can be assigned to a web server. To obtain an IP address and domain name combination, the user submits an application to a domain name provider or web-hosting service for a nominal fee. Once the information is processed, an IP address is assigned to the domain name. The IP address must be a public IP address.

A domain name must be unique. In other words, the chosen domain name cannot be in use by another person or company. You can check whether your desired domain is unique by using the **whois** utility on the InterNIC website (www.internic.net). If the domain name you enter is in use, the **whois** utility displays information such as the domain name's registrar, the names of the name servers on which the domain name is listed, the date the domain name was assigned, and the date the domain name expires.

Figure 13-3 shows the **whois** utility screen prior to a request for information. Figure 13-4 shows the detailed results of a search for the google.com domain name. The **whois** utility can conduct searches by the domain name, registrar name, or name server. The name server can be listed as a domain name or an IP address.

There are several ways to set up a web server. A web server can be established on the same server as the network server, a server dedicated to only web services, and a web-hosting company's website.

A web server can run on the same server as the network server, especially if the LAN has only one server. In fact, web-server services can be run from a workstation. For example, installing Internet Information Services (IIS) on a Windows workstation allows the workstation to run a single website that can be accessed by a maximum of ten simultaneous users.

Figure 13-3 The **whois** utility can be accessed through the InterNIC website.

Goodheart-Willcox Publisher

Figure 13-4 The results of a **whois** search.

Goodheart-Willcox Publisher

Copyright Goodheart-Willcox Co., Inc.

A dedicated server can be used to host web services. A *dedicated server* serves only one function. However, more than one website can be hosted from a single server.

A company or organization may choose to have a web-hosting company host its website. A *web-hosting company* sells space on its web server, allowing a company or organization to establish a website without the need of owning and supporting a web server.

Figures 13-5 and 13-6 illustrate the two most common scenarios of web hosting. Each has advantages and disadvantages. For a large website consisting of many pages and a large volume of traffic, it is probably less expensive to install a web server in-house. For a smaller website with a low volume of traffic, using a web-hosting company is more appropriate. Using a company that provides most of your web-hosting needs is called *outsourcing*. Look at the chart in Figure 13-7 to see how some of the factors of website operation compare between hosting your own website and outsourcing your website.

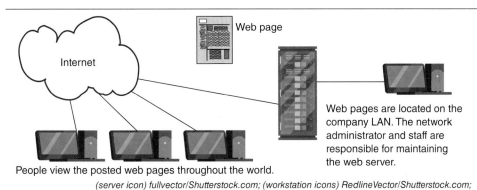

People view the posted web pages throughout the world.

Web pages are located on the company LAN. The network administrator and staff are responsible for maintaining the web server.

(server icon) fullvector/Shutterstock.com; (workstation icons) RedlineVector/Shutterstock.com; Goodheart-Willcox Publisher

Figure 13-5 When a web server is part of a company's LAN, the network administrator and staff are responsible for maintaining the server.

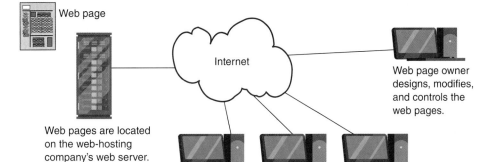

Web pages are located on the web-hosting company's web server.

People view the posted web pages throughout the world.

Web page owner designs, modifies, and controls the web pages.

(server icon) fullvector/Shutterstock.com; (workstation icons) RedlineVector/Shutterstock.com; Goodheart-Willcox Publisher

Figure 13-6 Web-hosting companies can provide web services. In this scenario, the web page owner is responsible for the content and design of web pages. The web-hosting company is responsible for supporting and maintaining the server.

Apache HTTP Server

The most widely used web-server software is Apache HTTP Server. The main reason for its popularity is its price. Programmers with a common interest developed the Apache HTTP Server software for free. The Apache HTTP Server software can be downloaded from the Apache Software Foundation website at www.apache.org, or it can be bought as a package with documentation and extra utilities for a modest price. Documentation and additional references are available at the Apache Software Foundation website. Once Apache is installed and started on a server, a manual can be accessed through http://localhost/manual/index.html. The manual is a complete

Figure 13-7 Comparison of outsourcing a website and hosting your own website.

Outsourcing Your Website	Hosting Your Own Website
Server space used is prorated.	Owner must purchase and install server hardware and software.
Technical support is provided.	An expert technician is required.
Connectivity is provided. Fee varies according to traffic volume.	Owner must obtain and pay for connectivity such as DSL, cable modem, T1 line, or other high-bandwidth connection.
Most services, such as administration and maintenance, are provided.	Frequent administration, maintenance, and security checks are needed.
Website design is not provided. Some companies offer a one-time design service for free on a limited number of pages.	Need web-page design software and personnel competent to use it.

Goodheart-Willcox Publisher

user guide with information about all aspects of installing and using Apache HTTP Server.

Apache HTTP Server software is generally associated with Linux and Unix systems. However, versions of Apache HTTP Server software are available for all the major network operating systems.

Internet Information Services (IIS)

The Internet Information Services (IIS) is the Microsoft Windows default web-server service. IIS supports website creation and management. Some service protocols supported by IIS include the Network News Transfer Protocol (NNTP), File Transfer Protocol (FTP), and Simple Mail Transfer Protocol (SMTP). These protocols are covered in detail later in this chapter.

IIS is not installed by default on a Microsoft server. Services such as IIS, FTP, SMTP, and NNTP must be installed as additional services. Figure 13-8 shows the **Windows Features** dialog box, which lists additional services to turn off or on. The checkbox for Internet Information Services (IIS) is filled, indicating that only part of the IIS feature is turned on. A check mark indicates that all of a feature is turned on.

Microsoft's original web-page program is called *FrontPage*. FrontPage is not as robust as other web page and website development tools. Microsoft subsequently moved to a tool called *Microsoft Expression*. Microsoft Expression does not require extensions (supportive software programs) to be installed on the host server as was required with FrontPage. Microsoft Expression is a complete suite of programs and utilities that are as powerful as any other web-page suite today. This tool has been around for many years and is relatively stable in terms of web-page software. To learn more about the Microsoft Expression web suite, visit www.microsoft.com/expression.

Figure 13-9 shows the default page for IIS, using Windows 10. The page shown will display on the Windows web server and from a workstation accessing the web server.

Tech Tip

IIS can be installed on a Windows workstation and support a maximum of 10 simultaneous connections. This is a great way to experiment with web-page designs and web-server technologies.

Copyright Goodheart-Willcox Co., Inc.

Figure 13-8 Internet Information Services and other services can be installed through the **Windows Features** dialog box.

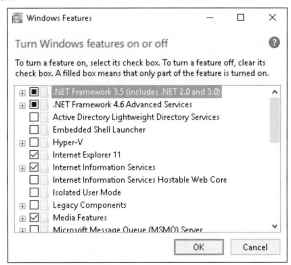

Goodheart-Willcox Publisher

Figure 13-9 Default IIS web page displayed on the web server or from a Windows workstation.

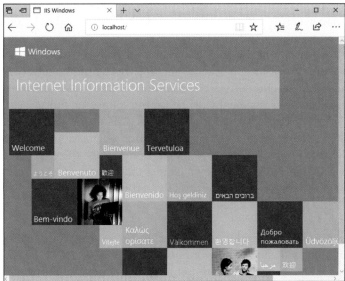

Goodheart-Willcox Publisher

Search Engines

A **search engine** is a software program that is designed to locate websites and pages by relevant terms entered into the search text box. Most web browsers incorporate a search engine, but web browsers and search engines are technically two different software applications. For example, Microsoft Bing and Google are the two most widely known and used search engines in the world. Google also offers specialized search engines. One that will be of particular interest to students is Google Scholar. Whereas search engines normally search every website they can reach, Google Scholar limits its searches to peer-reviews journals, university websites, and governmental websites. This means that Google Scholar will retrieve fewer results for a given search, but the results will be more likely to retrieve reliable sources.

Figure 13-10 shows Microsoft Edge (the web browser) with Google (the search engine) set as the default search engine. Keep in mind that Microsoft recently

Tech Tip

To determine if a software application is a web browser or a search engine, enter **C:** into the address bar. A web browser such as Microsoft Edge, Google Chrome, or Mozilla Firefox will display the contents of the **C** partition. If you enter **C:** into a search-engine text box, results will be displayed with web page and website locations related to the term **C:.**

Copyright Goodheart-Willcox Co., Inc.

Figure 13-10 The Microsoft Edge web browser with Google set as the default search engine.

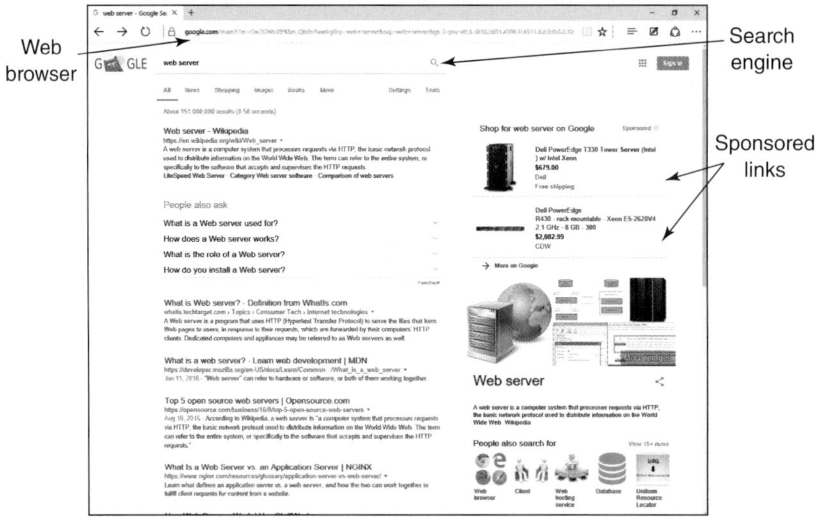

Web browser

Search engine

Sponsored links

Web server

Goodheart-Willcox Publisher

replaced Internet Explorer with Microsoft Edge. The web browser has an address bar in which you can enter a website URL or IP address. The search engine has a search text box in which to enter relevant key terms. Notice in Figure 13-10 the term web server is used to generate a list of corresponding web pages and websites.

The reason web browsers and search engines are free software applications is they display advertised links as part of an Internet search. Sponsored links or paid advertisements are used to generate money for the search engine company, thus providing the search-engine software application for free to users. The actual results relevant to the search term(s) begin just below the sponsored links.

Search engine companies maintain millions of listings in a database correlated to search terms. The exact method used by search engine companies to rate web pages and websites is a closely guarded secret. Even though the exact method is kept secret, there are some commonly known factors that influence search engine results.

One factor is that you can apply directly to the search engine company to have your website and web pages listed. Some companies will list the site for free while others charge a fee.

Another factor is a search engine searches the entire World Wide Web using software programs known as *spiders* or *bots*. The spiders or bots collect information about web page content such as terms found on the page and links to other web pages and websites. The search engine company collects the data and stores it in large server farms. When a user enters search terms or key words into a search-engine text box, the terms are compared to terms in the database.

Finally, a website can have a high ranking. One key to having a high ranking in a search engine is to have a web page that has many links to it from other websites. The more links to the page from other websites, the more popular the web page, hence, a higher ranking by the search engine company.

NET
1.1, 3.4

Website Communication

Website communication is based on the Hypertext Transfer Protocol (HTTP) and the hypertext markup language (HTML). The **Hypertext Transfer Protocol (HTTP)** is a protocol designed for communication between a web browser and a web server. **Hypertext markup language (HTML)** is a programming language used to create web pages. It can be interpreted by any type of computer with any type of web browser.

Copyright Goodheart-Willcox Co., Inc.

A **web browser** is a software program that permits the user to navigate the World Wide Web and then interpret and display web pages. The most common web browsers incorporate other software programs such as e-mail clients and security features. Some popular web browsers are Microsoft Edge (formerly Internet Explorer), Google Chrome, Apple Safari, and Mozilla Firefox. There are other, less well-known browsers such as Opera, for cxample.

HTML

HTML also provides a means for linking to other web pages or to an area on the same web page. A link to another web page or to an area on the same web page is called a **hyperlink**. A user simply clicks the hyperlink and the web browser automatically replaces the current web page with the web page designated in the hyperlink or "jumps" to a specified area within the web page.

A web page contains text and special symbols defined by HTML tags. HTML tags are also referred to as *markups*. An **HTML tag** is an instruction for how the text and graphics should appear when displayed in a web browser. For example, HTML tags determine the size, style, and color of the text font and identify the placement of graphics. A web browser interprets the HTML tags to make the text and graphics appear on the display as specified.

Figure 13-11 shows the Goodheart-Willcox Publisher web page as it appears in Microsoft Edge. Figure 13-12 shows a section of coding used to represent the page. In this image, one can see how the HTML tags and information combine to present the information in a web browser.

The HTML standard was developed by the World Wide Web Consortium (W3C). As discussed in Chapter 1, W3C is a nonprofit organization dedicated to the development of voluntary standards for the web. The consortium has spent many years developing the standards for SGML, HTML, and XML.

SGML

Standard generalized markup language (SGML) is the original standard for both HTML and XML. HTML is a compact version of SGML. XML was developed to

Figure 13-11 A web browser interprets the HTML tags in the web page coding to display the text and graphics.

Goodheart-Willcox Publisher

Copyright Goodheart-Willcox Co., Inc.

Figure 13-12 Example of coding used to create the Goodheart-Willcox Publisher home page.

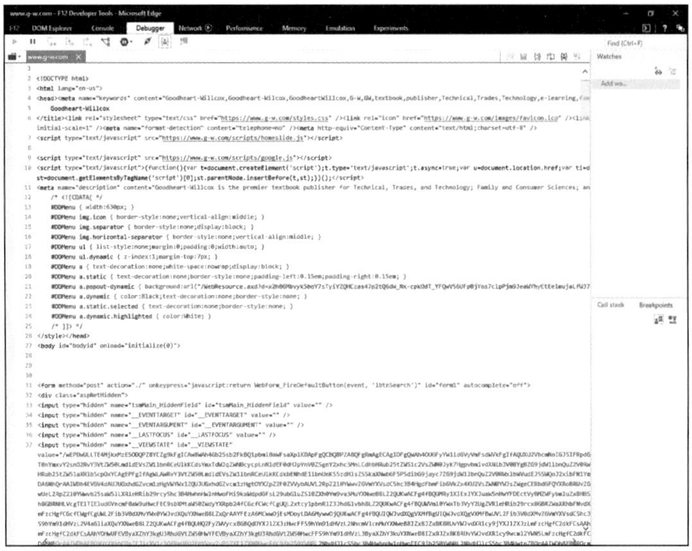

Goodheart-Willcox Publisher

enhance HTML. Today, *extensible hypertext markup language (XHTML)* is a variation of XML and is the recommended replacement for HTML.

XML

Extensible markup language (XML) is designed especially for large enterprise business applications running on web servers and is greatly enhanced compared to HTML. While XML is based on the same principles as HTML, it has one very important difference: XML allows the creation of custom tags. XML also identifies the data contained inside the tags, while HTML only identifies how to display the data identified by the tag. For example, HTML uses tags to identify the size, font, or color of a block of text. XML can do the same, but it can also identify the contents, such as a numerical calculation for a database or spreadsheet. This allows the contents to be easily accessed and manipulated by a database or spreadsheet program. XML was designed with business applications in mind. XML can be easily converted to HTML and displayed through a browser. This ensures downward compatibility for systems.

CSS

The latest markup language is CSS. **Cascading style sheets (CSS)** is a style-sheet language that defines the presentation and layout of all pages in a website. Think of CSS as an enhancement to HTML tags rather than a separate new language. A CSS script is a set of program instructions written as plain text and saved as a file on the website. When CSS is used as a separate script file, it can be referenced by any and all web pages in the entire website. The advantage of using CSS is a web designer can make changes to all web-page content or HTML tags in every page in the website from a single location. For example, the CSS file can contain a description of the navigation bar that appears on every web page in the site. By modifying the contents of the CSS file, the appearance of the navigation bar on every web page will be affected. Before CSS, a web designer would need to make changes to the navigation bar on each website page. CSS can save a web designer many hours of work caused by website changes.

Copyright Goodheart-Willcox Co., Inc.

JavaScript

JavaScript is a programming language that is designed to be embedded into an HTML web page and allows the user to interact with the web page. For example, an online order form is most often written in JavaScript. The information filled into the text boxes of the form are typically sent to a server and inserted into a database. The database information can then be acted on.

To learn more about programming languages for web pages, visit the W3Schools website at www.w3schools.com. W3Schools has an extensive collection of excellent tutorial programs. Try out the HTML tutorial. There is an interactive tutorial web page that allows users to modify web-page content and view the effect immediately. This is a great way to learn the basics of web-page programming and construction.

SOAP

Simple Object Access Protocol (SOAP) is a set of rules for web-based messages and is constructed from XML. It allows a client to freely interact with a web page on a web server, rather than download it. For example, a database stored on a web server can be accessed and manipulated by an authorized client without downloading any database records. Also, a program can be run on the web server while viewed by the client.

SOAP combined with XML and HTML technologies solves the problem of exchanging data and information between two incompatible systems such as Windows and UNIX. Normally, the two operating systems require a gateway or the installation of additional protocols to support communication. By using HTML, XML, and SOAP technologies, the two incompatible systems are able to communicate without additional modifications.

The use of SOAP to access and run applications on a web server has led to a phrase coined by Microsoft—*Web Services*. The phrase *Web Services* means that services can be provided through web pages.

File Transfer Protocol (FTP)

NET
1.1, 3.4

The **File Transfer Protocol (FTP)** supports file transfers between a client and a server and can be incorporated into a web server. FTP uses TCP packets and establishes a connection between the client and server. FTP is accessed using an FTP client that is either text-based or GUI-based. When using a text-based FTP client, a series of commands are issued at an FTP prompt similar to the way commands are issued at a DOS prompt. The following is a list of some common FTP commands and their functions:

bye	Exit the FTP program
cd/directory	Change the directory on the FTP site
get	Transfer a file from the FTP site to the client
help	Display FTP commands
lcd	Change the directory on the client
open	Open a connection to an FTP site
put	Transfer a file from the client to the FTP site
pwd	Display the current directory of the FTP site
quit	Close the FTP session

Copyright Goodheart-Willcox Co., Inc.

To start the FTP utility, go to the DOS prompt and enter the **ftp** command. Use the **help** command to display a list of FTP commands, as shown in Figure 13-13. To get help with a specific command, type **help** followed by the command. To exit the FTP program, enter the **bye** command.

Most web-page software has its own utility for uploading a file to the web server FTP directory. There are also many third-party utilities available.

Most web browsers can be used to access an FTP site by simply changing the protocol in the web browser's address bar from http: to ftp:. One important difference between most websites and an FTP site is that files can be uploaded to an FTP site but not to a website. However, files can be downloaded from both a website and an FTP site.

Figure 13-14 shows a computer connected to an FTP site using FileZilla. FileZilla is a free download and can be used as a robust FTP client for any FTP site. It also supports secure FTP, which will be examined in this chapter.

One of the main disadvantages of an FTP site is the lack of security. FTP does not encrypt passwords or the contents of transferred files. If security is a concern, another utility and protocol should be used to ensure secure data transfers. One such tool is Microsoft File Transfer Manager. This tool provides security and guarantees file delivery over the Internet. It is available as a free download from Microsoft.

Figure 13-13 A list of **ftp** commands can be displayed by entering **help** at the FTP command prompt.

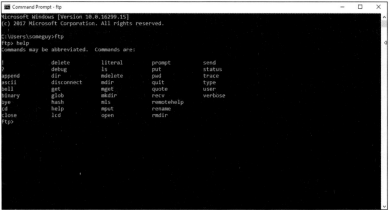

Goodheart-Willcox Publisher

Figure 13-14 Example of an FTP site displayed through FileZilla.

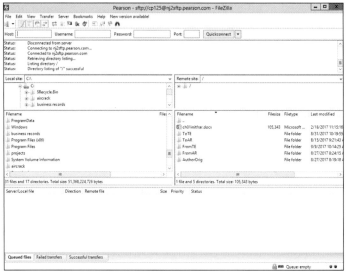

Goodheart-Willcox Publisher

FTP Variations

Two other variations of the FTP protocol are Trivial File Transfer Protocol and Secure File Transfer Protocol. **Trivial File Transfer Protocol (TFTP)** is a lightweight version of FTP. TFTP never requires the use of a username and password because it uses UDP packets for transferring data. Since UDP packets are used, a connection is never established between the client and server. The client is allowed to transfer files, but not to view the directory listing at the FTP site. TFTP uses fewer commands than FTP.

Secure File Transfer Protocol (SFTP) is a secure version of FTP. SFTP uses TCP packets and therefore establishes a connection using a username and password. It encrypts the username, password, and data to provide the highest level of security compared to FTP and TFTP. SFTP should be used when transferring sensitive data or when security is required.

Anonymous FTP Site

One of the easiest FTP sites to administer is an anonymous FTP site. An **anonymous FTP site** allows anyone to access the site and download or upload files. No password or any other form of authentication is required. Since no real form of authentication is required, the site is always at risk of being vandalized. It is better to require some form of authentication such as an e-mail address or to have a list of authorized usernames and passwords. With proper authentication required, an administrator can determine who accessed the site, when the site was accessed, and what files were downloaded or uploaded.

Another major problem with anonymous FTP sites is the unauthorized use of the site. If anyone can access the site using the *anonymous* username, he or she can store illegal files on the site. It is a common practice of crackers to use anonymous FTP sites to store their stolen files. They do not run the risk of being caught with stolen files on their own computer. They can gain access to their files on the anonymous site at any time in the future.

FTP sites established as secure sites should always have their security tested. Try accessing the FTP site from another computer using some of the commands mentioned earlier.

Internet Information Services can activate a log of activities at the website or FTP site. Common information contained in the IIS log file is client address, username, date and time of access, server name, IP address, and number of bytes downloaded or uploaded.

Tech Tip

A *cracker* is an unauthorized user who infiltrates the network to create problems or to disrupt or steal information. A *hacker* simply breaks in to see if he or she can but does no real damage.

Network News Transfer Protocol (NNTP)

Network News Transfer Protocol (NNTP) is designed to distribute news messages to NNTP clients and NNTP servers across the Internet. It is part of the TCP/IP suite of protocols. News articles are stored in a central NNTP server and distributed automatically to other NNTP servers and clients.

News articles are arranged in groups or categories referred to as **newsgroups**. A newsgroup is also referred to as a *discussion group*. There are many different newsgroups available. Each newsgroup is dedicated to a particular Microsoft product and contains a collection of messages posted by individuals. The messages consist of questions and answers. You can join a discussion or post a question to a newsgroup. Members of the group will post responses to your question. A complete listing of all responses is available for reading.

Copyright Goodheart-Willcox Co., Inc.

A client is required in order to access, download, and read the contents of an NNTP server. There are various newsreader clients designed for accessing and reading the messages posted on an NNTP server. Microsoft Outlook can be used to access a network news server and read and post messages.

Figure 13-15 shows an example of a newsgroup message being posted on one of Microsoft's newsgroups. The message concerns three quick fixes for stubborn PC problems. The message and link are being displayed in Microsoft Outlook. Notice in the left panel that the newsgroup messages are displayed separately from the e-mails. Originally, newsgroups distributed simple text-based articles. Today, newsgroup communication is greatly enhanced. Newsgroup communication provides links to web pages that contain the articles rather than displaying simple text messages.

Microsoft ended support of its newsgroups program in 2010 and replaced it with a more forum-based service called the Microsoft Community. Figure 13-16 shows the Microsoft Community web page. From this page, users can select a category or search the Community for a topic similarly to how topics were found on the newsgroup page. Microsoft still sends newsgroup messages to Outlook e-mails similar to what was shown in Figure 13-15.

Figure 13-15 Example of a newsgroup message displayed in Microsoft Outlook.

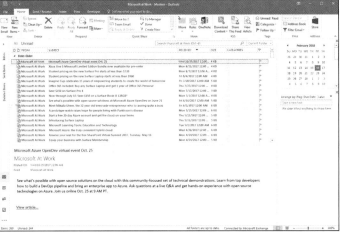

Goodheart-Willcox Publisher

Figure 13-16 Categories of posts and discussion available on the Microsoft Community web page.

Goodheart-Willcox Publisher

Copyright Goodheart-Willcox Co., Inc.

E-Mail

You are probably familiar with e-mail as a user but not with its underlying protocols and standards. Early in the history of networking, e-mail was viewed as a novelty rather than a necessity. Early e-mail messages contained text information only and not the rich formats viewed today that include various fonts, pictures, sounds, and multimedia.

In the simplest terms, an e-mail system consists of a mail server and an e-mail client. The mail server is responsible for forwarding e-mail to other servers and storing e-mail until a client can retrieve them. The user must use an e-mail client, also referred to as an *e-mail agent*, to communicate with the mail server and to retrieve the messages. An ISP or a private network, such as one run by a corporation, can provide a mail server. In other words, the e-mail service could be limited to a private network or could span the world using the Internet. In the following sections, the protocols most commonly associated with e-mail are covered. They are SMTP, POP, and IMAP.

Simple Mail Transfer Protocol (SMTP)

Simple Mail Transfer Protocol (SMTP) is part of the TCP/IP protocol suite and is designed to transfer plain-text e-mail from an e-mail client to a mail server and from one mail server to another. Figure 13-17 depicts a mail server that has been connected to the Internet, where it forwards messages to other mail servers. The PC uses an e-mail client with the POP or IMAP protocol to access messages on a mail server. The mail server uses the POP or IMAP protocol to communicate with and to download e-mail to the client.

1.1   NET

Figure 13-17 The SMTP protocol is used to send mail from an e-mail client to a mail server and from a mail server to a mail server. The POP3, IMAP, and HTTP protocols are used to retrieve e-mail from mail servers.

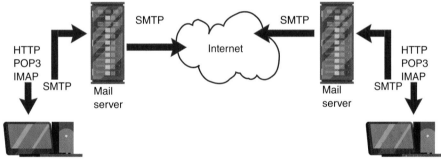

(server icons) fullvector/Shutterstock.com; (workstation icons) RedlineVector/Shutterstock.com;
Goodheart-Willcox Publisher

When creating an e-mail account, the mail server is designated as an SMTP server for sending e-mail and as a POP3 or IMAP server for retrieving e-mail. Two separate mail servers may be used—one for sending e-mail and the other for receiving e-mail—or one server may be used for sending and receiving e-mail. In either case, two server names typically need to be supplied when creating an e-mail account.

Figure 13-18 shows a typical Windows **Internet Connection** dialog box associated with establishing an e-mail account. Notice the requirements, such as selecting the type of incoming mail server, the name of the incoming mail server, and the name of the outgoing mail server. If the same server is used for incoming and outgoing e-mail, the same server name will appear in each text box. The protocol choices for the incoming mail server include POP3 and IMAP. The outgoing mail server is limited

Figure 13-18 Setting up an e-mail account with the Windows **Internet Connection**. Notice the choices for the type of incoming mail server. Also note that an incoming mail server and an outgoing mail server must be specified.

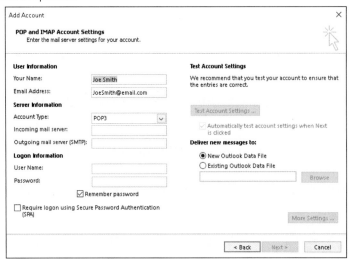

Goodheart-Willcox Publisher

to the SMTP protocol. Each of these protocols has a secure version that is encrypted with TLS: POP3S (port 995), IMAPS (port 993), and SMTPS (port 465).

Tech Tip

An e-mail server that hosts the POP or IMAP protocol can be called a *POP server* or an *IMAP server*. A server that hosts the SMTP protocol can be called an *SMTP server*.

Post Office Protocol (POP)

The **Post Office Protocol (POP)** is a simple protocol designed to access a mail server and download e-mail to an e-mail client. In contrast to IMAP, POP does not allow a user to store messages on the mail server. Stored e-mail resides on the user's local hard drive, not the mail server's hard drive. Typically, as soon as a POP mail account is opened, the server begins downloading e-mail to the PC. There are various versions of POP: POP, POP2, and POP3. Today, these protocols are simply referred to as *POP* or *POP3*. Many e-mail service providers are moving away from POP3 toward IMAP.

Internet Message Access Protocol (IMAP)

Internet Message Access Protocol (IMAP) is used to access messages stored on a mail server in similar fashion to POP. There are various releases of IMAP, such as IMAP, IMAP2, IMAP3, and IMAP4. When compared with POP, IMAP is a more sophisticated protocol because it can manipulate the e-mail while it is on the server. You can view the e-mail headers and content before downloading the e-mail. IMAP allows you to select the e-mail that you want to download rather than automatically downloading all of the e-mail for you. You can also store the e-mail on the mail server rather than on the client. One advantage of storing e-mail on the server is the server may be automatically backed up each day. Important e-mail can be retained even if your PC's hard drive fails.

The IMAP protocol also allows the user to access his or her e-mail from more than one PC. A user can access e-mail and then leave the e-mail on the server.

This means that a user can access e-mail from home, work, or while traveling. Copies of the e-mails can be stored on more than one computer, such as a home computer or laptop. With the POP protocol, all e-mail is downloaded to a PC and is deleted from the e-mail server. If a user accesses the mail server from another PC, the previously downloaded e-mail is no longer available. Any new e-mail on the mail server is downloaded instead. E-mail is spread across the total number of computers you use to access your e-mail, rather than stored in one central location.

The downside to the way IMAP handles e-mail storage is the mail server must provide sufficient space for all e-mail users. Storage space could be limited, which forces the e-mail user to remove some of his or her e-mail from the server to provide space for new e-mail. Also, a large e-mail, such as one with a graphic or sound attachment, might very well use all the storage space provided for the e-mail account, causing other e-mail delivery attempts to be rejected.

It may seem that all e-mail clients should use IMAP rather than POP. This is not always the case. For example, a corporate organization may choose to use POP rather than IMAP because POP is less resource-intensive than IMAP. POP e-mail would not burden the network server the way IMAP would. Also, IMAP would create more network traffic than POP because IMAP allows a greater number of port numbers.

Multipurpose Internet Mail Extensions (MIME)

Multipurpose Internet Mail Extensions (MIME) is a protocol that encodes additional information known as mail attachments to e-mail protocols that normally could not transfer attachments such as graphics. SMTP is designed only to transfer text material between servers and from clients. MIME allows e-mail attachments to be transferred as separate files using SMTP as the transport protocol. Not all mail servers support MIME, but most do. Some do not support MIME by design to reduce the amount of traffic on a network. Remember that mail attachments such as music and animation require a lot of bandwidth and can congest a network. Simple text messages do not cause severe congestion.

E-Mail Address Format

An e-mail address is based on the domain name system of addresses. The following are typical e-mail address formats:

- someone@email.com
- someone@NewAccounts.email.com
- someone@email.com.uk

The username or mailbox name in the example is *someone*. The host name follows the @ symbol. Then the type of domain is identified after the period. The type of domain in the example is .com for commercial. There are many domain types and names, such as .gov for government or .org for organization. For addresses outside the United States, there is an additional country code such as .uk for United Kingdom or .ca for Canada.

E-Mail Structure

Figure 13-19 shows an example of an e-mail structure. In the example, you can see how HTML commands, or tags, are used to form e-mail. The HTTP **<message>** tag is used with the attributes **to =**, **from =**, and **subject =**. These attributes form the e-mail header. The HTML **<text>** tag identifies the text portion of the e-mail.

Of course, e-mail clients are much more sophisticated than the previous example. The example is used to illustrate how HTTP commands are combined with

Copyright Goodheart-Willcox Co., Inc.

HTML tags to form a basic e-mail structure. Typical e-mail incorporates icons and visual elements from other programming languages to hide HTML coding. The same message would appear in an e-mail client as in the screen capture shown in Figure 13-20.

Figure 13-19 Example HTML commands, or tags, used to form an e-mail.

```
<message to="JoeSmith@email.com" from="Richard@rmroberts.com"
        subject="Chapter revision">
        <text>
        Good morning Joe
        Attached is the latest chapter revision for Chapter 13.
        Richard
        </text>
/message>
```

Goodheart-Willcox Publisher

Figure 13-20 E-mail client software hides the HTML coding from the user.

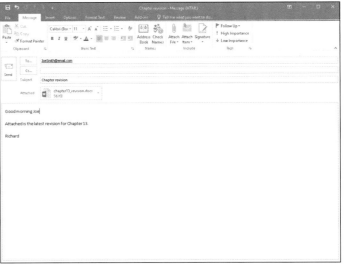

Goodheart-Willcox Publisher

Mail Filter

A **mail filter** blocks, or filters, unwanted e-mail messages such as spam. **Spam** is unwanted e-mail messages distributed to a large number of users. The distribution of unsolicited e-mail is called **spamming**. E-mails are sent as broadcasts to numerous mailboxes using a list of known mailboxes or programs that randomly generate mailbox addresses. A **spammer** often sends e-mail with some sort of advertisement as a probe. The spammer often includes a line that says something like, "If you received this e-mail by mistake or want to be removed from our mailing list, simply reply to this e-mail address." If the recipient responds to the e-mail, the spammer receives an e-mail reply with a legitimate e-mail address to add to his or her list of e-mail addresses. The spammer can use this e-mail address in the future or sell it. Many legitimate companies or organizations do offer a genuine removal from an e-mail list service. If you receive unsolicited e-mail from an unknown source, the best advice is do *not* reply!

Mail filters can be placed on servers or desktops. The filtering technique varies among the different mail filter systems available. Most e-mail clients contain some sort of filtering feature. For example, Microsoft Outlook allows you to identify undesirable sources of e-mail.

Microsoft Outlook has two features available called *block sender* and *message rule*. Block sender blocks messages based on the mailbox address of the sender. Message rule filters mail contents based on header or letter body contents, or both. The filter can be based on one or more words. For example, you can filter all incoming mail that contains the phrase "act now" or "immediate response required" in the message header or body. By guessing the most common sales terminology used, you can block unwanted spam, but you must be careful. The filter acts solely on the words or phrases present in the message. If a friend sends e-mail to you with the same phrase, your friend's e-mail will be filtered.

Mail Gateway

A **mail gateway** is a special software and device used to connect two normally incompatible e-mail systems. For example, two e-mail systems that cannot be directly translated require a gateway to act as an intermediate. The gateway translates e-mail protocols so they can be read by the other e-mail system. Sometimes the contents can be translated, but not the attachment. In other words, the textual contents of the message can be transferred between the two systems, but the attached graphic or audio file cannot.

Tech Tip

When troubleshooting e-mail systems, *always* attempt to send an e-mail that contains a short, plain text message and no fancy paper backdrops or attachment. Many times an e-mail problem between two different systems is a result of the enhanced e-mail or a lesser-known e-mail client. If the plain text e-mail is successfully delivered, it will ensure that the network infrastructure is intact and that the SMTP system is working correctly. You can then turn your attention to e-mail client compatibility.

Copyright Goodheart-Willcox Co., Inc.

Summary

Internet, Intranet, and Extranet

- The Internet is a worldwide network that anyone can use for communication.

- An intranet is typically a private, web-based network limited to a select set of clients.

- An extranet is a combination of a private and public web-based network.

Domain Name and URL Resolution

- A uniform resource locator (URL) is a user-friendly name that resolves to an IP address.

- A Domain Name System (DNS) server translates URLs to IP addresses.

- Microsoft Active Directory (AD) relies on the Lightweight Directory Access Protocol (LDAP) to communicate directory information between clients and servers.

Web Servers

- Web servers provide services, such as web page, file transfer, and e-mail, to clients.

- The **whois** utility provides information about domain name owners.

- Apache is the most widely used web-server software package.

Search Engines

- Search engines are software applications designed to located relevant web pages and websites based on search terms.

- A search engine searches the entire World Wide Web using software programs known as *spiders* or *bots* that collect information about web page content, which is collected and stored in large server farms. When a user enters search terms or key words into a search-engine text box, the terms are compared to terms in the database.

Website Communication

- Web-based communication is based on HTTP and HTML standards.

- The Hypertext Transfer Protocol (HTTP) is designed for communication between a web client and a web server.

- The hypertext markup language (HTML) is a programming language.

- Web browsers are designed to navigate the World Wide Web and to display web-page contents.

- XML is an enhanced markup language that supports client interaction with server applications.

- CSS is an enhancement to HTML tags that allows a web designer to make changes to each web page at one time rather than individually.

- JavaScript allows a visitor of a website to enter into a web-based form information that is then stored in a database.

- SOAP is a protocol designed to support XML and run applications on a web server.

Copyright Goodheart-Willcox Co., Inc.

File Transfer Protocol (FTP)

- The File Transfer Protocol (FTP) supports file transfers between a client and an FTP server.
- TFTP is a simpler version of FTP that uses fewer commands.
- SFTP securely transfers data by encrypting usernames, passwords, and data.
- An anonymous FTP site permits file transfers without the need of a required password or username.

Network News Transfer Protocol (NNTP)

- Network News Transfer Protocol (NNTP) distributes news messages to clients and servers across the Internet.
- Articles are grouped by *newsgroup*.

E-Mail

- Incoming mail server choices are typically limited to POP3, IMAP, and HTTP.
- An outgoing mail server is typically an SMTP server.
- One server may function as both the incoming and outgoing mail server.

Review Questions

1. What are the three types of networks that provide web-page distribution?
2. A(n) _____ is a network in which employees can only access a company web server from within the company.
3. A(n) _____ allows internal access to web pages and allows authorized personnel from outside the network to access the network's web pages.
4. What is the purpose of a DNS server?
5. What protocol is common to Microsoft Active Directory (AD)?
6. What is the purpose of a web server?
7. What does the **whois** utility do?
8. What are some things to consider when choosing to set up your own web server rather than choosing to use a web-hosting service?
9. Name two software packages that are designed to turn a server into a web server.
10. What does the acronym IIS represent?
11. What is the name of the default web-server software installed on a Microsoft server.
12. Describe how search engines collect their results.
13. What are two common web browsers?
14. What is the difference between HTML and HTTP?
15. What is a markup?
16. What is the purpose of HTML tags?
17. What does the acronym W3C represent?
18. What is the difference between HTML and XML?

Copyright Goodheart-Willcox Co., Inc.

19. SOAP is closely associated with which markup language?

20. What is an anonymous FTP site?

21. Describe a *newsgroup*.

22. What protocol is used to send e-mail to a mail server or to transfer e-mail from one mail server to another mail server?

23. What protocols download e-mail from a server?

24. Which e-mail protocol is used to download e-mail automatically without the option to store it on the mail server?

25. How does MIME enhance e-mail?

✦ Sample Network+ Exam Questions

1. Edward is configuring a web server. It is behind a firewall, so he wants to make sure the firewall allows the appropriate protocol through. What protocol is used to transport web page information from a web server to a client?

   A. HTML

   B. HTTP

   C. IPX/SPX

   D. SMTP

2. Terri is a network administrator for a university. She needs to configure a server so that users can download files from the server. Which protocol is designed to download files from a server?

   A. ATM

   B. FTP

   C. SNMP

   D. ICMP

3. A(n) _____ is a network in which only employees from within a company can access the company web server.

   A. internet

   B. intranet

   C. extranet

   D. LAN net

4. Ahmed is trying to open the appropriate ports on his network firewall. He has a web server behind the firewall and needs to open that port. The typical port number used for making a web-server connection is _____.

   A. 33

   B. 80

   C. 125

   D. 440

5. Charles is setting up an e-mail server for his company. His company wants to use a version of SMTP that is encrypted with TLS. Which port should he open on the firewall?

   A. 25

   B. 465

   C. 993

   D. 995

6. Which type of server is designed to receive e-mail messages from an e-mail client?

   A. DNS

   B. DHCP

   C. SMTP

   D. POP

7. Your company is setting up an e-mail system for the sales department. The sales department wants to be able to access and read its current e-mail as well as stored e-mail while traveling outside the office. Which type of e-mail server will best meet its needs?

   A. POP3

   B. FTP

   C. TFTP

   D. IMAP

8. Which is the correct e-mail format for a salesperson from the United Kingdom with a user name of Bjones?

   A. BJones@Sales.Homeoffice.com.uk

   B. BJones@uk.com/homeoffice.sales

   C. BJones@Sales/HomeOffice/com/uk

   D. BJones.HomeOffice.Sales.com@uk

9. What type of server translates URLs to IP addresses?

   A. DNS

   B. DHCP

   C. IMAP

   D. IIS

10. Reggie is trying to determine who owns a given website. He thinks the website is selling knockoff products from his company, and wants to determine who is behind this. Which program or utility would you use to determine who owns and operates a specific website?

    A. **netstat**

    B. **tracert**

    C. **whois**

    D. **ping**

Copyright Goodheart-Willcox Co., Inc.

Remote Access and Long-Distance Communication

Network+ Certification Exam Objectives

The Network+ Certification Exam covers the various types of media associated with the telecommunication industry. Typical questions are based on descriptions of the media and media performance limits. Be sure you are familiar with VPN and the associated protocols that support VPN.

Objectives

1.1: Protocols and Ports—RDP 3389

2.3: VPN Concentrator

2.5: Service Types

Transmission Mediums—Satellite

Characteristics of Service—MPLS, Frame Relay, PPPoE, PPP, DMVPN, SIP trunk

Termination—CSU/DSU

3.4: VPN—IPSec

RDP

Out-of-Band Management—Modem

Learning Outcomes

- Recall components of telecommunication systems.
- Compare remote connection technologies.
- Explain how dial-up networking is achieved.
- Recall the function and characteristics of a Virtual Private Network (VPN).

Copyright Goodheart-Willcox Co., Inc.

Key Terms

Bandwidth Allocation Protocol (BAP)

Basic Rate ISDN (BRI-ISDN)

Broadband ISDN (B-ISDN)

Channel Service Unit/Data Service Unit (CSU/DSU)

dial-up networking

Digital Subscriber Line (DSL)

dynamic multi-point virtual private network (DMVPN)

edge router

head-end

Integrated Services Digital Network (ISDN)

International Telecommunication Union (ITU)

Layer 2 Forwarding (L2F)

Layer 2 Tunneling Protocol (L2TP)

loading coil

local central office

local exchange carrier (LEC)

local loop

Multilink Point-to-Point Protocol (MLPPP)

Multi-Protocol Label Switching (MPLS)

point of presence (POP)

Point-to-Point Protocol (PPP)

Point-to-Point Protocol over Ethernet (PPPoE)

Point-to-Point Tunneling Protocol (PPTP)

Primary Rate ISDN (PRI-ISDN)

remote access server

Remote Desktop Protocol (RDP)

Serial Line Internet Protocol (SLIP)

sunspots

Synchronous Optical Network (SONET)

T-carrier

trunk line

upconverter

Virtual Private Network (VPN)

VPN concentrator

Overview

This chapter explains the requirements for communicating remotely with a network, between LANs, and to and from a MAN or a WAN. Remote communication relies on either public communication systems or private communication systems. The communication system we are most familiar with is the public telephone system.

Remote connection technology is at the very heart of a MAN and WAN. To understand a MAN and WAN, you must have an excellent understanding of remote-connection technologies, such as T1, ISDN, and SONET. This chapter explores remote-connection technologies and the different types of media used to transfer data across vast distances. We will begin the chapter with an introduction to the telecommunication system.

Introduction to Telecommunication Systems

The telecommunication industry has existed for almost one hundred years. This industry ran as an analog system for most of its existence, but it has been steadily converting to a completely digital system. The typical telephone system with which you are familiar consists mainly of two systems: local carriers and long-distance carriers.

Originally, local and long-distance carriers were the same entity. Rates were controlled to an extent by the government. The breakup, or deregulation, of telephone companies began as a series of legal disputes beginning in the late 1940s and ending in 1984 with the complete deregulation of the telephone industry. Large companies such as AT&T and Bell Telephone Company were separated into individual companies.

The two major service parts, local service and long-distance service, were also separated. This meant the customer would use one company for local telephone service, or local calls, and another for long-distance calls. Deregulation eliminated the monopolistic nature of the telecommunication industry. The concept was to make the market more competitive so that the consumer could benefit from the competition.

Deregulation created many local service and long-distance carriers. A local carrier is often referred to as a **local exchange carrier (LEC)**, or sometimes a *competitive local exchange carrier (CLEC)*, and is made of one or more local central offices. The **local central office** is where the customer's telephone lines connect to the switchgear. The local central office connects to long-distance carriers to provide long-distance access to individual residencies. Look at Figure 14-1. Notice that the **local loop** is the section of wiring between customer premises and the local central office. The local central office can be tied to other local central offices via trunk lines. A **trunk line** consists of hundreds of pairs of twisted-pair cable or fiber-optic cable.

The **point of presence (POP)** is the point where a telephone company line connects to a subscriber line. The subscriber line begins at the customer's premises. Before deregulation, the telephone company was responsible for all wiring and equipment provided to the customer. The telephone company provided, installed, and repaired telephones and telephone lines inside the customer's home or business. Today, as you know, you must purchase a telephone and are responsible for repairing any telephone lines and equipment inside your home or business.

Figure 14-1 A local loop is typically a low-bandwidth, twisted-pair line between the telephone company's Local Central Office and the customer premises.

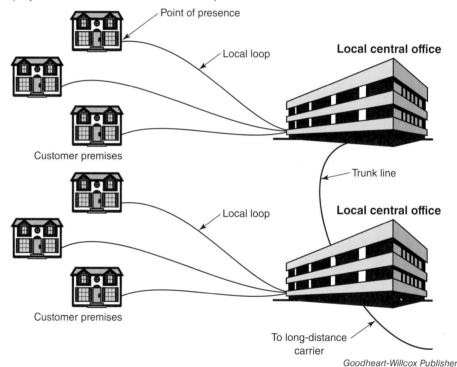

Goodheart-Willcox Publisher

Remote Connection Technologies and Media

The worldwide communication system is quite complex, offering a variety of media to use and many different long-distance providers. While a LAN usually has a limited scope of communication media, a MAN and a WAN have a large variety of communication media and technologies from which to choose.

Both public and private communication companies often control the media. Communication companies are referred to as *carriers* or *providers*. These companies provide and maintain the media for data transmission.

Small businesses and private residencies typically connect to their ISP via the local central office, as illustrated in Figure 14-2. Therefore, they usually use the

Copyright Goodheart-Willcox Co., Inc.

Figure 14-2 While typical residences use a low-bandwidth, twisted-pair line for telecommunication and Internet access, Internet service providers (ISPs) and enterprise businesses use a high-bandwidth line, such as T1.

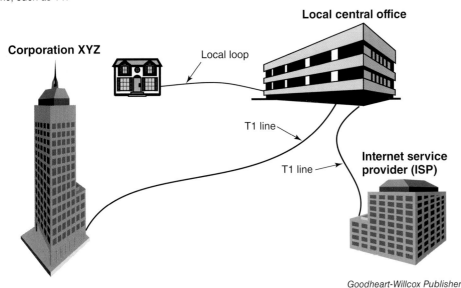

Goodheart-Willcox Publisher

low-bandwidth local loop between their site and the local central office. Enterprises or large businesses require high bandwidth for telecommunication and Internet access. They typically avoid the low-bandwidth local loop by using high-speed leased lines, such as a T1 line, to access other business locations and their ISP.

The geographic area of a residence or business often affects the choice or availability of remote connection media. Connecting to a remote network from an office in a metropolitan area does not typically present the same bandwidth limitations as connecting to a remote network in a rural or suburban area. Access to the local exchange carrier from a metropolitan area is usually accessible using media that provides a much higher bandwidth than is typically found in suburban residential or rural areas.

In a metropolitan area, there is the option of using leased lines, which provide private and high-bandwidth communication. Telecommunication companies make leased lines available between major metropolitan areas all over the world. In general, private communication systems are typically available in densely populated, metropolitan areas that contain numerous businesses, each with a need for high-speed communication. In contrast, public communication systems are typically located everywhere but do not always offer the same high bandwidth.

The following section discusses many different types of media available for communicating over long distances, such as PSTN, ISDN, cable, DSL, satellite, and T-carrier lines. Each medium covered is offered at various speeds and costs.

Public Switched Telephone Network (PSTN)

As previously discussed in Chapter 12, a public switched telephone network (PSTN) is an older telephone technology that uses twisted-pair cabling and analog signals rather than digital. Another name for a public switched telephone network (PSTN) is *plain-old telephone service (POTS).*

The public telephone system was originally analog. As digital electronics emerged, the telephone industry began switching the public telephone system equipment and lines to that which supports digital technology. Today, the public telephone

Copyright Goodheart-Willcox Co., Inc.

system is a mixture of digital and analog systems. While long-distance connections are usually digital, the short run between a residence or small business to the local loop is usually analog. Connections between the major telephone equipment are digital. It is possible, however, to have an entirely digital system that includes the local loop. Several options to achieve an entirely digital connection are discussed later in the chapter.

Typically, the PSTN is used when making a dial-up connection. A dial-up connection is a type of connection made using a traditional telephone line to reach a distant computer or network system. For example, a businessperson using a laptop will typically connect the laptop modem to a telephone jack and dial a telephone number. This will connect the laptop modem to the modem at the distant network. Home users use a dial-up connection to reach their ISP when accessing their ISP through the telephone line.

It is important to note that a remote connection to a distant network or other computer has a total bandwidth equal to its weakest link. The weakest link is typically the local loop. This is especially true when attempting to connect to a remote computer from a residence. The existing residential telecommunication technology is largely influenced by the original telecommunication technology.

The original telephone system was an analog system requiring 48 volts to communicate across telephone lines. The telephone lines were designed to carry voice, not digital data. The original line did not require the twist in the conductor pairs, which is required for a high data rate. The telephone lines were designed to carry a maximum frequency of 4 kHz. This frequency is more than adequate for voice communication. Historically, the first network systems were designed to run at these slow transmission rates to take advantage of the millions of miles of existing telephone cables. Although this speed is usable, it is unacceptable by today's standards.

Integrated Services Digital Network (ISDN)

NET
+ 2.5, 3.4

Integrated Services Digital Network (ISDN) provides the means for a fully digital transmission. It was developed in the 1980s. ISDN lines are commonly found in small businesses, but there are some homes that are wired with ISDN. ISDN requires an ISDN modem. The ISDN modem can be installed either internally in the PC as an expansion card or externally, connecting through a serial port.

There are three categories of ISDN from which to choose: basic rate, primary rate, and broadband. **Basic Rate ISDN (BRI-ISDN)** consists of three conductors: two B channels, referred to as *bearer channels*, and one D channel, referred to as the *delta channel*, as illustrated in Figure 14-3. The B channels carry data, voice, video, or a combination of voice and data. Each B channel carries a maximum of 64 kbps or a combined maximum data rate of 128 kbps. This data rate is approximately two

Figure 14-3 A Basic Rate ISDN (BRI-ISDN) cable consists of two 64-kbps B channels and one 16-kbps D channel. The two B channels can be combined for a total bandwidth of 128 kbps.

Basic Rate ISDN (BRI-ISDN) Cable

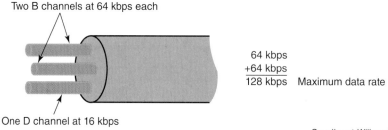

Two B channels at 64 kbps each

64 kbps
+64 kbps
128 kbps   Maximum data rate

One D channel at 16 kbps

Goodheart-Willcox Publisher

to five times faster than the traditional telephone modem, which is 56 kbps. The D channel has a maximum bandwidth of 16 kbps. The D channel carries control signals. The control signals are used to set up, maintain, and terminate transmission on the B channels.

Primary Rate ISDN (PRI-ISDN) consists of twenty-three B channels and one D channel. It has a total data rate of 1.544 Mbps. **Broadband ISDN (B-ISDN)** is designed to carry multiple frequencies. It has a total data rate of 1.5 Mbps. Remember that *broadband* refers to media that can carry multiple frequencies. Baseband refers to media that can carry only one frequency. Basic Rate ISDN and Primary Rate ISDN are digital technologies and can carry only one frequency; hence, they are both baseband. ISDN lines are not common today. While the Network+ Exam may still ask a few questions about ISDN lines, the concept has been largely de-emphasized.

Cable Internet Service

Cable Internet service uses the cable television distribution system to provide Internet access. Typically, cable Internet service requires a cable modem connection and a twisted-pair or USB connection. The cable modem connection connects to the F-type connector on the cable service coaxial cable. The RJ-45 or USB connection on the cable modem connects via twisted-pair or USB cable to the network interface card on the computer. The RJ-45 or USB connection on the cable modem may also connect to a hub, switch, gateway, or router to provide a shared Internet connection.

Tech Tip

A cable modem is also called a *transceiver.* The word *transceiver* is a combination of the words *transmit* and *receive.*

Cable Internet service is an asymmetrical form of communication. The term *asymmetrical* is used to describe cable Internet service communication because the uplink and downlink have two different transfer speeds. Upstream and downstream speeds can vary quite a bit. The term *downstream* is used to describe the data flow direction from the carrier or provider site to the customer. The term *upstream* is used for the data flow direction from the customer to the carrier. These speeds are advertised by the Data over Cable System Interface Specification (DOCSIS), which is the industry standard.

The speeds advertised by DOCSIS are theoretical speeds and are far from the actual speeds you can expect. In fact, it is difficult to obtain the actual speed because speed is affected by various factors, such as time of day, type of data downloaded, and overall distance from the cable provider.

The amount of bandwidth available is mostly influenced by how many other subscribers are using the cable service in the local area. The local area distribution point is referred to as the **head-end**, as shown in Figure 14-4. There can be hundreds of subscribers connected to the cable before accessing the head-end. As the volume of subscribers increases, the bandwidth decreases.

Actual bandwidth fluctuates according to the number of users online at the same time and the type of data downloaded. For example, in the middle of the night, a typical user should have remarkable download speeds because there are very few users online. In contrast, the late afternoon hours offer slower speeds due to the large number of users, typically just home from school or work. At that time, students are on the system doing homework or downloading music and games, and most people

Tech Tip

The DOCSIS standard was developed by a group of cable industry representatives before the IEEE 802.14 standard was developed. The IEEE 802.14 standard was an early attempt to standardize cable modems and high-speed access. It failed because of a lack of support by the manufacturers who opted to follow the DOCSIS standard.

Copyright Goodheart-Willcox Co., Inc.

are checking personal e-mail, social media, or financial accounts. All this traffic puts a stress on the bandwidth, thus decreasing it substantially.

As stated earlier, cable Internet service requires a special piece of equipment called a cable modem. The cable modem provides a connection to the cable television service media and to the network interface card in the PC. Figure 14-5 shows how a splitter can be used to share the cable television coaxial cable with the cable modem.

Figure 14-4 While cable Internet access offers a high-bandwidth Internet connection to residences, the total number of simultaneous Internet connections through the cable system affects the amount of bandwidth used by each residence.

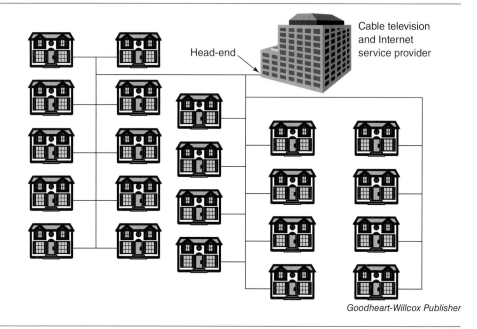

Goodheart-Willcox Publisher

Figure 14-5 The television cable service can provide Internet access. A cable modem is needed to connect the PC to the cable service.

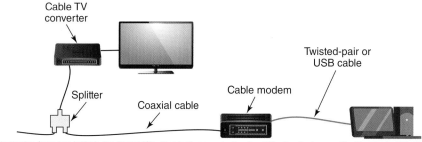

(clockwise from top left) Vadim Ermak/Shutterstock.com, dashadima/Shutterstock.com, RedlineVector/Shutterstock.com, Vadim Ermak/Shutterstock.com; Goodheart-Willcox Publisher

Not all cable companies can provide Internet service because Internet access requires special equipment to distribute Internet access through the cable company's distribution system. Original cable distribution equipment was designed for the downstream distribution of video and music and not designed to accept upstream communication. The cabling and the equipment at the cable company's distribution center usually have to be upgraded to provide Internet access. The original coaxial cable is replaced with hybrid fiber-coax cable. The fiber-optic portion supports the high bandwidth while the coaxial portion supports the control.

Digital Subscriber Line (DSL)

Digital Subscriber Line (DSL) refers to high-speed Internet access technology that uses existing local-loop telephone lines. It is much faster than ISDN and was designed to replace it. DSL comes in a variety of standards that vary in the techniques used to make data transmission faster.

Copyright Goodheart-Willcox Co., Inc.

DSL uses modulation techniques similar to those discussed in Chapter 4. Multiple frequencies are used as separate channels on the existing telephone local loop. The multiple channels combine to carry more data than the original telephone modem design. The original telephone modem design does not use multiple frequency signals. It uses only one.

Maximum distance for DSL is limited due to the high frequencies transmitted. The typical maximum distance for DSL is 1,000 to 18,000 feet and is measured from the DSL modem to the telephone company's local central office. The exact limit depends on the variation of DSL used and any special equipment that might exist on the telephone line, such as loading coils, or a change in the media. A **loading coil** is used to amplify voice signals, which are analog, and will not amplify DSL signals, which are digital. In fact, the loading coil reduces or blocks the higher frequency DSL signal.

Another factor is the length of the cable. Signal strength is affected in direct proportion to the length of the cable. A short cable can pass a much higher frequency than a long cable. This means that the longer the cable, the lower the applied DSL frequency, resulting in lower data transfer rates.

The media may also change between the subscriber location and the local central office. For example, the copper conductor may be changed to a fiber-optic cable at some point, which will prevent the application of DSL. The DSL technique is applied only to copper-core cable, not fiber-optic cable.

DSL varies in upstream and downstream bandwidth based on the transmission technique used. Some varieties of DSL are listed in Figure 14-6. The main points to remember about DSL is it is a high-speed Internet access technology that uses existing local-loop telephone lines, and the actual download rate is affected by the length of the cable. With the widespread adoption of cable Internet services, DSL lines are becoming less common in heavily populated areas. They can still be found in smaller communities.

Figure 14-6 DSL technologies.

DSL Type	Description	Upstream Data Rate	Downstream Data Rate	Maximum Distance between DSL Modem and Central Office
ADSL	Asymmetrical DSL	1.544 Mbps	1.5 Mbps–8 Mbps	12,000 ft.–18,000 ft.
SDSL	Symmetric DSL	1.544 Mbps	1.544 Mbps	10,000 ft.
HDSL	High bit-rate DSL	1.544 Mbps	1.544 Mbps	14,000 ft.
VDSL	Very high bit-rate DSL	1.5 Mbps–2.3 Mbps	13 Mbps–52 Mbps	1000 ft.–4500 ft.

Goodheart-Willcox Publisher

Satellite

2.5 NET

A satellite system can be used for Internet access and data communication, as demonstrated in Figure 14-7. A typical satellite system consists of a satellite dish at the satellite service-provider location, a satellite, and a satellite dish at the consumer location. Satellite system installations are available in consumer-grade and business-grade. The typical consumer-grade installation consists of a small dish for downloading and a landline, such as a traditional telephone line, for uploading. Before a user can connect to the Internet, an initial connection to the satellite Internet service provider must be made through a modem. Thereafter, the telephone line connection via the modem is used to communicate web-page requests and to send e-mail.

Copyright Goodheart-Willcox Co., Inc.

Figure 14-7 Typical satellite system components.

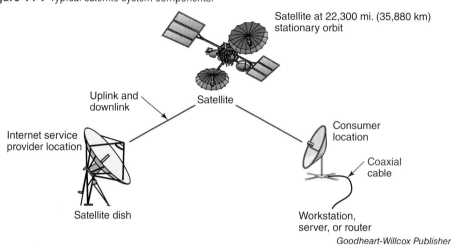

Goodheart-Willcox Publisher

Typical download speeds for consumer satellite communication are 400 kbps to 500 kbps. Upload speeds are limited to the particular land-based technology used for upload. For example, a telephone modem offers speeds of 56 kbps and an ISDN modem offers speeds of 1.54 Mbps and 128 kbps. Often, the only real advantage for consumer satellite technology is access from remote locations.

Business-grade satellite communication offer higher speeds, typically up to 1.5 Mbps in the US and up to 2 Mbps in Europe and other countries. The speed difference between the US and other countries is due to different wireless regulations. Business-grade satellite communication is designed with more-expensive equipment while consumer-grade satellite communication is designed with less-expensive equipment. Using less-expensive equipment for consumer-grade satellite communication allows satellite communication to be competitively priced among other Internet access technologies. Business-grade satellite communication, however, offers uplink and downlink capabilities. Uplink requires a radio transmitter to be integrated into a satellite dish. The radio transmitter is referred to as an **upconverter**.

The main advantages of using satellite communication is it is ideal for temporary connections such as sporting events or remote locations where landlines are not readily available. The disadvantages of satellite communication are latency, security, and interference. As discussed in Chapter 4, the satellite is located approximately 22,300 miles from Earth's surface and is in a geosynchronous orbit. The great distance the radio wave must travel causes the transmitted signal to experience propagation delay. The propagation delay for a signal transmitted from a satellite to a satellite dish is approximately 250 milliseconds. The propagation delay does not noticeably affect the downloading of web pages with text-based contents, but it is unacceptable for telephone support or full-duplex video conferencing.

Security is also a problem because all transmissions are based on radio transmissions, which can be easily intercepted. An encryption program is needed to secure sensitive data. Radio-wave transmissions to and from the satellite can be adversely affected by certain conditions.

Atmospheric conditions due to inclement weather affect satellite communication, causing data loss. Another phenomenon known as *sunspots* also affects communication. **Sunspots** are magnetic energy storms that occur at the surface of the sun. The magnetic fields produce charged particles that are released from the surface of the sun and projected into space. The charged particles can enter Earth's atmosphere and affect electronic communication systems. A sunspot transmits high levels of electromagnetic energy across the universe and affects to some degree all radio transmissions.

Copyright Goodheart-Willcox Co., Inc.

The radio frequency used for satellite transmission is classified as microwave. Microwaves have a high-frequency pattern with short wavelengths. The high frequency, short wavelength radio waves are easily disrupted by trees, buildings, bridges, and other such obstacles. A clear line of sight is required between the receiving satellite dish and the orbiting satellite. This is in contrast to low frequency radio waves like the one used for wireless networks. Wireless network radio waves can penetrate some objects that are not very dense. In summary, satellite communication requires a clear line of sight between the destination and source, unlike the satellite communication setup illustrated in Figure 14-8.

The same principle used to transmit data between the satellite and satellite dish can be used between a series of microwave satellite dishes. You can see microwave dishes located on towers all over the country. The microwave dishes are commonly used by telephone communication systems, especially in areas where laying cables is difficult or impossible.

Another location where microwave dish transmission is often used is across bodies of water, such as bays and wide rivers, or over large tracts of flat land. Again, the line of sight principle must be applied, and the series of dishes must be precisely aimed at one another.

T-Carrier

2.5 NET

A **T-carrier** is a leased line that follows one of the standards known as T1, fractional T1, T2, or T3. While T1 and T3 are relatively commonplace, T2 is uncommon. The T-carrier is a dedicated, permanent connection that is capable of providing high bandwidth. A T1 line consists of 24 channels, each with a data rate of 64 kbps or a total bandwidth of 1.544 Mbps. These channels are actually the equivalent of individual phone lines, also called *DS0 lines*. Each has a bandwidth of 64 kbps. A fractional T1 only uses part of a T1 line's full capability, using a certain number of DS0 lines. See Figure 14-9 for a summary of T-carrier standards. A T3 line will achieve bandwidths

Figure 14-8 There must be a clear line of sight between the satellite dish and the satellite. Trees, buildings, bridges, and such interfere with satellite radio transmissions.

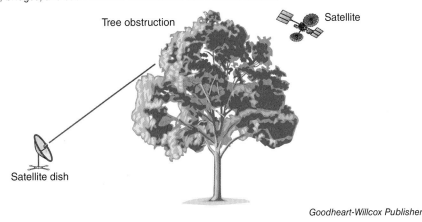

Goodheart-Willcox Publisher

Figure 14-9 T-carrier technologies.

T-Carrier Standard	Number of T1 Lines	Number of Channels	Maximum Data Rate
T1	1	24	1.544 Mbps
T2	4	96	6.312 Mbps
T3	28	672	44.736 Mbps
T4	168	4032	274.176 Mbps

Goodheart-Willcox Publisher

Copyright Goodheart-Willcox Co., Inc.

of 44.733 Mbps, combining 622 channels or DS0 lines. This is the equivalent of 28 T1 lines.

The European counterpart to a T1 leased line is E1, which has a maximum rate of 2.048 Mbps. The Japanese counterpart is J1. Notice in Figure 14-10 that data rates for T1, E1, and J1 differ.

T-carriers were developed to carry data and voice signals. You will often see T1 lines as a mixture of voice and data lines. To accomplish the task of sharing T1 media with different signals, a pair of multiplexers is used. One multiplexer is placed on each end of the T-carrier line. A *multiplexer* combines the different signal types (voice and data) into an organized manner and places the different signal types onto a single T1 line for transmission, as shown in Figure 14-11.

Figure 14-10 Comparison of T1, E1, and J1 lines.

USA		Europe		Japan	
T1	1.544 Mbps	E1	2.048 Mbps	J1	1.544 Mbps
T2	6.312 Mbps	E2	8.448 Mbps	J2	6.312 Mbps
T3	44.736 Mbps	E3	34.368 Mbps	J3	32.064 Mbps
T4	274.176 Mbps	E4	139.264 Mbps	J4	97.728 Mbps
NA	NA	E5	564.992 Mbps	J5	397.200 Mbps

Goodheart-Willcox Publisher

Figure 14-11 A multiplexer typically combines multiple lines of incoming data into a single series of data packets on a T1 line. A demultiplexer at the destination reverses the process.

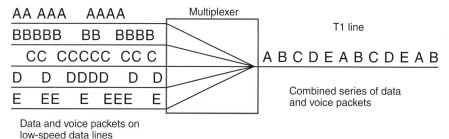

Goodheart-Willcox Publisher

When mixing voice and data, voice packets must be placed onto the T-carrier line in close proximity to one another. If voice packets are spaced too far apart (interspersed between data), the received voice transmission will have undesirable pauses. It is the multiplexer's responsibility to place the voice packets on the T-carrier line often enough so that there will not be any detectable sound gaps or pauses when reassembled at the destination multiplexer. It is not as critical for data packets to be placed in close proximately to one another.

Often, the multiplexer and a Channel Service Unit/Data Service Unit (CSU/DSU) are incorporated into a single unit. A **Channel Service Unit/Data Service Unit (CSU/DSU)** converts signals from the LAN into signals that can be carried by the T1 line, and vice versa. The Network+ Exam emphasizes the T-carrier lines and their European counterparts.

FDDI

The Fiber Distribution Data Interface (FDDI) is a dual-ring, fiber-optic arrangement. FDDI was covered earlier in Chapter 3 and is mentioned here because it is often used in a MAN distribution system because of its reliability and its high bandwidth. FDDI

Copyright Goodheart-Willcox Co., Inc.

can be used for distances of up to 62 miles. This distance is more than adequate for MAN installations.

SONET

Synchronous Optical Network (SONET) is similar in design to T-carrier technology except SONET bases its technology on fiber-optic cable. Because SONET is based on fiber-optic cable, it can provide a much higher bandwidth. SONET is the standard choice for connecting global-sized networks spanning across the nation and oceans. See Figure 14-12 for a summary of SONET levels.

Figure 14-12 SONET levels.

SONET Level	Maximum Data Rate
OC-1	51.84 Mbps
OC-3	145.52 Mbps
OC-12	622 Mbps
OC-24	1244 Mbps
OC-48	2488 Mbps
OC-192	9953 Mbps

Goodheart-Willcox Publisher

SONET is similar to T-carrier in that special termination equipment, such as a multiplexer, is needed at the customer location. SONET often uses multiplexer technology to carry a mix of data, voice, and video on the same channel.

SONET is designed as a ring topology similar to the dual-ring structure of FDDI. One ring is the primary communication ring, and the other ring serves as a backup. The backup ring ensures reliability. If the primary ring fails, data transmission is automatically switched to the backup ring.

Enterprise companies spanning long distances, such as across the nation or the globe, most often use SONET. Small or mid-size companies do not typically use SONET because it is quite expensive to lease when compared with other technologies. It has, however, the best design for reliability.

SONET speeds are measured by Optical Carrier (OC) values. OC-1, the baseline for all OC, has a bandwidth of 51.84 Mbps. OC-3 is 3 times the bandwidth of the baseline for OC, or 155.52 Mbps. There are many levels of OC, including OC-3, OC-12, OC-24, OC-48, OC-192, and OC-768.

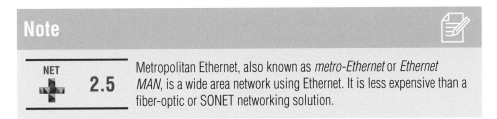

> **Note**
>
> **NET 2.5** Metropolitan Ethernet, also known as *metro-Ethernet* or *Ethernet MAN*, is a wide area network using Ethernet. It is less expensive than a fiber-optic or SONET networking solution.

X.25

X.25 is a packet-switching analog network technology developed in the 1970s. X.25 can support a maximum bandwidth of 56 kbps. For over twenty years, X.25 was used to transmit data over long distances. It was used almost exclusively for transmissions around the world because the International Telecommunication Union (ITU)

Copyright Goodheart-Willcox Co., Inc.

recognized it as a standard. The **International Telecommunication Union (ITU)** is responsible for standardizing communication on an international level. The ITU regulates radio, television, and satellite frequencies and standards and telephony standards. Although X.25 dominated worldwide communication, Frame Relay has been the first choice since the early 1990s.

X.25 is not usually available in the USA. However, knowledge about X.25 is required for working with WAN systems that connect all over the world. This protocol is often included in the list of protocols available in many different operating systems.

Frame Relay

Frame Relay uses digital media rather than analog like X.25. Frame Relay is a packet-switching technology similar to X.25. Both X.25 and Frame Relay are permanent virtual circuits. A *permanent virtual circuit (PVC)* typically uses numerous paths between two points. A packet-switching technology reduces data into smaller units (packets) and uses a number of different routes (switching) to transport the packets. Remember, a packet contains a destination and source address and a packet sequence number. The sequence number allows the packets to be arranged in their original order when they reach the destination.

Frame Relay technology is a shared, leased line, which means it can be leased at a reduced rate. This advantage can mean a significant cost reduction when compared with T-carrier, especially for expensive overseas communication. The fact that Frame Relay is a shared, leased line can also be viewed as a disadvantage, however. The available bandwidth could fluctuate from 56 kbps to 45 Mbps. For example, the bandwidth available to a user in the morning can be significantly reduced because of the traffic generated by personnel checking for data transactions from the night before. At another time of day, the full 1.544 Mbps bandwidth could be available. See Figure 14-13 for a summary of WAN connection technologies.

Dial-Up Networking

Remote connections can be made to distant networks using existing telephone lines. The term **dial-up networking** describes a network system in which a dial-up connection is used to access a remote access server. A **remote access server** is a server that is accessed remotely by users not on a LAN. To set up a dial-up network, a modem must be installed at the client location and on the remote access server. Remote access software must also be installed. The remote access software specific to Microsoft operating systems are Dial-Up Networking (DUN) and Remote Access Service (RAS). DUN is installed on the client side of the remote access network, and RAS is installed on the remote access server.

Look at Figure 14-14. A laptop at a distant location is connected to a telephone line. The laptop connects to the home-office network through the remote access server. Once a connection is established, the remote access user can check his or her office e-mail, print out customer orders, access files on his or her office desktop computer, and access the company database. There are three common ways to set up remote dial-in access on a server:

- Allow dial-in to the remote access server only.

- Allow dial-out from the remote access server only.

- Allow full-service dial-in and dial-out on the remote access server.

While dial-up networking may seem outdated, dial up is still used in some remote areas, as well as by some small businesses for credit card transactions.

Tech Tip

Windows 2000 Server, as well as Windows Server 2003, 2008 and 2016 use an enhanced version of RAS called *Routing and Remote Access Service (RRAS).*

Copyright Goodheart-Willcox Co., Inc.

Figure 14-13 Summary of WAN connection technologies.

WAN Connection Technology	Access Method	Data Rate	Comments
ATM	Direct connection	25 Mbps–622 Mbps	Virtually private.
Cable Internet Service	Direct connection	Downstream: 27 Mbps–37 Mbps (theoretical). 300 kbps– 500 kbps (actual) Upstream: 320 kbps–10 Mbps	TV Cable service. Requires a cable modem. Cable service uses MPEG-2 for data compression.
FDDI	Direct connection	100 Mbps	High reliability and bandwidth.
Fractional T1	Direct connection	64 kbps	T-carrier technology. Can use multiple channels to increase speed by increments of 64 kbps.
Frame Relay	Virtual connection	56 kbps–45 Mbps	Virtually private.
ISDN	Dial-up	64 kbps and 128 kbps	Requires a leased line and an ISDN modem. Can carry only one frequency.
PRI-ISDN	Direct connection	1.544 Mbps	Requires a leased line and an ISDN modem. Can carry only one frequency.
Public Switched Telephone Network (PSTN)	Dial-up	56 kbps	This is also known as Plain Old Telephone Service (POTS). Requires a telephone modem.
Satellite Internet Service	Direct connection	400 kbps–2 Mbps	May use a dial-up service to connect to the satellite Internet provider. Experiences propagation delay.
SONET	Direct connection	51 Mbps–9953 Mbps	Commonly used to span long distances such as across the nation and overseas.
T1	Direct connection	1.544 Mbps	T-carrier technology.
T3	Direct connection	44.736 Mbps	T-carrier technology.
X.25	Virtual connection	56 kbps	Packet switching, analog technology.
xDSL	Direct connection	1.544 Mbps–52 Mbps	Data rate depends on the version of DSL. Requires an xDSL modem. Limited distance from the DSL modem to the telephone company's Local Central Office is between 1,000 ft.–18,000 ft.

Goodheart-Willcox Publisher

Figure 14-14 A laptop computer can connect to the corporate office by using dial-up networking software. A server must be set up with remote access server software. Once this is accomplished, the remote client can access items such as the office computer, printer, company database, and e-mail.

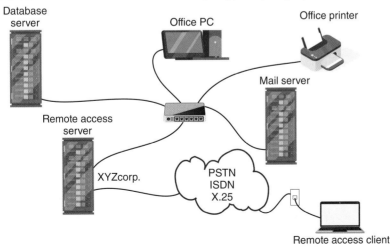

(server icons) fullvector/Shutterstock.com; (workstation icon) RedlineVector/Shutterstock.com; (printer icon) Vectors Bang/Shutterstock.com; (laptop icon) Jemastock/Shutterstock.com; (hub icon) Vadim Ermak/Shutterstock.com; Goodheart-Willcox Publisher

Copyright Goodheart-Willcox Co., Inc.

Dial-In Only

A *dial-in only* configuration allows remote access clients to connect to the network server, but it does not allow hosts on the network to dial out. This prevents personnel from surfing the World Wide Web, but allows the hosts on the network to accept incoming calls. This is a good business scenario that prevents workers from wasting time when they should be providing service to customers.

Dial-Out Only

Dial-out only access adds security to a network system by allowing calls to be placed from the network but not into the network. This prevents unauthorized persons from accessing the network through a telephone modem connection.

Full Service

Full service access allows the remote client to dial into the network and also allows network hosts to dial out to remote locations. This type of access is perfect for a small office environment or a limited number of users in an enterprise business environment. Security policies can control individual user access to telephone features in much the same way file-sharing access can be controlled. Specific users can be identified and granted various levels of modem use and specific hours or times of modem access.

Remote access can be configured to allow the business to bear the cost of a long-distance call. For example, a remote access client calls into the office server. The office server detects the incoming call but does not accept it. The call is terminated and the server immediately returns the call to the remote access client so that the server side bears the cost of the long-distance call rather than the remote access client.

A network may also be accessed remotely through an Internet connection if the network has a network server with a modem and the remote access service running. Not all offices have a network server. In this scenario, remote access must take place from telephone modem to telephone modem between a network PC and a remote access PC.

Remote Desktop Protocol (RDP)

The **Remote Desktop Protocol (RDP)** is a presentation protocol that allows Windows computers to communicate directly with Windows-based clients. The Remote Desktop Protocol is transmitted across any TCP/IP connection. RDP provides security by encrypting the contents of packets sent across the TCP/IP network. Port 3389 is the default port used for RDP and must be opened when a firewall is used.

RDP is an extension of the original Terminal Services technology, an earlier version of the presentation type protocol. Look at Figure 14-15. In this illustration, the

Figure 14-15 Terminal Services technology allows a Terminal Services Client to send keyboard and mouse control to the Terminal Services Server and the Terminal Services Server to send its display to the Terminal Services Client.

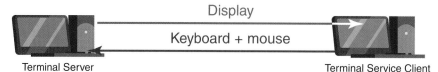

Terminal Server   Terminal Service Client

(workstation icons) RedlineVector/Shutterstock.com; Goodheart-Willcox Publisher

Copyright Goodheart-Willcox Co., Inc.

original Terminal Service technology allowed a Terminal Services Client to send keyboard and mouse control to the Terminal Services Server and the Terminal Services Server to send its display to the Terminal Services Client. For example, after the client establishes a connection with the Terminal Services Server, it sends commands via the keyboard or mouse to manipulate the directory and file structure. The Terminal Services Server sends the screen image to the client as the files are manipulated. The client experiences the session as though he or she were sitting at the server.

When using RDP with a Windows Professional system, the roles of Terminal Services Client and Terminal Server are simply called the *client* and *host*, respectively. The client uses the Remote Desktop Connection software to connect to the host. Keep in mind, however, that RDP sends in clear text, unencrypted. Therefore, unless you first connect a VPN and run the RDP through that, it is very unsecure.

Tech Tip

RDP is based on the International Telecommunication Union (ITU) T.120 protocol.

Remote Access Protocols

Dial-up access uses special protocols for negotiating a connection between a PC and a network, two networks, or two PCs. Some of the most common remote access protocols are briefly introduced in this section. You will see that many remote access protocols were developed to address the issues of security better. See Figure 14-16 for a summary of remote access protocols.

Figure 14-16 Summary of remote access protocols.

Remote Access Protocol	Full Name	Description
L2F	Layer 2 Forwarding	Enhances security and makes use of a VPN using the public Internet. L2F requires special equipment on the host side to support data transfers.
L2TP	Layer 2 Tunneling Protocol	Combines the features of L2F and PPTP.
MLPPP	Multilink Point-to-Point Protocol	Combines two or more physical links in such a way that they act as one, thus increasing the supported bandwidth. Works with ISDN lines, PSTN lines, and X.25 technology.
PPP	Point-to-Point Protocol	A synchronous protocol that supports multiple protocols such as IPX and AppleTalk. Enables a PC to connect to a remote network using a serial line connection, typically through a telephone line.
PPPoE	Point-to-Point Protocol over Ethernet	Supports multiple clients connected to an ISP over Ethernet.
PPTP	Point-to-Point Tunneling Protocol	Enhanced version of PPP that makes use of a VPN using the public Internet. It encapsulates the existing network protocol (IP, IPX, AppleTalk, and such) into the PPTP protocol.
SLIP	Serial Line Internet Protocol	An asynchronous protocol that supports only IP. Enables a PC to connect to a remote network using a serial line connection, typically through a telephone line.

Goodheart-Willcox Publisher

Copyright Goodheart-Willcox Co., Inc.

SLIP and PPP

Serial Line Internet Protocol (SLIP) and Point-to-Point Protocol (PPP) enable a PC to connect to a remote network using a serial line connection, typically through a telephone line. The **Serial Line Internet Protocol (SLIP)** protocol was introduced with Unix and supports only TCP/IP. **Point-to-Point Protocol (PPP)** is a vast improvement over SLIP and can support multiple protocols such as IPX and TCP/IP.

SLIP is strictly an asynchronous protocol while PPP is both asynchronous and synchronous. Remember from earlier chapters that *synchronous* transmission relies on a separate timing signal so that both the transmitting and receiving equipment are in step during the exchange of data. *Asynchronous* means that the data is transferred without a timing signal. Data is transferred from one point to another without being in step.

PPP is much easier to set up than SLIP because most of the required settings can be automatically negotiated. SLIP requires information such as the IP address to be entered manually. You will seldom encounter SLIP because it does not support authentication, encryption, or VPN connections.

PPTP

Point-to-Point Tunneling Protocol (PPTP) is an enhanced version of PPP designed to upgrade security and to make use of a virtually private network using the public Internet. The Internet is used by millions of people. While it is an excellent system of communication, it has many security issues. The term *virtually private* means that the network connection appears to be a private network.

When using PPTP, you can gain access to a corporate network by using a dial-up connection through an ISP and then negotiating data transfers over the public Internet. The term *tunneling* refers to encapsulating the existing network protocol into the PPTP protocol.

PPTP incorporates methods to encrypt data. The PPTP protocol also supports the necessary remote access service and network access authentication.

PPPoE

Point-to-Point Protocol over Ethernet (PPPoE) provides one or more hosts on an Ethernet network the ability to establish an individual PPP connection with an ISP. PPPoE frames the PPP protocol so that the PPP frame can travel over an Ethernet network.

Notice in Figure 14-17 that each computer using the PPPoE protocol has the ability to establish and maintain an individual connection with an ISP. With Internet Connection Sharing (ICS), one computer establishes a connection to the ISP and must remain on for the other computers to have the ability to connect to the Internet. With the PPPoE protocol, each PPPoE client has direct access to the ISP. The PPPoE clients are arranged as a typical Ethernet network and use a DSL or cable modem to connect to the ISP. The DSL or cable modem may be incorporated into a router or serve as an individual piece of equipment. A PPPoE access server is located at the ISP. The server provides individual connections as needed to each of the PPPoE clients.

The PPPoE connection has two stages: discovery and session. In the discovery stage, the PPPoE client attempts to discover the location of the PPPoE server. There may be more than one PPPoE server. The client must locate and establish a connection with only one PPPoE server. Typically, the PPPoE client and the PPPoE server

Copyright Goodheart-Willcox Co., Inc.

Figure 14-17 PPPoE is an effective means of creating individual high-speed connections for Internet access.

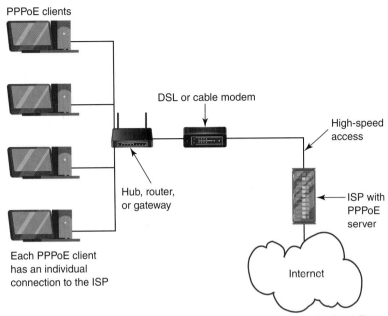

PPPoE clients

DSL or cable modem

High-speed access

Hub, router, or gateway

ISP with PPPoE server

Each PPPoE client has an individual connection to the ISP

Internet

(workstation icons) RedlineVector/Shutterstock.com; (router and modem icons)Vadim Ermak/Shutterstock.com; (server icon) fullvector/Shutterstock.com; Goodheart-Willcox Publisher

exchange network identification consisting of an IP address and MAC address. After addressees are exchanged, a connection is established and maintained indefinitely. The established connection is referred to as a *session*. Each session is independent of other connections to the PPPoE.

In Figure 14-17, all computers are on the same network. In another scenario, the computers connecting to the ISP may reside in an office building consisting of many different businesses. Individual users may need to be billed rather than the entire site. The MAC address provides a way of billing the user and establishing a user account for authentication purposes. The ISP can then provide billing based on a per-user, rather than per-site basis.

PPPoE establishes a virtual serial connection to the ISP in the same way a single PPP connection creates a true serial connection. In other words, when using PPPoE, each computer establishes a virtually private PPP connection to the Internet.

MLPPP

Multilink Point-to-Point Protocol (MLPPP), also known as *multilink dialing*, combines two or more physical links in such a way that they act as one, thus increasing the supported bandwidth. For MLPPP to operate, the access server and the client must have MLPPP enabled. MLPPP works with ISDN lines, PSTN lines, and X.25 technology.

MLPPP can use the **Bandwidth Allocation Protocol (BAP)**, which allows the number of lines used by MLPPP to change on demand. For example, if simple text is downloaded, a single line will suffice for the low-bandwidth data. If multimedia is downloaded to multiple workstations, such as for a videoconferencing, BAP will automatically increase the number of lines to support the increased bandwidth. Once the high-bandwidth data transmission has ended, the number of lines is

Copyright Goodheart-Willcox Co., Inc.

reduced to minimum. Remember, there is a high cost associated with telephone and leased lines. Controlling the number of lines used based on demand is cost-effective.

L2F

Layer 2 Forwarding (L2F) is a protocol similar to PPTP. It was developed by Cisco Systems and then released for use by other venders. One advantage of L2F is that it can work directly with ATM and Frame Relay, and it does not require TCP/IP. L2F also supports more than one connection. PPTP does not. However, L2F requires special equipment on the host side to support data transfer. The only requirement for PPTP is that the host is installed with a Microsoft server class of operating system.

L2TP

Layer 2 Tunneling Protocol (L2TP) combines the L2F and PPTP protocols. Microsoft and several other companies developed PPTP. Cisco Systems developed L2F. The Internet Engineering Task Force (IETF) wanted to create a protocol that had the best features of both L2F and PPTP protocols. Jointly, the IETF, Cisco Systems, Microsoft, and many others designed L2TP. L2TP has become an industry standard tunneling protocol that uses IPSec to encrypt the contents of the encapsulated PPP protocol.

NET 2.5

MPLS

Multi-Protocol Label Switching (MPLS) allows the network administrator to attach a label or header to an IP packet in order to route the packet to a specific destination. This protocol is designed for high-speed packet routing networks. Traditional routing protocols require that every router in the route inspect the contents, or at least a portion of the contents, of the Ethernet packet and then calculate or refer to a table to determine the best route for the packet. MPLS-enabled routers simply inspect the attached label and then forward the packet based on the contents of the label.

The MPLS label and route are predetermined by the network administrator, thus eliminating the need for a router CPU to calculate or search routing tables for the best route. The overall effect is reduced packet latency. The MPLS label contents also contain a priority code, which ensures quality of service. Thus, MPLS provides a faster means of distributing packets from one edge router to another. The term **edge router** refers to the router at the entrance and exit of a WAN.

The Internet Engineering Task Force (IETF) developed the standard for MPLS because of the need to provide a quicker method of routing packets across the Internet and large enterprise networks. The IETF design specifies a very small MPLS label of approximately three bytes. The MPLS label can be attached to IPv4 or IPv6 packets, ensuring compatibility now and in the future.

By design, MPLS is not intended for routing on a local area network but rather for moving packets from point to point across large network systems controlled by a single authority, for example, Sprint networks or an Internet provider such as Comcast. The MPLS label is removed upon entering a local area network. Traditional routing protocols such as IS-IS and OSPF can be used to forward the packet across the local network after the label has been removed.

The two main network applications for MPLS are traffic shaping and VPN support. MPLS traffic shaping is when the system administrator decides which route will be taken between distant nodes. A VPN can be created by the label attached to the packet.

The main advantage of MPLS when compared with ATM is MPLS is designed to work with existing IP network technology. ATM is not and requires special equipment

Copyright Goodheart-Willcox Co., Inc.

and support. Also, ATM is designed to create small packets of a fixed size (48 bytes). MPLS simply adds a small 4 header of four to eight bytes to the existing IP packet, which has no size limitation. The larger packets can be moved more efficiently across large IP networks.

The main advantage of MPLS when compared with Frame Relay is cost. Frame Relay generally requires leased lines, which can be very expensive. As stated earlier, MPLS can use existing Internet networks.

The concept of how MPLS works is simple. At each end of the MPLS portion of the WAN are routers referred to as *label edge routers*. Between the label edge routers are other MPLS routers called *label switch routers*. The network administrator inserts information into the label portion of the MPLS, specifying the destination for all MPLS packets. The label information is distributed throughout the network to all MPLS devices by the Label Distribution Protocol (LDP). The LDP distributes the information in advance so the label can be interpreted immediately on arrival and forwarded to the predetermined destination. The MPLS tag is added when the packet enters the WAN and is removed when the packet leaves the WAN and enters a local area network.

The administrator can control the packet flow through the WAN, thus "shaping" network traffic. Through the use of MPLS, the administrator can guarantee a specific minimum bandwidth and quality of service to customers. In other words, an Internet service provider can guarantee quality of service to specific customers when using MPLSs over private network systems.

MPLS is referred to as a "layer 2.5" protocol because it does not align with either layer 2 or layer 3 of the OSI model. It does, however, perform similar functions as layer 2 and layer 3 devices. To learn more about MPLS, visit www.mplsrc.com/mplsfaq.shtml.

VoIP

2.5 NET

Voice over IP (VoIP) has been discussed in several other chapters. It can also be considered a remote access protocol, however, if the VoIP is done with remote networks. When providing VoIP to businesses, the concept of SIP trunks becomes especially important. A *SIP trunk* is a way of providing VoIP and streaming media to customers who have a SIP-based private branch exchange (PBX).

Virtual Private Network (VPN)

A **Virtual Private Network (VPN)** is a simulated, independent network created by software over a public network. An example of a public network is the Internet. Since anyone can access and use a public network, there is a possibility of unauthorized access to any network connected to it. A VPN makes it possible to create a private connection over a public network with no additional cost. For example, a company may wish to use the Internet to connect to its many branch offices spread throughout the country. The main reason for using the Internet is it is inexpensive when compared with leased lines and other physical private connections. However, the company may wish to keep its data and transmissions secure while using the Internet for data transfers and communication. The answer to this dilemma would be to implement a VPN.

A VPN is created through a software package that provides security. Adding special equipment, such as a firewall, can further increase the security of the VPN. All operating systems support a form of VPN.

Most VPN software encapsulates transport protocol packets inside a secure protocol packet and encrypts the contents as well. In the early days of networking,

Tech Tip

Not all firewalls are equipment-based technologies. Some firewalls are strictly software packages.

Copyright Goodheart-Willcox Co., Inc.

security was not considered a real concern. The original TCP/IP protocol suite was not very secure. In fact, the early designs were made public to encourage the development of the Internet by the private sector. Today, security is a prime concern of all Internet users. Through the utilization of VPN technology, a secure link can be created through an unsecure public network like the Internet. VPN is not just limited to the Internet but is also used to create private links inside a private network system like a company network or a school network. Since most local area networks use the TCP/IP suite of protocols, security concerns still exist in the local network.

Four of the most common protocols used in a VPN are PPTP, L2F, L2TP, and IPSec. These protocols allow a VPN to provide four basic features common to all VPN connections: authentication, access control, confidentiality, and data integrity. When discussing VPNs, *authentication* is the process of assuring the person who is accessing the remote system is truly the person who is authorized to use the system. *Access control* is the act of allowing only authorized users access to the VPN. *Confidentiality* is the act of preventing anyone else from reading the data that flows through the VPN. *Data integrity* is the process of ensuring the data that leaves the source and arrives at the destination has not been tampered with. These topics are covered in further detail in Chapter 15.

A VPN concentrator is a good solution for any sort of VPN connection. A **VPN concentrator** is a device, normally a router, that also provides VPN connections for the network. Another method of implementing a VPN is a dynamic multi-point virtual private network. **Dynamic multi-point virtual private network (DMVPN)** refers to a secure network establishing VPN connections between multiple points.

IPSec is the most common VPN technology today. As discussed earlier, PPTP and L2TP can be used to create VPN's, but those have largely been supplanted by IPSec. IPSec works in one of two modes: tunneling or transport. In tunneling mode, the entire packet and the header is encrypted. It is then wrapped in an IPSec header. This prevents an eavesdropper from gathering even metadata about the data. In transport mode, the data is encrypted, but the original packet header is still used, and unencrypted.

Copyright Goodheart-Willcox Co., Inc.

Summary

Introduction to Telecommunication Systems

- The deregulation of the telecommunication industry allows for separate local telephone systems and long-distance telephone systems, which increases competition and reduces overall costs.

- The point of presence (PoP) is the point where the public telephone line ends and the customer premises telephone line and equipment begin.

- Since the deregulation of the telecommunication industry, residents and business owners are responsible for the telephone system on their side of the point of presence (PoP).

Remote Connection Technologies and Media

- There are many types of media available for communicating over long-distances, such as cable, DSL, ISDN, PSTN, satellite, SONET, and T1. Each is offered at various speeds and costs.

- Basic Rate ISDN (BRI-ISDN) consists of two B channels and one D channel with a total bandwidth of 128 kbps.

- Primary Rate ISDN (PRI-ISDN) consists of twenty-three B channels and one D channel with a total data rate of 1.544 Mbps.

- Broadband ISDN (B-ISDN) is the newest category of ISDN and is designed to carry multiple frequencies; hence, the term *broadband*.

- Cable Internet service offers data rates as high as 36 Mbps downstream and 10 Mbps upstream. However, 10 Mbps is a theoretical speed.

- Cable Internet service is defined by the Data over Cable System Interface Specification (DOCSIS) standard developed independently of IEEE 802.14.

- DSL is offered in many varieties, such as ADSL, SDSL, HDSL, and VDSL.

- The maximum allowable distance between a DSL modem and the local central office is typically 1,000 feet to 18,000 feet. This distance varies according to the type of DSL used and any special equipment that might exist on the telephone line, such as loading coils or a change in the media.

- DSL bandwidth varies from 1.5 Mbps to 52 Mbps depending on the DSL variation used and the distance from the local central office.

- Satellite communication is ideal for remote locations and offers various speeds based on cost of equipment and service.

- Consumer satellite-service bandwidth is typically 400 kbps to 500 kbps.

- Commercial satellite service bandwidth is a maximum 1.5 Mbps in the United States and 2 Mbps in Europe.

- Satellite communication use microwave technology and must have a clear line of site between the satellite and the satellite dish.

- T-carriers are leased lines and range from fractional T1 to T4. The most common T-carrier lines encountered in networking are fractional T1, T2, and T3.

- A T1 line consists of 24 channels with 64 kbps of bandwidth available per channel.

- T1 offers a maximum bandwidth of 1.544 Mbps, and T3 offers 44.736.

Copyright Goodheart-Willcox Co., Inc.

- Synchronous Optical Network (SONET) offers the highest bandwidth and the greatest distances.

- X.25 is an older telephone line technology that is rarely encountered in the United States but still exists in other parts of the world.

- Frame Relay is the replacement for X.25 and employs a permanent virtual circuit (PVC).

- Frame Relay and X.25 are packet switching technologies.

Dial-Up Networking

- Dial-up networking allows a user to access a network remotely using telephone lines.

- Dial-up networking requires a modem and remote access software to be installed on the client side of a remote connection and on a remote access server.

- Serial Line Interface Protocol (SLIP) is an older protocol used to support remote connections over telephone lines. It has been replaced by PPP and PPTP.

- Point-to-Point Tunneling Protocol (PPTP) encapsulates other protocols inside the PPTP packet, resulting in a secure connection.

- Multi-Protocol Label Switching (MPLS) can be used with IPv4- or IPv6-based networks as well as ATM, Frame Relay, or most any networking technology available today.

- MPLS provides a more efficient method of routing packets than traditional routing protocols.

- The main two applications of MPLS are network traffic shaping and support for VPN.

Virtual Private Network (VPN)

- A Virtual Private Network (VPN) is a secure connection over a public network system based on software, not hardware.

Review Questions

1. What is the name used for the telephone line running between customer premises and the local central office?

2. Where is the point of presence (POP) located?

3. What does the acronym ISDN represent?

4. How many channels are there in a BRI-ISDN cable assembly?

5. What is the maximum bandwidth of a BRI-ISDN service?

6. What is the maximum bandwidth for a telephone modem?

7. What is the purpose of the D channel in an ISDN cable assembly?

8. What is the maximum theoretical bandwidth for cable Internet access?

9. What factors influence the speed of a cable Internet service connection?

Copyright Goodheart-Willcox Co., Inc.

10. What is the difference between a T1 and a fractional T1 line?

11. How many T1 lines make up a T3 line?

12. Which has the highest bandwidth: a T1 connection or a telephone modem connection?

13. Which has the highest bandwidth: SONET or ISDN?

14. Which has the highest bandwidth: T1 or X.25?

15. What high-speed technology is used for long-distance communication especially overseas via underwater?

16. Which has a highest bandwidth: ISDN or consumer satellite service?

17. What does the acronym CSU/DSU represent?

18. With what type of media is a CSU/DSU associated?

19. Match the following:

i. ISDN	A. Fiber-optic system used for overseas connections
ii. DSL	B. Typically the slowest connection technology
iii. SONET	C. Two B channels and one D channel
iv. T3	D. Typically 45-Mbps bandwidth
v. Telephone modem	E. Digital telephone line

20. What is the main difference between SLIP and PPP?

21. In what situation is the PPPoE protocol used?

22. What is the main difference between PPTP and PPP?

23. What does the MPLS represent?

24. What are the two main applications for MPLS?

25. To which layer of the OSI model does MPLS align?

26. Which protocol is used to distribute MPLS label information to all MPLS-enabled routers?

27. What is the difference between a Virtual Private Network (VPN) and a network that uses a T1 line to connect two branch offices?

✚ Sample Network+ Exam Questions

1. Which technology provides the most bandwidth when connecting two networks located approximately 18 miles apart?

   A. PSTN

   B. DSL

   C. ISDN

   D. T1

2. Mary is establishing an ISDN connection to one of her company's remote offices. What is the typical bandwidth of one ISDN B channel?

   A. 56 kbps

   B. 64 kbps

   C. 128 kbps

   D. 1.5 Mbps

3. Josiah is trying to configure T1 access for a small bookkeeping company. What is the typical bandwidth for a T1 line?

   A. 56 kbps

   B. 64 kbps

   C. 128 kbps

   D. 1.544 Mbps

4. Abdel has noticed that his DSL line is getting far less than expected bandwidth. He is trying to troubleshoot this problem. What would most likely affect the bandwidth of a DSL line?

   A. The number of subscribers sharing the DSL line.

   B. The distance from the DSL modem to the DSL provider.

   C. The distance to the ISP.

   D. The amplitude of the signal modulation.

5. What network media does DSL use?

   A. Shielded twisted pair

   B. Coaxial cable

   C. Fiber-optic cable

   D. Telephone line

6. Ixia is setting up a VPN for her company. She needs to select a protocol for establishing a VPN. Which of the following protocols is commonly used to create a VPN?

   A. FTP

   B. HTTP

   C. PPTP

   D. SLIP

Copyright Goodheart-Willcox Co., Inc.

7. Which of the following protocols would be most appropriate for creating multiple, individual dial-up connections from an Ethernet network through a common DSL or cable modem to an ISP.

   A. PPP

   B. PPPoE

   C. SLIP

   D. TFTP

8. Frank needs to connect two offices. The offices transmit confidential information of their customers. For this reason, the connection must be very secure. Which medium provides the best security when transmitting data between two points?

   A. Satellite

   B. Internet

   C. T1 line

   D. IEEE 802.11a

9. Which of the following statements is true concerning X.25 and Frame Relay technologies?

   A. Frame Relay uses analog technology and X.25 does not.

   B. X.25 uses analog technology and Frame Relay does not.

   C. Frame Relay and X.25 both use analog technology.

   D. Frame Relay and X.25 both use digital technology.

10. Which communication medium is used for SONET?

    A. Wireless 2.5 GHz

    B. UTP

    C. RG-58

    D. Fiber-optic

Copyright Goodheart-Willcox Co., Inc.

CHAPTER 15 — Network Security

Network+ Certification Exam Objectives

The Network Security domain of the CompTIA Network+ Exam objectives has been expanded in recent years to include many of the latest security technologies. While an in-depth knowledge of any particular security technology is not required, you should be familiar with all of the objectives in the Network Security domain. It should be noted that each new version of Network+ has not only updated, but expanded the role of network security. This fact makes this chapter a pivotal chapter in your knowledge of networking.

Objectives

1.1: Protocols and Ports—SSH 22, SFTP 22

1.3: Segmentation and Interface Properties—DMZ

Access Control Lists

2.2: Firewall

2.3: Explain the Purposes and Use Cases for Advanced Networking Devices

3.2: Recover—Backups

3.4: VPN, SSH, VNC, HTTPS/Management URL

Remote File Access—SFTP

3.5: Identify Policies and Best Practices

4.1: Detection, Prevention

4.2: Authorization, Authentication, and Accounting—RADIUS, TACACS+, Kerberos, Single Sign-On, Local Authentication, Certificates, Auditing and Logging

Multifactor Authentication, Access Control

4.3: Given a Scenario, Secure a Basic Wireless Network

4.4: Summarize Common Networking Attacks

4.5: Given a Scenario, Implement Network Device Hardening

4.6: Explain Common Mitigation Techniques and Their Purposes

Switch Port Protection—Flood Guard, DHCP Snooping

5.2: Software Tools—Packet Sniffer, Protocol Analyzer, WiFi Analyzer, Command Line (netstat)

5.4: Security Type Mismatch

Learning Outcomes

- Differentiate between types of hackers.
- Give examples of common network security breaches and vulnerabilities.
- Explain the difference between an intrusion detection system and an intrusion prevention system.
- Provide examples of security methods and protocols.
- Describe methods for securing a wireless network.
- Compare RADIUS, Diameter, and TACACS+.
- List authentication methods.
- Compare authentication protocols.
- Summarize various methods of security implementation.
- Recall the purpose of various computer and network security tools.
- Give examples of security compliance requirements.

Copyright Goodheart-Willcox Co., Inc.

Key Terms

AAA proxy

application gateway

asymmetric-key encryption

authentication

authentication, authorization, and accounting (AAA)

backdoor

biometrics

certificate authority (CA)

Challenge Handshake Authentication Protocol (CHAP)

circuit-level gateway

content filter

demilitarized zone (DMZ)

Denial of Service (DoS)

Diameter

digital certificate

encryption

Extensible Authentication Protocol (EAP)

firewall signature identification

hashing

Health Insurance Portability and Accountability Act (HIPAA)

honey pot

Internet Protocol Security (IPSec)

intrusion detection system (IDS)

intrusion prevention system (IPS)

Kerberos

Lightweight Extensible Authentication Protocol (LEAP)

logic bomb

macro virus

malware

man in the middle (MITM)

media access control (MAC) filter

Microsoft Challenge Handshake Authentication Protocol (MS-CHAP)

packet filter

packet sniffer

Password Authentication Protocol (PAP)

Payment Card Industry Data Security Standard (PCI DSS)

phishing

port monitoring

Protected Extensible Authentication Protocol (PEAP)

protocol analyzer

proxy server

ransomware

Remote Authentication Dial-In User Service (RADIUS)

replay attack

rogue access point

Secure Copy Protocol (SCP)

Secure Shell (SSH)

Secure Sockets Layer (SSL)

smart card

Smurf attack

social engineering

spoofing

stateful packet inspection

stateless packet inspection

symmetric-key encryption

Terminal Access Controller Access-Control System Plus (TACACS+)

Transport Layer Security (TLS)

transport mode

Trojan horse

tunnel mode

virtual network connection (VNC)

virus

worm

Zero Configuration (Zeroconf)

Overview

This chapter presents the basics of network security. All network users need user and system policies that are set in place and enforced. Policies outline how users are to use and not use their workstations and the network. Basically, policies and procedure are a list of dos and don'ts for the users. Typically, this procedural list is referred to as an *acceptable use policy*.

In this chapter, you will receive a general overview of security systems and principles. Security often begins with authentication. This is simply the process of ensuring the user is indeed who he or she claims to be. There are many methods for authenticating a user, some specifically designed to make it extremely difficult to circumvent the authentication process. Regardless of which one is utilized, all authentication methods have the same final goal: to verify a user's identity.

Some examples of authentication methods include digital certificates, smart cards, and biometrics. We will look at these and other methods of authentication as well as security protocols and security methods, such as encryption, authorization, and accounting.

The field of network security is vast and complex. This chapter covers only the basics. A complete presentation of network security would require an entire course with a textbook completely dedicated to network security and an intensive series of lab activities.

Hacking

The term *hacker* truly describes any computer enthusiast who simply experiments with systems to learn about them. The term hacker does not necessarily imply criminal activity or behavior. There are three basic types of hackers: white-hat, black-hat, and gray-hat. *White-hat hackers* conduct themselves ethically and legally. Some are employed as penetration testers. *Black-hat hackers*, or *crackers*, are those who commit crimes with their hacking skills. It should be noted that this is actually a small segment of the hacking community. *Gray-hat hackers* are those who are generally white hat but occasionally drift into the black-hat arena. For the sake of clarity, anyone who gains access to a system he or she is not authorized to access is referred to in this text as an *intruder*.

Common Network Security Breaches

The topic of network security is very complex and would easily fill thousands of pages. In its simplest form, network security comprises two main elements: authentication and encryption. **Authentication**, or *local authentication*, is the process used to identify a user and ensure the user is who he or she claims to be. **Encryption** is a method of using an algorithm to encode data. Typically, authentication is accomplished through a combination of username and password. This method is probably the one with which you are most familiar. However, authentication alone is insufficient. Safeguards must be in place to protect a network fully.

In this next section, the most commonly encountered security breaches are covered to provide a basic understanding of network vulnerability. It may come as a surprise to learn that people, not equipment, generate most security breaches.

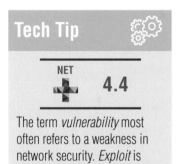

Tech Tip

The term *vulnerability* most often refers to a weakness in network security. *Exploit* is used to describe an attack that acted on a vulnerability.

Unprotected Network Shares

Many times employees will set up a network share to allow other employees to access or copy their files. What they do not realize is that setting up a network share with minimal to no security sets up a possible entry point for an attack from the outside. Many hacker tools can probe and access available shares on a network. This is a common way networks are compromised. Employees also create network shares with minimal to no security so that they might be able to access their own files from home. Network shares with minimal to no security, such as the one shown in Figure 15-1, and those with remote access enabled combine for a security breach waiting to happen.

Social Engineering

Social engineering is a term used to describe the manipulation of personnel through deceitful means to gain security information. One of the weakest security areas is the lack of security awareness of typical users and their respect for assumed authority. For example, consider the following scenario. A telephone rings on an administrator's desk and the following conversation takes place:

- **Caller:** Hello. This is Bob down at IMS operations conducting a security check. We believe we may have an intruder in our system.

- **Admin:** Yes. What can I do to help?

Copyright Goodheart-Willcox Co., Inc.

Figure 15-1 In this example, an employee has given the group **Administrators** full access to the **C:** drive.

Goodheart-Willcox Publisher

- **Caller:** Well Gene, I need to look at your PC files to see if there have been any possible intrusions. I need your username and password to inspect your system. It will only take a minute and will save me a lot of time rather than coming down there.

- **Admin:** Sure. My username is admin and the password is pa$$word.

The administrator's system has now been compromised by social engineering.

The forgoing scenario is a bit obvious, and frequently social engineering is not that blatant. However, any attempt to use social skills either to obtain illicit information from a user or to gain access to networks or facilities is social engineering. Consider phishing e-mails. In a fundamental sense, all phishing e-mails use social engineering to some extent. The e-mail is worded in a manner designed to entice the recipient into clicking on some link or opening some attachment that results in some type of security breach.

Open Ports

Ports, such as HTTP port 80, are used to connect to computers during communication sessions. Legitimate users normally use them for browsing a web page, network meetings, and performing file transfers and downloads. Open ports can also be a way for intruders to gain access to the network system. Open ports are one of the most common security problems for any site. All unused ports should be closed, and all

Copyright Goodheart-Willcox Co., Inc.

ports should be monitored for activity. A third-party utility or the **netstat** utility can be used to check for open ports. The **netstat** utility is covered later in this chapter.

Obviously, some ports need to be open or no services would be accessible. However, unnecessarily open ports, along with unnecessarily running services, present security vulnerabilities.

Zero Configuration (Zeroconf)

Zero Configuration (Zeroconf) is a standard developed by IEEE that recommends how to design a device that automatically detects other devices on the same network or on a nearby network segment without the need of intervention by an administrator or a DHCP or DNS server. Identification is based on MAC addresses, which are unique for each network device. *Network devices* are any devices that can be identified by a MAC address; this includes communication devices and electronic appliances.

Zeroconf devices must have a unique IP address, subnet mask, and gateway address issued automatically. The Zeroconf protocol must also be able to resolve duplicate IP addresses automatically and translate between IP addresses and host names.

The main reason for the development of Zeroconf protocol is to enable an easy method of networking devices without the intervention of an administrator. Microsoft operating systems as well as Mac OS 9 and later incorporate the Zeroconf standard. For example, the Microsoft wireless device protocol automatically configures a wireless network card when it is physically inserted into the computer.

The downside of Zeroconf is it makes a network less secure. A person could simply purchase a similar device and connect it to a network system to gain access. An example is a wireless device, such as a WAP, that uses a default SSID and automatic IP addressing. If the device is installed with the default settings and uses Zeroconf to configure the clients, anyone with a similar device installed can access the same network. From a security point of view, it is fortunate that Zeroconf has not become particularly popular.

Denial of Service (DoS)

Denial of Service (DoS) is the denial of access to a server by overloading it with false requests. It is one of the most common attacks on servers. A DoS attack overloads the server to the point that it crashes or is not able to complete legitimate user requests Aside from specific attacks, there are various types of DoS used: reflective, amplification, and distributed. *Reflective attacks*, as the name suggests, reflect other sources to the target. *Amplification attacks* amplify traffic. A *Distributed Denial of Service (DDoS) attack* is simply a DoS originating from multiple attacking machines. There have been a number of different ways of performing DoS attacks over the years. Examples include the Smurf attack and DHCP starvation.

Smurf Attack

The **Smurf attack** is a type of reflective DoS that uses a combination of IP spoofing and ICMP to saturate a target network with traffic. The attacker sends a modified ping to the broadcast address of a large network. The modified packet contains the source address of a target site. This causes all the machines on the target network to send replies to the target machine. If a flood of such packets is sent to the broadcast address of the target network, it will cause that network to flood the target machine and render it inaccessible.

Copyright Goodheart-Willcox Co., Inc.

DHCP Starvation

DHCP starvation is a DoS attack that seeks to exhaust the pool of available IP addresses, thus preventing users from connecting to the network. If enough requests flood onto a network, the attacker can completely exhaust the address space allocated by the DHCP servers for an indefinite period of time. There are tools such as *gobbler* that will do this automatically.

Man in the Middle (MITM)

Man in the middle (MITM) is a method of intercepting a network transmission, reading it, and then placing it back on route to its intended destination, as illustrated in Figure 15-2. It is a serious security breach. The contents may or may not be modified. This method can also be used for a replay attack. A **replay attack** occurs when the data in a network transmission is copied and stored. Later, information such as an IP or MAC address can be used to establish an unauthorized connection to the destination by impersonating the original source. Replay attacks are generally avoided by using a time stamp as part of the communication structure. The time stamp is used to verify the time of each transmission. If the time that is recorded in the time stamp exceeds a specific value, the entire packet is dropped because it is assumed to be bogus.

Spoofing

Spoofing is fooling a destination by using an IP address other than the true IP address of a source to create a fake identity, as demonstrated in Figure 15-3. For example,

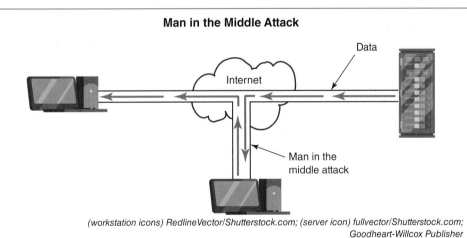

Man in the Middle Attack

Data

Internet

Man in the middle attack

(workstation icons) RedlineVector/Shutterstock.com; (server icon) fullvector/Shutterstock.com;
Goodheart-Willcox Publisher

Figure 15-2 A man in the middle attack occurs when a third party intercepts a data transmission with the intent to use vital information it contains for a later attack. Once the third party reads and stores the data transmission, it is placed back on route to its destination.

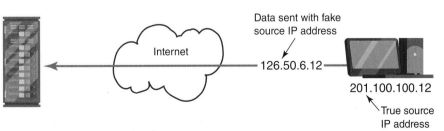

Spoofing

Data sent with fake source IP address

Internet

126.50.6.12

201.100.100.12

True source IP address

(workstation icons) RedlineVector/Shutterstock.com; (server icon) fullvector/Shutterstock.com;
Goodheart-Willcox Publisher

Figure 15-3 Spoofing is the act of using a fake IP address to gain access to a network.

Copyright Goodheart-Willcox Co., Inc.

to gain access to a network, an unauthorized person may try to use what they think is a valid IP address to fool a server. Another example is to use a fake IP address and ID when sending an unsolicited e-mail to someone. The e-mail can be used to solicit information or release a worm.

It is a good policy never to respond to an unsolicited e-mail. A common ploy is to send unsolicited e-mails to millions of possible legitimate e-mail addresses using a software program that generates possible e-mail addresses. In the e-mail, a line is included that states: "If this e-mail was sent by mistake and you wish to be removed from our e-mail list, please click the link below." The link is intended to generate a list of everyone who replies. The list is valuable because it contains a list of real e-mail addresses that can be sold or distributed to interested parties, such as advertisers. By responding to the removal link, you are actually verifying the e-mail address used was a genuine e-mail address.

Tech Tip

The terms *malware, virus*, and *worm* are often used interchangeably even though this is not technically correct.

Malware

Malware, short for *malicious software*, is a term given to software programs that are intended to damage, destroy, or steal data. Often, malware is disguised as something innocent but has devastating effects. For example, clicking an unsolicited link in an e-mail can trigger a line of code that will leave a computer or network vulnerable to infection. Malware comes in many forms including Trojan horses, viruses, worms, ransomware, and logic bombs.

Trojan Horse

A **Trojan horse** is a program designed to gain access to a computer while pretending to be something else. For example, a user downloads what he or she thinks is a free game. A real game may indeed be inside the download, and for a good Trojan horse design, it should be. However, in addition to the game program code is code of a malicious nature. The malicious code could contain a virus, worm, or what is known as a *backdoor*. A **backdoor** is a software access port to a computer infected by a Trojan horse. Another common purpose for a Trojan horse is to download a program that imitates the logon screen of a legitimate operating system. When the user logs on using the Trojan horse fake logon screen, the user's name and password is sent to an unauthorized user for later use in gaining access to the computer.

Virus

A **virus** is software that self-replicates. There are many different types of viruses, and some of the major categories will be discussed in this section. It is important to note that modern malware often combines elements of different categories. For example, a given malware infection could be a virus that also delivers a Trojan horse, and the Trojan horse then contains software to launch a DDoS attack.

Macro Virus

One of the most common and most easily written virus programs is a **macro virus**. Many legitimate software programs, such as word-processing packages, contain a special tool called a *macro writer*. The macro writer records and saves certain keystroke sequences as a convenience for the user. For example, a user can make a macro that inserts his or her return address into a document when he or she pressees a specific key sequence. The macro program is handy for reducing the amount of work involved for repetitive tasks. The same principle can be used to create viruses. A series of commonly used keystrokes can be linked to a virus. The macro is sent as an e-mail attachment and is launched when the e-mail recipient opens the attachment.

Copyright Goodheart-Willcox Co., Inc.

The macro virus may infect a template file like normal.dot and then execute when the user presses a certain combination of keys.

Stealth Virus

Often, virus creators want their viruses to go undetected by antivirus software. To accomplish this, they may use one or more stealth techniques. For example, *sparse infector* viruses will only do whatever illicit activity they are programmed to do intermittently. That makes it harder to detect the viruses. In other circumstances, the virus might be encrypted. There are many techniques a virus creator can use to make it harder to detect the virus.

Worm

A **worm** is essentially a rapidly spreading virus, as illustrated in Figure 15-4. Most of what is termed a virus today is actually a worm. A typical virus cannot spread automatically. There are many examples of famous worm programs, including ILOVEYOU, MyDoom and Storm Worm. Worms are typically spread through e-mail.

Figure 15-4 E-mail is the most common method of transmitting a worm. Using this method, the worm multiplies at an exponential rate.

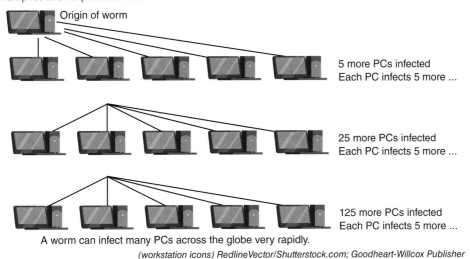

A worm can infect many PCs across the globe very rapidly.

(workstation icons) RedlineVector/Shutterstock.com; Goodheart-Willcox Publisher

Ransomware

Ransomware functions initially as a worm then either disables system services or encrypts user files. The perpetrator or originator of the malware then demands a ransom to release those files or services.

The first known ransomware attack was the 1989 PC Cyborg Trojan, which only encrypted filenames with a weak symmetric cipher. The notion of using public key cryptography for these attacks was introduced by Adam Young and Moti Yung in 1996.

One of the most widely known examples of ransomware is the infamous CryptoLocker. First discovered in 2013, CryptoLocker utilized asymmetric encryption to lock the users' files. Several varieties of CryptoLocker have since been detected.

Logic Bomb

A **logic bomb** is a type of malware that initiates malicious activity after some logical condition has been met. This can be a specific date or time or some condition occurring. One example of a condition-based logic bomb is one in which an employee of a company designs the bomb in a way that it deletes vital files should the employee's termination be processed.

DNS Poisoning

DNS poisoning occurs when an attacker tries to get fake entries into the target's DNS server. That way, when users on that network enter a domain, for example, xyzbank.com, their own DNS server redirects them to a phishing site. This is closely related to ARP poisoning. *ARP poisoning* involves obtaining a network's ARP table and spoofing responses from ARP addresses. This only works within a domain.

Evil Twin

In an evil twin attack, a rogue wireless access point is configured so it has the same MAC address as one of the existing legitimate access points. A rogue WAP will often then initiate a denial of service attack on a legitimate access point, making it unable to respond to users. This results in users being redirected to the evil twin. This is also a form of man in the middle (MITM) attack. In general, a MITM attack has occurred any time someone gets between two parties. This is also done in cryptography during the key-exchange process. If an attacker can get between the two parties during key exchange, he or she can compromise the encryption process.

Deauthentication

A deauthentication attack is also sometimes called *deassociation*. In this attack, the attacker causes the client to deauthenticate from a reliable source. This is often followed by trying to get the user to connect to an evil twin.

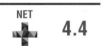

Phishing

Phishing (pronounced *fishing*) is a method of Internet fraud that involves using e-mail to steal a person's identity and other sensitive information, such as financial data. In a phishing attack, an e-mail is sent that appears to be from a legitimate enterprise in an attempt to solicit personal information. For example, a person may receive an e-mail that appears to be from the legitimate company eBay. The e-mail may even use the eBay artwork and logo. The contents of the e-mail requests the person's personal information, such as a bank account PIN, credit card number, password, Social Security number, and anything else that can be used for identity theft.

Another example is an e-mail that poses as a known and often accessed company, such as a credit card company. The e-mail states that a virus has compromised all user accounts and that the company must reconstruct all user account information. The e-mail contains a link to the company's website. The e-mail recipient is told in the e-mail to go to the website and enter the requested information. When the e-mail recipient clicks the included link, he or she is directed to an illegal site created to look like the website of the legitimate company. However, the domain name of the illegal site is slightly different than the domain name of the legitimate company. The bogus domain name goes undetected by the e-mail recipient because of slight changes in the characters. Notice in Figure 15-5 how similarly shaped characters and numbers have been substituted.

Based on the examples in Figure 15-5, one can see how easy it can be to create a fictitious website designed solely for extracting personal data. Also, be aware that rolling the mouse over a website link embedded in the text of an e-mail created with HTTP can automatically take you to a site that resembles the website indicated in the link. The link can be easily programmed to direct a user to a different website

Copyright Goodheart-Willcox Co., Inc.

Figure 15-5 A domain name can be disguised by making slight changes in the characters. Notice how a lowercase *l* looks similar to the number *1* and a capital *O* looks similar to the number *0*.

Legitimate Site	Bogus Site	Look At the Following in the Bogus Website:
www.paypal.com	www.paypa1.com	The number *1* used in place of the letter *l*.
firstfederal.com	www.firstfedera1.com	The letter *l* again.
www.payonline.com	www.pay0nline.com	The number *0* for the letter *O*.

Goodheart-Willcox Publisher

altogether. Never send personal information in response to e-mail, even if the e-mail looks legitimate. It is best to call the company first to confirm the legitimacy of the e-mail.

Insider Threat

Perhaps the most critical threat today is the insider. This threat manifests in two general ways. The first is simply user error. A user on a network mistakenly picks a bad password, clicks on a link, visits a bad website, or some other accidental occurrence. These activities have no malicious intent; they are just mistakes. However, they can pose a significant threat to a network.

The second issue is the intentional malicious activity by an insider. An inside employee can choose to manipulate critical data, damage network resources, or even plant a logic bomb or other malware. This can be done for financial reasons or because the employee is simply disgruntled.

Brute Force

Possibly the simplest of all security attacks is a brute-force attack. A brute-force attack, also known as brute-force cracking, is one in which the attacker tries various password or passphrases until one is accepted. For example, if an attacker wanted to gain access to a person's laptop, he or she could repeatedly try passwords until the correct one is found. If the correct phrase is never found, there is likely no trace the attack ever occurred. If the attack succeeds, access is granted to the network. Brute-force attacks can often be avoided by complex passwords, limiting the number of tries a person has to log in, and temporarily locking out users who exceed the number of password attempts.

Intrusion Detection and Intrusion Prevention Systems

An intrusion detection system (IDS) and intrusion prevention system (IPS) are designed to monitor host and network systems for unauthorized activity. All security protection systems, both software and hardware, can be classified as either IDS or IPS.

An **intrusion detection system (IDS)** is a passive system that only detects unauthorized activity, as illustrated in Figure 15-6. For example, Microsoft Event Viewer is a type of IDS system. It monitors activities on a host computer but does not prevent unauthorized activity.

An **intrusion prevention system (IPS)** is a reactive system that not only detects unauthorized activity, but also performs some function to stop the activity, shown in Figure 15-7. For example, most antivirus software programs not only detect unauthorized activity, such as an attempt to download and install malware, they can also remove malware.

Figure 15-6 An intrusion detection system (IDS) passively monitors all packets and detects unauthorized activity. It does not prevent unauthorized activity.

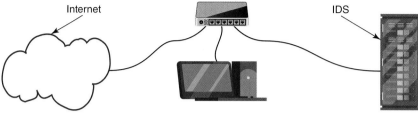

(workstation icon) RedlineVector/Shutterstock.com; (server icon) fullvector/Shutterstock.com; (hub icon) Vadim Ermak/Shutterstock.com; Goodheart-Willcox Publisher

Figure 15-7 An intrusion prevention system (IPS) actively monitors all packets by detecting unauthorized activity and performing some function to stop the activity.

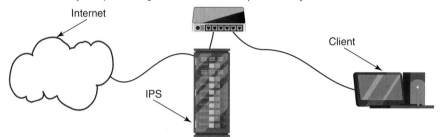

(workstation icon) RedlineVector/Shutterstock.com; (server icon) fullvector/Shutterstock.com; (hub icon) Vadim Ermak/Shutterstock.com; Goodheart-Willcox Publisher

The detection system can be either host-based or network-based. A host-based system is installed on an individual computer, where it monitors and prevents unauthorized activity. Network-based systems monitor and protect the entire network.

Both IDS and IPS can generate false positives. A *false positive* is when a file is detected and perceived as harmful to the system. The file is then quarantined or deleted, and a notice is sent to the system administrator. After reviewing the file, it is typically found to be a driver update that was downloaded with the intention of being installed automatically or some other equally harmless file. A perfect IDS/IPS solution does not exist, nor will one likely ever be attained.

Network IDS and IPS typically require some form of port monitoring. **Port monitoring** is when a particular port on a switch is connected directly to the IDS or IPS and monitors all activity through another port on the same switch. In other words, two ports carry identical packet information. One port is used to carry packets to other parts of the network while the other port (the mirror) analyzes the packets.

Another related security device is a honey pot. A **honey pot** is a fake system designed to look attractive to an attacker, for example, it may appear to be a financial database. However, all the data contained within it is fake. An intruder who bypasses other security measures will be attracted to this device. When they begin exfiltrating data, two things occur. The first is that all the data is fake, so no harm is done. The second is that a honey pot is usually configured with extensive monitoring. Often, all of the attacker's activities are logged and tracked.

NET
+ 4.6

Security Methods and Protocols

The two basic building blocks of secure network communication are authentication and encryption. These security methods are supported by security protocols. The concepts presented in this section are critical for a basic understanding of the sophisticated world of network security.

Copyright Goodheart-Willcox Co., Inc.

Cryptography

There are two basic types of cryptography in use today: *symmetric-key encryption* and *asymmetric-key encryption*. Symmetric means the same key is used to encrypt and decrypt the message. With asymmetric cryptography, a different key is used to encrypt the message than is used to decrypt the message. A *key* is a software code used to encode or decode data.

Symmetric-Key Encryption

Symmetric-key encryption, or *secret-key cryptography*, uses a key that only the sender and the receiver know. Both parties use the same key to perform encryption and decryption, as illustrated in Figure 15-8. The term *symmetric* is used because the same key is used for both coding and decoding the message.

Figure 15-8 The symmetric-key encryption system uses the same key to encrypt and decrypt data.

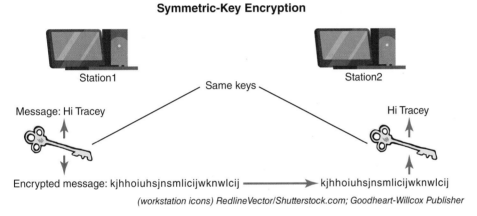

Symmetric-Key Encryption

(workstation icons) RedlineVector/Shutterstock.com; Goodheart-Willcox Publisher

Symmetric keys are typically used when large amounts of data are to be encrypted. The symmetric key encodes and decodes faster than more complex methods and can be just as secure. Symmetric algorithms are usually much faster than asymmetric and tend to use smaller keys. However, there is the issue of key exchange. How do you get the key to the other party? A few common symmetric ciphers are described here.

DES

DES is the oldest modern symmetric cipher, first published in 1976. It uses a 56-bit key to encrypt 64-bit blocks of code. It is a robust algorithm, but the key length is considered too short for modern usage. There is a variation called 3DES that uses three different DES keys to encrypt the message.

AES

Advanced Encryption Standard (AES) was the algorithm eventually chosen to replace DES. It is a block cipher that works on 128-bit blocks. It can have one of three key sizes of 128, 192, or 256 bits. This was selected by the United States government to be the replacement for DES and is now the most widely used symmetric-key algorithm. According to the US government, AES with a 256-bit key is secure enough for top-secret documents.

Blowfish

Blowfish is a symmetric block cipher. It uses a variable-length key ranging from 32 to 448 bits. Blowfish was designed in 1993 by Bruce Schneier. There is no copyright or patent on this algorithm, so it is very popular for use in open-source products.

Copyright Goodheart-Willcox Co., Inc.

Asymmetric-Key Encryption

Asymmetric-key encryption, or *public-key cryptography*, uses two keys: a private key and a public key, shown in Figure 15-9. Typically, the originator of the encryption system owns the private key. For example, a teacher who wishes to communicate with his or her students across the Internet while ensuring privacy would retain a private key. A public key is then issued to all students. A message is encoded using the private key and can only be decoded using the public key. The owner of the public key can send a message in return that can only be decoded by the private key.

Figure 15-9 The asymmetric key encryption system uses two different keys—one key for encrypting the data and the other for decrypting the data.

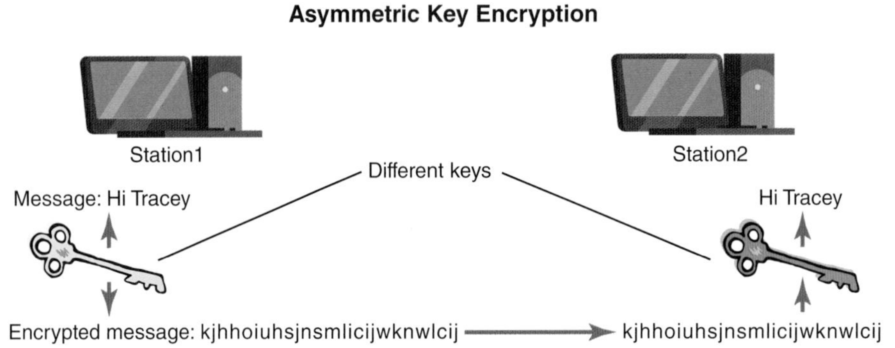

Asymmetric Key Encryption

Station1   Station2

Message: Hi Tracey   Hi Tracey

Different keys

Encrypted message: kjhhoiuhsjnsmlicijwknwlcij ⟶ kjhhoiuhsjnsmlicijwknwlcij

(workstation icon) RedlineVector/Shutterstock.com; Goodheart-Willcox Publisher

In this method, a message created with a private key can only be decoded with a public key, and a message encrypted with a public key can only be decoded with a private key. A message created with a public key cannot be decoded with another public key. This means that all the encryption and decryption is centered on the owner of the private key. It takes both the public and private keys to code and decode an encrypted message. Examples of asymmetric algorithms include RSA and Diffie-Hellman.

RSA

RSA is probably the most widely used asymmetric cipher today. This public key method was developed in 1977 by three mathematicians: Ron Rivest, Adi Shamir, and Len Adlema. The name *RSA* is derived from the first letter of each mathematician's last name. The secret to the math behind RSA is that it is very difficult to factor large numbers into their prime factors. RSA depends on this for security.

Diffie-Hellman

Diffie-Hellman was the first publicly described asymmetric algorithm. This is a cryptographic protocol that allows two parties to establish a shared key over an insecure channel. In other words, Diffie-Hellman is often used to allow parties to exchange a symmetric key through some unsecure medium, such as the Internet. It was developed by Whitfield Diffie and Martin Hellman in 1976.

Certificate Authority (CA)

NET
✚ 4.2

Typically, a service referred to as the **certificate authority (CA)** contains the security list of users authorized to access the private key owner's messages using a public key, as demonstrated in Figure 15-10. The private key owner consults the CA for this information before sending a message. The CA sends the requested information in the form of a digital certificate. A **digital certificate** is a file that commonly contains data such as the user's name and e-mail address, the public key value assigned to the user, the validity period of the public key, and issuing authority identifier information.

The encryption/decryption process is demonstrated in Figure 15-11. Suppose *Station1* wants to send an encrypted message to *Station2*. *Station1* applies for a digital certificate from a CA. The CA issues a digital certificate, which contains the user's public or private key and security identification information known only to *Station1* and the CA. *Station1* uses the private key to encrypt the message. *Station1* can now send a message to *Station2*. When *Station2* receives the message, it uses the public key to decode the encrypted message. If *Station2* sends an encrypted reply to *Station1* using the public key, *Station1* will decode the reply using the private key.

Figure 15-10 The CA issues a private key to the private key owner and then issues public keys to public key users approved by the private key owner.

Goodheart-Willcox Publisher

Figure 15-11 *Station1* applies for and receives a digital certificate from the CA. *Station2* uses the public key provided by the CA to decode the message and to verify the sender is really *Station1*. After verifying and receiving the message from *Station1*, *Station2* can send an encrypted reply to *Station1*.

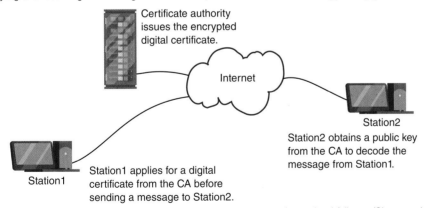

(workstation icons) RedlineVector/Shutterstock.com; (server icon) fullvector/Shutterstock.com;
Goodheart-Willcox Publisher

DigiCert is one of the largest commercial digital certificate companies in the world. A certificate from DigiCert can be obtained by applying for one at their website. Figure 15-12 shows a DigiCert security certificate. The list of protection services offered by this particular certificate is visible to the user. In Figure 15-13, some of the details about this certificate can be seen. Looking closely, a user can see the validity period of the certificate, the particular algorithm used, and the length of the public key, which is 2048 bits.

Figure 15-12 A digital certificate issued from DigiCert.

Goodheart-Willcox Publisher

Figure 15-13 Details of a digital certificate from DigiCert.

Goodheart-Willcox Publisher

Copyright Goodheart-Willcox Co., Inc.

Secure Sockets Layer (SSL)

3.4 NET

Secure Sockets Layer (SSL) is a security protocol used to authenticate clients and servers and to encrypt data between web servers and individuals. SSL was first introduced and developed by Netscape Communications Corporation. It was designed to secure transactions between web servers and individuals using the Internet for such purposes as credit card transactions. SSL has been well accepted, and as a result, there have been several revisions of the SSL protocol. SSL 3.0 is the latest version. Even though this version was released before the year 2000, it has not been supplanted by TLS.

Transport Layer Security (TLS)

3.4 NET

Transport Layer Security (TLS) is an Internet Engineering Task Force (IEFT) standard that was developed after SSL. It serves the same purpose as SSL. Both SSL and TLS are application layer protocols. Both are based on public key encryption technology. When used to support secure website connections, they both display https:// at the start of the URL. The *S* at the end of *https* means that the connection is secure and is using either SSL or TLS as the security mechanism.

The main difference between SSL and TLS is in the way they secure the connection. According to the SANS Technology Institute, TLS is more secure than SSL. Ironically, SSL is more popular than TLS. This is most likely because SSL was introduced first and has become the accepted de facto security protocol for website transactions.

Originally, SSL was designed to support secure website connections. Today, SSL and TLS security functions have been expanded to include applications, such as VoIP, e-mail, and remote connections.

Although the differences between the two protocols SSL and TLS are minor, the two protocols are not directly compatible. Users must use either SSL or TLS but not both at the same time. There are provisions that allow users to attempt a connection with one protocol and answer the request with the other protocol. A negotiation takes place between the client and server, and an agreement is reached where both the client and server will use either TLS or SSL to complete the secure connection. SSL and TLS are similar in the following ways:

- They are application layer protocols.
- They are based on public key cryptology.
- They are supported by all major Internet browsers.
- Neither one requires that the client have a preconfigured user account on the server.

To learn more about TLS and SSL, visit http://technet.microsoft.com/en-us/library/cc784450(WS.10).aspx.

Virtual Network Connection (VNC)

3.4 NET

A **virtual network connection (VNC)** is a term used to describe the broad category of remote connection systems that allow a user to connect to a network device, such as a server or a desktop computer, from a remote device, such as a laptop or cell phone. Typically, the user attaches to the remote network either wirelessly or through an Internet connection. Because the remote user is not actually a physical part of the network the user is accessing, the connection is considered "virtual."

Copyright Goodheart-Willcox Co., Inc.

Internet Protocol Security (IPSec)

Internet Protocol Security (IPSec) provides end-to-end security across the public Internet and private networks. It is one of the most widely used methods for configuring a virtual private network (VPN). IPSec was developed by the Internet Engineering Task Force (IETF) and was incorporated into many different vender security systems. IPSec is an optional security feature for IPv4, but it is not optional for IPv6.

IPSec consists of a wide collection of security protocols, hashes, and algorithms. **Hashing** is a technique that relies on an algorithm or encryption device based on mathematical algorithms for guessing a password. The security protocols, hashes, and algorithms can be implemented in various combinations to make IPSec more unique for a given vender. Some of the more common software applications are firewalls, VPNs, and authentication software.

There are two standard modes of IPSec implementation: transport mode and tunnel mode. In **tunnel mode**, the payload and the header, which contains routing information, is encrypted. In **transport mode**, only the payload is encrypted, as demonstrated in Figure 15-14. Transport mode is typically used for a host-to-host connection that already provides another form of security so that only the payload needs protection. Tunnel mode provides a greater degree of security and is commonly used for VPN applications.

Figure 15-14 Transport mode encrypts only the packet data. Tunnel mode encrypts both the IP header information and the data. Tunnel mode requires a gateway or router IP header address, which accounts for the additional IP header at the front of the packet.

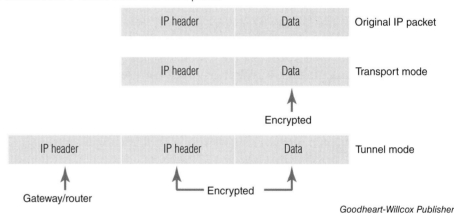

Goodheart-Willcox Publisher

Some of the more common security technologies that can be implemented with IPSec are ESP, IKE, AH, MDS, SHA-1, 3DES, AES, and more. The two common protocols associated with IPSec are Encapsulated Security Payload (ESP) and Authentication Header (AH). Authentication can also be verified using Kerberos; a preshared key, which is a key shared in advance of information exchanges; or digital certificate. IPSec VPNs typically use public and private keys for encryption. IPSec works at the network layer and is transparent to the user. Microsoft first started incorporating IPSec into Windows Server 2003.

Secure Shell (SSH)

Secure Shell (SSH) is a protocol that provides secure network services over an insecure network medium such as the Internet. SSH was originally designed for Unix systems to replace Remote Login (**rlogin**), Remote Shell (**rsh**), and Remote Copy (**rcp**). These utilities are known as *r commands* by Unix and Linux users. The r commands do not directly support encryption, which means files and commands are sent in plain text and can be intercepted and read by a protocol sniffer or analyzer. SSH is as-

Copyright Goodheart-Willcox Co., Inc.

sociated with TCP/IP port 22. It requires the use of a private and a public key as well as a password. The *r commands* do not require a password, but they do need to be issued by the root user. While the *r commands* require root privileges, which provide a level of system security, many security experts do not consider this a sophisticated means of authentication.

Today, the open-source SSH protocol can be used on any operating system that supports the TCP/IP suite. This means SSH can be used on Microsoft and Mac OS. Microsoft does not directly support SSH because it uses its own security mechanisms. However, a third-party software program that supports SSH can be installed.

Secure Copy Protocol (SCP)

Secure Copy Protocol (SCP) provides a secure way of transferring files between computers. It is the replacement for **rcp**. Similar to anonymous FTP, the **rcp** command does not require a password. Recall from Chapter 13 that an anonymous FTP site allows anyone to access the site and download or upload files.

SSH, SCP, and SFTP are all issued as commands in the Unix/Linux environment. Linux commands are case-sensitive, so they must be issued in lowercase form, such as **ssh**, **scp**, and **sftp**. There are third-party GUI programs that incorporate the open source SSH, SCP, and SFTP protocols so that the user does not need to issue text commands at the command prompt.

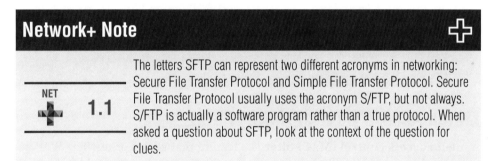

Network+ Note

NET 1.1

The letters SFTP can represent two different acronyms in networking: Secure File Transfer Protocol and Simple File Transfer Protocol. Secure File Transfer Protocol usually uses the acronym S/FTP, but not always. S/FTP is actually a software program rather than a true protocol. When asked a question about SFTP, look at the context of the question for clues.

Wireless Security

NET 4.2

Wireless devices are inherently insecure because the wireless medium, the radio wave, is an unbound medium. Wired networks can be installed inside walls, ceilings, floors, and metal conduits, which provide a degree of physical security. Someone attempting to tap into a wired network would at least need to access the inside of the building. A wireless network can extend beyond the physical limits of a building. This means that anyone can automatically have physical access to the network without entering the building if certain security measures are not set in place. For example, a small wireless network may have no security enabled or have only limited security provided by a wireless access point (WAP).

Although it is becoming less common, attackers sometimes will engage in war driving. *War driving* is the process of driving around looking for a Wi-Fi network that is vulnerable to infiltration. It can be useful to scan your own wireless network with a Wi-Fi analyzer to determine if vulnerabilities exist.

4.4, 5.2 NET

The original solution to wireless network security involves three mechanisms: service set identifier (SSID), media access control (MAC) filtering, and Wired Equivalent Privacy (WEP). Wireless network security has evolved at a remarkable rate. In less than seven years, four major security implementations have been developed: WPA, WPA2, 802.1x, and 802.11i. This section covers the original solution to wireless network security, SSID, MAC filtering, and WEP, plus the most recent security implementations, WPA, WPA2, 802.1x, and 802.11i.

4.2 NET

Tech Tip

NET 5.4 Devices must be using the same security settings in order to connect. If a device is using WPA, it cannot communicate with one using WPA2. This is called a *security type mismatch*.

Wireless Access Point Authentication

Wireless device authentication can be achieved in more than one way. A wireless access point (WAP) is the first authentication mechanism. However, not all wireless access points implement authentication based on username and password. Typically, a WAP is set by default to allow anyone with the same brand of wireless network device to connect automatically to the WAP, and thus to the wired network.

Wireless networks use a *service set identifier (SSID)* to identify the wireless network. The SSID is similar to a workgroup name. Multiple wireless networks can coexist within range of each other and operate independently by using different SSIDs. All wireless devices have a default SSID. To increase security, the SSID should be changed when the WAP is installed. In order to connect to a WAP, users must have the correct SSID; otherwise, they will receive an error message or connect to the wrong WAP.

Tech Tip

If a WAP has more sophisticated options, such as a username and password feature, it is referred to as a *wireless gateway* or *router*.

Media Access Control (MAC) Filter

A **media access control (MAC) filter** is a feature that allows or restricts WAP access based on the MAC address of a wireless network card. To set up a MAC filter, an administrator creates an access control list (ACL). The ACL contains a list of MAC addresses belonging to authorized wireless network devices. The ACL is stored in the WAP. When a wireless network device attempts to access the network through the WAP, the WAP checks the ACL to see if the wireless network device is authorized to access the network.

Wired Equivalent Privacy (WEP)

Wired Equivalent Privacy (WEP) was the first attempt to encrypt data transferred across a wireless network. It was part of the original IEEE 802.11 wireless standard. Not long after WEP was implemented, it was discovered that there were flaws in the encryption method. The WEP algorithm was not as complex as it was first thought to be. A determined hacker could crack the encryption in several hours. In fact, several tools are available on the Internet that can be used to crack WEP encryption keys.

WEP-secured networks can use open-system or shared-key authentication. *Open-system authentication* is arranged in a way that clients do not need to provide credentials to an access point during authentication. With shared-key authentication, a client sends a request to the access point, which replies with a clear-text challenge. The client then encrypts the clear-text and sends it back to the access point. If the decrypted response matches the original clear text, the client is connected.

While WEP might be adequate for a low-risk network, such as a home network that does not participate in financial transactions, it is inadequate for high-risk

Copyright Goodheart-Willcox Co., Inc.

networks, such as a business where financial transactions are commonplace. Creating a VPN, however, can compensate for WEP vulnerability. A VPN can incorporate an authentication and an encryption method, adding to the security set in place by WEP.

Wi-Fi Protected Access (WPA)

Wi-Fi Protected Access (WPA) was developed by the Wi-Fi organization and is not an IEEE standard. When vulnerabilities were discovered in the algorithm used for WEP, a more restrictive encryption was needed to protect data transferred across a wireless network. The Wi-Fi organization sponsored the development of Wi-Fi Protected Access (WPA) as a solution to the vulnerabilities discovered in WEP. WPA uses a more complex encryption technique to protect data. It has become the replacement for WEP. WPA is designed to be compatible with 802.11 devices and uses *Temporal Key Integrity Protocol (TKIP)* to change keys frequently. This makes the network more secure.

Wi-Fi Protected Access 2 (WPA2)

Wi-Fi Protected Access 2 (WPA2) was developed by the Wi-Fi organization as an enhanced version of WPA. It is designed to be compatible with the IEEE 802.11i standard. WPA2 uses *Counter Mode-Cipher Block Chaining Message Authentication Code Protocol (CCMP)*. The details of this protocol are beyond the scope of the Network+ Exam. However, you should be aware that it ensures confidentiality and integrity of messages.

802.11i

The IEEE ratified the IEEE 802.11i standard in June of 2004 to remedy the original security flaws in 802.11. The 802.11i standard specifies the use of a 128-bit Advanced Encryption Standard (AES) for data encryption. It also incorporates a mechanism for generating a fresh set of keys for each new connection. This results in enhanced security because the keys are constantly changed rather than reused. 802.11i is downward compatible with existing 802.11 devices. However, this does not mean that the security standards of the 802.11 devices are improved. It simply means that an 802.11i device will use WEP for security when communicating with an 802.11 device.

802.1x Authentication

802.1x provides port-based, network access control. Port-based network access control supports authentication for Ethernet network access. The term *port-based* refers to any location point represented as a point of access. Do not confuse the term *port-based* with the term *port*, which is used in conjunction with an IP address to identify a service, such as port 80 for HTTP. 802.1x is primarily used for client/server-based networks. It allows the network server to authenticate a wireless network device when the wireless network device attempts to connect to the wired network through a WAP. Older wireless network hardware does not support Advanced Encryption Standard (AES) and therefore cannot fully support the 802.1x enhancements.

802.1x requires three components: supplicant, authenticator, and authentication server, as illustrated in Figure 15-15. The *supplicant* is the wireless network device that is requesting network access. The WAP functions as the *authenticator* and does not allow any type of access to the network without proper authentication. A server running Remote Authentication Dial-In User Service (RADIUS) acts as the *authentication server*. **Remote Authentication Dial-In User Service (RADIUS)** is a service that allows remote access servers to authenticate to a central server.

Copyright Goodheart-Willcox Co., Inc.

Figure 15-15 The 802.1x standard provides centralized authentication for wireless LANs. It incorporates three components: supplicant, authenticator, and authentication server.

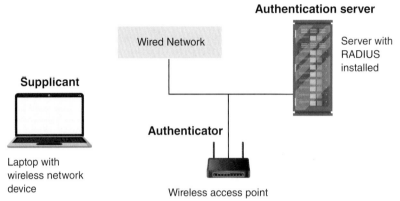

(server icon) fullvector/Shutterstock.com; (router icon) Vadim Ermak/Shutterstock.com; (laptop icon) Jemastock/Shutterstock.com; Goodheart-Willcox Publisher

802.1x provides a much easier way to manage numerous wireless access points. By using a server to provide centralized authentication, there is no need to maintain an ACL at each WAP. For example, a university campus might incorporate hundreds of wireless access points, which permit students and faculty to access the system from anywhere on campus. Every semester, new students and faculty need to be added to the ACL. 802.1x allows for a much easier security model by allowing an administrator to manage security from a centralized location.

To set up IEEE 802.1x on a wireless network client, IEEE 802.1x must be enabled within the wireless network properties menu. There are numerous authentication methods available from which to choose. Additionally, the exact number of security types, encryption types, and authentication methods available will vary according to the operating system version and network adapter manufacturer support. Many of these methods are proprietary designs by companies such as Microsoft, Cisco, and Intel. The authentication method selected must match the method used by the RADIUS server.

IEEE 802.1x authentication is enabled in the **Wireless Network Properties** dialog box. The exact number of security, encryption, and authentication types will vary according to operating system version and network adapter manufacturer support. If no security type is selected, no encryption types or authentication options will be available.

If encryption is disabled for the wireless client or the wireless client is part of a peer-to-peer network, an error message will display. The message says that if encryption is disabled for the wireless client, IEEE 802.1x cannot be used for authentication—nor can 802.1x be used on a peer-to-peer network. Remember, a peer-to-peer network does not have a server to verify authentication, which is one of the requirements of 802.1x.

Rogue Wireless Access Points

A **rogue access point** is an unauthorized wireless access point that is installed on a network system. Rogue access points provide a means to compromise the security of a network. Any network user could add a WAP to an existing network, thus allowing anyone to gain access to the network. Rogue access points can be prevented by using a wireless intrusion prevention system (WIPS). The WIPS will automatically conduct radio scans to identify the existence and location of the rogue access point. One method of preventing the successful use of a rogue access point is the use of an 802.1x system such as RADIUS, which requires authentication through a server.

Copyright Goodheart-Willcox Co., Inc.

Authentication, Authorization, and Accounting

2.3 NET

Authentication, authorization, and accounting (AAA), also known as *triple A*, is a security standard that consists of three parts: authentication, authorization, and accounting. Authentication is the process of verifying the identity of the user. It incorporates various authentication models typically designed around a username and user password. Authorization is the process of identifying which system resources a user may use. User share permissions are an example of authorization. Accounting is a system that tracks what resources a user accesses and keeps a record of user activity. An example is the Windows security log, shown in Figure 15-16.

Figure 15-16 Windows 10 security log as accessed through Computer Management. The security log can be used to track user activity.

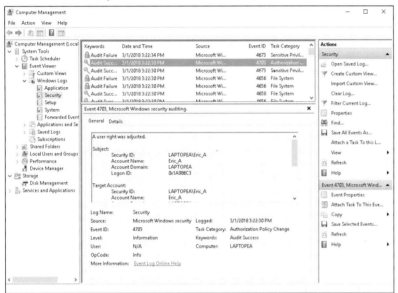

Goodheart-Willcox Publisher

Another form of accounting is the activity log used by Internet service providers that host web pages. The ISP uses logs to track total bandwidth and disk space used and to maintain a list of IP addresses that access each web page.

The triple-A security standard is the most common model used for network access today. The dominant client/server security models that support the AAA concept are RADIUS, TACACS+, and Diameter. Each of these security systems provide authentication, authorization, and accounting but in different ways.

RADIUS

2.3, 4.2 NET

RADIUS is the acronym for Remote Authentication Dial-In User Service and is an IETF standard that describes how to access client/server network systems. RADIUS is the default method of network security used by Microsoft and is incorporated into many of the Microsoft security features, such as Internet Authentication Service (IAS), Network Policy Server (NPS), and remote access service.

RADIUS systems authenticate users on a client/server network. The server is referred to as the *Network Access Server (NAS)*. Today, RADIUS is used for more than just dial-in access to a network. It is also used for wireless access and Internet access to the NAS. RADIUS provides a centralized location, typically a server that is used to store user account credentials. Many Internet service providers use RADIUS to store

> **Note**
>
> When using the Internet to research authentication, authorization, and accounting (AAA), you may be directed to Cisco and its AAA security model and not to the intent of the AAA identified in the CompTIA Network+ objectives. Cisco provides a security system for router and server access referred to as *Cisco IOS AAA* and *Cisco NX-OS*. The IOS is an acronym representing *Internetwork Operating System* and the NX-OS is an acronym representing *NeXt-generation Operating System*.

> **Note**
>
> Internet Authentication Service (IAS) is the Microsoft implementation of RADIUS for Windows Server 2003 and Network Policy Server (NPS) is the Microsoft implementation of RADIUS for Windows Server 2008 and 2016.

usernames and passwords and record user activity. A token is typically assigned to the user after authentication. The token is used to authorize the user account to various portions of the network that match the user permissions. The token is also used to track user activity.

RADIUS is referred to as a *port authentication standard*. Microsoft refers to it as an *802.1x security standard*. Some switches have an advanced feature referred to as *port authentication*. Port authentication is a method in which a switch restricts access through a specific switch port until access is authenticated by a RADIUS or TACACS+ server. To learn more about Microsoft RADIUS, visit the following Microsoft TechNet links:

- http://technet.microsoft.com/en-us/network/bb643123.aspx
- http://technet.microsoft.com/en-us/library/bb742381.aspx
- http://technet.microsoft.com/en-us/library/cc731320.aspx

Diameter

Note

Diameter is a play on words with RADIUS; both refer to measurements of a circle.

Diameter is an IETF standard and a next-generation authentication protocol designed to secure a connection between two or more devices. The Diameter standard is especially applicable to roaming devices such as cell phones. In contrast to RADIUS, Diameter does not require a client/server model and can be used in a peer-to-peer network for applications such as a cell phone peer-to-peer wireless network. Diameter allows for *attributes* to be added to the basic Diameter protocol structure. By adding attributes, Diameter is enhanced to meet AAA security requirements.

In its simplest form, Diameter is not directly compatible with RADUIS, but the IETF designed Diameter so that it can be compatible with a client/server application that uses a RADIUS server. For example, attributes can be added to the Diameter protocol that will allow a Diameter device to authenticate with a RADIUS server. Diameter can be compatible with a RADIUS server without the need to translate protocols or use a gateway. RADIUS typically requires the clients and server be configured manually, whereas Diameter supports automatic dynamic discovery through DNS.

When Diameter is extended to meet the AAA requirements, it can be used for not only authentication and authorization, but also accounting. Cell phone billing information can be included in the accounting portion of AAA. For example, a user with a Diameter-enabled portable communication device can make a secure connection with the home-office network. The user will authenticate through the network RADIUS server and be tracked not only by the client/server network but also by the cell phone service provider. You can think of it as a shared AAA environment.

The **AAA proxy** is any network device that acts as an intermediary to exchange security packets between the AAA server and the AAA client. For example, when a portable device such as a cell phone receives a request, it acts as the server by forwarding the authentication request to a RADIUS server for verification. The cell phone acting as a server will then act as a client to the RADIUS server when it receives verification. In this function, the cell phone acts as an AAA proxy server.

Diameter uses TCP packets only and uses IPSec and TLS for security. To learn more about Diameter, visit www.ibm.com/developerworks/library/wi-diameter/index.html.

TACACS+

NET+ 2.3, 4.2

Terminal Access Controller Access-Control System Plus (TACACS+) is a secure alternative to RADIUS. TACACS+ is often confused with TACACS and thought to be an improved version of TACACS. It is actually an entirely new system, not a derivative

Copyright Goodheart-Willcox Co., Inc.

of TACACS, which is a much older security system originally implemented for Unix servers. TACACS+ is a client/server proprietary AAA security system developed by Cisco Systems. The following table is a brief comparison of RADIUS and TACACS+:

RADIUS	TACACS+
Uses connectionless UDP	Uses connection-oriented TCP
Uses one database for authentication, authorization, and accounting	Uses separate databases for authentication, authorization, and accounting
Encrypts only the password	Encrypts the entire exchange of logon packets
Uses a token-based authentication method	Uses a token-based authentication method

Authentication Methods

Regardless of the protocol used, authentication comes in one of three main types:

- Type I: something you know. This is a password or PIN.
- Type II: something you have. This can be a key, swipe card, etc.
- Type III: something you are. This is biometrics.

Recently there have been two other methods of authentication added to this mix: somewhere you are and something you do. The *somewhere you are* method uses geolocation to authenticate. For example, a user might enter the right username and password, but instead of logging in from his or her office in Toronto, the login is coming from Nigeria, so the login is blocked. Geolocation is related to another technology called geofencing. *Geofencing* is the process of using GPS or RFID to create a virtual boundary. For example, if a company issues a tablet or laptop to an employee that is only meant to be used on company premises, geofencing prevents it from functioning off-campus.

The *something you do* method involves any sort of user activity. This is usually in addition to at least Type I authentication. This is a vague category and can encompass anything from keyboard typing habits, to how fast you read pages of data.

Strong authentication requires at least one mechanism from at least two categories. *Something you know*, for example a password, along with *something you have*, for example a swipe card, is considered strong authentication, or *two-factor authentication*. Today, authentication that is not two-factor is considered inadequate. A common concept in authentication is *single sign-on (SSO)*. This allows a user to log in and authenticate one time, and that authentication propagates to other subsystems. Whatever authentication process is used, it should be audited and logged.

Authentication Protocols

Chapter 14 introduced SLIP, PPP, and many variations of PPP, such as PPTP, PPPoE, and MLPPP. While PPP and SLIP are primarily concerned with remote connection security over dial-up telephone lines and ISDN, there are many protocols designed to provide secure connections over Ethernet networks and the Internet, such as PAP, CHAP, and Kerberos. This section takes a look at these protocols.

Password Authentication Protocol (PAP)

Password Authentication Protocol (PAP) is a basic password authentication technique used for HTTP and remote dial-up access. PAP sends the username and password in plain-text format, also referred to as *clear text*. The username and password are sent over the network and then compared to a database of usernames and

Copyright Goodheart-Willcox Co., Inc.

passwords to determine if they may access the server. PAP was developed when security on the Internet using TCP/IP was not a real problem. The clear text used inside the packet allows the password and username to be easily intercepted.

Note

PAP is basically obsolete because of the clear-text characteristic.

Challenge Handshake Authentication Protocol (CHAP)

The **Challenge Handshake Authentication Protocol (CHAP)** is an authentication protocol that sends an encrypted string of characters representing the username and password. It does not send the actual username and password. CHAP was designed to be used with PPP when making a remote connection to a server. **Microsoft Challenge Handshake Authentication Protocol (MS-CHAP)** is an enhanced version of CHAP that encrypts not only the username and password but also the data package. MS-CHAP must be used with Microsoft operating systems. It is not compatible with other operating systems.

CHAP works by using the PPP protocol to allow a computer to connect to a remote system. After a connection is established, the server, also known as the *authentication agent*, sends a challenge to the client, or peer. The authentication agent sends a key to the client so that it can encrypt its username and password. The client responds with an encrypted key representing the username and password. The server either accepts or rejects the client username and password based on a matching encryption key. The actual username and password are not sent. Only a key generated from the characters used in the username and password is sent.

The authenticating agent randomly generates challenges to verify it is still connected to an authorized peer and not to an impostor that has intercepted packets. CHAP prevents the replay attack by repeating the challenge at random intervals to detect an unauthorized connection. The technical names *authentication agent* and *peer* are used because CHAP can be used for more than server access, such as to authenticate two routers when using a tunneling protocol or VPN connection.

MS-CHAP began being phased out with the introduction of Windows Vista. The latest version used for authentication is MS-CHAPv2. *MS-CHAPv2* provides stronger encryption and supports two-way authentication. MS-CHAP only supports one-way authentication. One-way authentication only verifies with the authenticator who the client is. Two-way authentication takes it one step further and also verifies who the authenticator is to the client.

NET
4.2

Kerberos

The Massachusetts Institute of Technology (MIT) developed a security authentication system called Kerberos. The name Kerberos (also spelled *Cerberus*) comes from Greek mythology. It is the name of the mythical three-headed dog that guards the entrance to Hades. **Kerberos** allows two computers to communicate securely over a network that is not typically secure, such as the Internet. While Kerberos was developed and distributed as an open protocol, it has been incorporated into many proprietary software systems.

The details of how Kerberos works are beyond the scope of this book and the Network+ Exam. However, a general overview is necessary and helpful. Kerberos works by sending messages back and forth between the client and the server. The actual password, or even a hash of the password, is never sent. That makes it

Copyright Goodheart-Willcox Co., Inc.

impossible for someone to intercept it. Instead, the username is sent. The server then looks up the stored hash of that password and uses the hash as an encryption key to encrypt data and send it back to the client. The client then takes the password the user entered and uses that as a key to decrypt the data. If the user entered the wrong password, then it will never get decrypted. This is a clever way to verify the password without it ever being transmitted.

Extensible Authentication Protocol (EAP)

4.3 | NET

Extensible Authentication Protocol (EAP) is an Internet Engineering Task Force (IETF) standard used for network access and authentication in a client/server environment when IP is not available. For example, a dial-up connection to an Internet service provider uses a telephone line to make the connection using the Point-to-Point Protocol (PPP). There is no existing network. EAP was originally developed for use with PPP. Later EAP was adopted for use with wireless connections. Microsoft used EAP for applications such as PPP and dial-up, VPN, and site-to-site and remote access connections. EAP is also used for 802.1x wireless connections and for access and authentication to network switches.

There are numerous variations of the original EAP standard, such as EAP-MD5, EAP-TLS, EAP-IKEv2, EAP-AKA, EAP-FAST, and EAP-SIM. In this text, coverage is limited to only the most commonly encountered variations: PEAP and LEAP.

Protected Extensible Authentication Protocol (PEAP)

Protected Extensible Authentication Protocol (PEAP) is a proprietary protocol developed jointly by Cisco Systems and Microsoft. PEAP is an extension to the original EAP. EAP sends clear text messages, which can be intercepted. PEAP is an enhanced version of EAP, which first establishes a secure connection using Transport Layer Security (TLS). TLS provides encryption for the EAP connection and ensures data integrity.

Lightweight Extensible Authentication Protocol (LEAP)

Lightweight Extensible Authentication Protocol (LEAP) is a proprietary authentication system developed by Cisco Systems for its line of wireless access points. Cisco released this improved EAP standard before the IETF completed the 802.11i standard for wireless network security. One of the major improvements of Cisco LEAP security is the periodical reauthorization of the LEAP wireless connection, thus ensuring that the client is still the original authenticated client and that the connection has not been hijacked by an unauthorized person.

Security Implementations

This section covers the various ways an administrator can implement network security. Several recommended security practices for new network installations include installing the latest software updates and patches, setting up an account for daily administrative tasks, and changing the default administrator's name. A network administrator constantly needs to educate system users in routine security practices. Yearly seminars, e-mail alerts, and reminders at department meetings are all good efforts.

An administrator should add software or hardware devices that block open ports or filter incoming and outgoing traffic to secure the network. Physically securing the server and other vulnerable points of the network, such as wiring closets, hubs, and router, should also be seriously considered.

Copyright Goodheart-Willcox Co., Inc.

Software Installation Patches

Security begins immediately after the initial installation of the network operating system and associated software programs. There are hundreds of known vulnerabilities to operating systems and software packages. For example, when a network operating system such as Windows Server 2016 is installed and configured, it has many known vulnerabilities. Before the installation can be considered complete, the latest patch must be installed. Software patches contain many software fixes that close security holes and fix software bugs. Microsoft releases collections of patches and fixes referred to as a service pack.

NET
3.5, 4.5

Administrator Account

Many network operating systems are installed with a default administrator account. During installation, you are given the opportunity to enter a password of your choice for this account. A default username, such as *Administrator*, provides one half of authenticity to a potential intruder. To secure this potential breach, choose a new administrator name to use in place of the default administrator name, assign the account full administrative privileges, and then delete the default account. Administrators are one example of privileged user accounts. Any account that has more privilege than an average user requires additional security. One example of this increased security is a *privileged user agreement*, which is an agreement specifying how the account should be used.

For example, Windows Server has the default system administrator name of *Administrator*. A new account should be made with a new name, such as *Operat0r1$*. It should be created with full administrative privileges. After the new account has been created, the original account, *Administrator*, should be deleted from the system.

It is also recommended an account be established for the administrator to use to perform daily duties and that does not require a complete set of administrative powers. The idea behind using a limited administrator account is to protect the system in the event an intruder compromises the account. If an intruder were to gain access to the system using a Trojan horse, the intruder could use a password-stealing program to acquire the administrator's password when the administrator logs on to maintain the system. The intruder could use the administrator account to set up his or her own account that has administrative powers.

If an administrator uses an account with less-than-full administrative powers, the powers of an intruder are limited if the system is cracked. A user account cannot create another user account that is more powerful than his or her own. It can only create an account that has equal or lesser powers. By using a less-powerful account for daily business, the most powerful account is left in reserve for when it is really needed. Remember, if the intruder has power equal to the administrator, the intruder can delete everything the system administrator account has created.

Tech Tip

The ability to delete or rename the administrator account varies according to operating system and version.

NET
4.5, 4.6

Network Device Hardening

One common security measure is to make devices as secure as you can. This is often referred to as *hardening*. Most hardening is rather simple. It begins with changing default passwords. All devices come with default passwords. These must be changed, and *common passwords*, which are passwords that can be easily guessed or cracked, should not be used.

Next, the system must be kept updated. This includes updating the firmware on devices as well as patching and making sure the system stays updated. Any unnecessary services or unused ports (IP ports and physical ports) should also be disabled. When communicating with a device, always use a secure protocol like SSH instead of unsecure protocols like Telnet. Finally, if the device uses encryption, ensure that you are generating new keys from time to time.

An extra step that can be taken is to create a file hash of critical files, such as configuration files. This allows the current file on the device to be checked against the stored hash if you suspect someone has altered it. This process is also used for monitoring file integrity.

The switch ports on a network are also particularly vulnerable to a variety of attacks. There are snooping attacks, such as DHCP snooping and flooding attacks, that must be guarded against. The most common mitigation step is to ensure switchport protection. That means that one cannot connect to a port on a switch unless the MAC address of the device being connected has been previously authorized to connect to that specific port.

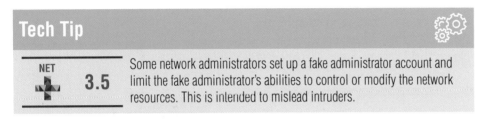

User Account Passwords

After installing the network operating system and patches, the next major item of concern is password protection. The network administrator can do much to ensure proper passwords and techniques are used. An administrator can educate system users on choosing a proper password and establish password policies. Educating users includes teaching them about poor and secure passwords. Establishing password policies includes setting defaults for password histories, age, and length.

Poor passwords contain common names, words, or sequential numbers or letters. The following are some examples of poor passwords:

- Jamie
- Reds
- password
- secret
- TopSecret
- love

- 12345
- abcde
- AbCdE
- A1B2C3
- 1q2w3e4r

Poor passwords match words commonly found in the dictionary or contain names familiar to the password's owner. Poor passwords also include keyboard combinations that are easy for the password owner to remember. Look at the password *1q2w3e4r* in the previous list. The *1q2w3e4r* password may look like a secure password. However, by locating the letters and numbers on your keyboard to reveal the pattern, you will see that it is not. Keyboard patterns are not secure, but they are better than most typical poor passwords.

Another common password that should be avoided is a Social Security number. A Social Security number is easily identified by its nine-number sequence. When a Social Security number is cracked, the intruder can gain access to other personal information. Never use your Social Security number as a password under any circumstance.

Copyright Goodheart-Willcox Co., Inc.

Secure passwords do not match words commonly found in a dictionary. Instead, they incorporate numbers and special characters, which makes them much more difficult to crack. The following are some examples of secure passwords:

- AceHat$_301
- Bob_$ecure4PC
- Open_Lock231!

NET
4.5

No password is 100 percent secure. However, there are passwords that are difficult to guess or hash. Passwords are so critical to authentication that network operating systems can control many of the important characteristics required of good passwords.

An administrator can set policies or default settings that can aid in password security. Figure 15-17 shows the Group Policy Management utility associated with Windows Server 2008. You can readily see the list of password policies available, such as history, age, length, and complexity.

Figure 15-17 Windows Server 2008 password policies for the domain.

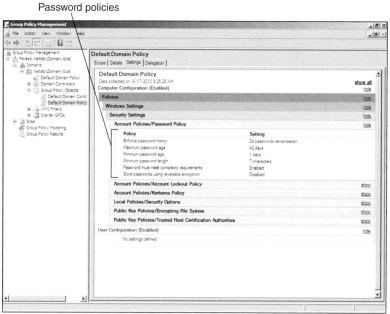

Goodheart-Willcox Publisher

Password History

As passwords are changed, the old passwords can be stored and used for comparison against the most recent password. For example, a user may be required to change his or her password every 90 days. This practice is compromised if the user constantly switches between two passwords, such as *MySecret* and *Secure*. Not only are these poor passwords, but by constantly switching between the two, there is little protection offered by changing the password. Some network operating systems, therefore, allow the administrator to set a minimum password history, which forces the user to use a new password that does not match any of their old passwords. For example, the history password policy can be set to store the last 24 passwords. By enforcing the password history, users are forced to use new passwords continually. However, this practice can also be easily compromised by simple techniques, such as adding a number to the end of a password and then simply incrementing the number by one each time a new password is required—for example, *MySecret1*, *MySecret2*, and *MySecret3*.

Password Age

Passwords should be changed frequently, but not so often that it becomes a real annoyance to the users. A good rule of thumb is to require passwords to be changed every 90 days.

Minimum Password Length

The exact password length depends on the company and network administrator's perception of the need for security. Passwords that are too long are not practical for most applications. A password should be of sufficient length to allow a variety of characters and symbols to be used but not so long that the support desk is constantly reassigning forgotten passwords.

A good rule of thumb is a minimum of eight characters. Administrators and special operators, such as department heads with administrative privileges to assign passwords to individual workgroups, should be required to use a password of at least 12 characters.

Other Password Security Measures

For additional password security, it is a recommended practice to move the location of the password storage file. Depending on the network operating system, it is also a good practice to relocate other security files from the default location. When security files are left in the default location, intruders can easily locate them. Also, when a database with username and password information is saved on a computer, the database should be encrypted and placed under an unassuming file name, such as *Tax Report Summaries* rather than *Personnel Security Passwords*.

Any password can be hacked, but not all intruders can hack all password methods. For example, an intruder can hack a highly secure password, but it can be very difficult and take even a month or more. A nonsecure password can be compromised very easily and in a very short time.

You can audit the network security passwords by using special software packages designed for this purpose. Many operating system websites provide such tools at no cost.

Firewall

A *firewall* is designed to monitor and pass or block packets as they enter or leave a network system, as shown in Figure 15-18. A firewall may consist of either hardware or software or a combination of both. Servers, routers, and individual computers may be used as firewalls.

Firewalls are designed to filter the inbound and outbound flow of network packets based on factors such as IP address, port numbers, software application, packet contents, and protocols. The exact selection of factors can vary according to the firewall design, purpose, and configuration.

Windows Firewall is very sophisticated and can filter both inbound and outbound packets. The Windows 10 Firewall and Windows Server 2016 Firewall are almost identical in design. Look at Figure 15-19, which shows the Windows 10 Firewall. As you can see, there are many default firewall settings that are directly coordinated

2.2   NET

Figure 15-18 A firewall inspects data packets and allows the packet to pass, or it blocks the packet.

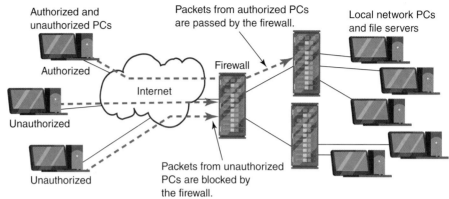

(workstation icons) RedlineVector/Shutterstock.com; (server icons) fullvector/Shutterstock.com;
Goodheart-Willcox Publisher

Figure 15-19 Windows Firewall with Advanced Security has many default firewall settings that are directly coordinated with the network location or environment, such as Public, Private, or Domain.

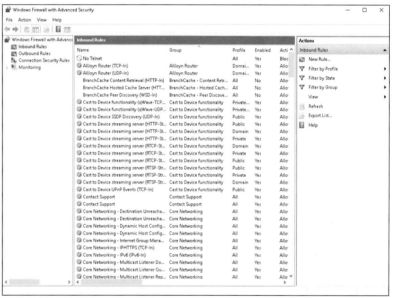

Goodheart-Willcox Publisher

with the network location. Most users do not comprehend how a sophisticated firewall system works. Microsoft simply asks the user to pick the type of environment he or she is in, such as Public, Private, or Domain. Then, Microsoft automatically configures Windows Firewall for the type of environment selected.

Users have the option to configure individual software program access and specific port access. Notice in Figure 15-19 that every software application and computer service is associated with a protocol such as TCP or UDP and a corresponding port number. The basic operation of all firewalls is based on filtering port numbers that are directly correlated to network services. For example, NetBIOS Name Resolution and UDP port 137 as shown in Figure 15-20.

Specific, well-known port numbers (0–1023) are correlated to specific services assigned by the IANA organization. Well-known port numbers are typically assigned to system services. Registered ports (1024–49151) are also assigned by IANA and are typically assigned to specific software applications. Dynamic or private ports (49152–65535) are not assigned and can be used for any purpose by any software designer. You may wish to review the list of typical port number assignments in

Copyright Goodheart-Willcox Co., Inc.

Figure 15-20 The firewall is configured to allow packets related to Network Discovery NetBIOS Name Resolution through assigned UDP port 137.

Goodheart-Willcox Publisher

Chapter 10. A complete list of port numbers can be found at: www.iana.org/ assignments/port-numbers. You can also conduct an Internet search using the phrase IANA.org port numbers.

There are several classifications of firewalls, such as packet filter, application gateway, content filter, and circuit level gateway. A typical firewall consists of two or more filtering techniques. Often, network devices are identified as performing firewall functions in addition to their intended purpose. For example, a network gateway can also perform functions associated with a firewall by filtering packets based on IP address, port number, or MAC address.

Packet Filter

A **packet filter** inspects each packet as it passes through the firewall and then accepts or rejects the packet based on a set of rules. The terms *stateful* and *stateless*, as applied to firewall technology, refer to the way the packets are inspected. When configured for **stateless packet inspection**, a firewall inspects individual packet attributes, such as IP address, port number, and protocols. It then applies a filter based on the individual packet attributes. The filter is based on static information. It does not take into account packet flow. For example, a malicious program can delete a section of packets or alter the sequence. A stateless packet inspection will not detect the missing packets. Stateless packet inspection aligns with layer 3 of the OSI model.

A firewall configured for **stateful packet inspection** applies a filter based on the sequence of packets. A stateful packet inspection can detect missing packets or an altered sequence of packets. For example, a firewall configured for stateful packet inspection could detect a MITM exploit, but a firewall configured for stateless packet inspection could not. Stateful packet inspection aligns with layer 3 and 4 of the

Copyright Goodheart-Willcox Co., Inc.

OSI model because it not only inspects packet contents related to layer 3 (network layer), it also inspects the packet sequence as related to layer 4 (transport layer).

Stateful packet inspection requires packets to be stored and the firewall CPU to process information before applying a filter. As a result, stateful packet inspection is slower than stateless packet inspection and can cause network latency. Stateless packet inspection is quicker because it simply compares packet data against a set of firewall rules and then applies the filter. Stateless packet inspection causes less network latency compared with stateful packet inspection. The following table summarizes stateful and stateless packet inspection.

Stateless Inspection	Stateful Inspection
Inspects individual packets	Inspects packet flow
Operates at OSI layer 3 (network layer)	Operates at OSI layer 3 (network layer) and layer 4 (transport layer)
Static inspection	Dynamic inspection
Fast	Slow and increased network latency

Application Gateway

An **application gateway** provides security for specific applications such as FTP and Telnet. The gateway is configured to accept traffic based on the exact match of the application permitted.

Content Filter

Many websites contain inappropriate material. A **content filter** is configured to block websites or packet contents that contain specific terms. Most content filtering packages require a subscription to a service that updates the filtering components on a routine basis. Content filtering can also incorporate protection from malware. Typically, a content filter is based on a list of search terms, such as *alcohol*, *cult*, and *drugs*. The exact list can be controlled by the system administrator. For example, the word *drug* may not be appropriate for a middle school, but would be appropriate for a medical college.

Circuit-Level Gateway

A **circuit-level gateway** monitors a connection until the connection is successfully established between the destination and source hosts. After the connection is established, packets can flow freely between the two hosts. Since the packet sequence is encoded, it is usually quite difficult for an intruder to access the stream of data moving between the hosts.

Firewall Signature Identification

Firewall signature identification works in similar fashion as antivirus protection and is often considered the same thing. Malware can often be classified by a collection of distinct attributes such as port number, payload size, and source address. When a packet is intercepted, it can be compared to specific attributes. When the attributes match, the packet is removed. The main weakness of signature identification is the same as it is for antivirus software. Both require constant updates of new signatures or definitions; this is referred to as *signature management*. New malware is created every day. There is no signature immediately available for new malware.

Copyright Goodheart-Willcox Co., Inc.

Demilitarized Zone (DMZ)

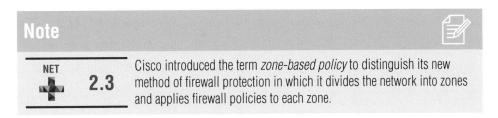

A **demilitarized zone (DMZ)** is an area of a network that permits access from a host located outside the local area network. Network administrators configure a firewall to allow Internet access to part of the network while restricting access to the private portion of the network. This configuring can be seen in Figure 15-21.

The DMZ is the portion of the network that permits access from the Internet. A DMZ can be created with a router or a server with three network adapters installed. One network adapter is connected directly to the Internet, another is connected to the DMZ, and the other is connected to the private section of the network.

> **Note**
>
> **NET 2.3**   Cisco introduced the term *zone-based policy* to distinguish its new method of firewall protection in which it divides the network into zones and applies firewall policies to each zone.

Figure 15-21 The DMZ is the portion of the network that permits access from the Internet.

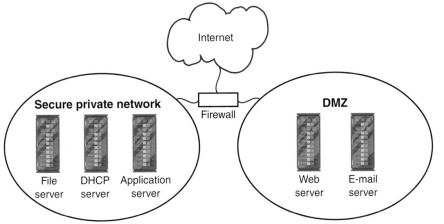

(server icons) fullvector/Shutterstock.com; Goodheart-Willcox Publisher

Unified Threat Management (UTM)

A very popular technology today is unified threat management (UTM). UTM combines several security technologies, allowing you to manage your firewall as well as proxy server, IDS, or other function. The combination of all of these in one package is very useful.

Layer 7 Firewall

While firewalls often work at lower layers of the OSI model, it is possible for them to work at other layers. These are often part of the next-generation firewalls (NGFW), which combine traditional firewall security with any number of other filtering functionalities.

Proxy Server

A **proxy server** is a firewall component that is typically installed on a server and resides between the Internet server and the LAN hosts. It appears as a destination host

Copyright Goodheart-Willcox Co., Inc.

while hiding the address of the true host inside the LAN. To anyone outside the network, only the proxy server is seen. Proxy servers replace the IP address of outgoing packets with the IP address assigned to the proxy server.

For incoming packets that are allowed to flow into the network, the reverse is true. The proxy server can be configured to allow packets to flow into and out of the network if they meet certain conditions. The conditions configured can be items such as specific IP addresses, certain protocols, and server names or URLs.

Proxy servers may also cache information such as frequently visited websites. By caching the websites and their IP addresses, connections can be made faster than when searching for the website. Proxy servers are sometimes referred to as *gateways*. Remember, there are many types of gateways. A gateway provides a connection between the network and some other service. A common example is a VoIP gateway, which provides Voice over IP access.

Securing Remote Access

Remote access is sometimes a necessity, especially for sales personnel who travel. Sales personnel typically need to attach to the office file server to check their e-mail, place customer orders, and check an order's status. While remote access is necessary, it can also pose as a vulnerable access point.

It is interesting to note that remote access can occur without the direct knowledge of network administrators. An employee can secretly attach a modem to his or her workstation so that he or she may access office files from home. Software such as pcAnywhere and Windows Remote Desktop Connection are designed for such capabilities. A hacker can gain access the exact way the employee did.

Most intruders are aware that telephone numbers assigned to an office run in successive numerical order. For example, if the business telephone number is 333-1234, it is probably a safe bet that other telephones in the business are assigned telephone numbers, such as 333-1235, 333-1236, 333-1237, and 333-1238. The pattern is easily revealed. This is also true for telephone number extensions.

When an employee attaches a telephone modem to his or her computer at work, he or she leaves a backdoor open to an intruder. As stated earlier, the employee most likely has created a file share on his or her workstation so the file share can be accessed from home or while traveling.

Physical Security

Physical security is an important aspect of network security. The phrase *physical security* refers to the location of the physical system. File servers should be placed in a secure room. A *secure room* is one that it is physically locked and can only be accessed by authorized personnel. This policy should apply to the file server room, wiring closets, point of presence location, and anywhere along data lines where someone can gain access. Devices that connect the workstations to the network, such as hubs and routers, must also be secured but generally not at such a high level as the file server and wiring closets.

Workstations should also be physically secured. Many users leave their workstation connected to the network when they go home for the day. When they leave, the workstation is still logged on to the network with their user account. This is an open invitation to unauthorized personnel. This is especially true in a large, open-office environment when 50 or more workers have open access to every computer in the office area. What if a sensitive document such as a salary schedule for the entire corporation was downloaded from an employee's workstation, reproduced, and posted on the company lounge bulletin board? Management would most likely

Copyright Goodheart-Willcox Co., Inc.

be upset. The network administrator could trace the event to a specific workstation using a standard event-monitoring utility. That employee would then have to explain this incident and hope his or her job can be saved in the process.

Any devices used, such as alarms or cameras, would also have to have tamper protection. This allows you to detect and prevent attempts to manipulate or disable your security measures. Beyond technological measures, security guards and employee name badges can be very helpful in securing a facility. Locks, including those with passcodes that record who went through the door, are excellent physical security measures. Key fobs can also be helpful, especially when used with smart locks.

Biometrics

Biometrics is the science of using unique physical features of a person to confirm that person's identification for authentication purposes. Some examples of unique physical features include fingerprints, speech, eye color patterns, and facial features. One or more of these physical traits can be scanned and encoded as data to be used for comparison when a person attempts to enter a secure area. Figure 15-22 shows an example of a fingerprint-based biometric device. Biometrics can also be used in conjunction with traditional authentication methods, such as usernames and passwords.

Figure 15-22 A biometric device that uses the fingerprint for authentication.

Precise Biometrics

It is assumed that because biometrics is unique it cannot be compromised. It is a well-known fact that even foolproof security models can be compromised. A group of college students once cracked a biometrics fingerprint scanner by getting a sample of a network user's fingerprint from a glass. Next, they made a mold of the fingerprint and poured a plastic substance similar to rubber into the mold. They used the rubber form of the fingerprint to crack a biometrics fingerprint scanner. As this story exemplifies, any security model can be broken. However, certain models are much more difficult to crack than others.

Smart Card

A **smart card** incorporates a special card into a security system. It is used in conjunction with a personal identification number (PIN). An example of a smart card is shown in Figure 15-23. A card reader is attached to the computer system via any standard port, such as a serial or USB port. Once the smart card is inserted into the card reader, the user is prompted for a PIN. After the correct PIN is entered, access to the computer system is granted. Smart card technology is not only designed for

4.1 NET

4.1 NET

4.1 NET

Copyright Goodheart-Willcox Co., Inc.

Figure 15-23 A smart card security system typically uses a smart card and a PIN for authentication.

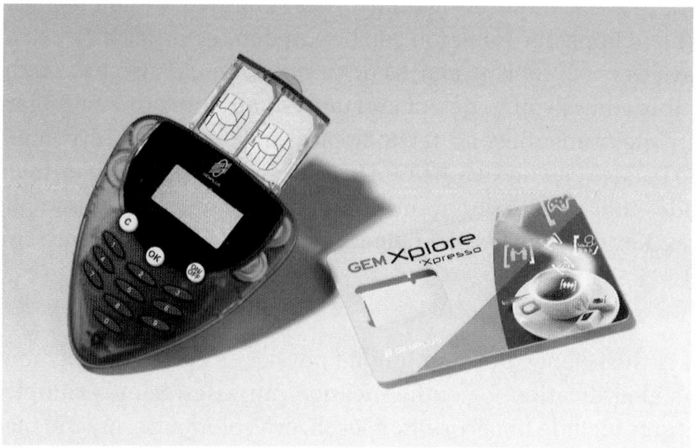

Gemplus

a single PC; it can also be used to access a network workgroup or domain. Access to the network is limited to the permissions assigned to the user account by the system administrator.

In addition to physical access control, the Network+ Exam discusses general physical security mechanisms. For example, video surveillance is highly recommended. This can be combined with motion detection. For valuable equipment such as company-owned laptops or smartphones, asset-tracking tags that identify the location of the asset can also be valuable. This can be done with radio frequency identifier (RFID) chips.

NET

1.3, 4.4, 4.6

Common Mitigation Techniques

In addition to the processes and devices already described in this chapter, there are other common mitigation techniques. One technique is the network design itself. For example, a network can be segmented. *Network segmentation* divides a network into different sections, each with different security needs. This can include a DMZ. As you may recall from earlier in this chapter, DMZs are zones between two firewalls. Often, public-facing devices, such as web servers, are placed in DMZs.

Virtual local area networks (VLANs) are used to segment a network further. In a VLAN, a group of ports on one or more switches is treated as a separate network, a virtual LAN. VLANs must be configured properly to prevent *VLAN hopping*. This is the process of jumping from one VLAN to another. The goal of VLAN hopping is for an attacker to gain access to traffic on other VLANs that would be inaccessible under typical circumstances. If the VLANs were configured securely, this would be very difficult. An easy way to secure a VLAN is to change the native VLAN.

Another security technique involves user accounts. User accounts have a variety of security measures. The first is the principle of least privileges. That means each account is only given just enough privileges to do its job. In addition to necessary privileges to do a job, *privileged user accounts*, such as domain administrator accounts, are given extra security measures. There is also the issue of *separation of roles*, often called *separation of duties*. This means that if there is some critical task, one that could be used to cause great harm to a system, no single user can do that task. At least two users must collaborate to do the task.

Access control lists (ACLs) are commonly used to limit access to any system, device, or data. It is also recommended that any network at least periodically be given a penetration test. A *penetration test* is a formal process, whereby someone uses actual hacking techniques to attempt to gain access. The techniques used, the results, and remediation steps are all documented.

Copyright Goodheart-Willcox Co., Inc.

Security Tools

There are numerous security tools available on the market that are designed to identify common network security weaknesses by probing the network and searching for vulnerabilities. The tools are similar to tools used by hackers and crackers to probe a network. Security tools can help you determine if a potential problem exists. One such tool is GFI LANguard.

In Figure 15-24, the GFI LANguard utility has revealed some potential problems that exist on a network. Since this information is taken from an actual site, the IP address has been blocked out for protection. As shown in the image, numerous possible security problems exist on this network. A person with some expertise could easily penetrate this site and cause a tremendous amount of damage. GFI LANguard is designed to check security problems on the local area network, but can be used by a hacker or cracker as well.

Figure 15-24 The GFI LANguard utility can be used to check for security problems on a local area network.

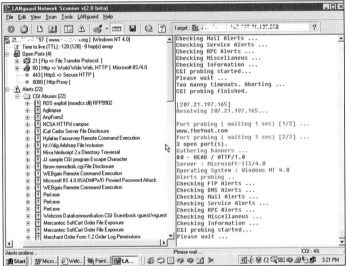

Goodheart-Willcox Publisher

Netstat Utility

The **netstat** utility can help determine which ports are open on a computer. To check for open ports using the **netstat** utility, enter **netstat -a** at the command prompt. A display will appear similar to the one in Figure 15-25, which shows the TCP protocol, the port number of each port currently opened, and the name of the computer associated with the protocol. Any port listed that is not being used should be closed. A utility that periodically detects open ports and alerts you to unauthorized intrusions should also be used.

4.2, 5.2   NET

Audit Tools

User authentication and encryption may not be a sufficient measure of security. A system of auditing user activities should also be established. Not all network attacks or probes come from outside the network. Many network attacks come from inside the network by employees. The activities of users or intruders can be recorded in a log, or the network can be configured to generate messages to alert the administrator of a possible attack. Activities such as repeated logon failures can typically indicate intruder activity.

The Event Viewer allows network activities to be monitored that may indicate an attempted or successful system intrusion. Look at the Event Viewer security log events of a Windows Server 2016 system in Figure 15-26. The security log lists log-on events, successes and failures, dates, and times. By clicking a failed event in the security log, specifics about the event are revealed in more detail. Notice the Audit Failure event that is highlighted in middle pane in Figure 15-26. It refers to a failed cryptographic operation.

Figure 15-25 An administrator can use the **netstat** utility to detect open ports on a computer.

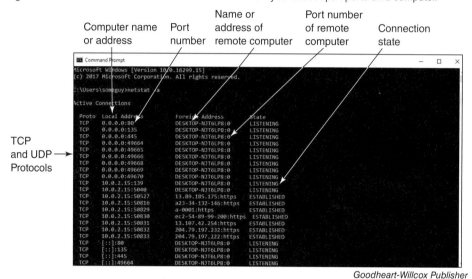

Goodheart-Willcox Publisher

Figure 15-26 The Event Viewer security log can be used to monitor the system for an attempted or successful system intrusion.

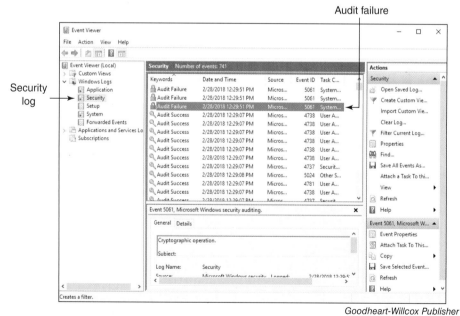

Goodheart-Willcox Publisher

Copyright Goodheart-Willcox Co., Inc.

Self-Hack Tools

Several companies have self-hack tools available. These tools are typically built into a security package and offered as an additional feature. For example, GFI LANguard is not only designed to provide security measures for a network; it can also test network security using common methods such as password cracking. GFI LANguard probes the LAN for open communication ports and general security weaknesses. It also provides a password-cracking tool.

Protocol Analyzer

A **protocol analyzer** is a special software application used to monitor a network and inspect frame/packet contents. Protocol analyzers are sometimes referred to as *protocol sniffers*. It can reveal information about protocols, such as the source and destination IP address, MAC address, port address, time of transmission, and the contents of unencrypted packets.

Figure 15-27 shows an e-mail transmission. Take a close look at the contents of the e-mail, which are translated on the right side of the screen. In the translation, you will see the password and the username issued to the recipient because the e-mail was not encrypted. The contents of this e-mail are revealed to anyone using a protocol analyzer or protocol sniffer on this network. Another excellent tool is the Fluke OptiView Protocol Analyzer. In fact, Fluke has an entire series of network analyzing tools to help you inspect a network system. Related to protocol analyzers are port scanners. These literally scan a target to see what ports are open and listening.

Figure 15-27 Notice how the contents of an unencrypted e-mail can be revealed to anyone using a protocol analyzer or protocol sniffer.

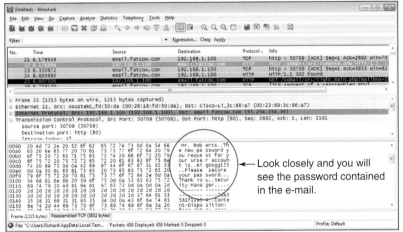

Goodheart-Willcox Publisher

Packet Sniffer

A **packet sniffer** is a network monitoring utility that captures data packets as they travel across a network. As shown in Figure 15-28, a packet sniffer provides a vast amount of information such as packet size, protocol, and the source and destination address expressed as an IP address and a MAC address. On the right side of the screen, you can see some of the information contained inside the decoded packet. The packet sniffer seen in Figure 15-28 can capture and perform a complete analysis of TCP, IP, ARP, and UDP protocols. This utility can be very useful in analyzing network problems. However, in the wrong hands, it can be a security threat.

Tech Tip

The terms *packet sniffer* and *protocol analyzer* are commonly used interchangeably. A packet sniffer is mainly designed as a tool to capture packet contents and header information and to provide limited information. A protocol analyzer provides these same functions and much more, such as analyzing network traffic patterns, producing graphical representations of protocol characteristics and the network infrastructure, and analyzing network problems.

Figure 15-28 A packet sniffer provides a vast amount of information about a packet.

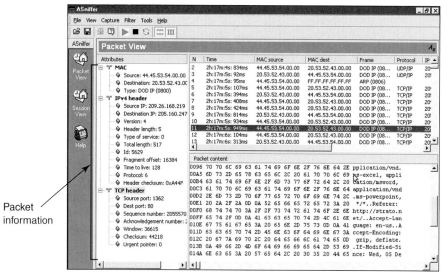

Packet information

Goodheart-Willcox Publisher

NET 3.2

System Backups

System backups are necessary for recovering lost data. However, a common system backup will restore *most* data lost from an attack, but will not restore *all* the data. Any data saved during routine operation, which has not been backed up since the last incremental backup, will be lost.

For example, assume a system is backed up every night at 7:00 p.m. The next day, the office opens at 8:00 a.m. and begins business for the day. At 2:00 p.m., an intruder enters the system and formats the hard drive of the file server and then releases a virus on the workstations. All data stored since 8:00 a.m. is lost and cannot be recovered.

Tech Tip

Network security is a rapidly growing field. It has its own special certification. The certification requires an intensive study of security far above the limited scope of this textbook. If you think you would like to become an expert in network security, visit the SANS organization website to find out more about the requirements. This certification is well respected and much in demand. CompTIA also offers a certification exam in cybersecurity: Security+.

Policies

Policies and procedures must cover many things. Included in the list of items you must have policies for are on-boarding and off-boarding procedures. These procedures determine how new employees will be set up on a network and how exiting employees will be removed. This may include signing a non-disclosure agreement (NDA).

These policies should also define expectations for remote access; best practices and safety guidelines; and how the company handles situations in which employees work with their own devices, commonly referred to as *bring your own device (BYOD)*.

The most common policy is an acceptable use policy (AUP). This often describes how systems should be used. A technology frequently used and referenced in an AUP, particularly in conjunction with BYOD, is network access control (NAC). This scans any device connecting to the network and determines if it meets the minimum security standards. If it does not meet the standards, the device is not allowed to connect to the network.

There should also be policies describing how to handle software usage, including licensing restrictions and international export controls. This is particularly important on encryption software. Related are guidelines for asset disposal. More often than not, computer equipment cannot simply be thrown away. This is due to both environmental and security concerns. For example, computer and electrical often contain heavy metals and carcinogens that can enter the atmosphere if improperly disposed. Additionally, a hard drive that is simply thrown in a dumpster can be retrieved and accessed. This is called *dumpster diving*. Therefore, policies should outline how to dispose equipment properly to ensure environmental stability and loss prevention.

Data Loss Prevention Policies (DLP) address how a company will prevent data from being obtained from the company. This might include forbidding the use of USB devices, or implementing intrusion-detection rules. *Captive portals* are an excellent way to ensure users are aware of policies and agree to them. A captive portal is a web page the user must access before accessing the network. They often include the user checking a box agreeing to the network policies.

Just as important as policies for end users are policies for the security staff. This includes incident response policies. These define exactly what to do should an incident arise. That includes any type of incident from a hacker infiltrating the network to a fire in the server room.

Data Security Compliance Requirements

There are several security standards and laws aimed at securing personal user data such as medical records, banking records, health records, and credit card information. The difference between a standard and a law is that a *standard* is voluntary, whereas a *law* is legally binding.

Both standards and laws typically require the network to be tested for security vulnerabilities. Most require network access and activity to be tracked, monitored, and recorded. They also require that network security features be tested on a regular basis. A policy and procedure guide should also be created and maintained, and all network users be instructed in security-related procedures, such as password and e-mail security.

3.5, 4.2 NET

Tech Tip

A standard can be incorporated into a contract, making it legally binding. For example, when a network construction contract states that "all work shall conform to the latest IEEE standards," then the standard has become the legally binding part of the contract.

Copyright Goodheart-Willcox Co., Inc.

A standard contains rules such as no wireless devices can be used in the company for processing customer information and the network must be scanned periodically to identify any rogue access point. As discussed earlier in this chapter, a rogue access point is one that has been installed without company authorization. For example, a credit manager installs a WAP so that he or she can use his or her own laptop from any location in the store to access user-account information. The WAP installed by the credit manager would be considered a rogue access point.

Another key requirement to data security compliance is the creation and enforcement of an incident response plan. An incident response plan contains step-by-step instructions to be followed immediately after a security incident has occurred. For example, on discovery of unauthorized access to the network, all network servers containing customer data will be shut down until the breach has been secured. The network will not be considered secure until notification has been distributed by the network security chief.

Health Insurance Portability and Accountability Act

The **Health Insurance Portability and Accountability Act (HIPAA)** is a set of standards designed to protect health records. All health-care organizations are required to protect patient-related records. This applies to all health-care organizations and insurance companies. HIPAA has three broad areas of compliance requirements: administrative safeguards, physical safeguards, and technical safeguards.

Administrative safeguards require that policies and procedures be designed, maintained, and implemented to ensure confidentiality of patient records. An administrative safeguard must also include an employee training component.

Physical safeguards require that all patient information must be physically secured. For example, patient information must be kept in a safe, secure area and only authorized personnel can access the data and only on a need-to-know basis. The information must be secured from access when no one is present.

Technical safeguards include mandates such as all exchange of patient data must be encrypted when transferred over public networks. There is an exception at the time of this writing concerning encryption. E-mail to and from a patient is not required to be encrypted unless requested by the patient. All access to the network must be authenticated. This means that, at a minimum, usernames and passwords are required for all users on an individual basis. Also, access from other health entities, such as insurance companies or other health professionals, must have their identities verified. Another aspect of technical safeguards is the establishment of policy and procedures to ensure security of patient records.

Payment Card Industry Data Security Standard

Payment Card Industry Data Security Standard (PCI DSS) is a set of credit card security standards designed to protect credit card information. This is not a law but rather a voluntary set of security standards. PCI DSS typically requires all data to be encrypted when transferred, a firewall to be installed and maintained, and a written policy and procedure manual to be used as a guide for personnel dealing with customer data security. Failure to comply with this standard could result in fines and a possible suspension of the ability to accept credit cards for any transactions.

Copyright Goodheart-Willcox Co., Inc.

Summary

Hacking

- A hacker is a computer enthusiast who experiments with systems to learn about them.
- There are three types of hackers: white-hat, black-hat, and gray-hat.

Common Network Security Breaches

- Authentication is the procedure of verifying a user's identity.
- Encryption is a method of using an algorithm to encode data.
- An unprotected network share establishes a possible entry point for an attack from outside a network.
- Social engineering is an activity that uses personal skills rather than technical knowledge to gain access to a network or secure area.
- Zeroconf outlines recommendations for designing a device that automatically detects other devices on the same network.
- A Denial of Service (DoS) attack overloads a server to the point of it crashing.
- Man in the middle is a method of intercepting a network transmission.
- Spoofing is fooling the destination by using an IP address other than the true IP address of a source to gain access to a system.
- Malware is a term given to software programs intended to damage, destroy, or steal data.
- Malware comes in many forms including Trojan horses, viruses, worms, ransomware, and logic bombs.
- DNS poisoning occurs when an attacker tries to get fake entries into the target's DNS server.
- An evil twin is a rogue wireless access point that is configured so it has the same MAC address as one of the existing legitimate access points.
- A deauthentication, or *deassociation*, attack causes the client to deauthenticate from a reliable source.
- In a phishing attack, an e-mail is sent that appears to be from a legitimate enterprise in an attempt to solicit personal information.
- Insider threats are perhaps the most critical threat.

Intrusion Detection and Intrusion Prevention Systems

- An intrusion detection system (IDS) and intrusion prevention system (IPS) are designed to monitor host and network systems for unauthorized activity.

Security Methods and Protocols

- There are two main types of key encryption methods: symmetric-key encryption and asymmetric-key encryption.
- A key is a software code used to encode or decode data.
- A symmetric key is a key classification that uses the same key to encrypt and decrypt data.

Copyright Goodheart-Willcox Co., Inc.

- An asymmetric key is a key classification that uses two different keys to encrypt and decrypt data.

- Digital certificates are issued by certificate authorities and are used to verify identities.

- The Secure Socket Layer (SSL) protocol was developed by Netscape to secure transactions between web servers and individuals using the Internet for such purposes as credit card transactions.

- Transport Layer Security (TLS) was developed after SSL by the Internet Engineering Task Force (IETF). It serves the same purpose as SSL but is more secure.

- A virtual network connection (VNC) describes a broad category of remote connection systems that allow a user to connect to a network device.

- IPSec is a protocol designed to secure IP packets on an unsecured network medium.

- Secure Shell (SSH) is a protocol that provides secure network services over an insecure network medium.

- Secure Copy Protocol (SCP) provides a secure way of transferring files between computers.

Wireless Security

- Wireless networks use a *service set identifier (SSID)* to identify the wireless network.

- A media access control (MAC) filter allows or restrict WAP access based on the MAC address of a wireless network card.

- Wired Equivalent Privacy (WEP) was the first attempt to encrypt data transferred across a wireless network. It was part of the original IEEE 802.11 wireless standard.

- When vulnerabilities were discovered in the algorithm used for WEP, the Wi-Fi organization developed the Wi-Fi Protected Access (WPA) encryption technique.

- Wi-Fi Protected Access 2 (WPA2) is an enhanced version of WPA.

- IEEE 802.11i is a standard that was developed to remedy the original security flaws in 802.11.

- 802.1x provides port-based, network access control, which supports authentication for Ethernet network access.

- 802.1x is composed of three components: supplicant, authenticator, and authentication server.

- A rogue access point is an unauthorized wireless access point that is installed on a network system.

Authentication, Authorization, and Accounting

- AAA represents Authentication, Authorization, and Accounting.

- RADIUS, Diameter, and TACTACS+ are all models of AAA.

Copyright Goodheart-Willcox Co., Inc.

Authentication Methods

- Regardless of authentication protocol used, there are three main types of authentication: *something you know, something you have*, and *something you are*.
- Two other methods were recently added: *somewhere you are* and *something you do*.
- Strong authentication requires at least one mechanism from at least two categories.

Authentication Protocols

- Password Authentication Protocol (PAP) was an early development of username and password authentication that transmits the username and password as clear text.
- The Challenge Handshake Authentication Protocol (CHAP) encrypts the username and password.
- Microsoft Challenge Handshake Authentication Protocol (MS-CHAP) is a Microsoft version of CHAP that can only be used with Microsoft operating systems.
- Kerberos was designed at the Massachusetts Institute of Technology (MIT) and is used to authenticate the client and the server.
- The Kerberos system uses two different keys similar to a public and private key for security.
- Extensible Authentication Protocol (EAP) is an IETF standard used for network access and authentication in a client/server environment when IP is not available.
- The most commonly encountered variations of EAP are Protected Extensible Authentication Protocol (PEAP) and Lightweight Extensible Authentication Protocol (LEAP).

Security Implementations

- After installing a network operating system, you should immediately apply any available software patches or service packs to the system.
- The default system-administrator username should be changed to lessen the chance of the system being cracked.
- A common security measure is to make devices as secure as possible; this is called device hardening.
- A strong password is composed of letters, numbers, and special symbols.
- Network operating systems typically incorporate password policy features such as password history, minimum length, age, and complexity.
- A firewall monitors data packets as they enter or exit the network system and blocks or passes them.
- Unified threat management (UTM) combines several security technologies, allowing you to manage your firewall as well as proxy server, IDS, or other function.
- A proxy server is a special firewall designed to hide clients inside the network from unauthorized personnel outside the network.

Copyright Goodheart-Willcox Co., Inc.

- Physical security of a network refers to the location of the physical, tangible system components.
- Workstations, server rooms, and any access point should be secured, and devices should have tamper protection.
- Biometrics is the use of physical characteristics for the basis of user authentication.
- A smart card integrates electronics into a card for authentication.

Security Tools

- The **netstat** utility can help determine which ports are open on a computer.
- A protocol analyzer is a tool that inspects protocol activity and contents.
- A packet sniffer is a type of network monitoring utility that inspects data packets.
- Policies and procedures should outline security measures, including remote access guidelines, best practices and safety guidelines, BYOD rules, an acceptable use policy (AUP), proper disposal of equipment, data loss prevention, and incident response.

Data Security Compliance Requirements

- The difference between a standard and a law is that a *standard* is voluntary, whereas a *law* is legally binding.

Review Questions

1. Summarize the differences between the three basic types of hackers.
2. _____ is the process used to identify a user and ensure the user is who he or she claims to be.
3. _____ is a method of using an algorithm to encode data.
4. The manipulation of personnel through deceitful means to gain security information is called _____.
5. When a server is overloaded with false requests so much that it crashes, what type of attack has occurred?
6. What is using a false IP address or identity called?
7. What is the purpose behind using a Trojan horse?
8. Where are macro writers commonly found?
9. Through what method are worms typically spread?
10. Describe DNS poisoning.
11. What is the purpose of intrusion detection and intrusion prevention systems?
12. What is the difference between symmetric-key encryption and asymmetric-key encryption?
13. Another name for symmetric-key encryption is _____.
14. List three examples of symmetric cyphers.

Copyright Goodheart-Willcox Co., Inc.

15. List two examples of asymmetric algorithms.

16. What is the purpose of a certificate authority (CA)?

17. Who developed SSL?

18. What is the purpose of SSL?

19. Which two protocols are specifically designed to make website transactions safe?

20. What is IPSec?

21. What is the difference between IPSec tunnel mode and transport mode?

22. What two protocols are common to IPSec?

23. What are the three original wireless device security mechanisms?

24. What encryption mechanism was developed as a replacement for WEP?

25. What is 802.11i?

26. What is 802.1x?

27. List the three components of an 802.1x configuration.

28. Identify three security technologies that meet the AAA requirements.

29. Which protocol could be considered as the next generation RADIUS?

30. Provide an example of *something you know*, *something you have*, and *something you are*.

31. What is *geofencing*?

32. Why is PAP considered an unsecured system of authorization?

33. What does the acronym CHAP represent?

34. Why is CHAP considered an improvement over PAP?

35. MS-CHAP is designed exclusively for _____ operating systems.

36. Of the three different protocols, PAP, CHAP, and MS-CHAP, which encrypts the contents of the packet?

37. What is Kerberos?

38. Before a network operating system installation can be considered complete, the latest _____ must be installed.

39. Why should the default name of an administrator account be changed?

40. Making network devices as secure as possible is often referred to as device _____.

41. Describe the characteristics of a poor password.

42. Describe the characteristics of a good password.

43. How is a firewall used to secure network access?

44. What factors are used by firewalls to filter inbound and outbound network traffic?

45. What is the difference between stateful and stateless firewall inspection?

46. In terms of network security, what is a *demilitarized zone (DMZ)*?

47. How is a proxy server used to secure network access?

Copyright Goodheart-Willcox Co., Inc.

48. What is biometrics?

49. What technology uses a plastic card with embedded electronics for identification?

50. What TCP utility displays open ports?

51. Why is a protocol analyzer used?

52. What is a packet sniffer?

53. Differentiate between a standard and a law.

✚ Sample Network+ Exam Questions

1. John is trying to ensure that new systems on his network are secure. What common security measure should be performed immediately after the new network operating system has been installed?

   A. Change the default administrator username and give it a difficult password to crack.

   B. Immediately write down the administrator username and password, and then delete the administrator account to prevent it from being penetrated by unauthorized persons.

   C. Access the BIOS settings and change the network administrator's password.

   D. Install a protocol analyzer to see if a cracker detected the installation.

2. Mary has been assigned the task of analyzing network traffic. Which of the following software packages or utilities is used to analyze the contents of individual packets on a network?

   A. **arp**

   B. Packet sniffer

   C. **tracert**

   D. **ping**

3. You are a network administrator for a small college. You are trying to select an authentication method for your network servers. Which of the following is the least secure authentication method?

   A. CHAP

   B. PAP

   C. Kerberos

   D. 802.1x

4. Which utility can record security events as they take place on a Windows network?

   A. Event Viewer

   B. Network Monitor

   C. Directory Service

   D. Device Manager

Copyright Goodheart-Willcox Co., Inc.

5. Terri is reviewing password security for her company. She is concerned about password security. Which is the best example of a secure password?

   A. BigDog

   B. Star$Read1345

   C. NtsysFive

   D. Pass123456789

6. Which security term is used to describe the act of trying to get information from a person through fraudulent means?

   A. Trojan

   B. Phishing

   C. Man in the middle

   D. DoS

7. Which is a centralized security method that uses a server for wireless authentication?

   A. WEP

   B. WAP

   C. WPA

   D. 802.1x

8. Mark is responsible for the wireless network at his company. He is training a new intern, and trying to explain all the various parts of the wireless network. Which of the following is used to identify a wireless network?

   A. MAC filter

   B. SSID

   C. EAP

   D. Subnet mask

9. Which is the most common means of spreading a computer worm?

   A. Uploading data from a disc

   B. Newly installed hardware devices

   C. Opening e-mail attachments

   D. Newly installed software utilities

10. Which protocol was designed to provide secure communication between a web server and a web browser?

   A. SSL

   B. FTP

   C. PPP

   D. RADIUS

Copyright Goodheart-Willcox Co., Inc.

Network+ Certification Exam Objectives

Questions concerning maintaining the network are drawn from such topics as patches, upgrades, and fixes; data backup strategies; antivirus procedures; disaster recovery; and fault tolerance. Maintaining the network requires knowledge about all aspects of networking and of some basic concepts associated with PC support.

Even if you do not have access to your own Windows server, you can still become very familiar with network maintenance because many of the tools discussed here are almost identical in Windows desktop operating systems.

Objectives

1.3: Performance Concepts—Traffic Shaping

1.5: Wired Topologies—Logical vs. Physical

2.3: Load Balancer

3.1: Given a Scenario, Use Appropriate Documentation and Diagrams to Manage the Network.

3.2: Compare and Contrast Business Continuity and Disaster Recovery Concepts.

3.3: Explain Common Scanning, Monitoring, and Patching Processes and Summarize Their Expected Outputs.

Learning Outcomes

- List methods for monitoring a server and a network.
- Explain how to maintain system software.
- Describe proper maintenance of system hardware.
- Identify methods for maintaining system integrity.
- Provide examples of tools used to maintain stable electrical power.

Copyright Goodheart-Willcox Co., Inc.

Key Terms

archive bit

average utilization

baseline

blackout

brownout

bug

cluster

cold spare

continuous UPS

differential backup

disaster recovery

electrical spike

electrical surge

frame size average

frame size peak

full backup

generator

hot spare

incremental backup

isolation transformer

lightning arrestor

logical diagram

mean time between failures (MTBF)

mean time to repair (MTTR)

peak utilization

physical diagram

power conditioning

service-level agreements (SLA)

service pack

Simple Network Management Protocol (SNMP)

standby UPS

swap file

uninterruptible power supply (UPS)

Overview

A network only comes to a user's attention after it fails or is slow to respond to requests. In reality, after a network is installed, it requires constant maintenance to be in near-perfect condition and to ensure data integrity. Only with constant maintenance will the network be in good condition to ensure user satisfaction and smooth company operation.

This chapter introduces some new concepts and reintroduces some concepts that have been taught much earlier. Earlier concepts are applied directly to network maintenance. Most of the maintenance of a network system is the result of constant monitoring by the network administrator. While the network technician may perform routine daily maintenance under the direction of the network administrator, the administrator is ultimately responsible for the type, extent, and frequency of the maintenance to be performed.

Network+ Note

Be aware that you may see questions on the Network+ Certification Exam similar to those found on the CompTIA A+ Exam.

Monitoring the Server and Network

A network system should be constantly monitored to determine when failures occur or to predict possible or imminent failure. Activity can be monitored, recorded, and expressed statistically to predict failure. For example, as a company grows, so will the amount of network traffic generated by the number of employees and customers. Statistical data based on network media bandwidth, total CPU activity, data storage space, and memory utilization can be monitored, and a predicted failure rate can be forecasted through data analysis.

The predictions are based on system history. For example, if a company consumes storage space at a rate of six percent per month, network storage will be compromised in less than 18 months. A server's CPU activity can be monitored, such as when and how often CPU utilization reaches 100 percent. Another example is

Copyright Goodheart-Willcox Co., Inc.

memory (RAM) activity. When exceeded, it typically causes more storage space activity. For example, operating systems use hard disk drive space to assist RAM. A block of hard disk drive space is used to augment RAM. When RAM is full, the operating system uses the block of hard disk drive space to supplement the RAM.

Hard drive disk space that supplements the RAM is referred to as a **swap file**, or *page file*. The swap file on the hard disk drive serves the same purpose as RAM. When the swap file is used, data processing slows because the hard disk drive cannot perform at the same high speed as the RAM. The slower swap file causes data processing to slow and affects the time it takes to retrieve data across the network. While the network is not the cause for the slowdown, the network appears to be responding slowly to the user.

NET
1.5, 3.1

Documentation and Diagrams

It is very difficult to maintain a network without a clear understanding of it. This requires extensive documentation and diagrams. The first step in documentation and diagramming begins with logical and physical diagrams. A **logical diagram** documents the flow of data. A **physical diagram** documents the actual wiring and devices on your network. Each of these diagrams should include network configuration data and baseline data, which will be discussed later in this chapter. Even diagrams of network racks are important. Rack diagrams detail the location of each device contained in the network rack.

General documentation is also helpful. For example, change-management documentation will let you know any changes that have been made to any system. This is closely related to *standard operating procedures*, which detail how to work with a given system, and how to conduct change management.

At a more basic level, inventory management is equally important. A large network quickly becomes unwieldy, and it can be difficult to know what equipment exists on the network. Inventory management begins with simply labeling devices, ports, etc. in a server room. Documenting the wiring and port locations is also important. If a network has an outside line coming into the building, such as a T1 or fiber-optic line, then the main distribution frame and any intermediate distribution frame should also be documented. IDF/MDF documentation will help to show the demarcation points for a network. Recall that the MDF, or *Main Distribution Frame*, is where outside lines, such as T3 or OC lines enter the premises. The IDF, or *Intermediate Distribution Frame*, is an extension of the MDF.

When diagramming a network, there are specific symbols used to document various devices. Some of these symbols are shown in Figure 16-1. These symbols should be used in all network diagrams. Since they are universal, any network administrator will understand their meaning.

Figure 16-1 Universal network diagram symbols should be used in documentation so any network administrator will be able to read and understand it.

Firewall   Router   Workgroup switch   Workstation

Goodheart-Willcox Publisher

NET
3.1, 3.3

Establishing a Baseline

The only way to determine objectively the performance of a network or server is to establish a baseline immediately after the network or server is installed. A **baseline**

Copyright Goodheart-Willcox Co., Inc.

is a measurement of performance characteristics that can be used at a later date to determine if the network or server is performing satisfactorily. Typically, a baseline can be established by software utilities specifically designed for such tasks. Many network operating systems have their own set of utilities that can perform routine baseline assessments. The Network+ Exam will likely ask you about forming a baseline.

One of the most important aspects of establishing a baseline is testing the network or server under normal and stressed conditions. Some software packages are designed to simulate network traffic so that the network can be stress-tested.

One of the best times to monitor a network or server is early in the morning. Start the monitoring process before the first shift of personnel arrives. At this time, activity should be at a minimum. As personnel report to their offices and start the workday, network traffic increases dramatically. For example, the mail server will experience the most activity when the greatest number of personnel check their e-mail and send return e-mails. The times that typically generate the most e-mail traffic are first thing in the morning, after the lunch break, and at the end of the workday.

It is important to understand that a baseline is not a collection of data at a particular point in time, but rather a collection of data over a period of time. A baseline should be established as soon as a new network or server is installed and operational. After, the baseline information should be routinely collected and reviewed to predict events that could affect network or server performance. By predicting events such as reaching an unacceptable level of collisions or running out of data storage space, preventive maintenance can be scheduled.

Network Baseline

Look at a sample form in Figure 16-2 for collecting and recording baseline information for a network. Baselines can be very detailed, but the one in the example is brief. It is meant only to present you with an idea of what type of data is gathered and why.

Peak utilization is the highest level of utilization experienced by the network. Peak utilization occurs when there is the most traffic on the network segment. This can happen several times during a day, such as first thing in the morning, lunchtime, and at the end of the day. This is normal and is mainly generated by users logging on

NET
3.3

Figure 16-2 A simple form like this example, or a more detailed form, can be created to record baseline information.

| Network Segment ID _____ | | |
| Date and Time Period _____ | | |

Segment	Value	Comments
Peak utilization		
Average utilization		
Frame size peak		
Frame size average		
Number of protocols		
Number of nodes		
Most active 10 nodes		
Collisions		
Packets dropped		

Goodheart-Willcox Publisher

Copyright Goodheart-Willcox Co., Inc.

to the network, opening files (especially large ones), and reading and sending e-mail. Peak utilization should not exceed 80 percent for long periods of time.

Average utilization is as the name implies—the average amount of utilization or traffic on a network in a given monitoring period. The average utilization for the network segment should not exceed 40 percent. Most new network segments will operate at 10 to 25 percent. The average and peak utilization is of major concern. When high rates occur, the network should be evaluated as to the cause. After the cause is determined, a plan for corrective action should be proposed.

Frame size peak is a record of the largest frame size recorded during the monitoring period. **Frame size average** is the average of all frame sizes during the monitoring period. Frame size varies, but the factors that affect frame size are the type of protocol and equipment used, the amount of traffic on the segment, and the type of data transmitted. An average TCP frame will be approximately 500 bytes. Very small TCP frames can indicate a problem.

Number of protocols is the number of different protocols transmitted in the network segment. A large number of different protocols can reflect an improperly configured network device such as a network adapter, router, switch, or wireless access point. There can also be existence of legacy devices on the network that are still configured for old Ethernet frame types or older protocols. Legacy devices typically broadcast more than one frame type until they receive a response from the other device or service they are requesting. For example, many devices automatically configure the network device for older network protocols to ensure backward compatibility. As such, you may see protocols related to NetBEUI, IPX/SPX, or AppleTalk. A large number of duplicate protocol frames and packets are generated across network segments caused by the network devices being configured for IPv4 and IPv6 by default. The number of protocols can be reduced by manually configuring devices and selecting only the appropriate protocols and services.

Number of nodes refers to the number of nodes communicating on the network segment. The number of nodes normally increases as time goes by. This is because economically healthy organizations grow. When comparing segment statistics over long periods of time (years), the number of nodes generating network traffic needs to be taken into account.

The *most active 10 nodes* entry is an indicator of possible network problem locations. For example, a workstation with a bad cable connection may be dropping an unusually large number of frames, which in turn causes new frames to be generated and transmitted. A node that must retransmit many frames will most likely be in the top 10 of this list.

The *collisions* entry represents frame or packet collisions on the network segment. Collisions are the primary indicator of a problem. There should be very few collisions on a healthy Ethernet segment. Less than one percent is not unusual. The *packets dropped* entry also indicates a problem. Dropped packets are often indicative of a cable or connection problem.

Excessive collisions and network traffic can be reduced through traffic-shaping techniques. When a network link is experiencing too many collisions or excessive traffic, routers or layer 3 switches can be installed to provide additional segment links. Another advantage to multiple segment paths is increased network reliability provided by link redundancy.

While a form was used in the example, many systems can typically collect data and export the data to spreadsheet format. The spreadsheet format can be incorporated into word-processing software or simply printed as a direct report with graphs. Most protocol analyzers can also record system baseline information.

Copyright Goodheart-Willcox Co., Inc.

Be aware that a server, not just network devices, can cause network bottlenecks. The three main causes of server bottlenecks are insufficient resources, unbalanced client loads, and incorrectly configured service(s). Insufficient server resources include too many users for the amount of server resources available. This is especially true of server memory and hard disk drive activity. To alleviate this type of problem, simply add more memory or configure more hard disk drives and map users to the additional drives.

When resource sharing is unbalanced, too many users are logging on to the same server when other servers are available. In this case, the default server logon for a portion of the users should be changed to balance the load.

A server may be incorrectly configured to handle the given client load. For example, a DHCP server may be configured with a limited IP address pool or with a long lease period duration. In this case, the administrator may need to increase the number of available IP addresses or shorten the lease period.

Server Baseline

Some of the most commonly monitored categories for establishing a server baseline are memory utilization, hard disk activity, CPU utilization, and server access activity. Memory utilization will determine if more memory needs to be installed in the server. Baselines include determining the amount of RAM available and paging swapfile activity. The page file is a section of a hard disk drive used to act as memory to supplement the available RAM. Legacy server systems depended on a paging file to augment the limited amount of installed RAM. In general, a maximum page file of 1.5 times the actual amount of RAM installed was created.

Beginning with Windows Server 2003 and Windows XP, the 64-bit operating system was introduced. Today, all modern servers are typically 64-bit systems. All 32-bit operating systems recognize 4 GB maximum of RAM. Any more RAM in a 32-bit system is wasted. However, 64-bit operating systems can recognize up to 16 TB (terabytes) of RAM. Page file size is not as critical for 64-bit systems because these systems can handle more physical memory than 32-bit systems, thus reducing the need for page files. In fact, Microsoft has no recommended size of page file for a 64-bit system. Microsoft even states that there may be no need at all for a page file if there is sufficient physical RAM installed on a 64-bit system.

Hard disk drive activity, or disk I/O activity, is monitored to determine when additional hard drives need to be installed. When a hard drive reaches approximately 80 percent capacity, additional storage should be installed.

CPU utilization determines if the CPU is overloaded with requests. CPU utilization should not exceed 85 percent. When the 85 percent threshold is reached, a faster CPU or additional CPUs should be installed. Additional servers can also be installed to share the processing load. When additional servers are configured for load balancing, they are often referred to as *server clusters* or *server farms*. It is very common to have two or more servers providing web services for a high demand website location. For example, Google uses a server farm, which is a collection of over 50,000 64-bit servers. The exact number of servers is constantly changing because the capability of individual servers is constantly changing. In 2016, it was estimated that Google's multiple data centers contained over 2,500,000 servers.

It is important to note that running performance-monitoring software applications adversely affects server performance. Server performance-monitoring tools use system resources such as RAM and CPU. A healthy server can handle performance-monitoring applications with no problem. However, if the server is already overburdened, the use of a performance-monitoring tool can cause a server to increase response time to network clients.

Note

The original release of Windows Server 2008 was the last iteration that could be installed as 32-bit or 64-bit. Starting with the second release of Windows Server 2008, only the 64-bit system is available.

NET

2.3, 3.2

Copyright Goodheart-Willcox Co., Inc.

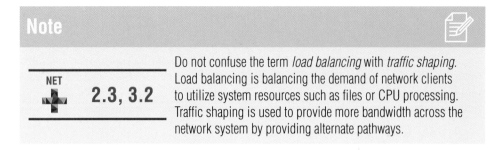

Note

NET **2.3, 3.2**

Do not confuse the term *load balancing* with *traffic shaping*. Load balancing is balancing the demand of network clients to utilize system resources such as files or CPU processing. Traffic shaping is used to provide more bandwidth across the network system by providing alternate pathways.

Monitoring Tools

Network events need to be monitored to detect and predict problems. The exact problems can vary a great deal, from simple user problems to detecting an intruder's attempts to break into the system. All major operating systems have monitoring utilities. There are also many good third-party tools available. Monitoring tools not only monitor events but also record the events into a log, which is then saved as a file. Event logs can be used to assist in analyzing system problems involving hardware, software, and security issues.

NET **3.3**

Performance Monitors

Most major operating systems come with some type of performance-monitoring utility. Microsoft Server provides Performance Monitor, which monitors network activity and system resources, as shown in Figure 16-3.

Figure 16-3 The Performance Monitor is part of the diagnostic tools available in Microsoft operating systems.

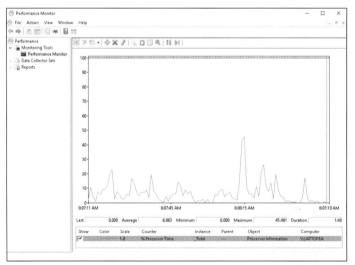

Goodheart-Willcox Publisher

A utility such as Performance Monitor provides a network administrator with the information needed for making objective decisions about the system. Performance Monitor can be configured to send alerts to the system administrator when resources are critical.

Performance Monitor can be used to predict system failure or to isolate the cause of poor performance. When used properly, an administrator can schedule routine hardware replacements, additions, and upgrades that will minimally affect user access. For example, if the CPU is at maximum performance for extended periods, a better CPU can be installed or more CPUs can be added during a period of low

Copyright Goodheart-Willcox Co., Inc.

usage, such as a weekend or evening. Scheduling routine repairs and upgrades prevents both unexpected and predictable network system failures. Many failures can be avoided by routine monitoring of system activities.

Windows Server operating systems have many of the same tools that are available in the Windows desktop operating systems. Figure 16-4 shows the screen capture of Windows Task Manager taken from a Windows 10 computer. It has the same appearance as the Task Manager in a Microsoft desktop system.

Windows Task Manager provides a quick view of system performance and can also show what software applications, processes, and services are running. For a more detailed view of performance factors, click the **Open Resource Monitor** button. Notice in Figure 16-5 a more detailed view of system resources and network performance is presented. The graphs at the top of the **Resource Overview** dialog box provide a picture of the CPU, disk, network, and memory performance.

Figure 16-4 Windows Task Manager can be used to display a quick view of system performance.

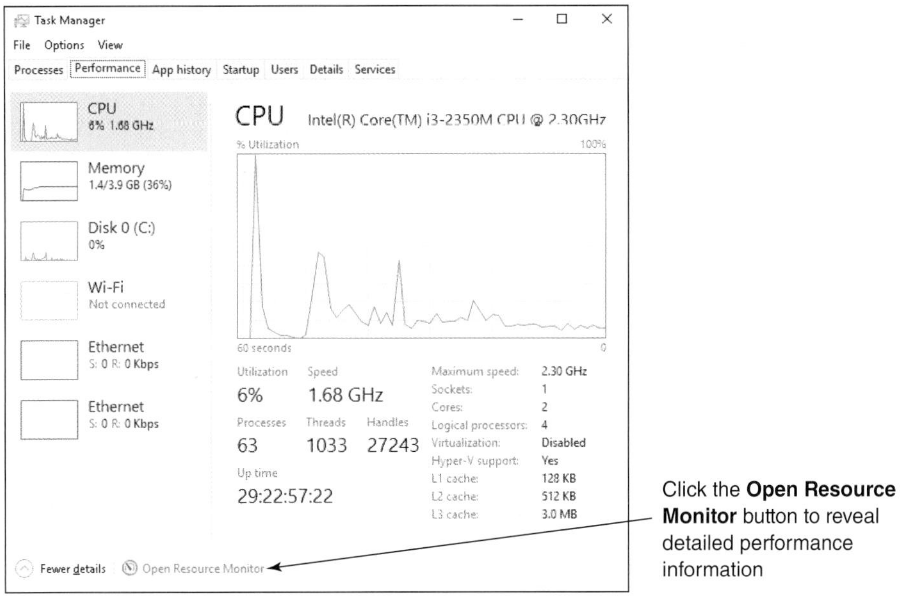

Click the **Open Resource Monitor** button to reveal detailed performance information

Goodheart-Willcox Publisher

Figure 16-5 By clicking the **Open Resource Monitor** button in Windows Task Manager, detailed performance information can be displayed.

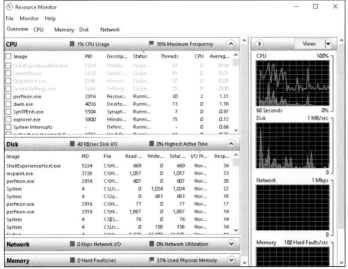

Goodheart-Willcox Publisher

Copyright Goodheart-Willcox Co., Inc.

Microsoft Network Monitor has evolved over the years from a simple introductory protocol analyzer into a full protocol analyzer with many features found only in very expensive third-party protocol analyzers. It can be used to establish a baseline of information about network performance. Microsoft Network Monitor is not installed by default but can be freely downloaded from the Microsoft website. It comes in both 32-bit and 64-bit versions and runs on Microsoft server and desktop systems. A screen capture of Microsoft Network Monitor is shown in Figure 16-6.

Figure 16-6 Microsoft Network Monitor is a protocol analyzer that can be used to monitor network performance.

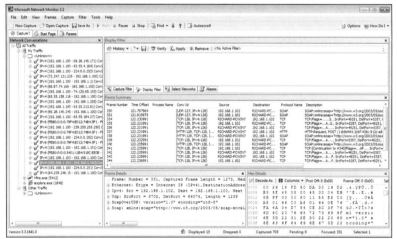

Goodheart-Willcox Publisher

The main difference between Microsoft Network Monitor and other protocol analyzers is the way they present data. Another significant difference is Microsoft Network Monitor identifies fewer protocols because it is designed to identify only Microsoft proprietary protocols and those belonging to the TCP/IP protocol suite.

Microsoft Network Monitor displays all active network connections and collects frames in a similar manner to Wireshark or any other protocol analyzer. The encapsulation of the protocols and packet contents are displayed. Filters can be applied so that specific protocol types or contents can be isolated from the total collection of packets and frames.

Microsoft Network Monitor could be used to establish a baseline for network performance; however, Performance Monitor does a better job of collecting and presenting raw data. At the time of this writing, Microsoft Network Monitor lacks many of the advanced features, such as graphically displaying statistical information and presenting written reports, found in other protocol analyzers Microsoft Network Monitor data captures can be opened by other protocol analyzers, such as Wireshark. Then, the features of the advanced protocol analyzer can be used to study the data.

Event Viewers

All major operating systems include some form of an event-monitoring utility. Microsoft provides in many of its operating systems a utility called *Event Viewer*. It is designed to record events that occur during the operation of the server or desktop system. Some typical events are the starting or stopping of a service, user logon activities, share access, file access, and hardware and software information. Event Viewer is an excellent utility for troubleshooting system failures.

Figure 16-7 shows some of the various system events recorded in the Event Viewer system log. Windows Server 2008 Event Viewer is very similar to Event Viewer in Windows Vista and Windows 7. Logs can be created for events related to

Copyright Goodheart-Willcox Co., Inc.

applications, security, setup, system, and forwarded events. In Figure 16-8, information is displayed about the failure of the Windows Update service.

Figure 16-7 Event Viewer is located under the **Diagnostics** section of Server Manager. Events relating to applications, security, setup, system, and forwarded events are collected and stored for viewing.

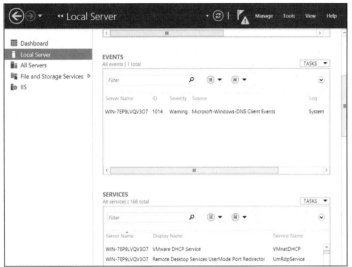

Goodheart-Willcox Publisher

Figure 16-8 The individual event can be opened as a separate window by double-clicking the event item in Event Viewer.

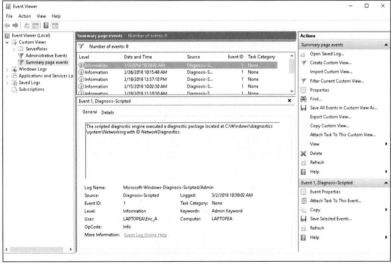

Goodheart-Willcox Publisher

Simple Network Management Protocol (SNMP)

The **Simple Network Management Protocol (SNMP)** was designed by the ITEF to support network management, allowing an administrator to manage and monitor network devices and services from a single location. SNMP is an application-layer protocol that uses UDP packets for delivery.

The ITEF SNMP protocol is not a complete, finished protocol but rather a framework that is used by third-party software companies. The third-party software designers finish the framework to perform a function, such as network monitoring of devices or remote configuration of network devices. SNMP applications are designed

Copyright Goodheart-Willcox Co., Inc.

to monitor and configure items on a network from a centralized location. Some items that can be configured and monitored are servers, routers, switches, IP video cameras, IP phones, and just about any device that uses the TCP/IP suite of protocols.

The SNMP agent is installed on the devices that are to be monitored by the network management system (NMS). The NMS collects the data and stores the data in a management information base (MIB).

Microsoft server and desktop operating systems do *not* enable SNMP by default. Figure 16-9 shows the Windows Server 2008 **Windows Features** dialog box. Notice that SNMP must be selected manually. This is because Microsoft has developed its own protocols used for network management.

Figure 16-9 SNMP can be enabled through the **Programs and Features** menu found in **Control Panel**.

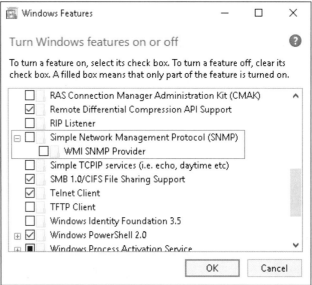

Goodheart-Willcox Publisher

Maintaining System Software

Software packages typically need routine maintenance. When software developers design their programs, they do the best job they can, but problems, or program errors, do occur. A software program error is referred to as a **bug**. Software patches, or fixes, are developed after the discovery of a bug or security problem. Software is usually updated through patches, service packs, and system upgrades.

Patches

Software patches for operating systems are released frequently. Patches should be tested on a limited number of computers or servers before installing them across the entire network. Patches can cause problems with your existing system because of unknown or untested hardware or software applications. Only after careful and thorough testing of the effects of a patch can it be installed on other computers in the network. Another reason for the caution is most patches cannot be uninstalled. If an unforeseen critical problem develops after a patch has been installed, one may be forced to do a backup of important data, wipe the system clean, and then perform a new operating system installation. When talking about hundreds or thousands of computers, this could be very time-consuming. Take note that the term *patch* is often incorrectly used synonymously with the term *hotfix*. A hotfix is an update to a very

Copyright Goodheart-Willcox Co., Inc.

specific, serious problem and may not always be released publicly. It also applies to a specific type of patch that can be implemented without having to stop or restart the system, similar to hot-swap technology.

Service Packs

Microsoft uses the term **service pack** to describe a collection of software patches or fixes. After every release of a major operating system, a series of service packs is provided free of charge to users to update the system. A typical service pack consists of program modifications that provide security fixes and updated drivers for new hardware technologies. For example, Windows NT 4.0 went through a series of six major service packs. The first service pack released for Windows XP was a collection of 324 fixes that dealt with network, hardware, security, and basic operating system issues. A detailed list of each fix included in the service pack can be downloaded. Details about the nature of each problem are also provided.

Windows 8.1 and Windows Server 2012 R2 contained over 130 changes. Microsoft provided a downloadable Excel spreadsheet that the technician could use to link to information about the fixes and changes, as shown in Figure 16-10. The technician can simply click on the link to access detailed information about the fix.

Keeping an operating system up-to-date with service packs and individual patches as they are released is good insurance against program security flaws and other problems as they are discovered. Service packs, like patches, should be tested before installing them on a network system.

Figure 16-10 Microsoft provided a spreadsheet containing a list of over 130 changes for Windows 8 and Windows Server 2012 in the release of R2. Links to details about each change were embedded into the spreadsheet.

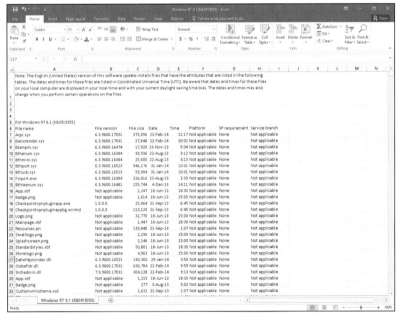

Goodheart-Willcox Publisher

Upgrades

A software upgrade is a major improvement or enhancement to existing software programs. For example, Windows Server 2012 was released in September 2012 and then released again in October 2013 as Windows Server 2012 R2. The *R2* represents *release number two* or *second release*. There were many changes to the operating

Copyright Goodheart-Willcox Co., Inc.

system and many more features added that it justified a new release rather than a service pack. Similarly, Windows Server 2008 was also given a second release. One of the most significant changes in this example was that Windows Server 2008 R2 is only available for 64-bit systems. The original Windows Server 2008 release was available for 32-bit and 64-bit systems. At the time of writing, Windows Server 2016 has not had any subsequent releases.

The term *upgrade* generally refers to changing from one operating system to another that uses the same basic core operating system features. A system upgrade occurs when the basic core of the operating system is still the same without significant changes. When there is a great difference between the old operating system and the new operating system, you cannot perform a system upgrade.

For diverse operating systems, you must perform a system migration. The term *migration* means combining two diverse operating systems or network systems into one system. For example, you cannot upgrade Windows Server 2008 32-bit to Windows Server 2008 R2, which is a 64-bit operating system. You must migrate it because of the significant changes to the basic structure, such as the 64-bit feature. There will be more about migration later in this chapter as applied to different network operating systems being merged into one network system.

Software Installations

Software developers do a good job of testing their software on numerous types of computers with various types of hardware and software configurations. However, new software programs should always be tested before they are installed on a network server or distributed to network clients. Often, a beta version of the software package is released so the developer can gain more knowledge about the software compatibility of the software package.

Microsoft and other software developers routinely allow users to have access to beta versions of an upcoming release of a software package. For example, Microsoft Windows Server 2016 was released as a beta version months before it was distributed through retail outlets. By releasing beta versions, thousands of copies of the software are able to be tested by many different users running various software packages and using many different types of hardware. Numerous flaws can be detected and remedied before releasing the software package.

The development of a new operating system can be quite involved. Hardware manufacturers work hand-in-hand with software developers to write driver programs to support their hardware. If the hardware drivers are developed in time, they are included in the beta version of the operating system so they can also be tested. After the release of new operating system hardware, developers must provide drivers for the system by packaging a disk or disc with the hardware device or offering free downloadable drivers from their website.

Before a new software package is installed on a server or client, it should be fully tested. A test network consisting of a few workstations and a server can be created using the same software and hardware that exists in the real network. The test network is separate from the real network and is used to test software package compatibility with hardware and software applications. A corporation or institution should have a lab or training room set aside that can be used for testing purposes.

Installing a new software system on a network can cause unpredictable problems. Some problems are not reversible. Any administrator or technician would want to avoid having to reformat the server hard drive, reinstall the operating system and software applications, and restore the data that was last backed up. During this time period, all personnel who use the network for work purposes would be idle. Production loss can be very expensive. Think about the hundreds or even thousands of

Copyright Goodheart-Willcox Co., Inc.

employees who are being paid while waiting for the network to be functional. Think about how many customers a business could lose.

Before installing any new hardware or software on a network system, you should also check the hardware or software compatibility list at both the hardware manufacturer's website and the operating system website, as shown in Figure 16-11.

Figure 16-11 A—Microsoft maintains a complete list of hardware- and software-compatible products at its website for all of its currently supported operating systems. B—A lengthy list of applications that are certified to be compatible with Microsoft Server 2016.

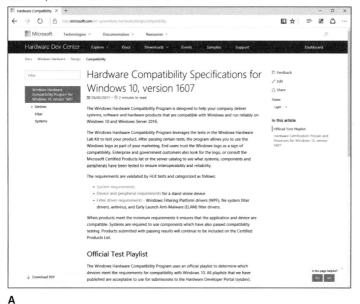

A

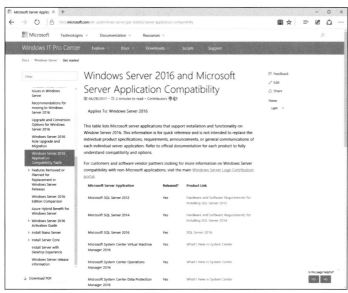

B

Goodheart-Willcox Publisher

Often, information on one website will conflict with another. For example, the operating system website might indicate that a hardware device is not compatible with the operating system. By going to the hardware manufacturer's website, you may find that a driver has been released for the hardware to allow it to work on that operating system. Conflicting information about hardware compatibility is a common occurrence.

Copyright Goodheart-Willcox Co., Inc.

Operating systems often offer patches or fixes for security problems as they are discovered. Security is an ongoing issue. Breaches in network security happen constantly. E-mail newsletters are offered free of charge at all leading operating system websites. Subscribing to and reading these newsletters often is a good way to become aware of the latest developments. It is increasingly important to stay ahead of intruders. Leading antimalware developers also provide newsletters. Not only do antimalware developers provide users with timely information, they typically release fixes within 24 hours of initial virus detection.

General Reviewing

There are a number of processes in a network that require review. Log reviewing is one of them. Logs are best reviewed with a Security Information Event Manager (SIEM). Such products aggregate logs, and provide alerts and notifications regarding issues. By reviewing logs and addressing SIEM alerts and notifications, administrators can be aware of potential issues before an issue becomes critical. For example, logs can determine if a system is failing or if an outside party has been port scanning a network. *Port scanning* is the process of sending client requests to a series of port addresses in an effort to find an active port. This is often the first step of a cyberattack or the first step in assessing your network.

Monitoring a network involves a number of metrics. Anomalous behavior cannot be detected if an administrator does not know what normal behavior is. The normal bandwidth or throughput for a given network segment must be known in order to tell if the bandwidth has decreased. The typical utilization of any network segment, service, or shared device should be known as well. It is also helpful to know what the normal percentage of packet drops is. This is related to understanding the error rate for all systems. Reviewing baselines for all of these metrics will provide an understanding of behavior that deviates from the norms. Packet and traffic analysis is an important part of this process. By analyzing packet traffic, metrics will be accumulated for the network.

However, reviewing and monitoring can only provide so much information about a network. Vulnerability scanning is needed to check for vulnerabilities that may still emerge but have yet to be exploited. There are a number of vulnerability scanners available that automate this process. Microsoft Baseline Security Analyzer (MBSA) is free to download from Microsoft. Nessus is perhaps the most common vulnerability scanner. It is not a free download, but it is quite comprehensive. You can learn more about Nessus at www.tenable.com.

Maintaining System Hardware

The proper maintenance of system hardware is cost-effective. A system failure during business hours can be very costly to the company. Whenever possible, all system hardware maintenance should be performed when business and clients will be least affected.

Scheduling Downtime

Scheduling downtime is an important aspect of maintenance. A small network with a single server should have maintenance performed after business hours to avoid the possibility of a system crash while workers are present. Maintenance that may possibly jeopardize the use of the network system should never be performed. Most maintenance, such as backups, upgrades, and virus updates, should be performed when the network is not being used. A notice should be sent to all users so they know

Copyright Goodheart-Willcox Co., Inc.

the network may be down. The notice should be sent even if the maintenance is going to be performed after regular business hours. Workers may be planning to work late or to work from home by accessing the network remotely.

Some businesses operate on a 24/7/365 schedule. In this case, two or more servers are routinely installed. One may be taken off-line to perform maintenance while the other carries the network. A special type of server installation is referred to as a *cluster*. A **cluster** is a group of servers that share the network demand. One of the servers can easily be taken off-line for maintenance without disrupting network activities.

A storage cluster is designed to ensure access to vital files and prevent loss of data. Notice in Figure 16-12 there are two servers sharing a common storage unit. The two servers share the same IP address and name. In a cluster configuration, the servers are referred to as *node 1*, *node 2*, etc. The client computers connect to the network through a switch or router. The cluster may also have two or more switches or routers for redundancy. If either of the nodes goes down or is taken off-line for maintenance, the other node will serve the clients. The shared storage is usually a RAID 5 configuration.

Figure 16-12 A two-node cluster and shared disk storage is used to form a simple storage cluster system.

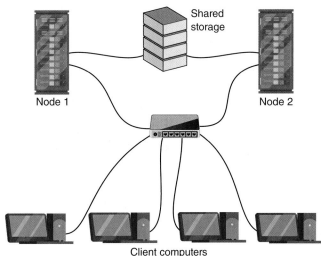

Client computers

(server icons) fullvector/Shutterstock.com; (hub icon) Vadim Ermak/Shutterstock.com;
(workstation icons) RedlineVector/Shutterstock.com; Goodheart-Willcox Publisher

Clustering provides a strong level of fault tolerance. On an individual server, this can be emulated with processes such as NIC teaming. *NIC teaming* is when multiple network interface cards work in conjunction. The primary reason for this is to provide increased throughput. However, it has the added effect that if one NIC goes down, the others can still function. A related function exists in many routers with port aggregation. *Port aggregation* allows two ports to be combined so that they function as one. This also increases throughput.

Virtual LANs

Backbones, additional servers, routers, switches, and other devices may be added to the network system. As a company grows, it will undoubtedly require more networking capacity. This means additional throughput capacity and additional workstations will be required. As a network system grows, other additional hardware may be required, such as routers and switches. Routers and switches are sometimes installed on existing systems as the number of workstations increases. The additional hardware is used to create Virtual LANs (VLANs). A VLAN theoretically increases the available bandwidth. The VLANs lower the number of devices on the network. Each VLAN acts as its own separate network, thus reducing the number of collision zones. While the bandwidth is not technically increased, the remaining devices on the network have more access to available bandwidth. Think of a VLAN as a high-occupancy-vehicle lane on a highway. It does not increase the speed limit on the highway, but it eliminates congestion in single-occupancy lanes.

Each VLAN has the same throughput as the original LAN. For example, it is possible to divide an existing 1000BaseT network consisting of 100 workstations into two separate VLANs by using switch technology. The network is divided according to workgroups. Workgroups often communicate within their own workgroup but seldom outside of the same workgroup. By dividing the network into two separate LANs, the bandwidth is technically doubled by creating two networks, each with 1000 Mbps bandwidth. However, this is not always practical. Bandwidth is based on the actual working conditions of two or more workgroups within the network.

Maintaining System Integrity

The completeness and accuracy of data is referred to as *system integrity* or *data integrity*. Maintaining system integrity requires protecting the data while the server is running. To protect data, fault tolerance and disaster recovery must be designed into the network. You should recall from Chapter 9 that fault tolerance is a system's ability to continue operation during a system hardware or software error. Fault tolerance strategies include some RAID systems and electrical power systems. Electrical power systems are covered in detail later in this chapter. **Disaster recovery** is the restoration of a system to normal operation after a disaster has occurred. It includes data backups; hot and cold spares; and hot, warm, and cold sites.

Network+ Note

For the Network+ Certification Exam, be sure you know the difference between *fault tolerance* and *disaster recovery* and can identify devices, systems, and strategies related to each. Remember, fault tolerance includes RAID systems, server clustering, and UPS units. Disaster recovery includes data backups and data backup media storage. RAID 0, however, does not provide fault tolerance.

Fault-Tolerant RAID Systems

RAID will only be quickly reviewed in this chapter. For a detailed explanation of each RAID system, review Chapter 9. While there are many different RAID styles, the predominant RAID systems that provide fault tolerance are RAID 1 and RAID 5.

RAID 1 consists of two disk drives with matching data on each drive. If one drive fails, the other has a complete copy of data. RAID 1 is also known as *disk mirroring*. RAID 5 combines parity and striping to provide an economical way to protect data should a hard disk drive fail. At least three hard disk drives are required for a RAID 5 configuration. Data blocks are striped across two hard disk drives, and parity for those two blocks is stored on a third hard disk drive. Parity and data blocks alternate across the drive system so that each hard disk drive consists of approximately two parts data blocks and one part parity. This method ensures equal restoration time if any of the three hard disk drives fail.

Copyright Goodheart-Willcox Co., Inc.

Tech Tip

RAID 0 does *not* offer fault tolerance. It is designed strictly for data storage speed.

Backup Data Methods

Even with fault-tolerant RAID systems, data can still be corrupted or damaged beyond repair. For example, a virus could infect each disk drive in the RAID system, or a natural disaster, storm, hurricane, tornado, flood, or a fire could destroy the entire computer system. A backup data method must be employed to restore valuable data in case any of these events occur. Backing up data is part of a disaster recovery system. Backups should be made at regular intervals. This way the data can be restored up to the last good backup.

The term *backup* refers to making copies of the data on a storage system. Backups can be made manually or automatically with software applications designed for such purposes. Copies of data can be made to most any type of data storage medium, such as hard disk drives, tapes, and network-attached storage devices. The most common storage device is a tape backup drive, but hard disk drives are becoming more prevalent for small storage systems. Three types of backups can be performed: full, incremental, and differential.

Full Backup

As the name implies, a **full backup** is a complete backup of all designated data. Not everything on a server needs to be backed up during a full backup, as only data need to be copied. If the hard disk drive is replaced because it failed, the operating system and applications can be reinstalled from discs. Data is the real concern. A full backup operation copies all identified data during a single backup period.

3.2 NET

Incremental Backup

An **incremental backup** copies only data that has changed since the previous backup, regardless of what type of backup it was. Compared to full backups, incremental backups are time-savers. A typical scenario of using the incremental backup method is to perform a full backup once a week and then incremental backups daily. In a week's time, this would equal seven backup sessions: one full backup and six incremental backups. This process saves time when compared with making daily full backups.

The only disadvantage is that when data is restored, the last full backup must first be restored and then each incremental backup in sequential order. If one incremental backup is restored out of sequence, the data restoration is flawed. See Figure 16-13. Keep in mind that large data systems may require more than one tape each day for differential as well as incremental backups. One tape was used in the example to keep the concept simple.

Figure 16-13 An incremental backup requires separate media for each incremental backup.

Goodheart-Willcox Publisher

Copyright Goodheart-Willcox Co., Inc.

Differential Backup

A **differential backup** backs up all data that has been changed since the last full backup. There is no need to use a series of tapes. One tape for the differential backup will do because all data changes since the last full backup are recorded, seen in Figure 16-14.

Figure 16-14 A differential backup can use the same media for each backup.

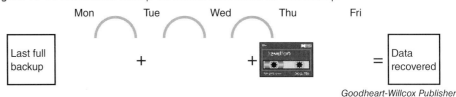

Goodheart-Willcox Publisher

A typical scenario of using the differential backup method is to perform a full backup once a week and a differential daily on the other days of the week. To restore data, the full backup is restored and then the last differential backup.

You may wonder how the technology knows if a full backup has been performed or an incremental or a differential change has occurred. A file attribute, called *archive*, provides this information. Remember that files have file attributes, such as *read-only* and *system*. The archive attribute is actually a bit that is set when changes are made in the file's contents. The **archive bit** identifies if a file has changed since the last full or incremental backup. By indicating which files have changed since the last full backup, the backup system can copy only the changed files. The archive bit is reset every time a full backup or an incremental backup is performed. The archive bit is not reset when a differential backup is performed or when a file is copied using commands such as **copy** and **xcopy**.

Remember, an incremental backup only copies files that have changed since the last full or incremental backup. Both full and incremental backups reset the archive bit. When the contents of a particular file changes by being opened and then closed during a business transaction, the archive bit is set, indicating that it should be backed up during the next backup operation.

A differential backup does not reset the archive bit. It simply copies all files that have changed since the last full backup. Note that differential and incremental backups are never mixed. Only one type of backup, incremental or differential, can be performed after a full backup.

Tech Tip

Tape drive media is vulnerable to damage through wear and electromagnetism. It is a good idea to alternate between two or more tapes when performing backups. For example, if performing a weekly full backup, you should overwrite a tape every other backup. This will increase the life of the tape and serve as a backup in case one of the tapes becomes damaged.

Data Backup and Restoration Methods

Backup data consists of a collection of many different files. Not all files are accessed on any given day. For example, if a bank maintains one file per customer, then that single file's content remains unchanged until the customer performs a bank transaction. A bank may have thousands or even millions of customers, which equates to millions of files. There is no need to back up every file every day, especially if the vast majority of files have not changed. In this scenario, performing a full backup once a week with incremental backups during the week is sufficient and will streamline the backup process. Small data systems, on the other hand, can perform a full backup every day or a full backup once a week followed by a daily differential backup.

Remember, when restoring data from an incremental backup, each incremental tape is needed as well as the last full backup. The incremental backups must be restored in the exact order they were created since the last full backup. When restoring data from a differential backup, only the last full backup and the last differential backup created are needed.

Storing Backup Data

Backups of critical information are a must, but what if the facility experiences a disaster, such as a fire, flood, severe storms, or vandalism? The backups must be stored in a secure, climate-controlled, off-site environment. Additional copies of the same backups may be kept on-site for easy access if needed, but critical data must be stored away from the site. Key points concerning data backup storage include the following:

- Store backups off-site in a secure, climate-controlled storage area with limited access.
- Avoid storing backups in direct sunlight, near electrical panels, or in equipment rooms.
- Avoid exposing backups to magnetic fields generated by electrical equipment, such as motors and speakers.

Never store magnetic tape, disc media, or any computer equipment in direct sunlight. Direct sunlight can damage sensitive magnetic media. The magnetic tracks on backup media can lose part or all of their magnetic qualities due to exposure to direct sunlight and the heat generated by the exposure. Backup media should never be stored in equipment rooms of buildings that contain electrical, HVAC (heating, ventilation, and air-conditioning), or other forms of electrical equipment and electrical motors. Storage areas need to be climate-controlled. Backup media, especially tapes, are easily damaged by excessive heat and humidity. Always store backup media in a secure area that has limited access by personnel. Someone can easily throw away a collection of backup media while on a routine cleanup assignment of a dusty storage area. Also, remember that backup media will prove to be of little value if the disaster that destroys the original data also destroys the backup copies.

Hot and Cold Spares

A **hot spare** is a backup component that can automatically replace a failed system component without the intervention of a technician. A hot spare is typically a spare disk drive that is part of a RAID system but not in regular use. It is a standby unit that activates when one of the disk drives in the RAID unit fails. On failure of any disk drive, the hot spare automatically replaces the failed disk drive. The disk controller will automatically begin rebuilding the lost data on the new disk drive. The process of rebuilding the data onto the new drive is only possible with a fault-tolerant RAID system, such as RAID 1 or RAID 5. Since hot spares automatically replace failed drives and rebuild lost data, they provide some level of fault tolerance and zero downtime for the server.

A failed hard disk drive can also be replaced by a cold spare. A **cold spare** is any compatible disk drive that is in storage and is used to replace a failed disk drive. If the server supports hot-swap drives, the cold disk drive can be hot-swapped with the

Copyright Goodheart-Willcox Co., Inc.

failed disk drive. As soon as the failed drive is hot-swapped with the cold spare, the disk controller will automatically begin to rebuild the data onto the new disk drive. The advantage of a hot spare over the cold spare is obvious. There is a minimum amount of server downtime when hot spares are used, as illustrated in Figure 16-15.

Hot, Cold, and Warm Sites

The terms *hot*, *cold*, and *warm* are used to describe the readiness of an off-site data storage facility to recover from a failure at the primary site. The fundamental differences between these sites are illustrated in Figure 16-16. A cold site refers to a data-storage facility where only backup data is stored. A warm site consists of hardware and data, but the data has not yet been loaded onto the hardware. A hot site is a data-storage facility where a backup of data is stored as well as a running system containing the most up-to-date data. A hot-site system is ready to serve users in case of a complete system failure at the original site. The only thing missing from the system is the last incremental or full backup.

Figure 16-15 Hot and cold spares. A—A hot spare requires no technician intervention. B—A cold spare requires a technician to install it into the system after removing the failed component.

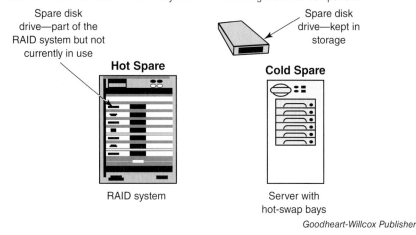

Goodheart-Willcox Publisher

Figure 16-16 Differences between a cold site, warm site, and hot site.

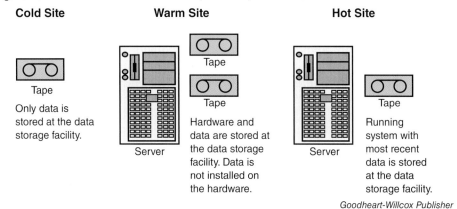

Goodheart-Willcox Publisher

The choice of off-site storage is directly related to cost and the value placed on the time it takes to recover from a data loss scenario. The cold site is the least expensive but takes the longest to set up and recover. The hot site offers the quickest recovery but is the most expensive to maintain.

Copyright Goodheart-Willcox Co., Inc.

Important Concepts

When considering disaster recovery and business continuity, there are several critical concepts one must keep in mind. **Mean time to repair (MTTR)**, also called *mean time to recover*, is the average time it would take to repair a system or device if it fails. This will help determine the type of RAID or backup needed. It will also help to determine if hot, cold, or warm sites are needed. Related to MTTR is **mean time between failures (MTBF)**, or *mean time before failure*. MTBF describes how long a system is likely to run before it fails.

Most organizations have **service-level agreements (SLA)**. These determine how fast, and in what manner, vendors will respond to an issue. The aforementioned MTTR and MTBF often help guide administrators to decide what SLA requirements should entail.

In addition to these important metrics, the equipment must be able to maintain high availability. *High availability* refers to the services and hardware are functioning most of the time and available to end users. The time of availability varies based on an individual company's requirements; however, 99.999 percent, or *five 9s*, is considered a very high, though difficult-to-achieve, standard for availability. At this level of availability, a system would be down for less than two hours in a given year.

Regardless of the metric for high availability, there are several technological steps that will support it. Hardware redundancy is a good first step. Servers should have redundant drives (recall discussions of RAID earlier in this book). However, redundant processors and circuits, dual power supplies, or other measures to ensure your servers are up and running can be implemented. It is also important to make backups, or *snapshots*, of your servers so they can be quickly restored in the event of a failure.

Maintaining Stable Electrical Power

A sufficient supply of electrical power is necessary to keep a server running. Most people assume the electrical power coming from a 120-volt outlet is a steady stream of 120-volt electricity. The fact is, the electrical power coming from the outlet is not a steady stream and, most times, is not exactly 120 volts. Commercial electrical power suffers from conditions such as surges, spikes, brownouts, and blackouts. This section contains a detailed discussion of electrical power conditions and the electrical power devices used to overcome the ill effects of these conditions.

Electrical Surges and Spikes

Electrical surges and spikes are common occurrences in commercial electrical power. An **electrical surge** is a higher-than-normal voltage level, typically caused by lightning. An **electrical spike** is a very short burst of abnormally high voltage, typically caused by electrical equipment. See Figure 16-17 for a visual comparison of the two. Electrical surges and spikes happen many times throughout the day and typically go unnoticed. The magnitude of the voltage level varies. Normally, electrical spikes are not of sufficient magnitude to harm most electrical systems, even delicate electronic equipment. Over the years, electronic designers have incorporated techniques that limit the effect of most electrical surges and spikes. Occasionally, though, they are of sufficient strength to damage equipment.

The most severe electrical surge is caused by lightning strikes. A thunderstorm need not be in close proximity to equipment to damage it. After lightning strikes a power line, the surge can travel over 20 miles before reaching its final destination. Equipment along the pathway of the electrical surge can be damaged. A **lightning**

Copyright Goodheart-Willcox Co., Inc.

Figure 16-17 An electrical surge is a higher-than-normal voltage level. An electrical spike is a very short burst of abnormally high voltage.

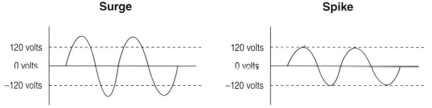

Goodheart-Willcox Publisher

arrestor is a special piece of electrical equipment designed to dampen the effects of an electrical surge caused by lightning. While they work most times, they do not always prevent the destruction associated with lightning. Most network systems are adequately protected from lightning damage by a high-quality uninterruptible power supply (UPS). UPS devices are discussed in detail later in this section.

Another cause of electrical surges through electrical systems is automobile accidents. Many times an automobile will strike a utility pole. When that happens, the power lines swing together causing the two lines to touch. This causes a momentary electrical explosion, which is followed by an electrical surge and occasionally a brownout or blackout condition.

Electrical equipment, such as motors, welders, and even electrical switches, cause electrical spikes. The spike is the result of an electrical phenomena referred to as inductive reactance. *Inductive reactance* is very common and is associated with the windings (coiled wire) inside motors, transformers, appliances, tools, and various other pieces of electrical equipment. When an electrical circuit that uses alternating current (AC) is opened or closed and the circuit has inductive properties (windings), an electrical spike is produced. The exact voltage level of the spike depends on the electrical characteristics of the circuit. In short, there are many electrical spikes during a normal 24-hour period. Most electrical spikes go unnoticed because of the way electrical systems are designed. The amount of information required to understand inductive reactance adequately is far beyond the scope of this book. In fact, it is one of the most difficult principles to master in the study of electronics. For now, just remember that electrical equipment, such as the items mentioned, can generate electrical spikes during normal usage.

Standards and best practices are used to reduce the effects of electrical spikes. For example, computer system electrical circuits are typically isolated from electrical circuits that provide power to lighting and electrical equipment. By isolating the electrical circuits serving computer equipment, the possibility of electrical spikes produced by equipment in the building is reduced. For example, commercial buildings, hospitals, and schools use a bright orange color to identify electrical outlets to be used strictly for computer or sensitive electronic equipment, such as hospital monitoring or life-support equipment. These outlets should never be used for equipment that can produce electrical noise or spikes, such as vacuum cleaners, drills, microwaves, and other common equipment found in the workplace. Many electrical appliances and power tools produce unwanted distortions in the AC signal, which may damage sensitive electronic equipment or corrupt data. A worker using a drill plugged into one of the designated orange outlets will produce thousands of small spikes that will affect equipment on the entire dedicated circuit.

Brownouts and Blackouts

Brownouts and blackouts are a classification of electrical energy loss dependent on the amount of voltage lost. A **brownout** is a partial loss of electrical energy while a

Copyright Goodheart-Willcox Co., Inc.

blackout is a total loss of electrical energy, as illustrated in Figure 16-18. For example, during a blackout, there is no voltage available. During a brownout, however, there is a measurable, lower-than-normal voltage level. A brownout sometimes appears to the naked eye as a dimming effect.

Figure 16-18 A brownout is a partial loss of electrical energy. A blackout is a total loss of electrical energy.

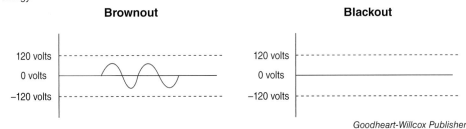

Goodheart-Willcox Publisher

Blackouts are routinely caused by equipment failure, automobiles striking utility poles, fires, and natural disasters, such as earthquakes, storms, tornadoes, and hurricanes. While a blackout can cause a loss of data, a brownout can actually damage electrical equipment. When a brownout occurs, the voltage level at the electrical equipment is lower than the equipment normally expects. Most electrical equipment will attempt to compensate for the lower voltage level by allowing the amperage to increase. The increased amperage will be in excess of what the system can safely handle. Normally, a fuse will blow or a breaker will trip, thus protecting the equipment. If not, the high electrical current (amperage) will damage components in the electrical system. The effects of blackouts and brownouts on the network server and other related equipment could be prevented by the use of an uninterruptible power supply (UPS).

Brownouts may occur on any power system. The main cause of brownouts is excessive consumption of electricity. Excessive consumption happens most often when there are severe weather conditions, such as extremely high or low temperatures. Electrical heating and cooling equipment requires large amounts of electrical energy during extreme temperature conditions. Most electrical devices specify that the ideal voltage for equipment should be within 10 percent of the indicated voltage level of the appliance or machine. For example, an electrical device rated for 120 volts AC requires a safe operating voltage level plus or minus 10 percent of 120 volts. That would be a range of 108 volts to 132 volts. Any voltage level outside this range could have serious side effects.

Uninterruptible Power Supply (UPS)

An **uninterruptible power supply (UPS)** is a device that ensures constant and consistent network performance by supplying electrical energy in case of a power failure or blackout. UPS systems are also designed to provide protection from electrical surges, spikes, and brownouts. A UPS provides a steady voltage level to equipment even when the input voltage level is higher or lower than needed. The exact length of time the UPS supplies power during a blackout depends on the amount of electrical load it must support and the size or amp-hour capacity of the batteries in the UPS unit. A UPS also provides power conditioning. **Power conditioning** is the process of eliminating spikes as well as any type of variation in the desired AC signal pattern.

There are two major categories of UPS units: standby and continuous. Many other names are used to describe UPS units, such as *off-line, online,* and *line-interactive.* Off-line and line-interactive refer to standby UPS units. Online refers to a continuous UPS unit. Manufacturers often coin these names. What is important to

Copyright Goodheart-Willcox Co., Inc.

understand are the characteristics of each. This will help you know which one is the correct style for your computer system's protection. For this chapter, the terms *standby* and *continuous* will be used to describe the two major categories.

A **standby UPS** waits until there is a disruption in commercial electricity before it takes over the responsibility of supplying electrical energy. A **continuous UPS** provides a steady supply of electrical energy at all times, even when there is no electrical problem. The reason for using a continuous UPS is to eliminate the possibility of data corruption. A standby UPS quickly takes over to supply electrical energy when commercial power is lost. The standby UPS can switch from standby mode to full operation in less than 5 milliseconds, or 5/1000 of a second. While that may seem fast, it is not fast enough to ensure error-free data during computer data processing. The best solution is to use a continuous UPS. Figure 16-19 illustrates how the two compare.

Both types of UPS systems use an inverter and a battery. The main difference is the continuous UPS provides a constant flow of electrical energy to equipment without the slightest interruption, Figure 16-19A. The standby UPS activates the switching mechanism when low or no voltage is detected. In Figure 16-19B, a pair of relay contacts indicates the switching mechanism. Some units use solid-state electronic switches, but even the electronic switches cause a slight interruption in power. Even though this may only take a few milliseconds and go unnoticed in conventional lighting, television, and other pieces of equipment, it is serious enough to lose valuable data during data transactions, such as saving, loading, or transferring.

Microsoft operating systems earlier than Windows Server 2000 and Windows XP provided options for managing UPS systems as part of the **Power Options** dialog box. For Windows Server 2000 and Windows XP and later Windows operating systems, UPS manufacturers supply their own software applications for configuration, monitoring, and notification. The typical UPS system connects to the computer through a USB port.

Figure 16-19 The two major categories of UPS units are continuous and standby. A—Continuous UPS supplies a constant flow of electrical power to the server. When the commercial power goes off, there is no momentary interruption of electrical power to the server because power is continuously supplied. B—Standby UPS does not provide a steady continuous supply of electrical power. There is always a momentary power interruption while switching to backup power.

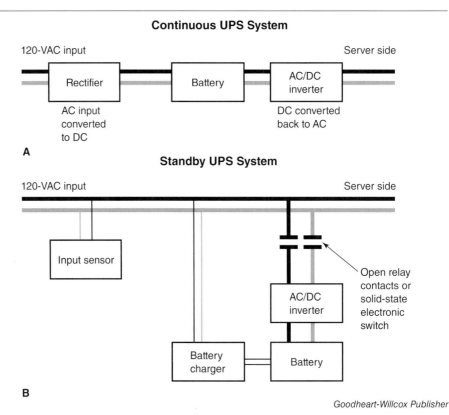

Goodheart-Willcox Publisher

Copyright Goodheart-Willcox Co., Inc.

Figure 16-20 shows a screen capture of the PowerChute software utility that is used to monitor and configure an APC UPS system. The monitoring option provides information such as the battery charge state and the amount of electrical energy consumed by the computer, expressed in watts. Configuration options such as voltage levels can be adjusted. In Figure 16-21, the default values for the maximum and minimum voltage levels are displayed. These levels can be adjusted up or down as desired.

Many other configuration options are available, such as automated notification to network clients when there is an AC power failure. The notification provides network users with ample time to close any open programs and shut down the computer before the UPS power supply is completely drained.

Figure 16-20 The PowerChute software utility provides options to monitor and configure the UPS.

Goodheart-Willcox Publisher

Figure 16-21 PowerChute can be used to configure the maximum and minimum voltage levels for the APC UPS system.

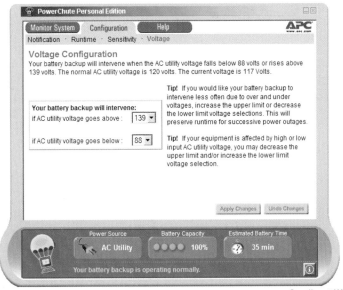

Goodheart-Willcox Publisher

Copyright Goodheart-Willcox Co., Inc.

Tech Tip

A UPS should be sized at approximately 130% of the average load, but not less than 110% of the expected maximum load.

Isolation Transformers

Dedicated electrical circuits used for supplying computer equipment typically have isolation transformers installed near the source or electrical panel. An **isolation transformer** is a device that uses a transformer to isolate a circuit from other circuits emanating from the same electrical source. For example, electrical circuits coming from the electrical panel feed regular purpose outlets used for coffee pots, copiers, paper shredders, pencil sharpeners, and other types of electrical equipment. An isolation transformer isolates the special computer equipment circuit from the other circuits. Transformers are normally used to raise or lower voltage levels in electrical or electronic systems. Refer to Figure 16-22 to see how an isolation transformer works.

Figure 16-22 An isolation transformer is used to isolate, or separate, dedicated power outlets from the other power outlets in an electrical distribution system. Isolation transformers suppress electrical voltage spikes.

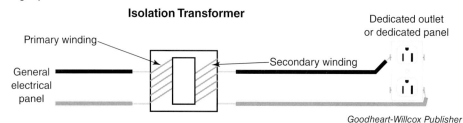

Goodheart-Willcox Publisher

The transformer consists of a primary, or input, winding and a secondary, or output, winding. The two windings are not electrically connected. They connect through a magnetic field produced in the primary winding. The magnetic field passes through the secondary winding, which in turn produces voltage in the output that mirrors the input voltage. One of the by-products of using an isolation transformer is its natural ability to suppress voltage spikes. The isolation transformer isolates the circuit on the output side of the transformer from the effects of spikes generated on the input side of the transformer. The isolation transformer will not eliminate very large spikes, but it will suppress the voltage level, which can damage computer equipment.

Generators

A **generator** is a device that creates and provides electricity. It is used for computer systems that require 24/7/365 uptime. A generator can maintain power for a few minutes to several hours, depending on the size of the unit. Critical systems, such as a system of computers used in an airfield control tower, require at least one generator. If severe weather took the commercial power out, the control tower could still monitor airplanes and provide information to pilots. Other systems that rely on computer technology and require generators are hospitals, police, fire, rescue, security, military, banking, high-rise buildings, and large enterprise businesses.

Copyright Goodheart-Willcox Co., Inc.

Summary

Monitoring the Server and Network

- A network system should be constantly monitored to determine when failures occur or to predict possible or imminent failure.

- Documentation and diagrams are essential for maintaining a network.

- A baseline of the system should be established and then routinely collected to predict events that may occur.

- Monitor the network performance and do periodic comparisons between the current indicators and the original baseline to spot trends.

Maintaining System Software

- Software programming flaws are referred to as *bugs*.

- Patches or fixes are used to correct bugs and security problems as they are discovered.

- Microsoft periodically releases collections of fixes and patches called *service packs*.

- Software patches, fixes, and service packs should be tested before applying them to the entire network.

Maintaining System Hardware

- A special type of server installation is referred to as a cluster, which allows one of the servers to easily be taken off-line for maintenance without disrupting network activities.

- Adding a switch to create two or more virtual LANs (VLANs) can increase an existing network's bandwidth.

Maintaining System Integrity

- Data integrity is the completeness and accuracy of data stored on the network system.

- Disaster recovery is the restoration of a system to normal operation after a disaster has occurred.

- Ensuring system integrity requires regular data backups and protecting the data while the server is running.

- The three backup types are full, incremental, and differential.

- A full backup makes a complete copy of the original data and resets the archive bit.

- An incremental backup copies changed files since the last incremental backup and then resets the archive bit.

- A differential backup copies changed files since the last full backup. It does not reset the archive bit.

Maintaining Stable Electrical Power

- A lightning arrestor is a special piece of electrical equipment designed to dampen the effects of an electrical surge caused by lightning.

Copyright Goodheart-Willcox Co., Inc.

- *Inductive reactance* is a very common electrical phenomena associated with the windings (coiled wire) inside motors, transformers, appliances, tools, and various other pieces of electrical equipment.
- A brownout is a partial loss of electrical energy while a blackout is a total loss of electrical energy.
- The two types of UPS units are standby and continuous.
- An isolation transformer is a device that uses a transformer to isolate a circuit from other circuits emanating from the same electrical source.

Review Questions

1. Why are networks monitored?
2. Why is a baseline established?
3. List types of information gathered for a network baseline.
4. What are some typical events that can be monitored on a server?
5. Problems in software programs are referred to as _____.
6. Software programs installed periodically to solve problems with security or hardware are called _____ or _____.
7. Microsoft periodically releases a major collection of software patches and fixes and refers to them as _____.
8. Why should patches be tested before installing them on a network system?
9. What should you do before installing a new software package on a network system?
10. What should you do before installing a new hardware device on a network server or client?
11. Explain how bandwidth is theoretically increased by installing a switch and creating two or more virtual LANs.
12. Which RAID system does *not* ensure data integrity?
13. What are the three types of system data backups?
14. Which backup system takes the least amount of time to perform for a daily backup?
15. Which backup system takes the most amount of time when restoring data?
16. Which backup system is performed using a series of individual tapes that must be reinstalled in the exact order they were created?
17. When is the archive bit for a file reset?
18. What device is used to protect a server from power blackouts and brownouts?

19. Will a UPS protect against voltage spikes and surges?

20. What are the two major classifications of UPS systems?

21. What is an isolation transformer?

✚ Sample Network+ Exam Questions

1. Imagine your network administrator has tasked you with ensuring a continuous and steady stream of power is available to devices on the network. Which device is required to provide a steady stream of continuous electrical power to a server?

   A. A power strip with surge protection.

   B. A generator rated for at least 12 kW.

   C. A standby UPS system rated for at least 2000 W.

   D. An online UPS system rated for at least 2000 W.

2. You need to design a fault-tolerant system for backing up critical data stored on a single network server. The system is in operation five days per week, Monday through Friday. You want to be able to restore the data as fast as possible after a hard disk drive failure. Which fault-tolerance system will best meet the requirement of restoring the lost data as quickly as possible?

   A. Perform a full backup Fridays and an incremental backup each day of the week.

   B. Perform a full backup each day of the week.

   C. Perform a full backup Friday and a differential backup each day of the week.

   D. Install a RAID 1 system in the server.

3. You notice that the network has slowed over the last several weeks. While in the server room, you notice that the hard disk drive activity light seems to be constantly blinking. What might be the most likely cause of both symptoms, the network speed appearing slower and an increase in hard disk drive activity?

   A. The CPU does not have sufficient processing speed to accommodate network requests and activity.

   B. The existing RAM is not of sufficient size to support the amount of network requests and activity.

   C. The power supply is heating up, causing a slowdown in processing speed.

   D. A loose or faulty cable is causing too many packets to be dropped, thus resulting in increased hard disk drive activity on the server.

4. Mary is responsible for software installation and upgrade for a large financial institution. She has just received an upgrade for the workstation operating system that she needs to install. What should be done before installing an operating system upgrade?

   A. Run **chkdsk** before you install the upgrade to provide more available disk space.

   B. Back up all critical files.

   C. Remove all existing applications before the system upgrade to ensure there will be no software conflicts during the initial boot. Then reinstall the applications.

   D. Stop all support services on the server so that they are not corrupted during the system upgrade.

5. Many more user workstations have been added to your existing Ethernet network since it was first installed. Over a period of time, demand has increased beyond the original design of the network. Which recommendation would best remedy the problem in the shortest amount of time with the least amount of cost?

   A. Install a new server with more RAM, at least two CPUs, and more hard disk space.

   B. Evaluate the system and install a switch that will separate the traffic flow by departments.

   C. Remove the logon and authentication requirement for network users to release more hard disk drive space, decrease CPU demand, and decrease most of the network traffic.

   D. Subdivide the network by department using hubs to block broadcasts from department to department and reduce the overall amount of broadcast across the entire network.

6. What does a file archive bit indicate?

   A. How many times the data has been copied.

   B. The file is not an original.

   C. A backup of the data has been made.

   D. A file accessible to legacy software programs.

7. Leticia is in the process of setting up a cold backup site for her company. Which of the following would be required for a cold backup site for the corporate accounting department?

    A. Copies of daily backup tapes.

    B. Equipment matching the corporate headquarters and backup copies of data.

    C. Operating software loaded on backup site computers and copies of data.

    D. Accounting software, operating system software, and backup copies of data loaded on the backup site computers.

8. Jarod is responsible for backups in his company. He is trying to select the proper backup method to use. Which backup technology only copies files that have changed since the last full backup and does not reset the file archive attribute?

    A. Incremental

    B. Differential

    C. Sequential

    D. Sparse

9. Which UPS system provides the best protection for a network server?

    A. Off-line

    B. Standby

    C. Continuous

    D. Generator

10. You are looking for a RAID level that will improve performance, but does not provide any fault tolerance. Which RAID system provides no fault tolerance protection?

    A. RAID 0

    B. RAID 1

    C. RAID 5

    D. RAID 1 and 5

CHAPTER 7

Fundamentals of Troubleshooting a Network

Network+ Certification Exam Objectives

Troubleshooting questions consume a major portion of the Network+ Certification Exam. This has been true for some time and is still true with the most recent version of the test. You must be familiar with common TCP/IP troubleshooting commands and proper troubleshooting procedures. The most common command-line utilities used in test items are **tracert**, **ping**, **nslookup**, **netstat**, **nbtstat**, **ipconfig**, **arp**, **dig**, **mtr**, and **route**. Knowing these network commands, along with the various flags for those commands, is critical to both the Network+ Certification Exam and to the practice of network troubleshooting itself.

You will also be asked about common network troubleshooting devices such as multimeter, OTD, OTDR, and tone probe. Most troubleshooting questions are scenario-type questions. These types of questions require more thought than standard fact-recollection questions. Generally, you will be provided with a situation and then asked what is the best approach or the most appropriate utility for solving the problem.

A portion of the troubleshooting questions will require knowledge of wireless systems. You will have a difficult time answering troubleshooting questions without some practical experience.

Objectives

1.1: Protocol Types—ICMP

5.2: Given a Scenario, Use the Appropriate Tool.

5.3: Given a Scenario, Troubleshoot Wired Connectivity and Performance Issues.

5.4: Attenuation, Power Levels, Signal-to-Noise Ratio

5.5: Given a Scenario, Troubleshoot Common Network Service Issues.

Learning Outcomes

- Apply the CompTIA network troubleshooting strategy when diagnosing network problems.
- List the stages of computer operation.
- Recall the startup process for Windows computers.
- Provide examples of Windows-based troubleshooting tools.
- Differentiate between system recovery strategies and methods.
- Explain how to troubleshoot dual-boot systems.
- List and describe items that can be used to ensure server integrity and performance.
- List tools used to troubleshoot network infrastructure.
- Describe methods for troubleshooting common network problems.
- Describe methods for troubleshooting common wireless problems.
- List TCP/IP utilities used to troubleshoot network problems.
- Describe additional, uncategorized network issues.

Key Terms

active partition
boot partition
dead drop
hardware abstraction layer (HAL)
master boot record (MBR)
signal bounce
system partition

Copyright Goodheart-Willcox Co., Inc.

Overview

This chapter presents commonly accepted troubleshooting utilities and techniques, and in many ways, serves as a review of all of the areas covered thus far. Troubleshooting requires not only knowledge about the various utilities and tools available, but also their applications. Practice using the utilities is essential to becoming proficient and skilled in troubleshooting.

Troubleshooting a network involves not only knowledge and skills for diagnosing a network problem but also knowledge and skills for diagnosing a PC. If you have not already completed a course in PC support and repair, it is highly recommended you do so. The need will become apparent while studying this chapter.

Much of this chapter is simply a brief review of already mastered knowledge but is presented in the context of troubleshooting. It is important that you bring these concepts together so you can apply them in a work setting.

CompTIA Network+ Troubleshooting Methodology

5.1   NET

This chapter introduces troubleshooting based on CompTIA's recommended troubleshooting procedures. Figure 17-1 lists the CompTIA procedures for troubleshooting a network problem. These steps are critical; use them regularly. The following sections discuss each procedure in detail and relate them to real-world troubleshooting situations.

Figure 17-1 CompTIA's network troubleshooting procedures.

> **Given a scenario, implement the following network troubleshooting methodology:**
> 1. Identify the problem
> 2. Establish a theory of probable cause
> 3. Test the theory to determine the cause
> 4. Establish a plan of action to resolve the problem and identify potential effects
> 5. Implement the solution or escalate, if necessary
> 6. Verify full system functionality and, if applicable, implement preventive measures
> 7. Document findings, actions, and outcomes

Goodheart-Willcox Publisher

1. Identify the Problem

Troubleshooting a network typically begins with answering a call to the help desk from a system user. The first thing you need to do to begin the troubleshooting process is identify the problem. This starts by gathering information. An accurate description is not always easy to obtain from a user because he or she does not understand root causes. Users will typically describe problems in vague terms and will not be able to establish any patterned behavior of the problem. Descriptions such as the following are common:

- The computer will not start.
- The computer keeps crashing.
- I cannot access my files.
- The computer is making a funny sound.
- My Adobe Dreamweaver program will not work.
- The printer will not work.

Copyright Goodheart-Willcox Co., Inc.

Most users cannot provide a true, technical description of a problem. Rather, they make general statements about the problem that is readily visible to them. You must be able to obtain information from the user without frustration while working with him or her through a dialogue that will help you better understand the problem. It is essential to maintain a good working relationship with the user at all times. It is not appropriate to laugh at the user's description or joke about the terminology he or she uses. Remember, they are not technical experts. After you have gathered information from the user, attempt to replicate the problem. Doing so will allow you to rule out user error and confirm that a true problem does in fact exist.

As a skilled technician, you can ask the user a series of simple questions to gather more information about the nature of the problem. A series of simple questions will typically lead you in the right direction. Some of these questions might include:

- Is this the first time the problem has occurred?

- When did the problem first occur?

- Is anyone else in the department having the same problem?

- Has anyone added new hardware or software to the system?

- What was the last change in the system?

This is similar to what a physician does when initially interacting with a patient. In a medical context, this is referred to as history of present illness (HPI). This is almost exactly what you are doing in network support. When a problem is first reported by a user or noticed by the IT staff, a series of questions needs to be asked and answered to better understand and isolate the problem. Correctly approaching the problem by analyzing the situation before attempting repairs can save valuable time and frustration. Once a problem is identified, the process toward solving it *always* begins with questions. Try to ask good questions that will yield detailed answers to help lead to a clear understanding of the problem.

One of the most important things you must ask yourself and others is, "What has changed?" This question can be asked in many different ways. For example, you may ask one or more of the following questions:

- What has happened recently that could have caused a problem?

- Was there a new software package installed recently?

- Was a new service started on the server?

- Was a new hardware device recently installed?

Any of the answers to these questions could help determine the cause of a network problem. Perhaps nothing has changed. The system failure may have occurred because of other reasons, such as hard disk drive failure, integrated circuit failure, or a corrupted system or file. A device failure and an unrelated event can easily confuse the troubleshooting process. Be aware that coincidences do occur.

While asking questions about the problem, you may discover that the user is actually experiencing more than one problem. For example, a user may report an inability to print, but you may discover that the user also has an inability to send e-mail. While the combination of these problems may likely point to a network connectivity issue, it is essential to approach each problem individually. Only then can you be sure to solve each error.

In a large networking environment, an incident report is typically completed by the person at the help desk. It may also be completed by the technician who will work with the problem. See Figure 17-2 for a sample of a help desk request form.

Copyright Goodheart-Willcox Co., Inc.

Figure 17-2 An example of an incident report form.

Help Desk Ticket Number _____

Caller: _____ Date: _____ Time: _____
Location:_____ Phone Number/Ext: _____
Department: _____ Tech. Assigned:_____

Complete Description _____
_____
_____
_____
_____
_____
_____
_____

Help Desk Action Taken _____
_____
_____
_____
_____

Follow-up Date: _____ Time: _____
_____
_____
_____

Goodheart-Willcox Publisher

There is a wide range of common problems in networks, but the following list includes some of the most common:

- *Attenuation.* Signals eventually lessen in amplitude; this is attenuation. It often means a cable is spanning a further distance than it should.

- *Latency.* Any delay in signal reception is latency. Some latency is normal.

- *Jitter.* A difference in delay of packets. This is sometimes called *packet delay variation (PDV),* which is a better definition.

- *Crosstalk.* When two wires are sending signals from one to the other.

- *EMI.* Electromagnetic interference is common in complex electrical environments.

- *Shorts.* Any type of wire can have a short.

Less common problems that still occur include:

- *Incorrect cable type.* This will usually show immediately when installing cable. Related to this problem is *incorrect pin-out,* meaning the wires inside the cabling sheath have not been terminated correctly, or a *bad port* error message, meaning the chosen port number is not valid. Any damaged cables or bent pins are also issues with the initial setup of cable and may occur when you first install a network segment.

5.3 NET

- *TX/RX reverse.* This refers to transmitters and receivers. It is another error that will show up when first installing. If the transmitter and receiver are mismatched, you will not get a signal.

- *VLAN mismatch.* When setting up a VLAN, any mismatch in the VLAN ports will cause a communication break.

2. Establish a Theory of Probable Cause

Troubleshooting requires a series of best guesses. Sometimes the solution to a problem is obvious, and other times the problem can be difficult to diagnose. Usually, someone else has encountered the same problem at some other location. There are thousands of documented problems and solutions available for review at no cost on the Internet. Once the symptoms have been clearly established, you can conduct a search using key words related to the symptoms. The search should produce a listing of document abstracts or articles from which to choose. User help forums can also yield valuable information at times.

Vendors of operating systems typically provide online support, which consists of free knowledge-base articles, free e-mail support, and limited live support. Figure 17-3 shows a screen capture of a Microsoft TechNet support web page for Windows Server 2016. The Microsoft TechNet website provides information about recent problems encountered by technicians. Solutions contain steps to follow to correct the problem.

Figure 17-3 Windows Server support website contains information to assist the technician when troubleshooting server problems. The website contains expert information about problems encountered and reported to Microsoft and solutions.

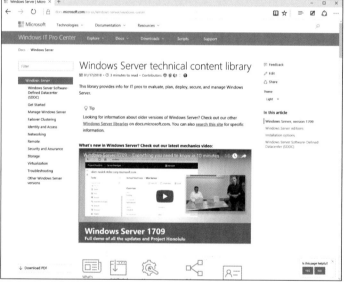

Goodheart-Willcox Publisher

Solutions for problems can come from numerous sources, such as websites from operating system manufacturers, hardware manufacturers, and other industry or commercial groups. Commercial websites offer mixed product support, focus groups, organizations, and more. One of the best ways for locating a possible solution to a networking problem is using an online search engine. The Internet has an extensive resource base waiting to be used. For example, Google is highly reliable for hits concerning technical information about networks. Chances are you will not only receive hits at a hardware or software manufacturer website, but also from many other reputable sources.

Technical support is also available by your specific operating system. The support can be provided via website or telephone and may be free or fee-based. Vendor diagnostic software CDs, especially for hardware tests, are also available.

Copyright Goodheart-Willcox Co., Inc.

Remember, you are establishing a theory of the probable cause of the problem. In this case, your theory is much like a scientific theory. It is not merely a guess but rather a full explanation based on the data you have. This can be accomplished by considering multiple approaches, including the obvious possible issues.

During this step of the troubleshooting process, you must consider whether a top-to-bottom approach or a bottom-to-top approach is better. A *top-to-bottom approach* means starting from broad-based network issues, where a *bottom-to-top approach* means starting with very small and specific issues. Once you have established a theory of the issue, the next logical step is to test the theory to determine the cause.

3. Test the Theory to Determine the Cause

This may sound simplistic, but you need to test the fix you made. For example, a user submits a help ticket because he or she is unable to access a specific printer. After talking to the user and gathering information, you suspect a new software package recently installed on a workstation has caused the problem. When the new software package was removed, the workstation user could access the printer once again. If the new software package really were the culprit, you should be able to duplicate the problem. Try installing the software package on a different workstation and see if the same problem develops. If the problem of connecting to the printer occurs on the new workstation, then the software did in fact cause the problem. Once you are able to confirm your theory, determine the next steps of resolving the problem.

If the second workstation did not experience a problem connecting to the printer, then a different problem may exist. For example, a loose network cable connection could cause an intermittent problem with the connection to the printer. You uninstall the suspected software package and the problem clears. While uninstalling the software package, the bad or loose connection reconnects and the printer is accessible once again. If you truly solved a problem, you should be able to duplicate it. If your theory is not confirmed by your actions, reestablish a new theory or escalate your solution.

Not all problems need to be replicated or tested. For example, obvious issues, such as a problem identified by a Windows message box, may provide you with the solution—a recent patch. Once the patch is installed, the error no longer occurs. The solution was obvious because it was identified for you, and the recommendation worked.

4. Establish a Plan of Action to Resolve the Problem and Identify Potential Effects

During your research about a probable cause, you will most likely also obtain information about possible solutions. You will need to assess the possible solutions to choose the one that is the most appropriate to the situation. This requires experience and broad knowledge of and familiarity with the network system.

Be sure to document your work as you progress through the process of diagnosing and implementing possible solutions. Documenting your work as you progress cannot be emphasized enough. Do *not* trust your memory. Writing down the steps you take is similar to leaving a trail for you to follow next time and will save you time and effort in the future. For example, if you have made any changes in system configurations, you need to write them down. A technician often loses track of time as they attempt to solve a network problem. As time goes by, they suddenly realize they have made many changes to the system configuration, and may have created additional problems or symptoms caused by those changes made. *Always* record the changes made and return the system configuration to its original settings before trying other changes.

Copyright Goodheart-Willcox Co., Inc.

You must realize the full ramifications of the corrective action you are taking. Before you apply a possible solution, you need to know the extent to which it will affect the existing system. For example, when all else fails to repair the workstation or server, you can always reinstall the operating system. However, reinstalling the operating system could produce adverse effects on the network or workstation.

You typically have two choices for reinstalling an operating system: perform a clean installation or perform a system upgrade. When you perform a clean installation, all data on the existing partition and possibly on the entire hard disk drive is lost! You must have backups of all data files available, as well as all application software and any required device drivers.

When performing a system upgrade, the original operating system files are replaced. Typically, data files, application software, and original drivers are not required. A bit of caution is necessary when performing an upgrade. You may see messages asking if you want to install the original version of a file or driver or leave the existing file intact. This message occurs when an original system has had patches or service packs installed since the original installation. When performing an upgrade, the existing files are compared to the files about to be installed.

When two file names match but their creation dates differ, the installation process will typically ask, "Do you want to leave the existing file or replace it with the original or older file?" You should answer, "No," and leave the latest copy of the file. The only exception to this rule is if you suspect the latest version is the cause of the system abnormality. In that case, you would install the original operating system as an upgrade and later add each service pack or patch one at a time until you reach the latest, which is the suspected cause of the abnormality. In most cases, a patch or service pack will not have adverse effects on a system. Always check the support documentation at the software vendor's website for the latest information when repairing a system.

5. Implement the Solution or Escalate If Necessary

After you have completed your action plan, implement your solution and determine its efficacy. If the solution did in fact resolve the problem, you can advance to the next step of the troubleshooting procedures. However, you will not be able to solve all problems on the first attempt. There may even be problems you are not able to solve at all. At times, it will be necessary to escalate the problem to a supervisor or someone with more expertise. This is especially true for a network technician with limited experience. For example, if you determine that the problem involves permission shares on a particular server and you do not have the skills or authority to make changes to the server shares, you will need to escalate the problem to your immediate supervisor. Never attempt to troubleshoot a network device or software package with which you are not thoroughly familiar. Never make configuration changes to any network device that you are not familiar with or when you do not have authority to make changes.

Network infrastructure problems that generally require escalation by an inexperienced network technician include switching loops, routing loops, route problems, proxy ARP, and broadcast storms. When these conditions are detected, they should be immediately escalated to your immediate supervisor.

Again, identifying the specific problem requires an experienced technician. The important thing is to remember not to be afraid to request the help of a more experienced person or supervisor. More damage can be done by attempting to correct a problem with which you are not thoroughly familiar.

Copyright Goodheart-Willcox Co., Inc.

6. Verify Full System Functionality and, If Applicable, Implement Preventive Measures

When a solution has been implemented and is deemed to have been effective, it is important to verify full system functionality. This verification ensures that you did not accidentally break, damage, or otherwise hinder any component of the computing system or networking architecture while implementing your solution to the previous problem. While it may sound silly, creating a new problem can be easier than you think. For example, assume a user requires the installation of a new network interface card. To do so, you will have to remove all cables and wires from the computer before swapping out NICs. If the cables and wiring are not reinstalled correctly, the computer will not be able to function effectively on the network.

7. Document Findings, Actions, and Outcomes

Network troubleshooting scenarios often start with an incident report filed with the help desk. The incident report typically includes an area for the technician to write down the implemented fix for the problem. This documentation will serve as a future reference.

Documentation is an important part of network administration. As such, it should be completed thoroughly and in a timely fashion. Documentation will save the company and personnel valuable time and money and should be considered by all technicians as a professional courtesy, as well as a necessity. Documentation should be shared with other workers especially in a large organization where workers do not get the opportunity to converse on a regular basis. The sharing of documentation can provide insight to other workers regarding problems they may encounter in the future. Documentation also acts as a history of the system. For example, if a network interface card is replaced by another brand or version, maintain a record of it. The record can be used to update equipment inventories and equipment descriptions.

Knowing what type of equipment is installed on the network is very important, especially when performing a migration to a new operating system. For example, when upgrading from Windows Server 2008 to Windows Server 2016, an accurate list of system hardware is invaluable. The list can be checked against the hardware compatibility list (HCL) to ensure that all hardware used on the existing system is compatible with the new operating system. Without a way to verify compatibility, a new operating system can be installed and problems may develop. These problems may require a long period of time troubleshooting only to find out later that a hardware compatibility problem was the issue. Always keep an up-to-date and complete set of documentation for the existing network and associated equipment.

Software programs, such as HelpSTAR, are available to help an administrator keep track of service requests, computer inventory, and history, as shown in Figure 17-4. HelpSTAR is specifically designed for the help desk. It is a practical way to keep track of calls to the help desk when working with a large network or supporting several companies. HelpSTAR can be used to initiate purchase orders and can keep an inventory of all new material and equipment as it is ordered for the network. By controlling the ordering process, the help desk also knows when the equipment needed to repair or replace a device is delivered and can match it to the correct job order. A service request can be initiated by e-mail or telephone request. The request is entered into the HelpSTAR database and assigned a reference number. The technician assigned to the problem can follow up by entering details about the progress and outcome of the incident.

Copyright Goodheart-Willcox Co., Inc.

Figure 17-4 The HelpSTAR program is a valuable tool in managing help desk requests.

Goodheart-Willcox Publisher

Stages of Computer Operation

> **Note**
>
> The information presented here consists of general guidelines based on the most likely causes and is not all-inclusive.

Troubleshooting the workstation and server involves a strong knowledge of PC operation, operating system software, and operating system boot sequences. If you are not knowledgeable about PC repair, it is strongly recommended that you take a computer-repair course. A computer-repair course will not only provide you with a background in PC hardware and repair, but with basic knowledge about the various desktop operating systems. This section assumes that you have a background in PC hardware and repair and are familiar with the various Microsoft desktop operating systems.

When troubleshooting a computer or server, you need to determine at which stage of computer operation the system failure occurs. You do this by observing computer operation beginning with the POST and continuing until after a successful system logon. There are three general areas of server/computer operation to consider: POST, operating system loading and initiation, and the time period after a successful logon.

During the POST

NET 5.5

The *power-on self-test (POST)* is the first stage of computer operation. Failure during the POST is generally an indication that there is a hardware failure. Some physical component is preventing the system from completing the startup operation. Failures during the POST are typically caused by such items as hard disk drives, RAM, CPU, motherboard, modem, and a failing power supply. Any essential computer hardware component can cause failure during the POST. If you suspect a POST failure caused by hardware, you should remove all nonessential components and attempt the boot process once more.

Loading and Initializing the Operating System

This phase of operation occurs immediately after completing the POST and continues to a successful user logon. During this period, the operating system loads and initiates system configuration files. A failure during this time usually indicates a corrupt operating system or driver file.

Copyright Goodheart-Willcox Co., Inc.

If the startup process fails here, you will see the infamous Microsoft blue-screen error. The blue-screen error provides some idea of the cause of the failure, typically with an alphanumeric error code. The error code can be used as an Internet search term to locate information concerning the failure. You can also conduct a search at Microsoft's website using the blue-screen error code.

This type of failure can typically be resolved by resetting certain aspects of the operating system. For example, Windows 10 has reset options available to users. **Windows 10 Resetting** lets you choose whether to keep your files or remove them. To get started, go to **Start**>**Settings**>**Update & security**>**Recovery**>**Get started** and choose an option. If for any reason, you are unable to open **Settings**, you can reset your PC from the sign-in screen. Use the [Windows key][L] key combination to access the sign-in screen, then hold the [Shift] key while you select **Power**>**Restart** in the lower-right corner of the screen. After your PC restarts, select **Troubleshoot**> **Reset this PC**.

After a Successful Logon

After a successful user logon, the most likely cause of a system failure is an installed software application or service. Software applications and services are started after a successful logon. An essential file that has been corrupted could cause a system to hang or even crash after logon. Any problems such as the computer freezing or a long delay before the user desktop appears are associated with the startup files and services. One of the best utilities to identify the offending software application is System Configuration (**msconfig.exe**), shown in Figure 17-5. The use of the System Configuration tool to troubleshoot a computer is covered later in this chapter.

Tech Tip

Malware can cause a system failure at any point of operation after the POST and, in some rare cases, during the POST. In general, malware affects the system after the POST.

Figure 17-5 System Configuration is an excellent tool for determining if a system failure is caused by application software or a service.

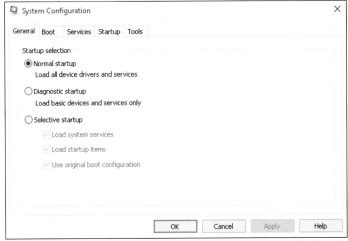

Goodheart-Willcox Publisher

The System Configuration tool provides many different options for correcting system problems caused by software applications during and after the system startup. It also provides access to the most common troubleshooting tools and provides a means of identifying suspected services.

Detailed Computer Startup Process

A good understanding of the computer startup process is an essential part of troubleshooting. Knowledge of the computer boot process will better enable you to determine in which general area of server/computer operation the problem failure is

Copyright Goodheart-Willcox Co., Inc.

occurring. Figure 17-6 compares the boot process phases of Windows XP and later operating systems. Both processes have remained the same since Windows Vista. Notice, however, that boot process phases three and four differ between Windows XP/Server 2003 and Windows Vista/7–10/Server 2008–2016, whereas boot process phases one, two, five, and six are similar. The following sections discuss each boot process phase. Figures 17-7 and 17-8 summarize the boot sequences for Windows XP/Server 2003 and Windows Vista/7–10/Server 2008–2016, respectively. The boot sequence is mostly the same across versions of Windows. The Network+ Exam will not require you to have a detailed knowledge of this. A general knowledge base is sufficient. This general knowledge of the boot process will apply to all versions of Windows.

Figure 17-6 Boot process phase comparison of Windows 2000 and later operating systems.

Phase	Windows 2000	Windows XP and Server 2003	Windows Vista, 7, 8, and 10, and Server 2008, 2012, and 2016
1	POST	POST	POST
2	Initial Startup	Initial Startup	Initial Startup
3	Bootstrap Loader	Boot Loader	Windows Boot Manager
4	Detect and Configure Hardware	Detect and Configure Hardware	Windows Boot Loader
5	Kernel Loading	Kernel Loading	Kernel Loading
6	Logon Phase	Logon Phase	Logon Phase

Goodheart-Willcox Publisher

Figure 17-7 Windows 2000/XP/Server 2003 boot sequence summary.

Windows 2000/XP/Server 2003 Boot Sequence

1. The BIOS performs the power-on self-test (POST).
2. The BIOS reads the master boot record and loads its code into memory.
3. The MBR loads the NT boot loader (ntldr) into memory.
4. The NT boot loader (ntldr) loads the kernel (ntoskrnl.exe) and the hardware abstraction layer (hal.dll) into RAM.
5. The kernel (ntoskrnl.exe) calls the ntdetect.com program.
6. The ntdetect.com program detects system hardware information and passes it to the NT boot loader (ntldr).
7. The NT boot loader (ntldr) passes hardware information to the NT kernel (ntoskrnl.exe).
8. The NT kernel (ntoskrnl.exe) loads the device drivers, initializes the HAL, and initializes the computer settings using the values stored in the system registry.
9. The NT kernel (ntoskrnl.exe) loads the session manager (smss.exe).
10. The session manager (smss.exe) runs an abbreviated version of Chkdsk and determines if the system volumes and partitions are in working order.
11. The Windows logon file (winlogon.exe) is executed and the logon dialog box appears.
12. After a successful logon, the Local Security Authority (LSA) process (lsass.exe) and service subsystem (services.exe) load and run.

Goodheart-Willcox Publisher

Note

Extensible Firmware Interface (EFI) is a new approach to the BIOS system. EFI is required on computers in order to use a new file-system directory structure referred to as *GUID*. In the future, EFI is expected to replace BIOS as it exists today. Many computers run a hybrid combination of BIOS and EFI.

1. Power-On Self-Test (POST)

When a computer has power first applied to the motherboard by pressing the power switch, the system firmware (BIOS or EFI) starts the boot process by performing a quick check of hardware components and verifying that all hardware devices listed in the configuration database are present and appear to be in working order. The hard disk drive and standard hardware devices such as memory are automatically detected and configured. All configuration data are then stored in CMOS.

Copyright Goodheart-Willcox Co., Inc.

Figure 17-8 Windows Vista/7–10/Server 2008–2016 boot sequence summary.

Windows Vista/7–10/Server 2008–2016 Boot Sequence

1. The BIOS performs the power-on self-test (POST).
2. The BIOS reads the master boot record and loads its code into memory.
3. The BIOS loads the Windows Boot Manager (bootmgr).
4. The Windows Boot Manager (bootmgr) displays a boot menu if more than one operating system is installed, and it starts the Windows Boot Loader (winload.exe).
5. The Windows Boot Manager (bootmgr) passes control to the Windows Boot Loader (winload.exe).
6. The Windows Boot Loader (winload.exe) loads the NT kernel (ntoskrnl.exe) and hardware abstraction layer (HAL) into RAM memory and then executes the kernel.
7. The NT kernel (ntoskrnl.exe) loads the session manager (smss.exe).
8. The session manager (smss.exe) runs an abbreviated version of Chkdsk and determines if the system volumes and partitions are in working order.
9. The Windows logon file (winlogon.exe) is executed and the logon dialog box appears.
10. After a successful logon, the Local Security Authority (LSA) process (lsass.exe) and service subsystem (services.exe) load and run.

Goodheart-Willcox Publisher

When POST completes, some adapters such as video cards or hard disk drives may carry out their own firmware diagnostics routine that is built into the device. This is independent from BIOS diagnostics.

2. Initial Startup

The initial startup phase is when the POST completes and then starts the operating system boot or bootstrap program. The POST routine looks for the boot device where the master boot record (MBR) is stored. The **master boot record (MBR)** contains information stored in the first sector of a hard disk that identifies an operating system location. The location of the boot device is stored by BIOS in CMOS memory. For example, the next boot device after POST may be a hard disk drive, CD or DVD drive, or a USB flash drive. The exact order can be changed in the BIOS setup program and then stored in the CMOS memory.

After identifying the location of the MBR, BIOS loads the MBR into RAM and then turns the boot routine over to the boot code located in the MBR. The MBR contains the boot code of the operating system and partition table used to locate the additional startup files. The MBR is located on the first sector of the active partition on the hard disk drive. Additional duties of the MBR are to identify the system file type (FAT16, FAT32, NTFS, etc.) and locate ntldr (NT boot loader file). The ntldr file loads any NT-based Windows operating system, which includes all versions of Windows since 2000. It is located on the active partition. On a Windows Vista and later system, the MBR loads the Windows Boot Manager (bootmgr). The ntldr is incorporated into the kernel but is only used to boot NT-based operating systems prior to Windows Vista.

Often the terms *active partition*, *boot partition*, and *system partition* are used interchangeably, but they actually have different technical meanings. The **active partition** describes the partition that contains the operating system files the computer should use to boot. The **system partition** contains the core files, such as ntldr and ntdetect.com, which are used to start the operating system. The **boot partition** contains the files needed to operate the computer. These files include device drivers, library files, services, commands, and utilities. These are stored in a separate directory, such as \windows and \winnt.

3. Boot Loader Phase

On most Windows computers, after the initial startup, the boot loader phase first loads the kernel (**ntoskrnl.exe**) into RAM but does not execute it yet. Next, the hardware abstraction layer (**hal.dll**) is loaded into RAM as well as the system registry hive. The **hardware abstraction layer (HAL)** is designed to prevent third-party software applications and programs from directly accessing hardware. Only the Microsoft operating system can directly communicate with system hardware such as the memory. Certain key services are started to support various device drivers that are required during the boot process. This differs slightly in some later Windows systems, where Windows Boot Manager (bootmgr) then passes control to the Windows Boot Loader (**winload.exe**). Windows Boot Loader then loads the NT kernel (**ntoskrnl.exe**) and hardware abstraction layer (HAL) into RAM memory and executes the kernel.

4. Detect and Configure Hardware

Next, on a Windows computer, ntldr calls the ntdetect.com program. The ntdetect.com program detects the system hardware information, such as the computer ID, adapters, video information, keyboard, ports, and hard disk drives. The ntdetect.com file passes this information back to the ntldr, which in turn passes the information to the NT kernel (**ntoskrnl.exe**).

5. Windows Boot Manager (Windows Vista and Later)

Starting with Windows Vista, after the initial startup, the BIOS loads the Windows Boot Manager (bootmgr). The Windows Boot Manager displays the boot menu, as demonstrated in Figure 17-9, when more than one operating system is present on a computer and starts the Windows Boot Loader (**winload.exe**).

Figure 17-9 The Windows Boot Manager will display a menu if more than one operating system is installed on the computer, allowing the user to select an operating system to which to boot.

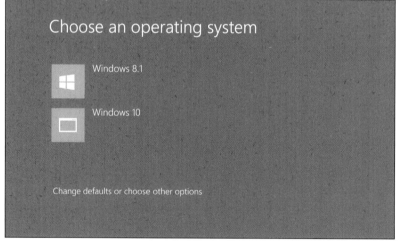

Goodheart-Willcox Publisher

6. Kernel Loading Phase

For all NT-based operating systems, the NT kernel (**ntoskrnl.exe**) is executed and takes over operation of the computer system. The NT kernel loads the device drivers, initializes the HAL, and initializes the computer settings using the values stored in the system registry.

The Windows kernel and HAL work together to communicate with software applications, drivers, and hardware. Driver files that do not require user security clearance are typically loaded. For example, the driver and services required to run the printer minimally is loaded at this time.

The kernel and HAL work together to process information stored in the registry, which is required to complete the boot process. The kernel also creates a new registry key that contains information about the drivers and devices loaded thus far and those loaded through the rest of the boot operation. This information is used for the

Copyright Goodheart-Willcox Co., Inc.

Last Known Good Configuration boot option when troubleshooting the system or attempting to recover from a system failure.

The session manager (**smss.exe**) is loaded and started by the kernel. This is when the boot process switches from text mode to graphics mode. The session manager will continue to run in the background until the computer is shut down.

The session manager starts and runs an abbreviated version of Chkdsk and determines if the system volumes and partitions are in working order. The session manager is also responsible for loading the page file or virtual memory. The page file supplements the amount of RAM installed on the computer.

Microsoft does not allow third-party software applications to access hardware and certain operating system files directly. However, when access is needed by the third-party software applications, the session manager manages the activities.

7. Logon Phase

The Windows logon file (**winlogon.exe**) is executed, and the logon dialog box appears. A user enters his or her logon name and password to proceed to the computer desktop.

After a successful logon, the local security authority (LSA) process (**lsass.exe**) loads and runs, and then the service subsystem (**services.exe**) loads and runs. The exact services loaded and started are determined by the computer configuration and the user credentials. Only the service the user is allowed access to or through will start. If there is only one default user and the computer is not connected to a network with a server, the user will be able to access and run all services for the computer. If a user has a limited account, he or she will only be able to run services allocated by the system administrator.

Startup programs are loaded and run at this point. If a computer user installs many programs over a period of time, it will take longer for the desktop to appear after completing the logon.

The boot process is not considered successful until an error-free logon has been completed. After a successful logon, the registry is updated and will become the registry reference for the **Last Known Good Configuration** boot option selected during the next startup process. Most problems encountered after a successful logon can be solved using System Restore or System Configuration tools.

Windows-Based Troubleshooting Tools

There are many tools and widely accepted procedures for recovering a failed NT-based operating system. Some of these utilities are briefly covered in this section. To master these troubleshooting concepts, practice using them. See Figure 17-10 for a complete list of diagnostic utilities and the Microsoft operating systems in which they are included. This section covers safe mode, System Restore, Last Known Good Configuration, Recovery Console, Roll Back Driver, and System Configuration. It also covers using an emergency repair disk.

Safe Mode

Safe mode is accessed through the **Advanced Boot Options** menu. Historically, this menu was activated by pressing the special function key [F8] during the system start-up on older systems. Newer systems that use EFI rather than BIOS have a different process. Conduct a search of a specific computer model for information regarding accessing safe mode on newer systems. In Windows 10, users can often select startup settings from **Start**>**Settings**>**Update & Security**>**Recovery**. Once the PC is restarted, the user will be given a number of startup options, as shown in Figure 17-11.

Copyright Goodheart-Willcox Co., Inc.

Figure 17-10 Common diagnostic utilities listed by various Microsoft NT-based operating systems.

Diagnostic Utility	Win XP	Win Vista	Win 7	Win 8	Win 10	Win Server 2003	Win Server 2008	Win Server 2012	Win Server 2016
System Restore	X	X	X	X	X	X	X	X	X
Roll Back Driver	X	X	X			X	X		
Recovery Console	X	X	X	X	X	X	X	X	X
System Recovery Options Menu		X	X	X	X		X	X	X
Safe Mode	X	X	X	X	X	X	X	X	X
System Configuration (msconfig)	X	X	X	X	X	X	X	X	X
System Information (msinfo32)	X	X	X	X	X	X	X	X	
DirectX Diagnostic Tool	X	X	X			X	X		
Registry Editor (regedit)	X	X	X	X	X	X	X	X	X
Registry Editor (regedit32)	X	**	**	**	**	X	**	**	**
Net	X	X	X	X	X	X	X	X	X
Dr. Watson	X	X	X	**	**	X	X	**	**
File Signature Verification	X	X	X	X	X	X	X	X	X
Network Diagnostics (netdiag)*	X	**	**	**	**	X	**	**	**
Network and Sharing Center		X	X	X	X	X	X	X	X
Performance Monitor	X	X	X	X	X	X	X	X	X
Reliability Monitor		X	X	X	X	X	X	X	X

*Note: Windows operating systems later than Windows XP and Server 2003 have only one registry editor. It is called regedit and performs registry edits for 16-, 32-, and 64-bit registries.

**Note: Network Diagnostics is now incorporated into Network and Sharing Center.

Goodheart-Willcox Publisher

Figure 17-11 Safe Mode is located in the **Advanced Boot Options** menu. When booting a computer in safe mode, Windows loads only standard video drivers and essential drivers that are needed for the keyboard, mouse, and storage devices.

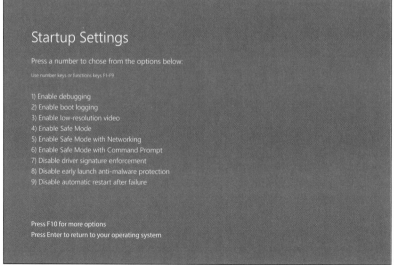

Startup Settings

Press a number to chose from the options below:

Use number keys or functions keys F1-F9

1) Enable debugging
2) Enable boot logging
3) Enable low-resolution video
4) Enable Safe Mode
5) Enable Safe Mode with Networking
6) Enable Safe Mode with Command Prompt
7) Disable driver signature enforcement
8) Disable early launch anti-malware protection
9) Disable automatic restart after failure

Press F10 for more options
Press Enter to return to your operating system

Goodheart-Willcox Publisher

Copyright Goodheart-Willcox Co., Inc.

During a safe mode boot, only standard video drivers are loaded and essential drivers that are needed for the keyboard, mouse, and storage devices. No network connection is made. Starting the computer in safe mode can help determine if there is a problem with the PC or with the network. If the system appears to be working correctly with the minimum set of drivers, you may be able to correct the suspected source of the problem. For example, if a recently loaded software or hardware device is suspected of causing the system boot failure, it can be deleted from the system, and an attempt to boot the computer system normally can be made.

System Restore

The System Restore utility does as the name implies. It restores the operating system to a condition established at a previous time. The System Restore utility can be accessed in Windows 10 through **Start**>**Control Panel**>**Recovery**>**Open System Restore** even if the computer is running in safe mode. Administrators may use the System Restore utility to roll the operating system back to a previous time when the system was working perfectly. For example, you may have installed a new pointing device and loaded the required drivers only to find the computer will not boot properly or freezes during the boot process. You can start the computer in safe mode, start the System Restore utility, and select an earlier time. The System Restore utility rolls back the registry but does not change the existing data files, e-mail, and other common file types that you would not want to be removed or changed. The System Restore utility does remove executable files, which means that programs that were installed after the rollback date may be inoperable.

For example, a user experienced no problem with his computer yesterday. Today, he starts his computer and he cannot access any of his software applications. A system restore may correct the problem. You would simply start the System Restore tool and then select an earlier date to which you want to restore the computer system, as demonstrated in Figure 17-12.

Figure 17-12 The System Restore tool can automatically reconfigure your computer with the registry settings from an earlier time.

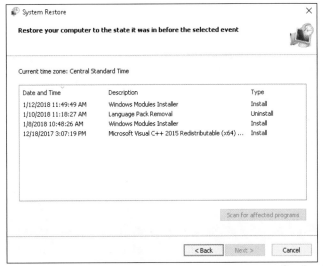

Goodheart-Willcox Publisher

If you can only start the computer in safe mode, you can access System Restore through Control Panel or from the **Start** menu. System Restore can also be accessed through the command prompt by entering **rstrui.exe**. Use caution when launching this program, however. The **rstrui.exe** program is often used as an attack path for

Copyright Goodheart-Willcox Co., Inc.

intruders. The known file size for this program in Windows XP/7/8/10 is approximately 380 kB. It can be helpful to navigate to the Windows\System32 subfolder that contains **rstrui.exe** and compare your file size to the previously referenced size before running the program. If the file size differs, it may be a malicious file.

Additionally, System Restore can be used to solve problems, such as when a computer suddenly starts to run slowly or develops problems associated with a recent download, a new driver or patch, or any recent change to the system configuration. System Restore does not change the contents of any user application files such as e-mails, pictures, documents, or other personal data. Any executable programs installed after the selected rollback date will not run properly because their registry settings will have been changed.

Last Known Good Configuration

The **Last Known Good Configuration** option in the **Advanced Boot Options** menu is essential for correcting most boot problems on a Windows system. Every time a Windows computer has a successful logon after a completed boot, a backup of the system registry is made. The backup is available for use when a computer fails to boot properly because of some change in the system. The change in the system could be the installation of a new or updated software driver or a change in some hardware configuration. If an error during the boot operation is detected, a message will display such as, "Restore the system to the last known good configuration." When the **Last Known Good Configuration** option is selected, the last copy of the registry made during a successful boot replaces the existing registry.

Emergency Repair Disk

All modern operating systems have what is called an *emergency repair disk* or *system repair disk*. An emergency repair disk is used to repair or replace items such as the master boot record, file allocation tables, system registry files, or system configuration files. There is one very important aspect to using an emergency repair disk. It can only restore the system to the way it was configured when the disk was made. If the emergency repair disk was made right after the original installation of the operating system, the system will be set up in its original state. Any modifications to the system since the emergency repair disk was made will be lost if the emergency repair disk is used to repair the system. The use of any new software systems that were installed may be lost, as well as hardware drivers and system updates or patches. An emergency repair disk should be made whenever changes to the system occur. This will ensure an updated system will be restored rather than the original system. More recent versions of Windows simply call this the System Repair Disk.

Recovery Console

Recovery Console is a last-resort recovery option in Windows. This option has been around for quite some time and still exists in Windows 10. When a system fails to start, the Recovery Console provides a command prompt that allows you to enter system commands in an attempt to recover the system. Recovery Console is not installed by default. Reboot the computer with the installation disc inserted into the drive to access Recovery Console. When the text-based portion of the installation process begins, simply press the letter *R* on the keyboard to start the Recovery Console. An administrator's password is required to access the Recovery Console command prompt. Once the command prompt appears, you could issue commands in an attempt to recover the operating system. For example, you could run the **chkdsk** command to resolve sector problems from the hard disk drive or run **fixboot** to

Copyright Goodheart-Willcox Co., Inc.

repair the boot sector. Look at Figure 17-13 to view some of the most common Recovery Console commands. To read a detailed explanation of installing and using Recovery Console, navigate to https://support.microsoft.com/en-us/help/216417/how-to-install-the-windows-recovery-console. To locate this site, you can also conduct an online search using the phrase Windows Recovery Console.

Roll Back Driver

The Roll Back Driver option has been part of Windows operating systems since Windows XP and still exists in Windows 10. The Roll Back Driver feature is available through the **Properties** dialog box of any hardware device installed on the computer. Figure 17-14 shows the **Properties** dialog box of a laptop touchpad. The dialog box contains buttons that allow you to view driver details, update the driver, roll back the driver, or uninstall the driver. To launch the Roll Back Driver feature, open Device Manager. From the list of devices, right-click the devices for which you want to roll back drivers, and select **Properties**>**Drivers**>**Roll Back Driver**>**Yes**.

Figure 17-13 Common Recovery Console commands.

Recovery Console Command	Description
chkdsk	Checks the hard disk drive platters for bad sectors.
diskpart	Displays and manages the partitions on a hard disk.
bootcfg	Modifies the boot.ini file.
fixboot	Writes a new boot sector on the system partition.
fixmbr	Repairs the master boot record.

Goodheart-Willcox Publisher

Figure 17-14 The **Roll Back Driver** feature is available through the **Properties** dialog box of any hardware device.

Goodheart-Willcox Publisher

The Roll Back Driver feature is a better alternative than using System Restore. System Restore rolls back all driver and configuration settings to the selected date. This can result in losing the configuration settings of devices you did not intend to

Copyright Goodheart-Willcox Co., Inc.

change. The Roll Back Driver feature only reverts to the last driver configured for a specific device. For example, if you suspect a newly installed driver or driver update is causing a problem with a hardware device, you can use the Roll Back Driver feature to return to the previous version of the driver.

System Configuration

Another handy tool for solving computer problems such as software application or services is the System Configuration tool. See Figure 17-15. It can be accessed by entering **msconfig.exe** at the command prompt. The System Configuration tool has three broad options under the default **General** tab. The three options are **Normal startup**, **Diagnostic startup**, and **Selective startup**. The **Normal startup** option, as the name implies, loads all device drivers and services as normal. When the **Diagnostic startup** option is selected, only basic devices and services are loaded. When the **Selective startup** option is selected, users can choose to load or not load system services or startup items. These options are broad and are selected to isolate the area of the problem quickly. For example, a startup item could cause the computer to have a very long boot. Many printer programs automatically install software applications that inspect a printer and check ink supply levels. They also perform routine diagnostics and even automatically check for newer drivers through an Internet connection. It is possible to have several programs installed on your computer that automatically start during the boot process and perform routine checks. The more programs that automatically start during the boot period, the longer the boot process will take. Problems such as this can be pinpointed by selecting which programs run during startup.

Figure 17-15 The System Configuration tool can be used to perform a diagnostic startup or a selective startup. You can use the tool to eliminate any or all services and software programs during computer startup.

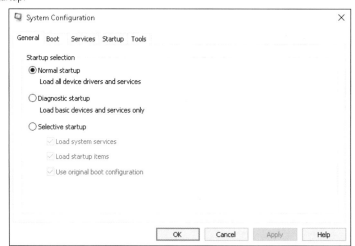

Goodheart-Willcox Publisher

The **Startup** tab enables users to view which items are run automatically during and after startup, as shown in Figure 17-16. You can enable or disable all items or simply select items by the corresponding check box. It is recommended that you first disable all items. If the problem is corrected, reintroduce items one by one until the offending item is identified.

From the **Services** tab, administrators can choose which services to allow to run during and after startup, as demonstrated in Figure 17-17. It is recommended to locate problems in the same manner as with startup items. First, disable all services

Copyright Goodheart-Willcox Co., Inc.

Figure 17-16 The System Configuration Startup tab in Windows 10 directs you to the Task Manager utility.

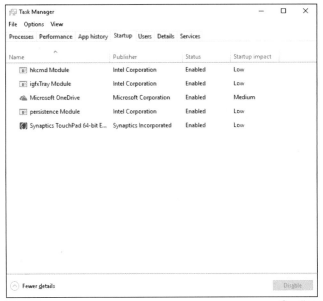

Goodheart-Willcox Publisher

Figure 17-17 The System Configuration Services tab allows you to view and then select suspect services.

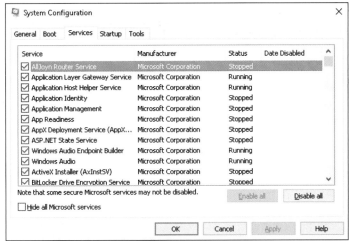

Goodheart-Willcox Publisher

and see how computer performance is affected. Then, reintroduce services until the problem service is identified. See Figure 17-18 for a description of all of the System Configuration tabs.

System Recovery Strategies and Methods

System recovery involves two major steps: recovering data and recovering the operating system. The best protection from a malware attack, breach, or unforeseen disaster is regular system and data backups. When other methods such as System Restore or System Configuration fail to repair the system, administrators can perform a new installation and then follow up with restoring lost data files from the most recent backup. This is why performing regular backups is emphasized.

Copyright Goodheart-Willcox Co., Inc.

Figure 17-18 Description of System Configuration tabs.

System Configuration Tab	Description
General	Performs broad diagnostics, such as eliminating all nonessential items from startup.
Boot	Provides access to boot configuration options associated with dual-boot or multiboot operating systems.
Services	Select which services to enable or disable during and after startup.
Startup	Select startup items to enable or disable during and after startup.
Tools	Provides access to many common troubleshooting and configuration tools.

Goodheart-Willcox Publisher

All Windows operating systems provide some form of backup program. Windows XP has the Backup Wizard, which will allow you to back up files. Windows Vista has Backup and Restore, which allows you to back up system files or create a complete PC backup, or disk image. Windows 7 has Backup and Restore, which allows you to create a system repair disc as well as create a system image. Windows 8 has File History, which allows for the backup of files saved in Libraries. This utility allows users to access Windows 7 file recovery features, such as the creation of a system image. Windows 10 has the System Image utility for creating an image of the system. Keep the following tips to aid in the recovery process:

- Always make a system image while the computer is running correctly.
- Perform system backups often or configure for automatic backups.
- Back up your system to a separate or external drive or to a network storage device.

Caution

Using the Windows Setup or installation disc to restore or recover the computer system can sometimes destroy all data stored on the computer. For this reason, this method should be used as a last resort.

Windows Installation Disc

Users can use the Windows Setup or installation disc to recover from a system failure. Begin the installation by placing the installation disc into the appropriate CD/DVD drive and rebooting the computer. Under normal circumstances, the existing operating system is detected during the installation process, and an option is given to perform a system repair. On rare occasions, the system can be so badly damaged that an existing operating system cannot be detected and a recovery option may not be presented.

After selecting the option to perform a system repair, menu items will be displayed. The menu items will vary, depending on the Windows operating system running. The following menu lists for Windows 7 and Windows 10 are very similar but not an exact match.

Windows 7

- Startup Repair
- System Restore
- System Image Recovery
- Windows Memory Diagnostic
- Command Prompt

Windows 10

- Restore from a restore point
- System Restore

Copyright Goodheart-Willcox Co., Inc.

- System Reset
- Reinstall Windows
- Command Prompt

The **Repair Your Computer** option is available in the **Startup Repair** menu located in the **Advanced Options** menu for operating systems that have the System Recovery program installed on a hard disk partition. In Windows 10, this repair option can be found in **Settings**>**Recovery**>**Advanced startup**, as demonstrated in Figure 17-19. Some computer systems do not have this option available. This option provides a list of recovery tools that can be used to repair startup problems, run diagnostics, or restore your system.

Tech Tip

To access the **Advanced Boot Options** menu, press [F8] within two seconds after the POST completes.

Figure 17-19 Selecting the **Startup Repair** option from the **Advanced Options** menu in Windows 10 will allow you to access recovery options.

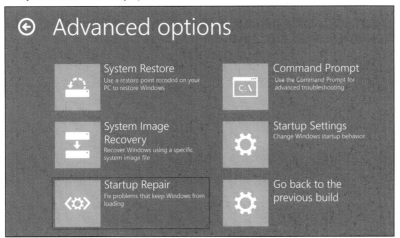

Goodheart-Willcox Publisher

Windows Backup and Restore

Windows Server has a similar option as Windows client for system image recovery located in its Backup and Restore tool. Figure 17-20 shows a screen capture of the Windows Backup and Restore tool. Notice that there are options to create a system image, create a system repair disc, and to restore from a backup. In this particular screen capture, note that a backup has never been performed, so the option to restore files from a backup is not available.

When using the **System Image Recovery** or **Windows Complete PC Restore** option from the **Advanced Boot Options** menu, the system restoration will match a previously made backup of the system. Therefore, all system backups and images must be kept current. A new backup or image should be made after every computer configuration change.

OEM and Repair Shop Disk Image

A computer can always be restored to new or factory condition by using the original installation disc or an image of the original system. There is one main problem with this method: all saved files and software applications will be lost. The result is a new system but no data unless a backup was recently made. Any previously created user accounts will need to be recreated, and the computer system such as e-mail and Internet access reconfigured. Ironically, when restoring the computer using a recent image, you may also be recreating the problem you were attempting to solve. For example, if the problem were caused by a virus, such as a logic time bomb, the virus

Figure 17-20 The Windows 7 Backup and Restore tool has options to create a system image, create a system repair disc, and to restore data from a backup.

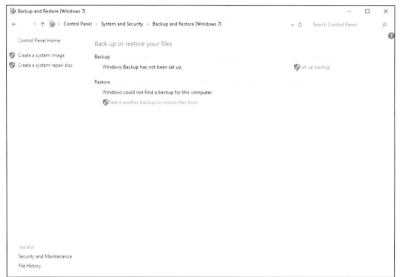

Goodheart-Willcox Publisher

may very well be on the image. Using the infected disk image will infect the computer once more.

A disk image is often used by the original equipment manufacturer (OEM) and computer repair shops when they configure their computers for resale. First, they make two separate partitions. They install the operating system and all software applications and drivers on the first partition. Then, an image of the first partition is made and stored on the second partition. The second partition is used to reimage the first partition to recover it from a disaster. Some manufacturers hide the second partition so that the user does not inadvertently damage the backup image.

Troubleshooting Dual-Boot Systems

Dual-boot and multiboot systems are becoming less common as people are more likely to use virtual machines to have multiple operating systems. However, they do still exist. In these instances, it is a common practice to install the new version as an optional system until the user has been trained on the new version.

The existence of two operating systems on one computer, however, can generate its own unique problems. A common problem is the corruption of the **boot.ini** file or the boot configuration data (BCD). The **boot.ini** file is used for Windows systems and the BCD has been used for all Windows systems starting with Vista.

The **boot.ini** and BCD file provide the user with a choice or selection of operating systems after the POST. An accidental modification or corruption of the **boot.ini** or BCD may prevent any of the operating systems to boot completely or cause only one of the operating systems to boot and not the others.

Look at the contents of a **boot.ini** file as it appears in the Windows System Configuration Utility. To see the **boot.ini** file, all hidden and system file attributes must first be removed. On a Windows 7 system, you can view and modify the BCD settings from the System Configuration **Boot** tab, as demonstrated in Figure 17-21. Notice the default **Timeout** setting of 30 seconds. If more than one operating system is installed on the computer, the Windows Boot Manager will appear for 30 seconds. When there is only one operating system installed on the computer, there will be a two-second delay. It is during this two-second interval that the function key [F8] can be pressed to interrupt the boot process causing the **Advanced Boot Options** menu to appear.

Copyright Goodheart-Willcox Co., Inc.

Figure 17-21 In Windows 10, the contents of the BCD can be viewed and modified from System Configuration.

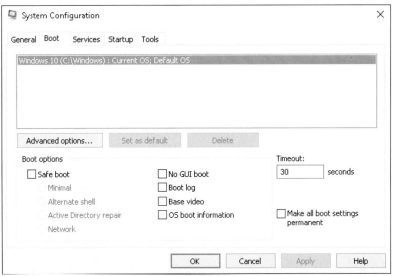

Goodheart-Willcox Publisher

If [F8] is not pressed within two seconds after completion of the POST, the operating system will quickly load the Windows Boot Loader and the kernel. Then, the session manager will load, which results in the familiar Windows GUI. The **Advanced Boot Options** menu cannot be accessed once the computer reaches this point; the computer must be restarted, and the [F8] key must be pressed before POST is finished to access the **Advanced Boot Options** menu.

When the **Advanced Boot Options** menu appears, select the **Command Prompt** option and enter the **bootrec** command, which is used to repair the MBR and the BCD. Any one of several commands can be issued to help repair a corrupt system on a Windows Vista or Windows 7, 8, or 10 computer. The following table lists the **bootrec** command with commonly used switches.

Bootrec Command	Description
bootrec /RebuildBCD	Resolves a corrupt BCD
bootrec /FixMBR	Resolves a corrupt MBR
bootrec /FixBoot	Writes a new boot sector on the system partition
bootrec /ScanOS	Scans for Windows 7 and Windows Vista compatible operating systems installed on the computer
bootrec /RebuildBCD	Scans for operating systems installed on the computer and adds them to the BCD

The practice of installing a dual-boot operating system is now being replaced by virtual PC and virtual server programs. A virtual PC and server allows two or more operating systems to be installed on the same computer. The main advantage of using a virtual computer is the ability to run two or more operating systems simultaneously on the same computer. In a dual-boot installation, either operating system can be run but not at the same time. A key disadvantage of the virtual computer is that it requires sufficient memory and CPU power to support multiple operating systems running simultaneously.

Server Data Integrity and Performance

5.5

Server failure is rare, but it does happen. If the correct precautions are taken when installing a server, the server can perform for years without failure. There are several items that can help ensure a long time between system failures and data loss. Some of these items include the following:

- UPS unit
- RAID system
- backup system
- antivirus/antimalware software
- service packs and patches

When configuring a server, it is important to install an uninterruptible power supply (UPS). It is also important to select a fault-tolerance type of RAID system that is appropriate for the company budget and type of data being stored. Since failure is often unavoidable, be sure to perform regular data backups or use an off-site storage facility service. Be sure to install patches and service packs as they become available. Remember to test the service pack or patch before installing it on the network server. Many patches and service packs can cause severe problems for the operating system and application programs. Referring to user forums, online bulletin boards, and communication from vendors can be prudent when handling this type of software as it may provide important information. Install an antivirus software package designed specifically for servers. In addition to a virus package for the server, it is also desirable to install virus protection on each workstation in the network. Do not overlook laptops used by the organization. Company laptop computers are also frequently attached to the network, which can infect the network system.

Detailed troubleshooting information covering each of the major network operating systems for servers is beyond the scope of this textbook. For troubleshooting information about a particular server network operating system, you can review the information available at Novell, Microsoft, Sun Micro Systems, IBM, Dell, Red Hat, and Hewlett-Packard. Expertise in one or more of these individual server network operating systems may be a certification you wish to obtain after completing this course of study.

Troubleshooting the Network Infrastructure

Network infrastructure consists of cabling and cabling devices, such as hubs, switches, and routers. One of the most commonly encountered infrastructure problems is a loose cable connection. The second most encountered network problem is forgotten user passwords. Many of the tools described in this section were previously explained earlier in the textbook.

Windows Network Diagnostic Utility

Windows XP introduced a network diagnostic tool known as Network Diagnostics. This continues with Windows 10. Originally, the Network Diagnostics utility was accessed by running **msinfo32** (System Information) from the **Run** dialog box off the **Start** menu. When the **System Information** window displays, select **Tools**>**Net Diagnostics**. Selecting the **Scan your system** option in the Network Diagnostics utility automatically runs a series of network diagnostics on the local computer. In Windows 10, users can access the Network Diagnostic utility, shown in Figure 17-22, by selecting **Start**>**Settings**>**Network & Internet**>**Status**>**Troubleshoot**, or **Control Panel**>**Network and Sharing Center**>**Troubleshoot problems**.

The Network Diagnostic utility combines many traditional network utilities. It can simultaneously check network connections, hardware, and networking services.

Copyright Goodheart-Willcox Co., Inc.

Some of the items it automatically checks are the network interface card, modem (if one exists), e-mail, WINS, DNS, and DHCP. Network Diagnostics is a versatile and powerful tool. Look at Figure 17-23 to see the results of a typical Network Diagnostics scan performed from a Windows workstation.

Figure 17-22 The Network Diagnostics utility can be accessed through the **Contol Panel**>**Troubleshooting**>**Network and Internet** menu.

Goodheart-Willcox Publisher

Figure 17-23 The results of a system scan in Network Diagnostics.

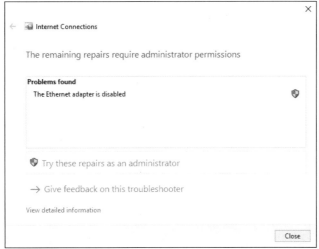

Goodheart-Willcox Publisher

When a particular device passes the test, the word *Pass* appears in bright green lettering to the right side of the device name. If it fails to pass a test, then the word *Failed* is presented in bright red lettering. The Network Diagnostic utility also identifies any items that were scanned but not configured in the workstation by displaying the words *Not Configured* in bright blue.

Network Diagnostics allows the user to customize the objects to scan and save the results to a file for viewing at a later date. Saving the results to a file allows a technician or any users to see what the original settings are and compare them to a scan later. A technician could also run a scan of the workstation, save the results to a file, and transfer the file across the network to a central location. At the central location, it can be added to a network documentation folder containing information about every workstation on the network. This makes network documentation much easier for the technician and the system administrator.

Copyright Goodheart-Willcox Co., Inc.

Network and Sharing Center

The Network and Sharing Center provides a centralized location to diagnose a network problem. Notice the **Diagnose** option shown in Figure 17-24. This option performs similar diagnostic tasks as the Network Diagnostics utility originally introduced in Windows XP. The main difference is a detailed report is not generated but rather a short message briefing you on the status of the network. Either the test passes or a message identifies the possible problem.

You can also consult Server Manager and generate a LAN Diagnostics report similar to that shown in Figure 17-25. The Server Manager can automatically generate a LAN Diagnostics report as well as a System Diagnostics report. The LAN Diagnostics feature is disabled by default so it will not use valuable network bandwidth. To record LAN Diagnostics events, the related service must be enabled.

Figure 17-24 The **Ethernet Status** dialog box accessed through the Network and Sharing Center contains an option to diagnose and repair the LAN connection.

Goodheart-Willcox Publisher

Figure 17-25 Server Manager has an option to generate a LAN Diagnostics report automatically.

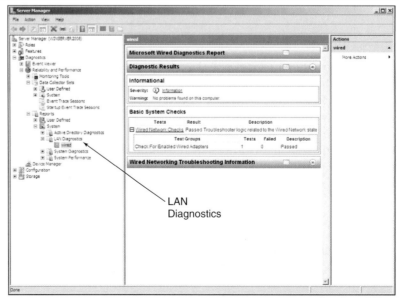

Goodheart-Willcox Publisher

Copyright Goodheart-Willcox Co., Inc.

As with many items in the Windows control panel, the functionality of Network and Sharing Center is consistent but has changed with newer versions of Windows. Notice in Figure 17-26 that the options in Windows 10 are rearranged as compared with those in Windows Vista and Windows Server 2008.

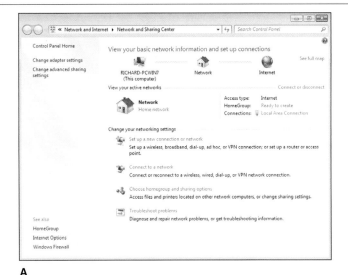

A

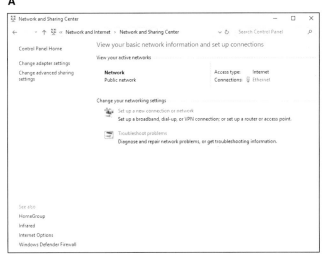

B

Figure 17-26 A—Windows 7 modified the look of the original Network and Sharing center. B—The look was again modified in Windows 10.

Goodheart-Willcox Publisher

A problem with the computer connection to the network is indicated in Network and Sharing Center by a yellow triangle containing an exclamation mark (!) or a red *X*. A problem with a connection to the Internet is indicated by a colorless globe icon, as shown in Figure 17-27.

When a problem is identified with the yellow triangle containing an exclamation mark (!) or red *X*, double-clicking the icon will yield more detailed information. After the problem is corrected, and after a short delay usually of no more than one or two minutes, the trouble-indicating icons will disappear. The network browser scans the local area network periodically to detect changes in the condition or to discover problems automatically.

Another great feature of the Network and Sharing Center is the ability to create a map of all devices connected in the local network. This allows users to identify how the network devices in the LAN relate to each other logically. Legacy devices, such as Windows XP and older switches, routers, and gateways, may not appear correctly in the map. The map relies on IPv6 and the Network Discovery protocols to create

Copyright Goodheart-Willcox Co., Inc.

Figure 17-27 The Network and Sharing Center immediately diagnoses problems with computer LAN connections.

Goodheart-Willcox Publisher

the map. Any device that does not support the Network Discovery feature or is only configured for IPv4 may not show up correctly in the map. There are downloadable patches or updates available for Windows XP and for some legacy network devices so that they will appear.

Network Cable Tester

Cables can be analyzed quickly using hardware tools such as a network cable tester. Cable testers go by many different names, such as *digital cable analyzer* and *cable analyzer*. A network cable tester performs a series of checks to verify cable integrity. Cable faults such as opens, shorts, and grounds can be quickly determined and located. Many cable testers can also check for crosstalk, radio interference, EMI, and excessive cable lengths. Some can also determine the exact location of a cable fault. Some of the more expensive models can record troubleshooting data and download it to a computer. The computer can store or print the information.

In testing with a cable tester, you may discover that a cable is improperly terminated. Provided there is enough extra cable length to do so, the connector can be cut off, and a new connector can be placed on the cable. For example, if an Ethernet cable were terminated with an incorrect pinout, the RJ-45 connector can be cut off with a pair of cutting pliers. Once the cable is cut, it can be terminated a second time by correctly aligning the twisted pairs to their correct termination points and using a crimper to seal the connector onto the cable. If the cable were used in a patch panel, a punch down tool would be needed. Punch down tools are explained in detail in Chapter 18.

Tone Generator and Tracer

A tone generator and tracer allow a technician to trace the exact location of cable runs hidden by walls, ceilings, or flooring. That can also be used to help identify unmarked cables. The tone generator and tracer are separate devices. The tone generator attaches to one end of a cable. It produces an analog or digital signal and transmits it through the cable. The tracer is designed with special circuitry that receives the signal and produces a tone if it is in close range of the cable. When a cable fault is encountered, the signal ends or changes pitch.

Copyright Goodheart-Willcox Co., Inc.

The fact that the tone generator and tracer are designed to trace the path of a conductor is an advantage over a cable analyzer, which does not have this feature incorporated. An old term still used by technicians to describe the tone generator and detector is *fox and hound*. The tone generator represents the fox and the tracer represents the hound. In essence, the hound (tracer) follows the fox (signal) until reaching the end of the cable.

Fiber-Optic Cables

Fiber-optic cable requires specialized tools for troubleshooting. Typically, an optical time domain reflectometer (OTDR), sometimes abbreviated as *OTD*, is used to locate faults in the fiber-optic cable core. The OTDR uses a light source to detect faults. The light source sends a pulse of light energy through the fiber-optic core. As the light pulse encounters defects in the core and connectors, the light reflects to the source, which also acts as a receiver. The amount of reflected light and the time it took to travel to the fault and back is instantly calculated. The intensity of the reflected light and the calculated time indicate the type of flaw and the location in meters where it occurred. A more in-depth explanation of the OTDR can be found in Chapter 3.

A light generator may also be needed for optical tests. Light generators emit a light that is sent down a fiber-optic cable. This tool allows administrators to find breaks or cracks in the fiber cabling. An additional tool to help diagnose fiber-optic cable is a light meter. Light meters measure the amount of light coming through a cable. This allows for the measurement of power levels and loss. Some even allow for the inspection of the connectors on a cable.

NIC Loopback Test

The network interface card loopback test typically employs the use of the **ping** command as part of its diagnostics. A loopback test checks a hardware device's ability to transmit and receive signals. It consists of diagnostic software and an adapter (connector) called a *loopback*. The loopback is plugged into the back of the network interface card. When the diagnostic software is run, the loopback completes the electrical circuit between the transmit and receive pins. Without a connection between the transmit and receive pins, a complete series of diagnostic tests cannot be run.

Multimeter and Spectrum Analyzer

Depending on the nature of the problem in your network, there are additional tools you may need to use in troubleshooting and repair. The first of these tools is a multimeter. A *multimeter* is a common and versatile tool used throughout electronics. It is used to test connectivity, resistance, current, and other electrical properties. Analog multimeters are equipped with a moving pointer on top of a scale to show the electrical readings, while digital multimeters often have a numeric display or graphical bar to output a reading. Multimeters come with probes that are placed on two ends of an electrical current and a dial to set resistance. These can be used to test most types of cable and determine whether a device is receiving electricity. Always follow the instructions of your individual tool and make sure there is no current running through the device you are testing.

Another common tool is a spectrum analyzer. A *spectrum analyzer* measures the magnitude of input signals compared to the full frequency range of the instrument. In other words, it measures the power of the spectrum of known or unknown signals. The result is a display of amplitude along a vertical axis with frequency along a horizontal axis. Spectrum analyzers come in a number of sizes, from large, desktop devices to small, handheld versions. The user plugs a radio frequency antenna into

5.2 NET

Tech Tip

A time domain reflectometer (TDR) is used to test copper core network cable and should not be confused with OTDR or OTD. The TDR works by sending an electronic pulse down the copper core cable and then reads signal bounce to locate cable faults.

5.2 NET

5.2 NET

the input of the analyzer and enters a *center frequency* into the device along with a *span*, or width of the frequency. The desired frequency will be displayed on the analyzer screen with noise on either side.

Indicator Lights

All network adapters and network devices, such as hubs and switches, are equipped with indicator lights. There is no standard interpretation of what the light patterns represent. To interpret the exact meaning of the light patterns, such as a flashing or steady light, consult the manufacturer's resources. However, there are some general assumptions that can be made. If none of the indicator lights are lit, a cable problem may exist. A cable problem may include a disconnected cable at the hub or switch or a bad connection at either end of the cable. There is also a possibility that the network card is bad, but this is rare. Generally, it is safe to assume network activity when the indicator lights are blinking. The more rapid the lights blink, the higher the rate of activity. A steady light can also indicate high activity.

Network Analyzer

Typically, the entire network infrastructure can be tested using a network analyzer. A network analyzer can be software or a combination of software and hardware. Network analyzers are typically the most expensive of all network-testing devices and often exceed the budget of IT departments with small LANs. The best network analyzers combine features found in all network testing software and hardware and have elaborate display capabilities.

Protocol Analyzer

Protocol analyzers are used to capture and monitor data frames traveling across the network media. While most protocol analyzers monitor only TCP/IP, more sophisticated protocol analyzers can monitor hundreds of different protocols. Protocol analyzers vary greatly in their features. Protocol analyzers can filter the data they gather by limiting the capture of data to one or more nodes, thus reducing the total amount of data that needs to be analyzed. Many of the more sophisticated protocol analyzers can chart their results in graph form. Protocol analyzers are commonly incorporated into network analyzers.

While protocol analyzers vary somewhat, all have similar functions and characteristics. Look at Figure 17-28 to view some of these features. Displayed are three viewing panes. The top pane displays the series of frames captured during the brief period the protocol analyzer was running. The frame that is highlighted contains the Simple Mail Transport Protocol (SMTP).

The middle pane displays detailed information about the highlighted frame, such as the IP address of the source and the destination, the time of the capture, and the type of protocol. The bottom pane displays the contents of the packet. The characters on the left side of the bottom pane display the contents as hexadecimal pairs. The ASCII equivalents of the hexadecimal pairs are on the right. Characters outside the range of the basic standard 128 characters are not displayed or are displayed as meaningless symbols. This particular SMTP-captured packet contains a plain-text e-mail message. A close inspection of these contents will show who sent the message. By scrolling through the pane, the entire contents of the message and the e-mail addresses of the sender and destination are displayed.

A technician in the workplace can use a protocol analyzer to analyze network conditions, observe network traffic patterns, and identify bottlenecks. Most protocol analyzers provide features to allow the user to filter packets by source, destination, protocol type, or by almost any characteristic of a frame or packet.

Copyright Goodheart-Willcox Co., Inc.

Figure 17-28 A protocol analyzer is used to capture frames and monitor frames of data traveling across the network media.

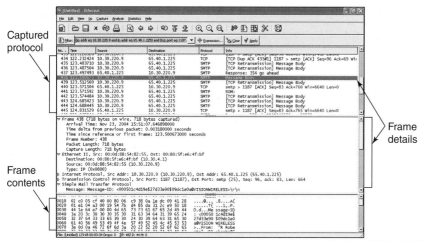

Goodheart-Willcox Publisher

Conditions such as switching loops, routing loops, route problems, proxy ARP, and broadcast storms generally can only be detected by a protocol analyzer. You must be familiar with a protocol analyzer to be able to recognize a looping condition. If a protocol analyzer is configured to a network and the same protocol repeats excessively between two or more devices, then a looping problem most likely exists. For example, if the predominate protocol is ARP, the network most likely has one of the above-mentioned problems. If a large number of corrupt packets is shown, a broadcast storm is likely taking place.

Wireless Network Tester and Analyzer

While not all protocol analyzers capture wireless protocols, many do. Wireless network analyzers often require hardware to perform a more in-depth analysis of the wireless infrastructure. Manufacturers often design wireless analyzers to check signal strength and measure radio and electromagnetic interference.

A freeware tool for checking a wireless network adapter and wireless access point is NetStumbler, shown in Figure 17-29. NetStumbler, also known as *Network Stumbler*, displays the signal-to-noise ratio picked up by the wireless device. This can be a very valuable aid if you suspect there might be radio signals (noise) interfering with the wireless network.

Troubleshooting the Most Common Network Problems

After all of the training and certification required to find employment, many technicians are disappointed to find that the most common networking problems consume about 90 percent of their time. In fact, most of the problems will be quite easy to solve with patience. This section presents some of the most common problems encountered. A technician that has a sound knowledge of PC repair and support can easily solve many of these problems.

Cannot Log on to the Network or Computer

The most common help desk request is assistance for logging on to the network. Some of the most common user logon problems are listed in Figure 17-30. A logon

Copyright Goodheart-Willcox Co., Inc.

Figure 17-29 The Network Stumbler utility can aid in detecting interference in a wireless network.

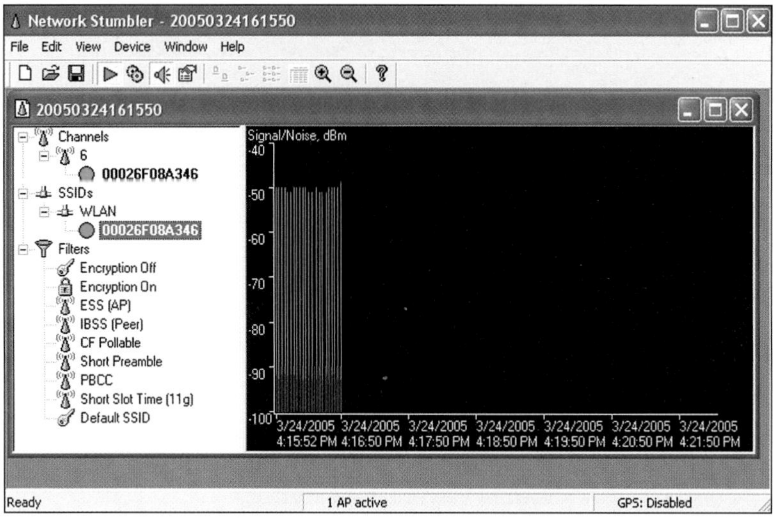

Goodheart-Willcox Publisher

Figure 17-30 Common logon problems and an explanation of how they happen.

Logon Problem	Explanation
Wrong password	Users forgot their latest password, which is a very common occurrence, especially if regular changing of passwords is required.
Typographical errors and spelling	Users often misspell their password or perform typographical errors while attempting to log on to the network.
[Caps Lock] key	The [Caps Lock] key is struck accidentally and remains on during the logon procedure. The password is case-sensitive, which results in the user being denied access.
[Num Lock] key	The user accidentally hits the [Num Lock] key, which causes the number pad function to change. If the user has a password that includes numbers and uses the number pad to enter the numbers, password errors will be generated when attempting to log on to the network. This is common with users that do accounting and use the number keypad frequently in their work.
Wrong domain or server	Users may inadvertently attempt to log on to the wrong server or domain when prompted by the logon dialog box. Depending on the network system, some users are capable of logging on to more than one domain controller or server and may have different usernames or passwords for each domain controller or server. While not a good practice, this is a real possibility.

Goodheart-Willcox Publisher

problem is without a doubt the most common problem encountered. Users generate the largest number of network failures, not the hardware or software. Do not blame the user. The fact that users produce so many problems is caused by a lack of user expertise. Users need training, and it is the responsibility of the network administrator to provide that training. The better you train the users, the less you will encounter common problems.

Loose or No Connection

After logon problems, the most commonly encountered network problem is loose cable connections. The number of times a connection problem has been cleared by

Copyright Goodheart-Willcox Co., Inc.

the removal and reinsertion of a cable from a hub, network interface card, or network device is significantly higher than anyone would assume. Connections of this type are mechanical connections, not soldered connections. Consequently, they can become loose or slightly oxidized.

Oxidation normally occurs at mechanical connection points where electrical energy flows through the connection. All metal oxidizes at various rates. The oxidation rate is accelerated when electrical energy flows through the connection. The amount of oxidation required for a connection failure need not be detectable by the human eye. There is no need for a heavy layer of electrical corrosion to exist. A microscopic, translucent layer of oxidation can render any electrical connection as an open circuit and produce a system failure.

For example, consider a situation in which a battery-operated electronic device, such as a television remote control, stopped working. Removing and reinserting the batteries, or even tapping the remote against a hand or object, may result in the device functioning again. In both cases, the sliding motion of the battery terminals across the remote control contacts removed the microscopic layer of oxidation, which is why the device was able to work properly.

The memory module shown in Figure 17-31 illustrates the excessive buildup of oxidation on metallic parts. Oxidation is particularly bothersome on low-voltage applications such as computers. A common pencil eraser has been used to remove a small section of oxidation from the memory module contacts that run along the edge. Pay particular attention to how shiny the copper contacts are now that oxidation has been removed.

Figure 17-31 The metal contacts of computer and network hardware are susceptible to oxidation. Note the oxidation on the contacts of this memory module.

Goodheart-Willcox Publisher

Oxidation can occur on any metal connection point in a computer, such as the contact edge of network interface cards and the pins of a CPU or hard disk drive. It can also occur on network cable connections.

A cable that does not provide a complete path back to the patch panel, resulting in a lack of connection is referred to as a **dead drop**. This phrasing comes from the fact that the network cable running through the building structure ceiling and wall is referred to as a *drop,* so consequently the phrase *dead drop* means the cable drop is dead, or does not make a connection.

The two main reasons for dead drops are security and new construction oversight. Many network administrators do not allow unassigned network outlets to be patched into the patch panel in the main utility room as a matter of system security. They feel that anyone could plug in a laptop computer to an existing network wall outlet and access the network system. While it is true that the unauthorized user does not have a server account, he or she still has gained physical access to the network system and is on his or her way to compromising network security.

The second most common reason for a dead drop is during construction of the new system, the network cable was never patched through at the patch panel, thus creating an open network circuit. This is easily remedied by simply making the appropriate patch at the patch panel.

Cannot Access a Share

There are several reasons a user may not be able to access a network share. Determine why by first making sure the user can connect to the share location by using the **ping** command with the IP address of the share location. The inability to access the share location through the **ping** command may indicate a network media problem or network device program. If connectivity with the share location is intact as indicated by the **ping** command, check that the user has rights or permissions to the share. This situation usually happens when the user or the share is new.

Cannot Print to Network Printer

Most printer problems are easy to resolve if the printer has worked correctly prior to the problem. Many users do not understand the basics of printer operation, especially if they have never used a networked printer. If a user is experiencing a printer problem, check that electrical power is supplied to the printer. This means that the printer is plugged in, the outlet has power, and the printer is turned on. Next, see if the printer will perform a self-test. All printers have a preprogrammed self-test that is activated through the printer menu selections or by a button combination or sequence. If necessary, consult the printer manual for instructions.

If the printer is connected to or managed by a server, check if there is sufficient disk space for the print job(s) currently waiting to print. Check if a print job has stopped because of some other problem, thus preventing any job sent to the printer to be processed. Make sure the person attempting to print has permissions or user rights to print. The user may be trying to use a printer he or she does not have permissions to use, especially if he or she is new. Check if the print server is down. Many of the reasons that a user cannot connect to a network printer would be the same as for connecting to a network share. Check if the DNS or WINS service/server is running.

Printer Is Printing Gibberish

Another common printing problem is a printer that has been working suddenly starts printing gibberish. The following is a list of common printer items to check:

- Does the cache or print spooler need to be cleared?
- Is the printer misidentified?
- Did the user attempt to connect to the wrong printer?

The print job in the cache or print spooler may have become corrupted, or the user may have used the wrong printer driver to print to the selected printer. Many times, it is quicker to dump all the files waiting to be printed, remove the printer drivers, reinstall the drivers, and reconfigure the printer share. It is impossible to know what has taken place before you arrived at the problem printer. Someone may have already attempted to fix the printer. That person would not typically be a technician, just someone who may have fixed a printer problem before and believes that he or she can most likely fix this one. They may have tried to change many of the settings

Copyright Goodheart-Willcox Co., Inc.

and even attempted to connect to a different printer share, thus sending the waiting files to a printer in a different location. Remember your people skills and be patient.

Computer Has a Virus or Worm

Worms are the real danger for computer networks. Worms are typically distributed by e-mail systems and use the list of e-mail contacts to spread the worm program. A good antivirus suite of programs that contain e-mail scanning services is essential to protect against worm attacks. There is no way to stop all virus or worm attacks. New viruses and worms are created daily. A system can be protected against known viruses and worms, but the protection package must remain up to date. E-mail alerts from virus protection vendors are often distributed to users as soon as a new virus or worm is identified.

Most viruses reported by users and inexperienced technicians are not really viruses at all. Many suspected viruses are actually the results of users and technicians misconfiguring software or hardware.

Cannot Obtain a Proper IPv4 Address

5.5 NET +

A network administrator may continue to add users and workstations to a large network system but inadvertently forget to expand the IP address pool at the DHCP server. Recall that an address pool is a range of IP addresses used by the DHCP server to assign to workstations. The total number of IP address assignments in a pool is referred to as the *scope*. If there are 250 addresses in the DHCP scope and more than 250 users, it is impossible for all workstations to be assigned an IP address. The DHCP scope must be expanded to allow for more users.

Also, the DHCP server may be off-line or the network path to the DHCP server may not be complete because of an open cable or device failure. When a computer cannot obtain an IP address from its DHCP server, the computer will automatically assign itself an IP address. This is called Automatic Private IP Addressing (APIPA). APIPA addresses range from 169.254.0.1 to 169.254.255.254. If the **ipconfig** command is run and the results show a corresponding APIPA in this range, it can be determined that the computer has not been able to obtain a DHCP IPv4 address. IPv6 automatically assigns a random IPv6 address at this time and does not rely on DHCP for an assignment. Eventually, dynamic IP addresses expire. This means that the IP address is no longer associated with a given device, and the address is recycled into the IP address pool. Address expiration, however, is not a problem, as the DHCP server will reissue an IP address. Static addresses do not expire.

A related problem is duplicate addresses. This occurs if two devices are given the same IP address. If that happens, neither device can communicate on the network. That can only occur if you have a static IP address. In fact, the issue of duplicate IP addresses is one reason DHCP is so widely used. Duplicate MAC addresses are incredibly rare. Since MAC addresses are assigned by the vendor at the factory, it is unlikely two devices with the same MAC address exist. If this happens, the most likely issue is that someone is spoofing a MAC address.

It is also possible, though rare, for an attacker, usually an insider, to configure his or her own rogue DHCP server. This means there is a DHCP server on the network that is not under the administrative control of the network administrator. These servers will function as a traditional DHCP server—offering IP addresses and DNS resolution, and providing access to the default gateway. However, if the information differs from the real DHCP server, users accepting addresses from it may experience network problems. The owner of the rogue server may also be able to sniff all packets being sent through it. These types of servers can be very hard to detect, especially without an intrusion detection system (IDS).

Copyright Goodheart-Willcox Co., Inc.

Cannot Connect to an Application Server

A common help desk request is that the user cannot access an application server, such as a mail server. After ruling out a user logon error and issuing the **ping** command to ensure a complete path to the application server exists, look for other causes of the problem. Are there any switches or routers between the user's workstation and the application server? Is the problem isolated to a single user, or is the problem shared by other users as well? Is the shared problem spread across the entire network or limited to a specific segment or department?

Many times all physical network equipment is working properly and there simply is too much demand for the application server. For example, a mail server would experience the most workload the first thing in the morning. The combination of the morning workload, a group of e-mails with several large attachments, and the workstation downloading updates would make it appear that the network is not performing or is performing very slowly. This type of condition can be verified with a protocol analyzer to see the traffic load. An overloaded network system could be remedied by adding additional network switches, which will reduce the size of collision domains.

Cannot Access VoIP Services

The most common reason users cannot access VoIP services is a VLAN switch failure or an incorrectly configured VLAN assignment. The most common reason for incorrect VLAN assignments is technician error when configuring the switch. Each port on the VLAN switch must be checked and verified to ensure it is assigned to the correct VLAN tag. If you are not familiar with the VLAN switch configuration, escalate the problem to a more qualified technician.

Duplex Mismatch

NET
5.3

Network devices operate in either half-duplex or full-duplex mode. When operating in full-duplex mode, the device can send and receive packets simultaneously. When configured as half-duplex mode, the device can send *or* receive but not send *and* receive packets simultaneously. Almost all network devices have the ability to auto-configure their mode of operation as either half-duplex or full-duplex. Typically, the two communicating devices are matched correctly; however, there will be times when the proper match fails and one device will be in full-duplex mode and the other device in half-duplex mode. The failure to automatically configure the duplex mode correctly can be caused by packet corruption for wired devices and radio interference for wireless devices.

When two devices with mismatched duplex are exchanging packets, the network segment appears to lose bandwidth or appears to have degraded performance. The full-duplex device is freely transmitting packets and not waiting on the half-duplex device. This condition causes packet collisions, and thus corrupt packets.

A simple fix is to reset network devices suspected of duplex mismatch, such as switches or computers. You can also manually configure both devices for either half- or full-duplex to correct this problem.

Cannot Access the Internet

Internet connection failure on a network can be caused by circumstances inside or outside the local network. The type of physical Internet access used by the network determines the exact method of troubleshooting. For example, if a telephone modem is used to access the Internet through an ISP, then a simple test such as dialing a cell phone number using the Internet connection modem will verify if the modem

Copyright Goodheart-Willcox Co., Inc.

is working. If a T1 line is used, you may need to call the provider to test the connection from its support office. In general, check if the problem is isolated to the Internet connection equipment, Internet service provider equipment, or a service on the LAN, such as the Internet Connection Sharing (ICS) service.

There are several common issues related to Internet access problems. Usually, the problem is directly related to Domain Name Service (DNS). Either the DNS server is down or the network adapter has been configured for the wrong DNS server or gateway. The DNS protocol uses UDP packets to transmit DNS information to the requesting client. UDP is not reliable and does not verify the delivery of the DNS packet. As a result, a corrupt DNS packet or failure to deliver the DNS packet can result in a failed Internet connection.

Be aware that some locations change their assigned web service provider. If the Internet connection information was stored in a local area network proxy server, router, or server cache, then the wrong address could be used when attempting to connect to a site on the Internet. Two possible remedies are the following:

- Purge the Internet DNS cache on all related network equipment.

- Use a protocol analyzer to determine if there is an excessive amount of corrupt packets caused by collisions on the network.

If there is excessive packet corruption, you will need to alleviate the problem by using traffic-management techniques such as increasing bandwidth or the addition of switches in the network.

Another important factor to consider is the network firewall configuration. If the problem is not with the DNS server, it might very well be caused by the system firewall. A user might be able to connect to an Internet location but may not be able to establish a connection with a service at that location. When the user cannot establish a service, he or she will generally report to the service desk that they are experiencing an Internet connection failure. However, the firewall is most likely configured to block the port related to the desired service. For example, a user might report that he or she cannot establish a connection to the Internet for his or her smartphone. Normally smartphones use port 110, the same port as POP3, which is used for the mail client. If the user is attempting to make a secure connection, such as with SSL, then port 995 is used. If port 995 is blocked, the user will not be able to establish a secure connection through the smartphone.

Remember, port numbers are directly correlated to specific services. If a required port number is blocked (filtered), the user cannot use the service, and it will appear as an Internet connection problem to the user. Of course, the firewall problem could be even more fundamental. Incorrect ACL settings can block communication. This means if the ACLs are not configured properly, legitimate users may be blocked.

Another reason for failure to connect to the Internet is when the network adapter is manually configured for the wrong or nonexistent gateway. It is not unusual for a network technician to make a typographical error, such as reversing the correct numbers of the default gateway address. This results in Internet access failure. Technicians often fail to catch their own mistakes. If the network adapter supports the capability, the system can be configured to find the gateway automatically, thus eliminating the need for a technician to enter the gateway IP address manually. This is a much more efficient method. Windows 10 will usually find the correct default gateway automatically, as do some older versions of Windows. On larger networks containing two or more subnets, it is very easy to assign the wrong default gateway to a computer. You can usually ping the default gateway to verify it is online and reachable from your location. After verifying the gateway, check your network adapter configuration carefully.

Tech Tip

NET
5.4

Power levels can affect wireless connectivity and performance. As the power level drops in a wireless device, it may begin to work more sporadically. Be sure to check battery and power levels as part of the troubleshooting process for these items.

Troubleshooting Common Wireless Problems

Due to the lack of a tangible network medium, the problems plaguing wireless networks are vastly different. These problems can also be more difficult to troubleshoot, especially if the person experiencing them works remotely. Fortunately, most users experience the same or similar problems. Four common problems associated with wireless networks are wrong ESSID, signal bounce, mismatched encryption configurations, and unbalanced signal-to-noise ratio.

ESSID Mismatch

When two or more wireless access points (WAPs) are used to support roaming and are connected to a common wired network, they must have matching SSIDs. The configuration of matching SSIDs to support device roaming is referred to as *Extended SSID (ESSID)*. An inexperienced technician might replace an existing WAP or add a new WAP and not change the default SSID to match the SSID of the other WAPs. When this happens, an ESSID mismatch has occurred and the roaming wireless device will not always be able to connect to the network.

At times, it is desirable to have a mismatch condition. You may want to create two different wireless network systems in the same wired network. For example, you could create two wireless networks, one for students and one for faculty. You could assign two different SSIDs for each of the wireless networks. In addition, you should also set up a passphrase or wireless key to prevent unauthorized persons from connecting to the wireless network. The SSID is not sufficient to prevent an unauthorized connection.

Signal Bounce

Signal bounce refers to a condition where the wireless signal reflects, or "bounces," off an object, such as a metal building, file cabinets, some types of glass, and certain building materials. Signal bounce can corrupt a wireless signal. Signal corruption caused by signal bounce can usually be eliminated by simply repositioning the wireless devices. Even moving a WAP a few feet can eliminate the problem. Ironically, signal bounce will actually improve a signal if its reflection is in close approximation to the original signal.

Encryption Enabled

When encryption is enabled on a wireless device, such as a WAP, all devices expected to communicate with the WAP must have a matching encryption passphrase or security key. Even if the wireless device is detected by the computer system and the SSID or ESSID matches, a user will still be unable to connect with the device if it is configured for encryption without a matching encryption passphrase or security key.

Other items to consider when troubleshooting wireless devices are wireless channels, frequency, maximum distance, and mismatch of IEEE standards. A review of Chapter 4 may be beneficial to generate a full understanding of wireless troubleshooting.

NET
5.4

Signal-to-Noise Ratio

Signal-to-noise ratio (SNR) describes the difference in decibels between a received signal and the background noise level that surrounds the signal. If the received signal

Copyright Goodheart-Willcox Co., Inc.

is too close to the noise level, data corruption and retransmission of data will occur. These retransmissions will ultimately affect network latency and bandwidth. Most wireless cards are not equipped to measure noise levels, so adapters or additional software is often needed. Typically, a signal with an SNR measurement of 20 decibels or greater is recommended for wireless data networks. This figure increases if applications such as video conferencing or VoIP are used. Often, signal boosters and the removal of other equipment from close proximity to a WAP can help improve signal-to-noise ratios.

Troubleshooting with TCP/IP Utilities

TCP/IP is the predominant network communication protocol in use. All major operating systems use TCP/IP for communicating across the Internet and a LAN. Microsoft NetBEUI and IPX/SPX are obsolete. An excellent understanding of TCP/IP utilities is essential for a network technician. There are several common TCP/IP utilities designed to diagnose problems with the TCP/IP protocol suite. Most of the commands are the same in all operating systems with only a few exceptions. Exceptions are pointed out in this section when appropriate.

Ping

The **ping** command is designed to send an echo request message to another node using the Internet Control Message Protocol (ICMP). The **ping** command is used to verify that a connection exists between the destination and the source. It is also used to verify that the TCP/IP protocol is configured properly. For example, you can issue the **ping localhost** command to verify that the TCP/IP protocol is configured for the host's network interface card. The following sequence will help troubleshoot a connection on a TCP/IP-based network:

> **1.1** NET

1. Ping the workstation. Use the **ping 127.0.0.1** or **ping localhost** command. This is used to verify that TCP/IP has been configured for the network interface card. Failure indicates a problem with the network interface card.

Tech Tip ⚙️

The switches available for the **ping** command can vary according to the operating system used.

2. Ping the assigned IP address. If a static address has been assigned to the desktop, ping that assigned IP address. If DHCP has been selected for an automatic IP address assignment, skip this step.

3. Ping another workstation on the LAN. Ping it by name and then by the assigned IP address. If the **ping** command returns successfully when the IP address is used but fails when the name of the distant workstation is used, it is a good sign of a DNS server or WINS server failure. *WINS* is used on older Windows systems to resolve NetBIOS computer names to IP addresses.

> **5.5** NET

4. Ping the default network server, gateway, or router. This will verify a complete cable connection from the workstation to the server, gateway, or router. The chosen device will vary according to each network design. Basically, you are verifying a connection to the outer edge of the LAN.

5. Ping the DNS server used for the network. This will verify that the server responsible for resolving domain names to IP addresses is accessible. Ping the DNS server when you are experiencing problems with Internet connections. This may not be necessary for a small network.

6. Ping a distant location, such as Google, Bing, or Microsoft, to verify that connections can be made outside the network. This is especially important when resolving Internet connection problems. You may experience a

Copyright Goodheart-Willcox Co., Inc.

timeout for the **ping** command. This is because many sites block the ping request for security reasons. The **ping** command appears as a probe of the network and may not be successful. You may need to try several well-known sites before one replies to your ping request. If either of the last two recommended ping steps fail, it may indicate that a DNS server problem exists.

In Figure 17-32, you can see a list of inbound and outbound firewall rules. The red circle with a diagonal line indicates that the inbound connection for ICMP has been blocked, thus preventing the ping echo request.

Figure 17-32 List of inbound and outbound firewall rules in Windows 10.

Inbound Rules

Outbound Rules

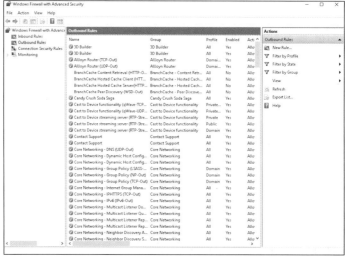

Goodheart-Willcox Publisher

There are some **ping** switches available that can modify its use. The **-n** switch is used to change the number of echo requests to be sent. The **-l** (el) switch may be used to increase the timeout value for special applications. For example, if you are pinging a site that requires a satellite connection, the time interval may need to be increased because of the inherently slow transmission times associated with satellite communication.

Copyright Goodheart-Willcox Co., Inc.

Pathping

The **pathping** command is a combination of the **ping** and **tracert** commands. It sends an ICMP echo request message to all routers and gateways along the path to the destination address, as demonstrated in Figure 17-33. The destination address can be expressed as an IP address, a URL or domain name, or FQDN. The disadvantage of the **pathping** command is it can take 5 to 10 minutes to obtain the final results. The advantage is the results are quite detailed when compared with **ping** or **tracert** and help to identify the exact device causing the bottleneck. The **pathping** command not only traces the router to the destination, it also continues to send out a series of pings over a period of time and after the initial route has been displayed. The additional series of pings are used to provide a statistical analysis of the route to each router or gateway along the path. The statistical information can be used to identify sources of network latency. Notice that in Figure 17-33 **pathping** generated a report after 300 seconds or approximately 5 minutes. The extended time period can better identify intermittent network bottlenecks that may be missed by **tracert**, **route**, or **ping**.

Tracert

The **tracert** command traces the route from the workstation to a remote location and displays information about the path taken by the **tracert** packets. Look at Figure 17-34 to see a typical **tracert** display. The utility displays a series of hops taken along the route from the workstation to the requested destination. The amount of time taken to reach each router along the route is displayed in milliseconds. The **tracert** command sends a series of **ping** packets from the source to the destination. At each router or gateway encountered along the path, an echo is sent back to the

5.3 NET+

Note

The **ping**, **tracert**, and **pathping** commands rely on ICMP echo requests to obtain their results. If a router or gateway is configured to filter echo requests, the command will not produce any result.

Tech Tip

Unix/Linux systems use a similar command as **pathping** called **mtr**.

Tech Tip

The Unix/Linux **tracert** command is **traceroute**.

Goodheart-Willcox Publisher

Figure 17-33 The **pathping** command is a combination of the commands **ping** and **tracert** and produces detailed information about the network route to the final destination.

Goodheart-Willcox Publisher

Figure 17-34 Typical display of the **tracert** command used with a DNS name. Notice that each router along the path to the destination is listed along with the time in milliseconds it took to reach the router.

Copyright Goodheart-Willcox Co., Inc.

source. Each additional **ping** packet increases the time-to-live to enable the packet to reach the final destination.

There are many third-party tools developed that provide a graphical presentation of a **tracert** result. Figure 17-35 shows various display formats from a graphical tool called NeoTrace.

Netstat

The **netstat** command displays information about active TCP/IP connections. The **netstat** command displays Ethernet statistics for IP, TCP, ICMP, and UDP for IPv4 and IPv6. When the **netstat** command is used without a switch, it lists all active TCP/IP connections. When used with the **/?** switch, the screen displays a summary of all the common **netstat** switches. Figure 17-36 displays a list of common **netstat** switches and a description of each.

Figure 17-35 The NeoTrace utility can display traced routes in various formats.

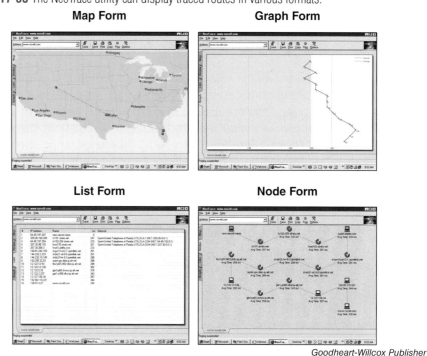

Map Form

Graph Form

List Form

Node Form

Goodheart-Willcox Publisher

Figure 17-36 Summary of **netstat** switches.

netstat switch	Description
-a	Displays all active TCP and UDP connections.
-e	Displays Ethernet statistics.
-f	Displays the Fully Qualified Domain Name (FQDN).
-n	Displays active TCP connections expressed numerically.
-p	Displays active connections for a specific protocol.
-s	Displays statistics by protocol.
-r	Displays contents of routing table.
/?	Displays help.

Goodheart-Willcox Publisher

Copyright Goodheart-Willcox Co., Inc.

Figure 17-37 illustrates the **netstat** command issued with the **-e** switch. The cumulative statistics for the host's Internet interface card are displayed. Notice that there are no discards or errors. This indicates that the network is working properly. A high number of discards or errors indicates a problem on the network.

Switches may also be used in combination to display very specific results. For example, the command **netstat -s -p ip** displays statistics pertaining only to the IP protocol. See Figure 17-38 for an example of a combination of switches in a command line.

Figure 17-37 The **netstat -e** command can be used to check if the network is working properly. A high number of discards or errors indicates a problem.

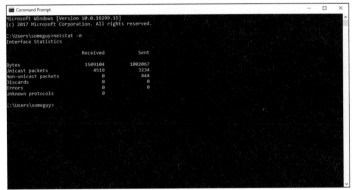

Goodheart-Willcox Publisher

Figure 17-38 The **netstat -s -p ip** command displays statistics relating to the IP protocol.

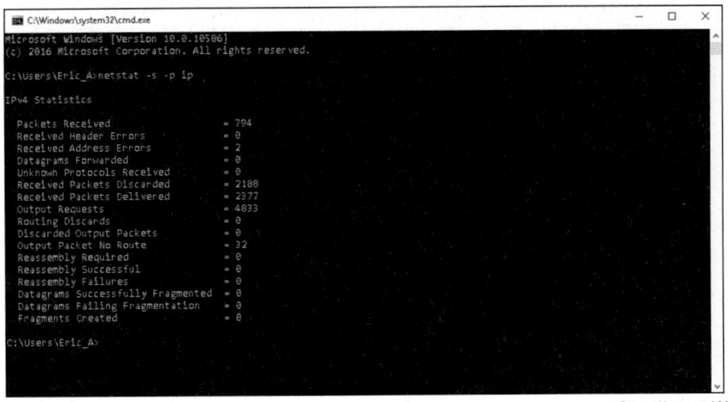

Goodheart-Willcox Publisher

The **netstat** command can be very handy as a troubleshooting tool. It is a way to collect statistics about TCP, IP, UDP, and ICMP. Of course, commercial analyzers display all this same data and more. Commercial network protocol analyzers can display statistics not only as raw data but also in bar, pie, or line chart form in a wide array of colors. These charts can be easily imported into a word-processing package to make formal presentations or written reports.

Nbtstat

The **nbtstat** command displays NetBIOS over TCP/IP statistics and information gathered from broadcasts, NetBIOS cache, and WINS services. It can be a very handy tool for verifying that the WINS server is functioning properly or that NetBIOS over TCP has been configured correctly for the network interface card. Look at the list of the common switches in Figure 17-39 that can be added to the **nbtstat** command to achieve the indicated results.

Copyright Goodheart-Willcox Co., Inc.

The application of a switch yields specific results. For example, by using the **nbtstat -c** command, you will display the contents of the cache of NetBIOS names, their host IP address, and the amount of time in seconds that the information will remain in the name cache. If there are no NetBIOS names stored in the cache, a message stating no names are stored will appear as demonstrated in Figure 17-40.

Figure 17-39 Issuing the **nbtstat** command at the command line displays a list of switches and their descriptions.

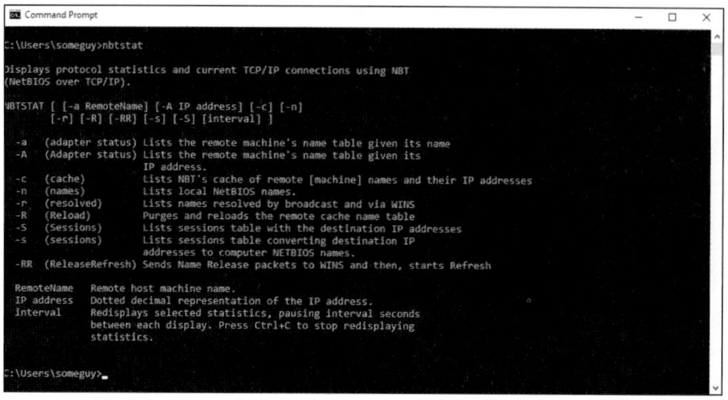

Goodheart-Willcox Publisher

Figure 17-40 The **nbtstat -c** command displays a list of NetBIOS names that are stored in a cache on the localhost.

Goodheart-Willcox Publisher

Notice the hexadecimal numbers located inside the greater-than and less-than symbols (< >) following the NetBIOS names in the list. The NetBIOS name actually contains 16 characters. The sixteenth character is a hexadecimal number used to provide additional programming information about the NetBIOS-named device. The hexadecimal number indicates if the device is a server or a workstation or if the name contains blank characters and other program-writing concerns. While a user can only enter 15 alphanumeric characters for a NetBIOS name, 16 characters are actually stored for each device. The user is unaware of the sixteenth character. To better illustrate the power of **nbtstat**, see the command examples listed in Figure 17-41.

ARP

The **arp** command is used to inspect the contents of the ARP table. The ARP table maps MAC addresses to IP addresses. The **arp** command can be useful when attempting to verify the physical address of another client or device on the local network. Simply ping the IP address or name of the other workstation or device and then check the ARP cache using the **arp -a** command.

Copyright Goodheart-Willcox Co., Inc.

Figure 17-41 Some **nbtstat** command examples.

Command	Description
nbtstat -n	This command displays the contents of the local computer NetBIOS name table.
nbtstat -a station24	This command displays the NetBIOS name table of the computer with the NetBIOS name of *Station24*.
nbtstat -A 192.168.0.23	This command displays the NetBIOS name table of the computer with the IP address 192.168.0.23.

Goodheart-Willcox Publisher

Ipconfig

Ipconfig is used on the Windows NT family of operating systems to identify the IP configuration of a computer. It reveals the assigned IP address, subnet mask, and default gateway. The equivalent command for Windows 98 and Windows 95 is **winipcfg**. On a Unix/Linux system, the equivalent command is the **ifconfig** command.

Nslookup

The **nslookup** command is used to display information about DNS servers. For example, by issuing the **nslookup** command from the command prompt, a reply would identify the name and IP address of the first available DNS server. The **nslookup** command can be used to verify that the DNS server is available and that there is a complete network media path to the DNS server.

When **nslookup** is used alone, it returns the network's default DNS server name and location. When used with a domain name, **nslookup** returns information about that domain, as shown in Figure 17-42. Notice that **nslookup** was used to gather information about the default Comcast server. It returned the complete default server name as well as the assigned IP address. To find out more about the **nslookup** command, issue the **/?** or **help** at the **nslookup** prompt.

Two Unix/Linux tools that perform a similar function as **nslookup** are **dig** (Domain Information Digger) and **host**. Both commands are run from the Unix/Linux command line. The **dig** and **host** commands are not supported by Windows operating systems.

Be aware there are many third-party tools that use the same name as these commands. Instead of the third-party tool using a command line, they typically provide a graphical user interface and display the retrieved information in a graphical form rather than a text-based form.

Route

The **route** command is used to view information contained in the local routing table. Figure 17-43 shows the results of issuing the **route print** command. The route command displays both IPv4 and IPv6 addresses, subnet masks, the default gateway, and the assigned IP address of the default gateway. The **netstat -r** command displays similar information to the **route print** command used in Figure 17-44.

Net

A very handy command line tool is the **net** command. This is the Microsoft command-line tool that can be used to investigate the local network. It is activated by typing net at the command prompt followed by a specific command. The commands are used to obtain information about the local network, such as a list of all the computers or shares on the LAN or statistics as related to the LAN. It can also be used to

Network+ Note

For the Network+ Exam, be sure you can identify which IP configuration tool command is used on each of the following operating systems: Windows NT-based, Windows 95 and 98, and Unix/Linux.

Figure 17-42 When the **nslookup** command is used alone, information about the network's default DNS server is given. When used with a domain name, information about that domain is given.

Goodheart-Willcox Publisher

Figure 17-43 The **route print** command displays the contents of the local routing table.

Goodheart-Willcox Publisher

Figure 17-44 The **netstat -r** command displays similar information as the route print command.

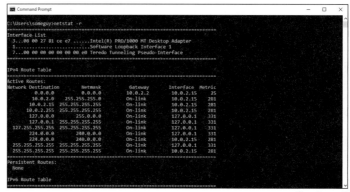

Goodheart-Willcox Publisher

start or stop a service. Entering net at the command line will display the commands and syntax to be used with this command, as demonstrated in Figure 17-45.

One of the most useful net commands is **net view**. This command will reveal all workstations and servers currently online in the LAN. You can also display information about the current user by typing and entering whoami at the command prompt. The command **hostname** will display the assigned host name of the computer. The **net stats workstation** command will display a list of network statistics for the workstation at which the command is issued, similar to Figure 17-46.

To view an extensive list of command-line tools, see http://technet.microsoft.com/en-us/library/bb490719.aspx and http://technet.microsoft.com/en-us/library/bb490890.aspx. You can also locate these web pages by conducting an Internet search using the search phrase Microsoft TechNet Net commands.

Copyright Goodheart-Willcox Co., Inc.

Figure 17-45 The **net** command can be used to view LAN information, such as the assigned computer name, username, and what shares are available.

Goodheart-Willcox Publisher

Figure 17-46 The **net stats workstation** command produces a list of workstation network statistics.

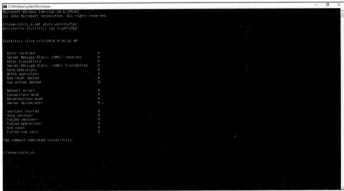

Goodheart-Willcox Publisher

Miscellaneous Issues

There are other common problems that do not necessarily fit into one of the preceding categories neatly, for example, untrusted SSL certificates. Untrusted SSL certificates are a significant security issue. When visiting a website, the browser will warn you if the SSL certificate cannot be verified. This means that the correct web server could not be confirmed by the client. However, the user can choose to proceed anyway. Connecting despite an untrusted or unverified SSL certificate can potentially expose the connection to interception through a man-in-the-middle attack. This problem can be easily mitigated by user education.

While it may seem like an odd problem, incorrect time is an issue that can have serious ramifications. Time should be synchronized among networked devices. Kerberos authentication depends on tickets with a short life span. If computers on a network do not have time synchronized, a legitimate ticket could be seen as expired, preventing users from authenticating to services. This can be resolved by setting the domain controller as the source for time synchronization as opposed to a hardware clock.

Incorrect ACL settings are also an issue. Access-control lists are meant to allow authorized personnel access and to restrict others. Any incorrect settings on any ACL could either allow unauthorized people to access resources or prevent legitimate users from gaining access.

NET
5.5

Copyright Goodheart-Willcox Co., Inc.

Summary

CompTIA Network+ Troubleshooting Methodology

- The seven steps to troubleshooting a network as outlined by CompTIA are: Identify the problem; establish a theory of probable cause; test the theory to determine the cause; establish a plan of action to resolve the problem and identify potential effects; implement the solution or escalate if necessary; verify full system functionality and, if applicable, implement preventive measures; document findings, actions, and outcomes.
- Asking questions is the easiest way to obtain important information that may help diagnose the problem.
- Always ask about items that have recently changed that could have caused the problem.

Stages of Computer Operation

- The three general areas of server/computer operation to consider when troubleshooting computer systems are during the POST, operating system loading and initiation, and after a successful logon.
- The most common reason for failure during the POST is a hardware failure.
- The most common reason for failure after the POST and before a successful logon is corruption of an essential operating system file or a driver failure.
- The most common reason for a system failure after a successful system logon is application software or a service.
- One of the best tools for identifying a problem software application or service is System Configuration (**msconfig.exe**).

Detailed Computer Startup Process

- The initial startup phase occurs when the POST completes and the operating system starts to load.
- The five major phases of the boot process are POST, initial startup phase, Windows Boot Loader or Boot Manager phase, Kernel loading phase, and logon phase.
- Extensible Firmware Interface (EFI) is a new approach to the BIOS system.
- EFI is required on computers to use a new file-system directory structure called *GUID*.
- The Windows Boot Manager used in Windows allows you to select which operating system to load when more than one operating system is installed.
- Press [F8] after the POST and before the operating system loads to access the **Advanced Boot Options** menu.
- The Windows Boot Manager and Boot Loader were introduced in Windows Vista and Windows Server 2008.

Windows-Based Troubleshooting Tools

- The **Safe Mode** option allows the computer to boot with a limited number of system drivers and memory space.

Copyright Goodheart-Willcox Co., Inc.

- System Restore replaces the current registry settings with an earlier set of registry settings.
- The **Last Known Good Configuration** option will attempt to load the operating system using the last set of registry data.

System Recovery Strategies and Methods

- A disk image is an exact copy of the operating system and all files sector by sector.
- The Windows 7 System Recovery Options items are **Startup Repair**, **System Restore**, **System Image Recovery**, **Windows Memory Diagnostic**, and **Command Prompt**.
- Windows 10 System Recovery Options include **Restore from a restore point**, **System Restore**, **System Reset**, **Reinstall Windows**, and **Command Prompt**.

Troubleshooting Dual-Boot Systems

- The System Configuration tool (**msconfig.exe**) can be used to select which startup programs and services run during the startup process.
- The Windows XP **boot.ini** file has been replaced with the Boot Configuration Data (BCD) starting with Windows Vista.

Server Data Integrity and Performance

- Ways to ensure data integrity of a network server and performance involve UPS units, RAID systems, frequent data backups, malware protection, and applying service packs and patches.

Troubleshooting the Network Infrastructure

- The Network Diagnostics utility is designed for Windows to diagnose common network problems and identify possible causes.
- Network and Sharing Center was first introduced in Windows Vista and Windows Server 2008 and provides a centralized location for network configuration and troubleshooting.
- In Network and Sharing Center, a red *X* indicates no connection and a yellow triangle containing an exclamation mark indicates a problem.

Troubleshooting the Most Common Network Problems

- The most common network errors are caused by human interaction with the network system.
- Additional, commonly encountered network problems include the inability of a user to log on to the network or computer, loose or no connection, inability to access shares, inability to print to a network printer, printer is printing gibberish, computer has a virus or worm, inability to obtain a proper IPv4 address, inability to connect to an application server, inability to access VoIP services, duplex mismatch, and inability to access the Internet.

Troubleshooting Common Wireless Problems

- Four common problems associated with wireless networks are wrong ESSID, signal bounce, mismatched encryption configurations, and unbalanced signal-to-noise ratio.

Copyright Goodheart-Willcox Co., Inc.

Troubleshooting with TCP/IP Utilities

- The command-line tools used to verify the network path are **ping** and **tracert**.
- The command-line tools used to verify the network path and identify possible bottlenecks by sending a series of ICMP echo requests over a period of time is **pathping**.

Miscellaneous Issues

- Additional problems on a network can include incorrect time and ACL settings.

Review Questions

1. List the seven steps recommended for network troubleshooting as outlined by CompTIA.
2. What is the start of any computer boot process?
3. When troubleshooting a computer or server, what three major stages of computer operation should you observe to determine at which stage the system failure occurred?
4. What is the final stage of the boot process?
5. What are the two types of system firmware?
6. Which Windows program replaced the boot loader (ntldr)?
7. What controls the sequence of boot device hardware, such as the hard disk drive, floppy disk, and CD-ROM?
8. What is the name of the Windows logon executable file?
9. Which two tools will solve most problems that occur after the system logon?
10. What executable file is loaded and run immediately after a successful logon?
11. List six troubleshooting tools used in Windows-based operating systems.
12. Which special function key is used to access the **Advanced Boot Options** menu?
13. Which **Advanced Boot Options** menu option will use the registry settings from the last successful boot?
14. What provides the best protection from viruses, worms, and unforeseen disasters?
15. List the menu items displayed in the Windows 10 system repair option from a Windows installation disc.
16. What is the advantage of using a virtual computer over a dual-boot or multiboot PC?
17. List items that will help maintain server integrity and performance.

Copyright Goodheart-Willcox Co., Inc.

18. Explain the term *loopback test*.

19. What is the most common problem encountered in a network?

20. What is a dead drop?

21. What would an assigned IP address of 169.254.0.12 indicate?

22. What is the most common problem that prevents a user from accessing VoIP services?

23. What condition occurs when one network device is configured for half-duplex and the other is configured for full-duplex?

24. What service is typically directly related to Internet access?

25. What wireless connection problem can usually be cleared by repositioning the wireless device?

26. What two wireless configuration options can prevent a user from establishing a connection?

27. What TCP/IP utility is designed to verify a connection between the source and destination quickly?

28. What network device could be responsible for preventing an ICMP echo request?

29. Which TCP/IP utility performs the same functions as **tracert** and also performs a statistical analysis of the path over a period of time?

30. What is the Unix/Linux command equivalent of the Windows NT **tracert** command?

31. Which TCP/IP utility is designed to list all routers along a path to a distant destination?

32. Which TCP/IP utility will display statistics for IP, TCP, ICMP, and UDP?

33. What command is used to view information contained in the local routing table?

34. What is an untrusted SSL certificate?

35. How can an incorrect time issue be resolved on a network?

✚ Sample Network+ Exam Questions

1. Teri is trying to troubleshoot cable connection issues with her network. Which command would she most likely use to verify a cable connection to the server on the LAN?

   A. **netstat**

   B. **ping**

   C. **ifconfig**

   D. **tracert**

Copyright Goodheart-Willcox Co., Inc.

2. Ethan has been trying to fix connectivity issues with a computer on his network. He believes there has been a change that has caused the problem. He wants to return to the last known good configuration. Where is the **Last Known Good Configuration** option located?

    A. It is located in the System Configuration collection of tools.

    B. It appears after inserting the operating system installation DVD immediately after the computer is rebooted.

    C. It is an option located in the **Advanced Boot Options** menu list.

    D. It is an option located off the **Start** menu under the **Administrative Tools**.

3. Michelle wants to limit what services start when her Windows workstation boots. Which tool can be used to select or limit startup programs in Windows?

    A. File Server Resource Manager

    B. **sysconfig**

    C. **msconfig**

    D. Network Policy Server

4. A workstation is connected to an Ethernet 100BaseT network. All workstations are configured for DHCP. You run **ipconfig** and see that the following IPv4 address is being used: 169.254.0.123. What would be the next most appropriate action?

    A. Replace the network adapter.

    B. Replace the network cable.

    C. Ping the DHCP server.

    D. Check the network adapter properties to see if a static IPv4 address has been assigned.

5. You are trying to determine what connections are active in your company's file server. Which network tool would you use to view all the active TCP and UDP ports?

    A. **ARP**

    B. **netstat**

    C. **nslookup**

    D. **ipconfig**

Copyright Goodheart-Willcox Co., Inc.

6. Carole has been assigned the task of troubleshooting cable problems. Which type of meter would be most appropriate for checking a 100BaseFX cable?

   A. Ohmmeter

   B. Ammeter

   C. Multimeter

   D. OTDR meter

7. You have just successfully booted a Linux server. Which command would be the most appropriate to check the server network adapter IP address assignment?

   A. **dig**

   B. **nslookup**

   C. **ipconfig**

   D. **pingpath**

8. You want to block outsiders from using ping to probe your network. Which protocol would you block using a firewall to prevent probes by the **ping** command?

   A. TFTP

   B. ICMP

   C. HTTP

   D. SSL

9. Which command would you issue from the command prompt to view the total number of packets sent and received from a workstation?

   A. **ping -w**

   B. **arp -a**

   C. **tracert -d**

   D. **netstat -e**

10. What is the first thing you should do when troubleshooting a network problem?

    A. Establish what has changed.

    B. Identify the symptoms and problems.

    C. Select the most probable cause.

    D. Implement an action plan.

Designing and Installing a New Network

Network+ Certification Exam Objectives

The Network+ Certification Exam does not cover in-depth specifications and standards or installing network systems. CompTIA typically limits its questions to the general installation topics provided in this chapter, such as TIA/EIA standards and architectural design elements. Be sure to know the common horizontal wiring cable standards for distances.

Objectives

2.1: Termination Points

2.5: Termination—Demarcation Point, Smart Jack

3.2: Availability Concepts—Fault Tolerance

5.2: Hardware Tools—Punch down Tool

Learning Outcomes

- Summarize the factors to consider when designing a network.
- List available tools that can help design a network.
- Describe the installation process of a new network.
- Identify required specifications of a network design.
- List organizations that develop important networking and electrical standards.

Copyright Goodheart-Willcox Co., Inc.

Key Terms

backbone
consolidation point (CP)
demarcation point
entrance facility
equipment room
horizontal cross connect
horizontal wiring
insulation-displacement connector
    (IDC)

main distribution frame (MDF)
main entrance room
multi-user telecommunication outlet
    assembly (MUTOA)
naming convention
network interface device (NID)
optical network terminal (ONT)
patch panel
punch down block

punch down tool
smart jack
telecommunication closet
telecommunication room
work area

Overview

This chapter introduces the concepts and related knowledge needed to design network systems. At this point in your networking course, you should be capable of designing a small-office/home-office (SOHO) network without assistance. Larger networks can be a challenge. System designers for large networks require years of training in all aspects of networking. The Microsoft Learning website (www.microsoft.com/learning/en/us/default.aspx) has a complete listing of Microsoft certifications as they relate to network installation, maintenance, and design.

This chapter is not intended to prepare you for a network infrastructure-design examination, but rather to provide you with an introduction to network design concepts. This chapter also reinforces concepts learned earlier in the textbook.

Tech Tip

Now that you have mastered the basics, you may wish to further your education after finishing this course by taking a course on network design. It can help to navigate the Internet for network-design certification exams and familiarizing yourself with their standards, objectives, and expectations.

Needs Assessment and Design

The first step of any design project is conducting a needs assessment. A *needs assessment* is a process used by companies or organizations for determining and addressing needs or for making organizational improvements. The process may be formal or informal, depending on the size of the project. For example, a needs assessment for a change in a small-office network can be as simple as interviewing the owner of the company on a one-on-one basis. However, a complex change involving hundreds or thousands of workstations and thousands of employees may involve a series of formal meetings with numerous personnel. It may also involve several surveys conducted over a long period of time. The scope of the needs assessment is dictated by the complexity of the project. Essentially, this is just determining exactly what a network actually needs. This prevents the building of an inadequate network or spending more money than was necessary.

There are many factors to consider when designing a new network or modifying an existing network. Figure 18-1 lists questions to consider when designing a network. The questions are organized by physical network structure, security, application, organizational structure, fault tolerance, and data integrity. The following sections take a closer look at some of these questions.

Figure 18-1 Questions to consider when designing a network. The questions are organized by physical network structure, security, application, organizational structure, and fault tolerance and data integrity.

Questions to Consider When Designing a Network
Physical Network Structure
• What type of business is performed at the site?
• What network requirements are necessary for business operations?
• How large is the geographic area to be networked?
• How many users will there be on the network?
• What types of resources are needed (Internet access, printers, and such)?
• Is remote access by sales personnel or other staff required?
• What services will be provided (e-mail, Internet, videoconferencing, and such)?
• How will the Internet be accessed (modem, DSL, ISDN, T1, fractional T1, satellite)?
• What type of electrical concerns should be considered?
• Where will equipment be placed?
• What is the total IT budget?
Security
• What level of security is required?
• What is the physical security level available and required?
• Will there be a firewall?
• Will there be a VPN?
• Will security procedures include passwords, shares, and encryption?
Application
• How much storage will each user require?
• What types of software application packages will be needed on the network (word processing, accounting, spreadsheet, database, and such)?
Organizational Structure
• How do different people, departments, or groups within the organization share data?
• How can services be divided and resources allocated to reduce network traffic?
• Should the security database be divided or replicated to reduce network traffic?
Fault Tolerance and Data Integrity
• How important is data integrity?
• How important is availability?
• What are the data recovery requirements?
• What are the data integrity requirements?
• What are the data redundancy requirements?
• What type of RAID level should be implemented?
• Should server clustering be implemented?
• What data backup method will be implemented?

Goodheart-Willcox Publisher

Physical Network Structure

Note

The term *network infrastructure* is often used to describe the physical aspects of the network, such as cabling and network devices.

The physical structure of a network is typically the first concern of the network designer. The physical structure consists of network devices and media. The number of users and geographic layout determine the type of network equipment and media needed. A company with ten employees working in a small office may only require a single hub to link workstations to the network. Cable length and network traffic will most likely not be an issue. A large company that spans several floors of a building and has many departments will typically need to divide the physical structure of the network into several LANs or virtual LANs to overcome cable length and network traffic issues. This type of network may require a fiber-optic backbone and many switches. A company that spans several geographic locations will need to use leased lines or implement a virtual private network (VPN).

Copyright Goodheart-Willcox Co., Inc.

Other factors that determine the type of network equipment and media needed are remote access to and from the network. A company sales force often requires remote access to the network while they are on the road or working from various locations within the state or country. For mobile employees, wireless access or a VPN connection over the Internet may be suitable. A router, firewall, and high-bandwidth Internet access device will be needed for employees working within the company who need to access the Internet.

Many businesses require a website for providing an online catalog of products and supporting online sales. The website can be configured as part of the network system or be outsourced to a web-hosting service. When outsourced, the business leases space from the web-hosting service, which provides hardware and software support on 24/7/365 basis. It also provides security.

Establishing a company website using a server inside the company network requires expertise and can be quite an expensive proposition. In general, small websites should be outsourced to be cost-effective. When a large website is required for a business, it may be less expensive for the business to host its own website by installing the necessary hardware and software and hiring additional personnel.

Security

Security is vital for a business of any size that provides online sales or remote access. A firewall is typically required to control traffic to and from the network and to block access to sensitive data. The type of firewall to be installed, such as firewall software or a firewall device, must be decided. Cost is typically a main factor when selecting a firewall.

A set of written security procedures needs to be established and enforced. This includes passwords, network access, and the physical security of server rooms and individual workstations. All personnel using the network need to be trained in security procedures. Obviously, security includes more than just a firewall and policies. Recall that security was covered in detail in Chapter 15.

Application

A network designer must note the types of applications network users will need. A company using only word-processing and spreadsheet programs will typically not require a large amount of hard drive space on the server for files. A company using a database program with a large database of customers will require a large amount of hard drive space. A network designer must determine the current size of the database and determine the future size due to growth.

Organizational Structure

Questions about organizational structure help determine the number of servers, directory structure, location of resources, and partition and volume configuration. It is important to note how the company is organized and how data is shared among departments or workgroups. The organizational structure of a company is typically reflected in the organizational structure of the security database, or directory. In a large company, services and resources must be allocated to reduce network traffic. A directory structure must be partitioned to do the same. Hard drive partitions and volumes within a server should also reflect how the company is organized and how data is shared. This will aid in security and system recovery. A network designer must also establish a naming convention for network objects such as users, printers, servers, and workstations as well as the types of attributes that will be filled in for each

Copyright Goodheart-Willcox Co., Inc.

user. The implementation of TCP/IP and domain names should be planned at this time.

TCP/IP

Typically, all networks use TCP/IP as their default protocol. How TCP/IP will be implemented for the network requires planning. A network designer must decide if the IP addresses will be assigned statically or dynamically. If dynamically assigned, the designer should determine which server will act as a DHCP server and document the IP address ranges of the IP address pools.

Online purchasing and catalogs are a part of most businesses. An assigned IP address will most likely be required. Also, most companies require a domain name to be used as their URL. To see if a domain name is in use by another company, a search can be conducted on the Internet. Most web-hosting sites provide a domain name search for free, such as that shown in Figure 18-2. After a unique name is found for the company, it can be purchased through a web-host provider. There is a recurring cost each year for the ownership of the name. Domain names can also be purchased from commercial vendors. Originally, URL names were purchased from the US government. As the demand increased, the government allowed commercial vendors to distribute the names for a reasonable cost—under governmental supervision, of course.

Figure 18-2 A domain name search engine provided by a domain name registration company.

Goodheart-Willcox Publisher

Number of Servers

A single server may be sufficient for the entire network, or several servers may be required. The overall requirements of the network structure determine the number of servers needed. Look at the following list of possible server roles:

- application server
- DHCP server
- DNS server
- file server
- firewall

Copyright Goodheart-Willcox Co., Inc.

- gateway
- mail server
- RADIUS server
- RAS server
- SQL server
- thin client terminal service server
- web server

There are many roles and services required by a network server based on the requirements of the business. A server may serve a single role or several. This is typically determined by a server's resources and physical location in the network.

Designing the Directory Structure

After all the information has been gathered concerning the structure of the organization (people, groups, services, software, workflow through the departments, and business requirements), the directory structure can be designed. There are tools that can be used to help design the directory structure. These tools are available from all the major network operating system vendors and third-party software developers.

All of the most common directory structure designs are based on the Lightweight Directory Access Protocol (LDAP). The most common directory structures based on LDAP are listed in Figure 18-3.

Figure 18-3 Common directory structures based on LDAP.

Operating System	Directory
Microsoft	Active Directory
IBM	Directory Server
Sun Microsystems	ONE Integrated Server
Open Source Unix/Linux	OpenLDAP

Goodheart-Willcox Publisher

LDAP has become the de facto standard for directory structures. LDAP was designed to overcome limitations of previous proprietary network designs. Many of the network designs were very complex and often required third-party software solutions for integrating different systems into a single unit. With the adoption of TCP/IP as the default Internet protocol of all major network systems and LDAP serving as the core for directory structures, networking systems from different companies are becoming easier to integrate.

LDAP is organized into major areas including the root, country, organization, organizational units, objects, and individuals. The exact name used for the components varies somewhat by each network operating system vendor. The name may be different, but the concept and function of the features are the same. A visual representation of LDAP organization can be seen in Figure 18-4.

The top of the directory structure is the root. Next is the country container, which is optional in most operating systems. The structure is then divided into organizations followed by organizational units. The last elements are objects. This structure closely resembles the Internet hierarchical structure.

This is a very brief summary of the LDAP directory structure. The amount of knowledge required to design an LDAP directory structure requires a complete course. You may wish to take a course on directory design later in your studies.

Tech Tip

Microsoft Visio includes templates to assist you in designing an LDAP directory structure.

Figure 18-4 LDAP organization.

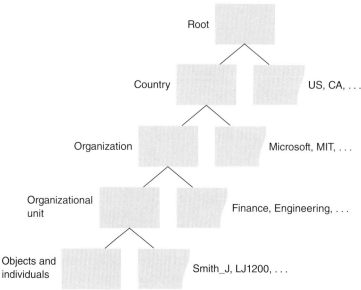

Goodheart-Willcox Publisher

Directory Structure Schema

The directory structure is composed of many different objects. Each object has a set of attributes associated with it. Some attributes are mandatory, such as logon name and full name, and some are optional, such as the user's home address and contact information. The network designer should determine and document a standard set of attributes for all users.

Naming Conventions

A **naming convention** is a standard naming format that is used when providing names for network objects. A naming convention should be established and a written policy developed, especially for a large network installation that involves many technicians. Establishing a naming convention for objects such as users, printers, and servers provides for consistency throughout the system. The consistency makes the system much easier to troubleshoot and locate objects.

A username may be established in several different ways. For example, various possible logon names for James Smith include the following:

- Jsmith
- SmithJ
- Smith_J
- J_Smith

The most commonly accepted form is last name, underscore, and the initial of the first name. While this is a common form, a more security conscious company may want a different naming convention that would be much harder for an outsider to guess, such as *Smith_J123*. When a username is easy to guess, the administrator has jeopardized half of the authentication process. Only the password needs to be guessed to access the network. This is why a naming convention that is more difficult to guess should be considered. In fact, a network administrator does not have to assign usernames that resemble the users' names unless dictated by the client or company.

A naming convention should be established that describes and identifies all equipment classified as an object. For example, thought should be given to how

Tech Tip

Remember, NetBIOS names are limited to 15 characters. If the network has Windows legacy operating systems, you may want to limit the number of characters in a name to 15. Otherwise, name-resolving problems can arise.

Tech Tip

Some systems have a more extensive set of rules for naming conventions. This can cause some system interoperability problems. For example, some Unix/Linux systems typically require that only lowercase letters be used for object names because object names are case-sensitive.

Copyright Goodheart-Willcox Co., Inc.

workstations, servers, printers, and other hardware are named. A workstation may reveal its location as part of the name, such as *WS-23-Bld4Rm110*. The location and the purpose of the server can be incorporated into the server name. This helps a technician readily identify a server in a large corporate environment or in a network that is spread across the country or world. Some examples of abbreviations that can be incorporated into object names include those in Figure 18-5.

Figure 18-5 Examples of abbreviations that can be incorporated into object names.

Classification	Name	Abbreviation
Business locations	California	CA
	Chicago	CHI
	Florida	FL
	Headquarters	HQ
	New York City	NYC
	Operations	OPS
Server role identification	Applications	APPS
	Backup server	BKUP
	Domain Name Server	DNS
	File server	FS
	Gateway (router, proxy server, firewall, etc.)	GW
	Web server	WEB
Workstation and printer identification	Building	BLD
	Color laser printer	CLP
	Department	DPT
	Inkjet	IJ
	LaserJet	LJ
	Room location number	RM
	Workstation	WS

Goodheart-Willcox Publisher

A server name may look like the following: *HQServer1*. The server may also follow the LDAP naming convention to match an Internet URL such as HQServer1.ABCcorp.com. This server is located at the headquarters of ABC Corporation and functions as a gateway to the Internet.

Workstations will also have a naming convention based on similar abbreviations. Room numbers, building identifiers, or departments can be incorporated into the name. For example, a workstation name for the 12th workstation in the accounting department in room 302 of building H might look like *WS12ACCBldH302* or *WS12_ACC_BLD_H302*. It is best to avoid using usernames to identify workstations because employees often leave the job or are promoted, which means the username no longer matches the workstation name.

It is important that all equipment or nodes on a network have a unique name. Be careful when designing a naming convention. It is easy to duplicate a workstation name while attempting to create a naming convention. For example, if you use a workstation number and room number and not a building identifier, you could easily create duplicate names if more than one building exists. A name such as *WS12RM11*, which uses only a workstation number and room number, can exist in more than one building. This results in duplicate names.

A network designer should also consider any naming restrictions. Is there a maximum number of letters that can be used? Are there any reserved symbols that cannot be used? Remember that the network may be remotely connected to another

Copyright Goodheart-Willcox Co., Inc.

network with a different naming requirement. When creating names for users, workstations, servers, printers, and other network objects, remember to be consistent. Create a maximum length, and keep the name compatible with other operating systems.

Figure 18-6 lists typical symbols that should be avoided when creating object names. These symbols are the most universally recognized as reserved symbols and cannot be used by most operating systems for file or object names. You will see these symbols typically listed by Microsoft as well as Unix/Linux. These special symbols should also be avoided for LDAP directory structures. The symbols have special programming functions and should be avoided; otherwise, unexpected results could occur.

Figure 18-6 Typical symbols that should be avoided when creating names in any of the major operating systems.

Symbol	Description
/	Forward slash
\	Backslash
:	Colon
;	Semicolon
,	Comma
*	Asterisk
[ ]	Brackets
< >	Greater and lesser than
|	Pipe
+	Plus sign
=	Equal sign
?	Question mark

Goodheart-Willcox Publisher

Partition and Volume Structure

The partitioning of storage devices is an important aspect to consider. You should not simply create one partition and place all files in it. The design should reflect the work activities of the company and reinforce security. For example, from a security aspect, a separate partition should be used to house the operating system and operating system boot files. The partition can be created to allow access to administrators. This will add an additional layer of security, in addition to typical user permissions. Work-related partitions can be used to isolate functions such as public shares, artwork, Internet downloads, workgroups, departments, or other features unique to the workplace. The partitioning design should be a reflection of the overall directory design.

The system structure of the hard disk drive must be designed before installing the network operating system. The two main concerns of partition design are security and data recovery. A partition should be designed to limit access and accommodate system recovery after failure. You can design the system to allow users to access only specific parts of the hard disk drive system. Limiting access strengthens the security of the network from unauthorized users inside and outside of an organization.

The hard disk drive system should also be organized to allow efficient system backups. For example, all data storage can be confined to a particular partition or volume. This will allow for easy backup of important system information. The drive that contains the data could easily be mirrored to provide a simple recovery system. The exact design of the partition or volume structure varies and depends mainly on the project administrator.

Copyright Goodheart-Willcox Co., Inc.

Fault Tolerance and Data Integrity

3.2 NET

The importance a company places on fault tolerance determines the type of RAID system needed or if server mirroring or clustering should be used. Do not forget that fault tolerance also includes the directory structure. A designer should determine how the directory structure is partitioned and replicated, not only to reduce network traffic, but also to provide for redundancy should one of the servers that hosts the directory database fail.

The importance a company places on data integrity determines the type of electrical system that should be employed. Remember, a dedicated electrical system used for computers and networks helps ensure data integrity by eliminating surges produced by office equipment. Many electrical devices, such as motor-driven devices that use a brush-type motor (kitchen appliances, office machines, vacuum cleaners, drills, saws, and such) produce voltage spikes during normal usage. These voltage spikes travel along the entire length of the circuit until they encounter suppression devices, such as transformers or voltage suppressers. If sensitive computer equipment share the same circuit as equipment that produce voltage spikes, computer equipment can be damaged.

The isolation of the electrical system starts in the electrical equipment room. Typically, a separate electrical panel is installed to serve only network equipment. The network equipment includes the computers throughout the facility. The electrical feed from the regular electrical supply to the dedicated network system panel typically uses isolation transformers to separate the two systems. The outlets used for computers are identified by a special color, such as orange.

Network Design Tools

There are many utilities and case studies available to help with network design. *Case studies* typically explain how an actual network was designed and implemented. Visiting the support website of the operating system used will often list available utilities and case studies. They can provide a valuable insight into how you might approach your design.

Microsoft Planning Tools

Planning a network system is not an easy task. To help with the planning, Microsoft, as well as other companies, offer tools to assist you when planning or designing a network system. One such item you may be interested in is Microsoft's *Infrastructure Planning and Design Guide Series*.

The *Infrastructure Planning and Design Guide Series* is part of the Solution Accelerators technical library on the TechNet website. Other guides available cover topics such as security, virtualization, server configuration, SQL server, and more, as shown in Figure 18-7.

Microsoft Assessment and Planning (MAP) Toolkit

The Microsoft Assessment and Planning (MAP) toolkit is a free, downloadable tool to help you update or migrate an existing network system. Included in the MAP toolkit are manuals and guides to help you use the kit, as demonstrated in Figure 18-8.

The MAP toolkit will automatically survey the existing network and inventory all virtual and non-virtual computers and servers. The toolkit needs to be configured before conducting the assessment. Certain information, such as the administrator name and password, must be supplied as well as the type of assessment desired. The toolkit will automatically discover network computers and servers after additional

Note

The guides and tools in this section are current at the time of this writing. When visiting the Microsoft support site for planning guides and tools, you may expect changes and updates as well as beta tools.

Copyright Goodheart-Willcox Co., Inc.

Figure 18-7 Microsoft's *Infrastructure Planning and Design Guide Series* can help you to plan or design a network system. This series is part of the Solution Accelerators technical library on the Microsoft TechNet website.

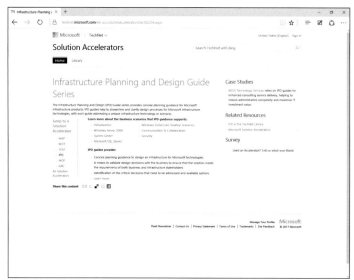

Goodheart-Willcox Publisher

Figure 18-8 The Microsoft Assessment and Planning Toolkit can help you plan a successful network upgrade or migration.

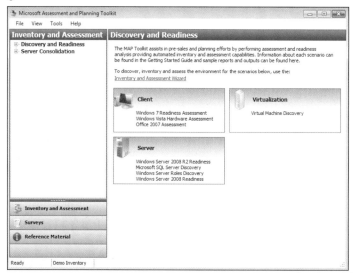

Goodheart-Willcox Publisher

information, such as a range of IP addresses and the Active Directory domain name, is provided.

The Microsoft Assessment and Planning Toolkit provides a summary of the inventory and assessment when completed, similar to that seen in Figure 18-9. Some of the items determined by the toolkit are how many computers in the network are ready for upgrade. A detailed report of the results can also be exported to one of Microsoft's Office software applications such as Excel or Word. Then, the results can easily be incorporated into a formal report.

To learn more about Microsoft planning tools and guides, visit http://technet.microsoft.com/en-us/solutionaccelerators/ee382254.aspx. This Microsoft website provides an entire series of free, downloadable guides for planning Active Directory domain services, file services, print services, Windows Server virtualization,

Copyright Goodheart-Willcox Co., Inc.

and more. To access this website, you can also use the search phrase Microsoft Active Directory Domain Services or Microsoft Infrastructure Planning and Design.

Microsoft Visio

Microsoft Visio is a powerful drawing tool used to diagram network systems and many other types of drawings, such as electrical, mechanical, floor plans, site plans, and LDAP structures. Figure 18-10 displays a sample Microsoft Visio drawing of a network. Various symbols or icons are available to incorporate into the drawing. This drawing is only two dimensional, but Microsoft Visio is capable of three-dimensional drawings as well. This is an extremely important tool for planning and documenting network systems. Network analyzer and troubleshooting software from Fluke can export information into a Microsoft Visio graphical format. Equipment manufacturers provide stencils and templates of their hardware devices so they can be incorporated easily into a Microsoft Visio drawing. The stencils are available for download.

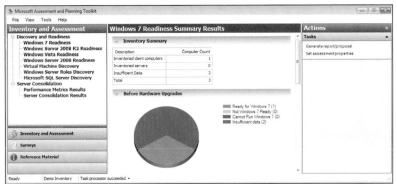

Goodheart-Willcox Publisher

Figure 18-9 The Microsoft Assessment and Planning Toolkit provides a summary expressed as a pie chart when the inventory is completed.

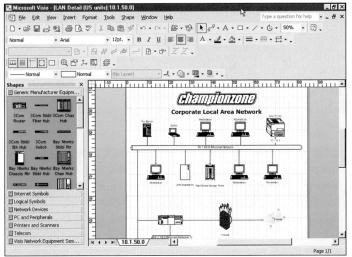

Goodheart-Willcox Publisher

Figure 18-10 A network designer can use the Microsoft Visio program to design the physical structure and directory structure of a network.

NetworkView

Similar to Microsoft Visio, *NetworkView* is a software application that allows network designers to create a map of a network. It can examine existing networks and document hardware located in the network system. It does this by sending out protocol probes to identify hardware IP addresses, names, operating systems, and more. An example of a NetworkView map is shown in Figure 18-11.

Copyright Goodheart-Willcox Co., Inc.

Figure 18-11 Some software programs, such as NetworkView, can examine an existing network and document hardware located in the network system.

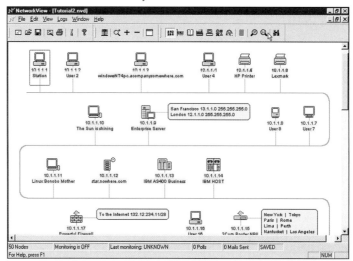

Goodheart-Willcox Publisher

The NetworkView software program identifies all TCP/IP nodes in a network, using DNS, SNMP, TCP ports, and MAC addresses. It draws a high-quality color map of any size that can be printed or saved for future use. This is an extremely valuable tool for identifying existing equipment in a network system that has incomplete or nonexistent drawings.

Installation Process

The installation of a network is a long process that requires teamwork and coordination. This process begins by a team coming together to schedule various aspects of installation. A large network requires a planning team with experts from a variety of network skills. Experts might include directory designers, hardware installers, cable installers, security experts, and web-hosting experts. Together, they put together a timeline for the installation process, which includes installation, implementation, documentation, and training.

Developing a Timeline

A *timeline* is a chronological listing of expected project progress and is essential for coordinating all project activities. The timeline must outline the entire project from beginning to end. It is a planning tool that allows everyone involved to chart the pace of the project and to determine if it will be completed on time.

A series of meetings should be scheduled with everyone involved in the project to discuss work accomplished and identify any problems as they arise. The meetings keep everyone informed and up-to-date, especially if circumstances require a change in the timeline. For example, a delay in delivery of a hardware item, such as a particular router or server, may require a change in the sequence of work activities. If it is expected that the server will be delivered late, the people responsible for installing the operating system and setting up the directory structure need to be notified.

Figure 18-12 shows an example of a timeline. There are several different styles of timelines. The timeline in the example is a Gantt chart. Notice that major tasks are listed. The duration of time they will take to perform is shown in a graphical form in the last column. Bars represent the time period allocated for the particular task. Notice that the time periods of some tasks run concurrently with the time period of

Copyright Goodheart-Willcox Co., Inc.

Figure 18-12 An example of a timeline for a network installation project.

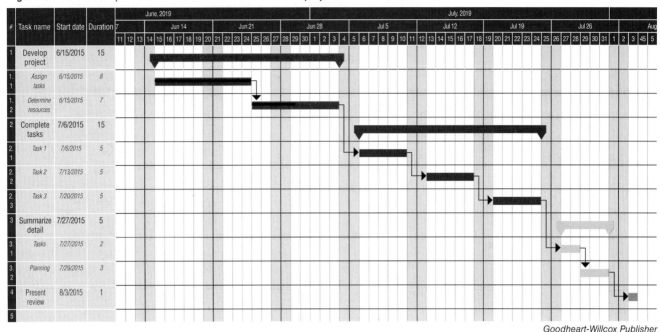

Goodheart-Willcox Publisher

other tasks. For example, task 1 and tasks 8–10 share some of the same time period. This means that while the conduit is installed at the job site, the server can be prepared away from the site.

Installation

Microsoft provides tools for automatic installation of multiple copies of software and operating systems. For example, original equipment manufacturers (OEMs) use an imaging toolkit to install operating systems automatically. One of the original kits used during the Windows XP era was called the *System Preparation tool* (sysprep.exe). Today, Microsoft provides the Windows Automated Installation Kit (AIK), which is a set of tools that automates the installation process. In short, a disk image is created containing the operating system, needed hardware drivers, and software applications. In essence, a clone is created of an "ideal" computer. Each computer must have identical hardware components. The disk image is then automatically copied and installed on all computers. This method saves thousands of technician-hours when creating or updating a large enterprise network. To learn more about Windows AIK, or other deployment options for Windows 10, visit https://docs.microsoft.com/en-us/windows/deployment/windows-deployment-scenarios-and-tools or conduct a search using the key terms Windows 10 Microsoft Windows Automated Installation Kit.

Implementation

After installing the network, the next step is implementation. Implementing and testing the network is a necessity that takes time. Most new, large networks will have problems, even those installed after many hours of planning. There are always oversights because it is impossible to predict every possible issue or aspect of usage. All sections of a network need to be tested to ensure there are no bottlenecks and the hardware and software are in working order. This is typically a combined effort involving the installation crew and business personnel.

Business personnel need to test the system by simulating or actually performing their job duties. Such duties may involve using printers, accessing the Internet, saving data to the backup location, engaging in a network videoconference, exchanging e-mail, and remotely accessing the network. Only after exhaustive testing can business personnel be sure the network hardware and software have been installed to expectation.

Documentation

Network documentation is vital to an organized approach of network installation and continued service. A set of network documents with specific procedures for security and other areas of network usage must be developed. Rules need to be established to ensure proper use of equipment and software and to prevent the company from being liable for actions taken by its employees.

For example, a set of policies needs to be established that clarify unauthorized use of the network and equipment. This is part of a network's *acceptable use policy*. Some examples of unauthorized use of the network are gambling, distribution of materials that are not part of the company or part of the user's job, harassment, and unauthorized downloading of graphic material, music, and software. In general, any illegal activity is prohibited. Personal uses of equipment, such as personal correspondence and printing personal documents, are typically unauthorized in many companies and are viewed as fraud against the company by the misuse of company time and resources.

Drawings of the finished network system are also needed. Note the word *finished*. Changes occur as the system is built. Thus, the finished product can be somewhat different from the original proposal. Too often, a network system is installed, but no drawings of the finished system exist. Only the original proposed plan exists. Changes do occur, especially in complex systems. Documentation of changes that occur after an installation is also important because the network administrator may be the only person who knows how the system was changed.

Training

An essential part of installing a network system is to design a training program for the network users. Each user must be trained in password and general security policies and procedures, remote access, e-mail fundamentals, and more.

The amount and depth of the training varies according to the size of the project. For example, a small modification to an existing network may require only a briefing. A large enterprise project may require training for hundreds of employees over a period of days, weeks, or months.

Company procedures and policies need to be developed before conducting training so they can be disseminated as part of the training. Involving a training professional in the development of the network can be of great assistance in this process. While network designers are good at their job, they do not often possess the skills and talents necessary to communicate technicalities to a broad audience of users.

Specifications for Network Design

A set of installation standards must be followed when installing a new network or modifying an existing network. A contract for a large installation typically includes a set of specifications or *specs*, as they are often referred to in trade jargon. Specifications are used to specify details or expectations about materials and craftsmanship that are acceptable for the installation of the system. The specifications ensure that the

Copyright Goodheart-Willcox Co., Inc.

owner and the contractor both know exactly what is expected. Without a set of specifications, there can be a wide variation of interpretation between what the owner expects and the finished product. Documentation that includes specifications reduces communication problems.

The overall size of a set of specifications can be quite lengthy. Most specifications reference other, previously established standards to reduce the size of the document. There is no need to call out details about wall outlets and electrical circuits installed for the network. The specifications simply reference established specifications. For example, a specification in a document might read, "All electrical work shall conform to the minimum standards established by the National Electrical Code (NEC)."

This section discusses standard organizations and some standards related to networking. It also defines some architectural design element terms, such as *main entrance room* and *horizontal cross connect*. It is important to be familiar with these terms because they are often used in the standards related to networking.

Different terms may be used to describe the same concept. This is because the terminology is often originated from conflicting industry standards and terminology developed by individual private companies. For example, the terms and acronyms used to describe the connection point where the customer and the commercial provider cable meets may include point of presence (POP), point of entry (POE), customer connection point (CCP), service delivery point (SDP), demarc, and demarcation point. In the electronics industry, different terminology for the same concept is common. Consider the source of the term before dismissing it as incorrect.

An important concept to remember for the Network+ Exam is the fact that up to the demarcation point, troubleshooting on one side of that point is the responsibility of the service provider, and on the other side, it is the responsibility of the network administrator.

The architectural design elements recognized by ANSI/TIA/EIA are demarcation point, network interface device, main entrance room, main distribution frame, entrance facility, equipment room, work area, horizontal cross connect, horizontal wiring, backbone, patch panel, punch down block, telecommunication room, and telecommunication closet. Figure 18-13 illustrates the general locations of some of these architectural design elements.

Tech Tip

The National Electrical Code (NEC) comprises hundreds of pages of specifications for wire sizes, conduit sizes, supports, and other materials that have been selected by an organization of electrical engineers, contractors, and fire and safety experts. Many years have been dedicated to researching the minimal, best standards that are adequate to ensure the safety of personnel.

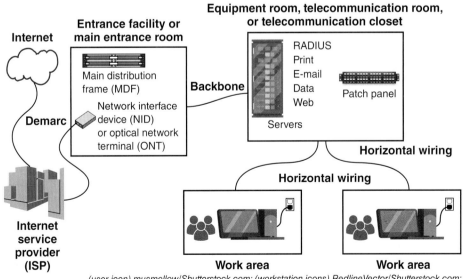

Figure 18-13 General locations of some of the architectural design elements recognized by ANSI/TIA/EIA.

(user icon) musmellow/Shutterstock.com; (workstation icons) RedlineVector/Shutterstock.com; (server icon) fullvector/Shutterstock.com; Goodheart-Willcox Publisher

Copyright Goodheart-Willcox Co., Inc.

Demarcation Point

The **demarcation point**, or *demarc*, is the spot where customer equipment or cable meets a telecommunication provider's cable or equipment. The demarcation point is where the customer and private/public telecommunication companies become responsible for the cable and equipment. If the private/public telecommunication company is directed to troubleshoot or make repairs on the customer side of the demarcation point, the customer is billed for the services. The customer is not responsible for any work performed on the private/public telecommunication side of the demarcation point.

Network Interface Device

A **network interface device (NID)** is a term used to describe a device that connects the commercial carrier local loop to the private customer's premises wiring. The NID can be considered the point of demarcation for the communication system. Two common NID devices are smart jack and optical network terminal.

The term *jack* was used to describe the connection point between the communication provider (telephone company) and the customer. A jack provides a simple and quick connection point. A **smart jack** is considered an intelligent connection point because it incorporates additional electronics that allow it to perform specific functions. For example, a smart jack can perform a loopback test remotely from the service provider without the need to send a technician to the smart jack location. The smart jack can also automatically perform diagnostics and generate a report of the probable cause of the problem. The self-diagnostics by the smart jack helps the provider determine if the problem exists on the customer premises or on the service provider's side of the connection. Smart jacks typically obtain electrical power from the telephone line connection, which means the jack does not need a separate power supply in most cases. Smart jacks are commonly used for T1 and DSL terminations.

An **optical network terminal (ONT)** is a fiber-optic cable termination point between the customer and the service provider. The ONT is more than just a simple fiber-optic cable connection point. Fiber-optic service can provide multiple services such as telephone, television, and Internet access. When the fiber-optic cable provides multiple services, the ONT acts as a multiplexer and demultiplexer unit. Combining signals on a fiber-optic cable is called *multiplexing*. The separation of the signals at the destination is referred to as *demultiplexing*.

The ONT typically obtains power from the customer site. There may also be a battery backup system to provide access even when the electrical power is out of service at the site. If the customer has a UPS system for the computer, then the customer can shut down the computer system safely, even if he or she is in the process of downloading or uploading data.

Main Entrance Room

The **main entrance room** is the room in which public or private telecommunication enters the building. In the past, the main entrance room not only housed the telecommunication equipment, but also the air-conditioning, heating, electrical, and other equipment. As the building industry evolved, the telecommunication room was eventually established in a separate room in the building. This is preferred for a multitude of reasons including access, security, and performance issues.

Main Distribution Frame (MDF)

The **main distribution frame (MDF)** is the cable connection point where the private telecommunication cables come into a building and then connect or distribute

---

Note

Both the smart jack and the optical network terminal (ONT) can be identified as the demarcation point.

Copyright Goodheart-Willcox Co., Inc.

to other areas in the building. The MDF typically consists of a cable rack and physical cable connections for the individual cable conductors. The MDF can function as a test point when troubleshooting. The MDF is usually located in the main entrance room.

Main distribution frame (MDF) and intermediate distribution frame (IDF) are relative terms. For example, when a multistory building requires telecommunication, there will be a combination of MDF and IDFs throughout the facility. Each floor would have an IDF that acts as the connection point from the MDF and distributes cable runs to all areas on that specific floor. The same terminology is often applied to network cable distribution.

Entrance Facility

The **entrance facility** is the room that is used as the entrance location for public or private communication cables. The entrance facility may also serve as a telecommunication room or equipment room. Many times, the location depends on the availability of rooms and spaces in an existing building or the design or the complexity of the equipment required.

Equipment Room

An **equipment room** contains the telecommunication equipment for the building such as the private branch exchange (PBX), servers, and telecommunication wiring system terminations. A private branch exchange (PBX) refers to a telephone system that is installed, maintained, and owned by the company in which it is installed. An equipment room may also serve the purpose of an entrance facility or a telecommunication room.

Work Area

The **work area** is where employees perform their normal office duties. The work area is given this designation because the standards are different from those for hallways, lounges, reception areas, storage areas, and various other areas in the building. When you consider the various rooms that might be found in a building, designating a work area as a special room is not unusual. The requirements for a work area are not the same as the requirements for a storage area or a reception area. However, if a reception area were also a work area, there would be different requirements than normal.

> ## Tech Tip
>
> The terminology for network facilities is based on telecommunication standards. The telecommunication industry existed long before computer network technology, and many of the terms used to describe network rooms are actually derived from that industry.

Horizontal Cross Connect

A **horizontal cross connect** provides a mechanical means of connecting horizontal cabling systems to other cables or equipment. For example, a horizontal cross connect is used to connect horizontal cabling to a backbone or to system equipment such as a router, switch, bridge, or server.

Horizontal Wiring

Horizontal wiring refers to the section of cable that runs from individual work areas to a telecommunication closet. A telecommunication closet contains connection

> ## Tech Tip
>
> Some specifications state that the total combined length of patch cables at each end of the horizontal run should be no more than 10 meters. However, a total combined length of patch cables over 10 meters is generally allowed as long as the maximum total distance for horizontal cabling does not exceed 100 meters.

Copyright Goodheart-Willcox Co., Inc.

equipment for the workstations in the immediate area. All work areas connect to the telecommunication closet horizontal cross connects. Horizontal cable distance is limited to 90 meters for the horizontal run from the telecommunication outlet to the telecommunication closet. The maximum total distance is 100 meters.

At least two outlets should be installed in each work area. One outlet is used for voice communication and the other for data communication. Typically, more than two outlets are installed as a combination of network and telephone outlets. Category 3 is the minimum recommendation for telephone wiring, but a higher category of wiring is permitted. The media for data communication can be any one of the following:

- Four-pair UTP Category 5/5e/6/6e (Category 5e or higher is recommended)
- Two-pair STP
- Two-strand, 62.5/125 μm fiber-optic cable

Backbone

A network **backbone** connects the telecommunication closets, equipment rooms, and main entrance facility. It is located between these areas and does not serve individual workstations. A backbone can run horizontally and vertically through a building. When a backbone is run vertically, it is sometimes referred to as a *riser* and typically passes through four-inch conduit sleeves in the floor or ceiling. A backbone cannot be run in elevator shafts. See Figure 18-14 for a list of the approved cable and distances for backbones. Note that when UTP and STP are used for telephone communication, the maximum distance is 800 meters. When UTP and STP are used for networks, the backbone is limited to 90 meters.

Figure 18-14 List of approved cable and distances for backbones.

Cable Type	Distance
UTP Category 3 or higher (Category 5, 5e, 6, or 6e recommended)	800 meters (voice)
	90 meters (data)
STP Category 3 or higher (Category 5, 5e, 6, or 6e recommended)	800 meters (voice)
	90 meters (data)
Multimode or 62.5/125 fiber-optic cable	2000 meters
Single-mode fiber-optic cable	3000 meters

Goodheart-Willcox Publisher

The most widely accepted material used for network backbones is fiber-optic cable. UTP can be used for small networks, but fiber-optic cable is the preferred media if it can be used within budget restraints. While coaxial cable has not been prohibited, it is not recommended for new installations as either backbone or horizontal wiring.

Patch Panel

A typical **patch panel** is a rack-mounted wiring device for network systems. The device has RJ-45 jacks on the front and a matching series of connections on the back, as demonstrated in Figure 18-15. Patch panel cables are used for making connections between the front of the patch panel and equipment. The back of the panel is where the horizontal run cable is terminated. A specialized type of patch panel is a *fiber-patch panel*. A fiber-patch panel, or *fiber-distribution panel*, is a panel designed for fiber-optic connections instead of UTP connections.

The individual wires of each cable are pushed into the connections on the back of the patch panel using a punch down tool. A **punch down tool** is used to push

NET
♣ 2.1

NET
♣ 5.2

Copyright Goodheart-Willcox Co., Inc.

individual twisted-pair wires into the connection and automatically trim conductor excess. It is specifically made for this type of cable wiring termination, as shown in Figure 18-16. The connections found on the back of patch panels are also found in outlets and punch down blocks. Punch down blocks are covered in the following section.

Figure 18-15 A patch panel serves as a connection point between cable runs and network equipment. A—Front view. B—Back view.

B

A

Goodheart-Willcox Publisher

Figure 18-16 A punch down tool is used to connect twisted-pair wire to the connections on the back of patch panels, RJ-45 outlets, and punch down blocks.

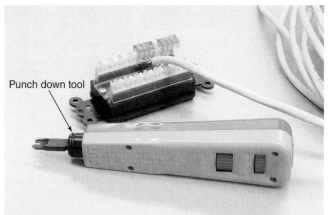

Punch down tool

Goodheart-Willcox Publisher

Patch panels are a convenient way to make connections and provide a means for easily modifying the cable connection system. The punch down tool uses a blade that corresponds to the termination style. For example, a 110 blade is used for a 110 block, and a 66 blade is used for a 66 block.

Punch Down Block

A **punch down block** is a network system-wiring device used to terminate communication cable for telephone systems. It is also used as an intermediate cable connection point for joining two cables. Punch down blocks are not typical network wiring devices; however, you may encounter them used to terminate DSL and cable modems.

Copyright Goodheart-Willcox Co., Inc.

There are two main types of punch down blocks: 66 and 110. Both types are shown in Figure 18-17. The 66 block is older than the 110 block and was originally designed for telephone communication. It is limited to Cat 3 or earlier types of twisted-pair cable. It does not support high frequencies. The 110 block was designed to support higher cable frequencies and is less prone to crosstalk. It is the preferred style for network cable such as Cat 5, Cat 5e, and Cat 6.

The cable termination for a 66 or 100 block is referred to as **insulation-displacement connector (IDC)**. During the installation process, the outer cable sheath is removed, and the insulation (plastic cover) is left on the individual conductors for the installation process. A punch down tool is used to push the conductor into the IDC. There is no need to remove the insulation from the conductor because the IDC pierces the insulation. The punch down tool not only pushes the conductor into place, it also cuts off excess conductor, as illustrated in Figure 18-18.

The number of punch down block terminals corresponds to the standard telecommunication cable design and is designated as pairs. For example, standard telecommunication cable designs are 25, 50, 100, and 300 pair. Note that the cables

Figure 18-17 Punch down blocks. A—66 block. B—110 block.

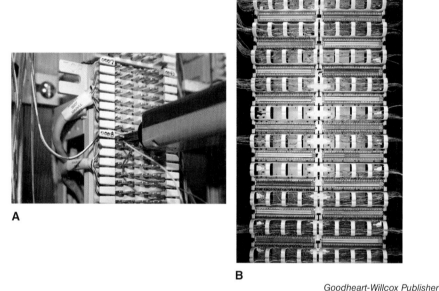

A

B

Goodheart-Willcox Publisher

Figure 18-18 When the punch down tool pushes the conductor into the IDC, the IDC pierces the conductor's insulation and the punch down tool cuts off the excess conductor. The punch down tool blade must match the type of punch down block being used.

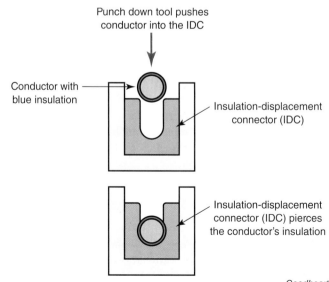

Punch down tool pushes conductor into the IDC

Conductor with blue insulation

Insulation-displacement connector (IDC)

Insulation-displacement connector (IDC) pierces the conductor's insulation

Goodheart-Willcox Publisher

Copyright Goodheart-Willcox Co., Inc.

are designated as pairs, which means the conductor count is by pair. Thus, a 25-pair cable has 50 conductors.

When two cables are terminated to a punch down block, the individual cable conductors can be connected by individual jumpers or by a bridge clip. A bridge clip is the preferred method of joining conductors at a punch down block location.

Telecommunication Room

A **telecommunication room** is a room or enclosed space that houses telecommunication equipment, such as cable termination and cross connect wiring. The telecommunication room serves as a transition point between the backbone and horizontal wiring. Sometimes, telecommunication rooms are referred to as *equipment rooms*. Exact terminology depends on the source of the technology reference. For example, a network technician may use the term *equipment room* while a telecommunication technician may use the term *telecommunication room*. There must be a minimum of one telecommunication room per floor of a multistory building.

Telecommunication Closet

A **telecommunication closet** is an enclosed space used to house telecommunication cable-termination equipment. It is the recognized transition point between the backbone and horizontal wiring. The telecommunication closet may also be referred to as a *telecommunication room*. The closet can be a small room about the size of a standard clothes closet, or it can be an enclosed cabinet that is placed securely inside a general office space. A telecommunication closet is typically placed in a centralized section of the work area and is used to house the horizontal cross connect for horizontal wiring. Many companies and organizations use the terms *telecommunication room* and *telecommunication closet* interchangeably.

Standards Organizations

There are many organizations that write standards for communication and network systems. The standards of these organizations are often incorporated into the contract specifications for the new network. Many of the standards appear to be redundant. However, the standards are not just for networks. Many of the standards are written for communication systems such as a telephone system. These communication systems overlap with network communication.

Many manufacturers publish their own set of standards, often exceeding the standards from the American National Standards Institute (ANSI), Electronic Industries Alliance (EIA), or Telecommunications Industry Association (TIA). This causes a lot of confusion for maximum cable ratings. For example, different manufacturers advertised Category 6 at various rates before it was ever a formal standard published by ANSI/TIA/EIA.

ANSI/TIA/EIA Standards

Network cabling, hardware, and structures are specified by a combination of standards. The set or combination of standards and recommendations used in the United States is a combination of ANSI, TIA, and EIA and is referred to as *ANSI/TIA/EIA*. While these are separate organizations, they come together for generally agreed-upon standards for telecommunication and networking, such as those in Figure 18-19.

Telecommunication is a worldwide media. The ANSI/TIA/EIA is the recognized authority for the United States. ANSI is the main organization responsible for overseeing and distributing information technology standards in the United States.

Copyright Goodheart-Willcox Co., Inc.

Figure 18-19 ANSI/TIA/EIA standards for telecommunication and networking.

Standard	Description
TIA/EIA 569-A	Commercial Building Standard for Telecommunications Pathways and Spaces
TIA/EIA 568-B.1-2000	Commercial Building Telecommunications Cabling Standard
TIA/EIA 606-A	Administration Standard for Commercial Telecommunications Infrastructure
TIA/EIA 607-A	Commercial Building Grounding and Bonding Requirements for Telecommunications
TSB-75	Additional Horizontal Cabling Practices for Open Offices

Goodheart-Willcox Publisher

TIA and EIA are international standards. To eliminate redundancy, the ANSI, TIA, and EIA formed a cooperative group to combine standards that cover common areas. The International Organization for Standardization (ISO) is the European standards organization with similar responsibilities to the ANSI/TIA/EIA. The OSI model was developed by the ISO. The Canadian Standards Association (CSA) is a Canadian standards organization. Standards may change from country to country. Also, these are minimum standards. They may be superseded by higher standards written by individual organizations such as bodies of government, the airline industry, and universities.

TIA/EIA 569-A

The 569-A standard for telecommunication pathways and spaces recommends how communication cables are to be installed. The term *telecommunication* is not limited to data networks, but rather to the broad range of communication, such as telephone and video. It is important to remember when reading standards that many pertain to communication systems and may not meet the requirements of a network standard such as 100BaseT or higher. Keep this in mind when references are made to Category 3 cable systems.

TIA/EIA 568-B

The 568-B standards describe the wiring standards for commercial buildings. They generally define the construction practices and design for the media, connection points, termination, and topology. Note that standards are not solely concerned with network systems, but rather with all types of general telecommunication systems like telephone wiring. Be careful when reading recommendations because Category 3 is still a recognized UTP for telephone wiring. An example of a 568-B standard is 568-B.1-2000 (commercial building telecommunication cabling), which was introduced in 2000 when the use of Category 5e cable for network use was approved.

TIA/EIA 606-A

The 606-A administration standard for commercial telecommunication infrastructure describes the telecommunication infrastructure design guidelines. This includes blueprint drawings, PBX records, equipment inventories, identification formats, color coding, and labelling.

TIA/EIA 607-A

The 607-A standard describes the grounding and bonding requirements for telecommunication in commercial buildings. To understand the concepts relating to grounding and bonding better, one must first understand some basic electrical concepts as they relate to personnel safety. Electrical systems carry electrical energy, which can be hazardous to personnel. When electrical equipment fails, electrical current attempts to find the best electrical path to the earth. The path can be provided intentionally for safety reasons or unintentionally, such as through people coming

Copyright Goodheart-Willcox Co., Inc.

in contact with the equipment. When people provide the path to earth, they can be severely shocked—sometimes fatally.

Electrical cables are insulated to prevent electrical energy from energizing the boxes, conduits, and devices that contain electrical wiring and equipment. To prevent electrical shock, the metal parts of the equipment are grounded and bonded. When equipment is grounded, a better path to earth can be made than through people coming in contact with the equipment.

The term *ground* or *grounding* means the intentional or accidental electrical path between an electronic device and the earth. The TIA/EIA 607-A standard specifies that equipment, such as boxes, conduits, and other metal devices associated with electrical and telecommunication equipment provide protection from electrical shock by grounding. When parts of the system are connected to the grounding system, they are described as bonded. *Bonding* means that a short copper jumper joins a noncurrent-carrying device to the electrical system ground. Proper grounding and bonding is a standard safety practice and a requirement by the NEC and the ANSI/TIA/EIA organizations.

The National Electrical Code (NEC) states that there can only be one main system ground for a facility. The main system ground serves as the main ground for all electrical-related equipment, such as the electrical system, telecommunication equipment, and network equipment. A grounding electrode rod is driven into the earth at the main electrical entrance of the building, as illustrated in Figure 18-20. A typical grounding electrode is made of copper or copper-clad steel approximately one-half inch in diameter and at least eight feet long. A grounding conductor made of either bare copper wire or green insulated wire is used to connect all required metallic devices in the system together. The building's steel structural support is also tied to the grounding system. The grounding conductor runs through each section of the facility, including the wiring closets.

Figure 18-20 A ground conductor is run throughout the entire facility, connecting all metal equipment and devices to the main electrical system ground located at the entrance facility.

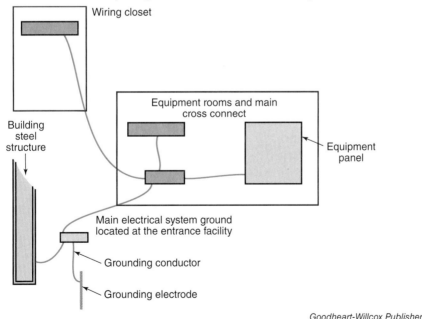

Goodheart-Willcox Publisher

TSB-75

The ANSI/TIA/EIA organization released TSB-75 to support the open office space design. TSB-75 is a supplement to the 568-A standard. ANSI/TIA/EIA often releases updated bulletins to support changes and exceptions to its standards rather than release an entirely new standard.

An open office space design requires a flexible wiring method that can easily support rewiring. Open office areas do not have permanent walls and typically consist of many office cubicles. The cubicle design is easily changed and rearranged. Many building owners who lease space to businesses prefer this style of construction. By using the open office design, the office area can be easily and quickly reorganized for many different types of businesses that require unique office floor arrangements. This type of design can also be used for convention centers and large assembly rooms, which often require the quick rearrangement of the floor plan.

TSB-75 states that a consolidation point (CP) and a multi-user telecommunication outlet assembly (MUTOA) can be used in open office spaces, as illustrated in Figure 18-21. A **multi-user telecommunication outlet assembly (MUTOA)** is a grouping of outlets that serves up to 12 work areas. This is not a cross connect, but rather a prefabricated set of connection points. The MUTOA is mounted on the permanent building structure or on furniture that is permanently secured to the floor. Patch cables run from the MUTOA to the equipment in the work area.

The **consolidation point (CP)** is a connection to the horizontal wiring system, which in turn, feeds to a wall outlet or an MUTOA. A patch cable can be plugged into the MUTOA and run directly to the equipment in the work area. Often, the patch cable is run through channels in the furniture to conceal the presence of the cabling and ensure office safety. A consolidation point uses twisted-pair cable with solid wire rather than stranded wire to connect to the outlets in the work area. See Figure 18-22 for visual representations of consolidation point and MUTOA systems.

Figure 18-21 An open office area has no permanent wall structures. It is designed to be a flexible office area. Several MUTOAs can be placed in the open office area to serve work areas. If the design changes, the MUTOA can be easily rearranged to accommodate the new office layout.

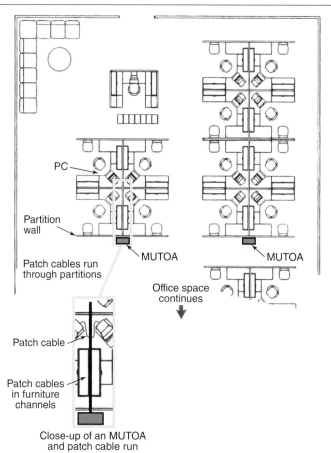

Goodheart-Willcox Publisher

Figure 18-23 lists the maximum recommended distances of cable lengths for horizontal wiring and patch cables. It is important to note that the overall length of the horizontal wiring is limited to 100 meters. The same distances are used for consolidation points. Certain equipment manufacturers provide their own distance charts that include modified distances based on conductor characteristics such as diameter. Also, note that the maximum length of a patch panel cable that can be used in a telecommunication room is seven meters.

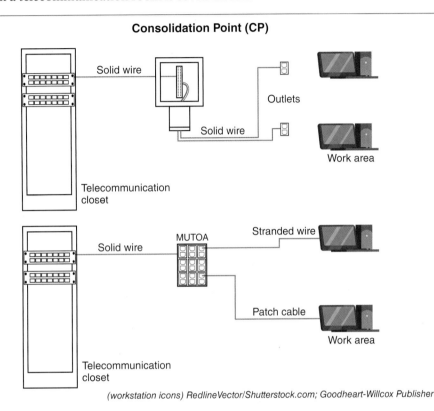

Consolidation Point (CP)

(workstation icons) RedlineVector/Shutterstock.com; Goodheart-Willcox Publisher

Figure 18-22 A Consolidation Point (CP) is a central point that provides connections for outlets in the work areas. An MUTOA is an assembly of outlets in a work area that equipment attaches to using patch cables.

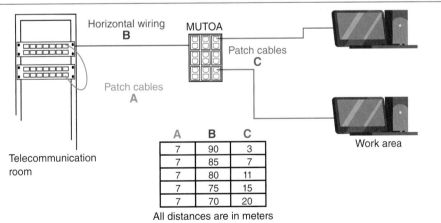

A	B	C
7	90	3
7	85	7
7	80	11
7	75	15
7	70	20

All distances are in meters

(workstation icons) RedlineVector/Shutterstock.com; Goodheart-Willcox Publisher

Figure 18-23 Maximum recommended distances of cable lengths for horizontal wiring and patch cables. Note that the total distance will never exceed 100 meters for the horizontal wiring length. Also note that the longest patch cable on the patch panel is 7 meters.

Network and Computer Electrical Requirements

The National Electrical Code (NEC) defines the electrical requirements and standards for networks. NEC specifies standards that ensure safety of personnel and serve as a guide to minimal equipment requirements. The NEC is used as a guide for electricians rather than for a certified network cable installer. Network system construction often requires the expertise of individuals from various backgrounds.

Copyright Goodheart-Willcox Co., Inc.

All electrical work requires a licensed journeyman electrician and an electrical contractor. Network technicians should never engage in the installation or modifications of electrical systems. Electrical systems are classified in three general groups according to the voltage levels encountered in the system, as outlined in Figure 18-24.

Figure 18-24 The three general groups in which electrical systems are classified. Note that they are classified according to the voltage levels encountered in the system.

Voltage	Application
< 50 volts	Signaling and communication
50 volts–600 volts	Residential and commercial wiring
> 600 volts	High-voltage wiring

Goodheart-Willcox Publisher

Telecommunication, video, and signaling systems fall into the category of fewer than 50 volts. Telecommunication wiring must never be in the same conduit or box as any system wiring of a higher voltage rating. The telecommunication system must be isolated from the higher voltage systems not only to prevent data corruption and interference, but also to ensure the safety of personnel using network equipment.

Tech Tip

The main components of the network wiring system use telecommunication terminology to describe the various sections of the network. Network standards are a subcategory of telecommunication, which existed long before networking systems. It is only natural that the existing terminology be used when describing the newer network wiring system.

BICSI

The Building Industry Consulting Service International (BICSI) is a worldwide nonprofit association dedicated to the education of skilled workers in the telecommunication infrastructure and related fields. The organization is referred to by its acronym, which rhymes with *Dixie*. In recent years, BICSI has expanded its educational offerings in network cabling, and it is a recognized authority for network cable and infrastructure installation. The organization offers training programs, publications, and testing for certification.

One such certification is in network cabling, which consists of a written examination and a performance examination. In the performance examination, candidates are required to make connections or splices using several different media, such as Category 5e, fiber-optic cable, and coaxial cable. The performance testing is performed under the direction of a BICSI-certified examiner, and the cables are sent to the BICSI organization where they are evaluated. Many building specifications state that only certified cable installers be used on the job. If you are interested in becoming a certified network-cable installer or simply want to know more, visit the BICSI website at www.bicsi.org. It is suggested you conduct research beyond the scope of this textbook to learn more about network design.

Tech Tip

Network cable installation is typically accomplished by BICSI-certified individuals. These individuals have passed the rigid BICSI Certification exam.

Copyright Goodheart-Willcox Co., Inc.

Summary

Needs Assessment and Design

- The first part of the design process is to conduct a needs assessment.
- Important factors to consider are physical network structure, security, application, organizational structure, fault tolerance, and data integrity.
- A network's physical structure is typically the primary concern of the designer.
- Questions about organizational structure help determine the number of servers, directory structure, location of resources, and partition and volume configuration.
- LDAP is the de facto directory standard used by network operating systems.
- A naming convention must be developed for all objects in the network environment to provide for easy identification.

Network Design Tools

- There are many utilities and case studies available to help with network design.
- The Microsoft Assessment and Planning (MAP) toolkit is a free, downloadable tool to help update or migrate an existing system.
- Microsoft Visio is a powerful drawing tool used to diagram network systems, electrical plans, mechanical plans, floor plans, site plans, and LDAP structures.
- NetworkView is a software application that allows for the creation of a network map.

Installation Process

- The installation process begins with the development of a timeline.
- A timeline is a chronological listing of the expected sequence of work from the beginning of the project until the end.
- Microsoft provides tools for automatic installation of multiple copies of software and operating systems.
- All sections of a network need to be tested after implementation to ensure there are no bottlenecks and the hardware and software are in working order.
- A set of network documents with specific procedures for security and other areas of network usage must be developed, and rules need to be established to ensure proper use of equipment and software.
- Each user must be trained in password and general security policies and procedures, remote access, e-mail fundamentals, and more.

Specifications for Network Design

- Specifications are a set of guidelines that explicitly describe the workmanship and materials that will be used in the project.
- An isolated electrical system should always be used for network equipment.

Copyright Goodheart-Willcox Co., Inc.

- The demarc or demarcation point identifies where the public/private telecommunication company cable terminates and the customer cabling begins.

- Smart jacks and optical network terminals (ONTs) are common demarc locations.

- The main distribution frame (MDF) is the cable connection point where the private telecommunication cables come into a building and then connect or distribute to other areas inside the building.

- Main distribution frame (MDF) and intermediate distribution frame (IDF) are relative locations as related to the distribution of telecommunication cables.

- Horizontal cable distance is limited to 90 meters for the horizontal run from the telecommunication outlet to the telecommunication room.

- The maximum distance for backbone wiring using UTP as a network medium is 90 meters.

- The maximum distance for a multimode fiber-optic cable backbone is 2000 meters.

- The maximum distance for a single-mode fiber-optic cable backbone is 3000 meters.

- Punch down blocks are used to distribute, terminate, and connect telecommunication cables.

Standards Organizations

- The main standard used for network design in the United States was developed jointly by several organizations and is referred to as ANSI/TIA/EIA.

- International Standards Organization (ISO) is the European standards organization similar to the ANSI/TIA/EIA.

- The Canadian Standards Association (CSA) is similar to ANSI/TIA/EIA.

- A consolidation point (CP) is a location in the horizontal wiring that provides an interconnection, which extends into the work areas.

- A multi-user telecommunication outlet assembly (MUTOA) is a grouping of outlets that serves up to 12 work areas.

- The maximum length of a patch panel cable that can be used in a telecommunication room is seven meters.

- All electrical work for a networking system must follow the recommendations of the National Electrical Code (NEC) standards.

- Network technicians should not engage in the installation of electrical devices.

- BICSI is a nonprofit organization dedicated to telecommunication installation, training, and education.

Copyright Goodheart-Willcox Co., Inc.

Review Questions

1. What is the first step in the network design process?
2. What are some of the roles and services provided by a network server? (Name at least 10).
3. On what protocol standard are all major directory structures based?
4. Why is a naming convention important?
5. List three software programs that help in the designing of a network.
6. What is a timeline, and how does it help with the installation of a network?
7. What is the purpose of specifications?
8. Name two network interface devices.
9. What is a smart jack?
10. What name is used to represent a fiber-optic building termination point located at the demarc?
11. List three services that are typically provided by an ONT device.
12. What is the name of the room where the telephone system enters the building?
13. Name two other uses or room designations that an equipment room may serve.
14. What do the acronyms MDF and IDF represent?
15. What is the purpose of the MDF?
16. Where is backbone cable located in a building?
17. What is a work area?
18. Describe a patch panel.
19. What tool is used to connect cable to the back of a patch panel?
20. How many telecommunication rooms must there be in a multistory building?
21. What do the three acronyms ANSI, TIA, EIA represent?
22. What is the difference between a multi-user telecommunication outlet assembly (MUTOA) and a consolidation point (CP)?
23. What is the maximum number of work areas a single MUTOA or Consolidation Point (CP) can serve?
24. Can an MUTOA be mounted behind a drop ceiling?
25. What characteristic does furniture need to allow a MUTOA or Consolidation Point (CP) to be attached to it?

Sample Network+ Exam Questions

1. A metal fabrication manufacturer is setting up a production plant that will incorporate network computer-controlled machinery. Welding is commonly used in the metal fabrication process and is automated. Which type of network cable would you recommend be used to counter the effects of EMI generated by the welding equipment on the plant floor.

   A. 24 AWG UTP

   B. 22 AWG UTP

   C. Multimode fiber-optic

   D. 1000BaseT

2. Ahmed is trying to make connections for his network cable. What type of tool is used to make 1000BaseT connections at telecommunication outlets in a work area?

   A. RG-58 crimper

   B. Punch down tool

   C. Electric soldering iron

   D. 24 AWG cable stripper

3. Martha is responsible for installing cable for a new network. She wants to ensure that she does not exceed cable lengths. What is the maximum length for a horizontal run of UTP cable from a telecommunication closet to the work area outlet?

   A. 800 meters

   B. 200 meters

   C. 100 meters

   D. 90 meters

4. What is the maximum length of a patch panel cable that can be used in a telecommunication room?

   A. 3 meters

   B. 5 meters

   C. 7 meters

   D. 9 meters

5. Juan is working with a new fiber-optic installation. What of the following is the best answer for the maximum distance of a single-mode, fiber-optic backbone?

   A. 100 meters

   B. 800 meters

   C. 2000 meters

   D. 3000 meters

Copyright Goodheart-Willcox Co., Inc.

6. Thomas is installing cables and wants to ensure that he adheres to well-known standards. Which standard describes how to install communication cables in telecommunication pathways and spaces?

   A. NEC

   B. TIA/EIA 569-A

   C. TIA/EIA 606-A

   D. TIA/EIA 607-A

7. What is the name of the Ethernet network passive device that is used in an equipment room to serve as a connection between horizontal cable runs and the equipment in the server room?

   A. Gateway

   B. Router

   C. Patch panel

   D. MUTOA

8. Trayvon is connecting workstations to the RJ-45 wall jacks. He needs to select the appropriate cable for this job. Which type of cable would most likely be used to provide connections between the workstation and the RJ-45 wall jack?

   A. Stranded core coaxial cable with a copper shield

   B. UTP with stranded copper wires

   C. STP with solid copper wires

   D. UTP with solid copper wires

9. You have been tasked with preventing electrical interference on your network. Which method provides the best protection from office equipment interference?

   A. Double insulate all electrical cables.

   B. Use only 120-VAC equipment in the office area.

   C. Use insulated RJ-45 connectors on all cable assemblies.

10. Mark works for a service provider. He frequently has to connect T1 or T3 lines to network demarc connection points. Which network device typically serves as the network system demarc?

    A. Router

    B. Gateway

    C. Smart jack

    D. Punch down block

CHAPTER 19

Network+ Certification Exam Preparation

 Network+ Certification Exam Objectives

As of this writing, the current Network+ Exam version is N10-007. As part of your test preparation, you should be able to install, configure, and troubleshoot basic network devices. You should also know the layers of the OSI model and be very familiar with all the common network protocols, especially those associated with the TCP/IP suite.

Be aware that some questions on the Network+ Certification Exam will be based on A+ Certification Exam knowledge. The CompTIA website states that all candidates for the Network+ Exam should have the A+ Certification or equivalent knowledge.

Learning Outcomes

- Summarize the domains of the CompTIA Network+ Certification Exam.
- Develop a strategy to prepare for the Network+ Exam.
- Complete the included Network+ practice exam.

Copyright Goodheart-Willcox Co., Inc.

Overview

This chapter is dedicated to helping you prepare for the CompTIA Network+ Certification Exam. Test preparation strategies and a practice exam are included in this chapter. The practice exam simulates what you may encounter when taking the Network+ Certification Exam. Every attempt has been made to simulate the Network+ Certification Exam closely by covering the exact areas to be tested at the approximate knowledge level required. However, there is no guarantee successfully passing this practice exam will ensure your success on the Network+ Certification Exam.

Note

At the time of this writing, CompTIA has changed its policy concerning the length of A+, Network+, and Security+ Certification from lifetime to three years. This took place January 1, 2011. Any certification obtained before January 1, 2011, will be good for a lifetime and, thus, will not need to be renewed.

Network+ Certification Exam

The CompTIA Network+ Exam consists of a maximum of 90 questions. The questions are multiple choice, drag-and-drop, and performance based. Students have 90 minutes to take the exam and must receive a score of 720 to pass. Test coverage includes wireless and wired network design, configuration, security, management, troubleshooting, and maintenance. The test is organized by industry-recognized objectives, referred to as *domains*.

The best way to prepare for the CompTIA Network+ Exam is to refer to the objectives. In this section, you will be provided with the CompTIA N10-007 domains. These domains will be discussed so you can familiarize yourself with what to expect from each testing area on the actual exam. Each domain has a wide range of topics. Clearly, CompTIA views all topics as having value. However, certain topics are more heavily emphasized on the test than others, and you should focus on those. This section describes the topics from each domain that are most important for you to know.

Network+ Note

The Network+ Certification Examination Objectives as well as the percentages listed are approximate and are subject to change.

Domain 1: Network Concepts (23%)

This domain covers network topologies, network protocols, ports, wireless technologies, and essentially all fundamental concepts used in networking. The test has recently added cloud technologies. Cloud is covered in a basic way, so you need only a general understanding of clouds and cloud terminology.

This domain also includes networking hardware. The way each device works is heavily emphasized on the Network+ Exam. Understanding what each device does and at which layer of the OSI model it operates will be critical. Also tested will be your knowledge of topologies, technologies, and classification.

Networking services such as DHCP and DNS are important parts of this domain. You should also have a general understanding of remote access protocols (TACACS/RADIUS), and VPNs. Network traffic topics such as routing, switching, and segmentation will be tested in this domain, as well.

Each version of the test for the past several years has given more emphasis on IPv6, so you should have a detailed knowledge of IPv6 before taking the test. Note, however, there are still many questions on IPv4.

Domain 2: Network Infrastructure (18%)

This domain emphasizes the various cable types, terminators, and connectors. It also covers the installation and configuration of basic network hardware such as routers and switches. More advanced network hardware such as VoIP PBX and multilayer switches are also covered. The test has recently added virtualization technology. You will need a general understanding of virtualization technology and the functions and mechanics of virtualization.

General knowledge about cables is always on the Network+ Exam. Particularly, details of T1, T3, E1, and E3 are covered. You should also have a general understanding of the other communication protocols (ISDN, ATM, etc.). Detailed knowledge of UTP connectors, cable times, and bandwidth is critical for the test. Expect some questions regarding coaxial (RG-6, RG-59, etc.) and fiber connectors (ST, SC, etc.).

Domain 3: Network Operations (17%)

Network diagrams and standards are covered in this domain. Remote access methods such as SSH and VPNs are also covered in this domain. Additionally, policies and best practices are covered here.

This domain requires you to be able to define the appropriate use of various networking tools and utilities. For example, you should understand what a port scanner is and what diagnostic utilities do. Expect emphasis on troubleshooting issues with bandwidth and bottlenecks.

Understand how to use backups, as well as how to handle updates. Basic understanding of technologies such as VLAN, trunking, port bonding, and port mirroring will be required. Expect an emphasis on wireless and be sure to have a strong understanding of the 802.11 standards. Additionally, expect basic coverage of mobile devices.

Domain 4: Network Security (20%)

You probably could have guessed that security is a critical domain. Make certain you can describe various attacks (e.g., DoS, Smurf, ransomware, Trojan horse, etc.), and ensure you have a general idea of how to mitigate those threats.

There will be some basic coverage of disaster recovery. Understand various acronyms (e.g., BCP, DRP, MTD, MTTR, etc.) their meanings, and what functions they serve. Wireless security is heavily emphasized and you should know it well. Make sure you can give a good description of WEP, WPA, and WPA2.

You should also understand vulnerabilities such as unsecure protocols and understand the differences between vulnerability scanning and penetration testing. Conversely, you should also know secure protocols, such as SSH, SFTP, and HTTPS.

Authentication is important; ensure you have a general understanding of CHAP, PAP, Kerberos, and other authentication protocols. You should also expect to see questions on cryptography and hashes.

Copyright Goodheart-Willcox Co., Inc.

There will be physical security questions, but they are not likely to be in-depth assessments. Familiarize yourself with the fundamentals. The same is true with forensics. You should understand the basics prior to taking the exam.

Domain 5: Troubleshooting and Tools (22%)

The Network+ Exam emphasizes troubleshooting processes and techniques. Specifically, it tests the CompTIA-recommended troubleshooting process covered in Chapter 17. Make certain that you can walk through basic problem scenarios and find the right solution. Most importantly expect several questions on the various troubleshooting utilities such as **ipconfig, ping**, and **nslookup**. You must know these well. Questions that ask about the switches and parameters for these utilities are sure to appear.

You should also be able to identify the various tools that have been discussed throughout this book. That means understanding the purpose of a given tool, how to use it, and when to use it.

Preparation Strategy

The secret to passing the Network+ Certification Exam is having an organized strategy for preparation. The most common mistake made by students is to sit down and simply study their notes and available materials. A student needs to approach exam preparation in the most effective and objective manner. The following is a list of key steps to exam success:

1. Schedule to take the Network+ Certification Exam.
2. Review and analyze the exam objectives.
3. Match exam objective details to resource materials.
4. Identify and practice laboratory activities that match the exam objectives.
5. Take practice exams.
6. Review problem areas.
7. Retake practice exams.

1. Schedule to Take the Network+ Certification Exam

It is best to schedule an exact date and time to take the exam. Give yourself a real and practical deadline. Vague deadlines do not work and will likely work against you. By procrastinating, you will lose the knowledge learned for the current exam. For example, do not simply say, "I plan to take the exam in the fall." Chances are you will still not be prepared by the time fall comes and will procrastinate by saying, "I plan to take the exam this winter." Remember, procrastination is not a luxury; in this case, it is your enemy.

You will have to pay to register the exam, but that can actually be a good motivator. Set an exact date for the exam. This way, you have committed both your financial and mental resources. Use your calendar to pick a date that gives you plenty of time to prepare by taking practice exams and reviewing. It is best not to wait until you think you are prepared to schedule the exam. In fact, scheduling the exam date should be one of the first things you do if you are serious about certification. Schedule the test, and then set up a specific, detailed schedule for study.

Network+ Note

When preparing for the Network+ Certification Exam, be sure to check the CompTIA website for the very latest Network+ Certification Examination Objectives. The objectives are constantly revised.

Copyright Goodheart-Willcox Co., Inc.

Network+ Note

Subnet calculations are not required for the Network+ Certification Exam, but it is required for other certification exams at the time of this writing. Also, note that changes in the exam composition can change. It is always a good idea to check the CompTIA website for any content changes.

2. Review and Analyze the Exam Objectives

The next step in the exam preparation strategy is to review and analyze the exam objectives outlined by the CompTIA organization. You need to know exactly what areas are required for certification. Networking is an extremely in-depth field that can easily fill volumes of books. The technical vocabulary alone spans over 10,000 words, not including all of the acronyms. Concentrate your studies on what is required for the Network+ Certification Exam. For example, if subnet calculations are not required, do not spend hours on this area of networking.

Too many people spend hours of study on areas that are not on the test. To avoid this mistake, make an outline of the current exam objectives and fill in related facts for each objective. A sample of such an outline is presented in Figure 19-1.

On your outline, write several facts about each item mentioned in the objective. Use several references for each item in addition to the textbook. A variety of reference materials will greatly enhance your understanding of the topics in the outline.

There are many websites that will provide you with a detailed outline for free or for a small charge. While this would be the most convenient way to make a complete exam outline, it is not a sound learning strategy. To better retain the information, you need to construct your own outline and research the facts and details yourself. This method will better prepare you for the exam. There are many ready-made study guides with inaccurate information and information outside the scope of the Network+ Certification Exam. Also, much of the material is out of date. You will do a more thorough job by constructing your own outline. This will ensure your study material is accurate, up to date, and in line with the current CompTIA objectives. By using multiple sources for information, you will be able to avoid inaccurate information.

Network+ Note

Since CompTIA recommends a Network+ candidate possesses CompTIA A+ equivalent knowledge, you may want to download and review the exam objectives for the A+ Certification Exams to use as an outline for review in addition to the Network+ outline.

3. Match Exam Objective Details to Resource Material

You should gather the content needed to fill in your outline from a variety of reputable sources. Use your textbook, laboratory manual, and the Internet. There are many fine resources available, especially at operating system vendor websites. For example, Microsoft has a wealth of material on WINS because it was vital to earlier network operating systems.

When researching facts for network interoperability, do not simply check the Microsoft website to see how to establish communication between a Microsoft system and a Linux system. Check the Linux site for its recommendations as well.

Copyright Goodheart-Willcox Co., Inc.

Figure 19-1 Sample study guide.

My Study Guide

1.1 Explain the purposes and uses of ports and protocols.

SSH 22 _____

_____

DNS 53 _____

_____

SMTP 25_____

_____

SFTP 22 _____

_____

FTP 20, 21 _____

_____

TFTP 69 _____

_____

TELNET 23 _____

_____

DHCP 67, 68 _____

_____

HTTP 80_____

_____

HTTPS 443_____

_____

SNMP 161_____

_____

_____

Goodheart-Willcox Publisher

Copyright Goodheart-Willcox Co., Inc.

Be careful of some sources, such as chat rooms or social media groups. Chat rooms and online groups that discuss particular exams often have a lot of inaccurate information. It is always better to use only reputable and authoritative websites.

4. Identify and Practice Laboratory Activities That Match the Exam Objectives

Many of the objectives, especially those related to troubleshooting, require the student to have knowledge acquired through experience. The laboratory activities presented in the *Network Fundamentals Laboratory Manual* are designed to provide you with needed experiences. You may want to review and repeat these laboratory activities. You should be able to perform all past laboratory activities with minimal assistance. Laboratory activity experiences are much easier to remember than textbook materials. For example, setting up a DHCP service and troubleshooting one will give you an in-depth knowledge and experience of the subject that is better and more valuable than simply memorizing facts.

Remember, becoming a network professional is not just about passing an exam. You need to know the subject area and be able to perform hands-on activities to obtain and keep a job in the industry. The industry does not pay you to answer questions, but rather to perform duties related to networking.

5. Take Practice Exams

Taking practice exams will help you to identify your areas for needed improvement in both subject matter and test-taking skills. All students have at least one area of weakness that could prevent them from passing the Network+ Certification Exam. Take the practice exam included in this chapter and have your instructor score it. After all of the questions are scored, you can analyze the areas in which you may need more study or laboratory experiences. Be careful of the many online exams offered for free on the Internet. Only use websites that your instructor recommends. Many of the websites have questions that do not exactly match the test objectives. Also, some of the provided answers are incorrect.

In general, most of the free practice exams are far more difficult than the actual Network+ Certification Exam. Many of the free Internet exam sites are marketing tools to sell you other exams from their website. The sample exams may actually be harder than the CompTIA exam. The reason is it enhances their sales if you do poorly on the sample exam. Use caution before purchasing any set of test questions.

6. Review Problem Areas

After taking a practice exam, review your problem areas. Do not simply take a practice exam and study a set of questions. You need to learn the material covered. Review the test items that were missed, and go back and study these areas. Use the outline you developed from the Network+ Certification Examination Objectives to help you prepare.

7. Retake Practice Exams

Retake practice exams by taking a different practice exam to see if you have improved in the needed areas. Repeat steps four through six until you have gained sufficient confidence that you can pass the CompTIA Network+ Certification Exam. Since your

Copyright Goodheart-Willcox Co., Inc.

testing date is already scheduled, all that will be left to do is to take, and hopefully pass, the Network+ Exam.

Network+ Certification Practice Exam

The following practice exam is structured according to the domains specified in the current Network+ Certification Examination Objectives. Before each set of questions for the domain, the objectives for that domain are listed. This practice exam is 50 questions and should be taken within approximately 45 minutes. After taking the exam, your instructor will score it.

Practice Exam Questions

The following exam questions are for you to test your knowledge. They are mixed, as they will be on the actual test, and not divided by domain. These are not the actual test questions from CompTIA, so do not memorize them. They are simply here to test your knowledge. However, every effort has been made to ensure these questions are in the format you can expect on the test, and cover the areas you are most likely going to see on the test.

1. John is selecting an Internet connection for his company. He wants bandwidth that is at least 40 Mbps. Which of the following should he choose?

   A. T1

   B. E1

   C. T3

   D. DS0

2. Which of the following devices uses the IEEE 1394 standard?

   A. parallel

   B. FireWire

   C. iSCSI

   D. USB 2.0

3. You are a network technician for a large bank. You are responsible for 450 users. A user is complaining about no network connection. Which should you do first?

   A. Check the LEDs on the NIC

   B. Install a new NIC

   C. Reset the router

   D. Re-install the OS

4. Shelly is a network administrator for a midsized college. She is examining the speed of various Internet connections. She is comparing T1 to T3. What is the maximum speed of a T1 Internet connection?

   A. 1.544 Mbps

   B. 2.048 Mbps

   C. 44.736 Mbps

   D. 274.176 Mbps

5. Juan is trying to teach a new network technician how to use network utilities. Which of the following would be the best for examining the relationship between IP addresses and MAC addresses?

   A. **arp**

   B. **nslookup**

   C. **tracert**

   D. **ipconfig**

6. Mary is reviewing various network topologies. Which of the following technologies is used when at least two machines have redundant connections?

   A. full mesh

   B. tree

   C. star

   D. partial mesh

7. Malik has been running several network commands attempting to diagnose connection problems. Which command most likely produced the following output?

   ```
   Default Server:  google-public-dns-a.google.com
   Address:  8.8.8.8

   >
   ```

   A. **nslookup**

   B. **ipconfig /d**

   C. **ipconfig /n**

   D. **arp**

8. You are a network administrator for a small company. You have been trying to determine why a particular user is having difficulty connecting to a specific website. You have executed several commands. Which command most likely produced the following output?

   ```
   1     5 ms     3 ms     2 ms   aca80001.ipt.aol.com [172.168.0.1]
   2     6 ms    15 ms     7 ms   185.108.243.33
   3     4 ms     5 ms     7 ms   192.168.194.1
   4     5 ms     4 ms    12 ms   static-185-29-95-0.mobily.com.sa [185.29.95.97]
   5     6 ms     8 ms     7 ms   ae2.0.igw.sbc.sr2.mobily.com.sa [86.51.2.62]
   6     *        *        *      Request timed out.
   7     9 ms     7 ms    19 ms   dam-adm-igw-br-02 [86.51.2.136]
   8     8 ms     7 ms     8 ms   adma-mgn-msr-02 [86.51.65.141]
   9   175 ms   185 ms   176 ms   pos-0-0-2-0.mgn.ashb.msr1.mobily.com.sa [86.51.65.67]
   10  193 ms   174 ms   197 ms   exchange-cust1.dc2.equinix.net [206.126.236.16]
   ```

   A. **ping -a**

   B. **pathping**

   C. **ping**

   D. **tracert**

Copyright Goodheart-Willcox Co., Inc.

9. Sharif has implemented a new wireless router. The router he implemented gets at least 500 Mbps. It also uses up to eight MIMO. Which 802.11 standard most closely aligns to Sharif's new router?

   A. 802.11n 2009

   B. 802.11n

   C. 802.11ad

   D. 802.11ac

10. Edward is examining cables and connecters used throughout his company's network. This includes backbones and segments. What type of cable uses an RJ-48C connector?

    A. fiber-optic

    B. coax (thinnet)

    C. coax (thicknet)

    D. T1

11. Digital Signal 0 (DS0) is a basic digital signaling rate of 64 kbit/s, corresponding to the capacity of one voice-frequency-equivalent channel. Which of the following is the number of DS0s used in a T1?

    A. 22

    B. 24

    C. 28

    D. 30

12. Users are complaining that they cannot connect to resources on the network. You check one of the computers and see it has an IP address of 169.254.3.2. The gateway and DNS servers are correct. What is the most likely problem?

    A. DHCP server unreachable

    B. Domain controller unreachable

    C. Network cable issue

    D. IP address conflict

13. Telnet (Telecommunication network) is a network protocol used on the Internet or local area networks. Which of the following is the default port for Telnet?

    A. 22

    B. 20

    C. 21

    D. 23

14. Jakub is taking inventory of cable in the network storage closet. He has found about 200 meters of RG58. Which cable type best described RG58?

    A. thinnet

    B. STP

    C. fiber-optic

    D. Ethernet over coax

15. You are configuring workstations using IPv6. Your IPv6 machine has M flag = 0 and O flag = 1. Which of the following is the most likely result?

   A. You will receive a dynamic IP address but not a gateway or DNS address.

   B. You will receive a gateway and DNS address dynamically but not an IP address.

   C. You will get dynamic IP, DNS, and gateway addresses.

   D. You will get nothing.

16. Missy is reading a network diagram. She is trying to interpret the various symbols on the diagram. What does the following symbol represent?

   A. router

   B. hub

   C. switch

   D. bridge

   E. gateway

17. Anson is examining IP addresses in his web-server log. Which of the following IP addresses is not routable?

   A. 201.35.44.1

   B. 172.16.16.1

   C. 126.14.254.1

   D. 192.10.20.1

18. Internet connectivity for a company is mission critical. The technician must be notified if the Internet router has failed. Which of the following is the best method to monitor this device?

   A. SFTP

   B. SLIP

   C. SMTP

   D. SNMP

19. After a technician came out and installed a new wireless router, one of the wired workstations began having problems connecting to the file server. This is only an intermittent problem. Which of the following actions should the technician perform first in an effort to resolve this problem?

   A. Change the router's SSID

   B. Move the router's location

   C. Check user permissions

   D. Check the cable ends

Copyright Goodheart-Willcox Co., Inc.

20. A technician is troubleshooting a printer problem in a SOHO environment. The printer is connected to the network and the computers can print using TCP/IP directly. The computers were able to print the day before, but now they cannot. Which of the following setups would aid in preventing this problem?

    A. Configure the printer to use an APIPA

    B. Change the printer setting to use multicast

    C. Assign the printer a static IP address

    D. Configure the printer on a public IP address

21. A user is having connectivity issues at multiple locations when using the RJ-45 port on the laptop. A technician wants to know if the CAT6 cable is the source of the problem. Which of the following should the technician use to troubleshoot the issue?

    A. cable tester

    B. toner probe

    C. protocol analyzer

    D. cable stripper

22. One end of a CAT5 cable is terminated following the 568B standard. The other end should be terminated using which standard to make a straight-through cable?

    A. 568B

    B. RJ-11

    C. RJ-45

    D. 568A

23. A technician receives a request to move several established phones; the technician can perform this request at the termination block by moving the wire connection. Which of the following tools is required to reconnect wires to the termination block?

    A. punch down tool

    B. snips

    C. butt set

    D. cable stripper

24. Adam is in charge of backups. He is using a type of backup that creates backup of all files that are new or modified since the last full backup. What is this called?

    A. incremental backup

    B. father-son backup

    C. differential backup

    D. full backup

25. David is working on a firewall solution. He is concerned specifically about DoS attacks. Which of the following solutions would specifically defend against that?

    A. packet-filtering firewall

    B. SPI firewall

    C. Windows Firewall

    D. application firewall

26. Which command displays Ethernet statistics for IP, TCP, ICMP, and UDP?

    A. **nbtstat**

    B. **arp**

    C. **netstat**

    D. **nslookup**

27. What type of attack depends on the attacker entering JavaScript into a text area that is intended for users to enter text that will be viewed by other users?

    A. SQL injection

    B. click jacking

    C. cross-site scripting

    D. blue jacking

28. Janine is looking for an algorithm that is often used to exchange keys over an insecure medium. Which of the following is used for exchanging secret keys over an insecure public network?

    A. Diffie-Hellman

    B. RSA

    C. IDEA

    D. MD5

29. Alice wants to send Bob a message. She is concerned about preventing Eve from intercepting and reading the message. Using asymmetric cryptography, what key should Alice use to encrypt the message?

    A. Bob's public key

    B. Bob's private key

    C. Alice's public key

    D. Alice's private key

30. Kelly is new to IPv6. She is trying to identify IPv6 addresses. Which of the following is an example of an IPv6 address?

    A. 12:AD:2B:DF:23:C4

    B. 323.244.454.100

    C. fe80::1c7d:22de:51cc:efcd

    D. 10.23.24.12.66.46

Copyright Goodheart-Willcox Co., Inc.

31. Which is an example of router convergence?

    A. All routers are connected to the same gateway.

    B. All routers share the same routing table information.

    C. All routers are connected to the same domain.

    D. A specified router designated as the "master router" is used to control all other router paths.

32. In the OSI model, which of the following layers would be the cause of a session time-out while browsing the web?

    A. Layer 2

    B. Layer 3

    C. Layer 5

    D. Layer 7

33. Which of the following cable types are the most widely used in a corporate gigabit network scheme?

    A. CAT5

    B. CAT6

    C. CAT1

    D. CAT3

34. A network technician is installing a small wireless network. A requirement is that individual users must authenticate using usernames and passwords. Which of the following technologies would support users authenticating with encrypted usernames and passwords?

    A. WPA TLS

    B. WPA PEAP

    C. 64-bit WEP

    D. 128-bit WEP

35. A client wants to extend the range of her wireless network without running wires throughout the small office. Which of the following could be implemented with the LEAST administrative effort?

    A. Install an 802.11n router and change all NICs to match

    B. Install an additional router to help with congestion

    C. Install a WAP in the middle of the office

    D. Install a repeater at the end of the office

36. Which represents a classless subnet mask that can be customized to a different length for each subnet based on its number of nodes?

    A. Class E networks

    B. VPN

    C. VLSM

    D CSM

Copyright Goodheart-Willcox Co., Inc.

37. What routing algorithm is based only on the number of hops required?

    A. BGP

    B. IGRP

    C. OSPF

    D. IRP

38. Your network needs a subnet that will have 35 nodes. What subnet mask should you use?

    A. 255.255.255.192

    B. 255.255.255.240

    C. 255.255.255.128

    D. 255.255.255.232

39. Which of the following data are included in a wireless access point's beacon frame?

    A. IP and MAC address

    B. SSID and WEP key

    C. WEP key and channel

    D. SSID and MAC address

40. Mark is working on setting up VoIP for the sales team at his company. Which protocol is used to establish and then terminate a VoIP session?

    A. FTP

    B. RTP

    C. RIP

    D. SIP

41. Martha is responsible for the company VPN. She is using IPSec. She wants the entire packet to be encrypted, including the header. Which mode should she use?

    A. tunnel

    B. transport

    C. secure

    D. masked

42. Users in your department complain about a slow Internet connection. You monitor the external interface of your company's border router and notice an unusually large quantity of ICMP Echo Reply packets. Of what type of attack is your company currently a victim?

    A. Smurf attack

    B. DDOS attack

    C. TCP hijacking attack

    D. TCP SYN flood attack

43. Emma is looking for a cryptographic hash function to use with message integrity in her company's e-mail system. She must select an algorithm to use. Which of the following is a cryptographic hash function?

    A. RSA

    B. SHA1

    C. RC4

    D. ECC

44. Jayne is the security administrator in charge of incident response at ACME brick. There has been a breach, and she wants to take the most critical first step in addressing the breach. Which of the following would be the best step for her to take?

    A. Eliminate all means of intruder access

    B. Contain the intrusion

    C. Determine to what extent systems and data are compromised

    D. Communicate with relevant parties

45. James is performing a port scan of a network as part of a security audit. He notices that the domain controller is using secure LDAP. Which of the following ports would lead him to that conclusion?

    A. 53

    B. 389

    C. 443

    D. 636

46. What is the default port for secure SMTP?

    A. 464

    B. 465

    C. 636

    D. 445

47. George is very concerned about server uptime. Which method should he implement to improve network system uptime?

    A. load balancing

    B. cache engine

    C. fault tolerance

    D. traffic shaping

48. You are responsible for a server cluster used for e-commerce. You need to have the best performance possible. Which method will improve overall network performance for high-bandwidth applications?

    A. load balancing

    B. port mirroring

    C. fault tolerance

    D. traffic shaping

Copyright Goodheart-Willcox Co., Inc.

49. Octavia is responsible for router configuration in her company's network. One of her concerns is switching loops. Which protocol is designed to prevent switching loops?

    A. FTP

    B. STP

    C. VLAN

    D. MS-CHAP

50. Which device would you use to prevent a single user on a local area network from slowing the network response because they are constantly downloading large volumes of data from the Internet?

    A. proxy server

    B. CSU/DSU

    C. bandwidth shaper

    D. bridge

Scoring the Exam

Ideally, you should answer at least 80 percent of the answers correctly. In this case, that means 40 out of 50 correct. After your instructor scores your practice exam, focus on the questions you answered incorrectly. More information can be obtained from those than your correct answers. Since these are your weakest areas, revisit the topics of focus in your incorrect questions for review and practice.

Network+ Note

Visit the Microsoft's support website and look at articles that will reinforce knowledge required for the Network+ Certification Exam. Pay particular attention to problems associated with the installation process. Also, look at the articles on troubleshooting tools provided by the operating systems. Many of these articles are a source of information for the Network+ Certification Exam.

Copyright Goodheart-Willcox Co., Inc.

Summary

Network+ Certification Exam

- The Network+ Certification Exam contains 90 questions.
- The maximum time allotted to answer the questions on the Network+ Certification Exam is 90 minutes.
- The N10-007 domains include Network Concepts, Network Infrastructure, Network Operations, Network Security, and Troubleshooting and Tools.
- Review and analyze all of the Network+ Certification Exam objectives to become familiar with the knowledge areas for which the exam tests.

Preparation Strategy

- Match the Network+ Certification Exam objective details to quality resource material.
- Identify and practice laboratory activities that match the Network+ Certification Exam objectives.
- Take practice exams, and then identify and review problem areas.

Review Questions

1. How many questions are on the Network+ Certification Exam?
2. What is the minimum passing score for the Network+ Certification Exam?
3. List the key points for an exam preparation strategy.
4. Why do you not want to depend on a commercial study guide to prepare for the exam?
5. What other CompTIA exam objectives may you want to use to help you prepare for the Network+ Certification Exam?

Copyright Goodheart-Willcox Co., Inc.

CHAPTER 20
Employment in the Field of Networking Technology

Learning Outcomes

- Compare networking technology careers.
- Identify available sources of career information.
- Recall general and college education requirements in an information technology field.
- Compare certification options.
- Describe the necessary steps in finding and retaining employment.

Key Terms

A+ Certification
business plan
consultant
cover letter
digital citizenship
engineer
entrepreneur
Linux+ Certification
LPIC-1 Certification
LPIC-2 Certification
LPIC-3 Certification

Microsoft Certified Solutions
   Associate (MCSA) Certification
Microsoft Certified Solutions
   Developer (MCSD) Certification
Microsoft Certified Solutions Expert
   (MCSE) Certification
Microsoft Office Specialist (MOS)
   Certification
Microsoft Technology Associate
   (MTA) Certification
network support specialist
Network+ Certification

PDI+ Certification
professionalism
programmer
reference
résumé
Security+ Certification
Server+ Certification
soft skills
systems analyst
web developer
web master

Copyright Goodheart-Willcox Co., Inc.

Overview

By successfully reaching this point in the textbook, you have likely determined if you do or do not want to pursue a career in networking technology. Networking is one of the fastest growing fields within the scope of computer technology. If you have the interest, desire, and ability, you can find a rewarding career in this field. It should also be noted that networking is the gateway to many other professions. Cybersecurity, digital forensics, and penetration testing all begin with a solid knowledge of networking.

Networking technology and related computer careers require a basic education in computers and networking as well as advanced education in the field. Technology is constantly advancing at a fast pace. New ideas become realities every day. As a professional in the computer and networking field, you will be required to update your skills continually through education and training. Commercial certification in one or more technology fields is often required and always encouraged.

To keep up with the rapid changes in networking technology, you must form some type of action plan. Your personal plan must include strategies for gaining initial training and certifications and keeping up to date with the changes and ways to expand your opportunities for advancement in the IT field. This chapter discusses ways to gain employment and advance your career. While you may already be employed in a networking, computer repair, or related job, this chapter may help you better define your career goals. First, it is important to look at some of the many different job titles in the IT industry.

Information Technology Industry Careers

There is a wide variety of careers in the information technology (IT) industry. Networking is the key to communication and information systems that play a major role in business and daily life. Think of all the things that depend on computer networks. For example, in the communication industry, telephone, television, and radio are linked to computer networks. The manufacturing industry uses computers and networks to design, build, inventory, and sell most everything it makes. Computer networks control robots and automate assembly lines. In the business world, computer networks make communication and business nearly instantaneous. Sharing information within and among companies and the Internet is commonplace. Tasks that, in the past, required days and months to complete are now completed automatically or within minutes. The entire banking industry relies on networked computers to calculate and track money exchanges and post records of interest, earnings, and mortgage statistics.

Network technology has also saturated the field of medicine. Surgeons can perform laser and other surgery through long-distance communication over networks, and patient medical records are computerized. MRI scans can be transmitted instantly across a network to any distant city where other doctors can evaluate them. Additionally, patients can now videoconference with a doctor for a variety of illnesses and conditions, as shown in Figure 20-1. In fact, there is now a separate field called healthcare information technology. Architects and engineers rely on computers to design structures around the world. Not only can they design the structure, they can take a virtual tour of the design from another country. Law enforcement, the military, and other governmental units are completely reliant on networking technology. Most nations now have network professionals in their militaries.

Figure 20-1 Network technology plays a vital role in the field of medicine. It can provide patients with the ability to videoconference with their doctors over a secure connection.

Rocketclips, Inc./Shutterstock.com

The need for people with networking and other computer skills has rapidly grown and will continue to grow. There are many careers in the IT industry from which to choose. Some of the many careers include the following:

- network support specialist
- network administrator
- systems analyst
- consultant
- technical salesperson
- web developer
- programmer
- software engineer
- entrepreneur

Network Support Specialist

As a **network support specialist**, you will be required to assist users and customers whenever they encounter a network problem. Often, a network support specialist is assigned to a help desk. They answer phone calls, interpret user problems, and recommend solutions or dispatch a technician to the user's workstation. Most of the support they provide is through the Remote Assistance utility found in Windows operating systems, similar to the technician shown in Figure 20-2. As a part of the role of support, network support specialists are often required to conduct training sessions for employees and write training manuals.

A network support specialist works under the direct supervision of a network administrator. The network administrator usually directs the network support specialists' activities for the day. Many network administrators started their careers as network support specialists.

A network support specialist must continuously learn about new software packages, operating systems, hardware, security, data storage, and other key elements of networking. New hardware systems, software packages, service packs, and security software are continuously developed. You will need to expand your knowledge in these areas to make yourself even more valuable as a network support specialist and to advance to network administrator.

Copyright Goodheart-Willcox Co., Inc.

Figure 20-2 A network support specialist is often assigned to a help desk. The network support specialist interprets user problems and can often provide support over the phone or remotely through a program like Remote Assistance.

goodluz/Shutterstock.com

Network Administrator

Most of the maintenance of a network system is the result of constant monitoring by a network administrator. Recall from Chapter 1 that a *network administrator* is the overall administrator who controls access to the network and its shares. This person is also ultimately responsible for the type, extent, and frequency of maintenance to be performed. While the network support specialist may perform routine maintenance, he or she does so under the direction of a network administrator. Network administrators are also responsible for the installation, configuration, and maintenance of a LAN, MAN, or WAN. They may perform many routine administrative functions, such as work with hardware and software vendors, make written and oral presentations about the state of the network, interview prospective employees, evaluate employee performance, coordinate work schedules, order supplies and equipment, and prepare budget reports. It is not unusual for this type of position to require a four-year degree in addition to one to two years of technical training and experience as a network specialist or technician.

Systems Analyst

A **systems analyst** is responsible for analyzing, evaluating, and recommending business software systems. Typically, a systems analyst is involved in designing systems and making recommendations rather than involved in day-to-day network operations. Many systems analysts work for hardware and software companies. A systems analyst works with clients by analyzing the client's business and making recommendations. He or she also designs network systems to match the needs of the client's business.

Some systems analysts work as independent contractors or consultants. As a consultant, they sell their expertise as a service to organizations that are about to install, upgrade, or modify a network system. A systems analyst must be able to communicate effectively with programmers, technicians, and engineers and with clients who have limited computer system knowledge. These positions usually require a four-year degree.

Copyright Goodheart-Willcox Co., Inc.

Consultant

Consulting is another growing business in the IT industry. A **consultant** works with clients on projects and makes recommendations based on his or her expertise, as demonstrated in Figure 20-3. The specific job a consultant does often depends on what work is needed. A client pays a consultant for his or her expertise and time. When the job is completed, the consultant is free to move on to a new job and client.

In the case of networking technology, it is recommended that a person become a consultant after extensive experience in the field. Consultants are expected to have answers to many challenges or be able to research them quickly. Consultants usually have vast expertise in one or more particular aspects of the IT industry, such as security, systems analysis, network design, and electronic marketing.

Figure 20-3 Companies often rely on consultants for their expertise in certain areas.

Monkey Business Images/Shutterstock.com

Technical Salesperson

Technical salespersons are always needed in the industry to represent manufacturers of hardware and software. Many technical salespeople originally started out as a technician and then moved into sales. They are typically required to obtain a certification directly related to their field of expertise. For example, if a technical salesperson is representing an antivirus software manufacturer, he or she will likely be required to obtain certification in cybersecurity or the specific product he or she is selling. A person seeking a career in technical sales needs an outgoing personality, must be well-groomed, and must like working with people. This is not a job for the shy or timid.

Tech Tip

The web page is often referred to as the *front end* while the support of the web server is referred to as the *back end*.

Web Developer

Web administration requires the design and implementation of web pages for internal and external websites. A **web developer** is responsible for converting written documents into HTML or other web-page programming languages. Web developers usually have to interpret the needs of their employers and convert those needs into web-page presentations. This job requires not only training in web-page programming languages, but also some expertise in networking technology. A web developer also requires some expertise in art and graphics. The ability to use a digital camera and video equipment and having video editing skills is beneficial.

Copyright Goodheart-Willcox Co., Inc.

There are many self-taught web-page designers. However, additional training in networking or server technology is likely needed to land a job as a web master, administrator, or technician. A **web master**, or *web administrator*, is responsible for maintaining websites and web servers and ensuring search engine optimization (SEO). This position requires expertise in web-programming languages, such as HTML, XML, CSS, JAVA, JavaScript, ActiveX, and familiarity with server management of IIS, Apache, Unix, Linux, and Microsoft systems. They are also well versed in transaction software and web-based security. Certification is typically a minimal job requirement. Web masters also have input on the website design and often respond to user comments.

Programmer

A **programmer** writes, tests, and modifies software programs. There are many programming languages from which to choose, and many programmers master more than one programming language. Some programming languages you may wish to learn are C, C++, Prolog, or JAVA. C and C++ are excellent programming languages to learn and a recommended starting point. Prolog is a programming language used in artificial intelligence and machines. One of the hottest programming languages today is JAVA. Other languages to consider are Visual Basic and XML.

Programmers vary from self-taught to college-educated. When college-educated, programmers are generally referred to as *software engineers*. Many programmers work as independent contractors who program or modify custom software packages to meet the needs of their employer. Some programmers are known as program analysts.

Engineer

An **engineer** is a degreed professional who possesses high-level skills necessary to solve problems related to his or her field of expertise. To become an engineer requires a four- to six-year college degree. Engineers require a strong background in mathematics, sciences, programming languages, and hardware. They typically advance to management and project leadership positions. If an engineer exhibits leadership skills, he or she often becomes the chief technology officer. Engineers often command the highest salaries in the IT job market. Those who earn a doctoral degree often become university-level engineering or computer science faculty. They also are employed in the area of research where they are responsible for developing new technologies.

Entrepreneur

An **entrepreneur** owns and operates a business. This person usually starts with an idea for filling a gap in a given marketplace or identifying where a new product or service is needed. An entrepreneur then develops a business plan. A **business plan** outlines the goals for the business and includes action plans and a timetable for meeting those goals. Business plans are required for entrepreneurs seeking financial support to open businesses. A good business plan is vital if the business is to succeed.

In addition to a sound business plan, a successful entrepreneur possesses certain skills. A successful entrepreneur has knowledge of the product or service he or she plans to provide. This knowledge allows the entrepreneur to make smart business decisions. An ideal entrepreneur also has sound management skills. These skills allow the entrepreneur to manage resources such as money, time, and employees. Resource management is critical to success. A serious lack of skill in any of these areas can lead to certain failure. The ability to think creatively and wisely are also

Copyright Goodheart-Willcox Co., Inc.

important skills for an entrepreneur to have. These skills allow him or her to control the business and move it in the right direction.

Entrepreneurial opportunities are vast in the IT industry. Along with the growth of networking technologies and products, growth has occurred in servicing these technologies and products. Installing, maintaining, and servicing networks is and will continue to be a sound business in the industry.

Career Information Sources

The major source of job information, especially information regarding information technology and networking, is the Internet. Many Internet sources contain job listings and job matching services. Nearly every college and school is connected to such a service. A valuable reference is the *Occupational Outlook Handbook*, which is published by the United States Bureau of Labor Statistics. Most school, community college, university, and public libraries have copies of this book. Information can be accessed digitally from the Bureau of Labor Statistics website, www.bls.gov.

A great amount of career and training information can be found on the Internet. Many company websites list employment opportunities, a brief job description, and the required skills and educational level for the job. The following are some careers you may find listed when searching these sources:

- analyst
- ATM engineer
- chief information officer
- customer service representative
- data communication engineer
- database specialist
- entry-level network technician
- industrial control engineer
- Internet systems administrator
- IT consultant
- network engineer
- network hardware specialist
- network installer
- network security specialist
- network support professional
- network training specialist
- programmer
- service/help desk technician
- software engineer
- systems engineer
- technical forensics technician
- technical sales and marketing professional
- technical writer
- telecommunication data specialist
- voice over IP (VoIP) engineer

Copyright Goodheart-Willcox Co., Inc.

- web developer

- web master

- website developer

School career counselors and local labor market offices are outstanding sources of career information as well. They can help you find information on particular careers and colleges, training programs, and military service opportunities. Career counselors and those who work in local labor market offices are typically well-informed and ready to help you in your search for a job or training. Additionally, schools typically have job information and placement services available.

Each person must ask himself or herself several questions before going further into the IT arena. Have you enjoyed this *Networking Fundamentals* textbook and the laboratory activities? The fact that you are studying networking shows that you likely already have a good background in computers and an interest in this area. Have you taken other classes in computer technology? Did you like them? Did you do well? Give serious thought to your responses to the above questions and guidelines. Your responses may be the start you need to achieve success in your chosen area.

General and College Education

The educational requirements for jobs in the IT industry vary. A minimum of a high school education is a solid foundation on which to build. Very few high school graduates enter the networking industry directly and are required to receive specialized education in the training programs maintained by large companies. Specialized training may also come from formal training in colleges, technical schools, or the military. To gain promotions, however, advanced certifications and degrees are required.

College is an excellent option for advancement in the IT industry. A college education in a field related to the IT industry is an excellent choice because of the demand for people with a college degree. A college education not only provides a technical background, it provides preparation for the business world through other classes, such as technical writing, business writing, and speech. These classes teach basic communication skills, which are just as important as IT skills.

If you plan to advance in the IT business world, you must master the skills of communication, both written and spoken. You may need to give presentations not only inside your company but also to prospective clients for your company. You need to have the skills to prepare written materials and make a presentation that represents your company. For example, your company may be bidding to contract a networking project for a firm. During the process of meeting with the firm, a single person or a team representing your company will need to make a presentation to attempt to gain the firm's business. If you plan to be a part of the team, you will need the very best communication skills. A technician who knows the technology and who can communicate well is always in demand, Figure 20-4.

There is a direct correlation between salary and education level. Research proves that as a person's education level increases, so does his or her salary level. While the direct correlation indicates college as a major factor, additional certifications are also a direct influence. An ideal situation for a person planning a future in the IT industry is to combine technological education with another field of study, such as business administration, finance, mathematics, science, electronics, medical, law enforcement, or any other field of interest. A combination of degrees greatly increases a person's employability.

Many community colleges offer courses and programs in the network technology field. You can take specific courses to learn more about a particular subject

Copyright Goodheart-Willcox Co., Inc.

Figure 20-4 In the networking field, you may be required to present a product or a system plan to a group of clients. The ability to communicate technical information to those without your expertise is crucial.

l i g h t p o e t/Shutterstock.com

without going for a degree. Alternative pathways, such as military training, are also available to gain a particular skill. The military offers many specialized areas of study in the networking and computer technology fields. The opportunities for education and for gaining valuable work experiences are excellent in the military.

As an IT professional, you will be learning the rest of your life. The total knowledge base related to the computer industry is practically limitless. Part of what you know now may be partially obsolete in just a few months. If you did not learn another thing from this point forward, many of your skills would be completely obsolete within a year or two.

Certification

Certification is a way to advance your knowledge and career in the IT industry. Many companies require certifications prior to hiring. When combined with work experience, certification can prove your abilities to an employer. It can also advance your career inside a company and provide you with job security.

Obtaining your CompTIA Network+ and A+ Certifications should just be the beginning. It is recommended that a person immediately begin advancing toward other CompTIA certifications, such as Security+, once the Network+ and A+ Certifications are obtained. Areas of specialization, such as network administration, as well as the Microsoft Certified Technical Specialist (MCTS) certification are also fruitful career paths a person can take after obtaining introductory certifications.

Microsoft, Cisco Systems, and many other companies offer certification exams in many advanced fields of study. One of the most demanding certifications offered by Microsoft is the Microsoft Certified Information Technology Professional (MCITP). To receive this certification, you must pass a series of exams to prove your knowledge and competency. Training preparation for this certification can be delivered in many ways, such as private schools, public schools, special seminars, online educational programs, and self-study. The following sections explore various certifications in greater detail.

Copyright Goodheart-Willcox Co., Inc.

CompTIA Certifications

The CompTIA organization offers certification in many areas. Receiving a CompTIA A+ and Network+ Certification is just the beginning. Some advanced CompTIA certifications available include Security+, Server+, Linux+, and PDI+.

A+

The **A+ Certification** is designed to test a person's knowledge related to PC support and repair. This certification requires passing two separate exams. The exams cover a broad range of topics as related to computers.

Over the years, the format of the test has changed. For example, for the original CompTIA A+ Certification, one exam covered hardware and another exam covered software. Later, the format was changed so that the first exam covered general knowledge as related to the PC, and the second exam matched an area of expertise, such as PC support technician, network support technician, or hardware support and repair. Currently, the A+ Certification exam consists of two similar exams. As of this writing, the main differences between these two exams are that one exam covers basic PC hardware and peripherals, mobile device hardware, network and troubleshooting hardware, and network connectivity. The other exam tests candidates on their knowledge of operating system configuration for Windows, iOS, Android, Apple OS X, and Linux; security; and cloud-computing fundamentals and operation.

CompTIA revises the A+ Certification Examination Objectives approximately every three years or sooner to keep pace with the rapidly changing field of PC repair. Minor changes in the test objectives can occur at any time between major revisions. Always check the CompTIA website for the very latest information about the A+ Certification Examination Objectives.

Network+

The **Network+ Certification** measures the skills necessary for an entry-level network support technician. The typical Network+ candidate should have the A+ Certification or equivalent knowledge. It is also recommended that the candidate have at least nine months of network experience before attempting the exam. The exam is vendor-neutral and is recognized by leading network organizations such as Cisco and HP as part of their certification process. It is an excellent starting point for students interested in further certification in the networking technology areas.

Security+

The **Security+ Certification** requires knowledge related to generally accepted security practices. Some of the areas covered are network infrastructure, cryptography, access control, malware, and wireless security. As with all the other CompTIA certifications, the exam is vendor-neutral. The Security+ Certification is an excellent choice for the next certificate after achieving the Network+ Certification. CompTIA recommends, but does not require, that the Security+ candidate have two years of experience and Network+ Certification.

Server+

The **Server+ Certification** tests a person's knowledge of network server hardware and software. Candidates are tested on installing, configuring, diagnosing, and troubleshooting network server hardware and network operating systems. The exam requires an in-depth knowledge of protocols, backup system standards, and system security.

Copyright Goodheart-Willcox Co., Inc.

Linux+

The **Linux+ Certification** tests a person's knowledge of the Linux operating system. It covers installing, configuring, administering, and troubleshooting the Linux operating system for a single PC and a network server.

PDI+

The **PDI+ Certification** measures a candidate's ability to configure and repair document-imaging devices such as printers, copiers, scanners, fax machines, and multifunctional machines. The test covers the theory of imaging as related to printing and scanning devices and also knowledge of basic electronics. The electronics knowledge required is not in-depth but rather limited to general information about relays, power supplies, diodes, transistors, common ICs, using a multimeter, and electrical safety. Also tested for on the exam is basic knowledge of networking fundamentals limited to simple network configuration and sharing. There are no prerequisites for this exam, but CompTIA recommends that the candidate have some work experience.

Microsoft Certifications

There are many different Microsoft certifications, each with various levels of certification. As new products are developed and released, these certifications evolve in scope and requirement. The entire scope of certifications can appear quite complex and confusing at first, but on further examination, there are only a few exams to start with based on the desired field of expertise. The first Microsoft certification you might consider after achieving CompTIA certification is the Microsoft Technology Associate (MTA).

MTA

The **Microsoft Technology Associate (MTA) Certification** is an entry-level certification that proves a person's basic technological knowledge and skills. There is no prerequisite for an MTA certification. While the MTA is considered entry-level and it is suggested this is the first certification obtained through Microsoft, it does not serve as a prerequisite for more advanced certifications, nor does it qualify as a Microsoft Certified Professional (MCP) exam.

MCSA

The **Microsoft Certified Solutions Associate (MCSA) Certification** is designed for those seeking entry-level employment in an IT field. This certification is often a prerequisite for more advanced certifications. The MCSA certification includes multiple exams. These individual exams allow candidates to take a more focused approach and certify in one specific area at a time. These areas include BI reporting, cloud platforms, data engineering with Azure, Linux on Azure, machine learning, Microsoft Dynamics 365, Microsoft Dynamics 365 for operations, Office 365, various SQL areas, universal Windows platform, web applications, Windows 10, Windows Server 2012, and Windows Server 2016.

MCSD

The **Microsoft Certified Solutions Developer (MCSD) Certification** confirms a person's knowledge of essential mobile or web-based applications and services. The MCSA certification serves as a prerequisite to this exam. This means candidates must hold the MCSA certification in order to fulfill the qualifications needed to obtain the

Copyright Goodheart-Willcox Co., Inc.

MCSD certification. Currently, only one area exists in the MCSD certification: app building.

MCSE

The **Microsoft Certified Solutions Expert (MCSE) Certification** is intended for those seeking to prove the ability to create and implement solutions across multiple platforms and technologies. Similar to the MCSA certification, candidates can choose a specific area in which they are seeking certification. These focused areas within the MCSE category include business applications, cloud platform and infrastructure, data management and analytics, mobility, and productivity.

MOS

The **Microsoft Office Specialist (MOS) Certification** is based on Microsoft Office products beginning with the 2000 versions. Today, this certification area is based on Microsoft Office 2016. Some of the areas offered for certification are Microsoft Word, Excel, PowerPoint, Outlook, and Access. The contents of the certification exams are based on a particular release version of the Microsoft Office product. For example, there are several versions of Microsoft Word certification exams, each based on the release date of the particular Microsoft Office product, such as 2003 and 2007.

There are three levels to the MOS Certification: Specialist, Master, and Expert. *Specialist certifications* demonstrate necessary skills to work in the Microsoft Office environment and use each program effectively. *Master certifications* verify a person's deep level of understanding of the Microsoft Office programs and above-average usage skills. *Expert certifications* prove advanced Microsoft Office skills. Currently, only Word and Excel are available for Expert-level certifications.

To learn more about the various Microsoft certifications, visit the Microsoft Learning website located at www.microsoft.com/learning/en/us/default.aspx. You can also locate this website by conducting an Internet search using the phrase Microsoft certification learning.

Cisco Certifications and Training

Cisco Corporation provides training opportunities at high schools and colleges all over the world. Cisco training sites are referred to as *academies*. The major emphasis at Cisco academies is network design, implementation, and troubleshooting as related to Cisco products.

Academy courses are designed as a combination of lecture, textbook, online learning, and hands-on laboratory activities. Some of the various certifications that can be earned at the Cisco academies are Cisco Certified Network Associate (CCNA), Cisco Certified Network Professional (CCNP), and Cisco Certified Entry Networking Technician (CCENT). There are also certifications available related to security, wireless devices, VoIP, VPN, and other specializations. The CCENT is one of the latest Cisco certifications and is designed for an entry-level job in networking, similar to the Network+ Certification. The biggest difference is that the Cisco CCENT requires basic knowledge and skills for programming switches and routers. You can locate the Cisco academy nearest you by visiting the Cisco website (www.cisco.com).

LPIC

The Linux Professional Institute (LPI) offers certification for Linux through a vendor-neutral exam. Other organizations, such as CompTIA, Red Hat Linux, IBM, HP, and Ubuntu have started to award Linux Professional Institute Certification (LPIC) credit toward their own certifications. There are three levels of LPI certification

Copyright Goodheart-Willcox Co., Inc.

exams: LPIC-1, LPIC-2, and LPIC-3. There are two exams each for LPIC-1 and LPIC-2 and one exam for LPIC-3. In the future, the LPIC-3 level is expected to require two exams.

LPIC-1

LPIC-1 Certification is an introductory-level certification that measures basic skills associated with installing, configuring, and managing a Linux operating system. Heavy emphasis is on using the command line to configure the operating system rather than the GUI. The LPIC-1 is a prerequisite to LPIC-2. It is also the certification level that is recognized for credit toward most other vendor-specific versions of Linux certification.

LPIC-2

LPIC-2 Certification is the second level of Linux certification and requires a more in-depth knowledge base than LPIC-1. Areas of emphasis are small, mixed networks and configuring a Linux Internet gateway and Internet server. The test also covers basic skills associated with installing and configuring Linux-based mail services, proxy server, news server, firewall, and web server. It is a prerequisite to LPIC-3.

LPIC-3

LPIC-3 Certification measures the Linux skill set for supporting a large, enterprise Linux network. Areas of emphasis are mixed environment interoperability, virtualization, mail and messaging, and in-depth security configuration. To learn more about the LPI organization, visit www.lpi.org.

Other Certifications

Many other companies have certification programs besides the ones outlined in the previous sections. Some of the companies are 3Com, Nortel Networks, HP, Red Hat, Sun Microsystems, and Oracle. More in-depth information about these certifications, such as exam outlines, study materials, available training, and prerequisites, can be found at the related websites. There are over 120 different companies and organizations that offer certifications and over 300 different types of certifications you may earn.

Many different certifications are available for network technicians and IT professionals. Individuals can customize their credentials by selecting different areas of certification similar to the way a university student selects classes for credit toward a degree. In fact, a collection of certifications can be similar to a university degree.

After finishing this course, it is suggested that you select a field of specialization. This is the time to begin training for a specialized certification. Two common areas are Microsoft and Cisco. These areas have shown the most interest of entry-level professionals and students. You may wish to seek employment before beginning your next level of training or train concurrently while employed. Going to school while employed is an excellent method to reinforce what you are learning in the classroom. Remember, there is a direct correlation between knowledge and earnings. The more you know, the more you will earn.

The IT industry demands continuing education of its workforce. If you choose to join the IT workforce, be prepared for a lifetime of study. New systems, protocols, software, and hardware are constantly introduced. Often, these new systems demand new expertise to install, service, and repair. You can continue your education in a number of ways, such as attending college classes, seminars, online courses, and self-study, as shown in Figure 20-5.

Copyright Goodheart-Willcox Co., Inc.

Burlingham/Shutterstock.com

Figure 20-5 Keeping up with the continuously changing field of computer and networking technology requires constant study. Some of the ways you can continue your education include attending college classes and seminars, taking online courses, and self-study.

You may choose not to pursue other certifications. This decision is acceptable, as long as you keep your skills current. You should subscribe to and read professional journals and newsletters in your area of work. Take as many courses as you possibly can, such as digital electronics, to enhance your networking and computer skills. If you are not willing to hone your skills continuously, then you should choose another, less demanding field of employment.

Employment

The three most important factors that will determine your ability to secure a position with an employer are your job history, technical expertise, and the job interview. A job history tells the employer a lot about your future as an employee, even if your job experiences are unrelated to the job for which you are applying. You may be just entering the IT profession. A solid recommendation from a past employer can make the difference. For example, if an applicant that has worked part-time while attending school for the last two years and a recommendation from the applicant's past employer shows a proven record of dependability, this applicant will have a great advantage. A person with no work experience leaves this aspect unknown.

Your training and work experiences show your technical expertise. If you have prior technical experiences, this can prove to be a real asset. Another applicant may have no technical employment history or any technical training. They may have simple, informal experience with a computer at home or have helped friends, and now they believe they can handle the job. This is where your training, experience, and especially your certification will put you ahead of the others.

Applying for a Job

While an in-person application may be suitable for many occupations and places of work, many companies would rather a candidate apply online through either an online job board or the company website. Applying for jobs online involves using job-search websites such as LinkedIn, Monster, Indeed, or CareerBuilder. Most of these sites will allow you to conduct a search for jobs using locations and keywords and apply for the jobs you want. Some may even allow a candidate to post employment documents, such as a résumé, cover letter, or certificate. The following section outlines the job-search process, which includes finding and applying for a job opening,

Copyright Goodheart-Willcox Co., Inc.

preparing a résumé, preparing a cover letter, and preparing for and executing a job interview.

Job Search Ideas

Finding a job can be a time-consuming and difficult task. The Internet has the most up-to-date information regarding job searches, as shown in Figure 20-6. You can often complete an application online. Many of these websites will allow candidates to post their résumés online, though you may be required to create a user account and profile. This allows employers to conduct searches and find résumés they feel match their needs. Sometimes, just having a résumé on the right website at the right time can help a person find gainful employment.

Figure 20-6 The Internet is a great place to conduct a job search. Many sites have search engines that allow you to enter a key word, job category, and location.

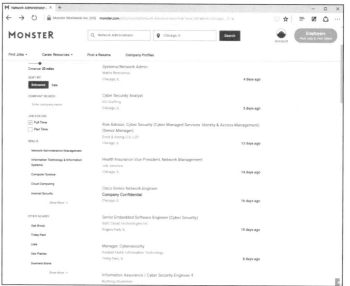

Goodheart-Willcox Publisher

Outside of the Internet, jobs can be found in a variety of places. The *Occupational Outlook Handbook* also has tips for conducting a job search. Start by talking to your parents, neighbors, teachers, or career counselors. These people may know of job openings that have not been advertised. Read the classified advertisements in the newspaper, especially in the Sunday editions. Additionally, private employment agencies might also provide leads, but they often charge a fee for a job placement.

Completing and Submitting a Job Application

Job applications will vary in appearance but seek to gather the same basic information. Besides routine information such as your name, address, telephone number, and Social Security number, the application typically requires information about your references and work experiences. It will also ask about police records or any crimes for which you may have been convicted. The application may ask you to write a short summary of why you want the position.

Whenever you fill out the job application, do your best to make it legible to the reader. Compare the two applications shown in Figure 20-7. If the job application is not legible, it will often not be reviewed very thoroughly. In fact, some personnel

Copyright Goodheart-Willcox Co., Inc.

Figure 20-7 Write neatly (application on the left) when filling out employment applications or taking tests. Poor penmanship (application on the right) can make a bad impression on a prospective employer.

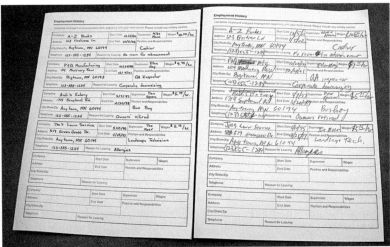

Goodheart-Willcox Publisher

offices will not even consider an application that is barely legible. When submitting a job application, include a copy of your résumé and a cover letter.

Preparing a Résumé

A **résumé** is a document that profiles a person's career goals, education, and work history. On your résumé, list all education and training you have had in reverse chronological order. List all past employment in sequence, and do not leave gaps in your employment history. If you stopped your employment to go to school, note that in your employment history. This makes sure your potential employer does not think you are leaving out an employer who may not give you a good reference. List any reason there may be a break in employment. Additional material that is optional as a part of your résumé can include copies of certifications, transcripts, or letters of reference. Typically, these will be verified if listed on your résumé. However, you should not include more than a few. Employers do not appreciate lengthy résumés.

A quality résumé can make a great impression on an employer. Use a good-quality paper and a cover sheet. Make sure you have produced a good-quality copy that they may keep. Never give a potential employer a poor-quality copy.

Preparing a Cover Letter

A **cover letter** is formal communication that accompanies a person's résumé or job application. It introduces the candidate to the employer and highlights why he or she is applying for the vacant position. The object of a cover letter is to highlight your skills and request an interview. Cover letters can be used to apply for a position, obtain information about any potential positions with the company, or introduce an applicant to an employer in the hopes the employer will remember the applicant when a position opens.

An ideal cover letter is no longer than one page and does not repeat information found on a résumé. It should be about you and why you are interested in working for a company. Cover letters should be submitted with a résumé and job application. Most companies request that cover letters be submitted electronically through the preferred application software or website. However, if you are submitting your résumé and application in person, it is appropriate to do the same with a cover letter.

Copyright Goodheart-Willcox Co., Inc.

Preparing for an Interview

After applying for a position and submitting a résumé and cover letter, with luck, you will be offered an interview. Always learn about the company or prospective employer before your interview. Many times, this information is available on the company's website. This preparation lets the employer know you are truly interested in the company and that you possess the personal initiative to research and learn.

Have a specific job or jobs in mind, generally at an entry level. Most companies do not begin a new employee in a high-level job until the new employee has proven his or herself to the company. Remember, in the networking field, you will have access to the highest level of company security. A trustworthy employee is critical.

Review your qualifications for the job. Make sure your qualifications match those desired by the employer. Do not waste the employer's time or your own by interviewing for a job that is far beyond your level. For example, if you are an entry-level technician, do not apply for a job as a network administrator.

Prepare to answer broad questions about yourself. It is wise to practice interviewing with someone who has knowledge about job interviews. A family member or friend who regularly does hiring for a company can be a great help, even if the hiring they do is not related to the field in which you are seeking employment. Practicing the interview will help you learn to control your natural nervousness.

You should plan to arrive early for your interview, but you should not arrive earlier than 15 minutes prior to the scheduled time of your interview. The company and interviewer have blocked off a certain amount of time for your interview. Arriving too early can be seen as rude, whereas showing up late for your interview displays a lack of care for the job, the company, and the interviewer. Get directions to the interview location and ensure you can find the building in advance. Make a practice run so that you will know exactly how to get to the interview and how long it will take to get there. Consider the traffic conditions for that time of day and have a backup plan in case you have difficulty with your transportation.

Personal Appearance at the Interview

Additionally, you should pay close attention to your physical appearance during a job interview. While some IT jobs allow a casual appearance, most employers require a more professional appearance. This is because technicians and administrators often interact with professionals within the company. A neat, clean, and professional appearance shows that you take pride in yourself and in your work. Even if the job is a backroom position, always dress appropriately for the interview. Blue jeans and a T-shirt are never appropriate.

Regardless of the job conditions, men and women should always dress up rather than down for an interview. This does not mean that you should dress for a party. Rather, you should dress for a formal business setting. Men should always wear a tie and a long-sleeved shirt at minimum. If you wear a suit or jacket, make sure it matches and fits properly. Women should always wear a suit or business dress. Guidelines for attire are shown in Figure 20-8.

Personal grooming is equally as important as attire. Refrain from wearing perfume or cologne, and style your hair in a professional manner. Fingernails should be clean and unbroken or uneven, and all tattoos should be covered. Similarly, all visible piercings should be downplayed.

Smile and use a firm handshake when you introduce yourself, as shown in Figure 20-9. This shows your confidence. Do not chew gum or eat candy during the interview, and refrain from smoking at any time when you are on the company premises. This is not a social visit. You may encounter your prospective supervisor on the premises prior to your interview.

Copyright Goodheart-Willcox Co., Inc.

Figure 20-8 Regardless of the job conditions, men and women should always dress up rather than down for an interview.

Appropriate Attire for a Job Interview	
Women	**Men**
• Wear a suit or dress with a conservative length	• Wear a conservative suit of a solid color
• Choose solid colors over prints	• Wear a long-sleeved shirt, either white or a light color
• Wear shoes with a moderate heel or flats	• Choose a tie of a solid color or conservative print
• Minimize jewelry and accessories	• Wear loafers or lace-up dress shoes with dark socks
• Wear a well-groomed hairstyle	• Avoid wearing jewelry outside
• Apply minimal makeup	• Wear a well-groomed hairstyle
• Avoid perfume or apply very lightly	• Avoid cologne
• Trim nails neatly; if using polish, choose conservative color with no decals	• Trim nails neatly
• Cover all tattoos	• Cover all tattoos

Goodheart-Willcox Publisher

Figure 20-9 Smile and use a firm handshake when introducing yourself.

Sata Production/Shutterstock.com

Information to Bring to an Interview

Common information required at an interview is your Social Security number, driver's license number, and a copy of your résumé and cover letter. It is customary to provide references for a job. A **reference** is a person who is familiar with an applicant's skills, talents, or personal traits and is willing to recommend the applicant for a position. References can be listed on a résumé or in their own, separate document. Regardless of the method, a copy of your references should be taken to the interview with your other employment documents. Your references should be professional, not personal. The quality of your references can mean a great deal to the employer. Some good references are teachers, past employers, supervisors, and fellow employees. Your immediate past employer may be required as a reference. Friends, family, and clergy are not considered good references. Get permission from people before using them as a reference. For each reference, provide a name, address, telephone number, and occupation. Also, note if the person was a past supervisor. You will need this information to complete a job application, which is typically required by the company's personnel office.

It is also a good idea to have a list of questions to ask the interviewer about the company. Your questions can reveal even more to the employer. Asking about how many breaks you will get during a day will send an undesirable message to the

Copyright Goodheart-Willcox Co., Inc.

employer. It is not *necessary* to ask questions, especially if the interview has been thorough. However, do not hesitate if you believe there is pertinent information you must know. You may ask questions about the position and the organization, but limit your questions to operation conditions that you do not understand. Many issues regarding a job can be obtained prior to the interview, especially if the information was posted.

Examples of topics about which a candidate may ask include the following:

- specific duties of the position
- to whom the position reports
- criteria for employee promotions
- how on-the-job training is conducted
- the working hours for this position
- when a hiring decision will be made
- anticipated start date

Topics to avoid when asking questions during an interview include the following:

- number of candidate interviews
- the interviewer's impression of the interview
- salary negotiation

Remember, if you are offered the job, there will be additional time at that point to make any clarifications or salary negotiations that you believe are necessary.

Completing a Job Interview

A major factor that determines your employment is the job interview. The job interview gives the employer a chance to assess the applicant both physically and mentally with a series of questions. At times, the way a question is answered is more important than the answer itself. For example, if an employer asks, "What would you do if you could not fix a networking problem?" The way you answer that question may tell the employer about your character, your confidence, and your ability to work with others. The employer is looking for certain traits in the individual the company is about to hire. Some common traits are honesty, confidence, dependability, and the ability to work well as a team member.

Employers may not ask the same questions for all applicants and will usually not be direct about the qualities they are seeking. The employer will ask questions to probe for the character and job-related qualities the company wants. For example, an employer may ask you to describe a time you had a problem with a fellow employee and how it was resolved. The answer to this question can tell an experienced interviewer a lot about the character of the applicant. Answer all questions to the best of your ability. If you do not know the answer, simply say so. Do not try to devise an answer. Express your willingness to learn any new topics with which you may not be familiar. The person conducting the interview is an expert. You will not fool them by trying to invent an answer, and you will find they will most likely respect your honesty.

Always address the persons who are conducting the interview as "Sir" and "Ma'am" unless the interviewers tell you otherwise. Even if you are personally acquainted with your prospective employer, treat him or her as a total stranger.

Copyright Goodheart-Willcox Co., Inc.

Do not become complacent or presume you have the job, and never use foul language, even in a joking manner. Read the following tips for a successful interview:

- Use proper English and avoid slang
- Speak slowly and concisely
- Use good manners
- Convey a sense of cooperation and enthusiasm
- Maintain appropriate posture and body language
- Smile
- Remember that the interview has not ended when you start asking questions

Testing at the Interview

Employer testing is a common part of the interviewing process. There may be times when you are notified of an employment test as part of the interviewing process. In these situations, try to obtain information about test content and format so you may study appropriately. An employer can tell a lot about your technical knowledge and communication skills through a test, especially if written responses are required. Written responses reveal a lot about an interviewee. When taking a test, be sure you understand all test directions. Verbally confirm them if you have questions before you begin. The following guidelines will improve your testing success:

- Read each question carefully
- Write legibly and clearly
- Budget your time wisely
- Do not dwell on one question

Keeping a Job

Obtaining a job is actually only part of finding gainful employment. The other, and at times more difficult, part is keeping the job. Remember, as an employee, you represent the company during your normal working hours or when on official company business. Since employees are extensions of the company, every employer looks for similar characteristics in their employees outside of skills. These characteristics include digital citizenship and various soft skills.

Digital Citizenship

Perhaps more important to information technology than any other industry, **digital citizenship** is the standard of appropriate behavior when using technology. Good digital citizenship focuses on using technology in a positive manner, rather than using it for negative or illegal purposes. It is necessary to learn to communicate effectively, ethically, and appropriately within a digital society.

Information posted online never really goes away. A *digital footprint* is a data record of all an individual's online activities. Even if something is deleted from the Internet, it remains in a person's digital footprint. Always consider what an employer would think of something before posting it online.

Cyberbullying is the use of electronic technology to harass or threaten a person. This includes social media, text messages, or e-mails. Cyberbullying is not only unethical, in many cases it can be prosecuted as a criminal act. Flaming and spamming are unethical actions that violate *netiquette*, or online etiquette. *Flaming* is purposefully

Copyright Goodheart-Willcox Co., Inc.

insulting someone and inciting an argument on the Internet, and *spamming* is the sending of unwanted mass e-mails or intentionally flooding an individual's social media site or e-mail inbox with unwanted messages.

Soft Skills

Soft skills are skills used to communicate and work well with others. Contrast these from *hard skills*, which are the essential, critical skills needed to perform required work-related tasks. Soft skills may also be referred to as *people skills* or *interpersonal skills*. These are the skills that virtually every employer looks for. Examples of essential soft skills in the workplace include professionalism, communication, punctuality, teamwork, and problem-solving skills.

Professionalism

Professionalism is the act of exhibiting appropriate character, judgment, and behavior by a person who is trained to perform a job. It is a person's conduct while at work or representing an employer. A professional employee arrives to work on time each day and performs job tasks in a productive manner. Professionals dress appropriately for their job, take responsibility for their behavior, and are good communicators. They also possess integrity, honesty, and a positive attitude.

Communication

Communication skills can be verbal or nonverbal. *Verbal communication* is speaking words to communicate. This allows information to be shared, requests to be made, direction to be given, and persuasion to be applied when action is needed. *Nonverbal communication* is any action, behavior, or attitude that sends a message. This can include body language; eye contact; touch; personal space; and paralanguage, which is the attitude projected with a tone or pitch of a person's voice.

Nonverbal communication also covers written communication. You can demonstrate good written communication skills by avoiding slang and using proper English. *Proper English* is language usage that follows the accepted rules for spelling, grammar, and punctuation. Even in the IT industry, you will encounter the need for professional writing, whether it is a work order, incident report, or e-mail to a client or supervisor. Sending correspondence that is littered with spelling errors or grammatical mistakes will make you, and by extension the company, look bad. It is essential to be able to communicate verbally, in writing, and to have awareness of one's nonverbal communication.

Copyright Goodheart-Willcox Co., Inc.

Punctuality

Punctuality means being on time. It is essential for you to be on time while at work. If you are scheduled to work at 8:00 a.m., then you should be in your designated work-space at that time. Parking your car or entering the building at that time technically constitutes a late arrival. Being constantly late or not showing up for a scheduled shift is inconsiderate and not tolerated in a professional workplace. It can also lead to volatile working relationships with your coworkers. If you know you are going to be late or miss work entirely, it is expected that your employer will be notified with enough time to make alternative plans.

Teamwork

Teamwork is the cooperative efforts by individual team members to achieve a goal. Being a good team player is an essential soft skill to career success. Members of a team ideally take pride in their work, share responsibilities and decision-making, and develop a sense of accomplishment when a project is completed. This only happens when the team members work together and focus on their assigned tasks. Showing you are a team player involves collaboration and compromising skills.

Problem-Solving

Problem-solving is the process of choosing a course of action after evaluating available information and weighing the costs, benefits, and consequences of alternative actions. It involves critical thinking and the ability to use prior knowledge, new data, and good judgment to solve problems. Applying a systematic problem-solving process is a necessary job skill. The steps of this process are shown in Figure 20-10.

Figure 20-10 Problem-solving is the process of choosing a course of action after evaluating available information and weighing the costs, benefits, and consequences of alternative actions.

Goodheart-Willcox Publisher

Copyright Goodheart-Willcox Co., Inc.

Summary

Information Technology Industry Careers

- There is a wide variety of careers available in the information technology industry; examples include network support specialist, network administrator, systems analyst, consultant, technical salesperson, web developer, programmer, software engineer, and entrepreneur.

Career Information Sources

- The major source of job information, especially information regarding information technology and networking, is the Internet.

- A valuable reference is the *Occupational Outlook Handbook*, which is published by the United States Bureau of Labor Statistics.

- School career counselors and local labor market offices are outstanding sources of career information as well.

General and College Education

- If you plan to advance in the IT business world, you must master the skills of communication.

- Very few high school graduates enter the networking industry directly and are required to receive specialized education in the training programs maintained by large companies.

- There is a direct correlation between the amount of education for a specific field and salary.

- An information technology (IT) position requires continuous education.

Certification

- Recognized commercial certifications are a way of proving your expertise in most computer-technology specialties, including networking.

- After gaining A+ Certification, Network+ Certification is a good next step in your career advancement.

- CompTIA offers A+, Network+, Server+, Linux+, PDI+, and many more certifications.

- The Linux Professional Institute (LPI) offers vendor-neutral Linux certifications.

- Microsoft, Cisco, and many other companies offer certifications based on exams regarding their respective operating systems and hardware.

- You must continually update your knowledge and skills to remain vital to the IT industry.

Copyright Goodheart-Willcox Co., Inc.

Employment

- When you are interviewing for a new job, be sure to take your Social Security card, driver's license, and a good-quality copy of your résumé.

- Be able to produce a list of at least three references, including addresses and phone numbers. Make sure you obtain permission to use associates as references.

- Be on time or 15 minutes early for your interview.

- Smile and show a sense of cooperation and enthusiasm when interviewed.

- If tested by the prospective employer, be sure you understand the instructions for the test.

- Digital citizenship is the standard of appropriate behavior when using technology.

- Soft skills are skills used to communicate and work well with others. These skills include professionalism, communication, punctuality, teamwork, and problem-solving skills.

Review Questions

1. List five occupations available in the IT industry.
2. Describe the job of a web master.
3. What is an entrepreneur?
4. Name four sources of career information.
5. Why is college an excellent option for advancement in the IT industry?
6. What is the correlation between education and salaries?
7. Why is continuing education required for an employee in the IT industry?
8. What certification options are available from CompTIA?
9. What certification options are available from Microsoft?
10. What items should accompany a job application?
11. What items should you bring to a job interview?
12. What information is needed concerning your references?

Appendix A

List of Networking Acronyms

A

AAA	authentication, authorization, and accounting
ABR	available bit rate
ACL	access control list
ACPI	Automatic Configuration and Power Interface
ACPICA	ACPI Component Architecture
AD	Active Directory
ADC	analog-to-digital converter
ADF	automatic document feeder
ADSL	asymmetric digital subscriber line
AEP	American Electric Power
AES	Advanced Encryption Standard
AH	Authentication Header
AM	amplitude modulation
AMI	alternate mark inversion
ANSI	American National Standards Institute
APIPA	Automatic Private IP Addressing
ARIN	American Registry for Internet Numbers
ARP	Address Resolution Protocol
ASCII	American Standard Code for Information Interchange
ASP	application service provider
ATM	asynchronous transfer mode
ATX	alien crosstalk
Auto-MDIX	automatic medium-dependent interface crossover
AWG	American Wire Gauge

B

BAP	Bandwidth Allocation Protocol
BCD	binary coded decimal
BDF	building distribution frame
BERT	bit-error rate test
BGP	Border Gateway Protocol
B-ISDN	broadband ISDN
BNC	British Naval Connector or Bayonet Neill-Concelman
BOOTP	Bootstrap Protocol
BPDU	Bridge Protocol Data Unit
BRI-ISDN	basic rate ISDN
BSS	basic service set

C

CA	Certificate Authority
CBR	constant bit rate
CDP	Cisco Discovery Protocol
CERN	*Centre European pour la Recherche Nucléaire*
CHAP	Challenge Handshake Authentication Protocol
CIDR	classless inter-domain routing
CIR	committed information rate
CLA	Certified Linux Administrator
CLDA	Certified Linux Desktop Administrator
CLE	Certified Linux Engineer
CLP	Certified Linux Professional
CNAME	canonical name
CP	consolidation point
CRAM-MDS	challenge-response authentication mechanism-message digest 5
CRC	cyclic redundancy check
CSMA/CA	carrier-sense multiple access with collision avoidance

Copyright Goodheart-Willcox Co., Inc.

CSMA/CD	carrier-sense multiple access with collision detection
CSS	cascading style sheets
CSU	channel service unit
CSU/DSU	channel service unit/data service unit
CUPS	common Unix printing system

D

DAC	digital-to-analog converter
dB	decibel
DDoS	distributed denial of service
DHCP	Dynamic Host Configuration Protocol
DLC	data link control
DMA	direct memory access
DMZ	demilitarized zone
DNS	Domain Name System *or* Domain Name Service
DOCSIS	data-over-cable service interface specification
DoS	denial of service
DSL	digital subscriber line
DSU	data service unit
DWDM	dense wavelength division multiplexing

E

E1	E-Carrier Level 1
EAP	Extensible Authentication Protocol
EBCDIC	Extended Binary Coded Decimal Interchange Code
EGP	Exterior Gateway Protocol
EIA	Electronic Industry Association
EIGRP	Enhanced Interior Gateway Routing Protocol
ELFEXT	equal level far-end crosstalk
EMI	electromagnetic interference
ESD	electrostatic discharge
ESP	encapsulated security packets
ESSID	extended service set identifier

F

FDDI	Fiber Distributed Data Interface
FDM	frequency division multiplexing
FEXT	far-end crosstalk
FHSS	frequency hopping spread spectrum
FIR	fast infrared
FLSM	fixed-length subnet mask
FM	frequency modulation
FQDN	Fully Qualified Domain Name
FTP	File Transfer Protocol

G

GBIC	gigabit interface converter
Gbps	gigabits per second
GUI	graphical user interface
GUID	globally unique identifier

H

HAL	hardware abstract layer
HDLC	high-level data link control
HIPAA	Health Insurance Portability and Accountability Act
HSRP	Hot Standby Router Protocol
HTML	hypertext markup language
HTTP	Hypertext Transfer Protocol
HTTPS	Hypertext Transfer Protocol Secure
Hz	hertz

I

IANA	Internet Assigned Numbers Authority
IBSS	independent basic service set
ICA	Independent Computing Architecture
ICANN	Internet Corporation for Assigned Names and Numbers
ICMP	Internet Control Message Protocol
ICS	Internet connection sharing
IDC	insulation-displacement connector
IDF	intermediate distribution frame
IDS	intrusion detection system
IEEE	Institute of Electrical and Electronics Engineers

Copyright Goodheart-Willcox Co., Inc.

IGMP	Internet Group Management Protocol
IGP	Interior Gateway Protocol
IGRP	Interior Gateway Routing Protocol
IIS	Internet Information Services
IKE	Internet Key Exchange
IMAP	Internet Message Access Protocol
InterNIC	Integrated Network Information Center
IP	Internet Protocol
IPP	Internet Printing Protocol
IPS	intrusion prevention system
IPSec	Internet Protocol Security
IT	information technology
IPv4	Internet Protocol version 4
IPv6	Internet Protocol version 6
IPX	Internetwork Packet Exchange
IRQ	interrupt request
ISATAP	Intra-Site Automatic Tunneling Address Protocol
iSCSI	Internet Small Computer System Interface
ISDN	Integrated Services Digital Network
IS-IS	Intermediate System to Intermediate System
ISO	International Organization for Standardization
ISP	Internet service provider
ITU	International Telecommunications Union

K

Kbps	kilobits per second

L

L2F	Layer 2 Forwarding
L2TP	Layer 2 Tunneling Protocol
LACP	Link Aggregation Control Protocol
LAN	local area network
LC	local connector
LDAP	Lightweight Directory Access Protocol
LDM	logical disk manager

LEAP	Lightweight Extensible Authentication Protocol
LEC	local exchange carrier
LED	light emitting diode
LLC	logical link control
LLDP	Link-Layer Discovery Protocol
LLDP-MED	Link-Layer Discovery Protocol–Media Endpoint Discovery
LLMNR	Link-Local Multicast Name Resolution
LLTD	Link-Layer Topology Discovery
LPR	Line Printer Request
LUN	logical unit number

M

MAC	media access control
MAN	metropolitan area network
MAU	multistation access unit
Mbps	megabits per second
MBR	master boot record
MCAS	Microsoft Certified Application Specialist
MCITP	Microsoft Certified Information Technology Professional
MCTS	Microsoft Certified Technical Specialist
MDF	main distribution frame
MDI	media dependent interface
MDIX	media dependent interface crossover
MIB	management information base
MIME	Multipurpose Internet Mail Extensions
MIMO	Multiple Input Multiple Output
MITM	man in the middle
MLPPP	Multilink Point-to-Point Protocol
MMF	multimode fiber
MOS	Microsoft Office Specialist
MPEG	Moving Picture Experts Group
MPLS	Multi-Protocol Label Switching
MS-CHAP	Microsoft Challenge Handshake Authentication Protocol
MSR	Microsoft Reserved
MT-RJ	mechanical transfer-registered jack

Copyright Goodheart-Willcox Co., Inc.

| MUTOA | multi-user telecommunication outlet assembly |
| MX | mail exchanger |

N

NAA	Network Address Authority
NAC	Network Access Control
NAS	network-attached storage
NAT	Network Address Translation
NBNS	NetBIOS Name Server
NCP	Network Control Protocol
NetBEUI	Network Basic Input/Output Extended User Interface
NetBIOS	Network Basic Input/Output System
NEXT	near-end crosstalk
NFS	Network File System
NIC	network interface card
NID	network interface device
nm	nanometer
NNTP	Network News Transfer Protocol
NOS	network operating system
NRZ	non-return to zero
NTFS	New Technology File System
NTP	Network Time Protocol
NWLINK	Microsoft IPX/SPX Protocol

O

OCx	Optical Carrier
OFD M	orthogonal frequency-division multiplexing
ONT	Optical Network Terminal
OS	operating system
OSI	Open Systems Interconnection
OSPF	Open Shortest Path First
OTDR	optical time domain reflectometer

P

PAN	personal area network
PAP	Password Authentication Protocol
PAT	port address translation
PC	personal computer

PCI DSS	Payment Card Industry Data Security Standard
PEAP	Protected Extensible Authentication Protocol
PKI	Public Key Infrastructure
PoE	Power over Ethernet
PoP	point of presence
POP	Post Office Protocol
POST	power-on self-test
POTS	plain old telephone system
PPP	Point-to-Point Protocol
PPPoE	Point-to-Point Protocol over Ethernet
PPTP	Point-to-Point Tunneling Protocol
PRI-ISDN	Primary Rate ISDN
PSTN	public switched telephone network
PVC	permanent virtual circuit

Q

| QoS | Quality of Service |

R

RADIUS	Remote Authentication Dial-In User Service
RAID	Redundant Array of Independent Disks
RARP	Reverse Address Resolution Protocol
RDP	Remote Desktop Protocol
RFC	Request for Comments
RFI	Radio Frequency Interface
RIP	Router Information Protocol
RIPng	RIP next generation
RJ	registered jack
RSA	Rivest, Shamir, Adelman
RSH	remote shell
RTP	Real-time Transport Protocol

S

SAN	storage area network
SAP	service access point
SAS	serial attached SCSI
SC	standard connector/subscriber connector

Copyright Goodheart-Willcox Co., Inc.

SCP — Secure Copy Protocol

SCSI — Small Computer Systems Interface

SDSL — symmetrical digital subscriber line

SFTP — Secure File Transfer Protocol

SGML — standard generalized markup language

S-HTTP — Secure HTTP

SIP — Session Initiation Protocol

SLIP — Serial Line Internet Protocol

SMB — Server Message Block

SMF — Single Mode Fiber

SMTP — Simple Mail Transfer Protocol

SNAT — Static Network Address Translation

SNMP — Simple Network Management Protocol

SOA — start of authority

SOAP — Simple Object Access Protocol

SOHO — small-office/home-office

SONET — Synchronous Optical Network

SOX — Sarbanes-Oxley

SPS — standby power supply

SPX — Sequenced Packet Exchange

SSH — Secure Shell

SSID — Service Set Identifier

SSL — Security Sockets Layer

ST — straight tip

STP — Spanning Tree Protocol

T

TA — terminal adaptor

TACACS — Terminal Access Controller Access-Control System

TACACS+ — Terminal Access Controller Access-Control System plus

TCP — Transmission Control Protocol

TCP/IP — Transmission Control Protocol/Internet Protocol

tcsh — Turbo C shell

TDM — Time Division Muliplexing

TDR — time domain reflectometer

Telco — telephone company

TFTP — Trivial File Transfer Protocol

TIA — Telecommunications Industry Association

TKIP — Temporal Key Integrity Protocol

TLS — Transport Layer Security

TTL — time to live

U

UBR — unspecified bit rate

UDP — User Datagram Protocol

UL — Underwriters Laboratories

UNC — Universal Naming Convention

UPS — uninterruptible power supply

URL — uniform resource locator

USB — Universal Serial Bus

UTP — unshielded twisted pair

V

VBR — variable bit rate

VBR-NRT — variable bit rate-non real time

VBR-RT — variable bit rate-real time

VDSL — variable digital subscriber line

VLAN — virtual local area network

VLSM — variable length subnet mask

VNC — virtual network connection

VoIP — Voice over IP

VPN — virtual private network

VTP — Virtual Trunking Protocol

Copyright Goodheart-Willcox Co., Inc.

W

W3C	World Wide Web Consortium
WAN	wide area network
WAP	wireless access point
WAP	wireless application protocol
WEP	Wired Equivalent Privacy
WINS	Windows Internet Naming Service
WPA	Wi-Fi Protected Access
WPA2	Wi-Fi Protected Access 2
WPAN	wireless personal area networks
WWW	World Wide Web

X

X.25	CCITT Packet Switching Protocol
XDSL	extended digital subscriber line
XML	extensible markup language

Z

Zeroconf	zero configuration

Copyright Goodheart-Willcox Co., Inc.

Appendix B

Binary Math

Binary math accurately represents digital circuitry. In digital electronics, a circuit is either on or off or a voltage condition is high or low. For example, a digital circuit may have two distinct conditions: 5 volts present or 0 volts present.

Binary math uses only two numbers (1 and 0) to represent an infinite range of numbers. The binary number system accomplishes this in a similar way the decimal number system does, by placing numbers into discrete, digit positions. The decimal number system fills these digits with values 0 through 9. The first digit position is commonly referred to as the *ones position*. The maximum value that can be entered here is 9. The second digit position must therefore be the *tens position*. If the maximum value of 9 is entered in both the ones and tens positions, the resulting number is 99. The third position must therefore be the *hundreds position*, and so on. Notice in Figure B-1 that each of the positions can be expressed as an exponent of the base 10.

Figure B-1

Digit Positions	1s	10s	100s	1,000s	10,000s	100,000s
Exponent	10^0	10^1	10^2	10^3	10^4	10^5
Range	0–9	10–90	100–900	1,000–9,000	10,000–90,000	100,000–900,000

Goodheart-Willcox Publisher

Note

The Range row indicates the allowed values for each digit position. Look at the number 2,753. This number includes the following:

2-1000s	2,000
7-100s	700
5-10s	50
3-1s	3
Total	2,753

Add the values together for a total of 2,753.

Binary numbers are expressed in similar fashion. However, instead of each digit position being 10 times greater than the position before it, the value of each position is double that of the position before it, as seen in Figure B-2.

Copyright Goodheart-Willcox Co., Inc.

Figure B-2

Digit Positions	1s	2s	4s	8s	16s	32s	64s	128s
Exponent	2^0	2^1	2^2	2^3	2^4	2^5	2^6	2^7
Range	1	2	4	8	16	32	64	128

Goodheart-Willcox Publisher

Look at the binary number 101011000001 and compare it to Figure B-3. This number includes the following:

1-2048s	2048
0-1024s	0
1-512s	512
0-256s	0
1-128s	128
1-64s	64
0-32s	0
0-16s	0
0-8s	0
0-4s	0
0-2s	0
1-1s	1
Total	2753

Figure B-3

2048s	1024s	512s	256s	128s	64s	32s	16s	8s	4s	2s	1s
1	0	1	0	1	1	0	0	0	0	0	1

Goodheart-Willcox Publisher

As you can see, 101011000001 is the binary equivalent of 2753.

To convert a binary number to a decimal number, simply record the decimal value assigned to that respective position for each position that contains a binary number *1*. Then, add the decimal numbers together, as illustrated in Figure B-4.

Figure B-4

32s	16s	8s	4s	2s	1s
1	0	1	1	0	1
32	+	8 +	4	+	1 = 45

Goodheart-Willcox Publisher

When converting a decimal number to a binary number, you simply reverse the previous operation. For example, to convert the decimal number 178 to a binary number, you must divide it by a series of powers of two. The phrase *powers of two*, or 2^n, means that you multiply a number by two to get the next number in the series before repeating the multiplication. The powers of two are 1, 2, 4, 8, 16, 32, 64, 128, 256, 512, 1024, 2048, and so on.

Copyright Goodheart-Willcox Co., Inc.

To convert the decimal number 178 to binary, start by finding the largest power of two that does not exceed 178. The largest power-of-two value that does not exceed 178 is 128. Place a 1 in the binary number position that represents 128, as seen in the following:

Powers of Two	128	64	32	16	8	4	2	1
Binary Digit	1							

Subtracting 128 from 178 leaves a difference of 50. Since the number 50 is less than the next-largest power of two (64), you must insert a 0 in the *64s* position.

Powers of Two	128	64	32	16	8	4	2	1
Binary Digit	1	0						

Next, since 50 is larger than the next-largest power of two (32), place a 1 in the *32s* position.

Powers of Two	128	64	32	16	8	4	2	1
Binary Digit	1	0	1					

Now, subtract 32 from 50. The difference is 18. The number 18 is larger than the next power-of-two value (*16*), so place a 1 in the *16s* position.

Powers of Two	128	64	32	16	8	4	2	1
Binary Digit	1	0	1	1				

Copyright Goodheart-Willcox Co., Inc.

Subtracting 16 from 18 leaves *2*, which is smaller than the next two powers of two (*8* and *4*). This means the next two positions in the binary number are both 0s.

Powers of Two	128	64	32	16	8	4	2	1
Binary Digit	1	0	1	1	0	0		

The next power of two is *2*, and the number remaining from the last step is also 2. Therefore, a 1 goes into the *2s* position.

Powers of Two	128	64	32	16	8	4	2	1
Binary Digit	1	0	1	1	0	0	1	

There are no decimal numbers remaining, so the *1s* position should be filled with 0. The binary equivalent of the decimal number 178 is 10110010.

Powers of Two	128	64	32	16	8	4	2	1
Binary Digit	1	0	1	1	0	0	1	0

Copyright Goodheart-Willcox Co., Inc.

Number Conversion Table

Decimal	Binary	Octal	Hexadecimal
0	000000	00	00
1	000001	01	01
2	000010	02	02
3	000011	03	03
4	000100	04	04
5	000101	05	05
6	000110	06	06
7	000111	07	07
8	001000	10	08
9	001001	11	09
10	001010	12	0A
11	001011	13	0B
12	001100	14	0C
13	001101	15	0D
14	001110	16	0E
15	001111	17	0F
16	010000	20	10
17	010001	21	11
18	010010	22	12
19	010011	23	13
20	010100	24	14
21	010101	25	15
22	010110	26	16
23	010111	27	17
24	011000	30	18
25	011001	31	19
26	011010	32	1A
27	011011	33	1B
28	011100	34	1C
29	011101	35	1D
30	011110	36	1E

(continued)

Copyright Goodheart-Willcox Co., Inc.

Decimal	Binary	Octal	Hexadecimal
31	011111	37	1F
32	100000	40	20
33	100001	41	21
34	100010	42	22
35	100011	43	23
36	100100	44	24
37	100101	45	25
38	100110	46	26
39	100111	47	27
40	101000	50	28
41	101001	51	29
42	101010	52	2A
43	101011	53	2B
44	101100	54	2C
45	101101	55	2D
46	101110	56	2E
47	101111	57	2F
48	110000	60	30
49	110001	61	31
50	110010	62	32
51	110011	63	33
52	110100	64	34
53	110101	65	35
54	110110	66	36
55	110111	67	37
56	111000	70	38
57	111001	71	39
58	111010	72	3A
59	111011	73	3B
60	111100	74	3C
61	111101	75	3D
62	111110	76	3E
63	111111	77	3F

Copyright Goodheart-Willcox Co., Inc.

Appendix D

Table of Standard ASCII Characters

Decimal	Character	Control Code (if applicable)
0	NUL	Null
1	SOH	Start of header
2	STX	Start of text
3	ETX	End of text
4	EOT	End of transmission
5	ENQ	Enquiry
6	ACK	Acknowledgment
7	BEL	Bell
8	BS	Backspace
9	HT	Horizontal tab
10	LF	Line feed
11	VT	Vertical tab
12	FF	Form feed
13	CR	Carriage return
14	SO	Shift out
15	SI	Shift in
16	DLE	Data link escape
17	DC1	Device control 1
18	DC2	Device control 2
19	DC3	Device control 3
20	DC4	Device control 4
21	NAK	Negative acknowledgment
22	SYN	Synchronous idle
23	ETB	End of transmit block
24	CAN	Cancel
25	EM	End of medium
26	SUB	Substitute
27	ESC	Escape
28	FS	File separator
29	GS	Group separator
30	RS	Record separator
31	US	Unit separator
32	SP	Space

Decimal	Character	Control Code (if applicable)
33	!	
34	"	
35	#	
36	$	
37	%	
38	&	
39	'	
40	(	
41	)	
42	*	
43	+	
44	,	
45	–	
46	.	
47	/	
48	0	
49	1	
50	2	
51	3	
52	4	
53	5	
54	6	
55	7	
56	8	
57	9	
58	:	
59	;	
60	<	
61	=	
62	>	
63	?	
64	@	
65	A	
66	B	
67	C	

(continued)

Copyright Goodheart-Willcox Co., Inc.

Decimal	Character	Control Code (if applicable)
68	D	
69	E	
70	F	
71	G	
72	H	
73	I	
74	J	
75	K	
76	L	
77	M	
78	N	
79	O	
80	P	
81	Q	
82	R	
83	S	
84	T	
85	U	
86	V	
87	W	
88	X	
89	Y	
90	Z	
91	[	
92	\	
93	]	
94	^	
95	_	
96	`	

Decimal	Character	Control Code (if applicable)
97	a	
98	b	
99	c	
100	d	
101	e	
102	f	
103	g	
104	h	
105	i	
106	j	
107	k	
108	l	
109	m	
110	n	
111	o	
112	p	
113	q	
114	r	
115	s	
116	t	
117	u	
118	v	
119	w	
120	x	
121	y	
122	z	
123	{	
124			
125	}	
126	~	
127	DEL	

Copyright Goodheart-Willcox Co., Inc.

Glossary

10Base2. Classification that specifies the use of RG-58 cable and a data rate of 10 Mbps. (2)

10Base5. First IEEE 802.3 classification developed for Ethernet. (2)

10BaseT. Classification specifies the use of the different categories of UTP cable. (2)

6to4. Mechanism that provides a means of communicating across the IPv4 Internet while preserving the original IPv6 assigned address of the network device. (10)

A

A+ Certification. Designed to test a person's knowledge related to PC support and repair; pronounced *A-plus.* (20)

AAA proxy. Network device that acts as an intermediary to exchange security packets between the AAA server and the AAA client. (15)

absorption. Occurs when intervening material absorbs some of the signal. (3)

access method. Method of gaining access to the network media. (6)

access port. Hub connection to which each network cable is connected. (1)

acoustical echo. Condition that takes place when a microphone and a speaker are in close proximity or the audio is improperly adjusted, causing feedback. (12)

ACPI Component Architecture (ACPICA). Extension to the original ACPI standard. (9)

Active Directory (AD). Windows Server standard used to manage large and small network systems. (7)

active hub. Enhanced passive hub; also called an *intelligent hub* or *switch.* (1)

active partition. Describes the partition that contains the operating system files the computer should use to boot. (17)

adaptive cut-through. Frame-forwarding technique that operates as cut-through until an unacceptable number of corrupt frames are detected. (11)

Address Resolution Protocol (ARP). Communication protocol that resolves an assigned IPv4 network address to a physical address (MAC address). (6)

Address Resolution Protocol (ARP). Used to map the host MAC address to the logical host IP address. (10)

ad hoc mode. Wireless network arrangement in which a wireless access point is not present. (4)

administrative server. Administers network security and activities. (1)

alien crosstalk (AXT). Measurement of noise introduced outside the cable jacket, typically caused by other network cables in close proximity. (2)

American National Standards Institute (ANSI). Private, nonprofit organization that does not develop standards, but rather prompts voluntary conformity and standardization. (1)

American Standard Code for Information Interchange (ASCII). Early attempt to standardize data codes. (5)

amplifier. Electronic device designed to raise a signal's amplitude. (2)

analog signal. Signal that has a continuous range of values, much like a wave. (2)

analog-to-digital converter (ADC). Computer chip designed to change an analog signal to a digital signal. (12)

anonymous FTP site. Allows anyone to access the site and download or upload files. (13)

ANT+. Function that can be added to base ANT protocols that allows for interoperability; pronounced *ant plus.* (4)

anycast address. IPv6 address that delivers packets to the nearest interface; mainly used for supporting router functions. (10)

application gateway. Provides security for specific applications such as FTP and Telnet. (15)

application layer. Interfaces directly to and performs common application services for the application processes; layer seven of the OSI model. (1)

archive bit. Identifies if a file has changed since the last full or incremental backup. (16)

asymmetric-key encryption. Encryption method that uses two keys: a private key and a public key; also known as *public-key cryptography.* (15)

asynchronous transfer mode (ATM). Protocol designed especially for transmitting data, voice, and video. (1)

asynchronous transmission. Data transmission method in which no reference signal is present. (5)

attenuation. Loss of signal strength. (1)

Note: The number in parentheses following each definition indicates the chapter in which the term can be found.

Copyright Goodheart-Willcox Co., Inc.

auditing. Service that tracks the events, use, and access of network resources and writes these actions to a log. (7)

authentication. Process used to identify a user and ensure the user is who he or she claims to be; also known as *local authentication*. (15)

authentication, authorization, and accounting (AAA). Security standard that consists of three parts: authentication, authorization, and accounting; also known as *triple A*. (15)

Automatic Configuration and Power Interface (ACPI). Standard for controlling the power options for computer hardware devices. (9)

automatic medium-dependent interface crossover (Auto-MDIX). Electronic chip technology incorporated into Gigabit Ethernet devices to automatically reassign pin functions and eliminate the need for a crossover cable. (2)

Automatic Private IP Addressing (APIPA). Feature that assigns an IP address from a special set of IP addresses that have been set aside by IANA when a DHCP server cannot be reached. (10)

available bit rate (ABR). ATM data transfer classification most appropriate for file transfer because it uses the available bit rate associated with the networking medium. (12)

average utilization. Measurement of the average amount of utilization or traffic on a network in a given monitoring period. (16)

AWG rating. Describes the size of a conductor's diameter. (2)

B

backbone. Connects the telecommunication closets, equipment rooms, and main entrance facility. (18)

backdoor Software access port to a computer infected by a Trojan horse. (15)

backplane. Simple motherboard designed with minimal components. (9)

bandwidth. Measurement of the network media's ability to carry data. (2)

Bandwidth Allocation Protocol (BAP). Allows the number of lines used by MLPPP to change on demand. (14)

bandwidth shaper. Used to prioritize network packets to ensure quality of service for time-sensitive applications such as VoIP; also known as a *traffic shaper*. (12)

baseband. Method of transmitting data in the form of a digital signal, using the entire bandwidth of a cable. (2)

baseline. Measurement of performance characteristics that can be used at a later date to determine if the network or server is performing satisfactorily. (16)

basic disk. Term applied to the old system of hard disk drive configuration. (7)

Basic Rate ISDN (BRI-ISDN). ISDN category that consists of three conductors: two B channels, referred to as *bearer channels*, and one D channel, referred to as the *delta channel*. (14)

basic service set (BSS). Group of wireless devices connected as a network. (4)

biometrics. Science of using unique physical features of a person to confirm that person's identification for authentication purposes. (15)

bipolar digital signal. Digital signal that fluctuates between a positive five-volt level and a negative five-volt level. (5)

bit rate. Number of bits used to represent the amplitude of the analog signal. (12)

blackout. Total loss of electrical energy. (16)

blade server. Extremely thin server designed to allow a large number of servers to be mounted in a small space. (9)

Bluetooth. Short-range, wireless system that is designed for limited distances. (4)

boot loader. Program that starts an operating system load process. (8)

boot partition. Contains the files needed to operate the computer. (17)

Border Gateway Protocol (BGP). Internet routing protocol that supports the exchange of routing information between autonomous networks. (11)

bridge. Can be used to divide the network into smaller segments, reducing the chance of collisions. (1)

broadband. Method of transmitting data in the form of several analog signals at the same time. (2)

Broadband ISDN (B-ISDN). ISDN category designed to carry multiple frequencies. (14)

broadcast frame. Frame in which the destination address is filled with all ones; intended for every computer on a network. (5)

broadcast storm. Occurs when the number of collisions reaches a point that the network is flooded with a continuous number of collisions and rebroadcasts. (6)

brouter. Combines router and bridge functions. (1)

brownout. Partial loss of electrical energy. (16)

bug. Software program error. (16)

bus topology. Network topology that uses a single cable or conductor to connect all nodes on the network. (1)

business plan. outlines the goals for the business and includes action plans and a timetable for meeting those goals. (20)

C

carrier wave. Electromagnetic wave of a set frequency that is used to carry data. (4)

Copyright Goodheart-Willcox Co., Inc.

carrier-sense multiple access with collision avoidance (CSMA/CA). Media access method that works much like CSMA/CD but tries to avoid, rather than detect, collisions. (2)

carrier-sense multiple access with collision detection (CSMA/CD). Media access method used by Ethernet networks to control and ensure data delivery. (2)

cascading style sheets (CSS). Style-sheet language that defines the presentation and layout of all pages in a website. (13)

cell. Area that is served by a radio access tower. (1)

cellular technology. Based on radio waves connecting to designated areas referred to as *cells*. (4)

centralized administration. Administration model in which the administrator does not have to go to each server to perform administrative tasks. (1)

certificate authority (CA). Service that contains the security list of users authorized to access the private key owner's messages, using a public key. (15)

Challenge Handshake Authentication Protocol (CHAP). Authentication protocol that sends an encrypted string of characters representing the user name and password. (15)

channel. Bandwidth of a carrier wave. (4)

channel bonding. Method whereby two or more links are combined. (4)

Channel Service Unit/Data Service Unit (CSU/DSU). Converts signals from the LAN into signals that can be carried by the T1 line, and vice versa. (14)

circuit switching. Data-routing method that establishes a permanent connection between two points for the duration of the data transfer period. (5)

circuit-level gateway. Monitors a connection until the connection is successfully established between the destination and source hosts. (15)

Cisco Discovery Protocol (CDP). Variation of LLDP designed to support equipment such as Cisco routers, switches, and telephones. (6)

Class A network. Can support up to 16 million hosts on each of 127 networks. (10)

Class B network. Supports up to 65,000 hosts on each of 16,000 networks. (10)

Class C network. Supports 254 hosts on each of 2 million networks. (10)

Classless Inter-Domain Routing (CIDR). Uses a special notation to identify which part of an IP address is the network portion. (11)

client/server network. Consists of computers connected via a network to one or more servers. (1)

cluster. Group of servers that share the network demand. (16)

coaxial cable. Consists of a copper-core conductor surrounded by an insulator referred to as a dielectric; also known as *coax cable*. (2)

codec. Term used to represent software, hardware, or combination of software and hardware that compress and decompress video and audio information; name stems from *compressor/decompressor*. (12)

cold spare. Any compatible disk drive that is in storage and is used to replace a failed disk drive. (16)

collision domain. Section of a network where collisions occur; also known as a *contention domain*. (6)

command prompt. Text-based interface in which commands are typed and entered in a command-line environment. (6)

command syntax. Correct manner and arrangement in which a command is to be typed. (6)

committed information rate (CIR). Guaranteed bandwidth a commercial carrier will provide to a subscriber. (12)

Common UNIX Printing System (CUPS). Daemon designed to support network printing using the Internet Printing Protocol (IPP). (8)

complex trust relationship. Type of trust relationship in which more than two domains have a full-trust relationship. (7)

consolidation point (CP). Connection to the horizontal wiring system. (18)

constant bit rate (CBR). ATM data transfer classification in which a steady stream of ATM cells move at a predictable rate. (12)

consultant. Works with clients on projects and makes recommendations based on his or her expertise. (20)

content filter. Configured to block websites or packet contents that contain specific terms. (15)

contiguous namespace. Namespace that uses the root domain name as part of its URL or as its complete name. (7)

continuous UPS. Type of UPS that provides a steady supply of electrical energy at all times, even when there is no electrical problem. (16)

convergence. State that occurs when all dynamic routing tables contain the same information; also known as *steady state*. (11)

copper-core cable. Consists of a copper wire surrounded by plastic or synthetic insulation. (1)

cover letter. Formal communication that accompanies a person's résumé or job application. (20)

crossed pair. Occurs when one of each of the two cable pairs has become part of the other pair's connection. (2)

crossover cable. Constructed with two pairs (four individual conductors) that are cross-connected; used to connect a computer to another computer. (2)

Copyright Goodheart-Willcox Co., Inc.

crosstalk. Interference that comes from neighboring conductors inside a wire's insulating jacket. (2)

cut-through. Method of frame forwarding in which the frame is forwarded immediately after receiving it; also known as a *low latency*. (11)

cyclic redundancy check (CRC). Based on the same principle for error detection as a parity check but uses mathematical algorithms to determine if any bits are corrupt. (5)

D

daemon. Program that runs in the background and waits for a client to request its services. (8)

data encryption. Encoding of data based on a mathematical formula, which converts the original data symbol into another symbol. (5)

data link layer. Describes how raw data is packaged for transfer from one network interface card to another; layer two of the OSI model. (1)

database server. Contains data files and software programs that query the data. (1)

dead drop. Cable that does not provide a complete path back to the patch panel, resulting in a lack of connection. (17)

decentralized administration. Networking administration model in which administration is spread across the entire network. (1)

decibel (dB). Unit of measurement that expresses the relationship of power between two electrical forces. (2)

dedicated server. Server that provides a single function. (1)

default gateway address. Address of the computer that provides a connection to the Internet. (10)

demarcation point. Point where customer equipment or cable meets a telecommunication provider's cable or equipment; also known as a *demarc*. (18)

demilitarized zone (DMZ). Area of a network that permits access from a host located outside the local area network. (15)

demodulation. Occurs when a receiver separates a voice wave from a carrier wave. (4)

Denial of Service (DoS). Denial of access to a server by overloading it with false requests. It is one of the most common attacks on servers. (15)

device file. Serves as a means of communication between a driver and a device. (8)

dial-up networking. Describes a network system in which a dial-up connection is used to access a remote access server. (14)

Diameter. IETF standard and a next-generation authentication protocol designed to secure a connection between two or more devices. (15)

differential backup. Backs up all data that has been changed since the last full backup. (16)

digital certificate. File that commonly contains data such as the user's name and e-mail address, the public key value assigned to the user, the validity period of the public key, and issuing authority identifier information. (15)

digital citizenship. Standard of appropriate behavior when using technology. (20)

digital encoding. Occurs when a network interface card converts data into a digital pattern acceptable to the network media. (5)

digital signal. Signal that has discrete values of *on* or *off*. (2)

Digital Subscriber Line (DSL). Refers to high-speed Internet access technology that uses existing local-loop telephone lines. (14)

digital-to-analog converter (DAC). Computer chip designed to change a digital signal to an analog signal. (12)

direct memory access (DMA) channel. Circuit that allows devices to communicate and transfer data to and from RAM without the need of CPU intervention. (9)

direct sequencing. Spread spectrum technique that transmits data on multiple channels sequentially. (4)

directional. Transmission of electromagnetic signals in a focused or aimed direction. (4)

disaster recovery. Restoration of a system to normal operation after a disaster has occurred. (16)

disjointed namespace. Any domain name that is a part of the Active Directory but does not follow the contiguous namespace requirement. (7)

disk mirroring. Act of writing the same information to two hard disk drives at the same time. (9)

disk quota. Amount of disk space assigned to specific users. (7)

disk striping. Involves dividing the data into separate sections and writing the data across several hard disk drives at the same time. (9)

dispersion. Distortion of a light wave pattern as it reflects off the core cladding. (3)

distance vector protocol. Routing protocol that shares its routing table with other routers. (11)

distinguished name. Uniquely identifies the location of the object in the Active Directory structure. (7)

domain. Logical grouping of users and equipment as defined by the network administrator. (7)

Domain Name System (DNS). Allows a name, called a *domain name*, to be associated with a network address. (10)

dotted decimal notation. Consists of writing each octet of an IP address separated by a period. (11)

driver. Software program that allows a PC to communicate with and transfer data to and from computer hardware. (1)

Copyright Goodheart-Willcox Co., Inc.

duplexing. Technique of placing each mirrored hard drive on a separate hard disk drive controller. (9)

dynamic addressing. Act of automatically assigning IP addresses. (10)

dynamic disk. New system of disk configuration and management introduced with NTFS 5.0. (7)

Dynamic Host Configuration Protocol (DHCP). Designed to replace the manual setup of IP addresses on a network. (10)

dynamic IP address table. Table in which IP addresses are generated automatically by a software program that communicates with nearby routers. (11)

dynamic IP assignment. Refers to an IP address that is issued automatically, typically when the computer boots and joins the network. (10)

dynamic multi-point virtual private network (DMVPN). Refers to a secure network establishing VPN connections between multiple points. (14)

dynamic VLAN. Created through software without the need of manual intervention. (11)

E

edge router. Refers to the router at the entrance and exit of a WAN. (14)

EFI partition. Partition that contains all programs required to boot the computer in the same way the BIOS boots the computer. (7)

electrical spike. Very short burst of abnormally high voltage. (16)

electrical surge. Higher-than-normal voltage level. (16)

electromagnetic wave. Form of energy that behaves like a wave and can travel through a vacuum. (3)

encapsulation. Process of adding information to a segment that identifies such things as the source address and destination addresses, end of the segment, and size of the segment. (5)

encryption. Method of using an algorithm to encode data. (15)

engineer. Degreed professional who possesses high-level skills necessary to solve problems related to his or her field of expertise. (20)

Enhanced Interior Gateway Routing Protocol (EIGRP). Cisco proprietary distance-vector protocol that is an improved version of IGRP. (11)

entrance facility. Room that is used as the entrance location for public or private communication cables. (18)

entrepreneur. Owns and operates a business. (20)

equal level far-end crosstalk (ELFEXT). Calculated by subtracting the effects of attenuation from the FEXT. (2)

equipment room. Contains the telecommunication equipment for the building. (18)

error correction. RAID technique that can use traditional error-checking code (ECC) or parity. (9)

EUI-64 identifier. Last 64 bits of an IPv6 address comprised of 24-bit manufacturer's ID and 40-bit unique ID. (10)

extended partition. Partition that can contain one or more logical drives. (7)

extended service set identifier (ESSID). Refers to two or more wireless access points or wireless devices using the same SSID. (4)

Extensible Authentication Protocol (EAP). Internet Engineering Task Force (IETF) standard used for network access and authentication in a client/server environment when IP is not available. (15)

extensible markup language (XML). Designed especially for large enterprise business applications running on web servers and is greatly enhanced compared to HTML. (13)

Exterior Gateway Protocol (EGP). Routing protocol designed to exchange information between different autonomous networks. (11)

external trust. Created when Windows Server 2016 configures a trust relationship with an older Windows Server operating system or another Windows Server 2016 computer or when the other domain is located in an entirely separate forest. (7)

extranet. Allows internal access to web pages while simultaneously allowing authorized personnel from outside the network to access the network's web pages. (13)

extrinsic loss. Signal loss caused by physical factors outside the normal core. (3)

F

fabric switch. Switch designed specifically for Fibre Channel networking. (9)

far-end crosstalk (FEXT). Measurement of reflective loss at the far end, or output end of the cable. (2)

fault tolerance. Ability of a RAID system to recover from a hard disk or hard disk controller failure without the loss of stored data. (9)

Fiber Distributed Data Interface (FDDI). Standard developed by ANSI that employs fiber-optic cable over great distances. (3)

fiber-optic cable. Uses a glass or clear, plastic core rather than copper. (1)

Fibre Channel. High-speed access method that typically uses fiber-optic cable as network media but may also use copper-core cable and wireless. (9)

file server. Used to store data files that can be accessed by a client. (1)

File Transfer Protocol (FTP). Supports file transfers between a client and a server and can be incorporated into a web server. (13)

filtering. Selective passing and blocking of frames. (11)

firewall signature identification. Works in similar fashion as antivirus protection and is often considered the same thing. (15)

Copyright Goodheart-Willcox Co., Inc.

firmware. Combination of a BIOS chip and software program. (9)

fixed-length subnet mask (FLSM). Subnet mask that has subnets that are equal in length and have an equal number of hosts. (11)

forest. Collection of domain trees that share a common Active Directory database. (7)

forest trust. Two-way trust relationship designed to share resources between two forests. (7)

fragment-free. Frame-forwarding method made up of a mixture of the store-and-forward and cut-through methods. (11)

frame. Packet that is encapsulated with information needed to travel the Internet. (5)

Frame Relay. Packet-switching protocol that typically uses leased lines such as T1 to carry data over long distances. (12)

frame size average. Average of all frame sizes during the monitoring period. (16)

frame size peak. Record of the largest frame size recorded during the monitoring period. (16)

free space. Space on a hard disk drive that has not been partitioned. (7)

frequency hopping. Spread spectrum technique that transmits data on multiple channels simultaneously. (4)

Fresnel reflection loss. Occurs due to the refraction property differences in the core material, the connector materials used for sealing the connector, and air. (3)

full backup. Complete backup of all designated data. (16)

full-duplex. Refers to communication that is bi-directional communication that occurs between two devices simultaneously. (2)

Fully Qualified Domain Name (FQDN). Complete name of a host. (10)

fusion splice. Joining of two fiber-optic cores using heat to fuse, or melt, the materials together. (3)

G

gateway. Device that connects a local area network to the Internet. (1)

generator. Device that creates and provides electricity. (16)

geosynchronous orbit. Occurs when a satellite's speed is synchronized with the earth's rotational speed. (4)

global address. Public address used to identify a local network; administered by IANA. (10)

global security policy. Security policy that affects users throughout the domain. (7)

globally unique identifier (GUID). New partitioning style that uses a partition table called *GUID partition table (GPT)*. (7)

graded-index multimode fiber-optic cable. Designed with a varying grade of core material. (3)

graphical user interface (GUI). Pictorial representation of commands and computer hardware that allows a user to access resources and programs with a click of a mouse button. (6)

group account. Collection of users that typically share a common job-oriented goal or similar function. (7)

H

H.323. Older telecommunication standard for audio, video, and data communications using IP or packet-type networks defined by the International Telecommunication Union (ITU). (12)

half-duplex. Refers to communication that is bi-directional but can only occur in one direction at a time. (2)

hard phone. Physical telephonic device. (12)

hardware abstraction layer (HAL). Designed to prevent third-party software applications and programs from directly accessing hardware. (17)

head-end. Local area distribution point. (14)

Health Insurance Portability and Accountability Act (HIPAA). Set of standards designed to protect health records. (15)

honey pot. Fake system designed to look attractive to an attacker. (15)

hop. Measure of how many network devices such as routers and gateways a packet must pass through until the packet reaches its destination. (11)

horizontal cross connect. Provides a mechanical means of connecting horizontal cabling systems to other cables or equipment. (18)

horizontal wiring. Refers to the section of cable that runs from individual work areas to a telecommunication closet. (18)

host. Computer on a network. (1)

hot spare. Backup component that can automatically replace a failed system component without the intervention of a technician. (16)

hot swapping. Removing components without shutting down the system. (9)

hot-swap technology. Allows a component to be removed or installed while the system is running. (9)

HTML tag. Instruction for how the text and graphics should appear when displayed in a web browser. (13)

hub. Central connection point where all network cables are concentrated. (1)

hybrid topology. Mixture of two or more network topologies. (1)

hyperlink. Link to another web page or to an area on the same web page. (13)

hypertext markup language (HTML). Programming language used to create web pages. (13)

Copyright Goodheart-Willcox Co., Inc.

Hypertext Transfer Protocol (HTTP). Protocol designed for communication between a web browser and a web server. (13)

I

impedance. Opposition to alternating current (AC). (2)

impedance mismatch. Refers to the effect of connecting two different electronic audio systems that have different electronic characteristics. (12)

incremental backup. Copies only data that has changed since the previous backup, regardless of what type of backup it was. (16)

independent basic service set (IBSS). Similar to an ad hoc network in that it does not use an access point and usually is a direct connection between two wireless devices. (4)

industrial, scientific, and medical (ISM) band. Band of radio frequencies associated with industrial, scientific, and medical devices. (4)

infrastructure as a service (IaaS). Provides at least part of the network infrastructure in a virtualized manner. (1)

infrastructure mode. Wireless network arrangement that contains one or more wireless access points. (4)

inode. Table entry that contains information such as permissions; file size; name of the owner; the time stamps of the file's creation, modification, and last access; and a pointer to where the file is stored. (8)

input/output (I/O) port. Small amount of memory assigned to a device that temporarily holds small amounts of data. (9)

Institute of Electrical and Electronics Engineers (IEEE). Professional organization that continually develops standards for the networking and communication industry; pronounced *I triple E*. (1)

insulation-displacement connector (IDC). Cable termination for a 66 or 100 block. (18)

integrated circuit card identifier (ICCID). Unique serial number assigned to a SIM card for international identification. (4)

Integrated Network Information Center (InterNIC). Governmental organization through which IP addresses were once regulated and assigned. (10)

Integrated Services Digital Network (ISDN). Provides the means for a fully digital transmission. (14)

interactive logon. Occurs when a user is verified and given access to the Active Directory. (7)

interference. Undesired electromagnetic signal imposed on a desired signal that distorts or corrupts the desired signal. (2)

Interior Gateway Protocol (IGP). Routing protocol confined to an autonomous network. (11)

Interior Gateway Routing Protocol (IGRP). Cisco proprietary, distance-vector protocol. (11)

Intermediate System to Intermediate System (IS-IS). IGP link state protocol. (11)

International Organization for Standardization (ISO). Organization interested in the standardization of computer equipment. (1)

International Telecommunication Union (ITU). Responsible for standardizing communication on an international level. (14)

Internet. Collection of interconnected networks from all around the world. (13)

Internet Corporation for Assigned Names and Numbers (ICANN). Private, not-for-profit organization that coordinates the assignment of domain names and IP addresses. (10)

Internet Message Access Protocol (IMAP). Used to access messages stored on a mail server in similar fashion to POP. (13)

Internet protocol (IP) address. Uniquely identifies each node on a network. (1)

Internet Protocol Security (IPSec). Provides end-to-end security across the public Internet and private networks. (15)

Internet Small Computer Systems Interface (iSCSI). Network storage standard developed by the Internet Engineering Task Force (IETF). (9)

interrupt request (IRQ). Circuit that communicates with the CPU. (9)

intranet. Private network that serves a specific group of users within a LAN. (13)

Intra-Site Automatic Tunneling Address Protocol (ISATAP). Developed jointly by Microsoft and Cisco Systems; designed to tunnel IPv6 addresses inside IPv4 packets at the data link layer. (10)

intrusion detection system (IDS). Passive system that only detects unauthorized activity. (15)

intrusion prevention system (IPS) Reactive system that not only detects unauthorized activity, but also performs some function to stop the activity. (15)

IPv6. Newest Internet addressing scheme is called. (10)

isolation transformer. Device that uses a transformer to isolate a circuit from other circuits emanating from the same electrical source. (16)

J

JavaScript. Programming language that is designed to be embedded into a HTML web page and allows the user to interact with the web page. (13)

jitter. Consists of small staggers or hesitations in the delivery sequence of audio or video data caused by latency or missing packets. (12)

journal file. This log of all file activity stored by a journaling file system. (8)

Copyright Goodheart-Willcox Co., Inc.

journaling file system. Type of file system that ensures file integrity whenever an unexpected system shutdown occurs. (8)

K

Kerberos. Security authentication system that allows two computers to communicate securely over a network that is not typically secure. (15)

kernel. Core of an operating system. (8)

L

latency. Amount of time it takes a signal to travel from its source to its destination. (2)

layer 1 device. Network device that makes no decisions about where a packet is sent but rather simply moves the packet along the network path such as through cabling, hubs, or repeaters. (1)

layer 2 device. Network device that makes decisions based on a MAC address or a logical name. (1)

Layer 2 Forwarding (L2F). Protocol developed by Cisco Systems that is similar to PPTP. (14)

Layer 2 Tunneling Protocol (L2TP). Protocol developed by Microsoft and several other companies that combines the L2F and PPTP protocols. (14)

layer 3 device. Network device that makes a decision about where to move the data based on a protocol. (1)

lightning arrestor. Piece of electrical equipment designed to dampen the effects of an electrical surge caused by lightning. (16)

Lightweight Extensible Authentication Protocol (LEAP). Proprietary authentication system developed by Cisco Systems for its line of wireless access points. (15)

link aggregation. Occurs when two or more network cables are paralleled to increase bandwidth and provide redundancy. (11)

Link-Layer Discovery Protocol (LLDP). Developed as an IEEE specification to identify devices connected on the local area network. (6)

Link-Layer Discovery Protocol–Media Endpoint Discovery (LLDP-MED). Enhanced version of LLDP used for routers, switches, Voice over Internet Protocol (VoIP) devices, and Power over Ethernet (PoE) devices. (6)

Link-Layer Topology Discovery (LLTD). Core protocol behind the Microsoft Network and Sharing Center Map function in older Microsoft operating systems. (6)

link-local. Portion of an organization's network. (10)

Link-Local Multicast Name Resolution (LLMNR). Protocol that serves the same function as a DNS server when a DNS server cannot be reached. (6)

link-state protocol. Routing protocol that performs its own calculations of the best route. (11)

Linux+ Certification. Tests a person's knowledge of the Linux operating system; pronounced *Linux-plus*. (20)

loading coil. Used to amplify voice signals, which are analog, and will not amplify DSL signals, which are digital. (14)

local area network (LAN). Network that is usually confined to a single building and managed by a single entity. (1)

local central office. Location where a customer's telephone lines connect to the switchgear. (14)

local exchange carrier (LEC). Local carrier made of one or more local central offices; also known as a *competitive local exchange carrier (CLEC)*. (14)

local loop. Section of wiring between customer premises and the local central office. (14)

local security policy. Security policy that affects local users. (7)

logic bomb. Type of malware that initiates malicious activity after some logical condition has been met. (15)

logical diagram. Documents the flow of data. (16)

Logical Disk Manager (LDM) partition. Partition that contains information about dynamic volumes and is created during the conversion from NTFS 4.0 to dynamic disk. (7)

logical drive. Partitioned hard disk drive that is assigned a drive letter. (7)

logical identification. Name that uniquely identifies the computer on the network. (1)

logical unit number (LUN). Identifies every additional device connected to a SCSI extender. (9)

logon right. Ability to log on to the network. (7)

loopback address. Reserved IP address of a network interface card. (10)

LPIC-1 Certification. Introductory-level certification that measures basic skills associated with installing, configuring, and managing a Linux operating system. (20)

LPIC-2 Certification. Second level of Linux certification and requires a more in-depth knowledge base than LPIC-1. (20)

LPIC-3 Certification. Measures the Linux skill set for supporting a large, enterprise Linux network. (20)

M

macro virus. One of the most common and most easily written virus programs. (15)

magnetic induction. Electronic phenomenon that occurs when a conductor is placed in close proximity to a current-carrying conductor and a magnetic field encircles the other conductor while inducing current; also known as *mutual induction*. (2)

mail filter. Blocks, or filters, unwanted e-mail messages. (13)

mail gateway. Special software and device used to connect two normally incompatible e-mail systems. (13)

Copyright Goodheart-Willcox Co., Inc.

main distribution frame (MDF). Cable connection point where the private telecommunication cables come into a building and then connect or distribute to other areas in the building. (18)

main entrance room. Room in which public or private telecommunication enter the building. (18)

malware. Term given to software programs that are intended to damage, destroy, or steal data; short for *malicious software.* (15)

man in the middle (MITM). Method of intercepting a network transmission, reading it, and then placing it back on route to its intended destination. (15)

Manchester encoding. Encoding scheme characterized by the digital pulse transitioning during the midpoint of the time period. (5)

master boot record (MBR). Contains information stored in the first sector of a hard disk that identifies an operating system location. (17)

maximum transmission unit (MTU). Refers to the largest network-layer data unit that can be sent at one time; the largest transmission unit. (2)

mean time between failures (MTBF). Describes how long a system is likely to run before it fails; also known as *Mean Time Before Failure.* (16)

mean time to repair (MTTR). Average time it would take to repair a system or device if it fails; also known as *Mean Time to Recover.* (16)

media. General term that identifies the material used to transport packets and data streams between nodes. (1)

media access control (MAC) address. Physical identification number of a device on a network. (1)

media access control (MAC) filter. Feature that allows or restricts WAP access based on the MAC address of a wireless network card. (15)

media converter. Changes one type of electrical signal into another or interfaces one cable type to another. (1)

memory address assignment. Large block of memory assigned to a device to transfer data between two locations. (9)

mesh topology. Network topology in which each node on the network connects to every other node on the network. (1)

metropolitan area network (MAN). Consists of two or more LANs connected with private or public communication lined within the same geographic area. (1)

Microsoft Certified Solutions Associate (MCSA) Certification. Designed for those seeking entry-level employment in an IT field. (20)

Microsoft Certified Solutions Developer (MCSD) Certification. Confirms a person's knowledge of essential mobile or web-based applications and services. (20)

Microsoft Certified Solutions Expert (MCSE) Certification. Intended for those seeking to prove the ability to create and implement solutions across multiple platforms and technologies. (20)

Microsoft Challenge Handshake Authentication Protocol (MS-CHAP). Enhanced version of CHAP that encrypts not only the username and password but also the data package. (15)

Microsoft Office Specialist (MOS) Certification. Based on Microsoft Office products beginning with the 2000 versions. (20)

Microsoft Reserved (MSR) partition. Required partition on every GPT disk. (7)

Microsoft Technology Associate (MTA) Certification. Entry-level certification that proves a person's basic technological knowledge and skills. (20)

modulation. Mixing of a carrier wave and data signal. (4)

module. Small program, such as a hardware driver or a kernel enhancement. (8)

mount point. Location in a directory structure where a device is mounted or inserted. (8)

Moving Picture Experts Group (MPEG). Industry standard that ensures compatibility between different cameras, displays, and other multimedia equipment. (12)

multicast address. IPv6 address that delivers packets to multiple addresses; also known as *many-to-one.* (10)

multicast frame. Frame that is intended for a preselected number of computers. (5)

multilayer switch. Enhanced switch designed to perform more than basic switch functions. (1)

Multilink Point-to-Point Protocol (MLPPP). Combines two or more physical links in such a way that they act as one; also known as *multilink dialing.* (14)

multimaster replication. Type of security database replication in which all domain controllers store a copy of the Active Directory database. (7)

multimode fiber-optic cable. Has a larger core diameter than single-mode fiber-optic cable. (3)

multiple-input-multiple-output (MIMO). Wireless networking technology that uses two or more streams of data transmission to increase data throughput and the range of the wireless network. (4)

Multi-Protocol Label Switching (MPLS). Allows a network administrator to attach a label or header to an IP packet in order to route the packet to a specific destination. (14)

Multipurpose Internet Mail Extensions (MIME). Protocol that encodes additional information to e-mail protocols that normally could not transfer attachments. (13)

Copyright Goodheart-Willcox Co., Inc.

multistation access unit (MAU). Allows for the quick connection and disconnection of token ring cables while maintaining the logic of the ring topology. (1)

multi-user telecommunication outlet assembly (MUTOA). Grouping of outlets that serves up to 12 work areas. (18)

N

namespace. Label that identifies a unique location in a structure such as the Internet. (7)

naming convention. Standard naming format that is used when providing names for network objects. (18)

near field communication (NFC). Set of communication protocols that allows mobile devices to exchange communication provided they are within a certain range of each other. (4)

near-end crosstalk (NEXT). Measurement of the reflected loss at the near end, or input end, of a cable. (2)

Neighbor Discovery. IPv6 data link layer mechanism used to identify network devices automatically, without the need of user intervention. (10)

network. Interconnected collection of computers, computer-related equipment, and communication devices. (1)

network address. Unique identifier for a node on a computer network. (1)

Network Address Authority (NAA). Naming standard developed by the International Committee for Information Technology Standards (ICITS). (9)

Network Address Translation (NAT). Specifically designed for implementing private network configurations by allowing unregistered private network addresses to communicate with legally registered IP addresses. (10)

network administrator. Overall administrator who controls access to the network and its shares. (1)

network authentication. Occurs when the security descriptor of the resource the user wishes to access is verified. (7)

Network File System (NFS). File-sharing protocol used by Unix and Linux operating systems. (7)

network interface card (NIC). Contains the electronic components needed to send and receive a digital signal. (1)

network interface device (NID). Term used to describe a device that connects the commercial carrier local loop to the private customer's premises wiring. (18)

network layer. Primarily responsible for addressing and navigating networks by using generated IP addresses; layer three of the OSI model. (1)

Network+ Certification. Measures the skills necessary for an entry-level network support technician; pronounced *network-plus*. (20)

Network News Transfer Protocol (NNTP). Designed to distribute news messages to NNTP clients and NNTP servers across the Internet. (13)

network operating system (NOS). Provides a communication system between the computers, printers, and other intelligent hardware that exists on the network. (1)

network share. Resource on the network that is shared among assigned users; also known as a *shared resource*. (7)

network support specialist. Required to assist users and customers whenever they encounter a network problem. (20)

network topology. Physical arrangement of computers, computer-related devices, communication devices, and cabling in a network. (1)

network-attached storage (NAS). Device or collection of devices that provides storage for network data. (9)

New Technology File System (NTFS). Native file format for Windows NT and Windows Server operating systems. (7)

newsgroups. News articles are arranged in groups or categories. (13)

node. Device that can be attached to a network and given a network address. (1)

noise. Electromagnetic interference. (2)

NTFS permission. Permission that can be applied to both the directory level and file level. (7)

O

object. Any physical or logical unit that is defined as part of the network. (7)

octet. Eight-bit (or one-byte) value. (10)

omni-directional. Transmission of electromagnetic signals in all directions. (4)

one-way trust relationship. Type of trust relationship in which the designated trusting domain allows the trusted domain to access its resources. (7)

open. Wiring fault that occurs when the circuit has an open spot along the length of the conductor. (2)

Open Shortest Path First (OSPF). Routing protocol that only exchanges the most recently changed information in the table. (11)

Open Systems Interconnection (OSI) model. Describes how hardware and software should work together to form a network communication system. (1)

optical network terminal (ONT). Fiber-optic cable termination point between the customer and the service provider. (18)

optical time domain reflectometer (OTDR). Device for testing and troubleshooting long runs of fiber-optic cable. (3)

organizational unit. Container that holds objects or other organizational units and is used to organize a network into manageable units. (7)

Copyright Goodheart-Willcox Co., Inc.

orthogonal frequency-division multiplexing (OFDM). Transmission technique used with wireless devices that use the 5-GHz radio band and can achieve a data rate as high as 54 Mbps. (4)

P

packet filter. Inspects each packet as it passes through the firewall and then accepts or rejects the packet based on a set of rules. (15)

packet sniffer. Network monitoring utility that captures data packets as they travel across a network. (15)

packet switching. Data-routing method that does not use a permanent connection but rather breaks the data transmission into smaller parts called *packets*. (5)

parallel processing. Program can be processed through more than one CPU simultaneously. (9)

parity check. Method of verifying the integrity of transmitted data. (5)

partition. Area of the hard disk drive that is to be allocated to an operating system. (7)

passive hub. Acts as a central connection point for network cables. (1)

Password Authentication Protocol (PAP). Basic password authentication technique used for HTTP and remote dial-up access. (15)

patch panel. Rack-mounted wiring device for network systems. (18)

Payment Card Industry Data Security Standard (PCI DSS). Set of credit-card security standards designed to protect credit card information. (15)

PDI+ Certification. Measures a candidate's ability to configure and repair document-imaging devices such as printers, copiers, scanners, fax machines, and multifunctional machines; pronounced *PDI-plus*. (20)

peak utilization. Measurement of the highest level of utilization experienced by the network. (16)

peer-to-peer network. Network in which all computers are considered peers or equals. (1)

permanent virtual circuit (PVC). Behaves like a hard-wired connection between a destination and source. (12)

permission. Ability to access a network share. (7)

personal area network (PAN). Very small Bluetooth network. (4)

personal unlocking key (PUK). Code used to reset a forgotten PIN. (4)

phishing. Method of Internet fraud that involves using e-mail to steal a person's identity and other sensitive information; pronounced *fishing*. (15)

physical diagram. Documents the actual wiring and devices on your network. (16)

physical drive. Hard disk drive inside the computer. (7)

physical layer. Where a user sees something tangible; consists of the cable and connectors used for constructing the network; layer one of the OSI model. (1)

platform as a service (PaaS). Provides access to operating systems in the same manner as SaaS. (1)

plenum-rated. Refers to cable that has a special type of insulation that will not give off toxic gases should the cable be consumed by fire. (2)

point of presence (POP). Point where a telephone company line connects to a subscriber line. (14)

Point-to-Point Protocol (PPP). Vast improvement over SLIP and can support multiple protocols such as IPX, AppleTalk, and TCP/IP. (14)

Point-to-Point Protocol over Ethernet (PPPoE). Provides one or more hosts on an Ethernet network the ability to establish an individual PPP connection with an ISP. (14)

Point-to-Point Tunneling Protocol (PPTP). Enhanced version of PPP designed to upgrade security and to make use of a virtually private network using the public Internet. (14)

port. Logical connection that matches a service with a computer. (5)

port monitoring. Occurs when a particular port on a switch is connected directly to the IDS or IPS and monitors all activity through another port on the same switch. (15)

port number. Associated with the TCP/IP protocol and is used to create a virtual connection between two computers running TCP/IP. (10)

Post Office Protocol (POP). Simple protocol designed to access a mail server and download e-mail to an e-mail client. (13)

power conditioning. Process of eliminating spikes as well as any type of variation in the desired AC signal pattern. (16)

Power over Ethernet (PoE). IEEE standard 802.3af; specifies the supply of small amounts of electrical power to network devices. (2)

power-on self-test (POST). Quick, initial check of the major components performed at startup to be sure that a minimum working system is available. (9)

presentation layer. Ensures character-code recognition; layer six of the OSI model. (1)

primary partition. Partition that stores a bootable copy of an operating system. (7)

Primary Rate ISDN (PRI-ISDN). ISDN category that consists of twenty-three B channels and one D channel. It has a total data rate of 1.544 Mbps. (14)

print server. Coordinates printing activities between clients and printers. (1)

professionalism. Act of exhibiting appropriate character, judgment, and behavior by a person who is trained to perform a job. (20)

Copyright Goodheart-Willcox Co., Inc.

programmer. Writes, tests, and modifies software programs. (20)

propagation delay. Amount of time it takes for data to be transmitted between the earth and satellite. (4)

Protected Extensible Authentication Protocol (PEAP). Proprietary protocol developed jointly by Cisco Systems and Microsoft. (15)

protocol. Group of computer programs that handle packet formatting and control data transmission. (1)

protocol analyzer. Software application used to monitor a network and inspect frame/packet contents. (15)

proxy server. Firewall component that is typically installed on a server and resides between the Internet server and the LAN hosts. (15)

public switched telephone network (PSTN). Older telephone technology that uses twisted-pair cable and analog signals; also known as *plain-old telephone service (POTS)*. (12)

punch down block. Network system-wiring device used to terminate communication cable for telephone systems. (18)

punch down tool. Used to push individual twisted-pair wires into the connection and automatically trim conductor excess. (18)

Q

Quality of Service (QoS). Protocol that gives time-sensitive packets a higher priority than data packets. (12)

R

radio interference. Interference that matches the frequency of a given carrier wave. (4)

radio waves. Electromagnetic waves with a frequency range of 10 kHz to 3,000,000 MHz. (4)

radio-frequency identification (RFID). Use of electromagnetic fields to identify and track objects equipped with active tags or chips. (4)

ransomware. Functions initially as a worm then either disables system services or encrypts user files. (15)

realm trust. Occurs when a trust relationship is created between a Windows Server 2016 domain and a non-Windows domain. (7)

Real-time Transport Protocol (RTP). Standard and protocol developed by IETF to stream voice and video in real time. (12)

receiver. Receives a modulated wave and demodulates it. (4)

Redundant Array of Independent Disks (RAID). System of disks arranged for speed, fault tolerance, or both. (9)

reference. Person who is familiar with an applicant's skills, talents, or personal traits and is willing to recommend the applicant for a position. (20)

reflected loss. Amount of signal reflected from the end of the cable. (2)

registrar. Each private company to which domain-name registration privileges is given. (10)

remote access server. Server that is accessed remotely by users not on a LAN. (14)

Remote Authentication Dial-In User Service (RADIUS). Service that allows remote access servers to authenticate to a central server. (15)

Remote Desktop Protocol (RDP). Presentation protocol that allows Windows computers to communicate directly with Windows-based clients. (14)

repeater. Amplifies or reshapes a weak signal into its original strength and form. (1)

replay attack. Occurs when the data in a network transmission is copied and stored. (15)

resistance. Opposition to direct current (DC). (2)

résumé. Document that profiles a person's career goals, education, and work history. (20)

Reverse Address Resolution Protocol (RARP). Used to find the MAC address of the host when the IP address is known. (10)

reversed pair. Occurs when two pairs of a cable assembly have reversed two connections. (2)

RG-6. Standard for cable television (CATV) systems and satellite systems. (2)

RG-8. Very rigid coaxial cable with a solid copper conductor in the center; also known as *thicknet*. (2)

RG-58. Coaxial cable that is smaller in diameter and easier to work with than thicknet cable; also known as *thinnet*. (2)

ring topology. Network topology that consists of a single cable that runs continuously from node to node. (1)

RIP next generation (RIPng). IPv6 version of RIP. (11)

rogue access point. Unauthorized wireless access point that is installed on a network system. (15)

rollover cable. Special cable in which the pin order is completely reversed on one end of the cable. (2)

router. Navigates packets across large networks using the most efficient route. (1)

Router Information Protocol (RIP). One of the oldest protocols ever developed for routers. (11)

router metric. Mechanism used to determine or measure the best route. (11)

routing. Process of selecting the "best route" through which to send packets. (11)

S

sampling frequency. Rate at which amplitude is measured per second. (12)

sampling rate. Number of times the sample is taken during a specific period. (12)

scattering. Loss of signal strength due to impurities in the core material. (3)

Copyright Goodheart-Willcox Co., Inc.

search engine. Software program that is designed to locate websites and pages by relevant terms entered into the search text box. (13)

Secure Copy Protocol (SCP). Provides a secure way of transferring files between computers. (15)

Secure File Transfer Protocol (SFTP). Secure version of FTP. (13)

Secure Shell (SSH). Protocol that provides secure network services over an insecure network medium such as the Internet. (15)

Secure Sockets Layer (SSL). Security protocol used to authenticate clients and servers and to encrypt data between web servers and individuals. (15)

security policy. Blanket policy that secures resources on the network. (7)

Security+ Certification. Requires knowledge related to generally accepted security practices; pronounced *security-plus*. (20)

segment. Smaller, deliverable piece of data that contains information to aid in reassembly. (5)

segmenting. Act of dividing a network into smaller sections to avoid collisions. (6)

Serial Attached SCSI (SAS). Next generation of SCSI. (9)

Serial Line Internet Protocol (SLIP). Protocol that was introduced with Unix and supports only TCP/IP. (14)

server. Computer that provides services to networked computers. (1)

server cluster. Group of individual servers connected both physically and logically to ensure constant service to clients. (7)

Server Message Block (SMB). Protocol that supports file sharing from a Windows operating system. (7)

Server+ Certification. Tests a person's knowledge of network server hardware and software; pronounced *server-plus*. (20)

service pack. Term used to describe a collection of software patches or fixes. (16)

service-level agreement (SLA). Determines how fast, and in what manner, vendors will respond to an issue. (16)

session. Logical connection with a Linux computer. (8)

Session Initiation Protocol (SIP). Standard and protocol specified by the Internet Engineering Task Force (IETF) and used for initiating, maintaining, and terminating the exchange of voice, multimedia, gaming, chat, and more. (12)

session layer. Establishes a connection between two different computers and provides a complete conversation context; layer five of the OSI model. (1)

share-level security. Provides password protection for a share and minimal share permissions. (7)

shell. User interface that interprets and carries out commands from the user similarly to the way a command interpreter interprets and carries out commands. (8)

short. Occurs in cabling when two conductors are improperly connected, resulting in a shorter circuit path. (2)

signal bounce. Refers to a condition where the wireless signal reflects, or "bounces," off an object. (17)

Simple Mail Transfer Protocol (SMTP). Part of the TCP/IP protocol suite designed to transfer plaintext e-mail from an e-mail client to a mail server and from a mail server to a mail server. (13)

Simple Network Management Protocol (SNMP). Designed by the ITEF to support network management, allowing an administrator to manage and monitor network devices and services from a single location. (16)

Simple Object Access Protocol (SOAP). Set of rules for web-based messages and is constructed from XML. (13)

simple volume. Volume that exists on a single drive; similar to a volume in Windows NT. (7)

simplex. Refers to communication that occurs in one direction only. (2)

single-mode fiber-optic cable. Much smaller in diameter than multimode cable. (3)

Small Computer Systems Interface (SCSI). Computer bus technology that allows for the connection of multiple devices to a single controller. (9)

smart card. Incorporates a special card into a security system; used in conjunction with a personal identification number (PIN). (15)

smart jack. Phone jack that is considered an intelligent connection point because it incorporates additional electronics that allow it to perform specific functions. (18)

Smurf attack. Reflective DoS that uses a combination of IP spoofing and ICMP to saturate a target network with traffic. (15)

snap-in. Tool or utility that is added to the Microsoft Management Console (MMC). (7)

social engineering. Used to describe the manipulation of personnel through the use of deceitful means to gain security information. (15)

socket. Combination of a port number and an IP address. (10)

soft phone. Virtual telephonic device. (12)

soft skills. Skills used to communicate and work well with others. (20)

software as a service (SaaS). Delivers specific applications in a virtualized manner; also known as *on-demand software*. (1)

spam. Unwanted e-mail messages distributed to a large number of users. (13)

spammer. Sends e-mail with some sort of advertisement as a probe. (13)

spamming. Distribution of unsolicited e-mail. (13)

Copyright Goodheart-Willcox Co., Inc.

spanned volume. Volume that combines two or more physical drives; similar to a Windows NT volume set. (7)

Spanning Tree Protocol (STP). Layer 2 protocol designed to manage networks based on MAC addresses. (11)

spatial multiplexing. Transmission of two or more streams of data in the same frequency channel. (4)

split pair. Occurs when two pairs of conductors are reversed in connection with another pair. (2)

spoofing. Fooling a destination by using an IP address other than the true IP address of a source to create a fake identity. (15)

spread spectrum. Transmission technique that uses multiple channels to transmit data either simultaneously or sequentially. (4)

standard generalized markup language (SGML). Original standard for both HTML and XML. (13)

standard. Set of recommendations or practices presented by an organization that defines specific aspects about a technology. (1)

standby UPS. Type of UPS that waits until there is a disruption in commercial electricity before it takes over the responsibility of supplying electrical energy. (16)

star topology. Network topology that involves running cables from each node to connect a single point. (1)

stateful packet inspection. Applies a filter based on the sequence of packets. (15)

stateless packet inspection. A firewall inspects individual packet attributes such as IP address, port number, and protocols. (15)

static addressing. Act of assigning IP addresses manually. (10)

static IP address table. Table in which IP addresses are entered manually. (11)

static IP assignment. Refers to an IP address that is entered manually for each host on the network. (10)

static VLAN. Created when physical ports on a switch are assigned manually to a particular VLAN. (11)

step-index multimode fiber-optic cable. General multimode fiber-optic cable that does not counter dispersion. (3)

storage area network (SAN). Separate, high-speed network that provides a storage facility for one or more networks. (9)

store-and-forward. Method of frame forwarding in which a switch reads the entire contents of the frame before forwarding the frame to its destination. (11)

straight-through cable. Constructed with each numbered pin connecting to the matching numbered pin on the opposite end of the cable; used to connect a computer to a hub. (2)

striped volume. Volume that increases the read/write access speed by spreading data across multiple hard disk drives. (7)

subdomain. Any level domain located beneath the secondary domain. (10)

subnet mask. Number similar to an IP address used to determine in which subnetwork a particular IPv4 address belongs. (10)

subnetting. Dividing a network into subnetworks, or subnets. (11)

subnetwork. Network within a network. (10)

subscriber identity module (SIM). Circuit that stores the international mobile subscriber identity (IMSI). (4)

sunspot. Magnetic energy storm that occurs at the surface of the sun. (14)

swap file. Hard drive disk space that supplements the RAM; also known as *page file*. (16)

switch. Filters network traffic or creates subnetworks from a larger network. (1)

symmetric-key encryption. Encryption method that uses a key that only the sender and the receiver know; also known as *secret-key cryptography*. (15)

Synchronous Optical Network (SONET). Similar in design to T-carrier technology except SONET bases its technology on fiber-optic cable. (14)

synchronous transmission. Data transmission method in which a digital signal is synchronized with a reference signal to ensure proper timing. (5)

system partition. Contains the core files used to start the operating system. (17)

systems analyst. Responsible for analyzing, evaluating, and recommending business software systems. (20)

T

tarball. Compressed file containing one or more software programs. (8)

T-carrier. Leased line that follows one of the standards known as T1, fractional T1, T2, or T3. (14)

telecommunication closet. Enclosed space used to house telecommunication cable-termination equipment. (18)

telecommunication room. Room or enclosed space that houses telecommunication equipment. (18)

Telecommunications Industry Association (TIA). Standards maintenance organization mainly concerned with fiber optics, user equipment, network equipment, wireless communication, and satellite communication. (1)

telephone gateway. Specialized piece of equipment that connects a packet-style network communication system to a telephone system using the H.323 protocol. (12)

Copyright Goodheart-Willcox Co., Inc.

Teredo. IPv6 transition technology configured by default in Windows Vista, 7, 8, and 10; considered a last-resort technology when ISATAP cannot be used. (10)

Terminal Access Controller Access-Control System Plus (TACACS+). Secure alternative to RADIUS. (15)

terminating resistor. Device installed to absorb the electrical signals when they reach the end of a segment. (2)

thin server. Server that has only the hardware and software needed to support and run a specific function. (9)

time period. Represents the rate of recurrence of an expected change in signal level. (5)

time to live (TTL). Maximum number of hops allowed. (2)

Transmission Control Protocol/ Internet Protocol (TCP/IP). Developed by the Defense Advanced Research Project Agency (DARPA) in the early 1970s to support communication over the Internet. (1)

transmitter. Generates a carrier wave and modulates information into the carrier wave. (4)

Transport Layer Security (TLS). Internet Engineering Task Force (IEFT) standard that was developed after SSL. (15)

transport layer. Ensures reliable data by sequencing packets and reassembling them into their correct order; layer four of the OSI model. (1)

transport mode. IPSec implementation in which only the payload is encrypted. (15)

tree. Collection of domains that share a common root domain name and Active Directory database. (7)

Trivial File Transfer Protocol (TFTP). Lightweight version of FTP. (13)

Trojan horse. Program designed to gain access to a computer while pretending to be something else. (15)

trunking. Technique of connecting different VLANs together using a single network link. (11)

trunk line. Consists of hundreds of pairs of twisted-pair cable or fiber-optic cable. (14)

trust relationship. Relationship between domains that allows users from one domain to access resources on another domain in which they do not have a user account. (7)

tunnel mode. IPSec implementation in which the payload and the header, which contains routing information, is encrypted. (15)

twisted pair. Type of cable that consists of four pairs of twisted conductors. (2)

two-way trust relationship. Type of trust relationship in which both domains are able to share resources with each other. (7)

U

unicast address. IPv6 address that delivers packets to a single network address. (10)

Unicode. Similar in principle to ASCII but uses 16 bits to represent individual characters. (5)

uniform resource locator (URL). User-friendly name associated with an IP address. (13)

uninterruptible power supply (UPS). Device that ensures constant and consistent network performance by supplying electrical energy in case of a power failure or blackout. (16)

unipolar digital signal. Digital signal that fluctuates between a positive five-volt and zero-volt level. (5)

unique-local. An entire organization's network or a portion of it. (10)

unspecified bit rate (UBR). ATM data transfer classification that does not guarantee any speed or meet requirements of any special application such as multimedia or telephony. (12)

upconverter. Refers to a radio transmitter integrated into a satellite dish for uplink. (14)

user-level security. Requires a user to authenticate through a security database to access a share. (7)

V

variable bit rate (VBR). ATM data transfer classification in which the ATM cell rate automatically adjusts to support time-sensitive data but using multiplexing techniques to provide a minimum CBR for time-sensitive audio and video transmissions while controlling the data rate of data that is not time sensitive. (12)

variable bit rate non-real-time (VBR-nrt). ATM data transfer classification that allows cells to move at a variable rate. (12)

variable bit rate real-time (VBR-rt). ATM data transfer classification that allows cells to move at a variable rate depending on the cell's contents to support real-time audio and video transfers. (12)

variable-length subnet mask (VLSM). Subnet mask that is not expressed in standard eight-bit or one-byte values. (11)

Virtual Local Area Network (VLAN). Broadcast domain created by one or more switches based on logical (IP) addresses. (11)

virtual network connection (VNC). Used to describe the broad category of remote connection systems that allow a user to connect to a network device such as a server or a desktop computer from a remote device. (15)

Virtual Private Network (VPN). Simulated, independent network created by software over a public network. (14)

Virtual Trunking Protocol (VTP). Proprietary protocol developed by Cisco Systems that automatically reconfigures multiple switches across an entire network. (11)

Copyright Goodheart-Willcox Co., Inc.

virtualization Act of creating a software-based, or *virtual*, environment. (9)

virus. Software that self-replicates. (15)

voice over IP (VoIP). Internet telephony protocol designed for high-performance data delivery and quality of service. (12)

volume. Accessible unit of hard disk drive space as seen through the Windows interface. (7)

volume set. Volume that consists of partitions from two or more hard disk drives. (7)

VPN concentrator. Device, normally a router, that also provides VPN connections for the network. (14)

W

web browser. Software program that permits the user to navigate the World Wide Web and then interpret and display web pages. (13)

web developer. Responsible for converting written documents into HTML or other web-page programming languages. (20)

web master. Responsible for maintaining websites and web servers and ensuring search engine optimization (SEO); also known as *web administrator*. (20)

web server. Server configured to provide web services. (13)

website. Location on the World Wide Web. (13)

wide area network (WAN). Consists of a large number of networks and PCs connected with private and public communication lines throughout many geographic areas. (1)

Wi-Fi. Name given to 802.11 network devices. (4)

Wi-Fi Protected Access (WPA). Protocol that combines authentication with encryption by using *Temporal Key Integrity Protocol (TKIP)*. (4)

Wi-Fi Protected Access 2 (WPA2). Developed by the Wi-Fi organization as an enhanced version of WPA. (4)

Windows Internet Naming Service (WINS). Server resolves NetBIOS names to IP addresses. (10)

windows manager. Controls the display and provides a GUI in a Unix/Linux system. (8)

Wired Equivalent Privacy (WEP). Intended to make a wireless network as secure as a wired network. (4)

wireless access point (WAP). Provides a connection between a wireless network and a cable-based network. (4)

wireless personal area network (WPAN). Typically a small Ethernet network consisting of personal wireless devices. (4)

wireless topology. Network topology that does not use cabling but rather infrared light or radio transmission to communicate between nodes. (1)

work area. Location where employees perform their normal office duties. (18)

workgroup. Group of computers that share resources such as files and hardware. (7)

World Wide Web Consortium (W3C). Organization that provides recommendations for language standards of web pages. (1)

worm. Rapidly spreading virus. (15)

X

X.25. Transport protocol that uses analog signals to transmit data across long distances. (12)

X client. Application, such as a word-processing program. (8)

X server. Program that communicates with the computer hardware. (8)

X Windows. System that provides a GUI for Unix and Linux systems. (8)

Z

Zero Configuration (Zeroconf). Standard developed by IEEE that recommends how to design a device that automatically detects other devices on the same network or on a nearby network segment without the need of intervention by an administrator or a DHCP or DNS server. (15)

Z-wave. Wireless communication protocol used for home automation. (4)

Copyright Goodheart-Willcox Co., Inc.

Index

4-7 switch. *See* multilayer switches
6to4, 321–322
10Base2, 67
10Base5, 68
10BaseT, 69
10GBaseW, 97–98
10 Gigabit Ethernet, 66
    802.3ae standard, 97–98
10Mbps Ethernet, 66–69

A

AAA (authentication, authorization, and accounting), 465–467
AAA proxy, 466
ABR (available bit rate), 377
absorption, 92
AC (alternating current), 53–54
acceptable use policy (AUP), 485, 594
access control, 438
access-control list (ACL), 573
access methods, 174–175
    CSMA/CA (carrier-sense multiple access with collision avoidance), 71, 129, 131
    CSMA/CD (carrier-sense multiple access with collision detection), 71
    Fibre Channel, 279–281
access ports, 8, 352
ACL (access-control list), 573
acoustical echo, 370–371
ACPI (Automatic Configuration and Power Interface), 271
ACPICA (ACPI Component Architecture), 271–272
Active Directory (AD). *See* AD DS
active hubs, 22–23
active partition, 537
ADC (analog-to-digital converter), 374
AD DS (Active Directory Domain Services), 208–218
    authentication, 214
    common names, 214
    hierarchical structure, 209–213
    replication of database, 214–216
    trust relationships, 216–218
adaptive cut-through, 346

Address Resolution Protocol (ARP), 152, 183, 326
ad hoc mode, 124
administration models, 12–14
administrative safeguards, 486
administrative servers, 13
administrator accounts, 470
AES (Advanced Encryption Standard), 140, 455, 463
alien crosstalk (AXT), 57
alternating current (AC), 53–54
American National Standards Institute (ANSI), 29. *See also* ANSI/TIA/EIA standards
American Standard Code for Information Interchange (ASCII), 155–157, 666–667
American Wire Gauge (AWG) ratings, 57–58
amplifier, 49
amplitude modulation, 48. *See also* modulation
analog signals, 48–50
analog-to-digital conversion, 365–368, 374
analog-to-digital converter (ADC), 374
anonymous FTP sites, 407
ANSI (American National Standards Institute), 29. *See also* ANSI/TIA/EIA standards
ANSI/TIA/EIA standards. 71, 77, 602–605
antenna classifications, 116–118
ANT+, 134
anycast address, 317
Apache, 249, 399–400
A+ Certification, 264, 284, 639
AppleTalk, 172
application gateway, 476
application layer (layer 7), 37
    data encoding and transmission, 162–163
applications, employment, 644–645
Application-Specific Integrated Circuit (ASIC), 350
arbitrated loop topology, 281
archive bit, 512
ARCnet, 178

arguments, for shell commands, 240–241
ARP (Address Resolution Protocol), 152, 183, 326
arp command, 248, 323, 326–327, 570
ARP poisoning, 452
ARP table, 327
ASCII (American Standard Code for Information Interchange), 155–157, 666–667
ASIC (Application-Specific Integrated Circuit), 350
asymmetric-key encryption, 456–457
asynchronous transfer mode. *See* ATM
asynchronous transmission, 148
ATM (asynchronous transfer mode), 18, 374–379
ATM switches, 376, 378–379
Attachment Unit Interface (AUI), 68
attenuation, 22, 91–92, 49, 529
attire, appropriate for interview, 646–647
audio. *See* voice and audio signals
auditing, 199
    tools, 481–482
AUI (Attachment Unit Interface), 68
AUP (acceptable use policy), 485, 594
authentication, 139, 214, 246, 438, 446, 465–469
    AAA (authentication, authorization, and accounting), 465–467
    methods, 467
    open-system, 462
    protocols, 467–469
    Unix/Linux, 246
    WAP (wireless access point), 462
authentication, authorization, and accounting (AAA), 465–467
authentication server, 463
authenticator, 463
Automatic Configuration and Power Interface (ACPI), 271
automatic medium-dependent interface crossover (Auto-MDIX), 72
Automatic Private IP Addressing (APIPA), 310–311
Auto-MDIX (automatic medium-dependent interface crossover), 72

Copyright Goodheart-Willcox Co., Inc.

Copyright Goodheart-Willcox Co., Inc.

circuit-level gateway, 476

circuit switching, 154

Cisco

certifications, 641

training academies, 351, 641

Cisco Discovery Protocol (CDP), 183

Class A, Class B, and Class C networks, 293–294

Classless Inter-Domain Routing (CIDR), 355–356

classless IP. *See* IPv6 addresses

clear text, 467

cleaving fiber-optic cables, 100–103

CLEC (competitive local exchange carrier), 420

client/server networks, 13–14, 190–191

cloud computing, 15

cluster, 509

CN (common name), 214

coaxial cables (coax), 58–62

codec (compressor/decompressor), 372

code-division multiple access (CDMA), 136

cold sites, 514

cold spares, 513–514

college education, 637–638

collision domains, 175–176

collisions, 175–176

command prompt, 173

commands, Unix/Linux, 240–241

command syntax, 173

committed information rate (CIR), 373–374

Common Internet File System (CIFS), 202

common name (CN), 214

Common Unix Printing System (CUPS), 247

communication, network, 16, 53.
See also transmission

communication skills, 637, 650

compatibility, 506–508

competitive local exchange carrier (CLEC), 420

complex trust relationships, 216

compression, of video, 372–373

compressor/decompressor (codec), 372

CompTIA

A+ Certification, 264, 284, 639

Linux+ Certification, 640

Network+ Certification, 613–628, 639

PDI+ Certification, 640

recommended troubleshooting procedures, 527–533

Security+ Certification, 639

Server+ Certification, 284, 639

computers, operation, 534–539

concentrator. *See* hubs

confidentiality, 438

connectionless communication, 153–154

connection-oriented communication, 153–154

connections

loose or missing, 558–560

troubleshooting problems, 550–557

connectors

coaxial cable, 60

fiber-optic, 99–100

twisted-pair cable, 71–74

consolidation point (CP), 604

constant bit rate (CBR), 375, 377

consultant, 634

content-address memory (CAM), 345

content filter, 476

contention domains. *See* collision domains

content switch, 351

contiguous namespace, 212

continuous UPS, 518

convergence, 347

conversion

analog and digital signals, 366–368, 374

number systems, 336

copper-core cables, 20, 57–65

termination standards, 71, 602

wiring faults, 77–79

copyleft, 237

Counter Mode-Cipher Block Chaining Message Authentication Code Protocol (CCMP), 140, 463

cover letter, 645

CP (consolidation point), 604

CPU (central processing unit), 264, 268

crackers, 407, 446

CRC (cyclic redundancy check), 33, 150

crimp tool, 73

crossed pair, 79

crossover cable, 71–72

crosstalk, 49, 54–57, 529

cryptography. *See* encryption

CSA (Canadian Standards Association), 602

CSMA/CA (carrier-sense multiple access with collision avoidance), 71, 129, 131

CSMA/CD (carrier-sense multiple access with collision detection), 71

CSS (cascading style sheets), 404

CSU/DSU (Channel Service Unit/Data Service Unit), 428

CUPS (Common Unix Printing System), 247

current, 53–54

cut-through, 346

cyclic redundancy check (CRC), 33, 150

D

DAC (digital-to-analog converter), 374

daemons, 234

daisy-chain hub configuration, 69–70

data

backup and restoration, 484, 511–515

codes, 155–158

digital signals, 48–50, 147–149

encoding, 147–149

frame structures by protocol, 158–161, 304–306

off-site storage, 513–514

OSI (Open Systems Interconnection) model and, 161–165

packaging, 149–153

security compliance, 485–486

transmission, 50–53, 153–155

database servers, 13

data encryption. *See* encryption

Data Encryption Standard (DES), 455

datagrams, 303. *See also* packaging of data; packets; UDP

data integrity, 438, 510–515, 549–550, 589

data link layer (layer 2), 33–34, 174–175

data encoding and transmission, 164–165

Data-Over-Cable Service Interface Specification (DOCSIS), 28, 423

Data Service Unit (DSU), 428

DC (direct current), 53–54

DDoS (Distributed Denial of Service) attacks, 448

dead drop, 559–560

deauthentication attack, 452

decentralized administration, 14

decibel (dB), 56

dedicated servers, 13, 399

default gateway address, 297

demarcation point (demarc), 596

demilitarized zone (DMZ), 477

demodulation, 112–114

Denial of Service (DoS) attacks, 448–449

DES (Data Encryption Standard), 455

designing a new network, 581–606

device file, 243

device hardening, 470–471

Copyright Goodheart-Willcox Co., Inc.

Copyright Goodheart-Willcox Co., Inc.

Copyright Goodheart-Willcox Co., Inc.

Copyright Goodheart-Willcox Co., Inc.

International Committee for Information Technology Standards (ICITS), 280

International Organization for Standardization. *See* ISO

International Telecommunication Union (ITU), 430

Internet, 395
  troubleshooting access problems, 562–563
  See also web servers and services

Internet Connection Sharing (ICS), 295

Internet Control Message Protocol (ICMP), 325

Internet Corporation for Assigned Names and Numbers (ICANN), 298

Internet Engineering Task Force. *See* IETF standards and technologies

Internet Information Services (IIS), 195, 400

Internet Message Access Protocol (IMAP), 410–411

Internet Protocol. *See* IP

Internet Protocol Security (IPSec), 460

Internet Small Computer Systems Interface. *See* iSCSI

InterNIC (Integrated Network Information Center), 298

interoperability, 226, 251–256
  troubleshooting problems, 255–256

interpersonal skills. *See* soft skills

interrupt request (IRQ), 272–273

interviews, employment, 646–649

intranet, 396. *See also* web servers and services

Intra-Site Automatic Tunneling Address Protocol (ISATAP), 322

intrusion detection system (IDS), 453–454

intrusion prevention system (IPS), 453–454

I/O (input/output) port, 273–274

IP (Internet Protocol), 17, 303
  addresses, 19–20, 292–297, 312–322
  frame structure, 304–306
  See also TCP/IP

IP addresses, 19–20, 292–297, 312–322

IP Address Management (IPAM), 310

IPAM (IP Address Management), 310

ipconfig command, 297, 309, 570

IPS (intrusion prevention system), 453–454

IPSec (Internet Protocol Security), 460

iptables command, 249

IPv4 addresses, 292–297, 311
  troubleshooting problems, 561

IPv6 addresses, 312–322
  Windows support, 323

IPX/SPX, 172

IQN (iSCSI-qualified name), 283

IRQ (interrupt request), 272–273

ISATAP (Intra-Site Automatic Tunneling Address Protocol), 322

iSCSI (Internet Small Computer Systems Interface), 281–284
  device name formats, 283–284

iSCSI-qualified name (IQN), 283

ISDN (Integrated Services Digital Network), 422–423

IS-IS (Intermediate System to Intermediate System), 349

ISM (industrial, scientific, and medical) band, 115

ISO (International Organization for Standardization), 28–29, 602
  27017 and 27018 cloud computing standards, 15

isolation transformers, 520

ITU (International Telecommunication Union), 430

J

JavaScript, 405

jitter, 369, 386, 529

job-search process, 643–649
  See also employment

journal file, 241

journaling file system, 241

Jumbo Frame, 66

K

Kerberos, 468–469

kernel, 233

kernel loading phase, 538–539

keys. *See* encryption

L

L2F (Layer 2 Forwarding), 436

L2TP (Layer 2 Tunneling Protocol), 436

label edge routers, 437

label switch routers, 437

LAN (local area network), 6

Last Known Good Configuration, 542

latency, 50, 369–370, 529

layer 1 devices, 38

layer 2 devices, 38

Layer 2 Forwarding (L2F), 436

Layer 2 Tunneling Protocol (L2TP), 436

layer 3 devices, 38

layer 3 switch, 350, 351

layer 7 firewall, 477

layer 7 switch. *See* multilayer switches

layers, OSI (Open Systems Interconnection) model, 32–37

LDAP (Lightweight Directory Access Protocol), 307
  directory structures, 585–586

LDM (Logical Disk Manager) partition, 226

LEAP (Lightweight Extensible Authentication Protocol), 469

lease period, for dynamic IP addresses, 309

LEC (local exchange carrier), 420

lifetimes, IPv6 addresses, 323

light, transmission of, 89–90

lightning arrestor, 515–516

Lightweight Directory Access Protocol. *See* LDAP

Lightweight Extensible Authentication Protocol (LEAP), 469

LILO (Linux Loader), 238–239

link aggregation, 356

Link-Layer Discovery Protocol. *See* LLDP

Link-Layer Discovery Protocol–Media Endpoint Discovery (LLDP-MED), 183

Link-Layer Topology Discovery (LLTD), 182

link-local, 316–317

Link-Local Multicast Name Resolution (LLMNR), 183

link-local unicast IPv6 address, 318

link-state protocol, 347

Linux, 234–238. *See also* Unix/Linux operating systems

Linux Loader (LILO), 238–239

Linux+ Certification, 640

Linux Professional Institute (LPI) certifications, 641–642

LLC (logical link control) sublayer, 33, 175

LLDP (Link-Layer Discovery Protocol), 18–19, 181–182
  Microsoft implementation, 19, 182

LLDP-MED (Link-Layer Discovery Protocol–Media Endpoint Discovery), 183

LLMNR (Link-Local Multicast Name Resolution), 183

LLTD (Link-Layer Topology Discovery), 182

Copyright Goodheart-Willcox Co., Inc.

Copyright Goodheart-Willcox Co., Inc.

Copyright Goodheart-Willcox Co., Inc.

private branch exchange (PBX), 597
privileged user accounts, 480
privileged user agreement, 470
problem-solving skills, 651
professionalism, 650
programmer, 635
propagation delay, 138
Protected Extensible Authentication
      Protocol (PEAP), 469
protocol analyzers, 139, 385, 483,
      556–557
protocol data unit (PDU). *See* packaging
      of data
protocols
      authentication, 467–469
      connectionless/unreliable, 153–154
      connection-oriented/reliable,
            153–154
      correlating to OSI model layers, 38,
            303–304
      dial-up networking, 432–437
      discovery, 18–19, 181–183, 314
      file-sharing, 201–202
      frame structures, 158–161, 304–306
      hardware, 173–178
      multimedia, 373–384
      networking, 16–19, 178–183
      network management, 503–504
      reliable, 153–154
      remote access, 247–249, 432–437
      routing, 347–350
      security, 459–461
      unreliable, 153–154
      *See also names of individual
            protocols*
protocol sniffers. *See* protocol analyzers
protocol stack. *See* OSI model
proxy servers, 397, 477–478
PSTN (public switched telephone
      network), 380, 421–422,
public-key cryptography. *See*
      asymmetric-key encryption
public switched telephone network
      (PSTN), 380 , 421–422
PUK (personal unlocking key), 136
punch down blocks, 599–601
punch down tool, 598–599
punctuality, 651
PVC (permanent virtual circuit), 373, 430

Q

QoS (Quality of Service) protocol, 382
quality of service, 314
Quality of Service (QoS) protocol, 382
queries, database, 14

questions
      network design and needs
            assessment, 582
      use in troubleshooting, 528

R

radio-frequency identification (RFID),
      134
radio interference, 114–115
radio-wave-based networking, 122–137
      Bluetooth, 133–134
      cellular technologies, 134–137
      modes, 124–125
      standards, 125–133, 463–464, 466
radio waves, 112–137
      interference, 114–115
      transmission techniques, 118–122
      wireless networking, 122–137
RADIUS (Remote Authentication Dial-In
      User Service), 463, 465–466
RAID systems, 275–278, 510
      levels, 276–278
ransomware, 451
RARP (Reverse Address Resolution
      Protocol), 326
r commands, 460–461
RDP (Remote Desktop Protocol),
      432–433
realm trusts, 218
Real-time Transport Control Protocol
      (RTCP), 384
Real-time Transport Protocol (RTP), 384
receiver, 112
recovery. *See* disaster recovery; system
      recovery
Recovery Console tool, 542–543
Redundant Array of Independent Disks.
      See RAID systems
Redundant Array of Inexpensive Disks.
      See RAID systems
references, using in job-search process,
      647
reflected loss, 54
registrar, 298
reliable communication, 153–154
remote access, 196, 419–438
remote access server, 430
Remote Authentication Dial-In User
      Service (RADIUS), 463, 465–466
Remote Desktop Protocol (RDP),
      432–433
repair disks, 542
repeaters, 22
replay attack, 449

replication, of AD DS (Active Directory
      Domain Services) database,
      214–216
reserved IPv4 addresses, 295–296
reserved symbols, 588
resistance, 54
resolution, video, 372
resolver, 300
résumé, 645
Reverse Address Resolution Protocol
      (RARP), 326
reversed pair, 79
RFID (radio-frequency identification),
      134
RG-6 cable, 62
RG-8 (thicknet) cable, 63
RG-58 (thinnet) cable, 63
ring topology, 8–9
RIP (Router Information Protocol), 348
RIPng (RIP next generation), 348–349
RIP next generation (RIPng), 348–349
Rivest, Ron, 456
RJ-45 connectors, 71–73
rogue WAP (wireless access point), 464
Roll Back Driver feature, 543–544
rollover cable, 74
root user, 243
route command, 248, 571
Router Information Protocol (RIP), 348
router metric, 347
routers, 26, 346–351
      versus multilayer switches, 350–351
routing, 346–351
      protocols, 347–350
RSA encryption, 456
RTCP (Real-time Transport Control
      Protocol), 384
RTP (Real-time Transport Protocol), 384

S

SaaS (Software as a Service), 15
safe mode, 539, 541
salesperson, technical, 634
Samba, 252–253
sampling frequency, 366–368
sampling rate, 366–368
SAN (storage area network), 278–279
SAS (Serial Attached SCSI), 271
satellite systems and communication,
      425–427
scattering, 92
scope ID, 320
SCP (Secure Copy Protocol), 461
SCSI (Small Computer Systems
      Interface), 268–271

Copyright Goodheart-Willcox Co., Inc.

Copyright Goodheart-Willcox Co., Inc.

Copyright Goodheart-Willcox Co., Inc.

Copyright Goodheart-Willcox Co., Inc.

Copyright Goodheart-Willcox Co., Inc.